Americans
in Paris
A Literary Anthology

Americans in Paris

A Literary Anthology

Adam Gopnik, *editor*

A Special Publication of
The Library of America

Introduction, headnotes, and volume compilation © 2004 by
Literary Classics of the United States, New York, NY. All rights
reserved. No part of this book may be reproduced commercially
by offset-lithographic or equivalent copying devices without the
permission of the publisher. Some of material in this volume is
reprinted with permission of holders of copyright and publication
rights. See page 609 for acknowledgments. Distributed to the
trade by Penguin Putnam Inc.

This book is set in Caslon 540.

Library of Congress Cataloging-in Publication Data:
Americans in Paris : a literary anthology / Adam Gopnik, editor.
    p. cm.
ISBN 1-931082-56-1 (alk. paper)
1. Americans—France—Paris—Literary collections. 2. Americans
—France—Paris—History—Sources. 3. American literature.
4. Paris (France)—Literary collections. 5. Paris (France)—
Description and travel. I. Gopnik, Adam. II. Title.
PS509.P28 A47   2004   2003066080

10 9 8 7 6 5 4 3 2 1

Printed in the United States of America

Americans in Paris: A Literary Anthology
is published in honor of

Florence Lacaze Gould
(1895–1983)

with support from

THE FLORENCE GOULD FOUNDATION

Contents

Introduction

The opening bars of the Gershwin rise, the rhythm is high-hearted, the percussion clacks and chimes, and though we know that the blues lie ahead, the first phrases still pierce our hearts as though struck by a jaunty woodpecker in a beret. There are songs about London and movies about Rome, but there is no circumstance quite so neatly mythological, no American tone so suggestive of its poem, no situation so neatly a *situation*, as that of the American in Paris. A musical comedy of the classic type set in London requires an occasion, a royal wedding, or a damsel in distress. The presence of an American in Paris is in itself an occasion for music, at least for other Americans. When a James hero walks into a London drawing room, our hearts sink for his embarrassments, but when he walks into a Paris hotel—no matter how poor his French may be, or how comic his prospects—our hearts lift a little at the promise of something that will be pleasurable in its unfolding. An American in Paris is, as they say, a story in itself: one need merely posit it to have the idea of a narrative spring up, even if there is no narrative to tell.

The idea keeps its hold on us for a simple reason. For two centuries, Paris has been attached for Americans to an idea of happiness, of good things eaten and new clothes bought and a sentimental education achieved. Paris suggests the idea of happiness as surely as an arrival in New York suggests hope and Los Angeles, in literature at least, hopelessness. It is the place we go to escape small-town, or even big-town, American life and be happy. The Parisian idea is also an idea of happiness divorced, perhaps, from any idea of virtue, or even of freedom. The islands of license and permission that Americans find are surrounded by canals of order. But the idea of happiness sought and found in Paris is, more than merely an occasional episode in "travel writing," one of the haunting small themes of American literature. Paris is "the wonderful place, the only real capital of the world," wrote that entirely American writer William Dean Howells, and many of his brothers and sisters agree with him.

One has only to compare the American idea of Paris to the idea of the Englishman in Paris—which figures very large in British writing—to sense how peculiarly willed our happiness in Paris is. The story of the

Englishman in Paris, though often liberating and beloved (as when Cyril Connolly sighs for Parisian hotels at the height of the Blitz), always has some note of the louche and the squalid, of the bordello and the bidet. It is like the idea of the American in Mexico: next door is where we go in search of a dirty weekend; across the ocean for a holy week. (It is the idea of the Englishman in New York, from Wodehouse to Quentin Crisp, which seems to have its song.) Distance enforces a romantic view. Harold Nicolson writes wearily in his diary in the 1930s that a friend "was going over to Paris on the Friday, so I decided to go with him, as it was more or less on my way," and the American is shocked. As casual as that? Paris remains a long way, not a short hop, or hope, away for us. Even in the age of air travel, for an American to go to Paris implicates a week, not a week-end, and seven days is what it takes to make a world. Given seven days, in fact, the visitor is almost obliged to make one.

This book is a history of the worlds Americans have made in the city where they have gone to be happy. It is in part, therefore, the history of an illusion. Every world America thinks up is a world we think we've discovered (It's India! cries Columbus, setting the tone), and the line between illusion and reality is even finer in Paris than it is elsewhere. Paris is our happy place because, against the logic of history and horror, we have insisted that it be so. A reasonable, sane, and healthy core of reasons does support the illusion, and renew it. Though we have been often at war in France, we have never been at war *with* France, and so, though ghosts rise at Normandy, they are not reproachful ghosts. They were trying to get to Paris, too. For most of its history, Paris was cheap, and you could get as much to drink there as you wanted when you couldn't get a single drink in Altoona or Poughkeepsie. The French love for writers and painters (and jazz musicians and dancers) is as real, and as tall, as the Eiffel Tower.

Still, happiness is multiple, and ours tends to cluster around two poles: one essentially bourgeois, the other bohemian. There are Americans who have come to Paris for the food, so to speak. They are in Paris to enjoy the haute-bourgeois civilization of comfort and pleasure and learning and formal beauty—to walk in the Luxembourg Gardens and study at the Bibliothèque and sketch at the Louvre, or, these days, to do a *stage* in a kitchen and come home with recipes. This type begins with Jefferson and encompasses Henry James and Edith Wharton and Malcolm Cowley and Matthew Josephson and every college student spending a junior year abroad, each one burning to learn something, and each one, in the end, learning—something. May Sarton captures this perfectly, remembering her first time in Paris, in the thirties:

> There were moments of immense excitement when after spending an hour browsing under the arches of the Odéon bookstall, I ran off with my prize "to burn it in myself" in the Luxembourg Gardens . . . There I sat in the shade of the chestnut trees, late into the autumn, while the leaves whirled up in eddies around me, cutting the pages, stopping to look out at the high plume of the fountain and the children sailing their boats in the round pond at its feet. . . . Everything I saw around me flowed out of the printed page . . .

The greatest image of this eager, isolated American Paris is John Singer Sargent's picture of the Boit daughters in their apartment: the curtains drawn against the Paris light, a slight air of mischief and melancholy combined. What are bright-eyed Daisys like us doing in this over-large apartment? Why, learning how to live in one.

In contrast are those who, usually arriving on the same boat or 747, come for the drink—for the dazzlement of new art and new experience, and, usually, for the actual drinks, too. They learn to fornicate in new ways, or in more ways with more kinds of people. They go to the Folies Bergères to be scandalized by the cancan or up to Montmartre to be shocked by the wild-man painters. This pattern is set very early by Franklin, who tried to have as much fun in Paris as he could, and went home with a reputation, and extends to Henry Miller and Jack Kerouac and beyond, to every backpacking summer kid around.

It is, of course, one of the truths of this history that the two kinds of visitors often end up swapping roles and tastes, like visitors to two sides of one buffet. The people who come for the drinks stay for the dinner, and the people who come for the dinner are often the ones who go home drunk. (Henry Miller and James Baldwin are instances of the first kind, arriving in high spirits and writing home in wisdom and sadness; and A. J. Liebling and James Thurber of the second kind, arriving for their own good and going home having learned in Paris never to be good again.)

This double life occurs partly because nobody can be a good student all the time, and even a libertine eventually gets worn out while learning how to be one. It also occurs because Parisian society, uniquely, contains both possibilities in a single package. The Parisian achievement was to have made, in the nineteenth century, two ideas of society: the Haussmannian idea of bourgeois order and comfort, and the avant-garde of *la vie de bohème*. These two societies, at famous and perpetual war in appearance, were at perpetual peace underneath, or, at least, more deeply dependent on each other than might be immediately apparent: "bourgeois" is the name the bohemian gives to his parents' apartment, "avant-garde" what the bourgeois calls his son's friends. This double existence is one of the special charms of Paris, and is evident in its greatest masters. Is Manet a bourgeois or a bohemian? Both, of course, and his life and art show that in French civilization the two are, to use a favorite metaphor of Henry Adams's, electro-magnetic—not just one field that looks like two, but one field that always produces the other.

As Americans search for these two things, pleasures of the flesh and instruction of the spirit, they come up, again and again, against two barriers. One is the simple restriction of language. People speak French in Paris, and only French. Reading British reminiscences of the thirties, one is startled to find that the upper classes all speak French, more or less nonchalantly, while the working classes, if they come at all, take it for granted that the first job is to learn the language. Americans are very poor with other people's languages, and very sure that it doesn't matter much. Again and again, the drama of learning French, failing to learn French, being less good at it than one should be occurs in these American histories, as it would not in a book of Italian or even Russian memoirs. (It is interesting to speculate on just how well, or not, the leading writers in this book spoke and wrote French: James was certainly in effect bilingual; but Hemingway's friends had their doubts about him, and Stein's French was, by some reports, shaky.)

This is not necessarily a bad thing; an accent and a stumbling tongue can sometimes help one "get" a foreign culture. Hercule Poirot solves the mystery because no one thinks he gets the point. But French for us is a struggle, a mountain to climb, and that mountain intrudes as part of the landscape in every Parisian scene described by an American; it is one of the reasons that our Paris is less narrowly serene than other people's. The barrier of language and the attempts to pass through it are often the material of comedy, and sometimes, as in Paul Zweig, of revelation: there is no more familiar or poignant moment than Zweig's sudden discovery, after being pathetically shut up in a cheap hotel room, reading, that he can now actually speak French! The fuss we make about French, either way, is one that a European, accustomed to an apartment house in Babel, would have found a little odd.

The other wall the American in Paris discovers is that French society, high and low, is open at the surface, closed at its core. Since the Grand Siècle, when Louis XIV drove French society off the land and forced the high livers to cohabit in small adjoining rooms at Versailles (and later in the Faubourg St. Germain, which replicated the urbanity and the close quarters), French high life has been uniquely polite, uniquely given to manners of appreciation and mutual admiration, if only from the necessity of forming an alliance with someone down the hall. A society built on cafés and dinner parties is always going to appear more open than one built on clubs and country weekends. Intimacy is the French keynote. There is simply no friendship in the world like French friendship—no friendship so intense, so nearly adolescent in its declarations of affection and intimacy, so needy in its demands on time and attention. "You have my love and esteem forever": this is not an exceptional but a routine and, in its own terms, heartfelt sentiment that one friend will inscribe in another's book.

But the friendship of the French is singular, and their obsessions and group identity remain home-bound. So while the fruits of social life, talk and food, are instantly, or almost instantly, offered (if not at home, then at a restaurant, that matchless French invention for semiprivate life) to a visiting American, the *roots* of social life, the sense of cohort and belonging, remain almost impossible for an American to put down in Paris. When an American does take deep root in France, it is nearly always by marriage, not by friendship or even simple duration. (Only Mary Cassat and Julian Green, on the long list of Americans in Paris, have become entirely "French," and Green was born half-French and became a French writer, a member of the Académie in fact and spirit, while Cassat had to "marry" Degas.) The theme of entrée offered and absolute acceptance evaded runs through this book. Even Edith Wharton, who knew the Faubourg St. Germain perfectly well, and for thirty years, did not really belong to it; she remained, as she cheerfully points out, a table-ender. The Faubourg, which Proust approached with such trembling reverence, was, or appeared to be, socially open to her, but it was only in the sense that the lions may leave a gazelle carcass socially open to the jackals: it is not that they are accepted; it is that they do not really count.

This is true up high, of course, but it is also true down low. What Wharton felt in the heart of Paris society was felt in the 1950s by James Baldwin, whose Paris, by his own account, was mostly a Paris of cheap hotels and sad cafés, and who writes that "it is perfectly possible to be enamored of Paris while remaining totally indifferent or even hostile to the French. . . . Unlucky indeed as well as rare, the traveler who thirsts to know the lives of the people—the people don't want him in their lives." Not entirely true, by the way, but true enough to haunt one's happiness just a little. There is no sadder, or more representative, image of the American in Paris than Henry James walking home alone to his chilly apartment after a Sunday with Flaubert, feeling both an exciting acceptance and his essential aloneness. Loneliness is nearly as strong a theme of the American Paris as happiness, with the two almost always plangently intertwined. We are happy because we are at last free of censorious eyes, and we are at last free of censorious eyes because nobody is looking.

Each wave of American invasion of Paris has had its own heroes and heroines, and though some asked, simply, what's this all about, the ones who came to stay asked, Why am I happy in Paris in a way that I am not happy in Altoona? Is it me, the place, or the time, or a little bit of all three?

Franklin and Jefferson set the tonic notes, the one as a happy libertine, the other as a good and watchful student. Their immediate successors in the early nineteenth century are perhaps the least known, though far from the least significant, of the Americans in Paris. The first, political American invasion, which began with the Revolution and extended into the nineteenth century, crested quickly, as the radically different paths that the two revolutions would travel—largely cautious and liberal in America, by turns violently radical and reactionary in France—became clear. Thomas Paine's great oration pleading for the life of Louis XVI is a reminder of the road not taken, and how much common sense this American radical did have. (What would have happened, one wonders, if the French had taken Paine's noble advice? Could the Revolution have survived the King?)

Americans kept coming, though. Henry James recalls, in his autobiography, how casually familiar his Albany uncles were with Paris. This next wave, which took in Mark Twain and P. T. Barnum alike—and Barnum's arrival in Paris to merchandise Tom Thumb was typical of a whole host of Americans arriving then as merchandisers, from Audubon with his birds to Catlin with his Indians—has a certain backwoods narrowness and skepticism at its core. Are these French really as hot as they pretend? Can they be duped as easily as Americans? At the same time, a note is heard that will run through to the present, of an unexpected, exclamatory delight. What a wonderful place! the American thinks, almost against his better Puritan judgment. This note, appearing in poets as unlikely as Longfellow and Emerson, balances the occasional philistinism that one finds even in Twain. The same note of pleasure is struck, from a less lofty perch, by the unfairly forgotten Nathaniel Parker Willis, who had already, by the early nineteenth century, invented the characteristically American tone of bewildered affection that one would have thought began with Thurber and Buchwald.

It is after the twin traumas of the decade beginning in 1861, the Civil War in America and the Commune in Paris, that something new in the relations of Paris and America happens. Paris becomes not a place you visit but a place where you can stay and still be an American writer. From then on, for almost a century, Paris remains a kind of literary laboratory, where American style gets made and proffered in refined form, from the curlicues of James and Wharton to the baroque comedy of Liebling and the sudden simplifications of Stein and Hemingway. There are few places where the evolution of American literary style can be seen in such a neat, perhaps over-lucid form.

This first permanent American Paris will always be associated with James and Wharton, for they were the first Francophiles, in the sense of accepting French cultural superiority not as a fact of life but, after the Franco-Prussian War, as a patriotic choice. James's European theme, the resistance of old Europe to young America, takes on a melodramatic, fairy-tale element in Paris: the French are *really* unknowable. Yet his novels are, no surprise, real novels, with remarkably few "episodes" and each chapter depending for its effect on what comes before and after. They resist excerpting—practically scream in pain when it's attempted—and the reader interested in the full complexities of Paris-America relations as James saw them should run out instantly and buy *The Ambassadors*, *The American*, and the lesser known but charming and prescient *The Reverberator*. (It concerns the coming of American "gossip" journalism to Paris.)

Still, James's central threads are present in both excerpts here. In "Occasional Paris" we have the marriage, special to James's nonfiction, of the agitated and the serene, the nervous and the ecstatic, and in " 'The

Velvet Glove'" a parable about the American courtship of Paris. Together, they suggest that Paris is romance itself, that is to say, approachable but unobtainable, to be wooed but possibly never won. (And when it is won— as in "'The Velvet Glove'" ironically, as in *The American* tragically—it suddenly turns to ashes and absurdity in your hand.)

Edith Wharton lived far longer in Paris than James, but used it less often as a literary venue. (When she does, as in her fine story "The Last Asset," or in *The Custom of the Country*, it is more often the American colony, rather than the French mainland, that she takes as a subject.) Nonetheless, she shares James's untroubled fascination with Paris as the ideal social mechanism. Paris for her seemed to represent, as the account of Parisian society in her memoir *A Backward Glance* makes plain, a social world as intricate and richly articulated as that of London, let alone New York, but wonderfully lacking the weight of Protestant guilt, of thwarted and repressed desire, that darkens her Anglo-Saxon pictures. It was possible to be respectable in Paris while remaining worldly—in fact, she implies, the Catholic dispensation of Paris, still felt as a cultural model if no longer in power as faith, with its emphasis on the public release of sin, makes it possible for the spiritual and the social to coexist. Among her favorite people in Paris were the worldly priests who shared her table. Though the artists and writers she knew in Paris were mostly of the second order, the small academic Emile Blanche and forgotten *boulevardier* playwrights, she had first-class taste, and saw that the French reverence for art was in itself a kind of religious faith coming-into-being. There are few more moving moments in literary history than Wharton's pressing on James a copy of Proust's first volume, and his instant assent in its vision.

The Great War, when it came, only increased their love of the place, Wharton writing with lucid emotion about the transformation of Paris by what seemed, at the time, to be a purifying rather than a merely scarifying event. For James, Paris remained the image not of the Great Good Place but of the Great Secret City, the citadel of romance, and therefore of mystery, and his idealization increased until, in 1915, at the height of the war, he could write, in words that, for all their involuted late-Jamesiness, ring still as high public speech: "I think that if there is a general ground in the world, on which an appeal might be made, in a civilized circle, with a sense of its being uttered only to meet at once and beyond the need of insistence a certain supreme recognition and response, the idea of what France and the French mean to the educated spirit of man would be the nameable thing."

For James and Wharton, the war marked the end of nineteenth-century mercantile Paris, and perhaps, they imagined, the rebirth of an ostensibly older, more spiritual one. (Henry Adams had a similar dream, fitfully.) What the war really brought to Paris was a lot of American kids. The landings and arrivals were multiple and complicated. "It would be interesting," Malcolm Cowley writes, "to list the authors who were ambulance or *camion* drivers in 1917. Dos Passos, Hemingway, Julian Green, William Seabrook, E. E. Cummings, Slater Brown, Harry Crosby, John Howard Lawson, Sidney Howard, Louis Bromfield, Robert Hillyer, Dashiell Hammett—one might almost say that the ambulance corps and the French military transport were college-extension courses for a generation of writers." (Others, like Thurber, arrived as code clerks, and still others arrived as soldiers with the U.S. Army in 1917.)

Cowley, penetratingly, points out what they got from coming to France as ambulance drivers: a soldier's courage and cynicism about rhetoric, and what he calls the "spectatorial" attitude, the habit of detachment, of seeming to stand aside. That detachment fills even apparently *engagé* writing, like Dos Passos's, and, in the hands of Hemingway, became the dominant note of the American stoical-courageous. "How you going to keep them down on the farm / after they've seen Paree?" the song asked after the war. Well, you couldn't, and the story of the twenties is largely that of how they failed to remain on the farm, what happened when they got to Paree, and why they ended up back on the farm afterward. (Or, at least, back in Greenwich Village, as good a farm as any.)

The American twenties in Paris presents a problem for the anxious anthologist. It was the decade when the idea of the American in Paris got fixed in the American imagination—the decade when Gershwin wrote his defining piece. But, as with vineyards, it is stress that makes for flavor, and there is something disappointingly flabby and crowded about the endless number of memoirs of that time that bombard the reader, feeding, as they do, on each other. The Lost Generation, as it was called, was perhaps not lost enough. In Paris, you always knew exactly where to find them: at a bar, alongside other Americans.

Some did shake free and got around to look at Paris. Matthew Josephson for instance, arriving as a dutiful student of the old generation

of French aesthetes, had the audacity to discover that the new, Dada generation looked to American commercial civilization as an inspiration, and
followed through on that discovery. His account of his life among the
Surrealists is a first-class comedy of cultural exchange, and it is a joy to
restore a portion of it to print. Some other good, surprising things, among
them Harry Crosby's diaries, still seem hot off the griddle, or anyway
chilled from the ice bucket.

But most of the literature is made much later; it is the fifties, not the
twenties, that is the great age of Lost Generation writing. Some of that
post-dated literature has the overpacked, incestuous crabbiness of all
small-colony literature. (Don't believe a word of it! I paid for those drinks
at the Select.) Some—but not all. To an impressive degree, the twenties-
in-Paris literature clings to the pre-fiesta chapters of *The Sun Also Rises*.
That book, along with James's novels, is the other dark body in this solar
system. It is not just that the figures, from Harold Loeb to Robert
McAlmon, whom Hemingway fixed in its pages, in that distinctive tone
of malicious simplicity, all come around to have their say. It is that something about those pages struck a moral tone for a generation, even if the
tone was only a tone, and not a morality, a pose more than a position.

Paris for Hemingway in the twenties was American, distastefully so,
and the whole thrust of the book is that it is the place you escape from, to
get to trout streams and noble, honor-bound Spain. Fitzgerald's shrewd
comment, that the book should have been called "A Romance and a
Guide Book," was exactly right; what young people look for in literature
is what you find in a good guide book—certainties of taste and a power of
disposition. Go there, not here; eat this, not that. Hemingway had a
thrilling power of exclusion, along with a gift for patient explanation—
Pernod brings you up and lets you down, you shouldn't order chicken
in a bad restaurant, etc.—and it is his gift as a taste-maker that seems to
have impressed, and scared, a generation, nothing like it until Holden
Caulfield let in Cole Porter and Swiss cheese sandwiches and ruled out
Errol Garner and apple brown Betty.

At the same time, Hemingway in Paris participated in the great cleaning up of American writing, the extreme paring down of American prose
style that was taking place in those years everywhere from Winesburg,
Ohio, to Harold Ross's *New Yorker* offices. It was in Paris, though, and particularly through the influence of Gertrude Stein on the young Hemingway, that this transformation was made most memorably. (Wilfrid Sheed

has written at length, in his book *Essays in Disguise*, on the influence of Stein's prose on Hemingway's, in one of the best examinations of Hemingway's style we have. Basically, Hemingway took Stein's stripped-down sentences and made them less "poetic," overlaying them with the narrative straightforwardness of newspaper writing.)

Was it just by chance that this cleansing took place in Paris? After all, neither Stein nor Hemingway could have found this urge to simplify in the French modernist writing they admired, which tended, if anything, to the elaborate and the allusive-by-cloudy-omission rather than the allusive-by-telegraphic-simplification. Hemingway gave Maupassant some credit, but Maupassant, though he is candid, is never especially simple. The kind of simplicity that Stein and Hemingway mastered did come from a peculiarly French-American connection, though—it came out of French painting, and in particular out of Cézanne and Matisse.

The deliberately childlike drawing of Matisse gave Stein a model of how much might be achieved in the apparent faux-naïf, just as Picasso's Cubism gave her a sense of the scrambled simple unit. Hemingway's claim to have been taught to write above all by Cézanne, though obviously at one level one of those things that writers say (sooner Cézanne than Sherwood Anderson, who's in there, too, God knows), is finally a plain truth. Those hours he spent at the Luxembourg Palace were as valuable as any an American has spent in France, and the small repeated bits, the monosyllabic vocabulary and paratactic rhythm, build up whole rooms and the emotions that go with them in something like the way Cézanne's simple patches realize a Provençal landscape. They both radiate the same feeling, too, of serenity gained through anxiety, sureness arrived at the hard way.

One has the feeling that, in the twenties, Paris was for Hemingway just another New York, where people were, where you worked and were expected to be. It was only much later, as the sad old man of the last books, that he made up his own Paris. *A Moveable Feast*, the ultimate fifties echo of the Paris twenties (the book was published posthumously in 1964), is one of those things of Hemingway's that one resists at first, a tourist trap, sentimental late Hemingway: "The Young Man and the *Sceau*." I know one discerning reader who insists that the good parts of *A Moveable Feast* must, for their purity of style (and heart), have been dug by the old man out of an old notebook. But it seems far more likely, and psychologically plausible, that the old man simply had something to write about, now, that worked in his style, which was never, or only pitifully, "epic" but always deeply sensual and evocative. The difference between the gentle, home-bound Paris of wife and child that he evokes so beautifully, and the relentless competitiveness in his relations with other writers that he perpetuates so nastily, even after most of them are dead and none of them rivals, is perhaps no more than a sign that a narcissist is happy only in his own extended skin. He still knew how to do it by remembering how he did it then. Fortunately the poison and the honey in the book are neatly separate, like layers in a pousse-café.

No survey of Paris in the twenties would be complete, as our grandfathers would have written, without mention of at least two great American women. Janet Flanner is Paris still in many American minds, for her fifty-year stint as the author of *The New Yorker*'s "Letter from Paris." Much of what Flanner did was to rewrite the French newspapers a week late. But though that is a comment on the pre-CNN times, it is no criticism of her method: her rewriting was peerlessly concise, stylish, and mind-opening. Few writers have grown as she did, and in public view, finding a tone of deepening seriousness from the twenties to the thirties as the world became more serious, and then finding an elegiac tone for the forties, when the world mourned, all without ever sounding like anyone but herself. Anita Loos, around the same moment as Flanner began, wrote, in *Gentleman Prefer Blondes*, one of the comic masterpieces of American literature, and her scenes in Paris, where Lorelei Lee decides that "Paris is devine," remain as fresh and funny as they were when they were written. (The manners of sexual predation have changed but not the matter.) Anita Loos and Gertrude Stein, by the way, make an interesting study in varieties of the American faux-naïf. Loos's Lorelei Lee and Stein's Alice B. Toklas are really two voices in the same chorus, the American girl who has an air of being more dryly perceptive and observant than she chooses to sound—who chooses to sound naïve and simple because that air is what dries out her observations. Being smarter than you sound, the American achievement, is anyway usually better than sounding smarter than you are, the French *faiblesse*.

With the Depression, another kind of exile began to gather and join the good students and glad revelers: the student of miserable diversions, the unhappy, or unglad, reveler. Henry Miller, who creates the type, is not exactly unglad—he's grateful for the revelations, and he has a lot of sex—

but the pleasures he takes are tinged by a misery that, though not strictly "political," is still of its time. A sense of bad faith, false values, and fundamental rot enters the picture. For the first time, a desire to have a Paris that is rotten, richly rotten, gets voiced. (The Lost Generation thought the world was rotten, but their Paris was pure, if often pure as vodka is pure, an undiluted stimulant.) In one way, of course, Miller's is simply a version—and, on the whole, a more "American," fundamentally sweet-tempered version—of the same literature of *pourriture* that ripened in Céline and, later, Genet. But Miller has another term in his equation, the America he has left, and what is striking is that for the first time he sees America as poisoned precisely because it pretends to be fresh, innocent, and antiseptic. The "innocence" of Americans becomes murderously naïve, in a way that is prescient of the literature of the fifties, when Miller, of course, really begins to matter to American writing. Even for those who find his method haphazard, his diatribe against the cheap American smile, like his loving evocation of the "shit" of Paris, remains startling, and a necessary human corrective to a literature at times too sugared. Miller is here, I will confess, as much because he must be as because I want him to be—which is not, I suppose, a bad description of his literary importance.

Parallel with Miller's arrival comes, in the thirties, a big wave of jazz musicians, with whom Miller has something in common, though their immersion in French low life is more unwilling than his. (Sidney Bechet would have been delighted to be playing the Elysée Palace from the word go.) If the American embrace of French painting is one of the secret engines of American writing in Paris, the French embrace of American jazz is its gas, what keeps it going. From Bechet himself through Coleman Hawkins and Ellington and on to Bud Powell and John Lewis, the French love of jazz, and understanding of it, has been one of the constant magnets of Paris for Americans. It is an experience more played than written, but Bechet's voice comes through in his autobiography, and when he speaks here for himself, he echoes with the voices of all those others.

The jazz influx, of course, puts one in mind of the wave of African-American writers arriving in Paris, beginning with Frederick Douglass and extending to James Weldon Johnson and on to Richard Wright and James Baldwin. As with the gay and lesbian experience of Paris, what black writers wanted from Paris, in the first instance, was freedom, the freedom to do their work and not be branded or shunned as a member of a particular group, or suffer the fear of an imprisoning mark. Like gay and lesbian

Americans, black Americans felt free in Paris to be themselves. If this was in a way one more illusion—James Baldwin wrote, ruefully, about the disillusioning reality of being a black man in Paris, the good city of equality that turns out to be just as treacherous as New York—it was a good one to have, and it lasted for a long time.

For some Americans, the grief of World War II was focused, perhaps to an unseemly degree, on the loss of Paris. There was "The Last Time I Saw Paris"; and *Casablanca* made having Paris seem continuous with the idea of happiness. "We fought our way back to Paris," Hemingway said afterward and the implicit italics fell on the word "back"— it was ours and we retook it. But though some of the troops stayed to write, it was the people coming in the second wave, after the war, who made a new American Paris. I have spoken to someone who was on the boat bringing the first returning American fashion professionals, Seventh Avenue merchants and fashion editors, and he described it as a kind of *extase* of gin rummy and starry expectations, none of them disappointed. The expectations were so high, in fact, the image made more glowing by the half-decade of absence, that a refusal to accept the corruption of the occupation set in. The "myth of the resistance," rhetorically alive in Paris, was just as heartfelt in America. We needed Paris to be eternal and unstained almost more than the French did.

Paris in the late forties and throughout the fifties emerged in the American imagination not as a rehabilitated victim but as a conquered paradise—a fabulous and unalterable Byzantium where we Crusaders were, blessed fate, the real rulers, with a fat dollar and a debt of gratitude to be repaid. The tone, best captured in Vincente Minnelli's movie version of *An American in Paris* and in the first half hour or so of Stanley Donen's *Funny Face*, is triumphant but not fatuously so, with a Paris seen from a position of assumed superiority, but seen also as a dazzlement. The feeling, which achieves a permanent form in Richard Avedon's fashion photographs of the period, is of earned joy.

Though perhaps best realized in those movies and images, this American moment in Paris had its writers, too. The decade was marked by the strange triumvirate of Irwin Shaw, James Jones, and Art Buchwald, who in their day were as instantly identified with Paris, and nearly as strong magnets for young Americans as Hemingway and Stein had been for an earlier generation. It is hard to do much with Jones today—a true primitive, he is at his best in his novels, where he has to be swallowed whole, awkwardness and all. Shaw wrote several short stories set in Paris, but to this reader, at least, they have today that quality of slightly secondhand Hemingway which infects so much of the American Abroad writing of the period. But for *Holiday* magazine he wrote, in the second person and at exuberant length, a kind of imaginary ideal day in Paris, which, if it has elements of cliché, also has, in its relentless detailing, the fascination, the commitment, of an ideal, or perhaps merely of an idyll. If there is accordion music in it—well, they were still playing accordions in Paris then. (And now, too, for that matter.) Buchwald, meanwhile, perfected a style of good-natured bemusement, neither condescending nor exasperated, and subsequent generations of humorists in Paris will blush to see how many of their subjects were sketched out in his genial broad outlines. And although Art Buchwald and Jack Kerouac might be thought to define polar ends of American writing in the fifties, the same heady whirl and buzz (in both cases in men by their own accounts not often happy) excites them both.

Schools and movements exist for busy anthologists to think up and for writers to get out of. The American poet and essayist Paul Zweig came to Paris at the height of this exuberant moment and, instead of making the rounds, burrowed deep into French life, a mole from Brighton Beach. He exchanged his American identity for that of a French Communist at the height of the Algerian war, even to the extent of collaborating for a time with the FLN, the Algerian terrorist organization. But his real preoccupations seem to have been sexual rather than political, and it is a pleasure to reintroduce this extraordinary and sadly overlooked American writer. Zweig writes with an adjectival density, a rhapsodic seeing, that recalls Updike's; both come from the same fifties aesthetic—where the academic example weighs heavily on the writer's shoulders, and sex is a way out into the real. Zweig adds to this mix a Bellow-like tartness, a depressive and self-consciously Jewish melancholy. His choice of Paris and of France is one of the bravest and most comically complete in the history of these transformations.

Between Meals: An Appetite for Paris, A. J. Liebling's 1962 memoir of a lifetime spent sporadically in Paris, is about memory, memory and food— Liebling evokes the parallel with Proust jocularly and defensively on his first page—and in one way might seem to be another instance of

American fifties triumphalism. Liebling was there to liberate the city in 1944, a journey he recounted in *The Road Back to Paris*, and he returned to eat in it. In another way, it is a further instance of twenties expatriate experience being written in the fifties: Liebling first came to Paris as a young student in 1928, on his dad's money, and a lot of the book, including one of our chapters, is about those years. But Liebling's eye and Liebling's language make the book something mysteriously *sui generis*: a great work of comic reporting. (Liebling has recently been taken to task by some for having too free a hand with the facts. Actually, he always signaled the terms on which his pieces or books should be read. I never believe that a word about Colonel Stingo is narrowly true, nor would I want it to be, for his is a tall tale and built under a baldachin of exaggeration; to fact-check it is to miss its splendor. But every word he writes about the war I am sure is true, because it signals that it is built on true things, and is one. If I found out that Molly never existed I would be disgusted; if I found out that Colonel Stingo really did I would be disappointed.)

Liebling's Paris is, of all the Parises included here, the best, or anyway the anthologist's favorite. Though he was in Paris in the twenties, Liebling knew no one in the Montparnasse American colony; nor, unlike Josephson and Cowley, did he know anyone in the French avant-garde. And we would not have been better off if he had. He knew *his* Paris, a young and greedy man's Paris of restaurants and passing encounters with waiters and whores (although his French was better than that of most of the famous authors included here). He matters, as all writers matter in the end, because of his line. Liebling could write rings around anyone, and he did; the rings and twists are the American baroque. Liebling is the master of the American baroque, as S. J. Perelman (who makes an appearance in these pages with a bit of funny, bitter French-American satire) is of the American rococo. A rococo style is built on ornament, a baroque style on curves and twists that extend around something, that enclose something. The matter in Perelman is almost nonexistent; in Liebling, it really counts. He makes strong statements in pretzel shapes; but, like real pretzels, they are made of solid bread. The baroque in Liebling is built on metaphor—metaphor large and small, metaphor offered when anyone else would offer straight declarative prose (he could do that, too, when he wanted to). Wodehouse is the only other writer who can reliably create three original metaphors on every page—with the difference that Wodehouse, an idyllist, was content if they were strange and funny, while Liebling, a novelist *manqué*, wanted them to be funny and revealing, strange and true. Liebling's metaphors are dazzling in Louisiana, but in Paris they have a particular gaiety, an unexpected force sweetened by the nostalgia, by the absence of any need to score points. Liebling's is also a postwar style, grown fat on good things, and expansive. In Hemingway, writing in the twenties, Gertrude Stein is just offstage, keeping time with a ruler. In Liebling, Tom Wolfe is just about to make an appearance.

Liebling's greatness does not depend on his subject. But it is true that, since Liebling, the American fascination with Paris has become more and more narrowly focused on food and eating it, and so we follow Liebling with an exceptional piece about Paris by M.F.K. Fisher, his austere food-loving opposite. The American new to Paris no longer asks the old hands where to go to look at pictures, since he assumes that there are no new pictures worth seeing; and no longer even asks where to go to learn to draw, since nobody learns to draw. Americans do not even ask where to go and have sex, since now they do that, too, in Altoona. But everyone wants to know where to eat, new places and old, and, if they have their doubts even about that church, still they recognize that it is the home of the church. Even Protestants are impressed by St. Peter's. By far the largest literature of Paris in Liebling's wake is food literature, and Julia Child and Patricia Wells have given to American readers more, perhaps, than the self-consciously literary writers have; the most vital traffic in cultural material now lies in telling how to roast a chicken. It is easy to sigh at this transformation, but it is hard to be really angry about it. One of the things that Paris teaches puritanical Americans is not to be so picky about other people's pleasures, including other Americans'.

To govern is to choose, a great man said, and to choose is to feel at least a little like a governor. The anthologist, making his exclusions and choices, has the thrill of a little dictator: you here, you're banished. But in truth many Americans who wrote beautifully or sensibly or significantly about Parisian life defeated my attempts to anthologize them. It was no lack of regard for Elliot Paul or Richard Wright or Samuel Putnam or Donald Ogden Stewart, to name four of four hundred we struggled with, that led me to leave them out.

I decided to limit this book to experiences before the late sixties, if in a couple of cases written afterward. Though obviously paying respects in full to the monuments of this history, I wanted also to "backload" the book with older material, almost all of it long out of print, that would be unfamiliar even to expert readers. This meant that more recent adventures in Paris might be left to the market and the bookstores, where they can more or less easily be found. A whisper of uncertainty rises, because the story, one fears, is incomplete without Diane Johnson or Edmund White. On the whole, though, it seemed more important to make the invisible accessible than to make the available canonical. The Library of America—my idea of it, anyway—is a place where the lost is found more even than one where the best is kept, and it ought to preserve the American past and let the present look after itself (until it becomes the past and, limping, needs the help of editors and anthologists).

But there is another, deeper reason for ending in the late sixties. It marked the end of something: 1968, and the "events" of May, was the last time that Paris was indisputably the center of the world. The two great events already underway then, the cleaning of Paris by Malraux and the removal of Les Halles, the food market, from central Paris to the suburbs, mark in retrospect the beginning of the "Venetian" Paris, the self-consciously museumed Paris. Since then the French influence on American life has turned mostly on literary theory and food, with academics and chefs taking over the roles of the old bourgeois and bohemian.

That the late sixties marked the end of something does not mean that it marked the end of everything. The transformation of Paris into a smaller and less central place, and the companion withdrawal of a large-scale American presence, has not been entirely unwelcome for writing. As the American colony has shrunk away, as the obvious significance of Paris has diminished, and as price and fashion have driven what bohemians remain to Prague and Budapest, in a curious way Americans are *more* engaged with specifically French manners than they have been since the nineteenth century. To be in Paris now is to be one more bourgeois in a bourgeois city, without an American colony to retreat into, and so how one gets married, and has affairs, and gets divorced, and raises a family, or learns the language, or just smokes becomes crucially dependent on how the French are doing these things. The drama of the American journey has lessened, perhaps, but the comedy of cultural misunderstanding has increased. Paris for Americans is no longer an exclamation point at the end of the world but a question mark at the fringe of our Empire, and if exclamation points provoke poetry, cultural interrogation produces comedy. If there is still juice in the American in Paris, then it is juice of another kind, and perhaps exactly juice and not wine.

Still, who can deny that Paris has contracted in the American imagination, just a little—or even, in a few cases, become a symbol not of happiness promised but of enmity unleashed? All the more reason to try to think again about why those of us who love it do. As I prepared this anthology, circumstances had me going back and forth to Washington, up and down the American East Coast, every weekend, and I packed all my books of Americans in Paris and read them on the train. Some were old friends, Liebling and Flanner, some have become friends since—Zweig and Josephson—but most, though friends for an hour or two, had to be put aside. All those memoirs of the time one spent as an art student at the Studio Julien before retreating back to Cleveland! And yet it was those books, which finally lacked the significance or the style to be included here, that in a sense were the most moving. They have a sequence of predictable epiphanies—the First Sighting, the First Meal, the First Morning—that have, as even predictable epiphanies should, something religious about them. If, from time to time, those unknown Americans in Paris were disillusioned, they were never disenchanted. They always return to the same places—the Luxembourg Gardens, the Tuileries—to imagine a civilization that lets you be, that gives a crucial margin of eccentric self-expression. Faulkner wrote home, after a day watching the kids in the Luxembourg, "Think of a country where an old man, if he wants to can spend his whole time with toy ships, and no one to call him crazy!" We think of that country because, in a sense, we have thought of that country—thought it up.

We keep coming back to Paris for those moments, those old men. As we age, and sadness and sickness begin to surround us, we fear that the city will give us less, not because it is different but because unclouded pleasure is harder to find. Friends sicken, mentors die, children age and find anxieties where once they found simple joy, the child with the baton in his hand is a boy with a needle of worry in his mind. The carousel looks smaller now; we might just as well stay home. . . . And then we don't, quite. "Paris is full of bumpers of consolation for Americans," the American painter Richard Overstreet, long an American in Paris, and the best of the kind (and to whom my own part in this anthology is dedicated, with love) once said. Those bumpers take the form of things that keep our minds at work. We are happy, above all, when we are absorbed, and we are absorbed when we are serious, and the secret of Paris, in the end, is that the idea of happiness it presents is always mingled, I do not always know how, with a feeling of seriousness.

That sense of serious happiness, of pleasure allied to education, is sometimes achieved by simply looking at the architecture, as it was for Hawthorne, sometimes by the mingling of sex with a student's purpose, as for Zweig—and often by literally going to school, as Edward Steichen and Lincoln Kirstein and Virgil Thomson all did in different ways. But this tincture of seriousness infiltrates our happiness, giving it dignity. In Paris, Americans achieve absorption without obvious accomplishment, a lovely and un-American emotion. (Liebling choosing between the Côtes du Rhone and the Chateauneuf du Pape seems charming but obvious to us, in a day when we all make that choice absentmindedly at the second-best wine shop on the way home from the subway. But in its day it was an *exemplum virtutis*, an instance of virtue.)

Even the commonplace literature of the First Morning, in this way, and its companion sacrament of the First Meal, is in the end a literature of pilgrimage. And at the end of any pilgrimage, the worst that mostly happens is that you get to go home. If one advantage of being an American is that the investment in the trip, emotional and financial, is large enough to make a world, to insist that *something* better happen, the other advantage is the clean break of return: the steamship waiting at the dock, the crowded 747 making the glaring day trip back into the mid-afternoon glare of Kennedy or LAX, home. Where Paris recomposes itself, again, into a symbol, a suggestion.

I write this, luckily back in Paris for a month, in a sublet apartment, where the furniture is pointed toward the golden dome of the Invalides, where the Emperor is buried. Upstairs, an American family has redone an identical apartment in high style, and everything looks toward the scintillating Eiffel Tower. Paris is as various as life: it all depends on how you arrange the furniture, and where you look out the window, and what you look out the window to see. Even as I'm sitting today by happy chance back in Paris, those weeks on the train seem curiously more true to the American idea of Paris, which is always in transit, always on its way. Paris is an idea of happiness we hope to get to, and the small miracle is that, when we get here, the images we get are not entirely wrong.

Enough. We need *someplace* to go and pretend to be happy in, damn it. There is no hierarchy of happiness; if this history teaches us anything it is that there is no one right way to find it. A set view, like a set menu, at least helps to organize the evening. If there is within this history of imagination also a history of pretenses, or illusions, it is still a history of love, which is always an illusion of a kind. The relationship between self-deception and self-transformation is complex and double-faced—these stories bear witness to that fact. But then it is always so: the journeys we take to fill our time and our coffee tables, and the pilgrimages we make to change our hearts, are hard to tell apart. Tourism, even the most degraded kind, still keeps some small savor of pilgrimage about it, just as a pilgrimage, no matter how pure, keeps a practical bit of tourism about it, a picnic lunch at Lourdes. In that sense, as the first and favorite goal of the American pilgrim, Paris is, and will always remain, at least a little bit devine.

Adam Gopnik
Paris, Rue de Grenelle, July 2003

Benjamin Franklin

Benjamin Franklin (1706–1790), America's nonpareil amateur scientist, diplomat, epigrammatist, and self-promoter, was the Moses of all American wanderers in Paris, the man who led the way. He arrived in Paris for the first time in 1767. At that moment, he was known primarily as an "electrician," a scientist researching the phenomenon of electricity—a role that, as recent biographers remind us, remained the fortunate basis of his reputation in France even a decade later, when he returned more famously as the American commissioner to France during the War of Independence. Fortunate, because it made him seem a man in touch with nature, rather than a politician doing the business of his government. Franklin was in fact far more artificial than the French ever wanted to believe, and the French more naïve than he chose to pretend (particularly in their sexual appetites). Yet it was this encounter—Mr. Natural meets the Worldlings—that set the basic rules of engagement for generations of Americans in Paris, from Fenimore Cooper to Catlin's Native Americans. Franklin never wrote an extended memoir of his stay, but in this letter home he sets down his first observations of his first visit, the first American in Paris before there were even Americans.

Letter to Mary Stevenson

DEAR POLLY   Paris, Sept. 14. 1767
    I am always pleas'd with a Letter from you, and I flatter myself you may be sometimes pleas'd in receiving one from me, tho' it should be of little Importance, such as this, which is to consist of a few occasional Remarks made here and in my Journey hither.

    Soon after I left you in that agreable Society at Bromley, I took the Resolution of making a Trip with Sir John Pringle into France. We set out the 28th past. All the way to Dover we were furnished with Post Chaises hung so as to lean forward, the Top coming down over one's Eyes, like a Hood, as if to prevent one's seeing the Country, which being one of my great Pleasures, I was engag'd in perpetual Disputes with the Innkeepers, Hostlers and Postillions about getting the Straps taken up a Hole or two

I

before, and let down as much behind, they insisting that the Chaise leaning forward was an Ease to the Horses, and that the contrary would kill
them. I suppose the Chaise leaning forward looks to them like a Willingness to go forward; and that its hanging back shows a Reluctance. They
added other Reasons that were no Reasons at all, and made me, as upon
a 100 other Occasions, almost wish that Mankind had never been endow'd
with a reasoning Faculty, since they know so little how to make use of it,
and so often mislead themselves by it; and that they had been furnish'd
with a good sensible Instinct instead of it.

At Dover the next Morning we embark'd for Calais with a Number of
Passengers who had never been before at Sea. They would previously
make a hearty Breakfast, because if the Wind should fail, we might not get
over till Supper-time. Doubtless they thought that when they had paid for
their Breakfast they had a Right to it, and that when they had swallowed
it they were sure of it. But they had scarce been out half an Hour before
the Sea laid Claim to it, and they were oblig'd to deliver it up. So it seems
there are Uncertainties even beyond those between the Cup and the Lip.
If ever you go to sea, take my Advice, and live sparingly a Day or two
before hand. The Sickness, if any, will be the lighter and sooner over. We
got to Calais that Evening.

Various Impositions we suffer'd from Boat-men, Porters, &c. on both
Sides the Water. I know not which are most rapacious, the English or
French; but the latter have, with their Knavery the most Politeness.

The Roads we found equally good with ours in England, in some
Places pav'd with smooth Stone like our new Streets for many Miles
together, and Rows of Trees on each Side and yet there are no Turnpikes.
But then the poor Peasants complain'd to us grievously, that they were
oblig'd to work upon the Roads full two Months in the Year without being
paid for their Labour: Whether this is Truth, or whether, like Englishmen,
they grumble Cause or no Cause, I have not yet been able fully to inform
myself.

The Women we saw at Calais, on the Road, at Bouloigne and in the
Inns and Villages, were generally of dark Complexions; but arriving at
Abbeville we found a sudden Change, a Multitude both of Women and
Men in that Place appearing remarkably fair. Whether this is owing to a
small Colony of Spinners, Woolcombers and Weavers, &c. brought hither
from Holland with the Woollen Manufacture about 60 Years ago; or to
their being less expos'd to the Sun than in other Places, their Business

keeping them much within Doors, I know not. Perhaps as in some other Cases, different Causes may club in producing the Effect, but the Effect itself is certain. Never was I in a Place of greater Industry, Wheels and Looms going in every House. As soon as we left Abbeville the Swarthiness return'd. I speak generally, for here are some fair Women at Paris, who I think are not whiten'd by Art. As to Rouge, they don't pretend to imitate Nature in laying it on. There is no gradual Diminution of the Colour from the full Bloom in the Middle of the Cheek to the faint Tint near the Sides, nor does it show itself differently in different Faces. I have not had the Honour of being at any Lady's Toylette to see how it is laid on, but I fancy I can tell you how it is or may be done: Cut a Hole of 3 Inches Diameter in a Piece of Paper, place it on the Side of your Face in such a Manner as that the Top of the Hole may be just under your Eye; then with a Brush dipt in the Colour paint Face and Paper together; so when the Paper is taken off there will remain a round Patch of Red exactly the Form of the Hole. This is the Mode, from the Actresses on the Stage upwards thro' all Ranks of Ladies to the Princesses of the Blood, but it stops there, the Queen not using it, having in the Serenity, Complacence and Benignity that shine so eminently in or rather through her Countenance, sufficient Beauty, tho' now an old Woman, to do extreamly well without it.

You see I speak of the Queen as if I had seen her, and so I have; for you must know I have been at Court. We went to Versailles last Sunday, and had the Honour of being presented to the King, he spoke to both of us very graciously and chearfully, is a handsome Man, has a very lively Look, and appears younger than he is. In the Evening we were at the *Grand Couvert*, where the Family sup in Publick. The Form of their sitting at the Table was this:

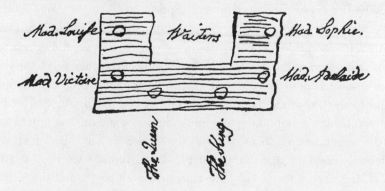

The Table as you see was half a Hollow Square, the Service Gold. When either made a Sign for Drink, the Word was given by one of the Waiters, *A boire pour le Roy*, or *A boire pour la Reine*, &c. then two Persons within the Square approach'd, one with Wine the other with Water in Caraffes, each drank a little Glass of what they brought, and then put both the Caraffes with a Glass on a Salver and presented it. Their Distance from each other was such as that other Chairs might have been plac'd between any two of them. An Officer of the Court brought us up thro' the Croud of Spectators, and plac'd Sir John so as to stand between the King and Madame Adelaide, and me between the Queen and Madame Victoire. The King talk'd a good deal to Sir John, asking many Questions about our Royal Family; and did me too the Honour of taking some Notice of me; that's saying enough, for I would not have you think me so much pleas'd with this King and Queen as to have a Whit less Regard than I us'd to have for ours. No Frenchman shall go beyond me in thinking my own King and Queen the very best in the World and the most amiable.

Versailles has had infinite Sums laid out in Building it and Supplying it with Water: Some say the Expence exceeded 80 Millions Sterling. The Range of Building is immense, the Garden Front most magnificent all of hewn Stone, the Number of Statues, Figures, Urns, &c in Marble and Bronze of exquisite Workmanship is beyond Conception. But the Waterworks are out of Repair, and so is great Part of the Front next the Town, looking with its shabby half Brick Walls and broken Windows not much better than the Houses in Durham Yard. There is, in short, both at Versailles and Paris, a prodigious Mixture of Magnificence and Negligence, with every kind of Elegance except that of Cleanliness, and what we call *Tidyness*. Tho' I must do Paris the Justice to say, that in two Points of Cleanliness they exceed us. The Water they drink, tho' from the River, they render as pure as that of the best Spring, by filtring it thro' Cisterns fill'd with Sand; and the Streets by constant Sweeping are fit to walk in tho' there is no pav'd foot Path. Accordingly many well dress'd People are constantly seen walking in them. The Crouds of Coaches and Chairs for that Reason is not so great; Men as well as Women carry Umbrellas in their Hands, which they extend in case of Rain or two much Sun; and a Man with an Umbrella not taking up more than 3 foot square or 9 square feet of the Street, when if in a Coach he would take up 240 square feet, you can easily conceive that tho' the Streets here are narrower they may be much less encumber'd. They are extreamly well pav'd, and the Stones being generally Cubes, when worn on one Side may be turn'd and become new.

The Civilities we every where receive give us the strongest Impressions of the French Politeness. It seems to be a Point settled here universally that Strangers are to be treated with Respect, and one has just the same Deference shewn one here by being a Stranger as in England by being a Lady. The Custom House Officers at Port St. Denis, as we enter'd Paris, were about to seize 2 Doz. of excellent Bourdeaux Wine given us at Boulogne, and which we brought with us; but as soon as they found we were Strangers, it was immediately remitted on that Account. At the Church of Notre Dame, when we went to see a magnificent Illumination with Figures &c. for the deceas'd Dauphiness, we found an immense Croud who were kept out by Guards; but the Officer being told that we were Strangers from England, he immediately admitted us, accompanied and show'd us every thing. Why don't we practise this Urbanity to Frenchmen? Why should they be allow'd to out-do us in any thing?

Here is an Exhibition of Paintings, &c. like ours in London, to which Multitudes flock daily. I am not Connoisseur enough to judge which has most Merit. Every Night, Sundays not excepted here are Plays or Operas; and tho' the Weather has been hot, and the Houses full, one is not incommoded by the Heat so much as with us in Winter. They must have some Way of changing the Air that we are not acquainted with. I shall enquire into it.

Travelling is one Way of lengthening Life, at least in Appearance. It is but a Fortnight since we left London; but the Variety of Scenes we have gone through makes it seem equal to Six Months living in one Place. Perhaps I have suffered a greater Change too in my own Person than I could have done in Six Years at home. I had not been here Six Days before my Taylor and Peruquier had transform'd me into a Frenchman. Only think what a Figure I make in a little Bag Wig and naked Ears! They told me I was become 20 Years younger, and look'd very galante; so being in Paris where the Mode is to be sacredly follow'd, I was once very near making Love to my Friend's Wife.

This Letter shall cost you a Shilling, and you may think it cheap when you consider that it has cost me at least 50 Guineas to get into the Situation that enables me to write it. Besides, I might, if I had staid at home, have won perhaps two shillings of you at Cribbidge. By the Way, now I mention Cards, let me tell you that Quadrille is quite out of Fashion here, and English Whisk all the Mode, at Paris and the Court.

And pray look upon it as no small Matter, that surrounded as I am by the Glories of this World and Amusements of all Sorts, I remember you and Dolly and all the dear good Folks at Bromley. 'Tis true I can't help it, but must and ever shall remember you all with Pleasure. Need I add that I am particularly, my dear good Friend Yours most affectionately.

Abigail Adams

Ur-WASP and waspish correspondent, Abigail Adams (1744–1818) married John Adams in 1764 and spent most of the Revolution in America, but left to join her husband in Paris after the signing of the Treaty of Paris. Though she remained there for only eight months she managed to write about many crucial subjects: manners and housekeeping, French theater, and, perhaps most memorably, Benjamin Franklin's flirtations.

————

Letters from Auteuil

TO MISS LUCY CRANCH

MY DEAR LUCY,   Auteuil, 5 September, 1784.
    I promised to write to you from the Hague, but your uncle's unexpected arrival at London prevented me. Your uncle purchased an excellent travelling coach in London, and hired a post-chaise for our servants. In this manner we travelled from London to Dover, accommodated through England with the best of horses, postilions, and good carriages; clean, neat apartments, genteel entertainment, and prompt attendance. But no sooner do you cross from Dover to Calais, than every thing is reversed, and yet the distance is very small between them.

    The cultivation is by no means equal to that of England; the villages look poor and mean, the houses all thatched, and rarely a glass window in them; their horses, instead of being handsomely harnessed, as those in England are, have the appearance of so many old cart-horses. Along you go, with seven horses tied up with ropes and chains, rattling like trucks; two ragged postilions, mounted, with enormous jack boots, add to the comic scene. And this is the style in which a duke or a count travels through this kingdom. You inquire of me how I like Paris. Why, they tell me I am no judge, for that I have not seen it yet. One thing, I know, and that is that I have smelt it. If I was agreeably disappointed in London, I am as much disappointed in Paris. It is the very dirtiest place I ever saw. There are some buildings and some squares, which are tolerable; but in

7

general the streets are narrow, the shops, the houses, inelegant and dirty, the streets full of lumber and stone, with which they build. Boston cannot boast so elegant public buildings; but, in every other respect, it is as much superior in my eyes to Paris, as London is to Boston. To have had Paris tolerable to me, I should not have gone to London. As to the people here, they are more given to hospitality than in England it is said. I have been in company with but one French lady since I arrived; for strangers here make the first visit, and nobody will know you until you have waited upon them in form.

This lady I dined with at Dr. Franklin's. She entered the room with a careless, jaunty air; upon seeing ladies who were strangers to her, she bawled out, "Ah! mon Dieu, where is Franklin? Why did you not tell me there were ladies here?" You must suppose her speaking all this in French. "How I look!" said she, taking hold of a chemise made of tiffany, which she had on over a blue lute-string, and which looked as much upon the decay as her beauty, for she was once a handsome woman; her hair was frizzled; over it she had a small straw hat, with a dirty gauze half-handkerchief round it, and a bit of dirtier gauze, than ever my maids wore, was bowed on behind. She had a black gauze scarf thrown over her shoulders. She ran out of the room; when she returned, the Doctor entered at one door, she at the other; upon which she ran forward to him, caught him by the hand, "Helas! Franklin;" then gave him a double kiss, one upon each cheek, and another upon his forehead. When we went into the room to dine, she was placed between the Doctor and Mr. Adams. She carried on the chief of the conversation at dinner, frequently locking her hand into the Doctor's, and sometimes spreading her arms upon the backs of both the gentlemen's chairs, then throwing her arm carelessly upon the Doctor's neck.

I should have been greatly astonished at this conduct, if the good Doctor had not told me that in this lady I should see a genuine Frenchwoman, wholly free from affectation or stiffness of behaviour, and one of the best women in the world. For this I must take the Doctor's word; but I should have set her down for a very bad one, although sixty years of age, and a widow. I own I was highly disgusted, and never wish for an acquaintance with any ladies of this cast. After dinner she threw herself upon a settee, where she showed more than her feet. She had a little lap-dog, who was, next to the Doctor, her favorite. This she kissed, and when he wet the floor, she wiped it up with her chemise. This is one of the Doctor's most intimate friends, with whom he dines once every week, and she with him. She is rich, and is my near neighbour; but I have not yet visited her. Thus you see, my dear, that manners differ exceedingly in different countries. I hope, however, to find amongst the French ladies manners more consistent with my ideas of decency, or I shall be a mere recluse.

You must write to me, and let me know all about you; marriages, births, and preferments; every thing you can think of. Give my respects to the Germantown family. I shall begin to get letters for them by the next vessel.

Good night. Believe me

Your most affectionate aunt, A. A.

———

TO MRS. WARREN

Auteuil, near Paris, 5 September, 1784.

Although I have not yet written to you, be assured, Madam, you have been the subject of some of my most pleasing thoughts. The sweet communion we have often had together, and the pleasant hours I have passed both at Milton and Braintree, I have not realized in Europe. I visit and am visited, but not being able to converse in the language of the country, I can only silently observe manners and men. I have been here so little while, that it would be improper for me to pass sentence or form judgments of a people from a converse of so short duration. This I may, however, say with truth, that their manners are totally different from those of our own country. If you ask me what is the business of life here? I answer, pleasure. The beau monde, you reply. Ay, Madam, from the throne to the footstool it is the science of every being in Paris and its environs. It is a matter of great speculation to me when these people labor. I am persuaded the greater part of those who crowd the streets, the public walks, the theatres, the spectacles, as they term them, must subsist upon bread and water. In London the streets are also full of people, but their dress, their gait, every appearance indicates business, except on Sundays, when every person devotes the day, either at church or in walking, as is most agreeable to his fancy. But here, from the gaiety of the dress and the places they frequent, I judge pleasure is the business of life. We have no days with us, or rather in our country, by which I can give you an idea of the Sabbath here, except commencement and election. Paris upon that day pours forth all her

citizens into the environs for the purposes of recreation. We have a beautiful wood cut into walks within a few rods of our dwelling, which, upon
this day, resounds with music and dancing, jollity and mirth of every kind.
In this wood booths are erected, where cake, fruit, and wine are sold. Here
milliners repair with their gauzes, ribbons, and many other articles, in the
peddling style, but for other purposes I imagine than the mere sale of their
merchandise. But every thing here is a subject of merchandise.

I believe this nation is the only one in the world which could make
pleasure the business of life and yet retain such a relish for it as never to
complain of its being tasteless or insipid; the Parisians seem to have
exhausted nature and art in this science, and to be "triste" is a complaint
of a most serious nature. In the family of Monsieur Grand, who is a Protestant, I have seen a decorum and decency of manners, a conjugal and family affection, which are rarely found, where separate apartments, separate
pleasures and amusements show the world that nothing but the name is
united. But whilst absolutions are held in estimation, and pleasure can be
bought and sold, what restraint have mankind upon their appetites and
passions? There are few of them left in a neighboring country amongst the
beau monde, even where dispensations are not practised. Which of the
two countries can you form the most favorable opinion of, and which is the
least pernicious to the morals? That where vice is licensed; or where it is
suffered to walk at large, soliciting the unwary and unguarded, as it is to a
most astonishing height in the streets of London, and where virtuous
females are frequently subject to insults. In Paris no such thing happens;
but the greatest decency and respect is shown by all orders to the female
character. The stage is in London made use of as a vehicle to corrupt the
morals. In Paris no such thing is permitted. They are too polite to wound
the ear. In one country vice is like a ferocious beast, seeking whom it may
devour; in the other like a subtle poison, secretly penetrating and working destruction. In one country, you cannot travel a mile without danger
to your person and property, yet public executions abound; in the other,
your person and property are safe; executions are very rare, but in a *law-
ful way, beware*; for with whomsoever you have to deal, you may rely upon
an attempt to overreach you. In the graces of motion and action this
people shine unrivalled. The theatres exhibit to me the most pleasing
amusement I have yet found. The little knowledge I have of the language
enables me to judge here, and the actions, to quote an old phrase, speak
louder than words. I was the other evening at what is called the French

Theatre (to distinguish it from several others,) it being the only one upon
which tragedies are acted. Here I saw a piece of the celebrated Racine, a
sacred drama, called Athalia. The dresses were superb, the house elegant
and beautiful, the actors beyond the reach of my pen. The character of the
high priest admirably well supported; and Athalia would have shone as
Sophonisba or Lady Macbeth, if the term *shine* may be applied to a character full of cruelty and horror. To these public spectacles (and to every
other amusement) you may go with perfect security to your person and
property. Decency and good order are preserved, yet are they equally
crowded with those of London; but in London, at going in and coming out
of the theatre, you find yourself in a mob, and are every moment in danger of being robbed. In short, the term John Bull, which Swift formerly
gave to the English nation, is still very applicable to their manners. The
cleanliness of Britain, joined to the civility and politeness of France, could
make a most agreeable assemblage. You will smile at my choice, but as I
am likely to reside some time in this country, why should I not wish them
the article in which they are most deficient?

It is the established custom of this country for strangers to make the
first visit. Not speaking the language lays me under embarrassments. For
to visit a lady merely to bow to her is painful, especially where they are so
fond of conversing as the ladies here generally are; so that my female
acquaintance is rather confined as yet, and my residence four miles from
Paris will make it still more so. There are four American ladies who have
visited me,—Mrs. Barclay, with whom I have a friendship, and whom I
can call upon at all times without ceremony, and who is an excellent lady;
a Mrs. Price, a Canadian lady; Mrs. Valnais, and Mrs. Bingham. Mrs. Bingham is a very young lady, not more than twenty, very agreeable, and very
handsome; rather too much given to the foibles of the country for the
mother of two children, which she already is.

As to politics, madam, the world is at peace, and I have wholly done
with them. Your good husband and mine would speculate upon treaties of
commerce, could they spend their evenings together, as I sincerely wish
they could, or upon what they love better, agriculture and husbandry,
which is become full as necessary for our country. This same surly John
Bull is kicking up the dust and growling, looking upon the fat pastures he
has lost, with a malicious and envious eye; and though he is offered admission upon decent terms, he is so mortified and stomachful, that, although
he longs for a morsel, he has not yet agreed for a single bite.

This village of Auteuil, where we reside, is four miles from Paris, and one from Passy;—a very pretty summer retreat, but not so well calculated for winter. I fear it will prove as cold as Milton Hill. If I was to judge of the winters here by what I have experienced of the fall, I should think they were equally severe as with us. We begin already to find fires necessary.

During the little time I was in England, I saw more of the curiosities of London than I have yet seen of Paris; so that I am not able to give you any account of any public buildings or amusements, except the theatres, of which I shall grow very fond as soon as I am mistress enough of the language to comprehend all the beauties of it. There are three theatres in Paris constantly open, but that upon which tragedies are acted is the most pleasing to me. Corneille, Racine, Crebillon, and Molière are very frequently given here; upon the stage the best pronunciation is to be acquired. There is a Mrs. Siddons in London, who is said to be the female Garrick of the present day. I had not the happiness to see her when I was in London, as she was then in Ireland; but I saw no actors upon their stage which by any means equal those which I have met with here. The people of this country keep up their intercourse with each other by dining together, after which they repair to the theatres and to the public walks.

I sigh (though not allowed) for my social tea parties which I left in America, and the friendship of my chosen few. Their agreeable converse would be a rich repast to me, could I transplant them round me in the village of Auteuil, with my habits, tastes, and sentiments, which are too firmly riveted to change with change of country or climate; and at my age, the greatest of my enjoyments consists in the reciprocation of friendship.

How is my good friend Charles? finely recovered, I hope. I do not despair of seeing him here; and at this house he may be assured of a welcome, whenever he wishes to try the air of France. Gay Harry, has he got any more flesh and health? Grave Mr. George is well, I hope, and fixed in some business to his mind. Let not my esteemed friend, the eldest of the brothers, think I have forgotten or neglected him by naming him last. His tenderness for his brothers, and his better health, will excuse me if I have been guilty of a breach of order. He will accept my good wishes for his health and prosperity without regard to place. Shall I ask General Warren how farming and husbandry flourish? I thought often of him, and the delight he would have received in a journey from Deal to London. The rich variety of grass and grain with which that country was loaded, as I rode through it, exhibited a prospect of the highest cultivation. All nature looked like a garden. The villages around Paris are pleasant, but neither the land nor the cultivation equals the neighboring nation.

When you see our good friend Madam Winthrop, be pleased to make my regards to her. You will also remember me to your neighbors at the foot of the hill; and let me hear from you by every opportunity, as the correspondence of my friends is the only compensation I am to receive for the loss of their society. Is Polly married? Happiness attend her and her partner if she is. To Mr. and Mrs. Otis, to one and all of my dear friends, be kind enough to remember me. The truth of one maxim of Rochefoucault I experience, that absence heightens, rather than diminishes, those affections which are strong and sincere.

12 December.

You will see, my dear Madam, by the date of the above, that my letter has lain by long, waiting a private conveyance. Mr. Tracy and Mr. Jackson design to return to London this week, and I shall request the favor of them to take charge of it. Since it was written there have been some changes in the political world, and the emperor has recalled his ambassador from the United Provinces. Every thing seems to wear a hostile appearance. The Dutch are not in the least intimidated, but are determined at all events to refuse the opening of the Scheldt to the emperor. This court is endeavoring to mediate between the emperor and the Dutch. When the affair was to be debated in the king's council, the queen said to the Count de Vergennes, "M. le Comte, you must remember that the emperor is my brother." "I certainly shall, Madam," replied the Count; "but your majesty will remember that you are queen of France."

Thus much for Politics. You ask about treaties of Commerce. Courts like ladies stand upon punctilios and choose to be addressed upon their own ground. I am not at liberty to say more.

This is the 12th of December and we have got an American snow storm; the climate is not so pleasant as I expected to find it. I love the cheerful sunshine of America and the clear blue sky. Adieu, my dear Madam, I have so much writing to do that I am, though unwillingly, obliged to close, requesting my son to copy for me. You will not fail writing soon to your friend and humble servant.

Thomas Jefferson

With Franklin one of the two pillars of the American experience in France, Thomas Jefferson (1743–1826), in his own words, merely succeeded Franklin as American minister to France, since no one could "replace" Benjamin Franklin. Yet Jefferson in his own way created a model of the American in Paris as significant (and in the long run as photogenic) as Franklin's. Where Franklin was the model American backwoods philosopher and (mostly theoretical) libertine, Jefferson was the model student, the first on a Junior Year Abroad. He bought the wine, admired the architecture (which he later copied), and befriended the intellectuals, including La Fayette and La Rochefoucauld. And he fell in love, though with a virtuous Englishwoman—the full hand, in fact. Even if, like most students, he left little impress on his masters, he did more even than Franklin to bring French manners and styles to America. But, a good Virginian neoclassicist, he kept an uneasy conscience suspicious about his own pleasures, as these two letters from 1785 and 1787 demonstrate.

Two Letters

TO CHARLES BELLINI

Paris, September 30, 1785

Dear Sir,—Your estimable favor, covering a letter to Mr. Mazzei, came to hand on the 26th instant. The letter to Mr. Mazzei was put into his hands in the same moment, as he happened to be present. I leave to him to convey to you all his complaints, as it will be more agreeable to me to express to you the satisfaction I received, on being informed of your perfect health. Though I could not receive the same pleasing news of Mrs. Bellini, yet the philosophy with which I am told she bears the loss of health, is a testimony the more, how much she deserved the esteem I bear her. Behold me at length on the vaunted scene of Europe! It is not necessary for your information, that I should enter into details concerning it. But you are, perhaps, curious to know how this new scene has struck a savage of the mountains of America. Not advantageously, I assure you. I find the general fate of humanity here, most deplorable. The truth of Voltaire's observation, offers itself perpetually, that every man here must be either the hammer or the anvil. It is a true picture of that country to which they say we shall pass hereafter, and where we are to see God and his angels in splendor, and crowds of the damned trampled under their feet. While the great mass of the people are thus suffering under physical and moral oppression, I have endeavored to examine more nearly the condition of the great, to appreciate the true value of the circumstances in their situation, which dazzle the bulk of spectators, and, especially, to compare it with that degree of happiness which is enjoyed in America, by every class of people. Intrigues of love occupy the younger, and those of ambition, the elder part of the great. Conjugal love having no existence among them, domestic happiness, of which that is the basis, is utterly unknown. In lieu of this, are substituted pursuits which nourish and invigorate all our bad passions, and which offer only moments of ecstacy, amidst days and months of restlessness and torment. Much, very much inferior, this, to the tranquil, permanent felicity with which domestic society in America, blesses most of its inhabitants; leaving them to follow steadily those pursuits which health and reason approve, and rendering truly delicious the intervals of those pursuits.

In science, the mass of the people is two centuries behind ours; their literati, half a dozen years before us. Books, really good, acquire just reputation in that time, and so become known to us, and communicate to us all their advances in knowledge. Is not this delay compensated, by our being placed out of the reach of that swarm of nonsensical publications, which issues daily from a thousand presses, and perishes almost in issuing? With respect to what are termed polite manners, without sacrificing too much the sincerity of language, I would wish my countrymen to adopt just so much of European politeness, as to be ready to make all those little sacrifices of self, which really render European manners amiable, and relieve society from the disagreeable scenes to which rudeness often subjects it. Here, it seems that a man might pass a life without encountering a single rudeness. In the pleasures of the table they are far before us, because, with good taste they unite temperance. They do not terminate the most sociable meals by transforming themselves into brutes. I have never yet seen a man drunk in France, even among the lowest of the people. Were I to proceed to tell you how much I enjoy their architecture, sculpture, painting, music, I should want words. It is in these arts they shine. The last of them, particularly, is an enjoyment, the deprivation of which with us, cannot be calculated. I am almost ready to say, it is the only thing which from my heart I envy them, and which, in spite of all the authority of the Decalogue, I do covet. But I am running on in an estimate of things infinitely better known to you than to me, and which will only serve to convince you, that I have brought with me all the prejudices of country, habit and age. But whatever I may allow to be charged to me as prejudice, in every other instance, I have one sentiment at least, founded in reality: it is that of the perfect esteem which your merit and that of Mrs. Bellini have produced, and which will for ever enable me to assure you of the sincere regard, with which I am, Dear Sir,

your friend and servant,

TO ANNE WILLING BINGHAM

Paris, February 7, 1787

I know, Madam, that the twelve month is not yet expired; but it will be, nearly, before this will have the honor of being put into your hands. You are then engaged to tell me, truly and honestly, whether you do not find the tranquil pleasures of America, preferable to the empty bustle of Paris. For to what does that bustle tend? At eleven o'clock, it is day, *chez madame*. The curtains are drawn. Propped on bolsters and pillows, and her head scratched into a little order, the bulletins of the sick are read, and the billets of the well. She writes to some of her acquaintance, and receives the visits of others. If the morning is not very thronged, she is able to get out and hobble round the cage of the Palais royal; but she must hobble quickly, for the *coeffeur's* turn is come; and a tremendous turn it is! Happy, if he does not make her arrive when dinner is half over! The torpitude of digestion a little passed, she flutters half an hour through the streets, by way of paying visits, and then to the spectacles. These finished, another half hour is devoted to dodging in and out of the doors of her very sincere friends, and away to supper. After supper, cards; and after cards, bed; to rise at noon the next day, and to tread, like a mill horse, the same trodden circle over again. Thus the days of life are consumed, one by one, without an object beyond the present moment; ever flying from the ennui of that, yet carrying it with us; eternally in pursuit of happiness, which keeps eternally before us. If death or bankruptcy happen to trip us out of the circle, it is matter for the buz of the evening, and is completely forgotten by the next morning. In America, on the other hand, the society of your husband, the fond cares for the children, the arrangements of the house, the improvements of the grounds, fill every moment with a healthy and an useful activity. Every exertion is encouraging, because to present amusement, it joins the promise of some future good. The intervals of leisure are filled by the society of real friends, whose affections are not thinned to cob-web, by being spread over a thousand objects. This is the picture, in the light it is presented to my mind; now let me have it in yours. If we do not concur this year, we shall the next; or if not then, in a year or two more. You see I am determined not to suppose myself mistaken.

To let you see that Paris is not changed in its pursuits, since it was honored with your presence, I send you its monthly history. But this relating only to the embellishments of their persons, I must add, that those of the city go on well also. A new bridge, for example, is begun at the Place Louis Quinze; the old ones are clearing of the rubbish which encumbered them in the form of houses; new hospitals erecting; magnificent walls of inclosure, and Custom houses at their entrances, &c. &c. &c. I know of no interesting change among those whom you honored with your acquaintance, unless Monsieur de Saint James was of that number. His bankruptcy, and taking asylum in the Bastile, have furnished matter of astonishment. His garden, at the Pont de Neuilly, where, on seventeen acres of ground he had laid out fifty thousand louis, will probably sell for somewhat less money. The workmen of Paris are making rapid strides towards English perfection. Would you believe, that in the course of the last two years, they have learned even to surpass their London rivals in some articles? Commission me to have you a phaeton made, and if it is not as much handsomer than a London one, as that is than a Fiacre, send it back to me. Shall I fill the box with caps, bonnets, &c.? Not of my own choosing, but—I was going to say, of Mademoiselle Bertin's, forgetting for the moment, that she too is bankrupt. They shall be chosen then by whom you please; or, if you are altogether nonplused by her eclipse, we will call an Assembleé des Notables, to help you out of the difficulty, as is now the fashion. In short, honor me with your commands of any kind, and they shall be faithfully executed. The packets now established from Havre to New York, furnish good opportunities of sending whatever you wish.

I shall end where I began, like a Paris day, reminding you of your engagement to write me a letter of respectable length, an engagement the more precious to me, as it has furnished me the occasion, after presenting my respects to Mr. Bingham, of assuring you of the sincerity of those sentiments of esteem and respect, with which I have the honor to be, Dear Madam, your most obedient and most humble servant,

Gouverneur Morris

Gouverneur Morris (1752–1816) arrived in Paris in February 1789, just in time for the Revolution, throughout which he served as American minister in France. Deeply conservative by nature and background, Morris had nevertheless joined the American patriotic cause at its key moment, and, still a very young man, sat from 1778 to 1779 in the Continental Congress. Greatly respected as a man of commerce, he went to France largely on private business, but his talents and contacts made him the natural successor to Jefferson as the key American in Paris, and in 1792 Washington appointed him official minister. It was a controversial appointment back home because of Morris's views, already known to be essentially aristocratic and reactionary. But it was exactly the tension between those views (he was active in trying to rescue Louis XVI from his house arrest in the Tuileries) and his public responsibilities as the representative of the other revolutionary democracy—as well as the tension between his own ideas of what a Republic ought to be like and the evidence before his eyes of what the nascent French democracy was becoming—that make his diary of the French Revolution one of the major documents of French, as well as American, history. His experience in France soured him for life, by the way, on the idea of democracy, and on his return to America he became a close-minded regionalist.

---

from

A Diary of the French Revolution

Sunday 12.—This Morning I begin to take Bark by itself and the Stomach is no longer out of Humour. Write all the Morning. Dine with the Maréchal de Castries who enquires very kindly the State of my Business. I tell him that I am about to conclude an indirect Agreement for 10,000 h^{ds} at 31$^{\#}$, instead of 20,000 at 36$^{\#}$, because *un mauvais Accomodement vaut mieux qu'un bon Procés.* He agrees in this Sentiment and is glad that my Voyage has not been wholly fruitless. He tells me that he is in Town for a few Days which he devotes to Business & therefore enquires how mine goes on. As I am going away he takes me aside and informs me that Mr Neckar is no longer in Place. He is much affected at this Intelligence, and indeed so am I. Urge him to go immediately to Versailles. He says he will not; that they have undoubtedly taken all their Measures before this Movement and therefore he must be too late. I tell him that it is not too late to warn the King of his Danger which is infinitely greater than he imagines. That his Army will not fight against the Nation, and that if he listens to violent Counsels the Nation will undoubtedly be against him. That the Sword has fallen imperceptibly from his Hand, and that the Sovereignty of this Nation is in the Assemblée Nationale. He makes no precise Answer to this but is very deeply affected. He tells me that if he stays longer in Town he will inform me, that we may see each other again. Call on Madame de La Suze who is not at Home, and then on Madame de Puisignieu who is just going out of Town; as He did not intend to depart untill ToMorrow Evening I presume that he has received Orders in Consequences of the new Arrangements. Call agreably to my Promise on Madame de Flahaut. Learn that the whole Administration is routed and M.ʳ Neckar banished. Much Alarm here. Paris begins to be in Commotion, and from the Invalid Guard of the Louvre a few of the Nobility take a Drum and beat to Arms. Mons.ʳ de Narbonne, the friend of Madame de Stahl, considers a civil War as inevitable and is about to join his Regiment, being as he says in a Conflict between the Dictates of his Duty and of his Conscience. I tell him that I know of no Duty but that which Conscience dictates. I presume that his Conscience will dictate to join the strongest Side. The little humpbacked Abbé Bertrand, after sallying out in a Fiacre, returns frightened because of a large Mob in the Rue S.ᵗ Honoré, and presently comes in another Abbé who is of the Parliament and who, rejoicing inwardly at the Change, is confoundedly frightened at the Commotions. I calm the Fears of Madame, whose Husband is mad and in a printed List, it seems, of the furious Aristocrats. Offer to conduct the Abbés safely Home, which Offer Bertrand accepts of. His Terror as we go along is truly diverting. As we approach the Rue S.ᵗ Honoré his Imagination magnifies the ordinary Passengers into a vast Mob, and I can scarcely perswade him to trust his Eyes instead of his Fears. Having set him down, I depart for M.ʳ Jefferson's; in riding along the Boulevards, all at once the Carriages, Horses and Foot Passengers turn about and pass rapidly. Presently after we meet a Body of Cavalry with their Sabres drawn, and coming Half Speed. After they have passed us a little Way they stop. When we come to the Place Louis Quinze observe the People, to the Number of perhaps an hundred,

picking up Stones, and on looking back find that the Cavalry are returning. Stop at the Angle to see the Fray, if any. The People take Post among
the Stone which lies scattered about the whole Place, being there hewn
for the Bridge now building. The Officer at the Head of this Party is
saluted by a Stone and immediately turns his Horse in a menacing Manner towards the Assailant. But his Adversaries are posted in Ground where
the Cavalry cannot act. He pursues his Route therefore and the Pace is
soon encreased to a Gallop amid a Shower of Stones. One of the Soldiers
is either knocked from his Horse or the Horse falls under him. He is taken
Prisoner and at first ill treated. They had fired several Pistols but without
Effect, probably they were not even charged with Ball. A Party of the
Swiss Guards are posted in the Champs Elisées with Cannon. Proceed to
M.ʳ Jefferson's. He tells me that M.ʳ Neckar received Yesterday about
Noon a Letter from the King, by the Hands of Monsieur de La Luzerne,
in which he orders him to leave the Kingdom, and at the same Time
Mons.ʳ de La Luzerne is desired to exact a Promise that he will not men-
tion the Matter to any Body. M.ʳ Neckar dines, and proposes to his Wife a
Visit to a female friend in the Neighbourhood. On the Route he commu-
nicates the Intelligence and they go to a Country Seat, make the needful
Arrangements and depart. M.ʳ de Montmorin immediately resigned, and
is now in Paris. In returning from M.ʳ Jefferson's I am turned off to the left
by the Vidette posted on the Road to the Place Louis Quinze. Go to Club.
A Gentleman just arrived from Versailles gives us an Account of the New
Administration. The People are employed in breaking open the Armor-
ers' Shops, and presently a large Body of the Gardes Françoises appear
with Bayonets fixed, in the Garden, mingled with the Mob, some of
whom are also armed. These poor Fellows have passed the Rubicon with
a Witness. Success or a Halter must now be their Motto. I think the Court
will again recede, and if they do, all farther Efforts will be idle. If they do
not, a Civil War is among the Events most probably. If the Representatives of the Tiers have formed a just Estimate of their Constituents, in ten
Days all France will be in Commotion. The little Affray which I have witnessed will probably be magnified into a bloody Battle before it reaches
the Frontiers, and in that Case an infinity of Corps Bourgeois will march
to the Relief of the Capital. They had better gather in the Harvest. Return
Home. This has been a pleasant Day and the Evening is cool.

Monday 13.—The Health begins to be reestablished. La Caze calls; I
desire him to urge M.ʳ Le Norm.ᵈ to get the Affair finished with the Farm.

Read him a Part of M.ʳ Ross's Letter. He asks my Advice and I treat the Question somewhat indignantly. Martin comes in and tells me that the Hôtel de Force is forced and all the Prisoners out. Presently after a Letter is brought to him, enclosing one to me from M.ʳ Nesbitt who is at the Temple and wishes to see me, but my Cocher tells me he cannot bring my Carriage, having already been stopped and turned back. In Effect, the little City of Paris is in as fine a Tumult as any one could wish. They are getting Arms wherever they can find any. Seize sixty Barrils of Powder in a Boat on the Seine. Break into the Monastery of S.ᵗ Lazar and find a Store of Grain which the holy Brotherhood had laid in. Immediately it is put into Carts and sent to the Market, and on every Cart a Friar. The Garde-meuble du Roy is attacked and the Arms are delivered up, to prevent worse Consequences. These however are more curious than useful. But the Detail of the Variety of this Day's Deeds would be endless. Dine at Home and La Caze dines with me. After Dinner dress and walk to the Louvre, having previously ornamented my Hat with a green Bow in Honor of the Tier, for this is the Fashion of the Day which every Body is obliged to comply with who means to march in Peace. It is somewhat whimsical that this Day of Violence and Tumult is the only one in which I have dared to walk the Streets, but as no Carriages are abroad but the Fiacres I do not hazard being crushed, and I apprehend nothing from the Populace. Madame de Flahaut is under great Apprehension, which I endeavor to appease. Capellis comes in, and when we are about to set off for the Palais royal we meet on the Stairs Mons.ʳ de —— from Versailles, who tells us the News there. Go to Club and sit awhile chatting on the State of Public Affairs. Mons.ʳ de Moreton tells us that the present Ministers are a Set of Rascals & Tyrants; that he knows them perfectly well; and one of them it seems is his Relation, for whom however he exhibits no Partiality. After a while Mons.ʳ de —— arrives from Versailles and tells us that the fashion at Court this Day is to believe that the Disturbances at Paris are very trifling. The Assemblée Nationale have addressed the King to recall the former Ministry, and to permit the Assembly to send a Deputation to Paris to recommend the forming des Corps Bourgeois for the Maintenance of Order in the City. To the first he replied that the Executive Power is his and he will appoint who he pleases to be his Ministers, and he disapproves of the second Measure. In Consequence of this the Assembly make some sharp Resolutions, whose Purport seems to be the devoting to public Infamy the present Administration and declaring his Majesty's Advisers to be guilty of high Treason. Thus the Court and popular Party are already pitted against each other. In ten Days I think it will be decided whether the Retreat of the Monarch will be immediate and only ruin his Counsellors, or whether it will be remote and his own Ruin involved in that of his Ministers. Some Horses are brought into the Garden of the Palais Royal. We go to see what they are, but cannot learn. We are told however by one of the Orators, that they have received a Deputation from the two Regiments quartered at St Denis, offering to join the Tiers if they will come out and receive them. My Companions urge them by all Means to go, but this Manœuvre must at least be deferred till ToMorrow. The Leaders here I think err in not bringing about immediately some pretty severe Action between the foreign and national Troops. The Consequences would, in my Opinion, be decisive. Return Home. The Weather has been cool and pleasant toDay but this Evening it approaches towards cold. Martin gives me another Note from Mʳ Nesbitt who wants more Money than I can spare. Indeed his Wants surprize me, for he has lived now for three Months on what I have advanced so that he appears to have made no Provision whatever for his Existence in this Country, or else his Friends are so kind as to neglect him entirely and leave the Weight of his Support upon my Shoulders.

Tuesday 14.—This Morning writing. Dress and wait a considerable Time for my Carriage. Send for it and find that the Coachman had determined on having a Holyday. As soon as it arrives, set off for the Temple. Am stopped twice to see if there be any Fire Arms in the Carriage. After waiting a long Time in the Temple, Martin at length finds out Mʳ Nesbitt. He wants to go by Flanders & Holland. For this Purpose 60 to 70 Guineas are necessary. Tell him that I cannot advance him this Money, that the present State of my Finances will not admit of it; offer however to endorse his Note for a hundred and advise him to apply to Mʳ Grand for the Advance of that Sum. Repeat my Opinion that he can go in Safety to Havre and embark there for America. Return Home late and dine. My Dinner is very bad and I feel a Chilliness which I do not like. After Dinner I have Fever. La Caze comes in and brings the Form of a Désistement which I had drawn, agreed to by the Farm. Sit down immediately, copy and sign it, which by no Means relieves the Headache; however Nature must submit sometimes to the Oppression of Circumstances. La Caze is to carry it to Le N.ᵈ and urge a Conclusion, which I hope will be affected ToMorrow. Go to M.ʳ Le Couteulx's. He is very anxious now to get the Affair finished. While sitting here a Person comes in and announces the taking of the Bastile, the Governor of which is beheaded and the Prevost des Marchands is killed and also beheaded; they are carrying the Heads in Triumph thro the City. The carrying of this Citadel is among the most extraordinary Things that I have met with; it cost the Assailants sixty Men it is said. The Hôtel Royal des Invalides was forced this Morning and the Cannon and small Arms &c.ᵃ, &c.ᵃ brought off. The Citizens are by these Means well armed; at least there are the Materials for about thirty thousand to be equipped with, and that is a sufficient Army. I find that the Information received last Night as to the Arrêté of the Assemblée Nationale is not just. They have only declared that the last Administration carry with them the Regret of the Chamber, that they will persist in insisting on the Removal of the Troops and that his Majesty's Advisers, whatever their Rank and Station, are guilty of all the Consequences which may ensue. Yesterday it was the Fashion at Versailles not to believe that there were any disturbances at Paris. I presume that this Day's Transactions will induce a Conviction that all is not perfectly quiet. From M.ʳ Le Couteulx's go to visit Madame de Flahaut who is in much Anxiety. Her Husband, she tells me, is foolhardy, and she apprehends much for his Safety. I am present at a family Scene in which she plays her Part extremely well and appeals to me for my Opinion on one of the Points. I answer that in Discussions of such delicate Nature it is a Rule with me not to interfere. The Question is whether he should leave the City. I advise him if he does, to go at NoonDay &c.ᵃ, &c.ᵃ. While he is sitting with us, Madame having on her Lap an Escritoire, by Way of exciting his Curiosity I scribble some wretched Lines which he asks me to translate for him. Nothing is easier but unluckily one of the Ideas is not calculated to please. It was thus:

> In fever, on your Lap I write,
> Expect then but a feeble Lay,
> And yet in every Proverb's Spite
> Tho 'tis in Verse, believe I pray
>
> No Lover I. Alas! too old
> To raise in you a mutual Flame.
> Then take a Passion rather cold
> And call it by fair Friendship's Name.

She tells me that he looked rather foolish at the Declaration of being too old to excite a Passion. I assure her my Object was only to excite Curiosity. She observes that I succeeded to my Wishes but that it was ridiculous in Monsieur to ask an Explanation because I could have given him the same Translation if the Lines had been entirely different. Return Home and take Tea, being ill. This has been a very cool Day.

Wednesday 15.—This Morning write to Le N^d to urge a Conclusion. La Caze comes in and I give him the Letter, which he is to carry immediately. He has not delivered the Désistement as I expected he would have done. He returns and tells me that Le N^d says it is impossible to do Business this Day, which I fear is true enough; he will try however, but this I doubt. La Caze tells us the King is to come to Town this Day &c^a, &c^a, which I do not believe a Word of. He leaves me and I write. Afterwards dress and wait a long Time for my Carriage, which at last am obliged to send for. Receive a Message from Madam de Flahaut; she wishes to see me this Morning. Walk thither and order my Carriage to follow me when it arrives. Find the Abbé Bertrand there. Sit a few Minutes and tell La Caze's News, with a *nota bene* that I do not believe it, then go for Mr Jefferson's. Am stopped near the Pont Royale and obliged to turn into the Rue St Honoré. Stopped again at the Church St Roch, and a Number of foolish Questions asked. Col^o Gardner comes to me; is very happy to be in Paris at the present Moment. So am I. Considers, as I do, the Capture of the Bastile to be an Instance of great Intrepidity. A few Paces from the Church I am again stopped & a vast Deal of Self Sufficiency in the Officer brings on an Alter-cation with my Coachman. As every Thing is turned into this Street and Interruptions of the Kind I experience are so frequent the *Embarras* is very great. I therefore turn back and come to the Hotel to dine. While I am at Dinner La Caze comes in. He contradicts his News of this Morning but says a Deputy is just arrived from the States General who brings an Account that the King has retreated &c^a, &c^a, &c^a. This I expected. We shall see. After Dinner go to Mr Jefferson's; meet with no Difficulty. Ask him for a Passport for Mr Nesbitt which he refuses, as I expected he would; however, having asked & even urged it I have done all which was in my Power. Go according to my Promise to Madame de Flahaut's. With her Nephew and the Abbé Bertrand we proceed along the Quai to the Tuilleries. Walk a little and sit some Time. She wants to see the Deputies of the Assemblée Nationale come to Town, owns that it is foolish but says that all Women have the like Folly. There is much *Réjouissance* in Town.

After placing Madame at Home her Nephew and I go to Club. I send away my Carriage and presently after receive a Message from her desiring the Loan of it. Send the Servants after the Coachman but it is too late; his Horses are put up and he is patroling as one of the Gardes Bourgeoises. The Duc D'Aiguillon and Baron de Menou are at Club, both of them Deputies of the Noblesse. I learn thro and from them the secret History of the Resolution of this Day. Yesterday Evening an Address was presented by the Assembly, to which his Majesty returned an Answer by no Means satisfactory. The Queen, Count D'Artois and Dutchess de Polignac had been all Day tampering with two Regiments who were made almost drunk and every Officer was presented to the King, who was induced to give Promises, Money, &c.ᵃ, &c.ᵃ, to these Regiments. They shouted Vive la Reine! Vive le Comte D'Artois! Vive la Duchesse de Polignac! and Their Music came and played under her Majesty's Window. In the mean Time the Maréchal de Broglio was tampering in Person with the Artillery. The Plan was to reduce Paris by Famine and to take two hundred Members of the National Assembly Prisoners. But they found that the Troops would not serve against their Country, of Course these Plans could not be carried into Effect. They took Care however not to inform the King of all the Mischiefs. At two o'Clock in the Morning the Duc de Liancourt went into his Bed Chamber and waked him. Told him all. Told him that he pawned his Life on the Truth of his Narration and that unless he changed his Measures speedily all was lost. The King took his Determination, the Bishop D'Autun (they say) was called on to prepare *un Discours*, which he did. The Orders were given for dispersing the Troops; and at the Meeting of the Assembly the King, accompanied by his two Brothers and the Captain of his Guard, came in and made his Speech. This produced very enthusiastic Emotions of Joy, and he was reconducted to the Château by the whole Assembly and by all the Inhabitants of Versailles. They tell me that the Baron de Bezenvald is dénoncé by the *Assemblée Nationale*, which Appellation the King recognizes in his Discours; that they will pursue the present Ministry &c.ᵃ, &c.ᵃ. I give my Opinion that after what is passed the Count D'Artois should not be suffered to stay in France. In this they agree. They say that they will *faire le Procés* of the Maréchal de Broglio & probably of the Baron de Breteuil. Sup with them, and the Claret being better than any I have tasted in France, I give them as a Toast the Liberty of the French Nation and then the City of Paris, which are drank with very good Will. Return Home. This has been a very fine Day. It is said that the King is to be in Town at Eleven o'Clock ToMorrow. But for what?—Bon Mot: the Baron de Bezenval is *dénoncé* on Account of some Letters he had written which were intercepted. The Duke de La Rochefoucault, appointed one of the Deputies from the Assemblée Nationale to the City of Paris, meets the Baron coming out of the King's Cabinet. '*Eh bien! Monsieur le Baron, avez vous encore des Ordres à donner pour Paris?*' The Baron takes it as a *Politesse*. '*Non, Monsieur le Duc, excepté qu'on m'envoie ma Voiture.*'—'*Aparemment c'est une Voiture de Poste, Monsieur le Baron.*'—Another. In the Procession Yesterday the King and Count D'Artois, walking together, were much crowded. One of the Deputies said to another: '*Voyez comme on presse le Roi et Monsieur le Comte D'Artois.*' The other answered: '*Il y a cette Différence pourtant, que le Roi est pressé par l'Amour de ses Peuples.*' To which the King, perhaps not hearing more than the last Words of the Conversation, replied in turning round: '*Oui, c'est juste.*'

Thursday 16.—This Morning La Caze calls and tells me it has been impossible to do any Thing Yesterday, the Farmers being out of Town, but as soon as they return it will be accomplished. Time however wears away. The King, who was to have been in Town this Day, does not come till ToMorrow, being sick. Write to M! Nesbitt. Dine at Home and after Dinner visit at the Marquis de La Fayette's. Thence go to Doctor M!Donald and Madame de La Suze's. Neither of the Three at Home. Call on Madame de Flahaut and thence go to Club. Nothing new. No Certainty as to the Administration. Sup, and drink Claret as a Remedy for my febrile Complaints. This has been a fine Day.

Friday 17.—This Morning my Coachman tells me that there are Placarts up forbidding any Carriages to run, as the King is to be in Town this Day between ten and eleven. Here then is another Day in which Nothing will be done. Dress immediately and go out. Get at a Window (thro the Aid of Madame de Flahaut) in the Rue S! Honoré, thro which the Procession is to pass. In squeezing thro the Crowd my Pocket is picked of a Handkerchief which I value far beyond what the Thief will get for it and I would willingly pay him for his Dexterity, could I retrieve it. We wait from eleven till four. It seems that his Majesty was escorted by the Militia of Versailles to the Point de Jour, where he entered the double File of Parisian Militia which extends from thence to the Hôtel de Ville; each Line composed of three Ranks, consequently it is a Body six deep extending that Distance. The Assemblée Nationale walk promiscuously together in the Procession. The King's Horse Guards, some of the Gardes de Corps, and all those who attend him have the Cockades of the City, viz: Red and Blue. It is a magnificent Procession in every Respect. After it is over, go to Dinner at the Traiteur's and get to a Beef Steak and bottle of Claret. A Deputy from Bretagne, whom I met with formerly at a Table d'hôte at Versailles, comes in and we seat him at our little Table. He tells me that the King Yesterday sent the Assembly a Letter of Recall for M.ʳ Neckar. That the Ministers have all resigned except the Baron de Breteuil, who says he never accepted. That the Count D'Artois, the Duke and Dutchess of Polignac, Mons.ʳ de Vaudreuil, and in short the whole Committee Polignac, have decamped last Night in Despair. I tell him that travelling may be useful to the Count D'Artois and therefore it would be well if he visited foreign Countries. We have a Conversation on the Commerce of their Islands in which I state to him what I conceive to be the true Principle on which their System should be founded. He desires farther Conversation when that Matter shall be agitated. Tell him I am going to London; he desires to have my Address that he may write to me. I promise to let him have it. He mentions Something which interests my Friend the Comtesse de Flahaut. I tell him sundry Truths, the Communication of which will be useful to her, and omit certain others which might prove injurious and thus make an Impression different from what he had received, but I fear the Folly of her Husband and the Madness of his Brother will ruin them both. It is impossible to help those who will not help themselves. I call on her and communicate what has passed, for her Government. Sit awhile with her and the Abbé Bertrand and then go to Club. The King this Day confirmed the Choice made of a Mayor. Gave his Approbation of the Regiment of City Guards &c.ᵃ, &c.ᵃ. He put in his Hat a large Cockade of the Red and Blue Ribbands and then, and not till then, received the general Shouts of Vive le Roi! This Day I think will prove an useful Lesson to him for the Rest of his Life, but he is so weak that unless he be kept out of bad Company it is impossible that he should not act wrongly. Sup at Club and drink Claret, from which within this two Days I have derived much Benefit. The Weather is fine.

Thomas Paine

How strange that at this time of endlessly renewed veneration for the Founding Fathers, Thomas Paine (1737–1809), a kind of lesser left-wing Ben Franklin, remains still just to one side of the pantheon. Best known as the author of the revolutionary pamphlet *Common Sense*, he remains perhaps the only American thinker to have played a crucial role in radical politics in three countries. After several earlier visits, he arrived in Paris for his longest stay in 1792—fleeing an England where he was being tried in absentia for his great work *The Rights of Man*. He was immediately voted French citizenship by the Convention and even elected as a representative, although, as it happened, he did not speak or write a word of French. Utterly fearless, almost to the point of irrationality, he immediately weighed in on what he grasped intuitively would be the great symbolic question of the time: whether or not to execute the King and his family, who had been captured trying to flee Paris the year before. Though a staunch and die-hard Republican, unlike the constitutional monarchist Gouverneur Morris, Paine spoke up movingly and passionately to spare the royal family, grasping that there could be no justification of "ends" or "means," even in a revolution, but only universal principles "of liberty and humanity." Rightly famous in his own time as the first master of an "American style," direct, popular, and unmediated, his speech in Paris remains one of the great plain-spoken statements of the American divergence from the French logic of pure radicalism. He was imprisoned by the Jacobins when they took power and sentenced to death by Robespierre. Saved from the guillotine more or less by accident—he remained furious at the conservative Morris for doing so little on his behalf—he nonetheless remained in France, writing and arguing, until 1802, when he returned to the U.S. to find himself largely neglected in the country he had done so much to make.

———

Shall Louis XVI. Have Respite?

SPEECH IN THE CONVENTION, JANUARY 19, 1793
(Read in French by Deputy Bancal.)

V ery sincerely do I regret the Convention's vote of yesterday for death.
      MARAT [*interrupting*]: I submit that Thomas Paine is incompetent

to vote on this question; being a Quaker his religious principles are opposed to capital punishment. [*Much confusion, quieted by cries for "freedom of speech," on which Bancal proceeds with Paine's speech.*]

I have the advantage of some experience; it is near twenty years that I have been engaged in the cause of liberty, having contributed something to it in the revolution of the United States of America. My language has always been that of liberty *and* humanity, and I know that nothing so exalts a nation as the union of these two principles, under all circumstances. I know that the public mind of France, and particularly that of Paris, has been heated and irritated by the dangers to which they have been exposed; but could we carry our thoughts into the future, when the dangers are ended and the irritations forgotten, what to-day seems an act of justice may then appear an act of vengeance. [*Murmurs.*] My anxiety for the cause of France has become for the moment concern for her honor. If, on my return to America, I should employ myself on a history of the French Revolution, I had rather record a thousand errors on the side of mercy, than be obliged to tell one act of severe justice. I voted against an appeal to the people, because it appeared to me that the Convention was needlessly wearied on that point; but I so voted in the hope that this Assembly would pronounce against death, and for the same punishment that the nation would have voted, at least in my opinion, that is for reclusion during the war, and banishment thereafter. That is the punishment most efficacious, because it includes the whole family at once, and none other can so operate. I am still against the appeal to the primary assemblies, because there is a better method. This Convention has been elected to form a Constitution, which will be submitted to the primary assemblies. After its acceptance a necessary consequence will be an election and another assembly. We cannot suppose that the present Convention will last more than five or six months. The choice of new deputies will express the national opinion, on the propriety or impropriety of your sentence, with as much efficacy as if those primary assemblies had been consulted on it. As the duration of our functions here cannot be long, it is a part of our duty to consider the interests of those who shall replace us. If by any act of ours the number of the nation's enemies shall be needlessly increased, and that of its friends diminished,—at a time when the finances may be more strained than to-day,—we should not be justifiable for having thus unnecessarily heaped obstacles in the path of our successors. Let us therefore not be precipitate in our decisions.

France has but one ally—the United States of America. That is the only nation that can furnish France with naval provisions, for the kingdoms of northern Europe are, or soon will be, at war with her. It unfortunately happens that the person now under discussion is considered by the Americans as having been the friend of their revolution. His execution will be an affliction to them, and it is in your power not to wound the feelings of your ally. Could I speak the French language I would descend to your bar, and in their name become your petitioner to respite the execution of the sentence on Louis.

THURIOT: This is not the language of Thomas Paine.

MARAT: I denounce the interpreter. I maintain that it is not Thomas Paine's opinion. It is an untrue translation.

GARRAN: I have read the original, and the translation is correct.

[*Prolonged uproar. Paine, still standing in the tribune beside his interpreter, Deputy Bancal, declared the sentiments to be his.*]

Your Executive Committee will nominate an ambassador to Philadelphia; my sincere wish is that he may announce to America that the National Convention of France, out of pure friendship to America, has consented to respite Louis. That people, by my vote, ask you to delay the execution.

Ah, citizens, give not the tyrant of England the triumph of seeing the man perish on the scaffold who had aided my much-loved America to break his chains!

MARAT [*"launching himself into the middle of the hall"*]: Paine voted against the punishment of death because he is a Quaker.

PAINE: I voted against it from both moral motives and motives of public policy.

James Gallatin

James Gallatin (1797–1876) was the son of Albert Gallatin, one of the American commissioners sent to Ghent in 1814 to negotiate an end to the War of 1812. Like Henry Adams a half century later working for his father when he was ambassador to the Court of St. James during the Civil War, young James was his father's secretary during the negotiations; he kept a diary throughout their time together in Europe from 1813 to 1827. (His father remained in Europe to become minister to France for the United States.) The diary was given by James to his grandson only in 1875, and it was not published until the 20th century. It gives a matchless, gossipy, at times touchingly ingenuous picture of what, given the events of the previous twenty years, seems to have been a remarkably self-satisfied social life in Paris right after the restoration of the monarchy.

————

from

The Diary of James Gallatin

July 11

I accompanied father to the palace to present his letters. I was amazed at our reception, both by the King and the Prince. Our audience was, of course, private.

Father presented me. Both the King and the Prince expressed themselves as most friendly towards the United States. "Monsieur," the Duc d'Angoulême, and the Duc de Berri were present. The King is old and very fat. Monsieur is rather handsome; the Duc d'Angoulême very stern but with a very kind face; the Duc de Berri very good-looking and very gay and smiling.

Very great etiquette is maintained. They say the King is more strict than even Louis XIV was. We cut a sorry sight in our plain black coats and breeches with all the splendours of the Court uniforms.

The King asked about mamma's health, how she had borne the journey—is really most kind and gracious. Court coaches were sent for us and took us back. Mr. Sheldon followed us in the second coach.

July 30: 21 Rue de l'Université

I have been all day interviewing servants—tall and short, fat and thin—until I can hardly speak. After sorting out what I considered the best, I had them drawn up for father's approval, which I am glad to say he gave.

Major-domo—Callon by name, a very fine person; two house footmen, Edouard and Alfred; two carriage footmen, Louis and Jean; Chef, Monsieur Ratifar, such a great personage (he brings his own kitchen staff); three maids, all pretty—I chose them. I don't know what mamma will say when she sees them. I hate to look at ugly women.

The house is really very fine *entre cours et jardin*. Furniture old but very good. We have to supply our own plate and linen. We have to make some alterations, so mamma and Frances have gone to the Lussacs at Versailles. I have my own valet, Lucien, aged twenty-five—a very important person he thinks himself, valet to a Secretary of Embassy. He will call me *"Excellence."*

August 2

All the morning choosing carriages and horses. Of the latter we got two pairs, very fine for the "Berline," which is all glass in front; this will be for Court and state occasions. A very strong "Brichka" for everyday use, a nice stout little pair for it. A cabriolet for me; any of the big horses will go in single.

August 6

We are really in very good order and the servants excellent. Madame Patterson Bonaparte has written from Geneva asking if she might be allowed to pay us a visit of a few days. She is on her way to America. She arrives on the 10th.

August 7

His Majesty has expressed a wish—in fact, a command—that mamma is to be received in private audience, and has fixed the 9th. Fortunately, she has all her frocks ready. She is to be received in the morning. All the *corps diplomatique* have called, and now it is nothing but returning visits. The de Broglies are still with Madame de Staël at Coppet, but are returning to Paris shortly. The Duc de la Rochefoucauld d'Enville (a distant relation) has been most kind, and has told father what he ought to do and what he ought not to do.

August 10

Mamma was most graciously received. Father accompanied her. She had to wear full Court dress at eleven in the morning. She was first received by the King, who spoke English to her, much to her relief. When she retired from the presence she was escorted by Madame de Duras to the apartments of the Duchesse d'Angoulême. It seems it was most trying. She has not yet recovered from the fatigue, as she is not strong.

August 11

Madame Patterson Bonaparte arrived this morning from Geneva. Her baggage nearly filled the antechamber. She is very lovely, but hard in expression and manner. I don't think she has much heart. Her son seems to be her one thought. She had a very long talk with father about his future (her son's); she is most ambitious for him. She even has a list of the different princesses who will be available for him to marry: as he is only ten years old, it is looking far ahead.

I have but little work to do here. I foresee I will soon be in mischief. Paris is indeed the paradise of young men.

August 12, 1816

Madame Bonaparte's conversation most brilliant. At supper last night she said that when in Paris just after the hundred days, she was at a ball at the British Embassy. She noticed she was much stared at, and that some of the ladies curtsied to her. She asked the Duke of Wellington what it meant, and he told her she was taken for Pauline Bonaparte as she was so strikingly like her, and that people were so amazed at thinking Pauline Bonaparte would have dared come back to France. The Ambassador came up to her at that moment to lead her to supper. This intrigued the company all the more. She is frightfully vain.

August 14

Father had an audience of the King this morning. He suddenly said: "I hear that Madame Jerome Bonaparte is with you. Pray express to her our regret she will not come to our Court, but that we know her reasons for not doing so." When father told her she was much gratified, and said, "That Corsican blackguard would not have been so gracious."

August 15

Madame Bonaparte left to-day for Havre to embark for America. She is such an interesting person, we will miss her. She gave mamma a ruby-velvet frock to cut up for Frances. To father she gave a really beautiful turquoise and diamond brooch. He will never wear it, so I will have it.

August 17

We are very busy with documents to be copied to send to America. The Duc de Richelieu had a very long conference with father yesterday. The latter likes him so much—admires all his fine qualities, particularly his great simplicity, frugality, and above all his honesty.

August 23

I drove my new "curricle" for the first time to-day. I do not know which was the most proud, myself, Lucien, or the horse. It is rather difficult to drive a spirited horse and to keep taking off one's hat every moment. I have to be on the *qui vive* not to fail to return a salute; I will do better when I get to know people's faces better, but now I find it most difficult. I saw many lovely ladies, and I flatter myself some of them saw me. I find they notice much more when I am driving than when I am on foot. Moral—always drive.

I have just come back from walking in the gardens of the Palais Royal. How pretty Frenchwomen are! I know I shall get into all sorts of scrapes. I don't remember if I noted our visit to Monsieur de Lafayette. He is stopping with a Mr. Parker some distance from Paris. He has permission to come to Paris but does not wish to do so at present. His greeting to father was most cordial. We are soon going to see him again. I now find it most difficult to keep up my diary; lately I have neglected it terribly. In the future I will have simply to write when I can find time and from memory. It is work all the morning, receiving for father all kinds and qualities of people; dining out, suppers, theatres, and all sorts and kinds of varied amusements. Hardly time to sleep.

I have made friends with a charming little *danseuse* of the opera, Rosette by name.

A week since I have been able to take up my pen. On Thursday father and mother were commanded to dine with the King—a very great honour it seems, and one reserved for princes and ambassadors. A rather amusing incident happened. After dinner a small reception was held. Amongst the ladies received was a Comtesse de Boigne. She is the daughter of the Marquis d'Osmond, ambassador in England. In a loud tone she expressed her astonishment at the presence of Monsieur Gallatin and his wife to the Prince de Condé. His answer to her was: "His Majesty cannot too highly honour Monsieur Gallatin, as, although representing a new country, his ancestors had served France for generations and one had been a most honoured and intimate friend of Henri IV." It seems this got to the King's ears, who was much annoyed, and when Madame de Boigne made her curtsy he turned his back on her. She called on mamma the next day, and was most gracious and asked too many questions. They say she is the mistress of the Duc d'Orléans, who is not allowed to come back to France.

Madame de Staël has arrived. I went with father to see her to-day; she looks very ill. She had heard of Madame de Boigne's behaviour and was very angry. She said, "That woman is effrontery itself," and "Truth never received her invitation to her christening." Madame Récamier was much amused and told many funny anecdotes about Madame de B. It seems her husband is an Indian nabob who has property at Chambéry. They do not live together but he allows her a large income.

Albertine de Broglie was delightful—so glad to see us and is so natural and unaffected. They are looking for a house, but are at present with her mother. . . .

December

Poor neglected diary! I have broken with Rosette and now dance with the *jeunes filles du monde*. It is not amusing as I take them back to their mothers when the dance is over. We hardly speak a word. How I hate all this etiquette! We dined yesterday at the Duc de Berri's. They were both most gracious; she is like a spoiled child and has very bad manners. The Duke of Wellington was a guest, and after dinner the Duc de Berri spoke most kindly to me. They say he has many friends in the *coulisse* of the opera. He is so gay and cheerful—such a contrast to his father and uncle. They say the Orléans family will soon return to the Palais Royale and they receive in the most informal manner. A great ball at the Duke of Wellington's.

It seems the Royal Family were most rude, but that the duke did not pay any attention and rather put them to shame. Some extraordinary English women were present.

January 1817

I am trying to collect my senses as it has been nothing but a whirl of gaiety. Father insisted upon having a supper Christmas Day: Madame de Staël, the de Broglies, Pozzo di Borgo, Baron Humboldt, Constant Rebecque, Monsieur la Place, the Duc de Richelieu, Chateaubriand, Duc and Duchesse de Clermont-Tonnerre, Rochefoucauld, his son, and a host of others. We sat down thirty-eight. Albert and Frances were allowed to appear on this occasion. Mamma had a huge Christmas-tree in one of the drawing-rooms. Small souvenirs for all. As Pozzo was cutting off some of the presents the tree caught fire: de Broglie pulled off his coat, I followed suit, and we smothered the fire before it did much damage. At midnight mamma had had prepared "egg nog" and "apple toddy," and we all drank each other's health in American fashion. Madame de Staël looks very ill. After all our guests had left I slipped off to the *Maison Dorée*—quite a different company. I managed to slip into the house at 6 o'clock without any of the servants seeing me.

What gaiety there is in Paris this season of the year! Everybody seems cheerful and happy, and all is so bright. Father and I dined on Sunday with the Prince and Prince Galitzin. Katinka Galitzin is pretty and full of fun; we get on capitally. She has much more liberty than French girls, being Russian. The son of the Duc de Caumont la Force is courting her. In the evening a reception at Court. Mamma had excused herself on the plea of illness, but the fact is her religious principles will not allow her to go to any big ball or Court on Sunday. It is a little awkward for father as most of the big Court functions are on Sunday. I forgot to mention the splendid ceremony at Notre Dame on Christmas Eve. The cathedral was in complete darkness save for a few dim lamps. As the bell rang twelve strokes a burst of light and the most beautiful singing I ever heard. The crowd was terrific; several women fainted. I was an hour getting out, so was late for a supper at the *Dorée. Toutes ces "petites dames!"*

What a gorgeous New Year! Visits, visits—nothing but visits. My pockets are empty. *Étrennes* for all the servants, presents to all the family, not forgetting my *coulisse* friends, has cleared me out.

Another Court function on Sunday, which, again on the plea of illness, mamma begged to be excused. His Majesty noticed her absence and most graciously inquired if she were seriously ill. Father, who is so absolutely frank, answered: "Sire, I regret that my wife's religious principles prevent her going to any entertainment on Sunday." The King, instead of being annoyed, answered, "Pray convey our respects to Madame Gallatin, and tell her we honour her principles and her courage." Father was much relieved.

January 9

To our immense surprise, a Court courier arrived this morning to say that his Majesty would in person call at 1.30. No time for any preparations. Father said, "We will receive his Majesty in absolute simplicity, as behoves our republic." He arrived with Monsieur in a very simple coach. Mamma, father, the children, and myself received him under the *perron* in the courtyard. He is very infirm—apologized for not getting out of the carriage. He handed mamma a large roll which was a very fine engraving of himself. Written in English is "To Madam Gallatin, with all the respect due to a woman who has principles. Signed, Louis." He greatly admired Frances, who really promises to be very beautiful. Her complexion, like mamma's, is absolutely perfect. After much bowing, &c. &c., he drove off. It seems no such honour has ever been conferred by him before. Everybody tells father the King pays more attention to him than to anybody else. Comte de Gallatin, our cousin, the Minister from Würtemberg, says he is very jealous. By the way, his story is an odd one. His father was in the service of the Duke of Brunswick when the duke was killed at the Battle of Jena. As he was dying he said to the King of Würtemberg, "I leave to you my most trusted friend." The King took him into his service and created him a Count. Unfortunately, this one only has daughters. We are on the most intimate terms with the family. Poor mamma is quite dazed—the whole system of living is so entirely different from that in America; this, coupled with her want of fluency in French, adds to her troubles. Fortunately, we have been able to obtain the services of an excellent housekeeper. Madame Berthal by name—a Russian who speaks every language under the sun. Nothing ever affects father; he is always pleased, and I have never seen him put out at anything. I really believe if he was given his breakfast at midnight, his dinner at 6 A.M., and his supper at midday he would hardly notice the difference. I have just been seeing the footmen, coachmen, &c., in their new liveries. For ordinary occasions, dark blue plush breeches, yellow waistcoats, and dark blue coats with silver buttons, black silk stockings; state liveries, light blue breeches, white silk stockings, yellow waistcoats, and light blue cloth coats with broad silver braid and silver buttons. The latter is exact, as dark blue does not exist in heraldry.

Father is a little doubtful, fearing Americans may object to so much show, but he feels the Court of France requires it.

Albert's black, Peter, whom we brought from America, showed the cook how to make buckwheat cakes. This came as a complete surprise. Poor mamma burst out crying when she saw them. Frances is taking dancing lessons. I have learnt to cut a "pigeon's wing" and had a great success at the Galitzin's on Sunday evening. . . . Our cousin, Count Gallatin, is most kind; he and his wife have told mamma all that is required of her at Court. We really are in a strange position. Father represents a new republic, and with all his aristocratic relations here much more is expected of mamma, but her manners are so simple and so utterly unaffected that father begs her not to change them in any way.

An accident happened to mamma's *berline* to-day. Turning from the Faubourg St. Honoré into the Rue des Écuries d'Artois, one of the hind wheels caught on the high kerb and was wrenched off. Fortunately, the horses are very quiet and were not frightened. Frances was a little cut by the glass of the window she was sitting by. The English Ambassadress was passing at the time, and very kindly insisted upon taking mamma to the Embassy, which is close by. After having Frances' face seen to she drove mamma home; it was most gracious of her.

I have made the acquaintance of a young American who is studying painting, Grayson by name. He is going to introduce me to the "*grisette* world"; I am looking forward to it. We go to one of the students' balls on Sunday night. I must keep this very quiet, as I fear father would be much annoyed. He does not mind how much I go out in the *grand monde* but he dislikes anything like low life. He never had a youth himself; he was penned up in Geneva, and when he went to America he lived a simple life in the wild parts. I would not care to do anything to annoy him.

My *grisette* ball was not a success—the fact is, it was not fit for any gentleman to go to; I am not particular but there are limits. The men were much worse than the women. How can they degrade themselves to such an extent! They left nothing to the imagination. I was determined to stop to the end, and even went to supper at a restaurant at the Halle. I will never forget the horrible orgie. There were Russian, Spanish, Italian, and Prussian students; they might have been wild beasts from their behaviour. This has been a lesson to me; I am glad of the experience and will profit by it.

At the Elysée Bourbon last evening there was a little singing vaudeville played by children which was very pretty; then supper, and we danced a *contre-danse*, which gave me a chance to cut my "pigeon's wings." I cut eight in succession when my turn came as advancing cavalier.

Madame de Boigne, in that horrid voice of hers, said, *"Très bien, mon jeune Américain."* How I dislike that woman! I cannot help it, she is nothing but pretension. I believe she thinks herself the most important person in France.

I dined at the Russian Embassy yesterday and made such a fool of myself. It was a delightful dinner, and I took in Princess Katinka Galitzin. There was a large *plat monté* of nougat. When it was passed to me the other guests had only taken off some of the ornaments. Princess K. wanted some of the nougat, so I boldly stuck it with a silver fork; I did not think it was so brittle—bang went the whole thing, scattering the nougat in all directions. If the floor had only opened! Bits of the nougat stuck in the ladies' hair, on their necks and shoulders. I was filled with confusion. Pozzo di Borgo exclaimed, *"Voila l'Américain qui attaque la citadelle de Russie."* This caused a general laugh and put everybody in a good humour. I have not got over it yet. I think the ladies forgave me as I am so young.

Mamma is so tiresome. When we were children, every Saturday night we had to take a powder and in the morning a black draught—always administered by mamma in person. She really forgets I am no longer a child; it is all very well for Frances and Albert. I had a bad headache for several days, and asked mamma's maid to give me a powder. To my horror, at 6 o'clock this morning (without knocking) in walked mamma with a black draught in her hand and a frilled nightcap on her head. No use resisting; but as she left the room I said, *"Merci, Madame l'Ambassadrice."* I don't think she quite liked the tone I said it in. . . .

Tuesday

I am in horrible disgrace. The Russian Ambassador gave mamma a beautiful cat. It is always in a large basket in her boudoir. Yesterday some people were coming to *déjeuner.* I was early and alone in the boudoir where we always assemble when *en petite committée.* Mamma had been sent a quantity of Madonna lilies which were in a vase. I do not know what possessed me, but I took one up and commenced to "annunciate" the cat in solemn tones. I had my back to the door, when I suddenly heard my name pronounced—"James," but in such a tone as only mamma can say it. I was saved for the moment by the Duc and Duchesse de Clermont-Tonnerre being announced. I hardly dared speak at table as I knew I was in disgrace. Dear mamma's French is very doubtful, and she never can get a name right. There was a pause in the general conversation. She turned to the duke and said, "How is Madame de Bidé," meaning Madame de Budé, the grandmother of the duchess. This was really too much for me. I exploded, and fortunately choked, and had hurriedly to leave the table. When I returned naturally I apologized, but I might have fallen into the middle of Stonehenge from the expression of their faces. Only dear father had a twinkle in his eye. He I know will get me out of this scrape.

Mamma sent for me before supper and I had a *mauvais quart d'heure*. I humbly apologized and was most repentant. I then threw my arms around her and gave her a good hug. She gave me six tracts, one for each day of the week; I promised to read them. The funniest fact of it is that Mourussa, the cat, gave birth to six kittens in the night. I only suggested to father that one might be called Annunciata. He did not answer but looked out of the window.

I am very sorry for mamma; I can see she is not happy. Father is so occupied that I do not think he notices it. It is hard for her: she speaks so little French, has really no friends whom she cares for, and her position is a very difficult one. The Court is so hemmed in by etiquette to which she is not accustomed. She does not understand the ways of Frenchwomen of the *grand monde* and is continually shocked. Indeed I am not surprised the only women she finds anything in common with are the ladies of the English Embassy and some of the English residents in Paris. There are few Americans, and those that are here are mostly in commerce and without education. I went with her two days ago to call on a Mrs. P., the wife of a very rich but common American. They have recently bought a very fine hotel in the Rue de Varennes; they sold all the beautiful old furniture and have refurnished it in execrable taste, but she is evidently very proud of it and insisted upon showing us all the reception-rooms. In one room there was a large bronze replica of a statue by "John of Bologna." For something to say, I admired it. She folded her arms and, with a palpable wink, said, "Bologny done it, but I am going to have pantaloons made for it when I receive." Mamma's face was a study. She relaxed into a smile when the poor woman offered her molasses candy and dough-nuts, saying she made them herself to remind her of home.

Now that the gaieties are over I am hard at work again; the continual writing, copying of documents, and so forth is very trying. Father cannot pin the Duc de Richelieu down to anything definite.

George Ticknor

George Ticknor (1791–1871), writer and historian, was, on his first and only visit to Paris in 1817, perhaps the first recognizably "modern" American in Paris: there on a visit without any political or diplomatic overtones, on his way, as it happened, to school in Germany—there for the conversation, and overwhelmed at every turn not by the futile search for political likeness but by the happy discovery of *différence*. Ticknor, rich by birth and immensely intelligent by nature—he entered Dartmouth at fourteen—somehow found his way, at least for a day or two, to some of the most recherché circles in Paris, including those of Mmes. de Staël and Récamier and the great and gloomy Chateaubriand. They welcomed him as a novelty, and as an audience, as their kind would welcome coming generations of American visitors, and the pleasure he took in their company still resonates in his letters. Ticknor went on to become a professor at Harvard, to write a major three-volume history of the reign of Ferdinand and Isabella, and to be a pillar of Boston intellectual society—the rare kind of scholar, as Hawthorne once noted, who was also a man of the world.

---

from

Life, Letters, and Journals

PARIS, *May 11, 1817.*—At last I have seen Mad. de Staël. Ever since I presented my letters, she has been so ill that her physicians refused her permission to see above three or four persons a day, and those such of her most familiar friends as would amuse without exciting her. Yesterday, however, her son called on me, and told me if I would come and dine with them to-day alone, his mother would see me, whether her physician gave her leave or not. I went, therefore, early, and was immediately carried to her room. She was in bed, pale, feeble, and evidently depressed in spirits; and the mere stretching out her hand to me, or rather making a slight movement, as if she desired to do it, cost an effort it was painful to witness.

Observing, with that intuition for which she has been always so famous, the effect her situation produced on me, she said: *"Il ne faut pas me juger de ce que vous voyez ici. Ce n'est pas mois,—ce n'est que l'ombre de ce que j'etais il y a quatre mois,—et une ombre qui peut-être disparaîtra bientôt.*" I told her that M. Portal and her other physicians did not think so. "*Oui*," said she, while her eye kindled in the consciousness that she was about to say one of those brilliant things with which she had so often electrified a drawing-room,—"*oui, je le sais, mais ils y mettent toujours tant de vanité d'auteur, que je ne m'y fie pas du tout. Je ne me releverai jamais de cette maladie. J'en suis sûre.*" She saw at this moment that the Duchess de Broglie had entered the apartment, and was so much affected by the last remark, that she had gone to the window to hide her feelings. She therefore began to talk about America. Everything she said was marked with that imagination which gives such a peculiar energy to her works, and which has made her so long the idol of French society; but whenever she seemed to be aware that she was about to utter any phrase of force and aptness, her languid features were kindled with an animation which made a strange contrast with her feeble condition. Especially when she said of America,—"*vous êtes l'avant garde du genre humain, vous êtes l'avenir du monde,*"—there came a slight tinge of feeling into her face, which spoke plainly enough of the pride of genius. As I feared to weary her with conversation, I asked her daughter if I should not go; but she said she was glad to see her mother interested, and wished rather that I should stay. I remained therefore half an hour longer,—until dinner was announced,—during which we talked chiefly of the prospects of Europe, of which she despairs.

When I rose to go she gave me her hand, and said, under the impression I was soon going to America, "*Vous serez bientôt chez vous,—et moi j'y vais aussi.*" I pretended not to understand her, and told her I was sure I should see her in Switzerland, much better. She looked on her daughter, while her eyes filled with tears, and said in English, "God grant me that favor," and I left her.

The impression of this scene remained upon us all during the dinner; but in the evening old M. St. Léon and MM. Lacretelle and Villemain (the latter I find to be one of the most eloquent professors in Paris) came in, and gave a gayer air to the party and conversation.

* * *

May 14.—This evening I passed delightfully at Benjamin Constant's. It matters little to me what may be thought of him as a politician. . . . . I care nothing for all his inconsistency, and forget it all when I am in his presence, and listen to the vivacity and wit of his conversation.

There were several distinguished men of letters there this evening. St. Léon, Lacretelle, Schlegel, etc,—two or three women who are at once wits and belles, etc. . . . . .

They were all assembled to hear the Baron de Humboldt read some passages out of an unpublished volume of his travels. This is precisely the sort of society that used to assemble in the coteries of the times of Louis XIV. and XV., and it required no great effort of the imagination to persuade me that I was at a *soirée* of those periods. Everything this evening was purely French; the wit, the criticism, the vivacity, even the good-nature and kindness, had a cast of nationality about them, and took that form which in France is called amiability, but which everywhere else would be called flattery. I was therefore amused, and indeed interested and excited; but the interest and excitement you feel in French society is necessarily transient, and this morning my strongest recollections are of Humboldt's genius and modesty, and his magical descriptions of the scenery of the Orinoco, and the holy solitudes of nature, and the missionaries.

May 16.—M. de Humboldt is certainly one of the most remarkable men I have seen in Europe,—perhaps the most so. I was sitting with him to-day, and, turning round, observed a large Mercator's Chart of the World suspended in front of the table at which he studies, and it seemed to me at the instant to be an emblem of the immensity of his knowledge and genius, which reach on all sides nearly to the limits of human acquirement, and on some have certainly extended to those limits. I have been most surprised at his classical knowledge, at his taste, and familiarity with the ancient and modern languages, for here he might be to a certain degree dispensed from the obligation of extending his researches very far; and yet I know few professed in the depths of "the humanities" who have more just and enlarged notions of classical antiquity; few scholars who understand Greek and Latin as well as he seems to; and no man of the world who speaks the modern languages with more fluency. And these all lie, as it were, out of the periphery of his real greatness; how great must he then be on those subjects to which he has devoted the concentrated efforts of his talents, and where I have not even the little knowledge and power necessary to estimate what he is!

May 17.—I went this morning to hear a lecture from Lacretelle; not because I have any desire to follow his course,—for I have long awakened from the dream in which I supposed I could find instruction in the branches I pursue, in the German way, from French lectures,—but because I wish to know what is the precise style adopted by these men, who are famous at home and even abroad. I have not been so well pleased with the manner of anybody, whose instructions I have heard, as with that of Lacretelle. He has a fine person, a fine voice, excellent command of language, which never permits him to hesitate, and a prompt taste, which never permits him to choose the wrong word. His memory too is remarkable; for, though his department is history, he never uses notes of any kind, and in relating to-day the story of Regulus, he repeated not less than thirty different numbers. I prefer him to the other lecturers I have heard, because there is more seriousness and dignity in his manner, less attempt at point and effect, and in general a greater desire to instruct than I have yet found,—though still even his manner is not simple enough to produce the just effects of instruction. He is, still, to a certain degree, a Frenchman talking brilliantly.

May 18.—This evening, by a lucky accident, I went earlier than usual to Miss Williams's, and found there, by another mere accident, Southey. . . . . There was little company present, and soon after I went in I found myself in a corner with him, from which neither of us moved until nearly midnight. He is, I presume, about forty-five, tall and thin, with a figure resembling the statues of Pitt, and a face by no means unlike his. His manners are a little awkward, but the openness of his character is so great that this does not embarrass him. He immediately began to talk about America, and particularly the early history of New England, with which he showed that sort of familiarity which I suppose characterizes his knowledge wherever he has displayed it. Of Roger Williams and John Eliot I was ashamed to find that he knew more than I did. Roger Williams, he thought, deserved the reputation which Penn obtained, and Eliot he pronounced one of the most extraordinary men of any country. Once, he said, he had determined to write a poem on the war and character of King Philip, and at that time studied the Indian history and manners, which he thinks highly poetical. So near has the Plymouth Colony come to being classical ground! While engaged in these researches, and as he was once travelling in a post-chaise to London, he bought at a stall in Nottingham, Mather's Magnalia, which he read all the way to town, and found it one of the most amusing books he had ever seen. Accident and other occupations interrupted these studies, he said, and he has never taken them up again. He had read most of our American poetry, and estimated it more highly than we are accustomed to, though still he did not praise it foolishly. Barlow's Columbiad, Dwight's Conquest of Canaan, McFingal, etc., were all familiar to him, and he not only spoke of them with discrimination, but even repeated some lines from them in support of his opinion of their merits. By accident we came upon the review of Inchiquin, which, he said, was written in a bad spirit; and he added that he had seldom been so chagrined or mortified by any event of his literary life, as by being thought its author, though he should rather have written the review than the New York answer to it. . . . . He talked with me about the Germans and their literature a good deal, and said if he were ten years younger he would gladly give a year to learn German, for he considered it now the most important language, after English, for a man of letters; and added with a kind of decision which showed he had thought of the subject, and received a good deal of information about it, that there is more intellectual activity in Germany now than in any other country in the world. In conversation such as this three hours passed very quickly away, and when we separated, I left him in the persuasion that his character is such as his books would represent it,—simple and enthusiastic, and his knowledge very various and minute.

May 28.—I dined to day again at Mad. de Staël's. There were few persons there, but she likes to have somebody every day, for society is necessary to her. To-day, however, she was less well, and saw none of us. At another time I should have regretted this; but to-day I should have been sorry to have left the party for any reason, since, beside the Duc de Laval, and M. Barante, whom I already knew, there were Chateaubriand and Mad. Récamier, two persons whom I was as curious to see as any two persons in France whom I had not yet met. The Duchess de Broglie, with her characteristic good-nature, finding how much I was interested in these new acquaintances, placed me between them at dinner, so that I had an opportunity to know something more of them. Mad. Récamier must now be forty or more, though she has not the appearance of so much, and the lustre of that beauty which filled Europe with its fame is certainly faded. I do not mean to say she is not still beautiful, for she certainly is, and very beautiful. Her figure is fine, her mild eyes full of expression, and her arm and hand most beautiful. I was surprised to find her with fair complexion, ... and no less surprised to find the general expression of her countenance anything but melancholy, and her conversation gay and full of vivacity, though at the same time, it should be added, always without extravagance.

Chateaubriand is a short man, with a dark complexion, black hair, black eyes, and altogether a most marked countenance. It needs no skill in physiognomy, to say at once that he is a man of firmness and decision of character, for every feature and every movement of his person announce it. He is too grave and serious, and gives a grave and serious turn to the conversation in which he engages; and even when the whole table laughed at Barante's wit, Chateaubriand did not even smile;—not, perhaps, because he did not enjoy the wit as much as the rest, but because laughing is too light for the enthusiasm which forms the basis of his character, and would certainly offend against the consistency we always require. It was natural for us to talk about America, and he gave me a long and eloquent description of his travels from Philadelphia to Niagara, and from Niagara across the unbroken forests to New Orleans; but I must confess he did not discover that eagerness and vanity on the subject which I think he does in his Martyrs and his Itinerary. . . . . On the contrary, he seemed rather to prefer to talk of Italy and Rome, of which his recollections seemed more lively than of any other part of his travels; and, indeed, I doubt not he would like to return there rather than to revisit any country he has yet seen, for he spoke of Rome as a "place where it is so easy to be happy." His conversation, like his character, seems prompt, original, decisive, and, like his works, full of sparkling phrases, happy combinations and thoughts, sometimes more brilliant than just. His general tone was declamatory, though not extravagantly so, and its general effect that of interesting the feelings and attention, without producing conviction or changing opinion.

* * *

June 2.—I called this morning on Chateaubriand. He is now poor, for his occupation is gone, and he lives in a *hôtel garni*, not far from my lodgings. We talked a good deal about our American Indians, and the prevalent notions of civilizing them; upon which he has the rational opinions that nobody can entertain, I suspect, but one who has seen them. He told me, too, a good deal about his journey across Greece that interested me, and a good deal that would prevent my undertaking a similar excursion, in the assurance that less could be learned from it than I had supposed.

June 5.—Chateaubriand called on me this morning, and asked me to visit him this evening. There were only three or four of his friends there, for Mad. de C—— is ill. He talked a great deal, but was not so much excited—or, as the French call it, *exalté*—as he was at Mad. de Staël's; and, if he was more reasonable in consequence, he was less amusing. His character, however, appeared more amiable to-night. He talked with good-nature and candor of the review in the *Mercure* that cut him up a few days ago so terribly; played with his cat as simply as ever Montaigne did; and went often to see how his wife did. I saw him, therefore, in a new point of view, and one which interested me for him a good deal.

* * *

June 16.—M. Villemain, of the Academy of Paris Faculty of Letters, is so famous an instructor that I have long intended to hear him, but have been prevented until this morning. He is now lecturing on French eloquence, in a desultory and amusing manner I should think, from what I have heard, and this morning he was on Rousseau's *Emile*. The number of his hearers could not have been less than three hundred and fifty, and I endeavored to find out what were the merits or attractions which give him such an extraordinary popularity. They are certainly neither a strong and vigorous eloquence, like Lacretelle's, nor amusing anecdotes and witticisms like those of Andrieux, nor severe instruction like what all good lectures should contain, for he evidently neither seeks nor possesses these merits; but it was what hits the French taste more than any or all three of them: it was an unhesitating fluency, though he spoke extemporaneously and without notes, a great choice of happy and sparkling phrases, though on a subject the most difficult to apply them discreetly, and an abundance of epigrammatic remarks, which seemed almost like arguments, because they struck the imagination so forcibly, and yet were nothing less. In short, it was a kind of amusement which ought to come rather under the great and indefinite class of what is called in France *spectacle*, than what in any country should be considered a part of public instruction. It was, however, fine of the sort.

The evening I passed delightfully at Chateaubriand's, with a few of his friends; most of whom were members of the House of Peers. He was in high spirits, excited, and even *exalté*, and poured out a torrent of rich and various eloquence, which made me almost think better of the language itself than I am accustomed to.

During the beginning of the evening the conversation turned upon the condition of Europe, and he burst upon the discussion by saying, *"Je ne crois pas dans la société Européenne,"* and supported his ominous proposition with a kind of splendid declamation, to which argument would have lent no force. "In fifty years," said he, "there will not be a *legitimate* sovereign in Europe; from Russia to Sicily, I foresee nothing but military despotisms; and in a hundred,—in a *hundred!* the cloud is too dark for human vision; too dark, it may almost be said, to be penetrated by prophecy. *There* perhaps is the misery of our situation; *perhaps* we live, not only in the decrepitude of Europe, but in the decrepitude of the world"; and he pronounced it in such a tone, and with such a look, that a dead silence followed it, and every person felt, I doubt not, with me, as if the future had become uncertain to him. In a few moments, from a natural impulse of selfishness, the question arose, what an individual should do in such a situation. Everbody looked to Chateaubriand. "If I were without a family, I would travel, not because I love travelling, for I abhor it, but because I long to see Spain, to know what effect eight years of civil war have produced there; and I long to see Russia, that I may better estimate the power that threatens to overwhelm the world. When I had seen these I should know the destinies of Europe, I think; and then I would go and fix my last home at Rome. There I would build my tabernacle, there I would build my tomb, and there, amid the ruins of three empires and three thousand years, I would give myself wholly to my God." Now there was not much fanaticism in this; it was the out-breathed despair of the heart of a poet, whose family has been exterminated by one revolution, and who has himself been sacrificed to another; and, though I do not think of the destinies of Europe and the world very much as he does, yet I shall, as long as I live, respect him for what I saw of his feelings to-night.

No American writer has climbed higher or fallen further than Henry Wadsworth Longfellow (1807–1882), and we may think of him, unfairly, as belonging to the high and dry New England aesthetes, or even as a doggerel rhymester. But in his own time his role as a translator, sometimes quite literally, of old Europe to young America was just as important. His translations of Dante and of the "Golden Legend" are still worth reading, and his sense of Europe, though revived throughout his life by his travels, rested primarily on the impressions he took in between 1826 and 1829 when he traveled in France, Spain, Italy, and Germany, arriving in Paris in the perfect month of July in 1826. He stayed in the Monsieur Le Prince on the Left Bank, somewhat unusually out of the Rue de Rivoli circles of most visiting Americans, and his letter home to his brother is a rhapsodic account of that great American experience, the first morning, and weeks in Paris. The surprisingly unsolemn, broken, dash-ridden catalogue of the Parisian "goings on" marks perhaps the first appearance of a style of rhapsodic and disjointed excitement at the sheer spectacle of Paris, an American poetic tone that one will find again later reproduced in the Parisian writing of such un-Longfellowish fellows as Hart Crane and Harry Crosby.

———

Letter to Stephen Longfellow, Jr.

Paris. July. 23rd. 1826.

My dear brother, Rue Mons. Le Prince. 49. St. Germain

After five weeks' residence in Paris I have settled down in something half-way between a Frenchman and a New Englander:—within,—all Jonathan—but outwardly a little of the Parlez-vous. That is to say, I have good home-feelings at heart—but have decorated my outward man with a long-waisted thin coat—claret-coloured—and a pair of linen pantaloons:—and on Sundays and other fête days—I appear in all the glory of a little hard French hat—glossy—and brushed—and rolled up at the sides—it makes my head ache to think of it. In this garb I jostle along amongst the crowds of the Luxembourg, which is the favorite promenade in St. Germain.

From what my own thoughts were, before I saw the Public Gardens of Paris, I imagine that you have no very correct idea of them: at least, I think that I can give you a more perfect conception of them by a short description of any one—say—for instance—the Luxembourg. This is a very extensive and beautiful garden—with long, shady gravel walks over which the tall old trees, which are all regularly planted, form perfect arches—and directly in the center, a valley or lower level of the ground in which are little plats of flowers—rows of orange trees, and a little pond with two beautiful white swans. You descend from the higher grounds to this little vale, which is an amphitheatre, open towards the palace—by flights of stone steps, which here and there interrupt the stone ballustrade around the brink. On the higher grounds, and in an oval,—parallel to this ballustrade, are placed the marble statues of the garden, each upon a high pedestal in a niche cut from the boughs of the trees. This part of the garden is the general lounge and promenade:—and is full of rush-bottomed chairs! Not to an absolute *plenum*,—but a row or two on each side of the walk, where the ladies sit to be looked at—and the gentlemen to look at them, whilst a crowd of both sexes run the gauntlet between them. Here the people gather every evening at about six o'clock and laugh and talk 'till the gates are closed—at 10. It is very pleasant, I assure you to take a high seat in the synagogue here, and review the multitude passing and repassing, in all the ridiculous peculiarity of French dress, and with all the ridiculous variety of French countenance. This must answer for the Luxembourg.

But after all the Boulevards are the most attractive places of resort of a warm summer's evening. These—you know consist of a wide fine street passing round the city like a girdle,—with excellent sidewalks, and a double row of trees on each side. The Italian Boulevards—that division of the whole, which lies to the north—are the oldest and the most frequented. The trees there have gained a noble height and overhang the pathway with their mingled branches, forming a delightful shade at noon-day and a high gloomy arch at night. At the Italian Boulevards are the most splendid Cafés in Paris. There the people of quality crowd in their coaches to taste ice-creams, &c. &c—and persons of every character and description throng the footpath—a living mass—wedged together and moving together, like the crowd in the aisle of a church on the 4th of July! [Memo—who delivered the Oration at Portland this summer?] You cannot conceive what "carryings on" there are there at all hours of the day and

evening! Musicians singing and playing the harp—jugglers—fiddlers,—
jewish cymbals and cat-calls—blind beggars and lame beggars,—and
beggars without any qualifying term, except importunity,—men with
monkeys—raree shows—venders of tooth-picks and cheap wares—Turks
in the oriental costume—Frenchmen with curling whiskers, and round-
plated straw-hats—long skirted coats and tight wrinkled trowsers—real
nankeen-ers—coblers—booksellers with their stalls—little *boutiques*
where no article is sold for more than 15 sous—&c—&c—&c.

At this Boulevard there are several minor theatres where parodies and
farces are performed. But a few months ago a most splendid opera was
brought forward, called "Mars and Venus," and a little while ago I
attended the parody of it at the Theatre of Varieties:—and saw Apollo in
a red hat and striped pantaloons—Vulcan was dressed up in a flame
coloured coat, and a monstrous heavy man played the part of Zephyr—
with a little sugar-loaf hat—blue-coat, tight white pantaloons and the
belly of an alderman! They are very fond of taking off John Bull at all the
little theatres in Paris, and I have seen his lordship represented by a
clumsy fellow of a Frenchman—in a flat hat and deer-skin breechess—
singing "Auld Lang Syn"—with most ludicrous trills and quavers.

I mentioned in one of my letters something about going to reside at
Montmorenci, near Paris. I have given up the idea—for one can live no
cheaper there than at Paris. Besides I am unwilling to leave Madame
Potet—it is such an excellent situation for one to learn the language—and
Madame takes such unwearied pains to instruct me. I am coming on
famously I assure you. Tell all my friends to write me soon, and with my
most affectionate remembrances to all the family—yourself remember
Harry.—

There is a book at home—Belknap's "Foresters"—which I borrowed
of Mr Cushman: with my respects to him—return it if you please.

Ralph Waldo Emerson

Ralph Waldo Emerson (1803–1842) is, like Longfellow, not an American one often associates with wide European horizons and Francophilia, transcendentalism seemingly the one thing that Americans don't search for in France. His account of his visit to Paris in 1833, in the course of a European trip intended to help him recuperate from the recent loss of both his wife and his Unitarian faith, is surprisingly modern in its undreamy account of a cosmopolitan city: "a loud modern New York of a place." "England has built London for its own use. France has built Paris for the world," he announced once, and his Paris is entirely metropolitan. He also recounts a key moment of private vision, when he visited the almost absurdly over-ordered Jardin des Plantes, and was overwhelmed by a mystical vision of a natural universe where all forms are a "property inherent in man the observer"—a vision of occult correspondence between mind and nature that would inspire most of his next poems and prose. If this confirms the skeptic's sense that Emerson's mysticism is the kind that would be born in a Parisian hothouse, it also reminds us that Americans can find in Paris things that no Frenchman would have imagined were there.

———

from

Journal, 1833

Paris, 20 June. My companions who have been in the belle ville before, & wished it to strike me as it ought, are scarce content with my qualified admiration. Certainly the eye is satisfied on entering the city with the unquestionable tokens of a vast, rich, old capital.

We crossed the Seine by the Pont Neuf & I was glad to see my old acquaintance Henry IV very respectably mounted in bronze on his own bridge but the saucy faction of the day has thrust a tricolor flag into his bronze hand as into a doll's & in spite of decency the stout old monarch is thus obliged to take his part in the whirligig politics of his city. Fie! Louis Philippe.

We were presently lodged in the Hotel Montmorenci on the Boulevard Mont Martre. I have wandered round the city but I am not well pleased.

I have seen so much in five months that the magnificence of Paris will not take my eye today. The gardens of the Louvre looked pinched & the wind blew dust in my eyes and (after a short time) before I got into the Champs Elysees I turned about & flatly refused to go farther. I was sorry to find that in leaving Italy I had left forever that air of antiquity & history which her towns possess & in coming hither had come to a loud modern New York of a place.

I am very glad to find here my cousin Ralph Emerson who received me most cordially & has aided me much in making my temporary establishment. It were very ungrateful in a stranger to be discontented with Paris, for it is the most hospitable of cities. The foreigner has only to present his passport at any public institution & the doors are thrown wide to him. I have been to the Sorbonne where the first scientific men in France lecture at stated hours every day & the doors are open to all. I have heard Jouffroy, Thenard, Gay Lussac.

Then the College Royale de France is a similar institution on the same liberal foundation. So with the College du Droit & the Amphitheatre of the Garden of Plants.

I have been to the Louvre where are certainly some firstrate pictures. Leonardo da Vinci has more pictures here than in any other gallery & I like them well despite of the identity of the features which peep out of men & women. I have seen the same face in his pictures I think six or seven times. Murillo I see almost for the first time with great pleasure.

July. It is a pleasant thing to walk along the Boulevards & see how men live in Paris. One man has live snakes crawling about him & sells soap & essences. Another sells books which lie upon the ground. Another under my window all day offers a gold chain. Half a dozen walk up & down with some dozen walking sticks under the arm. A little further, one sells cane tassels at 5 sous. Here sits Boots brandishing his brush at every dirty shoe. Then you pass several tubs of gold fish. Then a man sitting at his table cleaning gold & silver spoons with emery & haranguing the passengers on its virtues. Then a person who cuts profiles with scissors "Shall be happy to take yours, Sir." Then a table of card puppets which are made to crawl. Then a hand organ. Then a wooden figure called   which can put an apple in its mouth whenever a child buys a plum. Then a flower merchant. Then a bird-shop with 20 parrots, 4 swans, hawks, & nightingales. Then the show of the boy with four legs &c &c without end. All these are the mere boutiques on the sidewalk, moved about from place to place as the sun or rain or the crowd may lead them.

4 July. Dined today at Lointier's with Gen Lafayette & nearly one hundred Americans. I sought an opportunity of paying my respects to the hero, & inquiring after his health. His speech was as happy as usual. A certain Lieut. Levi   did what he could to mar the day.

13 July. I carried my ticket from Mr Warden to the Cabinet of Natural History in the Garden of Plants. How much finer things are in composition than alone. 'Tis wise in man to make Cabinets. When I was come into the Ornithological Chambers, I wished I had come only there. The fancy-coloured vests of these elegant beings make me as pensive as the hues & forms of a cabinet of shells, formerly. It is a beautiful collection & makes the visiter as calm & genial as a bridegroom. The limits of the possible are enlarged, & the real is stranger than the imaginary. Some of the birds have a fabulous beauty. One parrot of a fellow, called *Psittacus erythropterus* from New Holland, deserves as special mention as a picture of Raphael in a Gallery. He is the beau of all birds. Then the hummingbirds little & gay. Least of all is the Trochilus Niger. I have seen beetles larger. The *Trochilus pella* hath such a neck of gold & silver & fire! Trochilus Delalandi from Brazil is a glorious little tot—la mouche magnifique.

Among the birds of Paradise I remarked the Manucode or P. regia from New Guinea, the Paradisaea Apoda, & P. rubra. Forget not the Veuve à epaulettes or Emberiza longicauda, black with fine shoulder knots; nor the Ampelis cotinga nor the Phasianus Argus a peacock looking pheasant; nor the Trogon pavoninus called also Couroncou pavonin.

I saw black swans & white peacocks, the ibis the sacred & the rosy; the flamingo, with a neck like a snake, the Toucan rightly called *rhinoceros*; & a vulture whom to meet in the wilderness would make your flesh quiver, so like an executioner he looked.

In the other rooms I saw amber containing perfect musquitoes, grand blocks of quartz, native gold in all its forms of crystallization, threads, plates, crystals, dust; & silver black as from fire. Ah said I this is philanthropy, wisdom, taste—to form a Cabinet of natural history. Many students were there with grammar & note book & a class of boys with their tutor from some school. Here we are impressed with the inexhaustible riches of nature. The Universe is a more amazing puzzle than ever as you glance along this bewildering series of animated forms,—the hazy

butterflies, the carved shells, the birds, beasts, fishes, insects, snakes,—&
the upheaving principle of life everywhere incipient in the very rock
aping organized forms. Not a form so grotesque, so savage, nor so beautiful but is an expression of some property inherent in man the observer,—
an occult relation between the very scorpions and man. I feel the
centipede in me—cayman, carp, eagle, & fox. I am moved by strange
sympathies, I say continually "I will be a naturalist."

There's a good collection of skulls in the Comparative anatomy chambers. The best skull seemed to be English. The skeleton of the Balena
looks like the frame of a schooner turned upside down.

The Garden itself is admirably arranged. They have attempted to clas-
sify all the plants *in the ground*, to put together, that is, as nearly as may be
the conspicuous plants of each class on Jussieu's system.

Walk down the alleys of this flower garden & you come to the enclo-
sures of the animals where almost all that Adam named or Noah preserved
are represented. Here are several lions, two great elephants walking out
in open day, a camelopard 17 feet high, the bison, the rhinoceros, & so
forth all manner of four footed things in air & sunshine, in the shades of
a pleasant garden, where all people French & English may come & see
without money. By the way, there is a caricature in the printshops representing the arrival of the giraffe in Paris, exclaiming to the mob
"Messieurs, il n'y a qu'un bete de plus." It is very pleasant to walk in this
garden.

As I went out, I noticed a placard posted on the gates giving notice that
M. Jussieu would next Sunday give a public herborisation, that is, make
a botanical excursion into the country & inviting all & sundry to accompany him.

15 July. I have just returned from Pere le Chaise. It well deserves a visit
& does honour to the French. But they are a vain nation. The tombstones
have a beseeching importunate vanity and remind you of advertisements.
But many are affecting. One which was of dark slate stone had only this
inscription, 'Mon Pere.' I prefer the "Ci git" to the "Ici repose" as the
beginning of the inscriptions but take the cemetery through I thought the
classics rather carried the day. One epitaph was so singular, or so singular
to be read by *me*, that I wrote it off.

"Ici repose Auguste Charles Collignon mort plein de confiance dans
la bonte de Dieu à l'age de 68 ans et 4 mois le 15 Avril 1830. Il aima et

chercha à faire du bien et mena une vie douce et heureuse, en suivant autant qu'il put, la morale et les lecons des essais de Montaigne et des Fables de la Fontaine."—I notice that, universally, the French write as in the above, *"Here lies Augustus, &c."* & we write, *"Here lies the body of, &c"* a more important distinction than *roi de France* & *roi des Francais.*

I live at *pension* with Professor Heari at the corner of Rue Neuve Vivienne directly over the entrance of the Passage aux Panorames. If I had companions in the City it would be something better to live in the Café & Restaurant. These public rooms are splendidly prepared for travellers & full of company & of newspapers.

This Passage aux Panorames was the first Arcade built in Paris & was built by an American Mr Thayer. There are now probably fifty of these passages in the city. And few things give more the character of magnificence to the city than the suite of these passages about the Palais Royal.

Notre Dame is a fine church outside but the interior quite naked & beggarly. In general, the churches are very mean inside.

I went into the Morgue where they expose for 24 hours the bodies of persons who have been drowned or died in the streets, that they may be claimed by their friends. There were three corpses thus exposed, & every day there are some.

Young men are very fond of Paris, partly, no doubt, because of the perfect freedom—freedom from observation as well as interference,—in which each one walks after the sight of his own eyes; & partly because the extent & variety of objects offers an unceasing entertainment. So long as a man has francs in his pocket he needs consult neither time nor place nor other men's convenience; wherever in the vast city he is, he is within a stone's throw of a patissier, a cafe, a restaurant, a public garden, a theatre & may enter when he will. If he wish to go to the Thuilleries, perhaps two miles off, let him stop a few minutes at the window of a printshop or a bookstall, of which there are hundreds & thousands, and an Omnibus is sure to pass in the direction in which he would go, & for six sous he rides two or three miles. Then the streets swarm with Cabinets de Lecture where you find all the journals & all the new books. I spend many hours at Galignani's & lately at the English Reading Room in the Rue Neuve Augustine where they advertise that they receive 400 journals in all languages & have moreover a very large library.

Lastly the evening need never hang heavy on the stranger's hands, such ample provision is made here for what the newspapers call "nos

besoins recreatifs." More than twenty theatres are blazing with light &
echoing with fine music every night from the Academie Royale de la
Musique, which is the French Opera, down to the Children's Drama; not
to mention concerts, gardens, & shows innumerable.

The Theatre is the passion of the French & the taste & splendour of
their dramatic exhibitions can hardly be exceeded. The Journal in speaking of the opera last night, declares that "Mme D. was received by the
dilettanti of Paris with not less joy than the lost soul by the angels in
heaven." I saw the Opera Gustave performed the other night & have seen
nothing anywhere that could compare with the brilliancy of their scenic
decoration. The moonlight scene resembled nothing but Nature's; and as
for the masked ball, I think there never was a real fancy-ball that equalled
the effect of this.

At the Theatre Francais where Talma played & Madame Mars plays
I heard Delavigne's new piece Enfans d'Edouard excellently performed;
for although Madame Mars speaks French beautifully & has the manners
of a princess yet she scarcely excels the acting of the less famous performers who support her. Each was perfect in his part.

Paris is an expensive place. Rents are very high. All Frenchmen in all
quarters of their dispersion never lose the hope of coming hither to spend
their earnings, and all the men of pleasure in all the nations come hither,
which fact explains the existence of so many dazzling shops full of most
costly articles of luxury. Indeed it is very hard for a stranger to walk with
eyes forward ten yards in any part of the city.

I have been to the Faubourg St. Martin to hear the Abbe Chatel, the
founder of the Eglise Catholique Francaise. It is a singular institution
which he calls his church with newly invented dresses for the priests &
martial music performed by a large orchestra, relieved by interludes of a
piano with vocal music. His discourse was far better than I could expect
from these preliminaries.

Sometimes he is eloquent. He is a Unitarian but more radical than any
body in America who takes that name.

I was interested in his enterprize for there is always something
pathetic in a new church struggling for sympathy & support. He takes
upon himself the whole pecuniary responsibilities of the undertaking, &
for his Chapel in the Rue St Honoré pays an annual rent of 40,000 francs.
He gave notice of a grand funeral fête which is to be solemnized on the
anniversary of the Three Days at that Chapel.

In the printshops they have a figure of the Abbe Chatel on the same picture with Pere Enfant, & Le Templier.

I went this evening into Frascati's, long the most noted of the gambling houses or hells of Paris, & which a gentleman had promised to show me. This establishment is in a very handsome house on the Rue Richelieu.

Several servants in livery were waiting in the hall who took our hats on entering, & we passed at once into a suite of rooms in all of which play was going on. The most perfect decorum & civility prevailed; the table was covered with little piles of Napoleons which seemed to change masters very rapidly but scarce a word was spoken. Servants carry about lemonade, &c but no heating liquor. The house, I was told, is always one party in the game. Several women were present, but many of the company seemed to be mere spectators like ourselves. After walking round the tables, we returned to the hall, gave the servant a franc for our hats, & departed. Frascati has grown very rich.

Go to the Champs Elysées after sunset & see the manifold show. An orchestra, a roundabout, a tumbler, sugar-plum-gambling-tables, harpers, dancers, and an army of loungers.

I went to the Mazarine Library, & Mr Warden kindly introduced me to the seance of the Class of Science in the Institute, & pointed out to me the conspicuous men. I saw Biot, Arago, Gay Lusac, Jouffroy, & others. Several Memoirs were read & some debate ensued thereon.

Visited St Cloud.

Nathaniel Parker Willis

Willis (1806–1867), though hardly a name to conjure with in Franco-American history, seems in retrospect to have done more than any other single writer to set the tone of the American *journalist* in Paris—that tone of appreciative, high-hearted amusement (with a special concentration on food and sex) that runs right from him through to Waverly Root and Irwin Shaw to every issue of the *New York Times* travel section. He first went to Paris in the 1830s on behalf of the *New York Mirror*, as part of one of the first entirely professional exercises in foreign reporting an American had undertaken, an enterprise that kept him in Europe for most of the decade. When his dispatches were collected in 1835 as *Pencillings by the Way*, he became perhaps the most famous American journalist of his time. Unfairly forgotten now, Willis in his day was frequently and very unfairly attacked by his critics for what were seen as his affectations, but beloved by readers for an eye and voice that still seem, even today, preternaturally light, perceptive, and charming. Willis invented the casual voice in American journalism—*Dashes at Life with a Free Pencil*, as he wonderfully titled one of his books—and his account of a typical French breakfast, or of the Louvre in moonlight, or of following a bald French gourmet to his restaurant, or of French families in the Tuileries are still hard to beat for loose-limbed exactitude.

---

from

Pencillings by the Way

There are few things bought with money that are more delightful than a French breakfast. If you take it at your room, it appears in the shape of two small vessels, one of coffee and one of hot milk, two kinds of bread, with a thin, printed slice of butter, and one or two of some thirty dishes from which you choose, the latter flavored exquisitely enough to make one wish to be always at breakfast, but cooked and composed I know not how or of what. The coffee has an aroma peculiarly exquisite, something quite different from any I ever tasted before; and the *petit-pain*, a slender biscuit between bread and cake, is, when crisp and warm, a delightful accompaniment. All this costs about one third as much as the beefsteaks and coffee in America, and at the same time that you are waited upon with a civility that is worth three times the money.

It still rained at noon, and, finding that the usual dinner hour was five, I took my umbrella for a walk. In a strange city I prefer always to stroll about at hazard, coming unawares upon what is fine or curious. The hackneyed descriptions in the guidebooks profane the spirit of a place; I never look at them till after I have found the object, and then only for dates. The Rue Vivienne was crowded with people, as I emerged from the dark archway of the hotel to pursue my wanderings.

A walk of this kind, by the way, shows one a great deal of novelty. In France there are no shop-*men*. No matter what is the article of trade—hats, boots, pictures, books, jewellery, anything or everything that gentlemen buy—you are waited upon by girls, always handsome, and always dressed in the height of the mode. They sit on damask-covered settees, behind the counters; and, when you enter, bow and rise to serve you, with a grace and a smile of courtesy that would become a drawing-room. And this is universal.

I strolled on until I entered a narrow passage, penetrating a long line of buildings. It was thronged with people, and passing in with the rest, I found myself unexpectedly in a scene that equally surprised and delighted me. It was a spacious square enclosed by one entire building. The area was laid out as a garden, planted with long avenues of trees and beds of flowers, and in the centre a fountain was playing in the shape of a *fleur-de-lis*, with a jet about forty feet in height. A superb colonnade ran round the whole square, making a covered gallery of the lower story, which was occupied by shops of the most splendid appearance, and thronged through its long sheltered *pavés* by thousands of gay promenaders. It was the far-famed *Palais Royal*. I remembered the description I had heard of its gambling houses, and facilities for every vice, and looked with a new surprise on its Aladdin-like magnificence. The hundreds of beautiful pillars, stretching away from the eye in long and distant perspective, the crowd of citizens, and women, and officers in full uniform, passing and re-passing with French liveliness and politeness, the long windows of plated glass glittering with jewellery, and bright with everything to tempt the fancy, the tall sentinels pacing between the columns, and the fountain turning over its clear waters with a fall audible above the tread and voices of the thousands who walked around it—who could look upon such a scene and believe it what it is, the most corrupt spot, probably, on the face of the civilized world?

* * *

It is a queer feeling to find oneself a *foreigner*. One cannot realize, long at a time, how his face or his manners should have become peculiar; and, after looking at a print for five minutes in a shop window, or dipping into an English book, or in any manner throwing off the mental habit of the instant, the curious gaze of the passer by, or the accent of a strange language, strikes one very singularly. Paris is full of foreigners of all nations, and of course, physiognomies of all characters may be met everywhere; but, differing as the European nations do decidedly from each other, they differ still more from the American. Our countrymen, as a class, are distinguishable wherever they are met; not as Americans however, for, of the habits and manners of our country, people know nothing this side the water. But there is something in an American face, of which I never was aware till I met them in Europe, that is altogether peculiar. The French take the Americans to be English: but an Englishman, while he presumes him his countryman, shows a curiosity to know who he is, which is very foreign to his usual indifference. As far as I can analyze it, it is the independent self-possessed bearing of a man unused to look up to any one as his superior in rank, united to the inquisitive, sensitive, communicative expression which is the index to our national character. The first is seldom possessed in England but by a man of decided rank, and the latter is never possessed by an Englishman at all. The two are united in no other nation. Nothing is easier than to tell the rank of an Englishman, and nothing puzzles a European more than to know how to rate the pretensions of an American.

On my way home from the Boulevards this evening, I was fortunate enough to pass through the grand court of the Louvre, at the moment when the moon broke through the clouds that have concealed her own light and the sun's ever since I have been in France. I had often stopped, in passing the sentinels at the entrance, to admire the grandeur of the interior to this oldest of the royal palaces; but to-night, my dead halt within the shadow of the arch, as the view broke upon my eye, and my sudden exclamation in English, startled the grenadier, and he had half presented his musket, when I apologized and passed on. It was magically beautiful indeed! and, with the moonlight pouring obliquely into the sombre area, lying full upon the taller of the three *façades*, and drawing its soft line across the rich windows and massive pilasters and arches of the eastern and western, while the remaining front lay in the heavy black shadow of relief, it seemed to me more like an accidental regularity in some rocky glen of America, than a pile of human design and proportion. It is strange how such high walls shut out the world. The court of the Louvre is in the very centre of the busiest quarter of Paris, thousands of persons passing and repassing constantly at the extremity of the long arched entrances, and yet, standing on the pavement of that lonely court, no living creature in sight but the motionless grenadiers at either gate, the noises without coming to your ear in a subdued murmur, like the wind on the sea, and nothing visible above but the sky, resting like a ceiling on the lofty walls, the impression of utter solitude is irresistible. I passed out by the archway for which Napoleon constructed his bronze gates, said to be the most magnificent of modern times, and which are now lying in some obscure corner unused, no succeeding power having had the spirit or the will to complete, even by the slight labor that remained, his imperial design. All over Paris you may see similar instances; they meet you at every step: glorious plans defeated; works, that with a mere moiety of what has been already expended in their progress, might be finished with an effect that none but a mind like Napoleon's could have originally projected.

* * *

I think the most forcible lesson one learns at Paris is the value of time and money. I have always been told, erroneously, that it was a place to waste both. You could do so much with another hour, if you had it, and buy so much with another dollar, if you could afford it, that the reflected economy upon what you *can* command, is inevitable. As to the worth of time, for instance, there are some twelve or fourteen *gratuitous* lectures every day at the *Sorbonne*, the *School of Medicine* and the *College of France*, by men like Cuvier, Say, Spurzheim, and others, each, in his professed pursuit, the most eminent perhaps in the world; and there are the Louvre, and the Royal Library, and the Mazarin Library, and similar public institutions, all open to gratuitous use, with obsequious attendants, warm rooms, materials for writing, and perfect seclusion; to say nothing of the thousand interesting but less useful resorts with which Paris abounds, such as exhibitions of flowers, porcelains, mosaics, and curious handiwork of every description, and (more amusing and time-killing still) the never-ending changes of sights in the public places, from distinguished foreigners down to miracles of educated monkeys. Life seems most provokingly short as you look at it. Then, for money, you are more puzzled how to spend a poor pitiful franc in Paris (it will buy so many things you want) than you would be in America with the outlay of a month's income. Be as idle and extravagant as you will, your idle hours look you in the face as they pass, to know whether, in spite of the increase of their value, you really mean to waste them; and the money that slipped through your pocket you know not how at home, sticks embarrassed to your fingers, from the mere multiplicity of demands made for it. There are shops all over Paris called the *"Vingt-cinq-sous,"* where every article is fixed at that price—*twenty five cents!* They contain everything you want, except a wife and fire-wood—the only two things difficult to be got in France. (The latter, with or without a pun, is much the *dearer* of the two.) I wonder that they are not bought out, and sent over to America on speculation. There is scarce an article in them that would not be held cheap with us at five times its purchase. There are bronze standishes for ink, sand, and wafers, pearl paper-cutters, spice-lamps, decanters, essence-bottles, sets of china, table-bells of all devices, mantel ornaments, vases of artificial flowers, kitchen utensils, dog-collars, canes, guard-chains, chessmen, whips, hammers, brushes, and everything that is either convenient or pretty. You might freight a ship with them, and all good and well finished, at twenty-five cents the set or article! You would think the man were joking, to walk through his shop.

* * *

It is March, and the weather has all the characteristics of New-England May. The last two or three days have been deliciously spring-like, clear, sunny, and warm. The gardens of the Tuileries are crowded. The chairs beneath the terraces are filled by the old men reading the gazettes, mothers and nurses watching their children at play, and, at every few steps, circles of whole families sitting and sewing, or conversing, as unconcernedly as at home. It strikes a stranger oddly. With the *privacy* of American feelings, we cannot conceive of these out-of-door French habits. What would a Boston or New York mother think of taking chairs for her whole family, grown-up daughters and all, in the Mall or upon the Battery, and spending the day in the very midst of the gayest promenade of the city? People of all ranks do it here. You will see the powdered, elegant gentleman of the *ancien régime*, handing his wife or daughter to a straw-bottomed chair, with all the air of drawing-room courtesy; and, begging pardon for the liberty, pull his journal from his pocket, and sit down to read beside her; or a tottering old man, leaning upon a stout Swiss servant girl, goes bowing and apologizing through the crowd, in search of a pleasant neighbor, or some old compatriot, with whom he may sit and nod away the hours of sunshine. It is a beautiful custom, positively. The gardens are like a constant *fête*. It is a holiday revel, without design or disappointment. It is a masque, where every one plays his character unconsciously, and therefore naturally and well. We get no idea of it at home. We are too industrious a nation to have idlers enough. It would even pain most of the people of our country to see so many thousands of all ages and conditions of life spending day after day in such absolute uselessness.

Imagine yourself here, on the fashionable terrace, the promenade, two days in the week, of all that is distinguished and gay in Paris. It is a short raised walk, just inside the railings, and the only part of all these wide and beautiful gardens where a member of the *beau monde* is ever to be met. The hour is four, the day Friday, the weather heavenly. I have just been long enough in Paris to be an excellent walking dictionary, and I will tell you who people are. In the first place, all the well-dressed men you see are English. You will know the French by those flaring coats, laid clear back on their shoulders, and their execrable hats and thin legs. Their heads are fresh from the hair-dresser; their hats are *chapeaux de soie*, or imitation beaver; they are delicately rouged, and wear very white gloves; and those who are with ladies, lead, as you observe, a small dog by a string, or carry it in their arms. No French lady walks out without her lap-dog. These slow-paced men you see in brown mustaches and frogged coats are refugee Poles. The short, thick, agile-looking man before us is General ——, celebrated for having been the last to surrender on the last field of that brief contest. His handsome face is full of resolution, and unlike the rest of his countrymen, he looks still unsubdued and in good heart. He walks here every day an hour or two, swinging his cane round his forefinger, and thinking, apparently of anything but his defeat. Observe these two young men approaching us. The short one on the left, with the stiff hair and red mustache, is *Prince Moscowa*, the son of Marshal Ney. He is an object of more than usual interest just now, as the youngest of the new batch of peers. The expression of his countenance is more bold than handsome, and indeed he is anything but a carpet knight; a fact of which he seems, like a man of sense, quite aware. He is to be seen at the parties standing with his arms folded, leaning silently against the wall for hours together. His companion is, I presume to say, quite the handsomest man you ever saw. A little over six feet, perfectly proportioned, dark silken-brown hair, slightly curling about his forehead, a soft curling mustache, and beard just darkening the finest cut mouth in the world, and an olive complexion, of the most golden richness and clearness—Mr. —— is called the handsomest man in Europe. What is more remarkable still, he looks like the most modest man in Europe, too; though, like most modest *looking* men, his reputation for constancy in the gallant world is somewhat slender. And here comes a fine-looking man, though of a different order of beauty—a natural son of Napoleon. He is about his father's height, and has most of his features, though his person and air must be quite different. You see there Napoleon's beautiful mouth and thinly chiselled nose, but I fancy that soft eye is his mother's. He is said to be one of the most fascinating men in France. His mother was the Countess Waleski, a lady with whom the Emperor became acquainted in Poland. It is singular that Napoleon's talents and love of glory have not descended upon any of the eight or ten sons whose claims to his paternity are admitted. And here come two of our countrymen, who are to be seen constantly together—*Cooper* and *Morse*. That is Cooper with the blue surtout buttoned up to his throat, and his hat over his eyes. What a contrast between the faces of the two men! Morse with his kind, open, gentle countenance, the very picture of goodness and sincerity; and Cooper, dark and corsair-looking, with his brows down over his eyes, and his strongly lined mouth fixed in an expression of moodiness and reserve. The two faces, however, are not equally just to their owners—Morse is all that he looks to be, but Cooper's features do him decided injustice. I take a pride in the reputation which this distinguished countryman of ours has for humanity and generous sympathy. The distress of the refugee liberals from all countries comes home especially to Americans, and the untiring liberality of Mr. Cooper particularly, is a fact of common admission and praise. It is pleasant to be able to say such things. Morse is taking a sketch of the Gallery of the Louvre, and he intends copying some of the best pictures also, to accompany it as an exhibition, when he returns. Our artists do our country credit abroad. The feeling of interest in one's country artists and authors becomes very strong in a foreign land. Every leaf of laurel awarded to them seems to touch one's own forehead. And, talking of laurels, here comes *Sir Sidney Smith*—the short, fat, old gentleman yonder, with the large aquiline nose and keen eye. He is one of the few men who ever opposed Napoleon successfully, and that should distinguish him, even if he had not won by his numerous merits and achievements the gift of almost every order in Europe. He is, among other things, of a very mechanical turn, and is quite crazy just now about a six-wheeled coach, which he has lately invented, and of which nobody sees the exact benefit but himself. An invitation to his rooms, to hear his description of the model, is considered the last new bore.

And now for ladies. Whom do you see that looks distinguished? Scarce one whom you would take positively for a lady, I venture to presume. These two, with the velvet pelisses and small satin bonnets, are rather the most genteel-looking people in the garden. I set them down for ladies of rank, in the first walk I ever took here; and two who have just passed us, with the curly lap-dog, I was equally sure were persons of not very dainty morality. It is precisely *au contraire*. The velvet pelisses are gamblers from Frascati's, and the two with the lap-dog are the Countess N. and her unmarried daughter—two of the most exclusive specimens of Parisian society. It is very off—but if you see a remarkably modest-looking woman in Paris, you may be sure, as the periphrasis goes, that "she is no better than she should be." Everything gets *travestied* in this artificial society. The general ambition seems to be, to appear that which one is not. White-haired men cultivate their sparse mustaches, and dark-haired men shave. Deformed men are successful in gallantry, where handsome men despair. Ugly women dress and dance, while beauties mope and are deserted. Modesty looks brazen, and vice looks timid; and so all through the calendar. Life in Paris is as pretty a series of astonishment, as an *ennuyé* could desire.

But there goes the palace-bell—five o'clock! The sun is just disappearing behind the dome of the "Invalides," and the crowd begins to thin. Look at the atmosphere of the gardens. How deliciously the twilight mist softens everything. Statues, people, trees, and the long perspectives down the alleys, all mellowed into the shadowy indistinctness of fairy-land. The throng is pressing out at the gates, and the guard, with his bayonet presented, forbids all re-entrance, for the gardens are cleared at sundown. The carriages are driving up and dashing away, and if you stand a moment you will see the most vulgar-looking people you have met in your promenade, waited for by *chasseurs*, and departing with indications of rank in their equipages, which nature has very positively denied to their persons.

And now all the world dines and dines well. The *"chef"* stands with his gold repeater in his hand, waiting for the moment to decide the fate of the first dish; the *garçons* at the restaurants have donned their white aprons, and laid the silver forks upon the napkins; the pretty women are seated on their thrones in the saloons, and the interesting hour is here. Where shall we dine? We will walk toward the Palais Royal, and talk of it as we go along.

That man would "deserve well of his country" who should write a "Paris Guide" for the palate. I would do it myself if I could elude the immortality it would occasion me. One is compelled to pioneer his own stomach through the endless *cartes* of some twelve eating-houses, all famous, before he half knows whether he is dining well or ill. I had eaten for a week at Very's, for instance, before I discovered that, since Pelham's day, that gentleman's reputation has gone down. He is a subject for history at present. I was misled also by an elderly gentleman at Havre, who advised me to eat at *Grignon's*, in the *Passage Vivienne*. Not liking my first *coquilles aux huitres*, I made some private inquiries, and found that his *chef* had deserted him about the time of Napoleon's return from Elba. A stranger gets misguided in this way. And then, if by accident you hit upon the right house, you may be eating for a month before you find out the peculiar triumphs which have stamped its celebrity. No mortal man can excel in everything, and it is as true of cooking as it is of poetry. The *"Rochers de Cancale,"* is now the first eating-house in Paris, yet they only excel in fish. The *"Trois Fréres Provençaux,"* have a high reputation, yet their *cotelettes provençales* are the only dish which you can not get equally well elsewhere. A good practice is to walk about in the Palais Royal for an hour before dinner, and select a master. You will know a *gourmet* easily— a man slightly past the prime of life, with a nose just getting its incipient blush, a remarkably loose, voluminous white cravat, and a corpulence more of suspicion than fact. Follow him to his restaurant, and give the *garçon* a private order to serve you with the same dishes as the *bald* gentleman. (I have observed that dainty livers universally lose their hair early.) I have been in the wake of such a person now for a week or more, and I never lived, comparatively, before. Here we are, however, at the *"Trois Freres,"* and there goes my unconscious model deliberately up stairs. We'll follow him, and double his orders, and if we dine not well, there is no eating in France.

James Fenimore Cooper

As Leatherstocking's creator and the first great master of American wilderness and American rectitude, James Fenimore Cooper (1789–1851) is perhaps the most improbable of all the improbable American Francophiles. In fact, though, he knew Paris well and, in his own slightly grudging way, appreciated it. He had written his early novel *The Prairie* in Paris, where he was doing minor diplomatic service, and his *Gleanings in Europe*, published in 1837, was largely devoted to an account of his time in France. Fiercely judgmental and perhaps a tad too easily shocked, he nonetheless had a sharp eye for French manners—and emerges as one of the first Americans to look genuinely hard at Paris while remaining resolutely unimpressed by it.

---

from

Gleanings in Europe

I have had an odd pleasure in driving from one house to another, on particular evenings, in order to produce as strong contrasts as my limited visiting list will procure. Having a fair opportunity a few nights since, in consequence of two or three invitations coming in, for the evening on which several houses where I occasionally called were opened, I determined to make a night of it, in order to note the effect. As Susan did not know several of the people, I went alone, and you may possibly be amused with an account of my adventures: they shall be told.

In the first place I had to dress, in order to go to dinner at a house that I had never entered, and with a family of which I had never seen a soul. These are incidents which frequently come over a stranger, and, at first, were not a little awkward, but use hardens us to much greater misfortunes. At six, then, I stepped punctually into my *coupé*, and gave Charles the necessary number and street. I ought to tell you that the invitation had come a few days before, and, in a fit of curiosity, I had accepted it, and sent a card, without having the least idea who my host and hostess were, beyond their names. There was something *piquant* in this ignorance, and I had almost made up my mind to go in the same mysterious manner, leaving all to events, when happening, in an idle moment, to ask a lady of my acquaintance, and for whom I have a great respect, if she knew a *Madame Dambray*, to my surprise, her answer was—"Most certainly—she is my cousin, and you are to dine there to-morrow." I said no more, though this satisfied me that my hosts were people of some standing. While driving to their hotel, it struck me, under all the circumstances, it might be well to know more of them, and I stopped at the gate of a female friend, who knows every body, and who, I was certain, would receive me even at that unseasonable hour. I was admitted, explained my errand, and inquired if she knew a *M. Dambray*. *"Quelle question!"* she exclaimed—*"M. Dambray est Chancelier de France!"* Absurd, and even awkward, as it might have proved, but for this lucky thought, I should have gone and dined with the French Lord High Chancellor, without having the smallest suspicion of who he was!

The hotel was a fine one, though the apartment was merely good, and the reception, service and general style of the house were so simple that neither would have awakened the least suspicion of the importance of my hosts. The party was small and the dinner modest. I found the *chancelier* a grave dignified man, a little curious on the subject of America, and his wife, apparently a woman of great good sense, and, I should think, of a good deal of attainment. Every thing went off in the quietest manner possible, and I was sorry when it was time to go.

From this dinner, I drove to the hotel of the *Marquis de Marbois*, to pay a visit of digestion. M. de Marbois retires so early, on account of his great age, that one is obliged to be punctual, or he will find the gate locked at nine. The company had got back into the drawing-room, and as the last week's guests were mostly there, as well as those who had just left the table, there might have been thirty people present, all of whom were men but two. One of the ladies was Madame de Souza, known in French literature as the writer of several clever novels of society. In the drawing-room, were grouped, in clusters, the Grand Referendary, M. Cuvier, M. Daru, M. Villemain, M. de Plaisance, Mr. Brown, and many others of note. There seemed to be something in the wind, as the conversation was in low confidential whispers, attended by divers ominous shrugs. This could only be politics, and watching an opportunity, I questioned an acquaintance. The fact was really so. The appointed hour had come, and the ministry of M. de Villèle was in the agony. The elections had not been favourable, and it was expedient to make an attempt to reach the *old* end, by what is called a *new* combination. It is necessary to understand the general influence of political intrigues on certain *coteries* of Paris, to appreciate the effect of this intelligence, on a drawing-room filled, like this, with men who had been actors in the principal events of France, for forty years. The name of M. Cuvier was even mentioned as one of the new ministers. Comte Roy was also named, as likely to be the new premier. I was told that this gentleman was one of the greatest landed proprietors of France, his estates being valued at four millions of dollars. The fact is curious, as showing, not on vulgar rumour, but from a respectable source, what is deemed a first rate landed property in this country. It is certainly no merit, nor do I believe it is any very great advantage; but, I think we might materially beat this, even in America. The company soon separated, and I retired.

From the *Place de la Madeleine*, I drove to a house near the *Carrousel*, where I had been invited to step in, in the course of the evening. All the buildings that remain within the intended parallelogram, which will some day make this spot one of the finest squares in the world, have been bought by the government, or nearly so, with the intent to have them pulled down, at a proper time; and the court bestows lodgings, *ad interim*, among them, on its favourites. Madame de Mirbel was one of these favoured persons, and she occupies a small apartment in the third story of one of these houses. The rooms were neat and well arranged, but small. Probably the largest does not exceed fifteen feet square. The approach to a Paris lodging is usually either very good, or very bad. In the new buildings may be found some of the mediocrity of the new order of things; but in all those which were erected previously to the revolution, there is nothing but extremes in this, as in most other things. Great luxury and elegance, or great meanness and discomfort. The house of Madame de Mirbel happens to be of the latter class, and although all the disagreeables have disappeared from her own rooms, one is compelled to climb up to them, through a dark well of a staircase, by flights of steps not much better than those we use in our stables. You have no notion of such staircases as those I had just descended in the hotels of the *Chancelier* and the *Premier Président*,* nor have we any just idea, as connected with respectable dwellings, of these I had now to clamber up. M. de Mirbel is a man of talents and great respectability, and his wife is exceedingly clever, but they

---

*M. de Marbois was the first president of the Court of Accounts.

are not rich. He is a professor, and she is an artist. After having passed so much of my youth, on top-gallant-yards, and in becketting royals, you are not to suppose, however, I had any great difficulty in getting up these stairs, narrow, steep, and winding as they were.

We are now at the door, and I have rung. On whom do you imagine the curtain will rise? On a *réunion* of philosophers come to discuss questions in botany, with M. de Mirbel, or on artists, assembled to talk over the troubles of their profession, with his wife? The door opens, and I enter.

The little drawing-room is crowded; chiefly with men. Two card tables are set, and at one I recognize a party, in which are three dukes of the *vieille cour*, with M. de Duras at their head! The rest of the company was a little more mixed, but, on the whole, it savoured strongly of Coblentz and the *émigration*. This was more truly French than any thing I had yet stumbled on. One or two of the grandees looked at me as if, better informed than Scott, they knew that General La Fayette had not gone to America to live. Some of these gentlemen certainly do not love us; but I had cut out too much work for the night to stay and return the big looks of even dukes, and, watching an opportunity, when the eyes of Madame de Mirbel were another way, I stole out of the room.

Charles now took his orders, and we drove down into the heart of the town, somewhere near the general post-office, or into those mazes of streets that, near two years of practice, have not yet taught me to thread. We entered the court of a large hotel, that was brilliantly lighted, and I ascended, by a noble flight of steps, to the first floor. Ante-chambers communicated with a magnificent saloon, which appeared to be near forty feet square. The ceilings were lofty, and the walls were ornamented with military trophies, beautifully designed, and which had the air of being embossed and gilded. I had got into the hotel of one of Napoleon's marshals, you will say, or at least into one of a marshal of the old *régime*. The latter conjecture may be true, but the house is now inhabited by a great woollen manufacturer, whom the events of the day have thrown into the presence of all these military emblems. I found the worthy *industriel* surrounded by a groupe, composed of men of his own stamp, eagerly discussing the recent changes in the government. The women, of whom there might have been a dozen, were ranged, like a neglected parterre, along the opposite side of the room. I paid my compliments, staid a few minutes, and stole away to the next engagement.

We had now to go to a little, retired, house on the *Champs-Elysées*.

There were only three of four carriages before the door, and on ascending to a small, but very neat apartment, I found some twenty people collected. The mistress of the house was an English lady, single, of a certain age, and a daughter of the Earl of Dunmore, who was once governor of New York. Here was a very different set. One or two ladies of the old court, women of elegant manners, and seemingly of good information, several English women, pretty, quiet and clever, besides a dozen men of different nations. This was one of those little *réunions* that are so common in Paris, among the foreigners, in which a small infusion of French serves to leaven a considerable batch of human beings from other parts of the world. As it is always a relief to me to speak my own language, after being a good while among foreigners, I staid an hour at this house. In the course of the evening an Irishman of great wit and of exquisite humour, one of the paragons of the age in his way, came in. In the course of conversation, this gentleman, who is the proprietor of an Irish estate, and a Catholic, told me of an atrocity in the laws of his country, of which until then I was ignorant. It seems that any younger brother, or next heir, might claim the estate by turning Protestant, or drive the incumbent to the same act. I was rejoiced to hear that there was hardly an instance of such profligacy known.* To what baseness will not the struggle for political ascendancy urge us!

In the course of the evening, Mr. ——, the Irish gentleman, gravely introduced me to a Sir James De Bathe, adding, with perfect gravity, "a gentleman whose father humbugged the Pope—humbugged infallibility." One could not but be amused with such an introduction, urged in a way so infinitely droll, and I ventured, at a proper moment, to ask an explanation, which, unless I was also humbugged, was as follows.

Among the *détenus* in 1804, was Sir James Michael De Bathe, the father of Sir James Wynne De Bathe, the person in question. Taking advantage of the presence of the Pope at Paris, he is said to have called on the good-hearted Pius, with great concern of manner, to state his case. He had left his sons in England, and through his absence they had fallen under the care of two Presbyterian aunts; as a father he was naturally anxious to rescue them from this perilous situation. "Now Pius," continued my merry informant, "quite naturally supposed that all this solicitude was in behalf of two orthodox Catholic souls, and he got permission from Napoleon for the return of so good a father, to his own country, never

*I believe this infamous law, however, has been repealed.

dreaming that the conversion of the boys, if it ever took place, would only be from the Protestant Episcopal Church of England, to that of Calvin; or a rescue from one of the devil's furnaces, to pop them into another." I laughed at this story, I suppose with a little incredulity, but my Irish friend insisted on its truth, ending the conversation with a significant nod, Catholic as he was, and saying—"humbugged infallibility!"

By this time it was eleven o'clock, and as I am obliged to keep reasonable hours, it was time to go *the* party of the evening. Count Pozzo di Borgo, of the Russian Legation, gave a great ball. My carriage entered the line at the distance of near a quarter of a mile from the *hôtel*; *gendarmes* being actively employed in keeping us all in our places. It was half an hour before I was set down, and the *quadrilles* were in full motion when I entered. It was a brilliant affair, much the most so I have ever yet witnessed in a private house. Some said there were fifteen hundred people present. The number seems incredible, and yet, when one comes to calculate, it may be so. As I got into my carriage to go away, Charles informed me that the people at the gates affirmed that more than six hundred carriages had entered the court that evening. By allowing an average of little more than two to each vehicle, we get the number mentioned.

I do not know exactly how many rooms were opened on this occasion, but I should think there were fully a dozen. Two or three were very large *salons*, and the one in the centre, which was almost at fever heat, had crimson hangings, by way of cooling one. I have never witnessed dancing at all comparable to that of the quadrilles of this evening. Usually there is either too much or too little of the dancing master, but on this occasion every one seemed inspired with a love of the art. It was a beautiful sight to see a hundred charming young women, of the first families of Europe, for they were there of all nations, dressed with the simple elegance that is so becoming to the young of the sex, and which is never departed from here until after marriage, moving in perfect time to delightful music, as if animated by a common soul. The men, too, did better than usual, being less lugubrious and mournful than our sex is apt to be in dancing. I do not know how it is in private, but in the world, at Paris, every young woman seems to have a good mother; or, at least, one capable of giving her both a good tone, and good taste.

At this party I met the ——, an intimate friend of the ambassador, and one who also honours me with a portion of her friendship. In talking over the appearance of things, she told me that some hundreds of *applications for invitations* to this ball had been made. "Applications! I cannot conceive of such meanness. In what manner?" "Directly; by note, by personal intercession—almost by tears. Be certain of it, many hundreds have been refused." In America we hear of refusals to go to balls, but we have not yet reached the pass of sending refusals to invite! "Do you see Mademoiselle ——, dancing in the set before you?" She pointed to a beautiful French girl, whom I had often seen at her house, but whose family was in a much lower station in society than herself. Certainly—pray how came *she* here?" "I brought her. Her mother was dying to come, too, and she begged me to get an invitation for her and her daughter; but it would not do to bring the mother to such a place, and I was obliged to say no more tickets could be issued. I wished, however, to bring the daughter, she is so pretty, and we compromised the affair in that way." "And to this the mother assented!" "Assented! How can you doubt it—what funny American notions you have brought with you to France!"

P. T. Barnum

Barnum in Paris! What an odd idea—the searcher-out of suckers and rubes in a town that, by its own account, produces none. Phineas T. Barnum (1810–1891), the master American showman, was the inventor of most of what's wonderful and a lot of what's phony (and almost all of what's wonderfully phony) in American pop culture. Since he played that role in part by importing European "culture" to America, what was more natural than that he should run back to show the Europeans what the Americans had done with what they'd borrowed? In 1844, when he brought his educated dwarf "General" Tom Thumb to Paris, he had the kind of sensation that later would be caused by Josephine Baker and for some of the same reasons. American oddity = proof of American naturalness. Even the freaks in America were natural gentlemen. First published in his 1869 autobiography *Struggles and Triumphs*, his account of the diplomatic tact with which he finessed the question of Tom Thumb's appearing to the arch anti-Bonapartist King Louis Philippe in his normal impersonation of Napoleon is a byway and, given recent circumstances, maybe even a high-water mark in Franco-American diplomacy.

---

from

Struggles and Triumphs; or, Forty Years' Recollections

I stopped at the Hotel Bedford, and securing an interpreter, began to make my arrangements. The first difficulty in the way was the government tax for exhibiting natural curiosities, which was no less than one-fourth of the gross receipts, while theatres paid only eleven per cent. This tax was appropriated to the benefit of the city hospitals. Now, I knew from my experience in London, that my receipts would be so large as to make twenty-five per cent of them a far more serious tax than I thought I ought to pay to the French government, even for the benefit of the admirable hospitals of Paris. Accordingly, I went to the license bureau and had an interview with the chief. I told him I was anxious to bring a "dwarf" to

Paris, but that the percentage to be paid for a license was so large as to deter me from bringing him; but letting the usual rule go, what should I give him in advance for a two months' license?

"My dear sir," he answered, "you had better not come at all; these things never draw, and you will do nothing, or so little that the percentage need not trouble you."

I expressed my willingness to try the experiment and offered one thousand francs in advance for a license. The chief would not consent and I then offered two thousand francs. This opened his eyes to a chance for a speculation and he jumped at my offer; he would do it on his own account, he said, and pay the amount of one-quarter of my receipts to the hospitals; he was perfectly safe in making such a contract, he thought, for he had 15,000 francs in bank.

But I declined to arrange this with him individually, so he called his associates together and presented the matter in such a way that the board took my offer on behalf of the government. I paid down the 2,000 francs and received a good, strong contract and license. The chief was quite elated and handed me the license with the remark:

"Now we have made an agreement, and if you do not exhibit, or if your dwarf dies during the two months you shall not get back your money."

"All right," thought I; "if you are satisfied I am sure I have every reason to be so." I then hired at a large rent, the Salle Musard, Rue Vivienne, in a central and fashionable quarter close by the boulevards, and engaged an interpreter, ticket-seller, and a small but excellent orchestra. In fact, I made the most complete arrangements, even to starting the preliminary paragraphs in the Paris papers; and after calling on the Honorable William Rufus King, the United States Minister at the Court of France—who assured me that after my success in London there would be no difficulty whatever in my presentation to King Louis Philippe and family—I returned to England.

I went back to Paris with General Tom Thumb and party some time before I intended to begin my exhibitions, and on the very day after my arrival I received a special command to appear at the Tuileries on the following Sunday evening. It will be remembered that Louis Philippe's daughter, the wife of King Leopold, of Belgium, had seen the General at Buckingham Palace—a fact that had been duly chronicled in the French as well as English papers, and I have no doubt that she had privately expressed her gratification at seeing him. With this advantage, and with the prestige of our receptions by Queen Victoria and Prince Albert, we went to the Tuileries with full confidence that our visit and reception would be entirely satisfactory.

At the appointed hour the General and I, arrayed in the conventional court costume, were ushered into a grand saloon of the palace where we were introduced to the King, the Queen, Princess Adelaide, the Duchess d'Orleans and her son the Count de Paris, Prince de Joinville, Duke and Duchess de Nemours, the Duchess d'Aumale, and a dozen or more distinguished persons, among whom was the editor of the official *Journal des Debats*. The court circle entered into conversation with us without restraint, and were greatly delighted with the little General. King Louis Philippe was minute in his inquiries about my country and talked freely about his experiences when he wandered as an exile in America. He playfully alluded to the time when he earned his living as a tutor, and said he had roughed it generally and had even slept in Indian wigwams. General Tom Thumb then went through with his various performances to the manifest pleasure of all who were present, and at the close the King presented to him a large emerald brooch set with diamonds. The General expressed his gratitude, and the King, turning to me, said: "you may put it on the General, if you please," which I did, to the evident gratification of the King as well as the General.

King Louis Philippe was so condescending and courteous that I felt quite at home in the royal presence, and ventured upon a bit of diplomacy. The Longchamps celebration was coming—a day once devoted to religious ceremony, but now conspicuous for the display of court and fashionable equipages in the Champs Élysées and the Bois de Boulogne, and as the King was familiarly conversing with me, I ventured to say that I had hurried over to Paris to take part in the Longchamps display and I asked him if the General's carriage could not be permitted to appear in the avenue reserved for the court and the diplomatic corps, representing that the General's small but elegant establishment, with its ponies and little coachman and footman, would be in danger of damage in the general throng unless the special privilege I asked was accorded.

The King smilingly turned to one of the officers of his household and after conversing with him for a few moments he said to me:

"Call on the Prefect of Police to-morrow afternoon and you will find a permit ready for you."

Our visit occupied two hours, and when we went away the General was loaded with fine presents. The next morning all the newspapers noticed the visit, and the *Journal des Debats* gave a minute account of the interview and of the General's performances, taking occasion to say, in speaking of the character parts, that "there was one costume which the General wisely kept at the bottom of his box." That costume, however,— the uniform of Bonaparte—was once exhibited, by particular request, as will be seen anon.

Longchamps day arrived, and among the many splendid equipages on the grand avenue, none attracted more attention than the superb little carriage with four ponies and liveried and powdered coachman and footman, belonging to the General, and conspicuous in the line of carriages containing the Ambassadors to the Court of France. Thousands upon thousands rent the air with cheers for "General Tom Pouce." There never was such an advertisement; the journals next day made elaborate notices of the "turnout," and thereafter whenever the General's carriage appeared on the boulevards, as it did daily, the people flocked to the doors of the cafés and shops to see it pass.

Thus, before I opened the exhibition all Paris knew that General Tom Thumb was in the city. The French are exceedingly impressible; and what in London is only excitement, in Paris becomes furor. Under this pressure, with the prestige of my first visit to the Tuileries and the numberless paragraphs in the papers, I opened my doors to an eager throng. The élite of the city came to the exhibition; the first day's receipts were 5,500 francs, which would have been doubled if I could have made room for more patrons. There were afternoon and evening performances and from that day secured seats at an extra price were engaged in advance for the entire two months. The season was more than a success, it was a triumph.

It seemed, too, as if the whole city was advertising me. The papers were profuse in their praises of the General and his performances. *Figaro*, the *Punch* of Paris, gave a picture of an immense mastiff running away with the General's carriage and horses in his mouth. Statuettes of "Tom Pouce" appeared in all the windows, in plaster, Parian, sugar and chocolate; songs were written about him and his lithograph was seen everywhere. A fine café on one of the boulevards took the name of "Tom Pouce" and displayed over the door a life-size statue of the General. In Paris, as in London, several eminent painters expressed their desire to paint his portrait, but the General's engagements were so pressing that he found little time to sit to artists. All the leading actors and actresses came to the General's levees and petted him and made him many presents. Meanwhile, the daily receipts continued to swell, and I was compelled to take a cab to carry my bag of silver home at night.

The official, who had compromised with me for a two months' license at 2,000 francs, was amazed as well as annoyed at the success of my "dwarf." He came, or sent a man, to the levees to take account of the receipts and every additional thousand francs gave him an additional twinge. He seriously appealed to me to give him more money, but when I reminded him of the excellent bargain he supposed he was making, especially when he added the conditional clause that I should forfeit the 2,000 francs if I did not exhibit or if the General died, he smiled faintly and said something about a "Yankee trick." I asked him if he would renew our agreement for two months more on the same terms; and he shrugged his shoulders and said:

"No, Monsieur Barnum; you will pay me twenty-five per cent of your receipts when the two months of our contract expires."

But I did not; for I appealed to the authorities, claiming that I should pay only the ordinary theatrical tax, since the General's exhibition consisted chiefly of character imitations in various costumes, and he was more attractive as an actor than as a natural curiosity. My view of the case was decided to be correct, and thereafter, in Paris and throughout France, with few exceptions, I paid only the eleven per cent theatrical tax.

Indeed, in Paris, the General made a great hit as an actor and was elected a member of the French Dramatic Society. Besides holding his levees, he appeared every night at the Vaudeville Theatre in a French play, entitled "Petit Poucet," and written expressly for him, and he afterwards repeated the part with great success in other cities. The demands upon our time were incessant. We were invited everywhere to dinners and entertainments, and as many of these were understood to be private performances of the General, we were most liberally remunerated therefor. M. Galignani invited us to a soiree and introduced us to some of the most prominent personages, including artists, actors and editors, in Paris. The General was frequently engaged at a large price to show himself for a quarter of an hour at some fancy or charitable fair, and much money was made in this way. On Sundays, he was employed at one or another of the great gardens in the outskirts, and thus was seen by thousands of working people who could not attend his levees. All classes became acquainted with "Tom Pouce."

We were commanded to appear twice more at the Tuileries, and we were also invited to the palace on the King's birthday to witness the display of fireworks in honor of the anniversary. Our fourth and last visit to the royal family was by special invitation at St. Cloud. On each occasion we met nearly the same persons, but the visit to St. Cloud was by far the most interesting of our interviews. On this one occasion, and by the special request of the King, the General personated Napoleon Bonaparte in full costume. Louis Philippe had heard of the General in this character, and particularly desired to see him; but the affair was quite "on the sly," and no mention was made of it in the papers, particularly in the *Journal des Debats*, which thought, no doubt, that costume was still "at the bottom of the General's box." We remained an hour, and at parting, each of the royal company gave the General a splendid present, almost smothered him with kisses, wished him a safe journey through France, and a long and happy life.

George Catlin

Catlin (1796–1872) is best known as the first and finest painter of Native American life, so it is surprising to learn that most of his adult life, from 1839 until 1870, was spent in Europe—though what he was doing there, of course, was seeking attention and money for his "gallery" with its collection of Indian pictures. On the whole, he had greater success with it in London and Paris than in America itself, and in 1845 he took the "gallery" complete with a representative cross section of Iowa Indians with him to meet King Louis Philippe in Paris. Not surprisingly, these most "natural" of all the long line of "natural" Americans in Paris, from Ben Franklin to Tom Thumb to the great black jazz musicians, were a big hit with the French public and the French court. Catlin's 1845 report of this encounter of the most original Americans of all with the ancient but soon-to-disappear-for-good monarchy in France is slightly surreal in its collision of cultural styles, but nonetheless (as our grandfathers would have said) does credit to all parties.

------

from

Catlin's Notes of Eight Years' Travels and Residence in Europe

On the morning of the day for their reception the long stem of a beautiful pipe had been painted a bright blue and ornamented with blue ribbons, emblematical of peace, to be presented by the chief to the King. Every article of dress and ornament had been put in readiness, and, as the hour approached, each one came out from his toilet in a full blaze of color of various tints, all with their wampum and medals on, with their necklaces of grizzly bears' claws, their shields, and bows and quivers, their lances and war clubs, and tomahawks, and scalping-knives. In this way, in full dress, with their painted buffalo robes wrapped around them, they stepped into the several carriages prepared for them, and all were wheeled into the *Place Carousel*, and put down at the entrance to the palace. We were met on the steps by half a dozen huge and splendid-looking porters, in flaming scarlet livery and powdered wigs, who conducted us in, and, being met by one of the King's aides-de-camp, we were conducted by him into His Majesty's presence, in the reception-hall of the Tuileries.

The royal party were advancing towards us in the hall, and as we met them Mr. Melody and myself were presented; and I then introduced the party, each one in person, according to his rank or standing, as the King desired. A sort of *conversazione* took place there, which lasted for half an hour or more, in which I was called upon to explain their weapons, costumes, &c., and which seemed to afford great amusement to the royal personages assembled around and amongst us, who were: their Majesties the King and the Queen, the Duchess of Orleans and Count de Paris, the Princess Adelaide, the Prince and Princess de Joinville, the Duke and Duchess d'Aumale, and His Royal Highness the Duke de Brabant.

His Majesty, in the most free and familiar manner (which showed that he had been accustomed to the modes and feelings of Indians), conversed with the chiefs, and said to Jeffrey, "Tell these good fellows that I am glad to see them; that I have been in many of the wigwams of the Indians in America when I was a young man, and they treated me everywhere kindly, and I love them for it. Tell them I was amongst the Senecas near Buffalo, and the Oneidas; that I slept in the wigwams of the chiefs; that I was amongst the Shawnees and Delawares on the Ohio, and also amongst the Cherokees and Creeks in Georgia and Tennessee, and saw many other tribes as I descended the Ohio River the whole length, and also the Mississippi to New Orleans, in a small boat, more than fifty years ago." This made the Indians stare, and the women, by a custom of their country, placed their hands over their mouths, as they issued groans of surprise.

"Tell them also, Jeffrey, that I am pleased to see their wives and little children they have with them here, and glad also to show them my family, who are now nearly all around me. Tell them, Jeffrey, that this is the Queen; this lady is my sister; these are two of my sons, with their wives; and these little lads (the Count de Paris and the Duc de Brabant) are my grandsons; this one, if he lives, will be King of the Belgians, and that one King of the French."

The King then took from his pocket two large gold medals with his own portrait in relief on one side of them, and told me he wished to present them to the two chiefs with his own hand, and wished Jeffrey to explain to them that after presenting them in that way, he wished them to hand them back to him that he might have a proper inscription engraved on them, when he would return them, and silver medals of equal size to each of the others, with their names engraved upon them.

After the medals were thus presented and returned, the War-chief took out from under his robe the beautiful pipe which he had prepared, and advancing towards the King, and holding it with both hands, bent forward and laid it down at His Majesty's feet as a present.

We were now in charge of an officer of the household, who politely led us through the various magnificent halls of the palace, explaining everything as we passed, and at length introduced us into a room with a long table spread and groaning under its load of the luxuries of the season, and its abundance of the *"Queen's chickabobboo."* These were subjects that required no explanations; and all being seated, each one evinced his familiarity with them by the readiness with which he went to work. The healths of the King and the Queen were drank, and also of the Count de Paris, and the rest of the royal family. The *chickabobboo* they pronounced "first rate;" and another bottle being poured it was drank off, and we took our carriages, and, after a drive of an hour or so about the city, were landed again in our comparatively humble, but very comfortable, apartments.

Thus musing and moralizing on the events of the day, I left them to their conversation and their pipe, to attend myself where my presence was necessary, in arranging my collection, and preparing my rooms for their exhibitions. In this I had a real task—a scene of vexation and delay that I should wish never to go through again, and of which a brief account may be of service to anyone of my countrymen who may be going to Paris to open a public exhibition; at least, my hints will enable him, if he pays attention to them, to begin at the right time, and at the right end of what he has got to do, and to do it to the best advantage.

His first step is, for any exhibition whatever, to make his application to the chief of police for his license, which is in all cases doubtful, and in all cases also is sure to require two or three weeks for his petition to pass the slow routine of the various offices and hands which it must go through. If it be for any exhibition that can be construed into an interference with the twenty or thirty theater licenses, it may as well not be applied for or thought of, for they will shut it up if opened.

It is also necessary to arrange in time with the overseer of the poor, whether he is to take one-eighth or one-fifth of the receipts for the hospitals—for the *hospice*, as he is termed, is placed at the door of all exhibitions in Paris, who carries off one-eighth or one-fifth of the daily receipts every night. It is necessary also, if catalogues are to be sold in the rooms, to lodge one of them at least two weeks before the exhibition is to open in the hands of the commissaire de police, that it may pass through the office of the prêfect, and twenty other officers' hands, to be read, and duly decided that there is nothing revolutionary in it; and then to sell them, or to give them away (all the same), it is necessary for the person who is to sell, and who alone can sell them, to apply personally to the commissaire de police, and make oath that he was born in France, to give his age and address, &c., before he can take the part assigned him. It is then necessary, when the exhibition is announced, to wait until seven or eight guards and police, with muskets and bayonets fixed, enter and unbar the doors, and open them for the public's admission. It is necessary to submit to their friendly care during every day of the exhibition, and to pay each one his wages at night, when they lock up the rooms and put out the lights. In all this, however, though expensive, there is one redeeming feature. These numbers of armed police, at their posts, in front of the door, and in the passage, as well as in the exhibition rooms, give respectability to its appearance, and preserve the strictest order and quiet amongst the company, and keep a constant and vigilant eye to the protection of property.

During the time I was engaged in settling these tedious preliminaries, and getting my rooms prepared for their exhibition, the Indians were taking their daily rides, and getting a passing glimpse of most of the out-door scenes of Paris. They were admitting parties of distinguished visitors, who were calling upon them, and occasionally leaving them liberal presents, and passing their evenings upon their buffalo skins, handing around the never-tiring pipe, and talking about the King, and their medals, and curious things they had seen as they had been riding through the streets. The thing which as yet amused the Doctor the most was the great number of women they saw in the streets leading dogs with ribbons and strings. He said he thought they liked their dogs better than they did their little children. In London, he said he had seen some little dogs leading their masters, who were blind, and in Paris they began to think the first day they rode out that one half the Paris women were blind, but that they had a great laugh when they found that their eyes were wide open, and that instead of their dogs leading them, they were leading their dogs. The Doctor seemed puzzled about the custom of the women leading so many dogs, and although he did not in any direct way censure them for doing it, it seemed to perplex him, and he would sit and smile and talk about it for hours together. He and Jim had at first supposed, after they found that the ladies were not blind, that they cooked and ate them, but they were soon corrected in this notion, and always after remained at a loss to know what they could do with them.

On one of their drives, the Doctor and Jim, supplied with a pencil and a piece of paper, had amused themselves by counting, from both sides of the omnibus, the number of women they passed leading dogs in the street, and thus they made some amusement with their list when they got home. They had been absent near an hour, and driving through many of the principal streets of the city, and their list stood thus:

Women leading one little dog 432
Women leading two little dogs 71
Women leading three little dogs 5
Women with big dogs following (no string) 80
Women carrying little dogs 20
Women with little dogs in carriages 31

The poor fellows insisted on it that the above was a correct account, and Jim, in his droll way (but I have no doubt quite honestly), said that "it was not a very good day either."

I was almost disposed to question the correctness of their estimate until I took it into my head to make a similar one, in a walk I was one day taking, from the Place Madeleine, through a part of the Boulevard, Rue St. Honoré and Rue Rivoli, and a turn in the garden of the Tuileries. I saw so many that I lost my reckoning, when I was actually not a vast way from the list they gave me as above, and quite able to believe that their record was near to the truth. While the amusement was going on about the ladies and the little dogs, Daniel, who had already seen many more of the sights of Paris than I had, told the Indians that there was a *dog hospital* and a *dog market* in Paris, both of them curious places and well worth their seeing. This amused the Doctor and Jim very much. The Doctor did not care for the *dog market*, but the *hospital* he *must* see. He thought the hospital must be a very necessary thing, as there were such vast numbers; and he thought it would be a good thing to have a hospital for their mistresses also. Jim thought more of the market, and must see it in a day or two, for it was about the time they should give a feast of thanksgiving, and "a *dog feast* was always the most acceptable to the Great Spirit." It was thus agreed all around that they should make a visit in a few days to the dog market and the dog hospital.

Jim got Daniel to enter the above list in his book as a very interesting record, and ordered him to leave a blank space underneath it, in order to record anything else they might learn about dogs while in Paris.

* * *

The first evening party they were invited to attend in Paris was that of the lady of Mr. Greene, the American banker. They were there ushered into a brilliant blaze of lamps, of beauty, and fashion, composed chiefly of Americans, to whom they felt the peculiar attachment of countrymen, though of a different complexion, and anywhere else than across the Atlantic would have been strangers to.

They were received with great kindness by this polite and excellent lady and her daughters, and made many pleasing acquaintances in her house. The old Doctor had luckily dressed out his head with his red crest, and left at home his huge head-dress of horns and eagles' quills, which would have been exceedingly unhandy in a squeeze, and subjected him to curious remarks amongst the ladies. He had loaded on all his wampum and other ornaments, and smiled away the hours in perfect happiness, as he was fanning himself with the tail of a war eagle, and bowing his head to the young and beautiful ladies who were helping him to lemonade and blanc mange, and to the young men who were inviting him to the table to take an occasional glass of the *"Queen's chickabobboo."* Their heavy buffalo robes were distressing to them (said the Doctor) in the great heat of the rooms, "but then, as the ladies were afraid of getting paint on their dresses, they did not squeeze so hard against us as they did against the other people in the room, so we did not get so hot as we might have been."

It amused the Doctor and Jim very much to see the gentlemen take the ladies by the waist when they were dancing with them, probably never having seen waltzing before. They were pleased also, as the Doctor said, with "the manner in which the ladies showed their beautiful white necks and arms, but they saw several that they thought had better been covered." The many nice and sweet and frothy little things that the ladies gave them in tea-saucers to eat, with little spoons, were too sweet, and they did not like them much; and in coming away they were sorry they could not find the good lady to thank her, the crowd was so great; but the chickabobboo (champagne), which was very good, was close to the door, and a young man with yellow hair and moustaches kept pouring it out until they were afraid, if they drank any more, some of the poor fellows who were dancing so hard would get none.

It has been said, and very correctly, that there is no end to the amusements of Paris; and to the Indians, to whose sight everything was new and curious, the term no doubt more aptly applied than to the rest of the world. Of those never-ending sights there was one now at hand which was promising them and "all the world" a fund of amusement, and the poor fellows were impatient for its arrival. This splendid and all-exciting affair was the King's fête on the 1st of May, 184–, his birthday, as some style it, though it is not exactly such; it is the day fixed upon as the annual celebration of his birth. This was, of course, a holiday to the Indians, as well as for everybody else, and I resolved to spend the greater part of it with them.

Through the aid of some friends I had procured an order to admit the party of Indians into the apartments of the Duke d'Aumale in the Tuileries, to witness the grand concert in front of the palace, and to see the magnificent fireworks and illumination on the Seine at night. We had the best possible position assigned us in the wing of the palace overlooking the river in both directions, up and down, bringing all the bridges of the Seine, the Deputies, and Invalides, and other public buildings, which were illuminated, directly under our eyes. During the day Mr. Melody and Jeffrey and Daniel had taken, as they called it, "a grand drive" to inspect the various places of amusement and the immense concourse of people assembled in them. Of these, the Barrières, the Champs Elysées, &c., they were obliged to take but a passing glance, for to have undertaken to stop and to mix with the dense crowds assembled in them would have been dangerous, even to their lives, from the masses of people who would have crowded upon them. The Indians themselves were very sagacious on this point, and always judiciously kept at a reasonable distance on such occasions. It was amusement enough for them during the day to ride rapidly about and through the streets, anticipating the pleasure they were to have in the evening, and taking a distant view from their carriages of the exciting emulation of the Maypole and a glance at the tops of the thousand booths and "flying ships" and "merry-go-rounds" of the Champs Elysées.

At 6 o'clock we took our carriages and drove to the Tuileries, and, being conducted to the splendid apartments of the Duke d'Aumale, who was then absent from Paris, we had there, from the windows looking down upon the Seine and over the Quartier St. Germain, and the windows in front, looking over the garden of the Tuileries and Place Concorde, the most general and comprehensive view that was to be had from any point that could have been selected. Under our eyes in front, the immense area of the garden of the Tuileries was packed with human beings, forming but one black and dotted mass of some hundreds of thousands who were gathered to listen to the magnificent orchestra of music, and to see and salute, with "Vive le Roi!" "Vive la Reine!" and "Vive le Comte de Paris!" the royal family as they appeared in the balcony. Though it appeared as if every part of the gardens was filled, there was still a black and moving mass pouring through Rue Rivoli, Rue Castiglione, Rue Royale, and Place Concorde, all concentrating in the garden of the Tuileries. This countless mass of human beings continued to gather until the hour when their Majesties entered the balcony, and then, all hats off, there was a shout, as vast and incomputable as the mass itself, of "Vive le Roi! Vive le Roi! Vive la Reine! Vive le Comte de Paris!" The King then, with his chapeau in his hand, bowed to the audience in various directions; so did Her Majesty the Queen and the little Comte de Paris. The band then struck up the national air, and played several pieces, while the royal family was seated in the balcony, and the last golden rays of the sun, that was going behind the Arc de Triomphe, was shining in their faces. Their Majesties then retired as the twilight was commencing, and the vast crowd began to move in the direction of the Seine, the Terrace, and Place Concorde, to witness the grand scene of illumination and "feu d'artifice" that was preparing on the river.

As the daylight disappeared, the artificial light commenced to display its various characters, and the Indians began to wonder. This scene was to be entirely new to them, and the reader can imagine better than I can explain what was their astonishment when the King's signal rocket was fired from the Tuileries, and in the next moment the whole river, as it were, in a blaze of liquid fire, and the heavens burst asunder with all their luminaries falling in a chaos of flames and sparkling fire to the earth! The incessant roar and flash of cannons lining the shore of the river, and the explosion of rockets in the air, with the dense columns of white, and yellow, and blue, and blood-red smoke, that were rising from the bed of the river, and all reflected upon the surface of the water, heightened the grandeur of its effect, and helped to make it unlike anything on earth, save what we might imagine to transpire in and over the deep and yawning crater of a huge volcano in the midst of its midnight eruption.

This wonderful scene lasted for half an hour.

Margaret Fuller

Margaret Fuller (1810–1850) survives in popular literary memory as a kind of lesser lady Emerson—the salon-keeper and mistress of the Boston "conversations" of the 1830s that did much to marry New England piety with political radicalism. But in truth her criticism and journalism can have a hard-edged precision that Emerson himself achieved only fitfully. Fulfilling a lifelong dream, she sailed for Europe in 1846 and spent three winter months in Paris—another American transcendentalist who found she flourished in the worldly city. While there she met George Sand and attended a meeting of the National Assembly. Her quick eye showed her both the virtues of French political life—its quick-wittedness and the relative absence of the kind of fatuous orotundity then (and now) so commonplace back home—while still impressing on her, quite presciently, the need for the "radical reform" that would indeed come two years later, though in France the liberal revolution would hardly achieve its liberal goal. She soon left France for Italy, where she would make her startling marriage to a minor Italian aristocrat, fight for the Italian national cause, and write her history of the Roman revolution—a book tragically lost to American literature when the boat carrying her, along with her husband, baby, and manuscript, sank off the coast of Fire Island on their return voyage in 1850. (Her account of her Paris sojourn appeared in the *New-York Daily Tribune* on May 15, 1847, one of some three dozen letters she had sent home from abroad.)

---

from

Things and Thoughts in Europe

I bade adieu to Paris the twenty-fifth of February, just as we had had one fine day. It was the only one of really delightful weather, from morning till night, that I had to enjoy all the while I was at Paris, from the thirteenth November till the twenty-fifth February. Let no one abuse our climate; even in Winter it is delightful, compared to the Parisian Winter of mud and mist.

This one fine day brought out the Parisian world in its gayest colors. I never saw anything more animated or prettier, of the kind, than the promenade that day in the *Champs Elysées*. Such crowds of gay equipages, with *cavaliers* and their *amazons* flying through their midst on handsome and swift horses! On the promenade what groups of passably pretty ladies, with excessively pretty bonnets, announcing in their hues of light green, peach blossom and primrose the approach of Spring, and charming children—for French children are charming. I cannot speak with equal approbation of the files of men sauntering arm in arm; one sees few fine-looking men in Paris: the air half-military, half dandy, of self-esteem and *savoir-faire*, is not particularly interesting; nor are the glassy stare and fumes of bad cigars exactly what one most desires to encounter, when the heart is opened by the breath of Spring zephyrs and the hope of buds and blossoms.

But a French crowd is always gay, full of quick turns and drolleries; most amusing when most petulant, it represents what is so agreeable in the character of the nation. We have now seen it on two good occasions, the festivities of the new year and just after we came was the *mardi gras*, and the procession of the *Fat Ox*, described, if I mistake not, by Eugene Sue. An immense crowd thronged the streets this year to see it, but few figures and little invention followed the emblem of plenty; indeed few among the people could have had the heart for such a sham, knowing how the poorer classes have suffered from hunger this Winter. All signs of this are kept out of sight in Paris. A pamphlet, called "The Voice of Famine," stating facts, though in the tone of vulgar and exaggerated declamation, unhappily common to productions on the Radical side, was suppressed almost as soon as published, but the fact cannot be suppressed that the people in the Provinces have suffered most terribly amid the vaunted prosperity of France.

While Louis Philippe lives, the gases, compressed by his strong grasp, may not burst up to light; but the need of some radical measures of reform is not less strongly felt in France than elsewhere, and the time will come before long when such will be imperatively demanded. The doctrines of Fourier are making considerable progress, and wherever they spread the necessity of some practical application of the precepts of Christ, in lieu of the mummeries of a worn-out ritual, cannot fail to be felt. The more I see of the terrible ills which infests the body politic of Europe, the more indignation I feel at the selfishness or stupidity of those in my own country who oppose an examination of these subjects—such as is animated by the hope of prevention. The mind of Fourier is, in many respects, uncongenial to mine. Educated in an age of gross materialism, he is tainted by its faults; in attempts to reorganize society, he commits the error of making soul the result of health of body, instead of body the clothing of soul—but his heart was that of a genuine lover of his kind, of a philanthropist in the sense of Jesus—his views are large and noble,—his life was one of devout study on these subjects, and we should pity the person who, after the briefest sojourn in Manchester and Lyons—the most superficial acquaintance with the population of London and Paris,—could seek to hinder a study of his thoughts or be wanting in reverence for his purposes. But always, always, the unthinking mob has found stones on the highway to throw at the prophets.

Amid so many great causes for thought and anxiety, how childish has seemed the endless gossip of the Parisian press on the subject of the Spanish marriage—how melancholy the flimsy falsehoods of M. Guizot— more melancholy the avowal so naïvely made, amid those falsehoods that to his mind expediency is the best policy. This is the policy, said he, that has made France so prosperous.—Indeed, the success is correspondent with the means though in quite another sense than that he meant. I went to the *Hotel des Invalides*, supposing I should be admitted to the spot where repose the ashes of Napoleon, for though I love not pilgrimages to sepulchres, and prefer paying my homage to the living spirit, rather than to the dust it once animated, I should have liked to muse a moment beside his urn, but as yet the visiter is not admitted there. But in the library one sees the picture of Napoleon crossing the Alps, opposite to that of the present King of the French. Just as they are they should serve as frontispieces to two chapters of history.—In the first, the seed was sewn in a field of blood indeed, but the seed of all that is vital in the present period. By Napoleon the career was really laid open to talent, and all that is really great in France now consists in the possibility that talent finds of struggling to the light. Paris is a great intellectual center, and there is a Chamber of Deputies to represent the people very different from the poor, limited Assembly politically so called. Their tribune is that of literature, and one needs not to beg tickets to mingle with the audience. To the actually so-called Chamber of Deputies I was indebted for two pleasures. First and greatest, a sight of the manuscripts of Rousseau treasured in their Library. I saw them and touched them—those manuscripts just as he has celebrated them, written on the fine white paper, tied with ribbon—yellow and faded age has made them, yet at their touch I seemed to feel the fire of youth, immortally glowing, more and more expansive, with which his soul has pervaded this century. He was the precursor of all we most prize; true, his blood was mixed with madness, and the course of his actual life made some detours through villanous places, but his spirit was intimate with the fundamental truths of human nature, and fraught with prophecy: there is none who has given birth to more life for this age; his gifts are yet untold; they are too present with us; but he who thinks really must often think with Rousseau, and learn him even more and more: such is the method of genius to ripen fruit for the crowd by those rays of whose heat they complain.

The second pleasure was in the speech of M. Berryer, when the Chamber was discussing the address to the King. Those of Thiers and Guizot had been, so far, more interesting, as they stood for more that was important—but M. Berryer is the most eloquent speaker of the House. His oratory is, indeed, very good, not logical, but plausible, full and rapid, with occasional bursts of flame and showers of sparks, though indeed no stone of size and weight enough to crush any man was throw out by the crater. Although the oratory of our country is very inferior to what might be expected from the perfect freedom and powerful motive for development of genius in this province, it presents several examples of persons superior in both force and scope and equal in polish to M. Berryer.

Nothing can be more pitiful than the manner in which the infamous affair of Cracow is treated on all hands. There is not even the affectation of noble feeling about it. La Mennais and his coadjutors published in *La Reforme* an honorable and manly Protest, which the public rushed to devour the moment it was out of the press—and no wonder! for it was the only crumb of comfort offered to those who have the nobleness to hope that the confederation of nations may yet be conducted on the basis of divine justice and human right. Most men who touched the subject, apparently weary of feigning, appeared in their genuine colors of the calmest, most complacent selfishness. As described by Körner in the prayer of such a man:

> "O God, save me
> Thy wife, child, and hearth,
> Then my harvest also;
> Then will I bless thee,
> Though thy lightning scorch to
>   blackness all the
> rest of human kind."

A sentiment which finds its paraphrase in the following vulgate of our land:

> "O Lord, save me,
>   My wife, child, and brother Sammy,
>   Us four *and no more*."

The latter clause indeed, is not quite frankly avowed as yet by politicians.

It is very amusing to be in the Chamber of Deputies when some dull person is speaking. The French have a truly Greek vivacity; they cannot endure to be bored. Though their conduct is not very dignified, I should like a corps of the same kind of sharp-shooters in our legislative assemblies when honorable gentlemen are addressing their constituents and not the assembly, repeating in lengthy, windy, clumsy paragraphs what has been the truism of the newspaper press for months previous, wickedly wasting the time that was given us to learn something for ourselves, and help our fellow creatures. In the French Chamber, if a man who has nothing to say ascends the tribune, the audience swarm with the noise of a myriad bee-hives; the President rises on his feet, and passes the whole time of the speech in taking the most violent exercise, stretching himself to look imposing, ringing his bell every two minutes, shouting to the Representatives of the Nation to be decorous and attentive, in vain. The more he rings, the more they won't be still. I saw an orator in this situation, fighting against the desires of the audience, as only a Frenchman could—certainly a man of any other nation would have died of embarrassment rather—screaming out his sentences, stretching out both arms with an air of injured dignity, panting, growing red in the face, the hubbub of voices were stopped an instant. At last he pretended to be exhausted, stopped and took out his snuff-box. Instantly there was a calm. He seized the occasion, and shouted out a sentence; but it was the only one he was able to make heard. They were not to be trapped so a second time. When any one is speaking that commands interest, as Berryer did, the effect of this vivacity is very pleasing; the murmur of feeling that rushes over the assembly is so quick and electric—light, too, as the ripple on the lake. I heard Guizot speak one day for a short time. His manner is very deficient in dignity—has not even the dignity of station; you see the man of cultivated intellect, but without inward strength, nor is even his panoply of proof.

I saw in the Library of Deputies some books intended to be sent to our country through M. Vattemare. The French have shown great readiness and generosity with regard to his project, and I earnestly hope that our country, if it accept these tokens of good-will, will show both energy and judgment in making a return. I do not speak from myself alone, but from others whose opinion is entitled to the highest respect, when I say it is not by sending a great quantity of documents of merely local interest, that would be esteemed lumber in our garrets at home, that you pay respect to a nation able to look beyond the binding of a book. If anything is to be sent, let persons of ability be deputed to make a selection honorable to us and of value to the French. They would like documents from our Congress—what is important as to commerce and manufactures; they would also like much what can throw light on the history and character of our Aborigines. This project of international exchange could not be carried on to any permanent advantage without accredited agents on either side, but in its present shape it wears an aspect of good feeling that is valuable and may give a very desirable impulse to thought and knowledge. M. Vattemare has given himself to the plan with indefatigable perseverance, and I hope our country will not be backward to accord him that furtherance he has known how to conquer from his countrymen.

Harriet Beecher Stowe

Stowe (1811–1896), famous as the one American writer to have indubitably done something big (changing the course of American history with the publication of the anti-slavery novel *Uncle Tom's Cabin* in 1851), deserves to be at least a little bit better known for being a good American writer. And a sharp observer. She went to Paris in 1852 as part of what would now be called a book tour for *Uncle Tom's Cabin*, and while there wrote down her experiences. Even though they appeared under the slightly fatuous title of *Sunny Memories of Foreign Lands* (1854), her observations of what was becoming that set-piece American subject, The Pictures In The Louvre, are admirably original in her championing of the then not-quite-OK Rubens over the then entirely-too-OK Raphael.

———

from

Sunny Memories of Foreign Lands

MY DEAR L.:—

At last I have come into dreamland; into the lotos-eater's paradise; into the land where it is always afternoon. I am released from care; I am unknown, unknowing; I live in a house whose arrangements seem to me strange, old, and dreamy. In the heart of a great city I am as still as if in a convent; in the burning heats of summer our rooms are shadowy and cool as a cave. My time is all my own. I may at will lie on a sofa, and dreamily watch the play of the leaves and flowers, in the little garden into which my room opens; or I may go into the parlor adjoining, whence I hear the quick voices of my beautiful and vivacious young friends. You ought to see these girls. Emma might look like a Madonna, were it not for her wicked wit; and as to Anna and Lizzie, as they glance by me, now and then, I seem to think them a kind of sprite, or elf, made to inhabit shady old houses, just as twinkling harebells grow in old castles; and then the gracious mamma, who speaks French, or English, like a stream of silver—is she not, after all, the fairest of any of them? And there is Caroline, piquant, racy, full of conversation—sharp as a quartz crystal: how I like to hear her talk! These people know Paris, as we say in America, "like a book." They have studied it æsthetically, historically, socially. They have studied French people and French literature,—and studied it with enthusiasm, as people ever should, who would truly understand. They are all kindness to me. Whenever I wish to see any thing, I have only to speak; or to know, I have only to ask. At breakfast every morning we compare notes, and make up our list of wants. My first, of course, was the Louvre. It is close by us. Think of it. To one who has starved all a life, in vain imaginings of what art might be, to know that you are within a stone's throw of a museum full of its miracles, Greek, Assyrian, Egyptian, Roman sculptors and modern painting, all there!

I scarcely consider myself to have seen any thing of art in England. The calls of the living world were so various and *exigeant*, I had so little leisure for reflection, that, although I saw many paintings, I could not study them; and many times I saw them in a state of the nervous system too jaded and depressed to receive the full force of the impression. A day or two before I left, I visited the National Gallery, and made a rapid survey of its contents. There were two of Turner's masterpieces there, which he presented on the significant condition that they should hang side by side with their two finest Claudes. I thought them all four fine pictures, but I liked the Turners best. Yet I did not think any of them fine enough to form an absolute limit to human improvement. But, till I had been in Paris a day or two, perfectly secluded, at full liberty to think and rest, I did not feel that my time for examining art had really come.

It was, then, with a thrill almost of awe that I approached the Louvre. Here, perhaps, said I to myself, I shall answer, fully, the question that has long wrought within my soul, What is art? and what can it do? Here, perhaps, these yearnings for the ideal will meet their satisfaction. The ascent to the picture gallery tends to produce a flutter of excitement and expectation. Magnificent staircases, dim perspectives of frescoes and carvings, the glorious hall of Apollo, rooms with mosaic pavements, antique vases, countless spoils of art, dazzle the eye of the neophyte, and prepare the mind for some grand enchantment. Then opens on one the grand hall of paintings arranged by schools, the works of each artist by themselves, a wilderness of gorgeous growths.

I first walked through the whole, offering my mind up aimlessly to see if there were any picture there great and glorious enough to seize and control my whole being, and answer, at once, the cravings of the poetic and artistic element. For any such I looked in vain. I saw a thousand beauties, as also a thousand enormities, but nothing of that overwhelming, subduing nature which I had conceived. Most of the men there had painted with dry eyes and cool hearts, thinking only of the mixing of their colors and the jugglery of their art, thinking little of heroism, faith, love, or immortality. Yet when I had resigned this longing; when I was sure I should not meet there what I sought, then I began to enjoy very heartily what there was.

In the first place, I now saw Claudes worthy of the reputation he bore. Three or four of these were studied with great delight; the delight one feels, who, conscientiously bound to be delighted, suddenly comes into a situation to be so. I saw, now, those atmospheric traits, those reproductions of the mysteries of air, and of light, which are called so wonderful, and for which all admire Claude, but for which so few admire Him who made Claude, and who every day creates around us, in the commonest scenes, effects far more beautiful. How much, even now, my admiration of Claude was genuine, I cannot say. How can we ever be sure on this point, when the praise and glory of that family. I was predetermined not to like them for two reasons: first, that I dislike allegorical subjects; and second, that I hate and despise that Medici family and all that belongs to them. So no sympathy with the subjects blinded my eyes, and drew me gradually from all else in the hall to contemplate these. It was simply the love of power and of fertility that held me astonished, which seemed to express with nonchalant ease what other painters attain by laborious efforts. It occurred to me that other painters are famous for single heads, or figures, and that were the striking heads and figures with which these pictures abound to be parcelled out singly, any one of them would make a man's reputation. Any animal of Rubens, alone, would make a man's fortune in that department. His fruits and flowers are unrivalled for richness and abundance; his old men's heads are wonderful; and when he chooses, which he does not often, he can even create a pretty woman. Generally speaking his women are his worst productions. It would seem that he had revolted with such fury from the meagre, pale, cadaverous outlines of womankind painted by his predecessors, the Van Eyks, whose women resembled potato sprouts grown in a cellar, that he altogether overdid the matter in the opposite direction. His exuberant soul abhors leanness as Nature abhors a vacuum; and hence all his women seem bursting their bodices with fulness, like overgrown carnations breaking out of their green calyxes. He gives you Venuses with arms fit to wield the hammer of Vulcan; vigorous Graces whose dominion would be alarming were they indisposed to clemency. His weakness, in fact, his besetting sin, is too truly described by Moses:—

> "But Jeshurun waxed fat and kicked;
>   Thou art waxen fat, thou art grown thick,
>   Thou art covered with fatness."

Scornfully he is determined upon it; he will none of your scruples; his women shall be fat as he pleases, and you shall like him nevertheless.

In this Medici gallery the fault appears less prominent than else-where. Many of the faces are portraits, and there are specimens among them of female beauty, so delicate as to demonstrate that it was not from any want of ability to represent the softer graces that he so often becomes hard and coarse. My friend, M. Belloc, made the remark that the genius of Rubens was somewhat restrained in these pictures, and chastened by the rigid rules of the French school, and hence in them he is more gen-erally pleasing.

I should compare Rubens to Shakspeare, for the wonderful variety and vital force of his artistic power. I know no other mind he so nearly resem-bles. Like Shakspeare, he forces you to accept and to forgive a thousand excesses, and uses his own faults as musicians use discords, only to enhance the perfection of harmony. There certainly is some use even in defects. A faultless style sends you to sleep. Defects rouse and excite the sensibility to seek and appreciate excellences. Some of Shakspeare's finest passages explode all grammar and rhetoric like skyrockets—the thought blows the language to shivers.

As to Murillo, there are two splendid specimens of his style here, as exquisite as any I have seen; but I do not find reason to alter the judgment I made from my first survey.

Here is his celebrated picture of the Assumption of the Virgin, which we have seen circulated in print shops in America, but which appears of a widely different character in the painting. The Virgin is rising in a flood of amber light, surrounded by clouds and indistinct angel figures. She is looking upward with clasped hands, as in an ecstasy: the crescent moon is beneath her feet. The whole tone of the picture—the clouds, the drapery, her flowing hair—are pervaded with this amber tint, sublimated and spiritual. Do I, then, like it? No. Does it affect me? Not at all. Why so? Because this is a subject requiring earnestness; yet, after all, there is no earnestness of religious feeling expressed. It is a *surface* picture, exquisitely painted—the feeling goes no deeper than the canvas. But how do I know Murillo has no earnestness in the religious idea of this piece? How do I know, when reading Pope's Messiah, that *he* was not in earnest—that he was only most exquisitely reproducing what others had thought? Does he not assume, in the most graceful way, the language of inspiration and holy rapture? But, through it all, we feel the satisfied smirk of the artist, and the fine, sharp touch of his diamond file. What is done from a genuine, strong, inward emotion, whether in writing or painting, always mesmerizes the paper, or the canvas, and gives it a power which every body must feel, though few know why. The reason why the Bible has been omnipotent, in all ages, has been because there were the emotions of GOD in it; and of paintings nothing is more remarkable than that some preserve in them such a degree of genuine vital force that one can never look on them with indifference; while others, in which every condition of art seems to be met, inspire no strong emotion.

Yet this picture is immensely popular. Hundreds stand enchanted before it, and declare it imbodies their highest ideal of art and religion; and I suppose it does. But so it always is. The man who has exquisite gifts of expression passes for more, popularly, than the man with great and grand ideas who utters but imperfectly. There are some pictures here by Correggio—a sleeping Venus and Cupid—a marriage of the infant Jesus and St. Catharine. This Correggio is the poet of physical beauty. Light and shadow are his god. What he lives for is, to catch and reproduce flitting phases of these. The moral is nothing to him, and, in his own world, he does what he seeks. He is a great popular favorite, since few look for more in a picture than exquisite beauty of form and color. I, indeed, like him, so far as it is honestly understood between us that his sphere is to be earth, and not heaven; were he to attempt, profanely, to represent heavenly things, I must rebel. I should as soon want Tom Moore to write me a prayer book.

A large saloon is devoted to the masters of the French school. The works of no living artists are admitted. There are some large paintings by David. He is my utter aversion. I see in him nothing but the driest imitation of the classics. It would be too much praise to call it reproduction. David had neither heart nor soul. How could he be an artist?—he who coolly took his portfolio to the guillotine to take lessons on the dying ago-nies of its victims—how could he ever paint any thing to touch the heart?

In general, all French artists appear to me to have been very much injured by a wrong use of classic antiquity. Nothing could be more glori-ous and beautiful than the Grecian development; nothing more unlike it than the stale, wearisome, repetitious imitations of it in modern times. The Greek productions themselves have a living power to this day; but all imitations of them are cold and tiresome. These old Greeks made such beautiful things, because they did *not* imitate. That mysterious vitality which still imbues their remains, and which seems to enchant even the fragments of their marbles, is the mesmeric vitality of fresh, original con-ception. Art, built upon this, is just like what the shadow of a beautiful woman is to the woman. One gets tired in these galleries of the classic band, and the classic headdress, and the classic attitude, and the endless repetition of the classic urn, and vase, and lamp, as if nothing else were ever to be made in the world except these things.

Again: in regard to this whole French gallery, there is much of a cer-tain quality which I find it very difficult to describe in any one word—a dramatic smartness, a searching for striking and peculiar effects, which render the pictures very likely to please on first sight, and to weary on longer acquaintance. It seems to me to be the work of a race whose senses and perceptions of the outward have been cultivated more than the deep inward emotions. Few of the pictures seem to have been the result of strong and profound feeling, of habits of earnest and concentrated thought. There is an abundance of beautiful little phases of sentiment, pointedly expressed; there is a great deal of what one should call the pic-turesque of the *morale*; but few of its foundation ideas. I must except from these remarks the very strong and earnest painting of the Méduse, by Géricault, which C. has described. That seems to me to be the work of a man who had not seen human life and suffering merely on the outside, but had felt, in the very depths of his soul, the surging and earthquake of those mysteries of passion and suffering which underlie our whole exis-tence in this world. To me it was a picture too mighty and too painful—whose power I confess, but which I did not like to contemplate.

On the whole, French painting is to me an exponent of the great dif-ficulty and danger of French life; that passion for the outward and visible, which all their education, all the arrangements of their social life, every thing in their art and literature, tends continually to cultivate and increase.

Hence they have become the leaders of the world in what I should call the minor artistics—all those little particulars which render life beautiful. Hence there are more pretty pictures, and popular lithographs, from France than from any other country in the world; but it produces very little of the deepest and highest style of art.

In this connection I may as well give you my Luxembourg experience, as it illustrates the same idea. I like Paul de la Roche, on the whole, although I think he has something of the fault of which I speak. He has very great dramatic power; but it is more of the kind shown by Walter Scott than of the kind shown by Shakspeare. He can reproduce historical characters with great vividness and effect, and with enough knowledge of humanity to make the verisimilitude admirably strong; but as to the deep knowledge with which Shakspeare searches the radical elements of the human soul, he has it not. His Death of Queen Elizabeth is a strong Walter Scott picture; so are his Execution of Strafford, and his Charles I., which I saw in England.

As to Horace Vernet, I do not think he is like either Scott or Shakspeare. In him this French capability for rendering the outward is wrought to the highest point; and it is outwardness as pure from any touch of inspiration or sentiment as I ever remember to have seen. He is graphic to the utmost extreme. His horses and his men stand from the canvas to the astonishment of all beholders. All is vivacity, bustle, dazzle, and show. I think him as perfect, of his kind, as possible; though it is a *kind* of art with which I do not sympathize.

The picture of the Décadence de Rome indicates to my mind a painter who has studied and understood the classical forms; vitalizing them, by the reproductive force of his own mind, so as to give them the living power of new creations. In this picture is a most grand and melancholy moral lesson. The classical forms are evidently not introduced because they are classic, but in subservience to the expression of the moral. In the orgies of the sensualists here represented he gives all the grace and beauty of sensuality without its sensualizing effect. Nothing could be more exquisite than the introduction of the busts of the departed heroes of the old republic, looking down from their pedestals on the scene of debauchery below. It is a noble picture, which I wish was hung up in the Capitol of our nation to teach our haughty people that as pride, and fulness of bread, and laxness of principle brought down the old republics, so also ours may fall. Although the outward in this painting, and the classical, is wrought to as fine a point as in any French picture, it is so subordinate to the severity of the thought, that while it pleases it does not distract.

But to return to the Louvre. The halls devoted to paintings, of which I have spoken, give you very little idea of the treasures of the institution. Gallery after gallery is filled with Greek, Roman, Assyrian, and Egyptian sculptures, coins, vases, and antique remains of every description. There is, also, an apartment in which I took a deep interest, containing the original sketches of ancient masters. Here one may see the pen and ink drawings of Claude, divided into squares to prepare them for the copyist. One compares here with interest the manners of the different artists in jotting down their ideas as they rose; some by chalk, some by crayon, some by pencil, some by water colors, and some by a heterogeneous mixture of all. Mozart's scrap bag of musical jottings could not have been more amusing.

On the whole, cravings of mere ideality have come nearer to meeting satisfaction by some of these old mutilated remains of Greek sculpture than any thing which I have met yet. In the paintings, even of the most celebrated masters, there are often things which are excessively annoying to me. I scarcely remember a master in whose works I have not found a hand, or foot, or face, or feature so distorted, or coloring at times so unnatural, or something so out of place and proportion in the picture as very seriously to mar the pleasure that I derived from it. In this statuary less is attempted, and all is more harmonious, and one's ideas of proportion are never violated.

My favorite among all these remains is a mutilated statue which they call the Venus de Milon. This is a statue which is so called from having been dug up some years ago, piecemeal, in the Island of Milos. There was quite a struggle for her between a French naval officer, the English, and the Turks. The French officer carried her off like another Helen, and she was given to Paris, old Louis Philippe being bridegroom by proxy. *Savants* refer the statue to the time of Phidias; and as this is a pleasant idea to me, I go a little further, and ascribe her to Phidias himself.

The statue is much mutilated, both arms being gone, and part of the foot. But there is a majesty and grace in the head and face, a union of loveliness with intellectual and moral strength, beyond any thing which I have ever seen. To me she might represent Milton's glorious picture of unfallen, perfect womanhood, in his Eve:—

> "Yet when I approach
> Her loveliness, so absolute she seems,
> And in herself complete, so well to know
> Her own, that what she wills to do or say
> Seems wisest, virtuousest, discreetest, best.
> All higher knowledge in her presence falls
> Degraded; wisdom, in discourse with her,
> Loses discountenanced, and like folly shows.
> Authority and reason on her wait,
> As one intended first, not after made
> Occasionally; and to consummate all,
> Greatness of mind, and nobleness, their seat
> Build in her, loveliest, and create an awe
> About her, like a guard angelic placed."

Compared with this matchless Venus, that of Medici seems as inane and trifling as mere physical beauty always must by the side of beauty baptized, and made sacramental, as the symbol of that which alone is truly fair.

With regard to the arrangements of the Louvre, they seem to me to be admirable. No nation has so perfectly the qualifications to care for, keep, and to show to best advantage a gallery of art as the French.

During the heat of the outburst that expelled Louis Philippe from the throne, the Louvre was in some danger of destruction. Destructiveness is a native element of human nature, however repressed by society; and hence every great revolutionary movement always brings to the surface some who are for indiscriminate demolition. Moreover there is a strong tendency in the popular mind, where art and beauty have for many years been monopolized as the prerogative of a haughty aristocracy, to identify art and beauty with oppression; this showed itself in England and Scotland in the general storm which wrecked the priceless beauty of the ecclesiastical buildings. It was displaying itself in the same manner in Germany during the time of the reformation, and had not Luther been gifted with a nature as strongly æsthetic as progressive, would have wrought equal ruin there. So in the first burst of popular enthusiasm that expelled the monarchy, the cry was raised by some among the people, "We shall never get rid of kings till we pull down the palaces;" just the echo of the old cry in Scotland, "Pull down the nests, and the rooks will fly away." The populace rushed in to the splendid halls and saloons of the Louvre, and a general encampment was made among the pictures. In this crisis a republican artist named Jeanron saved the Louvre; saved the people the regret that must have come over them had they perpetrated barbarisms, and Liberty the shame of having such outrages wrought in her name. Appointed by the provisional government to the oversight of the Louvre, and well known among the people as a republican, he boldly came to the rescue. "Am I not one of you?" he said. "Am I not one of the people? These splendid works of art, are they not ours? Are they not the pride and glory of our country? Shall we destroy our most glorious possession in the first hour of its passing into our hands?"

Moved by his eloquence the people decamped from the building, and left it in his hands. Empowered to make all such arrangements for its renovation and embellishment as his artistic taste should desire, he conducted important repairs in the building, rearranged the halls, had the pictures carefully examined, cleaned when necessary, and distributed in schools with scientific accuracy. He had an apartment prepared where are displayed those first sketches by distinguished masters, which form one of the most instructive departments of the Louvre to a student of art. The government seconded all his measures by liberal supplies of money; and the Louvre is placed in its present perfect condition by the thoughtful and cherishing hand of the republic.

These facts have been communicated to me from a perfectly reliable sources. As an American, and a republican, I cannot but take pleasure in them. I mention them because it is often supposed, from the destructive effects which attend the first advent of democratic principles where they have to explode their way into existence through masses of ancient rubbish, that popular liberty is unfavorable to art. It never could be so in France, because the whole body of the people are more thoroughly artistic in their tastes and feelings than in most countries. They are almost slaves to the outwardly beautiful, taken captive by the eye and the ear, and only the long association of beauty with tyranny, with suffering, want, and degradation to themselves, could ever have inspired any of them with even a momentary bitterness against it.

Nathaniel Hawthorne

The great Nathaniel Hawthorne (1804–1864), apart from his fine and gloomy and permanent novels and all his other significance, reaches us as well, if on a lesser level, often now in his more artless and unself-conscious nonfiction. He was already fifty when he first left for Europe, becoming the American consul in Liverpool as a reward for writing *The Life of Franklin Pierce*—ah, America—and his notebooks record a journey to the Continent in 1858–59. If he insisted, perhaps a touch disingenuously, that he had "no sympathies" toward the French, still, his eye for a scene, and for the emotional meaning of architecture, is as arresting as one would expect from Nathaniel Hawthorne. His is the first American view of what Paris had become by the end of the Second Empire, and what it had never been before: a city built to be lovely. The beautiful surface of Paris had been made.

---

from

The French Notebooks

Hôtel du Louvre, Jany 8th, Friday.

It was so awfully cold that I really felt little or no curiosity to see Paris; and besides I had a cold in my head, which, probably, was the reason that my nose fell a-bleeding, the morning after our arrival. On this latter account, it was necessary that my wife and Miss Shepard should go without me to get our luggage (which had been registered through from London) passed through the Custom House. Until after one °clock, therefore, I knew nothing of Paris except the lights which I had seen beneath our window, the evening before, far, far downward, in the narrow Rue St Honoré; and the rumble of the wheels, which continued later than I was awake to hear it, and began again before light. I could see, too, tall houses, that seemed to be occupied in every story, and that had windows on the steep roofs; one of these houses is six stories high. This Rue St. Honoré is one of the old streets in Paris, and is that in which Henry IV was assassinated; but it has not, in this part of it, the aspect of antiquity.

After my wife's return, we all went out and walked along the Rue de Rivoli, in quest of our dinners; for we had determined, in consideration of the many mouths we have to feed, not to dine at the Restaurant of the Hotel, but at some less splendid one in the vicinity. We are here right in the midst of Paris, and close to whatever is best known to those who hear or read about it; the Louvre being right across the street; the Palais Royal but a little way off; the Tuilleries joining on to the Louvre; the Place de la Concorde just beyond, verging on which is the Champs Elysées. We looked about us for a suitable dining-place, and soon found the Restaurant des Echelles, (I am not sure that I spell it correctly) where we entered at a venture, and were courteously received by a waiter. It has a handsomely furnished saloon, much set off with gilding and mirrors; and (like, I presume, most of the eating-houses in this vicinity) it appears to be frequented by Englishmen or Americans, its carte—a bound volume—being printed in English as well as French. It was too late for dejeuners, and too early for dinner; so that there was but one other guest in the salôn. The waiter joined two tables together, to accommodate our large party; and the children immediately fell to work upon the long rolls of delicious bread which were placed at every plate. He recommended some cold *paté de foie gras*; and I think we all, except Julian and Rosebud, ate some and found it very good; and for the young people, we ordered some mutton-chops, of which Julian made no complaint, except that there was not half enough for his dinner. I really think he would eat a whole sheep. I had, moreover, a bottle of rather thin claret, which I found excellent for quenching thirst, and wholly ineffective on the brain. I had scarcely begun to eat and drink, before my nose set to bleeding again; and thus my blood must be reckoned among the rivers of human gore which have been shed in Paris, and especially on the Place de la Concorde, where the guillotine used to stand.

I think the above-mentioned dishes made up our dinner, for which I paid eleven francs, and thought it a very reasonable charge. It was now nearly four °clock, and too late to visit the Louvre, or to do anything else but walk a little way along the street. The splendor of Paris, so far as I have seen, takes me altogether by surprise; such stately edifices, prolonging themselves in unwearying magnificence and beauty, and, ever and anon, a long vista of a street, with a column rising at the end of it, or a triumphal arch, wrought in memory of some grand event. The light stone, or stucco, wholly untarnished by smoke and soot, puts London to the blush, if a blush could be seen through its dingy face; but, indeed, London is paltry, despicable, not to be mentioned in the same day, nor compared even for the purpose of ridiculing it, with Paris. I never knew what a palace was, till I had a glimpse of the Louvre and the Tuilleries;—never had any idea of a city gratified, till I trod these stately streets. The life of the scene, too, is infinitely more picturesque than London, with its monotonous throng of smug faces and black coats; whereas, here, you see soldiers and priests; policemen in cocked hats; Zouaves, with turbans, long mantles, and bronzed, half-Moorish faces; and a great many people whom you perceive to be outside of your experience, and know them ugly to look at, and fancy them villainous. Truly, I have no sympathies towards the French people; their eyes do not win me, nor do their glances melt and mingle with mine. But they do grand and beautiful things, in the architectural way; and I am grateful for it. The Place de la Concord is the most splendid square, large enough for a nation to erect trophies of all its triumphs there; and one side of it is the Tuilleries, on the opposite side the Champ Elyssée, and on a third the Seine, adown which we saw large cakes of ice floating beneath the arches of a bridge. The Champ Elysée, so far as I saw it, had not a grassy soil beneath its trees, but the bare earth, white and dusty. The very dust, if I saw nothing else, would assure me that I was out of England. We had time only to take this little walk, when it began to grow dusk; and being so pitilessly cold, we hurried back to our Hôtel. Thus far, I think, what I have seen of Paris is wholly unlike what I expected, but very like an imaginary picture which I had conceived of Saint Petersburg; new, bright, magnificent, and desperately cold. A great part of this architectural splendor is due to the present Emperor, who has wrought a great change on the aspect of the city within a very few years. A traveller, if he look at the thing selfishly, ought to wish him a long reign, and arbitrary power; since he makes it his policy to illustrate his capital with palatial edifices, which are better for a stranger to look at than for his own people to pay for.

Mark Twain

If Franklin and Jefferson invented the two basic American types in Paris—the happy libertine and the good student—it was Mark Twain (Samuel Clemens, of course, 1835–1910) who put the first counter-spin on both propositions: the American as disappointed libertine and failed student. In *The Innocents Abroad* (1869), his long, mostly very funny account of the long trip he took in 1867 with his wife and friends, he invents the tradition of American disappointment. He wants to have a good time, to become a libertine, to get a great shave (odd intense pleasure!), and a great meal, but circumstances and Parisian greed and duplicity prevent him. Apart from pioneering this form of comedy—the Bad Parisian Experience that will continue to define the "typical" tourist experience and enliven American humor from Donald Ogden Stewart to, most memorably, S. J. Perelman—his observations on the Louvre are a kind of masterpiece of the American Disabused. (His distaste for Rubens' sucking up to his patrons makes an interesting comparison to Stowe's keen appreciation of him, and shows the difference between a sincere good writer and an honest great one.) He is depressingly shocked (for his wife's benefit?) by the can-can, but at least admits slyly that, shocked or not, he looked through his fingers. Later on, Twain would make something of a fetish out of French-bashing, one of the very few major American writers who ever has, but it is plain, in these first pages, that the place knocked him out, too.

---

from

The Innocents Abroad

By Lyons and the Saone (where we saw the lady of Lyons and thought little of her comeliness;) by Villa Franca, Tonnere, venerable Sens, Melun, Fontainebleau, and scores of other beautiful cities, we swept, always noting the absence of hog-wallows, broken fences, cowlots, unpainted houses and mud, and always noting, as well, the presence of cleanliness, grace, taste in adorning and beautifying, even to the disposition of a tree or the turning of a hedge, the marvel of roads in perfect repair, void of ruts and guiltless of even an inequality of surface—we bowled along, hour after hour, that brilliant summer day, and as nightfall approached we entered a wilderness of odorous flowers and shrubbery, sped through it, and then, excited, delighted, and half persuaded that we were only the sport of a beautiful dream, lo, we stood in magnificent Paris!

What excellent order they kept about that vast depot! There was no frantic crowding and jostling, no shouting and swearing, and no swaggering intrusion of services by rowdy hackmen. These latter gentry stood outside—stood quietly by their long line of vehicles and said never a word. A kind of hackman-general seemed to have the whole matter of transportation in his hands. He politely received the passengers and ushered them to the kind of conveyance they wanted, and told the driver where to deliver them. There was no "talking back," no dissatisfaction about overcharging, no grumbling about any thing. In a little while we were speeding through the streets of Paris, and delightfully recognizing certain names and places with which books had long ago made us familiar. It was like meeting an old friend when we read *"Rue de Rivoli"* on the street corner; we knew the genuine vast palace of the Louvre as well as we knew its picture; when we passed by the Column of July we needed no one to tell us what it was, or to remind us that on its site once stood the grim Bastile, that grave of human hopes and happiness, that dismal prison-house within whose dungeons so many young faces put on the wrinkles of age, so many proud spirits grew humble, so many brave hearts broke.

We secured rooms at the hotel, or rather, we had three beds put into one room, so that we might be together, and then we went out to a restaurant, just after lamp-lighting, and ate a comfortable, satisfactory, lingering dinner. It was a pleasure to eat where every thing was so tidy, the food so well cooked, the waiters so polite, and the coming and departing company so moustached, so frisky, so affable, so fearfully and wonderfully Frenchy! All the surroundings were gay and enlivening. Two hundred people sat at little tables on the sidewalk, sipping wine and coffee; the streets were thronged with light vehicles and with joyous pleasure seekers; there was music in the air, life and action all about us, and a conflagration of gaslight every where!

After dinner we felt like seeing such Parisian specialties as we might see without distressing exertion, and so we sauntered through the brilliant streets and looked at the dainty trifles in variety stores and jewelry shops. Occasionally, merely for the pleasure of being cruel, we put unoffending Frenchmen on the rack with questions framed in the incomprehensible jargon of their native language, and while they writhed, we impaled them, we peppered them, we scarified them, with their own vile verbs and participles.

We noticed that in the jewelry stores they had some of the articles marked "gold," and some labeled "imitation." We wondered at this extravagance of honesty, and inquired into the matter. We were informed that inasmuch as most people are not able to tell false gold from the genuine article, the government compels jewelers to have their gold work assayed and stamped officially according to its fineness, and their imitation work duly labeled with the sign of its falsity. They told us the jewelers would not dare to violate this law, and that whatever a stranger bought in one of their stores might be depended upon as being strictly what it was represented to be.—Verily, a wonderful land is France!

Then we hunted for a barber-shop. From earliest infancy it had been a cherished ambition of mine to be shaved some day in a palatial barber-shop of Paris. I wished to recline at full length in a cushioned invalid chair, with pictures about me, and sumptuous furniture; with frescoed walls and gilded arches above me, and vistas of Corinthian columns stretching far before me; with perfumes of Araby to intoxicate my senses, and the slumbrous drone of distant noises to soothe me to sleep. At the end of an hour I would wake up regretfully and find my face as smooth and as soft as an infant's. Departing, I would lift my hands above that barber's head and say, "Heaven bless you, my son!"

So we searched high and low, for a matter of two hours, but never a barber-shop could we see. We saw only wig-making establishments, with shocks of dead and repulsive hair bound upon the heads of painted waxen brigands who stared out from glass boxes upon the passer-by, with their stony eyes, and scared him with the ghostly white of their countenances. We shunned these signs for a time, but finally we concluded that the wig-makers must of necessity be the barbers as well, since we could find no single legitimate representative of the fraternity. We entered and asked, and found that it was even so.

I said I wanted to be shaved. The barber inquired where my room was. I said, never mind where my room was, I wanted to be shaved—there, on the spot. The doctor said he would be shaved also. Then there was an excitement among those two barbers! There was a wild consultation, and afterwards a hurrying to and fro and a feverish gathering up of razors from obscure places and a ransacking for soap. Next they took us into a little mean, shabby back room; they got two ordinary sitting-room chairs and placed us in them, with our coats on. My old, old dream of bliss vanished into thin air!

I sat bolt upright, silent, sad, and solemn. One of the wig-making villains lathered my face for ten terrible minutes and finished by plastering a mass of suds into my mouth. I expelled the nasty stuff with a strong English expletive and said, "Foreigner, beware!" Then this outlaw strapped his razor on his boot, hovered over me ominously for six fearful seconds, and then swooped down upon me like the genius of destruction. The first rake of his razor loosened the very hide from my face and lifted me out of the chair. I stormed and raved, and the other boys enjoyed it. Their beards are not strong and thick. Let us draw the curtain over this harrowing scene. Suffice it that I submitted, and went through with the cruel infliction of a shave by a French barber; tears of exquisite agony coursed down my cheeks, now and then, but I survived. Then the incipient assassin held a basin of water under my chin and slopped its contents over my face, and into my bosom, and down the back of my neck, with a mean pretense of washing away the soap and blood. He dried my features with a towel, and was going to comb my hair; but I asked to be excused. I said, with withering irony, that it was sufficient to be skinned—I declined to be scalped.

I went away from there with my handkerchief about my face, and never, never, never desired to dream of palatial Parisian barber-shops any more. The truth is, as I believe I have since found out, that they have no barber shops worthy of the name, in Paris—and no barbers, either, for that matter. The impostor who does duty as a barber, brings his pans and napkins and implements of torture to your residence and deliberately skins you in your private apartments. Ah, I have suffered, suffered, suffered, here in Paris, but never mind—the time is coming when I shall have a dark and bloody revenge. Some day a Parisian barber will come to my room to skin me, and from that day forth, that barber will never be heard of more.

* * *

The next morning we were up and dressed at ten o'clock. We went to the *commissionaire* of the hotel—I don't know what a *commissionaire* is, but that is the man we went to—and told him we wanted a guide. He said the great International Exposition had drawn such multitudes of Englishmen and Americans to Paris that it would be next to impossible to find a good guide unemployed. He said he usually kept a dozen or two on hand, but he only had three now. He called them. One looked so like a very pirate that we let him go at once. The next one spoke with a simpering precision of pronunciation that was irritating, and said:

"If ze zhentlemans will to me make ze grande honneur to me rattain in hees serveece, I shall show to him every sing zat is magnifique to look upon in ze beautiful Parree. I speaky ze Angleesh pairfaitemaw."

He would have done well to have stopped there, because he had that much by heart and said it right off without making a mistake. But his self-complacency seduced him into attempting a flight into regions of unexplored English, and the reckless experiment was his ruin. Within ten seconds he was so tangled up in a maze of mutilated verbs and torn and bleeding forms of speech that no human ingenuity could ever have gotten him out of it with credit. It was plain enough that he could not "speaky" the English quite as "pairfaitemaw" as he had pretended he could.

The third man captured us. He was plainly dressed, but he had a noticeable air of neatness about him. He wore a high silk hat which was a little old, but had been carefully brushed. He wore second-hand kid gloves, in good repair, and carried a small rattan cane with a curved handle—a female leg, of ivory. He stepped as gently and as daintily as a cat crossing a muddy street; and oh, he was urbanity; he was quiet, unobtrusive self-possession; he was deference itself! He spoke softly and guardedly; and when he was about to make a statement on his sole responsibility, or offer a suggestion, he weighed it by drachms and scruples first, with the crook of his little stick placed meditatively to his teeth. His opening speech was perfect. It was perfect in construction, in phraseology, in grammar, in emphasis, in pronunciation—every thing. He spoke little and guardedly, after that. We were charmed. We were more than charmed—we were overjoyed. We hired him at once. We never even asked him his price. This man—our lackey, our servant, our unquestioning slave though he was, was still a gentleman—we could see that—while of the other two one was coarse and awkward, and the other was a born pirate. We asked our man Friday's name. He drew from his pocket-book a snowy little card, and passed it to us with a profound bow:

A. BILLFINGER,
Guide to Paris, France, Germany,
Spain, &c., &c.,
Grande Hotel du Louvre.

"Billfinger! Oh, carry me home to die!"

That was an "aside" from Dan. The atrocious name grated harshly on my ear, too. The most of us can learn to forgive, and even to like, a countenance that strikes us unpleasantly at first, but few of us, I fancy, become reconciled to a jarring name so easily. I was almost sorry we had hired this man, his name was so unbearable. However, no matter. We were impatient to start. Billfinger stepped to the door to call a carriage, and then the doctor said:

"Well, the guide goes with the barber-shop, with the billiard-table, with the gasless room, and may be with many another pretty romance of Paris. I expected to have a guide named Henri de Montmorency, or Armand de la Chartreuse, or something that would sound grand in letters to the villagers at home; but to think of a Frenchman by the name of Billfinger! Oh! this is absurd, you know. This will never do. We can't say Billfinger; it is nauseating. Name him over again: what had we better call him? Alexis du Caulaincourt?"

"Alphonse Henri Gustave de Hauteville," I suggested.

"Call him Ferguson," said Dan.

That was practical, unromantic good sense. Without debate, we expunged Billfinger *as* Billfinger, and called him Ferguson.

The carriage—an open barouche—was ready. Ferguson mounted beside the driver, and we whirled away to breakfast. As was proper, Mr. Ferguson stood by to transmit our orders and answer questions. Bye and bye, he mentioned casually—the artful adventurer—that he would go and get his breakfast as soon as we had finished ours. He knew we could not get along without him, and that we would not want to loiter about and wait for him. We asked him to sit down and eat with us. He begged, with many a bow, to be excused. It was not proper, he said; he would sit at another table. We ordered him peremptorily to sit down with us.

Here endeth the first lesson. It was a mistake.

As long as we had that fellow after that, he was always hungry; he was always thirsty. He came early; he stayed late; he could not pass a restaurant; he looked with a lecherous eye upon every wine shop. Suggestions to stop, excuses to eat and to drink were forever on his lips. We tried all we could to fill him so full that he would have no room to spare for a fortnight; but it was a failure. He did not hold enough to smother the cravings of his superhuman appetite.

He had another "discrepancy" about him. He was always wanting us to buy things. On the shallowest pretenses, he would inveigle us into shirt stores, boot stores, tailor shops, glove shops—any where under the broad sweep of the heavens that there seemed a chance of our buying any thing. Any one could have guessed that the shopkeepers paid him a per centage on the sales; but in our blessed innocence we didn't, until this feature of his conduct grew unbearably prominent. One day, Dan happened to mention that he thought of buying three or four silk dress patterns for presents. Ferguson's hungry eye was upon him in an instant. In the course of twenty minutes, the carriage stopped.

"What's this?"

"Zis is ze finest silk magazin in Paris—ze most celebrate."

"What did you come here for? We told you to take us to the palace of the Louvre."

"I suppose ze gentleman say he wish to buy some silk."

"You are not required to 'suppose' things for the party, Ferguson. We do not wish to tax your energies too much. We will bear some of the burden and heat of the day ourselves. We will endeavor to do such 'supposing' as is really necessary to be done. Drive on." So spake the doctor.

Within fifteen minutes the carriage halted again, and before another silk store. The doctor said:

"Ah, the palace of the Louvre: beautiful, beautiful edifice! Does the Emperor Napoleon live here now, Ferguson?"

"Ah, doctor! you do jest; zis is not ze palace; we come there directly. But since we pass right by zis store, where is such beautiful silk—"

"Ah! I see, I see. I meant to have told you that we did not wish to purchase any silks to-day; but in my absent-mindedness I forgot it. I also meant to tell you we wished to go directly to the Louvre; but I forgot that also. However, we will go there now. Pardon my seeming carelessness, Ferguson. Drive on."

Within the half hour, we stopped again—in front of another silk store. We were angry; but the doctor was always serene, always smooth-voiced. He said:

"At last! How imposing the Louvre is, and yet how small! how exquisitely fashioned! how charmingly situated!—Venerable, venerable pile—"

"Pairdon, doctor, zis is not ze Louvre—it is—"

"*What* is it?"

"I have ze idea—it come to me in a moment—zat ze silk in zis magazin—"

"Ferguson, how heedless I am. I fully intended to tell you that we did not wish to buy any silks to-day, and I also intended to tell you that we yearned to go immediately to the palace of the Louvre, but enjoying the happiness of seeing you devour four breakfasts this morning has so filled me with pleasurable emotions that I neglect the commonest interests of the time. However, we will proceed now to the Louvre, Ferguson."

"But doctor," (excitedly,) "it will take not a minute—not but one small minute! Ze gentleman need not to buy if he not wish to—but only *look* at ze silk—*look* at ze beautiful fabric." [Then pleadingly.] "*Sair*—just only one *leetle* moment!"

Dan said, "Confound the idiot! I don't want to see any silks to-day, and I *won't* look at them. Drive on."

And the doctor: "We need no silks now, Ferguson. Our hearts yearn for the Louvre. Let us journey on—let us journey on."

"But *doctor!* it is only one moment—one leetle moment. And ze time will be save—entirely save! Because zere is nothing to see, now—it is too late. It want ten minute to four and ze Louvre close at four—*only* one leetle moment, doctor!"

The treacherous miscreant! After four breakfasts and a gallon of champagne, to serve us such a scurvy trick. We got no sight of the countless treasures of art in the Louvre galleries that day, and our only poor little satisfaction was in the reflection that Ferguson sold not a solitary silk dress pattern.

I am writing this chapter partly for the satisfaction of abusing that accomplished knave, Billfinger, and partly to show whosoever shall read this how Americans fare at the hands of the Paris guides, and what sort of people Paris guides are. It need not be supposed that we were a stupider or an easier prey than our countrymen generally are, for we were not. The guides deceive and defraud every American who goes to Paris for the first time and sees its sights alone or in company with others as little experienced as himself. I shall visit Paris again some day, and then let the guides beware! I shall go in my war-paint—I shall carry my tomahawk along.

* * *

In Paris we often saw in shop windows the sign, *"English Spoken Here,"* just as one sees in the windows at home the sign, *"Ici on parle francaise."* We always invaded these places at once—and invariably received the information, framed in faultless French, that the clerk who did the English for the establishment had just gone to dinner and would be back in an hour—would Monsieur buy something? We wondered why those parties happened to take their dinners at such erratic and extraordinary hours, for we never called at a time when an exemplary Christian would be in the least likely to be abroad on such an errand. The truth was, it was a base fraud—a snare to trap the unwary—chaff to catch fledglings with. They had no English-murdering clerk. They trusted to the sign to inveigle foreigners into their lairs, and trusted to their own blandishments to keep them there till they bought something.

We ferreted out another French imposition—a frequent sign to this effect: "ALL MANNER OF AMERICAN DRINKS ARTISTICALLY PREPARED HERE." We procured the services of a gentleman experienced in the nomenclature of the American bar, and moved upon the works of one of these impostors. A bowing, aproned Frenchman skipped forward and said:

"Que voulez les messieurs?" I do not know what Que voulez les messieurs means, but such was his remark.

Our General said, "We will take a whisky-straight."

[A stare from the Frenchman.]

"Well, if you don't know what that is, give us a champagne cock-tail."

[A stare and a shrug.]

"Well, then, give us a sherry cobbler."

The Frenchman was checkmated. This was all Greek to him.

"Give us a brandy smash!"

The Frenchman began to back away, suspicious of the ominous vigor of the last order—began to back away, shrugging his shoulders and spreading his hands apologetically.

The General followed him up and gained a complete victory. The uneducated foreigner could not even furnish a Santa Cruz Punch, an Eye-Opener, a Stone-Fence, or an Earthquake. It was plain that he was a wicked impostor.

An acquaintance of mine said, the other day, that he was doubtless the only American visitor to the Exposition who had had the high honor of being escorted by the Emperor's body guard. I said with unobtrusive frankness that I was astonished that such a long-legged, lantern-jawed, unprepossessing looking spectre as he should be singled out for a distinction like that, and asked how it came about. He said he had attended a great military review in the *Champ de Mars*, some time ago, and while the multitude about him was growing thicker and thicker every moment, he observed an open space inside the railing. He left his carriage and went into it. He was the only person there, and so he had plenty of room, and the situation being central, he could see all the preparations going on about the field. By and by there was a sound of music, and soon the Emperor of the French and the Emperor of Austria, escorted by the famous *Cent Gardes*, entered the inclosure. They seemed not to observe him, but directly, in response to a sign from the commander of the Guard, a young lieutenant came toward him with a file of his men following, halted, raised his hand and gave the military salute, and then said in a low voice that he was sorry to have to disturb a stranger and a gentleman, but the place was sacred to royalty. Then this New Jersey phantom rose up and bowed and begged pardon, then with the officer beside him, the file of men marching behind him, and with every mark of respect, he was escorted to his carriage by the imperial *Cent Gardes*! The officer saluted again and fell back, the New Jersey sprite bowed in return and had presence of mind enough to pretend that he had simply called on a matter of private business with those emperors, and so waved them an adieu, and drove from the field!

Imagine a poor Frenchman ignorantly intruding upon a public rostrum sacred to some six-penny dignitary in America. The police would scare him to death, first, with a storm of their elegant blasphemy, and then pull him to pieces getting him away from there. We are measurably superior to the French in some things, but they are immeasurably our betters in others.

Enough of Paris for the present. We have done our whole duty by it. We have seen the Tuileries, the Napoleon Column, the Madelaine, that wonder of wonders the tomb of Napoleon, all the great churches and museums, libraries, imperial palaces, and sculpture and picture galleries, the Pantheon, *Jardin des Plantes*, the opera, the circus, the Legislative Body, the billiard-rooms, the barbers, the *grisettes*—

Ah, the *grisettes*! I had almost forgotten. They are another romantic fraud. They were (if you let the books of travel tell it,) always so beautiful—so neat and trim, so graceful—so naive and trusting—so gentle, so winning—so faithful to their shop duties, so irresistible to buyers in their prattling importunity—so devoted to their poverty-stricken students of the Latin Quarter—so light hearted and happy on their Sunday picnics in the suburbs—and oh, so charmingly, so delightfully immoral!

Stuff! For three or four days I was constantly saying:

"Quick, Ferguson! is that a *grisette*?"

And he always said, "No."

He comprehended, at last, that I wanted to see a grisette. Then he showed me dozens of them. They were like nearly all the Frenchwomen I ever saw—homely. They had large hands, large feet, large mouths; they had pug noses as a general thing, and mustaches that not even good breeding could overlook; they combed their hair straight back without parting; they were ill-shaped, they were not winning, they were not graceful; I knew by their looks that they ate garlic and onions; and lastly and finally, to my thinking it would be base flattery to call them immoral.

Aroint thee, wench! I sorrow for the vagabond student of the Latin Quarter now, even more than formerly I envied him. Thus topples to earth another idol of my infancy.

We have seen every thing, and to-morrow we go to Versailles. We shall see Paris only for a little while as we come back to take up our line of march for the ship, and so I may as well bid the beautiful city a regretful farewell. We shall travel many thousands of miles after we leave here, and visit many great cities, but we shall find none so enchanting as this.

Some of our party have gone to England, intending to take a roundabout course and rejoin the vessel at Leghorn or Naples, several weeks hence. We came near going to Geneva, but have concluded to return to Marseilles and go up through Italy from Genoa.

I will conclude this chapter with a remark that I am sincerely proud to be able to make—and glad, as well, that my comrades cordially indorse it, to wit: by far the handsomest women we have seen in France were born and reared in America.

I feel, now, like a man who has redeemed a failing reputation and shed lustre upon a dimmed escutcheon, by a single just deed done at the eleventh hour.

Let the curtain fall, to slow music.

Elihu Washburne

The American politician and diplomat Elihu Washburne (1816–1887) was born in Maine, and helped promote the fortunes of Ulysses S. Grant early in the Civil War. When Grant became president in 1869, he made Washburne secretary of state, which, given Washburne's lack of experience, was seen as one of Grant's more hair-raising appointments. However Washburne wisely resigned within two weeks to become minister to France, where he remained until 1877. After the French disasters in the Franco-Prussian War in 1870, the Emperor fled, and Paris was taken over by the far-left "Communards," who came under attack from what remained of the reactionary French government, and army, at Versailles. It was the bloodiest and most fraught episode in modern French history, and Washburne was the only foreign diplomat to remain in Paris through the siege of the city and the fall of the Commune. His eyewitness report was published in *Recollections of a Minister to France, 1869–1877* (1889).

The Proclamation of the Republic

It was evident, during the very first days of September, that matters in Paris were drifting to a crisis. It was a strange and indefinable feeling that existed among the population of Paris on Saturday, September 3d. Everybody was groping in the dark for news of military operations. The people alarmed, discouraged, maddened, at all the disasters which had fallen upon their arms, were preparing for great events. I went down to the Chamber of Deputies, at the Palais Bourbon at five o'clock in the afternoon. On leaving the Chamber, a diplomatic colleague whispered tremblingly in my ear that all was lost to the French, that the whole army had been captured at Sedan, and that the Emperor had been taken prisoner. A session of the Chamber of Deputies was called to meet at midnight. The startling news had fallen like a thunderbolt over all Paris. The Boulevards were thronged by masses of excited men, filled with rage and indignation. The police authorities strove in vain to disperse them.

The ministry had issued a proclamation which recognized the gravity of the situation, and which was brought by my secretary of legation,

Colonel Hoffman, to my residence at midnight. I at once foresaw that stupendous events were on the verge of accomplishment. The news of the full extent of the catastrophe which befell the army of MacMahon was not made public in Paris until about midnight on Saturday, September 3d, though Palikao had, in the evening session of the Chamber, given out enough news to prepare the people for almost anything. That Saturday night session of the *Corps Législatif* was represented as having been solemn and agitated. The hour designated for its meeting was at midnight, but the President did not take his chair until one o'clock on Sunday morning. M. Schneider, the President, came into the Chamber without the beating of the drum which ordinarily announced his entry. The silence was death-like; but few of the deputies of the Right were in their seats, though the members of the Left were almost all present. Count de Palikao, the Minister of War, took the floor and said that in the presence of the serious news which had been received, he deemed it better not to take any action at that time, but to postpone everything until twelve o'clock of that day. After Palikao had made this suggestion, M. Jules Favre arose and said that he should not propose any serious opposition to that motion, but he asked leave to give notice of a proposition which he had to submit, and which he would discuss at the meeting at twelve o'clock (on Sunday). The proposition which he read was as follows:

1. Louis Napoleon Bonaparte and his dynasty are declared fallen from the powers which the constitution has confided to them.

2. There shall be named by the legislative body a commission vested with powers and composed of —— members, and you will designate yourself the number of members who shall compose this commission, who will make it their first duty to repel the invasion and drive the enemy from the territory.

3. M. Trochu shall be maintained in his functions of governor-general of the City of Paris.

There was no discussion whatever on these propositions, and after a very brief session of ten minutes the Chamber adjourned.

It was easy to foresee that the sitting of the *Corps Législatif* on Sunday was likely to become historic. I went early to the hall of the *Corps Législatif*. When I arrived there I found a few troops stationed in the neighborhood, and there was not a large number of people in the immediate vicinity. Indeed, I was quite surprised at the tranquillity which seemed everywhere to reign in the quarter of the Palais Bourbon, which is the name of the building occupied by the *Corps Législatif*. Taking my seat in the diplomatic tribune, at a quarter before twelve, there was not a single person in the hall of the deputies, though the galleries were all well filled. Instead of the session opening at noon, it was precisely one o'clock when M. Schneider entered and took the chair of the President. The deputies then came rapidly into the hall. Count de Palikao was the first of the ministers to come in, and he was soon followed by the Prince de La Tour d'Auvergne and MM. Chevreau and Brame. Soon after, all the other ministers took their places on the ministerial benches. The members of the Left came in almost simultaneously, Gambetta hurrying along among the first, haggard with excitement. The venerable Raspail took his seat; Garnier-Pagès hurried across the area in front of the President's chair, in a state of intense agitation. Arago, Simon, Picard, Ferry, Estancelin, Guyot-Montpayroux entered and took their seats. Thiers, the little, brisk and vigorous old man, walked quietly to his place. The President sat in his chair quietly, and seemed in no hurry to call the Chamber to order. The members became impatient and clamorous. There was loud talk and violent gesticulation. At precisely twenty minutes after one o'clock, M. Schneider swung his bell, and the gruff voice of the *huissier* was heard above the din, *"Silence, messieurs! s'il vous plaît."* After some unimportant proceedings the floor was assigned to Count de Palikao, the Minister of War, who, in behalf of the Council of Ministers, submitted the following:

ART. 1. A council of government and of National Defence is instituted. This council is composed of five members. Each member of the council is named by the absolute majority of the *Corps Législatif*.

2. The ministers are named under the countersign of the members of this council.

3. The General Count de Palikao is named lieutenant-general of this council.

Done in a council of ministers the 4th of September, 1870.

For the Emperor, and in virtue of the powers which he has confided to us.

EUGÉNIE.

After that project had been read, M. Thiers arose and submitted another proposition which was as follows:

Considering the circumstances, the Chamber names a commission of government and National Defence. A Constituent Assembly will be convoked as soon as the circumstances will allow.

The proposition of Favre being already before the Chamber, "urgency" was voted on these three propositions, and they were sent to a committee for examination, under the rules of the Chamber. This voting of urgency, according to the rules of the Chamber, brings the matter before it for immediate consideration. At one o'clock and forty minutes in the afternoon, the sitting was suspended to await the report of the committee to which these three propositions had been submitted, and then all the members left the hall, going into a large lobby-room, called *la salle des pas perdus.*

As it was supposed that the sitting would not be resumed for an hour or more, I left the diplomatic gallery and descended into the court of the building facing upon the street which runs parallel with the Seine. There I found a great many people who had been admitted by virtue of tickets. The street in front of the building had been kept quite clear by the military, though there was an enormous multitude of the National Guard and the people on the Place de la Concorde, on the opposite side of the river. The Pont de la Concorde seemed to be sufficiently guarded by the military to prevent their crossing over. All at once I saw quite a number of people on the steps of the Palais Bourbon, and soon they commenced to raise loud cries of *"Vive la République!" "Déchéance!" "Vive la France!"*

At this moment I was called away by the messenger of the legation, who brought me an urgent message from Madame MacMahon, who wanted a safe-conduct from me to enable her to pass the Prussian lines to visit her wounded husband at Sedan. I had asked my friend, the Honorable George Eustis, Jr., of Louisiana, who was a perfect master of the French language, to accompany me to the *Corps Législatif,* and he was with me at the time my messenger came in to get this *laissez-passer* for Madame MacMahon. Leaving the diplomatic tribune, we went into an antechamber, where I could find writing-materials, to prepare the document which was sought for. I had no sooner sat myself down to the table than the cry was raised that the people had invaded the building. It seemed but a moment before the flood was rushing in, even into the antechamber where Mr. Eustis and myself were. The crowd and confusion were so great that I found it impossible to prepare the requisite paper, so we made our way into the court-yard. There was presented a most extraordinary spectacle. A part of the regiment of the line had been brought hurriedly into the yard, and had formed across it, and were loading their muskets. Behind them, and in the street, and rushing through the gates and up the front steps of the building, was a vast mass of excited people and the National Guard, who had fraternized—the guards having their muskets butt-end upward as a token of friendship. It was evident that there had been collusion between the people who were on the steps of the Palais Bourbon, and the people and the National Guard in the Place de la Concorde, on the other side of the river, for it was upon the signal of the people on the steps, that the guard and the people broke through the military force that was holding the bridge. As the crowd mounted the steps of the Palais Bourbon, it was received with terrific cheers and shouts of *"Vive la République!"* and *"Déchéance!"*

Making our way into the street, Mr. Eustis and myself managed to pass through the crowd and to reach the building of the Agricultural Club, in the immediate neighborhood, and from the balcony of which we could see all that was going on. And now the soldiers of the guard, many of them with their hats on the ends of their muskets, accompanied by an indiscriminate mass of men, women and children, poured over the Pont de la Concorde and filled the entire space, all in one grand fraternization, singing the Marseillaise and shouting *"Vive la République!"* The Municipal Guard, with its shining helmets and brilliant uniform, was forced back, inch by inch, before the people, until, finally, all military authority became utterly powerless. During this time the National Guard and the people had invaded the Hall of the Deputies, which they found vacant. M. Schneider and about a dozen of the members rushed in. The President in vain made appeals for order, and finally covered himself by putting on his hat, according to the immemorial usage of the French assemblies under such circumstances. Gambetta addressed a few energetic words to the invaders, and, a little order being restored, quite a number of deputies entered the hall. But, at three o'clock, a grand irruption into the Chamber took place. M. Jules Favre then ascended the tribune and was listened to for a moment. "Let there be no scenes of violence," he said, "let us reserve our arms for the enemy and fight to the last. At this moment, union is necessary, and for that reason we do not proclaim the republic." The President then precipitately left his seat, and it turned out that it was for the last time. The irruption into the Chamber continued.

The floor and the seats of the deputies, on which a few members of the Left only remained, were filled with a motley crowd in blouses and coarse woollen shirts, or in the uniform of the National Guard or the Guard Mobile. They wore caps and *képis* of all colors and shapes, and carried muskets with their muzzles ornamented with sprigs of green leaves. The tumult became indescribable, and some of the invaders seized on the pens and paper of the deputies and commenced writing letters, while different persons were going up to the President's chair and ringing his bell continually. The crowd in the hall now demanded the *"déchéance"* of the Emperor, which was declared, and then it was proposed to go to the Hôtel de Ville and proclaim the republic. The cry was therefore raised, *"À l'Hôtel de Ville,"* mingled with other cries, *"Cherchez Rochefort,"* etc., and then this vast multitude commenced moving away from the Palais Bourbon.

The crowd having soon sufficiently dispersed, we were enabled to make our way back again to the *Corps Législatif,* and to enter the diplomatic tribune. The hall was filled with dust, and was in the greatest possible confusion. A rough-looking man was in the President's chair, surrounded by a number of men still more rough in appearance. The soldiers and the people were occupying the seats of the deputies indiscriminately, writing letters, looking over documents, and talking and laughing, all in the best humor. In the hall, at this time, I recognized Garnier-Pagès, Raspail and a few other members of the Left.

Leaving the Chamber, we went at once to the Hôtel de Ville. The number of people assembled there was enormous, and we found the same fraternization existing between them and the National Guard as elsewhere. The building had been invaded by the people, and all the windows fronting on the square were filled with rough and dirty-looking men and boys. Soon we heard a terrific shout go up. Rochefort was being drawn in a cab by a multitude through the crowd. He was ghastly pale; he stood up in the vehicle, covered with sashes of red, white and blue, waving his hat in answer to the acclamations. As he was slowly hauled through the multitude to the main door of the Hôtel de Ville, the delirium seemed to have reached its height, and it is impossible to describe the frantic acclamations which were heard. At precisely four o'clock and forty-five minutes in the afternoon, as I marked it by the great clock in the tower of the Hôtel de Ville, at one of the windows appeared Gambetta; a little behind him stood Jules Favre and Emmanuel Arago; and then and there, on that historic spot, I heard Gambetta proclaim the republic of France. That proclamation was received with every possible demonstration of enthusiasm. Lists were thrown out of the window, containing the names of the members of the provisional government. Ten minutes afterwards,

Raspail and Rochefort appeared at another window and embraced each other, while the crowd loudly applauded them.

During this time the public were occupying the Tuileries, from which the Empress had just escaped. Sixty thousand human beings had rolled toward the palace, completely levelling all obstacles; the vestibule was invaded, and in the court-yard, on the other side of the Place du Carrousel, were to be seen soldiers of every arm, who, in the presence of the people, removed the cartridges from their guns, and who were greeted by the cries, "Long live the nation!" "Down with the Bonapartes!" "To Berlin!" etc. During all of this time there was no pillage, no havoc, no destruction of property, and the crowd soon retired, leaving the palace under the protection of the National Guard.

Some discussion had been raised at the Hôtel de Ville about changing the flag, but Gambetta declared that the tri-color was the flag of 1792–3, and that under it France had been, and yet would be, led to victory. From the Hôtel de Ville, Mr. Eustis and myself went back to the Chamber of Deputies, to find it still in the possession of the people. From there I returned to my legation, which I reached at half-past six o'clock in the evening. At eight o'clock, I rode down to the *Corps Législatif* to see what the situation there was, but on my arrival I found everything closed and the lights extinguished. The doors leading to the Hall of the Deputies had been shut and seals put upon them. I then drove through some parts of the city, and found everything remarkably quiet. The day had been pleasant and the night was beautiful beyond description. Before returning to my lodgings, I called upon Lord Lyons, the British Ambassador, to talk over the events of the day which we had witnessed, and which we were certain would become one of the most memorable in the history of France. In a few brief hours of a Sabbath day I had seen a dynasty fall and a republic proclaimed, and all without the shedding of one drop of blood.

Henry James

If Franklin is the Moses of the American experience in Paris, then Henry James (1843–1916) is our Solomon, the guy who built the first great literary kingdom out of the experience, and supported it all on beautifully twisted columns. In his long and immensely productive life, James lived in Paris only briefly—from November 1875 to December 1876—a mostly lonely and unsuccessful year, before he fled for London and the comforts of a familiar language (and the illusion of a more attainable society). But his sense of Paris and his love for it was so complex, and his sense of the American experience there so rich as a symbol and subject, that he returned again and again throughout the 1880s and 90s. Early in his career James tried, and mostly failed, to be a snappy Parisian correspondent along the lines of a Willis, but in "Occasional Paris" (first published in 1878) he achieved a masterful account of Parisian manners, offering an analysis, and ultimately a defense, of the "habit of comparison" so dear to American writers in Paris. His long story "'The Velvet Glove'" (1909) is one of the less known of his great, half-magical late stories, but Edith Wharton, who played a role in its genesis (she took James on the late-night Parisian journey that he re-used in his account of the dubious assignation of American writer and French aristocratic woman), thought it one of his best, and she was right. It must be read—or at least can be read—or at least I choose to read it—as a kind of allegory of the American pursuit of the city itself; it presents itself as a miraculously attainable erotic attraction, only to reveal itself, at the end, as a mercenary and self-interested "jade." But then the James hero, like the American in Paris, chooses to keep his illusions at the end.

Occasional Paris

It is hard to say exactly what is the profit of comparing one race with another, and weighing in opposed groups the manners and customs of neighbouring countries; but it is certain that as we move about the world we constantly indulge in this exercise. This is especially the case if we happen to be infected with the baleful spirit of the cosmopolite—that uncomfortable consequence of seeing many lands and feeling at home in none. To be a cosmopolite is not, I think, an ideal; the ideal should be to be a concentrated patriot. Being a cosmopolite is an accident, but one must make the best of it. If you have lived about, as the phrase is, you have lost that sense of the absoluteness and the sanctity of the habits of your fellow-patriots which once made you so happy in the midst of them. You have seen that there are a great many *patriæ* in the world, and that each of these is filled with excellent people for whom the local idiosyncrasies are the only thing that is not rather barbarous. There comes a time when one set of customs, wherever it may be found, grows to seem to you about as provincial as another; and then I suppose it may be said of you that you have become a cosmopolite. You have formed the habit of comparing, of looking for points of difference and of resemblance, for present and absent advantages, for the virtues that go with certain defects, and the defects that go with certain virtues. If this is poor work compared with the active practice, in the sphere to which a discriminating Providence has assigned you, of the duties of a tax-payer, an elector, a juryman or a diner-out, there is nevertheless something to be said for it. It is good to think well of mankind, and this, on the whole, a cosmopolite does. If you limit your generalisations to the sphere I mentioned just now, there is a danger that your occasional fits of pessimism may be too sweeping. When you are out of humour the whole country suffers, because at such moments one is never discriminating, and it costs you very little bad logic to lump your fellow-citizens together. But if you are living about, as I say, certain differences impose themselves. The worst you can say of the human race is, for instance, that the Germans are a detestable people. They do not represent the human race for you, as in your native town your fellow-citizens do, and your unflattering judgment has a flattering reverse. If the Germans are detestable, you are mentally saying, there are those admirable French, or those charming Americans, or those interesting English. (Of course it is simply by accident that I couple the German name here with the unfavourable adjective. The epithets may be transposed at will.) Nothing can well be more different from anything else than the English from the French, so that, if you are acquainted with both nations, it may be said that on any special point your agreeable impression of the one implies a censorious attitude toward the other, and *vice versâ*. This has rather a shocking sound; it makes the cosmopolite appear invidious and narrow-minded. But I hasten to add that there seems no real reason why even the most delicate conscience should take alarm. The consequence of the cosmopolite spirit is to initiate you into the merits of all peoples; to convince you that national virtues are numerous, though they may be very different, and to make downright preference really very hard. I have, for instance, every disposition to think better of the English race than of any other except my own. There are things which make it natural I should; there are inducements, provocations, temptations, almost bribes. There have been moments when I have almost burned my ships behind me, and declared that, as it simplified matters greatly to pin one's faith to a chosen people, I would henceforth cease to trouble my head about the lights and shades of the foreign character. I am convinced that if I had taken this reckless engagement, I should greatly have regretted it. You may find a room very comfortable to sit in with the window open, and not like it at all when the window has been shut. If one were to give up the privilege of comparing the English with other people, one would very soon, in a moment of reaction, make once for all (and most unjustly) such a comparison as would leave the English nowhere. Compare then, I say, as often as the occasion presents itself. The result as regards any particular people, and as regards the human race at large, may be pronounced agreeable, and the process is both instructive and entertaining.

So the author of these observations finds it on returning to Paris after living for upwards of a year in London. He finds himself comparing, and the results of comparison are several disjointed reflections, of which it may be profitable to make a note. Certainly Paris is a very old story, and London is a still older one; and there is no great reason why a journey across the channel and back should quicken one's perspicacity to an unprecedented degree. I therefore will not pretend to have been looking at Paris with new eyes, or to have gathered on the banks of the Seine a harvest of extraordinary impressions. I will only pretend that a good many old impressions have recovered their freshness, and that there is a sort of renovated entertainment in looking at the most brilliant city in the world with eyes attuned to a different pitch. Never, in fact, have those qualities of brightness and gaiety that are half the stock-in-trade of the city by the Seine seemed to me more uncontestable. The autumn is but half over, and Paris is, in common parlance, empty. The private houses are closed, the lions have returned to the jungle, the Champs Elysées are not at all "mondains." But I have never seen Paris more Parisian, in the pleasantest sense of the word; better humoured, more open-windowed, more naturally entertaining. A radiant September helps the case; but doubtless the matter is, as I hinted above, in a large degree "subjective."

For when one comes to the point there is nothing very particular just now for Paris to rub her hands about. The Exhibition of 1878 is looming up as large as a mighty mass of buildings on the Trocadéro can make it. These buildings are very magnificent and fantastical; they hand over the Seine, in their sudden immensity and glittering newness, like a palace in a fairy-tale. But the trouble is that most people appear to regard the Exhibition as in fact a fairy-tale. They speak of the wonderful structures on the Champ de Mars and the Trocadéro as a predestined monument to the folly of a group of gentlemen destitute of a sense of the opportune. The moment certainly does not seem very well chosen for inviting the world to come to Paris to amuse itself. The world is too much occupied with graver cares—with reciprocal cannonading and chopping, with cutting of throats and burning of homes, with murder of infants and mutilation of mothers, with warding off famine and civil war, with lamenting the failure of its resources, the dulness of trade, the emptiness of its pockets. Rome is burning altogether too fast for even its most irresponsible spirits to find any great satisfaction in fiddling. But even if there is (as there very well may be) a certain scepticism at headquarters as to the accomplishment of this graceful design, there is no apparent hesitation, and everything is going forward as rapidly as if mankind were breathless with expectations. That familiar figure, the Parisian *ouvrier*, with his white, chalky blouse, his attenuated person, his clever face, is more familiar than ever, and I suppose, finding plenty of work to his hand, is for the time in a comparatively rational state of mind. He swarms in thousands, not only in the region of the Exhibition, but along the great thoroughfare—the Avenue de l'Opéra—which has just been opened in the interior of Paris.

This is an extremely Parisian creation, and as it is really a great convenience—it will save a great many steps and twists and turns—I suppose it should be spoken of with gratitude and admiration. But I confess that to my sense it belongs primarily to that order of benefits which during the twenty years of the Empire gradually deprived the streets of Paris of nine-tenths of their ancient individuality. The deadly monotony of the Paris that M. Haussmann called into being—its huge, blank, pompous, featureless sameness—sometimes comes over the wandering stranger with a force that leads him to devote the author of these miles of architectural commonplace to execration. The new street is quite on the imperial system; it must make the late Napoleon III. smile with beatific satisfaction as he looks down upon it from the Bonapartist corner of Paradise. It stretches straight away from the pompous façade of the Opera to the doors of the Théâtre Français, and it must be admitted that there is something fine in the vista that is closed at one end by the great sculptured and gilded mass of the former building. But it smells of the modern asphalt; it is lined with great white houses that are adorned with machine-made arabesques, and each of which is so exact a copy of all the rest that even the little white porcelain number on a blue ground, which looks exactly like all the other numbers, hardly constitutes an identity. Presently there will be a long succession of milliners' and chocolate-makers' shops in the basement of this homogeneous row, and the pretty bonnets and bonbonnières in the shining windows will have their ribbons knotted with a *chic* that you must come to Paris to see. Then there will be little glazed sentry-boxes at regular intervals along the curbstone, in which churlish old women will sit selling half a dozen copies of each of the newspapers; and over the hardened bitumen the young Parisian of our day will constantly circulate, looking rather pallid and wearing very large shirt-cuffs. And the new avenue will be a great success, for it will place in symmetrical communication two of the most important establishments in France—the temple of French music and the temple of French comedy.

I said just now that no two things could well be more unlike than England and France; and though the remark is not original, I uttered it with the spontaneity that it must have on the lips of a traveller who, having left either country, has just disembarked in the order. It is of course by this time a very trite observation, but it will continue to be made so long as Boulogne remains the same lively antithesis of Folkestone. An American, conscious of the family-likeness diffused over his own huge continent, never quite unlearns his surprise at finding that so little of either of these two almost contiguous towns has rubbed off upon the other. He is surprised at certain English people feeling so far away from France, and at all French people feeling so far away from England. I travelled from Boulogne the other day in the same railway-carriage with a couple of amiable and ingenuous young Britons, who had come over to spend ten days in Paris. It was their first landing in France; they had never yet quitted their native island; and in the course of a little conversation that I had with them I was struck with the scantiness of their information in regard to French manners and customs. They were very intelligent lads; they were apparently fresh from a university; but in respect to the interesting country they were about to enter, their minds were almost a blank. If the conductor, appearing at the carriage door to ask for our tickets, had had the leg of a frog sticking out of his pocket, I think their only very definite preconception would have been confirmed. I parted with them at the Paris station, and I have no doubt that they very soon began to make precious discoveries; and I have alluded to them not in the least to throw ridicule upon their "insularity"—which indeed, being accompanied with great modesty, I thought a very pretty spectacle—but because having become, since my last visit to France, a little insular myself, I was more conscious of the emotions that attend on an arrival.

The brightness always seems to begin while you are still out in the channel, when you fairly begin to see the French coast. You pass into a region of intenser light—a zone of clearness and colour. These properties brighten and deepen as you approach the land, and when you fairly stand upon that good Boulognese quay, among the blue and red douaniers and soldiers, the small ugly men in cerulean blouses, the charming fishwives, with their folded kerchiefs and their crisp cap-frills, their short striped petticoats, their tightly-drawn stockings, and their little clicking sabots— when you look about you at the smokeless air, at the pink and yellow houses, at the white-fronted café, close at hand, with its bright blue letters, its mirrors and marble-topped tables, its white-aproned, alert, undignified waiter, grasping a huge coffee-pot by a long handle—when you perceive all these things you feel the additional savour that foreignness gives to the picturesque; or feel rather, I should say, that simple foreignness may itself make the picturesque; for certainly the elements in the picture I have just sketched are not especially exquisite. No matter; you are amused, and your amusement continues—being sensibly stimulated by a visit to the buffet at the railway-station, which is better than the refreshment-room at Folkestone. It is a pleasure to have people offering you soup again, of their own movement; it is a pleasure to find a little pint of Bordeaux standing naturally before your plate; it is a pleasure to have a napkin; it is a pleasure, above all, to take up one of the good long sticks of French bread—as bread is called the staff of life, the French bake it literally in the shape of staves—and break off a loose, crisp, crusty morsel.

There are impressions, certainly, that imperil your good-humour. No honest Anglo-Saxon can like a French railway-station; and I was on the point of adding that no honest Anglo-Saxon can like a French railway-official. But I will not go so far as that; for after all I cannot remember any great harm that such a functionary has ever done me—except in locking me up as a malefactor. It is necessary to say, however, that the honest Anglo-Saxon, in a French railway-station, is in a state of chronic irritation—an irritation arising from his sense of the injurious effect upon the genial French nature of the possession of an administrative uniform. I believe that the consciousness of brass buttons on his coat and stripes on his trousers has spoiled many a modest and amiable Frenchman, and the sight of these aggressive insignia always stirs within me a moral protest. I repeat that my aversion to them is partly theoretic, for I have found, as a general thing, that an inquiry civilly made extracts a civil answer from even the most official-looking personage. But I have also found that such a personage's measure of the civility due to him is inordinately large; if he places himself in any degree at your service, it is apparently from the sense that true greatness can afford to unbend. You are constantly reminded that you must not presume. In England these intimations never proceed from one's "inferiors." In France the "administration" is the first thing that touches you; in a little while you get used to it, but you feel somehow that, in the process, you have lost the flower of your self-respect. Of course you are under some obligation to it. It has taken you off the steamer at Folkestone; made you tell your name to a gentleman with a sword, stationed at the farther end of the plank—not a drawn sword, it is true, but still, at the best, a very nasty weapon; marshalled you into the railway-station; assigned you to a carriage—I was going to say to a seat; transported you to Paris, marshalled you again out of the train, and under a sort of military surveillance, into an enclosure containing a number of human sheep-pens, in one of which it has imprisoned you for some half-hour. I am always on the point, in these places, of asking one of my gaolers if I may not be allowed to walk about on parole. The administration at any rate has finally taken you out of your pen, and, through the medium of a functionary who "inscribes" you in a little book, transferred you to a cab selected by a logic of its own. In doing all this it has certainly done a great deal for you; but somehow its good offices have made you feel sombre and resentful. The other day, on arriving from London, while I was waiting for my luggage, I saw several of the porters who convey travellers' impedimenta to the cab come up and deliver over the coin they had just received for this service to a functionary posted *ad hoc* in a corner, and armed with a little book in which he noted down these remittances. The *pour-boires* are apparently thrown into a common fund and divided among the guild of porters. The system is doubtless an excellent one, excellently carried out; but the sight of the poor round-shouldered man of burdens dropping his coin into the hand of the official arithmetician was to my fancy but another reminder that the individual, as an individual, loses by all that the administration assumes.

After living a while in England you observe the individual in Paris with quickened attention; and I think it must be said that at first he makes an indifferent figure. You are struck with the race being physically and personally a poorer one than that great family of largely-modelled, fresh-coloured people you have left upon the other side of the channel. I remember that in going to England a year ago and disembarking of a dismal, sleety Sunday evening at Folkestone, the first thing that struck me was the good looks of the railway porters—their broad shoulders, their big brown beards, their well-cut features. In like manner, landing lately at Boulogne of a brilliant Sunday morning, it was impossible not to think the little men in numbered caps who were gesticulating and chattering in one's path, rather ugly fellows. In arriving from other countries one is struck with a certain want of dignity in the French face. I do not know, however, whether this is anything worse than the fact that the French face is expressive; for it may be said that, in a certain sense, to express anything is to compromise with one's dignity, which likes to be understood without taking trouble. As regards the lower classes, at any rate, the impression I speak of always passes away; you perceive that the good looks of the French working-people are to be found in their look of intelligence. These people, in Paris, strike me afresh as the cleverest, the most perceptive, and, intellectually speaking, the most human of their kind. The Paris *ouvrier*, with his democratic blouse, his expressive, demonstrative, agreeable eye, his meagre limbs, his irregular, pointed features, his sallow complexion, his face at once fatigued and animated, his light, nervous organisation, is a figure that I always encounter again with pleasure. In some cases he looks depraved and perverted, but at his worst he looks refined; he is full of vivacity of perception, of something that one can appeal to.

It takes some courage to say this, perhaps, after reading *L'Assommoir*; but in M. Emile Zola's extraordinary novel one must make the part, as the French say, of the horrible uncleanness of the author's imagination.

L'Assommoir, I have been told, has had great success in the lower walks of Parisian life; and if this fact is not creditable to the delicacy of M. Zola's humble readers, it proves a good deal in favour of their intelligence. With all its grossness the book in question is essentially a literary performance; you must be tolerably clever to appreciate it. It is highly appreciated, I believe, by the young ladies who live in the region of the Latin Quarter—those young ladies who thirty years ago were called grisettes, and now are called I don't know what. They know long passages by heart; they repeat them with infinite gusto. "Ce louchon d'Augustine"—the horrible little girl with a squint, who is always playing nasty tricks and dodging slaps and projectiles in Gervaise's shop, is their particular favourite; and it must be admitted that "ce louchon d'Augustine" is, as regards reality, a wonderful creation.

If Parisians, both small and great, have more of the intellectual stamp than the people one sees in London, it is striking, on the other hand, that the people of the better sort in Paris look very much less "respectable." I did not know till I came back to Paris how used I had grown to the English *cachet*; but I immediately found myself missing it. You miss it in the men much more than in the women; for the well-to-do Frenchwoman of the lower orders, as one sees her in public, in the streets and in shops, is always a delightfully comfortable and creditable person. I must confess to the highest admiration for her, an admiration that increases with acquaintance. She, at least, is essentially respectable; the neatness, compactness, and sobriety of her dress, the decision of her movement and accent suggest the civic and domestic virtues—order, thrift, frugality, the moral necessity of making a good appearance. It is, I think, an old story that to the stranger in France the women seem greatly superior to the men. Their superiority, in fact, appears to be conceded; for wherever you turn you meet them in the forefront of action. You meet them, indeed, too often; you pronounce them at times obtrusive. It is annoying when you go to order your boots or your shirts, to have to make known your desires to even the most neat-waisted female attendant; for the limitations to the feminine intellect are, though few in number, distinct, and women are not able to understand certain masculine needs. Mr. Worth makes ladies' dresses; but I am sure there will never be a fashionable tailoress. There are, however, points at which, from the commercial point of view, feminine assistance is invaluable. For insisting upon the merits of an article that has failed to satisfy you, talking you over, and making you take it; for

defending a disputed bill, for paying the necessary compliments or supplying the necessary impertinence—for all these things the neat-waisted
sex has peculiar and precious faculties. In the commercial class in Paris the
man always appeals to the woman; the woman always steps forward. The
woman always proposes the conditions of a bargain. Go about and look for
furnished rooms, you always encounter a concierge and his wife. When
you ask the price of the rooms, the woman takes the words out of her husband's mouth, if indeed he have not first turned to her with a questioning
look. She takes you in hand; she proposes conditions; she thinks of things
he would not have thought of.

What I meant just now by my allusion to the absence of the
"respectable" in the appearance of the Parisian population was that the
men do not look like gentlemen, as so many Englishmen do. The average Frenchman that one encounters in public is of so different a type from
the average Englishman that you can easily believe that to the end of time
the two will not understand each other. The Frenchman has always, comparatively speaking, a Bohemian, empirical look; the expression of his
face, its colouring, its movement, have not been toned down to the neutral complexion of that breeding for which in English speech we reserve
the epithet of "good." He is at once more artificial and more natural; the
former where the Englishman is positive, the latter where the Englishman is negative. He takes off his hat with a flourish to a friend, but the
Englishman never bows. He ties a knot in the end of a napkin and thrusts
it into his shirt-collar, so that, as he sits at breakfast, the napkin may serve
the office of a pinafore. Such an operation as that seems to the Englishman as *naif* as the flourishing of one's hat is pretentious.

I sometimes go to breakfast at a café on the Boulevard, which I formerly used to frequent with considerable regularity. Coming back there
the other day, I found exactly the same group of habitués at their little
tables, and I mentally exclaimed as I looked at them over my newspaper,
upon their unlikeness to the gentlemen who confront you in the same attitude at a London club. Who are they? what are they? On these points I
have no information; but the stranger's imagination does not seem to see
a majestic social order massing itself behind them as it usually does in
London. He goes so far as to suspect that what is behind them is not
adapted for exhibition; whereas your Englishmen, whatever may be the
defects of their personal character, or the irregularities of their conduct,
are pressed upon from the rear by an immense body of private proprieties

and comforts, of domestic conventions and theological observances. But it is agreeable all the same to come back to a café of which you have formerly been an habitué. Adolphe or Edouard, in his long white apron and his large patent-leather slippers, has a perfect recollection of "les habitudes de Monsieur." He remembers the table you preferred, the wine you drank, the newspaper you read. He greets you with the friendliest of smiles, and remarks that it is a long time since he has had the pleasure of seeing Monsieur. There is something in this simple remark very touching to a heart that has suffered from that incorruptible dumbness of the British domestic. But in Paris such a heart finds consolation at every step; it is reminded of that most classic quality of the French nature—its sociability; a sociability which operates here as it never does in England, from below upward. Your waiter utters a greeting because, after all, something human within him prompts him; his instinct bids him say something, and his taste recommends that it be agreeable. The obvious reflection is that a waiter must not say too much, even for the sake of being human. But in France the people always like to make the little extra remark, to throw in something above the simply necessary. I stop before a little man who is selling newspapers at a street-corner, and ask him for the *Journal des Débats*. His answer deserves to be literally given: "Je ne l'ai plus, Monsieur; mais je pourrai vous donner quelquechose à peu près dans le même genre—la *République Française*." Even a person of his humble condition must have had a lurking sense of the comicality of offering anything as an equivalent for the "genre" of the venerable, classic, academic *Débats*. But my friend could not bear to give me a naked, monosyllabic refusal.

There are two things that the returning observer is likely to do with as little delay as possible. One is to dine at some *cabaret* of which he retains a friendly memory; another is to betake himself to the Théâtre Française. It is early in the season; there are no new pieces; but I have taken great pleasure in seeing some of the old ones. I lost no time in going to see Mademoiselle Sarah Bernhardt in *Andromaque. Andromaque* is not a novelty, but Mademoiselle Sarah Bernhardt has a perennial freshness. The play has been revived, to enable her to represent not the great part, the injured and passionate Hermione, but that of the doleful, funereal widow of Hector. This part is a poor one; it is narrow and monotonous, and offers few brilliant opportunities. But the actress knows how to make opportunities, and she has here a very sufficient one for crossing her thin white arms over her nebulous black robes, and sighing forth in

silver accents her dolorous rhymes. Her rendering of the part is one more
proof of her singular intelligence—of the fineness of her artistic nature.
As there is not a great deal to be done with it in the way of declamation,
she has made the most of its plastic side. She understands the art of
motion and attitude as no one else does, and her extraordinary personal
grace never fails her. Her Andromaque has postures of the most poetic
picturesqueness—something that suggests the broken stem and droop-
ing head of a flower that had been rudely plucked. She bends over her
classic confidant like the figure of Bereavement on a bas-relief, and she
has a marvellous manner of lifting and throwing back her delicate arms,
locking them together, and passing them behind her hanging head.

The *Demi-Monde* of M. Dumas *fils* is not a novelty either; but I quite
agree with M. Francisque Sarcey that it is on the whole, in form, the first
comedy of our day. I have seen it several times, but I never see it without being forcibly struck with its merits. For the drama of our time it
must always remain the model. The interest of the story, the quiet art
with which it is unfolded, the naturalness and soberness of the means
that are used, and by which great effects are produced, the brilliancy and
richness of the dialogue—all these things make it a singularly perfect
and interesting work. Of course it is admirably well played at the Théâtre
Français. Madame d'Ange was originally a part of too great amplitude for
Mademoiselle Croizette; but she is gradually filling it out and taking possession of it; she begins to give a sense of the "calme infernal," which
George Sand somewhere mentions as the leading attribute of the character. As for Delaunay, he does nothing better, more vividly and gallantly,
than Olivier de Jalin. When I say gallantry I say it with qualification; for
what a very queer fellow is this same M. de Jalin! In seeing the *Demi-
Monde* again I was more than ever struck with the oddity of its morality
and with the way that the ideal of fine conduct differs in different nations.
The *Demi-Monde* is the history of the eager, the almost heroic, effort of a
clever and superior woman, who has been guilty of what the French call
"faults," to pass from the irregular and equivocal circle to which these
faults have consigned her into what is distinctively termed "good society." The only way in which the passage can be effected is by her mar-
rying an honourable man; and to induce an honourable man to marry her,
she must suppress the more discreditable facts of her career. Taking
her for an honest woman, Raymond de Nanjac falls in love with her, and
honestly proposes to make her his wife. But Raymond de Nanjac has

contracted an intimate friendship with Olivier de Jalin, and the action of the play is more especially De Jalin's attempt—a successful one—to rescue his friend from the ignominy of a union with Suzanne d'Ange. Jalin knows a great deal about her, for the simple reason that he has been her lover. Their relations have been most harmonious, but from the moment that Suzanne sets her cap at Nanjac, Olivier declares war. Suzanne struggles hard to keep possession of her suitor, who is very much in love with her, and Olivier spares no pains to detach him. It is the means that Olivier uses that excite the wonderment of the Anglo-Saxon spectator. He takes the ground that in such a cause all means are fair, and when, at the climax of the play, he tells a thumping lie in order to make Madame d'Ange compromise herself, expose herself, he is pronounced by the author "le plus honnête homme que je connaisse." Madame d'Ange, as I have said, is a superior woman; the interest of the play is in her being a superior woman. Olivier has been her lover; he himself is one of the reasons why she may not marry Nanjac; he has given her a push along the downward path. But it is curious how little this is held by the author to disqualify him from fighting the battle in which she is so much the weaker combatant. An English-speaking audience is more "moral" than a French, more easily scandalised; and yet it is a singular fact that if the *Demi-Monde* were represented before an English-speaking audience, its sympathies would certainly not go with M. de Jalin. It would pronounce him rather a coward. Is it because such an audience, although it has not nearly such a pretty collection of pedestals to place under the feet of the charming sex, has, after all, in default of this degree of gallantry, a tenderness more fundamental? Madame d'Ange has stained herself, and it is doubtless not at all proper that such ladies should be led to the altar by honourable young men. The point is not that the English-speaking audience would be disposed to condone Madame d'Ange's irregularities, but that it would remain perfectly cold before the spectacle of her ex-lover's masterly campaign against her, and quite fail to think it positively admirable, or to regard the fib by which he finally clinches his victory as a proof of exceptional honesty. The ideal of our own audience would be expressed in some such words as, "I say, that's not fair game. Can't you let the poor woman alone?"

———

"The Velvet Glove"

He thought he had already, poor John Berridge, tasted in their fulness the sweets of success; but nothing yet had been more charming to him than when the young Lord, as he irresistibly and, for greater certitude, quite correctly figured him, fairly sought out, in Paris, the new literary star that had begun to hang, with a fresh red light, over the vast, even though rather confused, Anglo-Saxon horizon; positively approaching that celebrity with a shy and artless appeal. The young Lord invoked on this occasion the celebrity's prized judgment of a special literary case; and Berridge could take the whole manner of it for one of the "quaintest" little acts displayed to his amused eyes, up to now, on the stage of European society—albeit these eyes were quite aware, in general, of missing everywhere no more of the human scene than possible, and of having of late been particularly awake to the large extensions of it spread before him (since so he could but fondly read his fate) under the omen of his prodigious "hit." It was because of his hit that he was having rare opportunities—of which he was so honestly and humbly proposing, as he would have said, to make the most: it was because every one in the world (so far had the thing gone) was reading "The Heart of Gold" as just a slightly too fat volume, or sitting out the same as just a fifth-act too long play, that he found himself floated on a tide he would scarce have dared to show his favourite hero sustained by, found a hundred agreeable and interesting things happen to him which were all, one way or another, affluents of the golden stream.

The great renewed resonance—renewed by the incredible luck of the play—was always in his ears without so much as a conscious turn of his head to listen; so that the queer world of his fame was not the mere usual field of the Anglo-Saxon boom, but positively the bottom of the *whole* theatric sea, unplumbed source of the wave that had borne him in the course of a year or two over German, French, Italian, Russian, Scandinavian footlights. Paris itself really appeared for the hour the centre of his cyclone, with reports and "returns," to say nothing of agents and emissaries, converging from the minor capitals; though his impatience was scarce the less keen to get back to London, where his work had had no such critical excoriation to survive, no such lesson of anguish to learn, as it had received at the hand of supreme authority, of that French authority which was in such a matter the only one to be artistically reckoned with. If his spirit indeed had had to reckon with it his fourth act practically hadn't: it continued to make him blush every night for the public more even than the inimitable *feuilleton* had made him blush for himself.

This had figured, however, after all, the one bad drop in his cup; so that, for the rest, his high-water mark might well have been, that evening at Gloriani's studio, the approach of his odd and charming applicant, vaguely introduced at the latter's very own request by their hostess, who, with an honest, helpless, genial gesture, washed her fat begemmed hands of the name and identity of either, but left the fresh, fair, ever so habitually assured, yet ever so easily awkward Englishman with his plea to put forth. There was that in this pleasant personage which could still make Berridge wonder what conception of profit from him might have, all incalculably, taken form in such a head—these being truly the last intrenchments of our hero's modesty. He wondered, the splendid young man, he wondered awfully, he wondered (it was unmistakable) quite nervously, he wondered, to John's ardent and acute imagination, quite beautifully, if the author of "The Heart of Gold" would mind just looking at a book by a friend of his, a great friend, which he himself believed rather clever, and had in fact found very charming, but as to which—if it really wouldn't bore Mr. Berridge—he should so like the verdict of some one who knew. His friend was awfully ambitious, and he thought there was something in it— with all of which might he send the book to any address?

Berridge thought of many things while the young Lord thus charged upon him, and it was odd that no one of them was any question of the possible worth of the offered achievement—which, for that matter, was certain to be of the quality of *all* the books, to say nothing of the plays, and the projects for plays, with which, for some time past, he had seen his daily post-bag distended. He had made out, on looking at these things, no difference at all from one to the other. Here, however, was something more—something that made his fellow-guest's overture *independently* interesting and, as he might imagine, important. He smiled, he was friendly and vague; said "A work of fiction, I suppose?" and that he didn't pretend ever to pronounce, that he in fact quite hated, always, to have to, not "knowing," as he felt, any better than any one else; but would gladly look at anything, under that demur, if it would give any pleasure. Perhaps the very brightest and most diamond-like twinkle he had yet seen the star of his renown emit was just the light brought into his young

Lord's eyes by this so easy consent to oblige. It was easy because the presence before him was from moment to moment referring itself back to
some recent observation or memory; something caught somewhere,
within a few weeks or months, as he had moved about, and that seemed
to flutter forth at this stir of the folded leaves of his recent experience very
much as a gathered, faded flower, placed there for "pressing," might drop
from between the pages of a volume opened at hazard.

He had seen him before, this splendid and sympathetic person—
whose flattering appeal was by no means *all* that made him sympathetic;
he had met him, had noted, had wondered about him, had in fact imagi-
natively, intellectually, so to speak, quite yearned over him, in some
conjunction lately, though ever so fleetingly, apprehended: which circumstance constituted precisely an association as tormenting, for the few
minutes, as it was vague, and set him to sounding, intensely and vainly,
the face that itself figured everything agreeable except recognition. He
couldn't remember, and the young man didn't; distinctly, yes, they had
been in presence, during the previous winter, by some chance of travel,
through Sicily, through Italy, through the south of France, but his
Seigneurie—so Berridge liked exotically to phrase it—had then (in ignorance of the present reasons) not noticed *him*. It was positive for the man
of established identity, all the while too, and through the perfect lucidity
of his sense of achievement in an air "conducting" nothing but the loud-
est bang, that this was fundamentally much less remarkable than the fact
of his being made up to in such a quarter now. That was the disservice, in
a manner, of one's having so much imagination: the mysterious values of
other types kept looming larger before you than the doubtless often
higher but comparatively familiar ones of your own, and if you had anything of the artist's real feeling for life the attraction and amusement of
possibilities so projected were worth more to you, in nineteen moods out
of twenty, than the sufficiency, the serenity, the felicity, whatever it might
be, of your stale personal certitudes. You were intellectually, you were
"artistically" rather abject, in fine, if your curiosity (in the grand sense of
the term) wasn't worth more to you than your dignity. What *was* your dignity, "anyway," but just the consistency of your curiosity, and what
moments were ever so ignoble for you as, under the blighting breath of
the false gods, stupid conventions, traditions, examples, your lapses from
that consistency? His *Seigneurie*, at all events, delightfully, hadn't the least
real idea of what any John Berridge was talking about, and the latter felt

that if he had been less beautifully witless, and thereby less true to his right figure, it might scarce have been forgiven him.

His right figure was that of life in irreflective joy and at the highest thinkable level of prepared security and unconscious insolence. What was the pale page of fiction compared with the intimately personal adventure that, in almost any direction, he would have been all so stupidly, all so gallantly, all so instinctively and, by every presumption, so prevailingly ready for? Berridge would have given six months' "royalties" for even an hour of his looser dormant consciousness—since one was oneself, after all, no worm, but an heir of all the ages too—and yet without being able to supply chapter and verse for the felt, the huge difference. His *Seigneurie* was tall and straight, but so, thank goodness, was the author of "The Heart of Gold," who had no such vulgar "mug" either; and there was no intrinsic inferiority in being a bit inordinately, and so it might have seemed a bit strikingly, black-browed instead of being fair as the morning. Again while his new friend delivered himself our own tried in vain to place him; he indulged in plenty of pleasant, if rather restlessly headlong sound, the confessed incoherence of a happy mortal who had always many things "on," and who, while waiting at any moment for connections and consummations, had fallen into the way of talking, as they said, all artlessly, and a trifle more betrayingly, against time. He would always be having appointments, and somehow of a high "romantic" order, to keep, and the imperfect punctualities of others to wait for—though who would be of a quality to make such a pampered personage wait very much our young analyst could only enjoy asking himself. There were women who might be of a quality—half a dozen of those perhaps, of those alone, about the world; our friend was as sure of this, by the end of four minutes, as if he knew all about it.

After saying he would send him the book the young Lord indeed dropped that subject; he had asked where he might send it, and had had an "Oh, I shall remember!" on John's mention of an hotel; but he had made no further dash into literature, and it was ten to one that this would be the last the distinguished author might hear of the volume. Such again was a note of these high existences—that made one content to ask of them no whit of other consistency than that of carrying off the particular occasion, whatever it might be, in a dazzle of amiability and felicity and leaving *that* as a sufficient trace of their passage. Sought and achieved consistency was but an angular, a secondary motion; compared with the air of complete freedom it might have an effect of deformity. There was no placing this figure of radiant ease, for Berridge, in any relation that didn't appear not good enough—that is among the relations that hadn't been too good for Berridge himself. He was all right where he was; the great Gloriani somehow made that law; his house, with his supreme artistic position, was good enough for any one, and to-night in especial there were charming people, more charming than our friend could recall from any other scene, as the natural train or circle, as he might say, of such a presence. For an instant he thought he had got the face as a specimen of imperturbability watched, with wonder, across the hushed rattle of roulette at Monte-Carlo; but this quickly became as improbable as any question of a vulgar *table d'hôte*, or a steam-boat deck, or a herd of fellow-pilgrims cicerone-led, or even an opera-box serving, during a performance, for frame of a type observed from the stalls. One placed young gods and goddesses only when one placed them on Olympus, and it met the case, always, that they were of Olympian race, and that they glimmered for one, at the best, through their silver cloud, like the visiting apparitions in an epic.

This was brief and beautiful indeed till something happened that gave it, for Berridge, on the spot, a prodigious extension—an extension really as prodigious, after a little, as if he had suddenly seen the silver clouds multiply and then the whole of Olympus presently open. Music, breaking upon the large air, enjoined immediate attention, and in a moment he was listening, with the rest of the company, to an eminent tenor, who stood by the piano; and was aware, with it, that his Englishman had turned away and that in the vast, rich, tapestried room where, in spite of figures and objects so numerous, clear spaces, wide vistas, and, as they might be called, becoming situations abounded, there had been from elsewhere, at the signal of unmistakable song, a rapid accession of guests. At first he but took this in, and the way that several young women, for whom seats had been found, looked charming in the rapt attitude; while even the men, mostly standing and grouped, "composed," in their stillness, scarce less impressively, under the sway of the divine voice. It ruled the scene, to the last intensity, and yet our young man's fine sense found still a resource in the range of the eyes, without sound or motion, while all the rest of consciousness was held down as by a hand mailed in silver. It was better, in this way, than the opera—John alertly thought of that: the composition sung might be Wagnerian, but no Tristram, no Iseult, no Parsifal and, no Kundry of them all could ever show, could ever "act" to the music, as our friend had thus the power of seeing his dear contemporaries of either sex (armoured *they* so otherwise than in cheap Teutonic tinsel!) just continuously and inscrutably sit to it.

It made, the whole thing together, an enchantment amid which he had in truth, at a given moment, ceased to distinguish parts—so that he was himself certainly at last soaring as high as the singer's voice and forgetting, in a lost gaze at the splendid ceiling, everything of the occasion but what his intelligence poured into it. This, as happened, was a flight so sublime that by the time he had dropped his eyes again a cluster of persons near the main door had just parted to give way to a belated lady who slipped in, through the gap made for her, and stood for some minutes full in his view. It was a proof of the perfect hush that no one stirred to offer her a seat, and her entrance, in her high grace, had yet been so noiseless that she could remain at once immensely exposed and completely unabashed. For Berridge, once more, if the scenic show before him so melted into the music, here precisely might have been the heroine herself advancing to the foot-lights at her cue. The interest deepened to a thrill, and every-thing, at the touch of his recognition of this personage, absolutely the most beautiful woman now present, fell exquisitely together and gave him what he had been wanting from the moment of his taking in his young Englishman.

It was there, the missing connection: her arrival had on the instant lighted it by a flash, Olympian herself, supremely, divinely Olympian, she had arrived, could *only* have arrived, for the one person present of really equal race, our young man's late converser, whose flattering demonstra-tion might now stand for one of the odd extravagant forms taken by ner-vous impatience. This charming, this dazzling woman had been one member of the couple disturbed, to his intimate conviction, the autumn previous, on his being pushed by the officials, at the last moment, into a compartment of the train that was to take him from Cremona to Mantua—where, failing a stop, he had had to keep his place. The other member, by whose felt but unseized identity he had been haunted, was the uncon-sciously insolent form of guaranteed happiness he had just been engaged with. The sense of the admirable intimacy that, having taken its precau-tions, had not reckoned with his irruption—this image had remained with him; to say nothing of the interest of aspect of the associated figures, so stamped somehow with rarity, so beautifully distinct from the common occupants of padded corners, and yet on the subject of whom, for the romantic structure he was immediately to raise, he had not had a scrap of evidence.

If he had imputed to them conditions it was all his own doing: it came from his inveterate habit of abysmal imputation, the snatching of the ell wherever the inch peeped out, without which where would have been the tolerability of life? It didn't matter now what he had imputed—and he always held that his expenses of imputation were, at the worst, a compliment to those inspiring them. It only mattered that each of the pair had been then what he really saw each now—full, that is, of the pride of their youth and beauty and fortune and freedom, though at the same time particularly preoccupied: preoccupied, that is, with the affairs, and above all with the passions, of Olympus. Who had they been, and what? Whence had they come, whither were they bound, what tie united them, what adventure engaged, what felicity, tempered by what peril, magnificently, dramatically attended? These had been his questions, all so inevitable and so impertinent, at the time, and to the exclusion of any scruples over his not postulating an inane honeymoon, his not taking the "tie," as he should doubtless properly have done, for the mere blest matrimonial; and he now retracted not one of them, flushing as they did before him again with their old momentary life. To feel his two friends renewedly in presence—friends of the fleeting hour though they had but been, and with whom he had exchanged no sign save the vaguest of salutes on finally relieving them of his company—was only to be conscious that he hadn't, on the spot, done them, so to speak, half justice, and that, for his superior entertainment, there would be ever so much more of them to come.

II

It might already have been coming indeed, with an immense stride, when, scarce more than ten minutes later, he was aware that the distinguished stranger had brought the Princess straight across the room to speak to him. He had failed in the interval of any glimpse of their closer meeting; for the great tenor had sung another song and then stopped, immediately on which Madame Gloriani had made his pulse quicken to a different, if not to a finer, throb by hovering before him once more with the man in the world he most admired, as it were, looking at him over her shoulder. The man in the world he most admired, the greatest then of contemporary Dramatists—and bearing, independently, the name inscribed if not in deepest incision at least in thickest gilding on the rich recreative roll—this prodigious personage was actually to suffer "presentation" to him at the good lady's generous but ineffectual hands, and had in fact the next instant, left alone with him, bowed, in formal salutation, the massive, curly, witty head, so "romantic" yet so modern, so "artistic" and ironic yet somehow so civic, so Gallic yet somehow so cosmic, his personal vision of which had not hitherto transcended that of the possessor of a signed and framed photograph in a consecrated quarter of a writing-table.

It was positive, however, that poor John was afterward to remember of this conjunction nothing whatever but the fact of the great man's looking at him very hard, straight in the eyes, and of his not having himself scrupled to do as much, and with a confessed intensity of appetite. It was improbable, he was to recognise, that they had, for the few minutes, only stared and grimaced, like pitted boxers or wrestlers; but what had abode with him later on, none the less, was just the cherished memory of his not having so lost presence of mind as to fail of feeding on his impression. It was precious and precarious, that was perhaps all there would be of it; and his subsequent consciousness was quite to cherish this queer view of the silence, neither awkward nor empty nor harsh, but on the contrary quite charged and brimming, that represented for him his use, his unforgettable enjoyment in fact, of his opportunity. Had nothing passed in words? Well, no misery of murmured "homage," thank goodness; though something must have been said, certainly, to lead up, as they put it at the theatre, to John's having asked the head of the profession, before they separated, if he by chance knew who the so radiantly handsome young woman might be, the one who had so lately come in and who wore the pale yellow dress, of the strange tone, and the magnificent pearls. They must have separated soon, it was further to have been noted; since it was before the advance of the pair, their wonderful dazzling charge upon him, that he had distinctly seen the great man, at a distance again, block out from his sight the harmony of the faded gold and the pearls—to speak only of that—and plant himself there (the mere high Atlas-back of renown to Berridge now) as for communion with them. He had blocked everything out, to this tune, effectually; with nothing of the matter left for our friend meanwhile but that, as he had said, the beautiful lady was the Princess. What Princess, or the Princess of what?—our young man had afterward wondered; his companion's reply having lost itself in the prelude of an outburst by another vocalist who had approached the piano.

It was after these things that she so incredibly came to him, attended by her adorer—since he took it for absolute that the young Lord was her adorer, as who indeed mightn't be?—and scarce waiting, in her bright simplicity, for any form of introduction. It may thus be said in a word that this was the manner in which she made our hero's acquaintance, a satisfaction that she on the spot described to him as really wanting of late to her felicity. "I've read everything, you know, and 'The Heart of Gold' three times": she put it all immediately on that ground, while the young Lord now smiled, beside her, as if it were quite the sort of thing he had done too; and while, further, the author of the work yielded to the consciousness that whereas in general he had come at last scarce to be able to bear the iteration of those words, which affected him as a mere vain vocal convulsion, so not a breath of this association now attended them, so such a person as the Princess could make of them what she would. Unless it was to be really what *he* would!—this occurred to him in the very thick of the prodigy, no single shade of possibility of which was less prodigious than any other. It was a declaration, simply, the admirable young woman was treating him to, a profession of "artistic sympathy"—for she was in a moment to use this very term that made for them a large, clear, common ether, an element all uplifted and rare, of which they could equally partake.

If she was Olympian—as in her rich and regular young beauty, that of some divine Greek mask over-painted say by Titian, she more and more appeared to him—this offered air was that of the gods themselves: she might have been, with her long rustle across the room, Artemis decorated, hung with pearls, for her worshippers, yet disconcerting them by having, under an impulse just faintly fierce, snatched the cup of gold from Hebe. It was to him, John Berridge, she thus publicly offered it; and it was his over-topping *confrère* of shortly before who was the worshipper most disconcerted. John had happened to catch, even at its distance, after these friends had joined him, the momentary deep, grave estimate, in the great Dramatist's salient watching eyes, of the Princess's so singular performance: the touch perhaps this, in the whole business, that made Berridge's sense of it most sharp. The sense of it as *prodigy* didn't in the least entail his feeling abject—any more, that is, than in the due dazzled degree; for surely there would have been supreme wonder in the eagerness of her exchange of mature glory for thin notoriety, hadn't it still exceeded everything that an Olympian of such race should have found herself bothered, as they said, to "read" at all—and most of all to read three times!

With the turn the matter took as an effect of this meeting, Berridge was more than once to find himself almost ashamed for her—since it seemed never to occur to her to be so for herself: he was jealous of the type where she might have been taken as insolently careless of it; his advantage (unless indeed it had been his ruin) being that he could inordinately reflect upon it, could wander off thereby into kinds of licence of which she was incapable. He hadn't, for himself, waited till now to be sure of what he would do were *he* an Olympian: he would leave his own stuff snugly unread, to begin with; that would be a beautiful start for an Olympian career. He should have been as unable to write those works in short as to make anything else of them; and he should have had no more arithmetic for computing fingers than any perfect-headed marble Apollo mutilated at the wrists. He should have consented to know but the grand personal adventure on the grand personal basis: nothing short of this, no poor cognisance of confusable, pettifogging things, the sphere of earth-grubbing questions and two-penny issues, would begin to be, on any side, Olympian enough.

Even the great Dramatist, with his tempered and tested steel and his immense "assured" position, even he was not Olympian: the look, full of the torment of earth, with which he had seen the Princess turn her back, and for such a purpose, on the prized privilege of his notice, testified sufficiently to that. Still, comparatively, it was to be said, the question of a personal relation with an authority so eminent on the subject of the passions—to say nothing of the rest of his charm—might have had for an ardent young woman (and the Princess was unmistakably ardent) the absolute attraction of romance unless, again, prodigy of prodigies, she were looking for her romance very particularly elsewhere. Yet where could she have been looking for it, Berridge was to ask himself with private intensity, in a manner to leave her so at her ease for appearing to offer *him* everything?—so free to be quite divinely gentle with him, to hover there before him in all her mild, bright, smooth sublimity and to say: "I should be so very grateful if you'd come to see me."

There succeeded this a space of time of which he was afterward to lose all account, was never to recover the history; his only coherent view of its being that an interruption, some incident that kept them a while separate, had then taken place, yet that during their separation, of half an hour or whatever, they had still somehow not lost sight of each other, but had found their eyes meeting, in deep communion, all across the great peopled room; meeting and wanting to meet, wanting—it was the most extraordinary thing in the world for the suppression of stages, for confessed precipitate intensity—to use together every instant of the hour that might be left them. Yet to use it for what?—unless, like beautiful fabulous figures in some old-world legend, for the frankest and almost the crudest avowal of the impression they had made on each other. He couldn't have named, later on, any other person she had during this space been engaged with, any more than he was to remember in the least what he had himself ostensibly done, who had spoken to him, whom he had spoken to, or whether he hadn't just stood and publicly gaped or languished.

Ah, Olympians were unconventional indeed—that was a part of their high bravery and privilege; but what it also appeared to attest in this wondrous manner was that they could communicate to their chosen in three minutes, by the mere light of their eyes, the same shining cynicism. He was to wonder of course, tinglingly enough, whether he had really made an ass of himself, and there was this amount of evidence for it that there certainly *had* been a series of moments each one of which glowed with the lucid sense that, as she couldn't like him as much as *that* either for his acted clap-trap or for his printed verbiage, what it must come to was that she liked him, and to such a tune, just for himself and quite after no other fashion than that in which every goddess in the calendar had, when you came to look, sooner or later liked some prepossessing young shepherd. The question would thus have been, for him, with a still sharper eventual ache, of whether he positively *had*, as an effect of the miracle, been petrified, before fifty pair of eyes, to the posture of a prepossessing shepherd—and would perhaps have left him under the shadow of some such imputable fatuity if his consciousness hadn't, at a given moment, cleared up to still stranger things.

The agent of the change was, as quite congruously happened, none other than the shining youth whom he now seemed to himself to have been thinking of for ever so long, for a much longer time than he had ever in his life spent at an evening party, as the young Lord: which personage suddenly stood before him again, holding him up an odd object and smiling, as if in reference to it, with a gladness that at once struck our friend as almost too absurd for belief. The object was incongruous by reason of its being, to a second and less preoccupied glance, a book; and what had befallen Berridge within twenty minutes was that they—the Princess and he, that is—had got such millions of miles, or at least such thousands of years, away from *those* platitudes. The book, he found himself assuming, could only be *his* book (it seemed also to have a tawdry red cover); and there came to him memories, dreadfully false notes sounded so straight again by his new acquaintance, of certain altogether different persons who at certain altogether different parties had flourished volumes before him very much with that insinuating gesture, that arch expression, and that fell intention. The meaning of these things—of all possible breaks of the charm at such an hour!—was that he should "signature" the ugly thing, and with a characteristic quotation or sentiment: that was the way people simpered and squirmed, the way they mouthed and beckoned, when animated by such purposes; and it already, on the spot, almost broke his heart to see such a type as that of the young Lord brought, by the vulgarest of fashions, so low. This state of quick displeasure in Berridge, however, was founded on a deeper question—the question of how in the world he was to remain for himself a prepossessing shepherd if he should consent to come back to these base actualities. It was true that even while this wonderment held him, his aggressor's perfect good conscience had placed the matter in a slightly different light.

"By an extraordinary chance I've found a copy of my friend's novel on one of the tables here—I see by the inscription that she has presented it to Gloriani. So if you'd like to glance at it—!" And the young Lord, in the pride of his association with the eminent thing, held it out to Berridge as artlessly as if it had been a striking natural specimen of some sort, a rosy round apple grown in his own orchard, or an exceptional precious stone, to be admired for its weight and lustre. Berridge accepted the offer mechanically—relieved at the prompt fading of his worst fear, yet feeling in himself a tell-tale facial blankness for the still absolutely anomalous character of his friend's appeal. He was even tempted for a moment to lay the volume down without looking at it—only with some extemporised promise to borrow it of their host and take it home, to give himself to it at an easier moment. Then the very expression of his fellow-guest's own countenance determined in him a different and a still more dreadful view; in fact an immediate collapse of the dream in which he had for the splendid previous space of time been living. The young Lord himself, in his radiant costly barbarism, figured far better than John Berridge could do the prepossessing shepherd, the beautiful mythological mortal "distinguished" by a goddess; for our hero now saw that his whole manner of dealing with his ridiculous tribute was marked exactly by the grand simplicity, the prehistoric good faith, as one might call it, of far-off romantic and "plastic" creatures, figures of exquisite Arcadian stamp, glorified rustics like those of the train of peasants in "A Winter's Tale," who thought nothing of such treasure-trove, on a Claude Lorrain sea-strand, as a royal infant wrapped in purple: something in that fabulous style of exhibition appearing exactly what his present demonstration might have been prompted by.

"The Top of the Tree, by Amy Evans"—scarce credible words floating before Berridge after he had with an anguish of effort dropped his eyes on the importunate title-page—represented an object as alien to the careless grace of goddess-haunted Arcady as a washed-up "kodak" from a wrecked ship might have been to the appreciation of some islander of wholly unvisited seas. Nothing could have been more in the tone of an islander deplorably diverted from his native interests and dignities than the glibness with which John's own child of nature went on. "It's her pen-name, Amy Evans"—he couldn't have said it otherwise had he been a blue-chinned penny-a-liner; yet marking it with a disconnectedness of intelligence that kept up all the poetry of his own situation and only crashed into that of other persons. The reference put the author of "The Heart of Gold" quite into *his* place, but left the speaker absolutely free of Arcady. "Thanks awfully"—Berridge somehow clutched at that, to keep everything from swimming. "Yes, I should like to look at it," he managed, horribly grimacing now, he believed, to say; and there was in fact a strange short interlude after this in which he scarce knew what had become of any one or of anything; in which he only seemed to himself to stand alone in a desolate place where even its desolation didn't save him from having to stare at the greyest of printed pages. Nothing here helped anything else, since the stamped greyness didn't even in itself make it impossible his eyes should follow such sentences as: "The loveliness of the face, which was that of the glorious period in which Pheidias reigned supreme, and which owed its most exquisite note to that shell-like curl of the upper lip which always somehow recalls for us the smile with which wind-blown Astarte must have risen from the salt sea to which she owed her birth and her terrible moods"; or "It was too much for all the passionate woman in her, and she let herself go, over the flowering land that had been, but was no longer their love, with an effect of blighting desolation that might have

proceeded from one of the more physical, though not more awful, convulsions of nature."

He seemed to know later on that other and much more natural things
had occurred; as that, for instance, with now at last a definite intermission
of the rare music that for a long time past, save at the briefest intervals,
had kept all participants ostensibly attentive and motionless, and that in
spite of its high quality and the supposed privilege of listening to it he had
allowed himself not to catch a note of, there was a great rustling and shifting and vociferous drop to a lower plane, more marked still with the quick
clearance of a way to supper and a lively dispersal of most of the guests.
Hadn't he made out, through the queer glare of appearances, though they
yet somehow all came to him as confused and unreal, that the Princess
was no longer there, wasn't even only crowded out of his range by the
immediate multiplication of her court, the obsequious court that the
change of pitch had at once permitted to close round her; that Gloriani had
offered her his arm, in a gallant official way, as to the greatest lady present,
and that he was left with half a dozen persons more knowing than the others, who had promptly taken, singly or in couples, to a closer inspection of
the fine small scattered treasures of the studio?

He himself stood there, rueful and stricken, nursing a silly red-bound
book under his arm very much as if he might have been holding on tight
to an upright stake, or to the nearest piece of furniture, during some
impression of a sharp earthquake-shock or of an attack of dyspeptic dizzi-
ness; albeit indeed that he wasn't conscious of this absurd, this instinctive
nervous clutch till the thing that was to be more wonderful than any yet
suddenly flared up for him—the sight of the Princess again on the threshold of the room, poised there an instant, in her exquisite grace, for recovery of some one or of something, and then, at recognition of him, coming
straight to him across the empty place as if he alone, and nobody and nothing else, were what she incredibly wanted. She was there, she was radiantly *at* him, as if she had known and loved him for ten years—ten years
during which, however, she had never quite been able, in spite of undis-
couraged attempts, to cure him, as goddesses *had* to cure shepherds, of his
mere mortal shyness.

"Ah no, not *that* one!" she said at once, with her divine familiarity; for
she had in the flash of an eye "spotted" the particularly literary production he seemed so very fondly to have possessed himself of and against
which all the Amy Evans in her, as she would doubtless have put it, clearly

wished on the spot to discriminate. She pulled it away from him; he let it go; he scarce knew what was happening—only made out that she distinguished the right one, the one that should have been shown him, as blue or green or purple, and intimated that her other friend, her fellow-Olympian, as Berridge had thought of him from the first, really did too clumsily bungle matters, poor dear, with his officiousness over the red one! She went on really as if she had come for that, some such rectification, some such eagerness of reunion with dear Mr. Berridge, some talk, after all the tiresome music, of questions really urgent; while, thanks to the supreme strangeness of it, the high tide of golden fable floated him afresh, and her pretext and her plea, the queerness of her offered motive, melted away after the fashion of the enveloping clouds that do their office in epics and idylls.

"You didn't perhaps know I'm Amy Evans," she smiled, "or even perhaps that I write in English—which I love, I assure you, as much as you can yourself do, and which gives one (doesn't it? for who should know if not you?) the biggest of publics. I 'just love'—don't they say?—your American millions; and all the more that they really *take* me for Amy Evans, as I've just wanted to be taken, to be loved too for myself, don't you know?—that they haven't seemed to try at all to 'go behind' (don't you say?) my poor dear little *nom de guerre*. But it's the new one, my last, 'The Velvet Glove,' that I should like you to judge me by—if such a *corvée* isn't too horrible for you to think of; though I admit it's a move straight in the romantic direction—since after all (for I might as well make a clean breast of it) it's dear old discredited romance that I'm most in sympathy with. I'll send you 'The Velvet Glove' to-morrow, if you *can* find half an hour for it; and then—and *then*—!" She paused as for the positive bright glory of her meaning.

It could only be so extraordinary, her meaning, whatever it was, that the need in him that would—whatever it was again!—meet it most absolutely formed the syllables on his lips as: "Will you be very, *very* kind to me?"

"Ah 'kind,' dear Mr. Berridge? 'Kind,'" she splendidly laughed, "is nothing to what—!" But she pulled herself up again an instant. "Well, to what I want to be! Just *see*," she said, "how I want to be!" It was exactly, he felt, what he couldn't *but* see—in spite of books and publics and pen-names, in spite of the really "decadent" perversity, recalling that of the most irresponsibly insolent of the old Romans and Byzantines, that could

lead a creature so formed for living and breathing her Romance, and so
committed, up to the eyes, to the constant fact of her personal immersion
in it and genius for it, the dreadful amateurish dance of ungrammatically
scribbling it, with editions and advertisements and reviews and royalties
and every other futile item: since what was more of the deep essence of
throbbing intercourse itself than this very act of her having broken away
from people, in the other room, to whom he was as nought, of her having,
with her *crânerie* of audacity and indifference, just turned her back on
them all as soon as she had begun to miss him? What was more of it than
her having forbidden them, by a sufficient curt ring of her own supremely
silver tone, to attempt to check or criticise her freedom, than her having
looked him up, at his distance, under all the noses he had put out of joint,
so as to let them think whatever they might—not of herself (much she
troubled to care!) but of the new champion to be reckoned with, the
invincible young lion of the day? What was more of it in short than her
having perhaps even positively snubbed for him the great mystified
Sculptor and the great bewildered Dramatist, treated to this queer experience for the first time of their lives?

It all came back again to the really great ease of really great ladies, and
to the perfect facility of everything when once they were great enough.
That might become the delicious thing to him, he more and more felt, as
soon as it should be supremely attested; it was ground he had ventured on,
scenically, representationally, in the artistic sphere, but without ever
dreaming he should "realise" it thus in the social. Handsomely, gallantly
just now, moreover, he didn't so much as let it occur to him that the social
experience would perhaps on some future occasion richly profit further
scenic efforts; he only lost himself in the consciousness of all she invited
him to believe. It took licence, this consciousness, the next moment, for
a tremendous further throb, from what she had gone on to say to him in
so many words—though indeed the words were nothing and it was all a
matter but of the implication that glimmered through them: "Do you *want*
very much your supper here?" And then while he felt himself glare, for
charmed response, almost to the point of his tears rising with it: "Because
if you don't——!"

"Because if I don't—?" She had paused, not from the faintest shade
of timidity, but clearly for the pleasure of making him press.

"Why shouldn't we go together, letting me drive you home?"

"You'll come home with me?" gasped John Berridge while the perspiration on his brow might have been the morning dew on a high lawn of Mount Ida.

"No—you had better come with *me*. That's what I mean; but I certainly will come to you with pleasure some time if you'll let me."

She made no more than that of the most fatuous of freedoms, as he felt directly he had spoken that it might have seemed to her; and before he had even time to welcome the relief of not having then himself, for beastly contrition, to make more of it, she had simply mentioned, with her affectionate ease, that she wanted to get away, that of the bores there she might easily, after a little, have too much, and that if he'd but say the word they'd nip straight out together by an independent door and be sure to find her motor in the court. What word he had found to say, he was afterward to reflect, must have little enough mattered; for he was to have kept, of what then occurred, but a single other impression, that of her great fragrant rustle beside him over the rest of the ample room and toward their nearest and friendliest resource, the door by which he had come in and which gave directly upon a staircase. This independent image was just that of the only other of his fellow-guests with whom he had been closely concerned; he had thought of him rather indeed, up to that moment, as the Princess's fellow-Olympian—but a new momentary vision of him seemed now to qualify it.

The young Lord had reappeared within a minute on the threshold, that of the passage from the supper-room, lately crossed by the Princess herself, and Berridge felt him there, saw him there, wondered about him there, all, for the first minute, without so much as a straight look at him. He would have come to learn the reason of his friend's extraordinary public demonstration—having more right to his curiosity, or his anxiety or whatever, than any one else; he would be taking in the remarkable appearances that thus completed it, and would perhaps be showing quite a different face for them, at the point they had reached, than any that would have hitherto consorted with the beautiful security of his own position. So much, on our own young man's part, for this first flush of a presumption that he might have stirred the germs of ire in a celestial breast; so much for the moment during which nothing would have induced him to betray, to a possibly rueful member of an old aristocracy, a vulgar elation or a tickled, unaccustomed glee. His inevitable second thought was, however, it has to be confessed, another matter, which took a different turn—for, frankly, all the conscious conqueror in him, as Amy Evans would again have said, couldn't forego a probably supreme consecration. He treated himself to no prolonged reach of vision, but there was something he nevertheless fully measured for five seconds—the sharp truth of the fact, namely, of how the interested observer in the doorway must really have felt about him. Rather disconcertingly, hereupon, the sharp truth proved to be that the most amused, quite the most encouraging and the least invidious of smiles graced the young Lord's handsome countenance—forming, in short, his final contribution to a display of high social candour unprecedented in our hero's experience. No, he wasn't jealous, didn't do John Berridge the honour to be, to the extent of the least glimmer of a spark of it, but was so happy to see his immortal mistress do what she liked that he could positively beam at the odd circumstance of her almost lavishing public caresses on a gentleman not, after all, of negligible importance.

III

Well, it was all confounding enough, but this indication in particular would have jostled our friend's grasp of the presented cup had he had, during the next ten minutes, more independence of thought. That, however, was out of the question when one positively felt, as with a pang somewhere deep within, or even with a smothered cry for alarm, one's whole sense of proportion shattered at a blow and ceasing to serve. "Not *straight*, and not too fast, shall we?" was the ineffable young woman's appeal to him, a few minutes later, beneath the wide glass porch-cover that sheltered their brief wait for their chariot of fire. It was there even as she spoke; the capped charioteer, with a great clean curve, drew up at the steps of the porch, and the Princess's footman, before rejoining him in front, held open the door of the car. She got in, and Berridge was the next instant beside her; he could only say: "As you like, Princess—where you will; certainly let us prolong it; let us prolong everything; don't let us have it over—strange and beautiful as it can only be!—a moment sooner than we must." So he spoke, in the security of their intimate English, while the perpendicular imperturbable *valet-de-pied*, white-faced in the electric light, closed them in and then took his place on the box where the rigid liveried backs of the two men, presented through the glass, were like a protecting wall; such a guarantee of privacy as might come—it occurred to Berridge's inexpugnable fancy—from a vision of tall guards erect round Eastern seraglios.

His companion had said something, by the time they started, about their taking a turn, their looking out for a few of the night-views of Paris that were so wonderful; and after that, in spite of his constantly prized sense of knowing his enchanted city and his way about, he ceased to follow or measure their course, content as he was with the particular exquisite assurance it gave him. *That* was knowing Paris, of a wondrous bland April night; that was hanging over it from vague consecrated lamp-studded heights and taking in, spread below and afar, the great scroll of all its irresistible story, pricked out, across river and bridge and radiant *place*, and along quays and boulevards and avenues, and around monumental circles and squares, in syllables of fire, and sketched and summarised, further and further, in the dim fire-dust of endless avenues; that was all of the essence of fond and thrilled and throbbing recognition, with a thousand things understood and a flood of response conveyed, a whole familiar possessive feeling appealed to and attested.

"From you, you know, it *would* be such a pleasure, and I think—in fact I'm sure—it would do so much for the thing in America." Had she gone on as they went, or had there been pauses of easy and of charmed and of natural silence, breaks and drops from talk, but only into greater confidence and sweetness?—such as her very gesture now seemed a part of; her laying her gloved hand, for emphasis, on the back of his own, which rested on his knee and which took in from the act he scarce knew what melting assurance. The emphasis, it was true—this came to him even while for a minute he held his breath—seemed rather that of Amy Evans; and if her talk, while they rolled, had been in the sense of these words (he had really but felt that they were shut intimately in together, all his consciousness, all his discrimination of meanings and indications being so deeply and so exquisitely merged in that) the case wasn't as surely and sublimely, as extravagantly, as fabulously romantic for him as his excited pulses had been seeming to certify. Her hand was there on his own, in precious living proof, and splendid Paris hung over them, as a consecrating canopy, her purple night embroidered with gold; yet he waited, something stranger still having glimmered for him, waited though she left her hand, which expressed emphasis and homage and tenderness, and anything else she liked indeed—since it was all then a matter of what he next heard and what he slowly grew cold as he took from her.

"You know they do it here so charmingly—it's a compliment a clever man is always so glad to pay a literary friend, and sometimes, in the case of a great name like yours, it renders such a service to a poor little book like mine!" She spoke ever so humbly and yet ever so gaily—and still more than before with this confidence of the sincere admirer and the comrade. That, yes, through his sudden sharpening chill, was what first became distinct for him; she was mentioning somehow her explanation and her conditions—her motive, in fine, disconcerting, deplorable, dreadful, in respect to the experience, otherwise so boundless, that he had taken her as having opened to him; and she was doing it, above all, with the clearest coolness of her general privilege. What in particular she was talking about he as yet, still holding his breath, wondered; it was something she wanted him to do for her—which was exactly what he had hoped, but something of what trivial and, heaven forgive them both, of what dismal order? Most of all, meanwhile, he felt the dire penetration of two or three of the words she had used; so that after a painful minute the quaver with which he repeated them resembled his drawing, slowly, carefully, timidly, some barbed dart out of his flesh.

"A 'literary friend'?" he echoed as he turned his face more to her; so that, as they sat, the whites of her eyes, near to his own, gleamed in the dusk like some silver setting of deep sapphires.

It made her smile—which in their relation now was like the breaking of a cool air-wave over the conscious sore flush that maintained itself through his general chill. "Ah, of course you don't allow that I *am* literary—and of course if you're awfully cruel and critical and incorruptible you won't let it say for me what I so want it should!"

"Where are we, where, in the name of all that's damnably, of all that's grotesquely delusive, are we?" he said, without a sign, to himself; which was the form of his really being quite at sea as to what she was talking about. That uncertainty indeed he could but frankly betray by taking her up, as he cast about him, on the particular ambiguity that his voice perhaps already showed him to find most irritating. "Let *it* show? 'It,' dear Princess——?"

"Why, my dear man, let your Preface show, the lovely, friendly, irresistible log-rolling Preface that I've been asking you if you wouldn't be an angel and write for me."

He took it in with a deep long gulp—he had never, it seemed to him, had to swallow anything so bitter. "You've been asking me if I wouldn't write you a Preface?"

"To 'The Velvet Glove'—after I've sent it to you and you've judged if you really can. Of course I don't want you to perjure yourself; but"—and she fairly brushed him again, at their close quarters, with her fresh fragrant smile—"I do want you so to like me, and to say it all out beautifully and publicly."

"You want me to like you, Princess?"

"But, heaven help us, haven't you understood?"

Nothing stranger could conceivably have been, it struck him—if he was right now—than this exquisite intimacy of her manner of setting him down on the other side of an abyss. It was as if she had lifted him first in her beautiful arms, had raised him up high, high, high, to do it, pressing him to her immortal young breast while he let himself go, and then, by some extraordinary effect of her native force and her alien quality, setting him down exactly where she wanted him to be—which was a thousand miles away from her. Once more, so preposterously face to face with her for these base issues, he took it all in; after which he felt his eyes close, for amazement, despair and shame, and his head, which he had some time before, baring his brow to the mild night, eased of its crush-hat, sink to confounded rest on the upholstered back of the seat. The act, the ceasing to see, and if possible to hear, was for the moment a retreat, an escape from a state that he felt himself fairly flatter by thinking of it as "awk-ward"; the state of really wishing that his humiliation might end, and of wondering in fact if the most decent course open to him mightn't be to ask her to stop the motor and let him down.

He spoke no word for a long minute, or for considerably more than that; during which time the motor went and went, now even somewhat faster, and he knew, through his closed eyes, that the outer lights had begun to multiply and that they were getting back somewhere into the spacious and decorative quarters. He knew this, and also that his retreat, for all his attitude as of accommodating thought, his air—*that* presently and quickly came to him—of having perhaps gathered himself in, for an instant, at her behest, to turn over, in his high ingenuity, some humbug-ging "rotten" phrase or formula that he might place at her service and make the note of such an effort; he became aware, I say, that his lapse was but a half-retreat, with her strenuous presence and her earnest pressure and the close cool respiration of her good faith absolutely timing the moments of his stillness and the progress of the car. Yes, it was wondrous well, he had all but made the biggest of all fools of himself, almost as big a one as *she* was still, to every appearance, in her perfect serenity, trying to make of him; and the one straight answer to it *would* be that he should reach forward and touch the footman's shoulder and demand that the vehicle itself should make an end.

That would be an answer, however, he continued intensely to see, only to inanely importunate, to utterly superfluous Amy Evans—not a bit to his at last exquisitely patient companion, who was clearly now quite taking it from him that what kept him in his attitude was the spring of the quick desire to oblige her, the charming loyal impulse to consider a little what he could do for her, say "handsomely yet conscientiously" (oh the loveliness!) before he should commit himself. She was enchanted—*that* seemed to breathe upon him; she waited, she hung there, she quite bent over him, as Diana over the sleeping Endymion, while all the conscientious man of letters in him, as she might so supremely have phrased it, struggled with the more peccable, the more muddled and "squared," though, for her own ideal, the so much more *banal* comrade. Yes, he could keep it up now—that is he could hold out for his real reply, could meet the rather marked tension of the rest of their passage as well as she; he should be able somehow or other to make his wordless detachment, the tribute of his ostensibly deep consideration of her request, a retreat in good order. She *was*, for herself, to the last point of her guileless fatuity, Amy Evans and an asker for "lifts," a conceiver of twaddle both in herself and in him; or at least, so far as she fell short of all this platitude, it was no fault of the really affecting folly of her attempt to become a mere magazine mortal after the only fashion she had made out, to the intensification of her self-complacency, that she might.

Nothing might thus have touched him more—if to be touched, beyond a certain point, hadn't been to be squared—than the way she failed to divine the bearing of his thoughts; so that she had probably at no one small crisis of her life felt so much a promise in the flutter of her own as on the occasion of the beautiful act she indulged in at the very moment, he was afterward to recognise, of their sweeping into her great smooth, empty, costly street—a desert, at that hour, of lavish lamplight and sculptured stone. She raised to her lips the hand she had never yet released and kept it there a moment pressed close against them; he himself closing his eyes to the deepest detachment he was capable of while he took in with a smothered sound of pain that this was the conferred bounty by which Amy Evans sought most expressively to encourage, to sustain and to reward. The motor had slackened and in a moment would stop; and meanwhile even after lowering his hand again she hadn't let it go. This enabled it, while he after a further moment roused himself to a more confessed consciousness, to form with his friend's a more active relation, to possess him of hers, in turn, and with an intention the straighter that her glove had by this time somehow come off. Bending over it without hindrance, he returned as firmly and fully as the application of all his recovered wholeness of feeling, under his moustache, might express, the consecration the bareness of his own knuckles had received; only after which it was that, still thus drawing out his grasp of her, and having let down their front glass by his free hand, he signified to the footman his view of their stopping short.

They had arrived; the high, closed *porte-cochère*, in its crested stretch of wall, awaited their approach; but his gesture took effect, the car pulled up at the edge of the pavement, the man, in an instant, was at the door and had opened it; quickly moving across the walk, the next moment, to press the bell at the gate. Berridge, as his hand now broke away, felt he had cut his cable; with which, after he had stepped out, he raised again the glass he had lowered and closed, its own being already down, the door that had released him. During these motions he had the sense of his companion, still radiant and splendid, but somehow momentarily suppressed, suspended, silvered over and celestially blurred, even as a summer moon by the loose veil of a cloud. So it was he saw her while he leaned for farewell on the open window-ledge; he took her in as her visible intensity of bright vagueness filled the circle that the interior of the car made for her. It was such a state as she would have been reduced to—he felt this, was certain of it—for the first time in her life; and it was he, poor John Berridge, after all, who would have created the condition.

"Good-night, Princess. I sha'n't see you again."

Vague was indeed no word for it—shine though she might, in her screened narrow niche, as with the liquefaction of her pearls, the glimmer of her tears, the freshness of her surprise. "You won't come in—when you've had no supper?"

He smiled at her with a purpose of kindness that could never in his life have been greater; and at first but smiled without a word. He presently shook his head, however—doubtless also with as great a sadness. "I seem to have supped to my fill, Princess. Thank you, I won't come in."

It drew from her, while she looked at him, a long low anxious wail. "And you won't do my Preface?"

"No, Princess, I won't do your Preface. Nothing would induce me to say a word in print about you. I'm in fact not sure I shall ever mention you in any manner at all as long as ever I live."

He had felt for an instant as if he were speaking to some miraculously humanised idol, all sacred, all jewelled, all votively hung about, but made mysterious, in the recess of its shrine, by the very thickness of the accumulated lustre. And "Then you don't like me—?" was the marvellous sound from the image.

"Princess," was in response the sound of the worshipper, "Princess, I adore you. But I'm ashamed for you."

"Ashamed——?"

"You *are* Romance—as everything, and by what I make out every one, about you is; so what more do you want? Your Preface—the only one worth speaking of—was written long ages ago by the most beautiful imagination of man."

Humanised at least for these moments, she could understand enough to declare that she didn't. "I don't, I don't!"

"You don't need to understand. Don't attempt such base things. Leave those to us. Only live. Only be. *We'll* do the rest."

She moved over—she had come close to the window. "Ah, but Mr. Berridge——!"

He raised both hands; he shook them at her gently, in deep and soft deprecation. "Don't sound my dreadful name. Fortunately, however, you can't help yourself."

"Ah, *voyons*! I so want——!"

He repeated his gesture, and when he brought down his hands they closed together on both of hers, which now quite convulsively grasped the window-ledge. "Don't speak, because when you speak you really say things—! You *are* Romance," he pronounced afresh and with the last intensity of conviction and persuasion. "That's all you have to do with it," he continued while his hands, for emphasis, pressed hard on her own.

Their faces, in this way, were nearer together than ever, but with the effect of only adding to the vividness of that dire non-intelligence from which, all perversely and incalculably, her very beauty now appeared to gain relief. This made for him a pang and almost an anguish; the fear of her saying something yet again that would wretchedly prove how little he moved her perception. So his eyes, of remonstrant, of suppliant intention, met hers close, at the same time that these, so far from shrinking, but with their quite other swimming plea all bedimmed now, seemed almost to wash him with the tears of her failure. He soothed, he stroked, he reassured her hands, for tender conveyance of his meaning, quite as she had just before dealt with his own for brave demonstration of hers. It was during these instants as if the question had been which of them *could* most candidly and fraternally plead. Full but of that she kept it up. "Ah, if you'd only think, if you'd only try——!"

He couldn't stand it—she was capable of believing he had edged away, excusing himself and trumping up a factitious theory, because he hadn't the wit, hadn't the hand, to knock off the few pleasant pages she asked him for and that any proper Frenchman, master of the *métier*, would so easily and gallantly have promised. Should she so begin to commit herself he'd, by the immortal gods, anticipate it in the manner most admirably effective—in fact he'd even thus make her further derogation impossible. Their faces were so close that he could practise any rich freedom—even though for an instant, while the back of the chauffeur guarded them on that side and his own presented breadth, amplified by his loose mantle, filled the whole window-space, leaving him no observation from any quarter to heed, he uttered, in a deep-drawn final groan, an irrepressible echo of his pang for what might have been, the muffled cry of his insistence. "You *are* Romance!"—he drove it intimately, inordinately home, his lips, for a long moment, sealing it, with the fullest force of authority, on her own; after which, as he broke away and the car, starting again, turned powerfully across the pavement, he had no further sound from her than if, all divinely indulgent but all humanly defeated, she had given the question up, falling back to infinite wonder. He too fell back, but could still wave his hat for her as she passed to disappearance in the great floridly framed aperture whose wings at once came together behind her.

Frederick Douglass

Douglass (1817–1895), father of African-American letters and liberation, came to Paris late in life, in 1887, but while there laid, in this letter home, a kind of cornerstone for the approaching 20th-century black American fascination with Paris as a potential paradise—a place where, as James Weldon Johnson would later write, a black man could have "the sense of just being a human being." Douglass also saw in the classical statuary in the Louvre evidence of the antiquity and nobility of Africans. Like Emerson finding divine order in the humdrum order of the Jardin des Plantes, Douglass's is one more case of an American seeing in a Paris museum what he needed to see.

Letter from Paris

Hotel Britanique.
Avenue Victoria.
Paris: November 19, 1887

Dear Friends Hayden and Watson:
I do not forget that I promised on parting with you in Boston to let you have a line from me during my stay abroad. Nothing has occurred during my absence thus far which could be of special interest to you or to my American friends. I have everywhere been received in this country and in England with civility, courtesy and kindness and as a man among men as I expected to be. I have felt however that my presence here even in silence, has a good influence in respect of the standing of the Colored race before the world. The lepros distilment of american prejudice against the negro is not confined to the United States. America has her missionaries abroad in the shape of Ethiopean singers, who disfigure and distort the features of the negro and burlesque his language and manners in a way to make him appear to thousands as more akin to apes than to men. This mode of warfare is purely american and is carried on here in Paris, as it is in the great cities of England and in the States. So that to many minds, as no good was thought to come out of Nazireth so no good is expected of the Negro. In addition to these Ethiopian Buffoons and serinaders who

presume to represent us abroad, there are malicious american writers who take pleasure in assailing us, as an inferior and good for nothing race of which it is impossible to make anything. These influences are very bountiful and not only tend to avert from us the sympathy of civilized Europians, but to bring us under the lash and sting of the world's contempt. I have thus far done little to counteract this tendency in public—but I have never failed to bear my testimony when confronted with it in private—with pen and tongue. When I shall return to England, as I hope to do, in the spring—I shall probably make a few speeches in that country in vindication of the cause and the character of the colored race in america in which I hope to do justice to their progress and make known some of the difficulties with which as a people they have had to contend. Notwithstanding what I have said of the malign influences I mentioned the masses of the people both in France and in England are sound in their convictions and feelings concerning the colored race. The best elements of both countries are just and charitable towards us. I had the great pleasure yesterday of an interview with a member I may say a venerable and highly distinguished member of the French senate, M. Schoelcher, the man who in the final hours of the Revolution of 1848 drew up the decree and carried through the measure of Emancipation to the slaves in all the French Colonies. Senator Schoelcher is now over eighty years old, but like many other Europian statesmen is still able to work. He attends the Senate daily and in addition to his other labors he is now writing the life of Toussaint, the hero of Haytian Independence and liberty. A splended testimonial of the gratitude of the Emancipated people of the French Colonies is seen in his house in the shape of a figure of Liberty in Bronze breaking the chains of the slave. The house of this venerable and philanthropic senator has in it many of the relics of slaveholding barbarism and cruelty. Besides broken fetters and chains which had once gulled the limbs of slaves, he showed me one more collar with four huge prongs placed upon the necks of refracting slaves designed to entangle and impede them in the bushes, if they should attempt to run away. I had seen the same hellish equipment in the States—but did not know until I saw them here, that they were also used in the French Islands. Monsieur Schoelcher spoke much in praise of Thomas Jefferson—but blamed Washington. The latter could have, (he said), abolished slavery and that it was his fault that slavery was fastened upon the american Republic. I spoke to him of Alexander Dumas. He said he was a clever writer, but that he was nothing in morals or politics—he never said one word for his race. So have nothing to thank Dumas for.

Victor Hugo the whiteman could speak for us, but this brilliant colored man, who could have let down sheets of fire upon the heads of tyrants and carried freedom to his enslaved people, had no word in behalf of liberty or the enslaved. I have not yet seen his statue here in Paris. I shall go to see it, as it is an acknowledgement of the genius of a colored man, but not because I honor the character of the man himself.

I have seen much here in Paris in the way of ancient and modern sculpture and painting which deeply interested me. The Louvre and the Luxombourgh abound in them. I have long been interested in Ethnology—especially of the North African races. I have wanted the evidence of greatness under a colored skin to meet and beat back the charge of natural, original and permanent inferiority of the colored races of men. Could I have seen forty years ago, what I have now seen, I should have been much better fortified to meet the Notts and Gliddens of america in their arguments against the negro as a part of the great african race. Knowledge on this subject comes to me late, but I hope not too late to be of some services—for the battle at this point is not yet fought out and the victory is not yet. Yesterday through the kind offices of Mr. Theodore Stanton who procured tickets for us, I had the pleasure with him and Mrs. Douglass of sitting in a favored part of the gallery of the French house of Deputies and listening to the deliberations of that august body. Answering to our house of Representatives but with powers more enlarged. It presents a fine appearance and though somewhat noisy it was in point of manners an improvement on our house of Representatives. I saw no one squirting tobacco, smoking, or his feet above the level of his head as is sometimes seen in our National Legislature.

Colored faces are scarce in Paris. I sometimes get sight of one or two in the course of a day's ramble. They are mostly from Hayti and the French Colonies. They are here as students and make a very respectable appearance. I met the other day at the house of Pere Hyacinthe a Mr. Janveir of Hayti a young man of the color of our well remembered friend Samuel R. Ward who is one of the finest scholars and most refined Gentlemen in Paris. I was very much delighted to find such a noble specimen of the possibilities of the colored race and to find him so highly appreciated by cultivated ladies and gentlemen of Paris. If a race can produce one such man it can produce many.

I am not ignorant of what is transpiring in the states. To days cable gram tells of the Death of Ex President Arthur an able man and while it must be regretted that he has fallen in the midst of his years, there is nothing in his career as President of the U.S. that proves him to have had any sympathy with the oppressed colored people of the south. I see that Mr. Blaine is likely to be the Republican Candidate in 1888. All I have to say is that whether he or another shall be chosen as our standard-bearer I see nothing better for us then to follow the Republican flag. We have not gained all that we had a right to expect under it, but under it we gained all that we have.

Please remember me kindly to the Wendell Phillips Club. I shall not soon forget the pleasant Evening and the happy send off the members of that Club gave me on the 11th Sept.

With kindest regards to yourselves and your families.

Always truly yours

Frederick Douglass.

Henry Adams

American literature's eccentric genius uncle, Henry Adams (1838–1918) showed himself in his work, and particularly in *Mont St. Michel and Chartres*, to be an almost absurdly fanatic admirer of all things French and medieval. (How many generations of American visitors must have been seduced by his words out to the generally touristy and depressing, if impressive, old sea-blown monastery?) So it is perhaps not surprising that, in his letters home during his frequent trips to Paris, he enjoyed playing at disparaging the modern capital of the country, as he does very entertainingly in this letter. Born to the leading American political family, he accompanied his father, Charles, to England, where he served as ambassador to the Court of St. James throughout the Civil War; the young Henry came home, on his own account, in search of political power, or at least influence, only to find himself a relic. He spent the rest of his life traveling, trying to act as an *eminence grise* to figures already gray, and privately publishing his novels and his matchless memoir, *The Education of Henry Adams*. "Playing at disparaging," because with Adams a note of slightly flirtatious disingenuous irony colors everything he writes. Not really misanthropic at all, he liked to pretend being so, just as—perhaps the most intellectually conceited man who has ever lived, and with reason—he liked to play at being a naïf, constantly "educated" by experience. It is hard to believe that his time in Paris was ever *quite* as bleak and dentist-bound as he makes it sound here, just as, in general, it is hard to know in all his writing—or, given the quality of the performance, to care—when he is being entirely serious, and when he is just being Henry Adams.

Letter to John Hay

Paris, 21 December, 1891.

Mon Cher

I expect a letter from you soon. That is the reason why I select this vast canvas of paper. I wish to do honor to the letter which ought to be entering my republic. Also I have nothing to do this evening. I have been here a week, which has just served to exhaust all the theatres, and the night is so cold that I shiver at the idea of beginning on the Cafés Chantants. For the first time in my life I am in Paris without society of any kind, as solitary as the sun or the moon. I converse with no one but my dentist and my book-seller, and when I am not squirming in the dentist's chair, I am burrowing on the archives of the Ministère des Affaires Etrangères, discovering blunders that adorn my history. Would that you were here! You would be bored to extinction, which would make you excellent company for me.

Naturally, with such inducements, I have taken arduously to improving my mind, and to picking up the lost pieces of broken crockery scattered over twenty neglected years of French manufacture. As yet, the painting and the sculpture have made me only sea-sick; with all the goodwill in the world I have not been able to face the terrors of French art, but I will still try, mon ami,—I will try. In the theatre I have done better. To be sure, the theatre is weaker than I ever knew it before, and I am, I find, a severer critic than one should be; but I have got pleasure out of Réjane, and I find Jane Hading fairly satisfactory. The Palais Royal and the Variétes are very amusing—almost as much so as they used to be. Generally the acting averages well, but I am pained to see that no distinctly first-rate actor or actress is on the stage, and as yet nothing approaching a first-rate new play has met my anxious eyes. At the Français—a theatre which irritates my sensitive nerves—I have seen the old Monde où l'on S'ennuie, and was considerably overcome at finding that, with all its wit, it impressed me as being saved from failure only by the visible efforts of the actors; its intrigue is excessively commonplace, and it hangs together very loosely. At the Vaudeville I have seen the reprise of Nos Intimes, and felt to the full extent the admitted weakness of its last Act. At the Variétés, the Cigale and Nitouche were delightful, but there too the last Acts were not good enough for the first. All these plays are reprises, and some of them from a long way back. The new plays are faulty the other way; they are better constructed; the climax is well worked up, and the last Act is the strongest; but, oh, my blessed virgin, what situations! Nothing so revolting and horrible ought to be allowed to be seen. I have not been to the Théatre Libre, where I observe by the Figaro that a rape and abortion are to be given on the stage at an approaching performance, but I would as lieve see either or both as see some of the situations I have seen. At the same time I am not so much impressed by indecency as I expected; in fact it seems to me no worse than in old times.

Curiously enough the thing that pleases me most in Paris is the newspapers. Think of that! I can read them. They are uncommonly well written, especially the feuilletons which seem to me better than ever. Jules Lemaitre is delightful. Anatole France is always good. Sarcey you know of old. I kept his yesterday's comments on Ibsen, thinking that I would send them to you, as they seemed to express our views with excellent fooling; but I don't know;—shall I, or shall I not? These things hardly keep their aroma through a sea-voyage. I know of nothing else to send, unless it is Jules Lemaitre's last volume of causeries. Books by the score are poured out, but Maupassant and Loti are the fashions of the day, and you know them both. I am keeping the Goncourts' journal for my next long voyage.

The Opéra here strikes me as poor both at the Grand and the Comique. I have endured Ambroise Thomas until flesh, to ignore blood entirely, rebelled. Lohengrin is better, but that damned swan bores one at last; and why should we not at least have Wagner in some less familiar form! Melba I heard only in Hamlet which is an intolerably commonplace opera. On the other hand Paris is immensely strong in concerts, and on Sunday one can choose between three big orchestras of the first class, all playing Beethoven, Wagner and Berlioz, and all crowded with audiences so respectable that Boston is fin de siècle compared with them.

As for the restaurants—well! I am shaving fiftyfour and things don't taste as they used to do. Perhaps the Café Anglais is as good as ever; but I should say that the cuisine had fallen off. Not but what it is good; only it wants go. I have made superhuman efforts to try all the restaurants far up the boulevards, where foreigners are unknown, and I much prefer them; but the cuisine is the same old story, or even more so. I prefer Delmonico.

December 25. Forgive me! it was not a rape; it was a "prise de possession." I enclose an account of it in this morning's paper.

I can tell you nothing of the world of society. I have seen absolutely no one. The last time I went to the Legation, I was told that the minister was about to depart for Spain. I did not see him because he was not at the office. I did see Gussy Jay; also I called on his wife. This represents my whole acquaintance. If anyone else is here whom I ought to call upon, I do not know it. I trust that whenever you come here to educate Helen and Alice, you will find society such as the world elsewhere cannot offer. For my own part, Apia and Papeete were socially gay compared with Paris.

I have an idea for the amusement of our future lives. Let us get possession of an evening newspaper, and write alternate feuilletons once a week. I think I could do it for a time with some enjoyment, if I were exempted from writing under my own name. If we were indecent enough, we could always make a success, and French literature would supply us with indecencies to perpetuity. Reflect on this! I am sure it has possibilities.

No letter from you. Gredin, va! While you are butterflying in the salons of Washington, I am grubbing in the desolation of Paris, and you do not give me a thought. If you have nothing to say, why not say it? À revoir! My love to all yours.

Ever   Henry Adams.

Richard Harding Davis

Davis (1864–1916) was, in his day, the most famous foreign correspondent in America. Born in Philadelphia, he became managing editor of *Harper's Weekly* in 1890 and began making trips to various parts of the world. As a foreign correspondent he covered all the wars of his day and published several books about them, some of doubtful accuracy. No kind of writer, really, he was still a gifted observer and had the kind of fearlessness that made him belong more to the aggressively inquisitive reporting of the 20th century than to the bemused and reflective style (a la Willis) of the 19th. Drawn from his book *About Paris* (1895), this hardboiled and skeptical account of Paris low life, and particularly of the legendary Aristide Bruant's café, marks one of the first appearances in American writing about Paris not merely of bohemia but of sinister and "criminal" life in Paris as a significant subject.

---

from

The Show-Places of Paris

In Paris there are virtually no slums at all. The dangerous classes are there, and there is an army of beggars and wretches as poor and brutal as are to be found at large in any part of the world, but the Parisian criminal has no environment, no setting. He plays the part quite as effectively as does the London or New York criminal, but he has no appropriate scenery or mechanical effects.

If he wishes to commit murder, he is forced to make the best of the well-paved, well-lighted, and cleanly swept avenue. He cannot choose a labyrinth of alleyways and covered passages, as he could were he in Whitechapel, or a net-work of tenements and narrow side streets, as he could were he in the city of New York.

Young men who have spent a couple of weeks in Paris, and who have been taken slumming by paid guides, may possibly question the accuracy of this. They saw some very awful places indeed—one place they remember in particular, called the Château Rouge, and another called

Père Lunette. The reason they so particularly remember these two places is that these are the only two places any one ever sees, and they do not recall the fact that the neighboring houses were of hopeless respectability, and that they were able to pick up a cab within a hundred yards of these houses. Young Frenchmen who know all the worlds of Paris tell you mysteriously of these places, and of how they visited them disguised in blue smocks and guarded by detectives; detectives themselves speak to you of them as a fisherman speaks to you of a favorite rock or a deep hole where you can always count on finding fish, and every newspaper correspondent who visits Paris for the first time writes home of them as typical of Parisian low life. They are as typical of Parisian low life as the animals in the Zoo in Central Park are typical of the other animals we see drawing stages and horse-cars and broughams on the city streets, and you require the guardianship of a detective when you visit them as much as you would need a policeman in Mulberry Bend or at an organ recital in Carnegie Hall. They are show-places, or at least they have become so, and though they would no doubt exist without the aid of the tourist or the man about town of intrepid spirit, they count upon him, and are prepared for him with set speeches, and are as ready to show him all that there is to see as are the guides around the Capitol at Washington.

I should not wish to be misunderstood as saying that these are the only abodes of poverty and the only meeting-places for criminals in Paris, which would of course be absurd, but they are the only places of such interest that the visitor sees. There are other places, chiefly wine-shops in cellars in the districts of la Glacière, Montrouge, or la Villette, but unless an inspector of police leads you to them, and points out such and such men as thieves, you would not be able to distinguish any difference between them and the wine-shops and their *habitués* north of the bridges and within sound of the boulevards. The paternal municipality of Paris, and the thought it has spent in laying out the streets, and the generous manner in which it has lighted them, are responsible for the lack of slums. Houses of white stucco, and broad, cleanly swept boulevards with double lines of gas lamps and shade trees, extend, without consideration for the criminal, to the fortifications and beyond, and the thief and bully whose interests are so little regarded is forced in consequence to hide himself underground in cellars or in the dark shadows of the Bois de Boulogne at night. This used to appeal to me as one of the most peculiar characteristics of Paris—that the most desperate poverty and the most heartless of crimes continued in neighborhoods notorious chiefly for their wickedness, and yet which were in appearance as well-ordered and commonplace-looking as the new model tenements in Harlem or the trim working-men's homes in the factory districts of Philadelphia.

The Château Rouge was originally the house of some stately family in the time of Louis XIV. They will tell you there that it was one of the mistresses of this monarch who occupied it, and will point to the frescos of one room to show how magnificent her abode then was. This tradition may or may not be true, but it adds an interest to the house, and furnishes the dramatic contrast to its present wretchedness. It is a tall building painted red, and set back from the street in a court. There are four rooms filled with deal tables on the first floor, and a long counter with the usual leaden top. Whoever buys a glass of wine here may sleep with his or her head on the table, or lie at length up-stairs on the floor of that room where one still sees the stucco cupids of the fine lady's boudoir. It is now a lodging-house for beggars and for those who collect the ends of castaway cigars and cigarettes on the boulevards, and possibly for those who thieve in a small way. By ten o'clock each night the place is filled with men and women sleeping heavily at the tables, with their heads on their arms, or gathered together for miserable company, whispering and gossiping, each sipping jealously of his glass of red wine.

There is a little room at the rear, the walls of which are painted with scenes of celebrated murders, and the portraits of the murderers, of anarchists, and of their foes the police. A sharp-faced boy points to these with his cap, and recites his lesson in a high singsong, and in an *argot* which makes all he says quite unintelligible. He is interesting chiefly because the men of whom he speaks are heroes to him, and he roars forth the name of "Antoine, who murdered the policeman Jervois," as though he were saying Gambetta, the founder of the republic, and with the innocent confidence that you will share with him in his enthusiasm. The pictures are ghastly things, in which the artist has chiefly done himself honor in the generous use of scarlet paint for blood, and in the way he has shown how by rapid gradations the criminal descends from well-dressed innocence to ragged viciousness, until he reaches the steps of the guillotine at Roquette. It is a miserable chamber of horrors, in which the heavy-eyed absinthe-drinkers raise their heads to stare mistily at the visitor, and to listen for the hundredth time to the boy's glib explanation of each daub in the gallery around them, from the picture of the vermilion-cheeked young woman who caused the trouble, to an imaginative picture of Mont-faucon covered with skulls, where, many years in the past, criminals swung in chains.

The café of Père Lunette is just around several sharp corners from the Château Rouge. It was originally presided over by an old gentleman who wore spectacles, which gave his shop its name. It is a resort of the lowest class of women and men, and its walls are painted throughout with faces and scenes a little better in execution than those in the Château Rouge, and a little worse in subject. It is a very small place to enjoy so wide-spread a reputation, and its front room is uninteresting, save for a row of casks resting on their sides, on the head of each of which is painted the portrait of some noted Parisian, like Zola, Eiffel, or Boulanger. The young proprietor fell upon us as his natural prey the night we visited the place, and drove us before him into a room in the rear of the wine-shop. He was followed as a matter of course by a dozen men in blouses, and as many bare-headed women, who placed themselves expectantly at the deal tables, and signified what it was they wished to drink before going through the form of asking us if we meant to pay for it. They were as ready to do their part of the entertainment as the actors of the theatre are ready to go on when the curtain rises, and there was nothing about any of them to suggest that he or she was there for any other reason than the hope of a windfall in the person of a stranger who would supply him or her with money or liquor. A long-haired boy with a three days' growth of hair upon his chin, of whom the proprietor spoke proudly as a poet, recited in verse a long descriptive story of what the pictures on the wall were intended to represent, and another youth, with a Vandyck beard and slouched hat, and curls hanging to his shoulder, sang Aristide Bruant's song of "Saint Lazare." All of the women of the place belonged to the class which spends many months of each year in that prison. The music of the song is in a minor key, and is strangely sad and eerie. It is the plaint of a young girl writing to her lover from within the walls of the prison, begging him to be faithful to her while she is gone, and Bruant cynically makes her designate three or four feminine friends as those whose society she particularly desires him to avoid. The women, all of whom sang with sodden seriousness, may not have appreciated how well the words of the song applied to themselves, but you could imagine that they did, and this gave to the moment and the scene a certain touch of interest. Apart from this the place was dreary, and the pictures indecent and stupid.

There is much more of interest in the Café of Aristide Bruant, on the Boulevard Rochechouart. Bruant is the modern François Villon. He is the poet of the people, and more especially of the criminal classes. He sings the virtues or the lack of virtue of the several districts of Paris, with the life of which he claims an intimate familiarity. He is the bard of the bully, and of the thief, and of the men who live on the earnings of women. He is unquestionably one of the most picturesque figures in Paris, but his picturesqueness is spoiled in some degree by the evident fact that he is conscious of it. He is a poet, but he is very much more of a *poseur*.

Bruant began by singing his own songs in the café chantant in the Champs Élysées, and celebrating in them the life of Montmartre and the Place de la République, and of the Bastille. He has done for the Parisian bully what Albert Chevallier has done for the coster of Whitechapel, and Edward Harrigan for the East Side of New York, but with the important difference that the Frenchman claims to be one of the class of whom he writes, and the audacity with which he robs stray visitors to his café would seem to justify his claims. There is no question as to the strength in his poems, nor that he gives you the spirit of the places which he describes, and that he sees whatever is dramatic and characteristic in them. But the utter heartlessness with which he writes of the wickedness of his friends the souteneurs rings false, and sounds like an affectation. One of the best specimens of his verse is that in which he tells of the Bois de Boulogne at night, when the woods, he says, cloak all manner of evil things, and when, instead of the rustling of the leaves, you hear the groans of the homeless tossing in their sleep under the sky, and calls for help suddenly hushed, and the angry cries of thieves who have fallen out over their spoils and who fight among themselves; or the hurried footsteps of a belated old gentleman hastening home, and followed silently in the shadow of the trees by men who fall upon and rob him after the fashion invented and perfected by le Père François. Others of his poems are like the most realistic paragraphs of *L'Assommoir* and *Nana* put into verse.

Bruant himself is a young man, and an extremely handsome one. He wears his yellow hair separated in the middle and combed smoothly back over his ears, and dresses at all times in brown velvet, with trousers tucked in high boots, and a red shirt and broad sombrero. He has had the compliment paid him of the most sincere imitation, for a young man made up to look exactly like him now sings his songs in the cafés, even the characteristically modest one in which Bruant slaps his chest and exclaims at the end of each verse: "And I? I am Bruant." The real Bruant sings every night in his own café, but as his under-study at the Ambassadeurs' is frequently mistaken for him, he may be said to have accomplished the rather difficult task of being in two places at once.

Bruant's café is a little shop barred and black without, and guarded by a commissionnaire dressed to represent a policeman. If you desire to enter, this man raps on the door, and Bruant, when he is quite ready, pushes back a little panel, and scrutinizes the visitor through the grated opening. If he approves of you he unbars the door, with much jangling of chains and rasping of locks, and you enter a tiny shop, filled with three long tables, and hung with all that is absurd and fantastic in decoration, from Cheret's bill-posters to unframed oil-paintings, and from beer-mugs to plaster death-masks. There is a different salutation for every one who enters this café, in which all those already in the place join in chorus. A woman is greeted by a certain burst of melody, and a man by another, and a soldier with easy satire, as representing the government, by an imitation of the fanfare which is blown by the trumpeters whenever the President appears in public. There did not seem to be any greeting which exactly fitted our case, so Bruant waved us to a bench, and explained to his guests, with a shrug: "These are two gentlemen from the boulevards who have come to see the thieves of Montmartre. If they are quiet and well-behaved we will not rob them." After this somewhat discouraging reception we, in our innocence, sat perfectly still, and tried to think we were enjoying ourselves, while we allowed ourselves to be robbed by waiters and venders of songs and books without daring to murmur or protest.

Bruant is assisted in the entertainment of his guests by two or three young men who sing his songs, the others in the room joining with them. Every third number is sung by the great man himself, swaggering up and down the narrow limits of the place, with his hands sunk deep in the pockets of his coat, and his head rolling on his shoulders. At the end of each verse he withdraws his hands, and brushes his hair back over his ears, and shakes it out like a mane. One of his perquisites as host is the privilege of saluting all of the women as they leave, of which privilege he avails himself when they are pretty, or resigns it and bows gravely when they are not. It is amusing to notice how the different women approach the door when it is time to go, and how the escort of each smiles proudly when the young man deigns to bend his head over the lips of the girl and kiss her good-night.

The café of the Black Cat is much finer and much more pretentious than Bruant's shop, and is of wider fame. It is, indeed, of an entirely different class, but it comes in here under the head of the show-places of Paris at night. It was originally a sort of club where journalists and artists and poets met round the tables of a restaurant-keeper who happened to be a patron of art as well, and fitted out his café with the canvases of his customers, and adopted their suggestions in the arrangement of its decoration. The outside world of Paris heard of these gatherings at the Black Cat, as the café and club were called, and of the wit and spirit of its *habitués*, and sought admittance to its meetings, which was at first granted as a great privilege. But at the present day the café has been turned over into other hands, and is a show-place pure and simple, and a most interesting one. The café proper is fitted throughout with heavy black oak, or something in imitation of it. There are heavy broad tables and high wainscoting and an immense fireplace and massive rafters. To set off the sombreness of this, the walls are covered with panels in the richest of colors, by Steinlen, the most imaginative and original of the Parisian illustrators, in all of which the black cat appears as a subject, but in a different rôle and with separate treatment. Upon one panel hundreds of black cats race over the ocean, in another they are waltzing with naiads in the woods, and in another they are whirling through space over red-tiled roofs, followed by beautiful young women, gendarmes, and boulevardiers in hot pursuit. And in every other part of the café the black cat appears as frequently as did the head of Charles I. in the writings of Mr. Dick. It stalks stuffed in its natural skin, or carved in wood, with round glass eyes and long red tongue, or it perches upon the chimney-piece with back arched and tail erect, peering down from among the pewter pots and salvers. The gas-jets shoot from the mouths of wrought-iron cats, and the dismembered heads of others grin out into the night from the stained-glass windows. The room shows the struggle for what is odd and bizarre, but the drawings in black and white and the watercolors and oil-paintings on the walls are signed by some of the cleverest artists in Paris. The inscriptions and rules and regulations are as odd as the decorations. As, for example, the one placed half-way up the narrow flight of stairs which leads to the tiny theatre, and which commemorates the fact that the café was on such a night visited by President Carnot, who—so the inscription adds, lest the visitor should suppose the Black Cat was at all impressed by the honor—"is the successor of Charlemagne and Napoleon I." Another fancy of the Black

Cat was at one time to dress all the waiters in the green coat and gold olive leaves of the members of the Institute, to show how little the poets and artists of the café thought of the other artists and poets who belonged to that ancient institution across the bridges. But this has now been given up, either because the uniforms proved too expensive, or because some one of the Black Cat's *habitués* had left his friends "for a ribbon to wear in his coat," and so spoiled the satire.

Three times a week there is a performance in the theatre up-stairs, at which poets of the neighborhood recite their own verses, and some clever individual tells a story, with a stereopticon and a caste of pasteboard actors for accessories. These latter plays are very clever and well arranged, and as nearly proper as a Frenchman with such a temptation to be otherwise could be expected to make them. It is a most informal gathering, more like a performance in a private house than a theatre, and the most curious thing about it is the character of the audience, which, instead of being bohemian and artistic, is composed chiefly of worthy bourgeoisie, and young men and young women properly chaperoned by the parents of each. They sit on very stiff wooden chairs, while a young man stands on the floor in front of them with his arms comfortably folded and recites a poem or a mono-logue, or plays a composition of his own. And then the lights are all put out, and a tiny curtain is rung up, showing a square hole in the proscenium, covered with a curtain of white linen. On this are thrown the shadows of the pasteboard figures, who do the most remarkable things with a natu-ralness which might well shame some living actors.

Isadora Duncan

For someone whose artistic practice passed away long ago (and whose performances, to judge by the few surviving jumpy films, would probably strike us
as kittenish and mannered now), Isadora Duncan (1877–1927) remains a
remarkably constant presence in our memories. After a childhood in San
Francisco, her vision of a revived form of "classical" Grecian dancing brought
her in 1903 to Europe, which she soon conquered. She settled in Paris in 1905,
and her discovery there of sex and her openly avowed appetite for physical
passion made her a genuine feminist heroine, of an oddly earnest American
kind. She is a kind of dancing bridge between the awed bourgeois fascination
with France of the Wharton-James era, and the coming avant-garde wave of
the Stein-Hemingway generation. Her account of her life in Paris, from her
autobiography *My Life* (1927), is still immensely winning in its details of love
made and love missed.

---

from

My Life

There was always a deficit between our expenditure and our earnings,
but it was a period of peace. But this peaceful atmosphere had made
Raymond restless. He left for Paris and in the spring he bombarded us
with telegrams imploring us to come to Paris, so one day Mother and I
packed up our belongings and took the Channel boat.

After the fogs of London we arrived on a spring morning at Cherbourg.
France seemed to us like a garden and from Cherbourg to Paris we leaned
out of our third-class window all the way. Raymond met us at the station.
He had let his hair grow long over his ears, and wore a turned-down collar and a flowing tie. We were somewhat astonished at this metamorpho-
sis but he explained to us that this was the fashion of the Latin Quarter
where he lived. He took us to his lodging where we met a little midinette
running down the stairs, and he regaled us on a bottle of red wine which,
he said, cost thirty centimes. After the red wine we set out to look for a

studio. Raymond knew two words of French and we walked along the streets saying *"Chercher atelier."* What we did not know was the *atelier* does not only mean a studio in France, but any kind of workshop. Finally, at dusk we found a studio in a courtyard, at the extraordinary price of fifty francs a month, furnished. We were overjoyed, and paid a month in advance. We could not imagine why it was so cheap, but that night we found out. Just as we had composed ourselves to rest, terrific earthquakes seemed to shake the studio and the whole thing seemed to jump into the air and then fall flat. This was repeated over and over again. Raymond went down to inspect and found that we were refuged over a night *imprimerie*. Hence the cheapness of the studio. It somewhat damped our spirits but, as fifty francs meant a great deal to us in those days, I proposed that it sounded like the sea and that we should pretend that we were at the seaside. The concierge provided the meals, twenty-five centimes for lunch and one franc a head for dinner, including wine. She used to bring up a bowl of salad and say with a polite smile, "Il faut tourner la salade, Monsieur et Mesdames, il faut tourner la salade."

Raymond gave up the midinette and devoted himself to me and we used to get up at five o'clock in the morning, such was our excitement at being in Paris, and begin the day by dancing in the gardens of the Luxembourg, walk for miles all over Paris and spend hours in the Louvre. Raymond had already got a portfolio of drawings of all the Greek vases, and we spent so much time in the Greek vase room that the guardian grew suspicious and when I explained in pantomime that I had only come there to dance, he decided that he had to do with harmless lunatics, so he let us alone. I remember we spent hours and hours sitting on the waxed floor, sliding about to see the lower shelves, or standing on tip-toe saying, "Look, here is Dionysus," or "Come here, here's Medea killing her children."

Day after day we returned to the Louvre, and could hardly be forced to leave at closing time. We had no money, we had no friends in Paris, but we wanted nothing. The Louvre was our Paradise, and I have since met people who saw us then—me in my white dress and Liberty hat, and Raymond in his large black hat, open collar and flowing tie—and say we were two bizarre figures, so young and so absolutely absorbed in the Greek vases. At the closing hour we walked back through the dusk, lingering before the statues in the Tuileries gardens, and when we had dined off white beans, salad and red wine, we were about as happy as any one could be.

Raymond was very clever with his pencil. In a few months he had copied all the Greek vases in the Louvre. But there exist certain silhouettes, which were afterwards published, which were not from Greek vases at all, but me, dancing in the nude, photographed by Raymond, which were passed off as Greek vases.

Besides the Louvre, we visited the Cluny Museum, the Carnavalet Museum, and Notre Dame, and all the other museums of Paris. I was especially entranced by the Carpeau group before the Opéra, and the Rude on the Arc de Triomphe. There was not a monument before which we did not stand in adoration, our young American souls uplifted before this culture which we had striven so hard to find.

Spring lengthened into summer and the great Exhibition of 1900 was opened, when, to my great joy, but to the discomfiture of Raymond, Charles Hallé appeared one morning at our studio in the Rue de la Gaieté. He had come over to see the Exhibition, and after that I was his constant companion. And I could not have had a more charming or intelligent guide. All day we roamed through the buildings and in the evening we dined at the Eiffel Tower. He was kindness itself, and when I was tired he would put me into a rolling chair, and I was often tired, for the art of the Exhibition did not seem to me at all equal to the art of the Louvre, but I was very happy, for I adored Paris and I adored Charles Hallé.

On Sundays we took a train and went into the country, to wander through the gardens of Versailles or the forest of Saint-Germain. I danced for him in the forest, and he made sketches of me. And so the summer passed. It was not so happy, of course, for my poor mother and Raymond.

One great impression remained with me of the Exhibition of 1900— the dancing of Sadi Yacca, the great tragic dancer of Japan. Night after night Charles Hallé and I were thrilled by the wondrous art of this great tragedian.

Another, even greater impression, that has remained with me all my life, was the "Rodin Pavillon," where the complete works of the wonderful sculptor were shown for the first time to the public. When I first entered this Pavillon I stood in awe before the work of the great master. Without, at that time, knowing Rodin, I felt that I was in a new world, and each time I came I was indignant at the vulgar people who said "Where is his head?" or "Where is her arm?" I often turned and apostrophised the crowd, rating them soundly. "Don't you know," I used to say, "that this is not the thing itself, but a symbol—a conception of the ideal of life."

Autumn approached, and the last days of the Exhibition. Charles Hallé had to return to London, but before going he presented to me his nephew, Charles Noufflard. "I leave Isadora in your care," he said, when he was going. Noufflard was a young man of about twenty-five, more or less blasé, but he was completely captivated by the naïveté of this little American girl who had been confided to his care. He set out to complete my education in French art, telling me much about the Gothic, and making me appreciate for the first time the epochs of Louis XIII, XIV, XV and XVI.

We had left the studio in the Rue de la Gaieté and, with the remainder of our little savings, we took a large studio in the Avenue de Villiers. Raymond arranged this studio in a most original manner. Taking sheets of tin foil, he rolled them and placed them over the gas jets, allowing the gas to flare through them like old Roman torches, thereby considerably increasing our gas bills!

In this studio my mother revived her music and, as in our childhood's days, for hours and hours she would play Chopin, Schumann and Beethoven. We had no bedroom or a bathroom in our studio. Raymond painted Greek columns round the walls and we had a few carved chests in which we kept our mattresses. At night we took them from the chests and slept upon them. At this time Raymond invented his famous sandals, having discovered that all shoes were obnoxious. He was of an inventive disposition and he spent three-quarters of the night working out his inventions and hammering, while my poor mother and I had to sleep on the chests as best we could.

Charles Noufflard was a constant visitor and one day he brought to our studio two of his comrades, a pretty youth called Jacques Beaugnies, and a young literary man called André Beaunier. Charles Noufflard was very proud of me and delighted to show me to his friends as a phenomenal American product. Naturally I danced for them. I was then studying the music of Chopin's Preludes, Waltzes and Mazurkas. My mother played extremely well, with the firm, strong touch of a man, and with great feeling and insight, and she would accompany me for hours. It was then that Jacques Beaugnies had the idea of asking his mother, Madame de St. Marceau, the wife of the sculptor, to have me dance one evening for her friends.

Mme. de St. Marceau had one of the most artistic and chic salons in Paris and a rehearsal was arranged in the studio of her husband. At the piano sat a most remarkable man, with the fingers of a wizard. I was instantly attracted to him.

"Quel ravissement!" he exclaimed, "quel charme! Quelle jolie enfant!" And, taking me in his arms he kissed me on both cheeks, in French fashion. He was Messager, the great composer.

The evening of my début arrived. I danced before a group of people so kind, so enthusiastic, that I was quite overcome. They scarcely waited for the end of a dance to call out, "Bravo, bravo, comme elle est exquise! Quel enfant!" and at the end of the first dance a tall figure, with piercing eyes, rose and embraced me.

"Quel est ton nom, petite fille?" he asked.

"Isadora," I replied.

"Mais ton petit nom?"

"When I was a little girl they called me Dorita."

"Oh, Dorita," he cried, kissing my eyes, my cheeks and my mouth, "tu es adorable," and then, Madame de St. Marceau took my hand and said,

"This is the great Sardou."

In fact that room held all who counted in Parisian life, and, when I left, covered with flowers and compliments, my three cavaliers, Noufflard, Jacques Beaugnies and André Beaunier, escorted me home beaming with pride and satisfaction because their little phenomenon had been such a success.

Of these three young men the one who was to become my greatest friend was not the tall and pleasant Charles Noufflard, or the good-looking Jacques Beaugnies, but the rather under-sized pale-faced André Beaunier. He was pale and round-faced and wore glasses, but what a mind! I was always a *"cèrèbrale,"* and although people will not believe it, my love affairs of the head, of which I had many, were as interesting to me as those of the heart. André, who was at that time writing his first books, "Petrarch" and "Simonde," came every day to see me, and it was through him that I became acquainted with all the finest French literature.

By this time I had learned to read and converse fairly easily in French, and André Beaunier would read aloud to me in our studio for long afternoons and evenings. His voice had a cadence in it that was exquisitely sweet. He read to me the works of Molière, Flaubert, Théophile Gautier, Maupassant, and it was he who first read to me Maeterlinck's "Pélleas et Mélisande," and all the modern French books of the day.

Every afternoon there was a timid knock at the door of the studio. It was André Beaunier, always with a new book or magazine under his arm. My mother could not understand my enthusiasm for this man, who was not her *beau idéal* of what a lover should be, for, as I have said before, he was fat and small with small eyes and one had to be a "cerebrale" to understand that those eyes were sparkling with wit and intelligence. Often, when he had read to me for two or three hours, we went off on the top of a Seine 'bus and rode down to the Ile de la Cité to gaze at Notre Dame in the moonlight. He knew every figure of the façade and could tell me the history of every stone. Then we would walk home and now and then I would feel the timid pressure of André's fingers on my arm. On Sundays too, we would take a train and go out to Marly. There is a scene in one of Beaunier's books in which he describes these walks in the forest—how I used to dance before him down the paths, beckoning to him like a nymph or dryad bubbling with laughter.

He confided to me all his impressions and the sort of literature which he wished to write, which would certainly never have been of the "best seller" description, but I believe that the name of André Beaunier will go down the centuries as one of the most exquisite writers of his time. On two occasions André Beaunier showed great emotion. One was on the death of Oscar Wilde. He came to me white and trembling in a terrible state of depression. I had read and heard vaguely about Oscar Wilde but knew very little about him. I had read some of his poems and loved them and André told me something of his story, but when I questioned him as to the reason why Oscar Wilde was imprisoned, he blushed to the roots of his hair and refused to answer.

He held my hands and just trembled. He stayed with me very late and kept on saying, "You are my only confidante," and he left me under the strange impression that some uncanny calamity had befallen the world. Again shortly after, he appeared one morning with a white tragic countenance. He would not confide to me what was the reason of his emotion, but remained silent with set face and eyes staring before him and on leaving kissed me on the forehead in such a significant manner that I had a premonition that he was going to his death and remained in painful anxiety until—three days later—he returned in brilliant spirits and confessed he had fought a duel and wounded his adversary. I never knew for what reason the duel took place. In fact I knew nothing of his personal life. He generally appeared at five or six each afternoon and then he read to me or took me for walks according to the weather or our mood. Once we sat at the opening where four roads cross in the Bois de Meudon. He named the right-hand, Fortune, the left Peace . . . and the road straight ahead Immortality and "Where we are sitting?" I asked. "Love," he replied in a low voice—"Then I prefer to remain here," I exclaimed delighted—but he only said: "We can't remain here," and rose and walked very fast down the road straight ahead.

Very disappointed and puzzled I trotted after him calling out: "But why, but why, why do you leave me?" But he didn't speak again all the way home and left me abruptly at the door of my studio.

This quaint and passionate friendship had lasted over a year when in the innocence of my heart I had dreamt to give it another expression. One evening I plotted to send Mother and Raymond to the Opera and to be alone—that afternoon I clandestinely bought a bottle of champagne. That evening, I set a little table with flowers, champagne, two glasses—and I donned a transparent tunic and wreathed my hair with roses and thus awaited André, feeling just like Thaïs. He arrived, seemed very astonished and terribly embarrassed—he would hardly touch the champagne. I danced for him, but he seemed distrait and finally left abruptly saying he had a great deal of writing to finish that evening. I was left alone with the roses and the champagne and I wept bitterly.

When you recollect that at that time I was young and remarkably pretty, it's difficult to find an explanation of this episode and indeed I have never found one—but then I could only think in despair: *"He doesn't love me."* And as a result of hurt vanity and pique, I began a violent flirtation with one of the others of my trio of admirers who was tall and blond and handsome and as enterprising as André was backwards in embraces and kisses. But this experiment also ended badly, for one night after a real champagne dinner in a *Cabinet particulier* he took me to a hotel room booked as Mr. and Mrs. X. I was trembling but happy. At last I would know what love was. I found myself in his arms, submerged in a storm of caresses, my heart pounding, every nerve bathed in pleasure, my whole being flooded in ecstatic joy— I am at last awakening to life, I exulted—when suddenly he started up and falling on his knees beside the bed in undescribable emotion cried: "Oh—why didn't you tell me? What a crime I was about to commit— No, no you must remain pure. Dress, dress at once!"

And, deaf to my laments, he put my coat around me and hurried me to a cab—and all the way home swore at himself in such a savage manner that I was very frightened.

What crime, I asked myself, was he about to commit? I felt dizzy, ill and upset, again left at my studio door in a state of great discouragement. My young blond friend never returned; he left shortly after for the Colonies and when I met him years later, he asked: "Have you ever forgiven me?" "But, for what—?" I questioned. . . .

Such were my first youthful adventures at the borders of the strange land of Love, which I longed to enter and which was denied to me for many years by this too religious and awe-inspiring effect which I produced upon my lovers—but this last shock had a decided effect upon my emotional nature, turning all its force toward my Art which gave me the joys which Love withheld.

Edward Steichen

Edward Steichen (1879–1973), the godfather of American photography, who would eventually become the first curator of photography at the Museum of Modern Art in New York City, divided his time between Paris and America throughout the 1890s, and was as at home in both as he was, unusually, at home and successful as both a painter and a photographer. (During World War I, however, he changed his name from the French-sounding Edouard to the all-American Edward.) In this selection from his memoir *A Life in Photography* (1963) he tells how he set out to photograph Rodin and his Balzac, and records the strange, and typically French, pedagogic mix of encouragement and disparagement that young American artists got for generations at the legendary Académie Julien.

———

from

A Life in Photography

After a day or two in Le Havre, Björncrantz and I got on our bicycles and photographed and sketched our way along the winding curves and bends of the Seine River to Paris. It was a wonderful introduction to France in the spring, with the orchards and meadows in bloom.

One of our fellow passengers on the ship had a sister living in Montmartre, and he had given us her address. The sister, who was the *concierge* of the building, had a spare room in the attic for rent. We took the room, washed up, and made tracks for the Rodin exhibition just outside the gates to the Paris World's Fair of 1900.

In the spring of 1898, the Milwaukee papers had carried stories about a sensational art controversy raging in Paris. It seemed that, seven years before, the sculptor Auguste Rodin had been commissioned by the Society of Men of Letters to make a statue of Balzac for the city of Paris. In the Salon of 1898, Rodin exhibited the plaster cast of the finished statue, and in the opening hours of the exhibition, crowds gathered around the statue, and vehement discussions took place pro and con. When the

Society of Men of Letters decided to refuse the statue, the newspapers enjoyed a heyday with the scandal, intensifying the feeling in Paris. The Balzac statue was called a monstrosity by some and by others a sack of flour with a head stuck on top.

When I saw it reproduced in the Milwaukee newspaper, it seemed the most wonderful thing I had ever seen. It was not just a statue of a man; it was the very embodiment of a tribute to genius. It looked like a mountain come to life. It stirred up my interest in going to Paris, where artists of Rodin's stature lived and worked.

Another French artist who had lighted up my imagination was Claude Monet. In the Milwaukee public library I had read an article about him. Here was a landscape painter, it said, who went out and painted landscapes on the scene, instead of painting them from memory in his studio. The article went on to say that Monet let light and air into landscape painting. As I read, it seemed to me that he worked on canvas the way I tried to work with a camera.

Björncrantz and I arrived at the Rodin exhibition late in the afternoon, just before closing hour. The light was dim. In the center of the gallery stood the Balzac, looking positively gigantic. In one corner of the gallery, I saw, talking earnestly to several people, a stocky man with a massive head, almost like a bull's. I felt, instinctively, that this must be the master himself, and I made up my mind I was going to photograph him someday.

A few days later, I went to the Louvre and had an experience for which I was totally unprepared. I made my firsthand acquaintance with the Old Masters. What a fabulous collection of painting and sculpture! Then there was the Luxembourg museum of living artists. That signified modern art, most of it very uninteresting, but one room contained a collection of the Impressionists, whom I had read and dreamed about. Here were Monet and Degas and Manet, Pissarro and Sisley. The Monets stirred me most. They dealt with something that was still well out of the domain of photography, the magic and color of sunlight.

Altogether, the first week in Paris was overwhelming. Everywhere I turned, I found a new experience, a revelation.

* * *

In Paris, I had found a studio that an American illustrator was vacating, and I now found myself a resident of the Rive Gauche at 83 boulevard du Montparnasse. It was a long, low studio building, and I had a large, well-lighted studio on the second floor.

I enrolled as a student at the Julian Academy. I appeared there on a Monday morning with my portfolio, drawing paper, and charcoal, and took up a position in one of the classrooms. We had a magnificent, tall, Italian athlete for a model. He assumed a grandiose pose of simulated action, legs spread as if climbing, one foot on a box, and a long staff in his hand. For the first time I was going to have a whole week in which to make a drawing, instead of the half-hour periods for sketching that we had had in Milwaukee. I was stirred by the project and the model, and I commenced to sketch in the action of the pose, working slowly and deliberately.

On Wednesday, Jean-Paul Laurens, the instructor, came round to criticize the work. He sat down near me at the place of a young man from Poland. This man had a large sheet of paper braced up on a chair in front of him, but he had been working on a small image, not more than ten inches high, in the middle of the paper. I had looked occasionally from my work to his with surprise. He was more concerned with smoothing out the surfaces than anything else. Jean-Paul asked him whether he was drawing the figure in front of us. The boy nodded his head, and Jean-Paul exploded, "Well, why don't you do it! This soft smooth thing has none of the spirit of the magnificent specimen of a man in front of you. You should fill the paper, sketch in the action and outline of the pose. Get the force and vigor, the bone structure and the anatomy of the model and not this soft nothingness you have on the paper."

As Jean-Paul got up and approached the easel where I was working he turned, grabbed the young man he had been criticizing so harshly, pulled him around, and told him to look at my drawing. He said, "This is the way to do it. See this outline . . . all the action and vitality has been reproduced. And look at that hand. That's the way Michelangelo drew a hand!"

I had gooseflesh all over. My hair commenced to rise. Everybody in the classroom looked round to see who the new Michelangelo was. After Jean-Paul departed, the young Pole packed up his drawing paper and went home. We never saw him again. I just stood staring at my drawing. It started to swim in front of me, and I was afraid to touch it, afraid I would spoil the miraculous thing I had done. Occasionally, some one of the Frenchmen who had been at the school a long time would come and look casually over my shoulder, grunt, and walk on. By Wednesday, one of these expert pupils had finished a drawing and moved into the young Pole's place to begin a new one. But I went at my drawing in a very gingerly manner. Nothing would have induced me to touch that hand.

When Friday came, Jean-Paul made the rounds for the final criticism. He sat down at the place of my new neighbor, the star student, rubbed his hands, and said, "Very good, very good." He suggested a hairline off the calf of one leg, and then, with a little rubber stamp, he made a purple mark, "JPL," on the drawing. It meant that this was one of the best drawings of the week.

Then he stood up next to me. He looked at my drawing and said, "Are you doing this from that model there?"

I said, "Yes sir."

"Well, why don't you do something with it? Put some modeling into it. Put some texture on it."

He paused for a moment. Then he said, "Look at that. That is not a hand, that is a block of wood!" He looked at that hand just as he had looked at the young Pole's drawing on Wednesday.

Out of a corner of my eye, I saw wry smiles on some of my colleagues' faces. All I could do was take it. I couldn't answer back and complain that he had approved the hand two days before.

The following week, I came back with oil color and canvas and started to paint. On Wednesday, when Jean-Paul entered the classroom, I quietly took my painting off the easel and left the room until he was gone. Then I brought it back and continued working. I did the same on Friday. But I decided to follow the young Polish lad's footsteps and call it quits with the Julian Academy. The kind of work that was admired there was cold, lifeless, slick, smoothly finished academic drawing. I was not interested, and after two weeks at the Julian Academy, my professional art training came to an end.

I took up photography actively again, sometimes painted or photographed a model, and spent a great deal of time in the Louvre. After the first overwhelming impact, I began studying the individual pictures and schools more closely and found myself wondering repeatedly whether such and such a painting could also be done by photography. One Titian particularly intrigued me, "Man with a Glove." It had been painted with great precision, but it also had style and an allure that I found hard to explain. About this time, F. Holland Day arrived from London with the photographs from the New American School exhibition. He had brought them to Paris with the idea of showing them there. I invited him to share my studio with me, and he seemed pleased to do so.

I painted a portrait of Day and sent it to the Salon National des Beaux-Arts. It was accepted and hung in one of the important galleries.

One day, I dressed up in one of Day's stocks, draped his mantle around my shoulders, picked up a palette and brush, and posed in the mirror for what I thought was going to be photography's answer to "Man with a Glove." I experimented with prints from the negative, first with the original gum-print process, then with other colloids, glues, and gelatins, sometimes in combination, sometimes separately. I worked out several formulas that gave interesting results and considerable leeway in controlling the results. It took me almost a year to master the technique and get the kind of print I wanted (plate 1).

When Day's exhibition opened at the Photo Club of Paris, it was greeted with some degree of the shock that had met the exhibition in London, but with none of the vituperation or wry humor. Robert Demachy, the leading pictorial photographer in France, referred to my work as that of the *"Enfant Terrible"* of the New American School.

The event that made 1901 memorable to me was the opportunity to realize my dream of knowing Auguste Rodin. I had been asked, tentatively, to photograph the two charming children of Fritz Thaulow, a popular Norwegian landscape painter living in Paris. He invited me to lunch at his home, a beautiful house on the boulevard Malesherbes, and with a portfolio of my prints strapped on my bicycle I pedaled across Paris. I showed the prints and received the order to photograph the children. During the luncheon, I mentioned my excitement at seeing the Rodin exhibition and confessed how eager I was to meet the sculptor. Thaulow said, "We know him well. We are friends. Since you have your bicycle, we will all bicycle out to Meudon this afternoon to see him." Meudon is one of the suburbs of Paris.

On the way out, Fritz said to Madame Thaulow, "Now, Rose will probably ask us for dinner, but we will be adamant and refuse to put her to that trouble." Rose was Madame Rodin. I secretly hoped she would be more adamant in her insistence than the Thaulows would be in their refusal.

Rose met us and said that Rodin was still in town but would be out soon, and she made us comfortable in the garden.

1. Self-Portrait with Brush and Palate. Paris. 1901

Late in the afternoon, there appeared over the brow of the hill a
stocky figure walking rapidly towards the house. I recognized Rodin from
the brief glimpse I had had at the exposition. There were the usual formal introductions, and then Rodin and Rose both insisted that we stay
for dinner. When Rodin insisted, that's all there was to it. We stayed.
Japanese paper lanterns were strung up in the trees. Rose set the table and

disappeared into the kitchen for a while. Then we sat down to a marvelous dinner, which was accompanied by wines that Rodin brought up from the cellar.

After dinner, with the liqueur and cigars, Fritz said to me, "Now bring out your portfolio." I did so with fear and trembling. Rodin went through the prints slowly, pausing now and then to look at one for some time, and giving grunts of approval and, sometimes, words. When it was all over, I blurted out that the great ambition of my life was to do a portrait of him. He clapped his hand on my shoulder and said to Thaulow, "You see, Fritz, enthusiasm is not dead yet."

He assured me that I could photograph him whenever I desired. I asked if it would be possible to visit him in his studio first in order to make plans for the picture. This pleased him, and he said I could come any time and often, especially on Saturday afternoons, when he usually did not work but received friends and visitors.

And so, practically every Saturday for a whole year, I visited and studied Rodin while he walked among his works. Finally, having decided just what I wanted to do, I made an appointment and went down with my camera. I asked him to stand next to the statue of the "Victor Hugo" and face "Le Penseur." But since the studio was filled to capacity with large blocks of sculptured marble and with plaster, bronze, and clay being worked on, there was not enough room for me to get Rodin, the "Victor Hugo," and "Le Penseur" on one plate. So I made an exposure that included Victor Hugo with Rodin. Then I moved my camera over and photographed "Le Penseur" separately, explaining to Rodin that I was going to join them both in one picture later. In those days, I had only one lens, a rapid rectilinear lens of relatively long focus. If I had had a wide-angle lens, I probably would have made the whole thing in one shot.

I didn't know enough about the technical problems to solve the job of uniting the two pictures at once, and at first I printed only the negative of Rodin standing near Victor Hugo. Later, I worked out a technique by which I could combine the two negatives and make one print, as it is shown in plate 2.

When I showed Rodin the combined print, he was elated. And Judith Cladel, who later wrote a wonderful biography of Rodin, looked at the photograph, and said to Rodin, "Ah, it is Rodin. It is you between God and the devil." He replied simply, "Mais oui," and laughed heartily. He was quite proud of the picture and showed it to everybody.

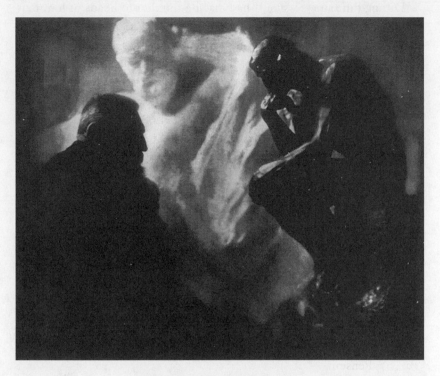

2. Rodin—Le Penseur. Paris. 1902.

3, 4. Auguste Rodin. Paris. 1902.

During the same session, I had made a number of heads of him that were more like conventional portraits (plates 3 and 4), but the silhouette of that massive head appeals to me as more like the Rodin who created the Balzac than any of the others. It is probably more of a picture *to* Rodin than it is *of* Rodin, because after all, it associates the genius of the man with that expressed by his work. Today, one bronze cast of "Le Penseur" has an honored place in front of the Pantheon in Paris and another looks down on the ground where Rodin and Rose are buried at Meudon.

James Weldon Johnson

One of the heroic figures of early 20th-century American history, James Weldon Johnson (1871–1938) is best known as the head of the NAACP throughout the 1920s, but he was also a diplomat, novelist, poet, songwriter, and memoirist. In this section from his late-in-life memoir *Along This Way* (1933), he tells of his first trip to Paris in 1905 and the miraculous moment of feeling, in France, both black and free; there are few more moving episodes in the entire history of Americans in Paris than Johnson and his companions' pleasure in being called "Messieurs" ("Gentlemen") by a Parisian hotel doorman.

———

from

Along This Way

From the day I set foot in France, I became aware of the working of a miracle within me. I became aware of a quick readjustment to life and to environment. I recaptured for the first time since childhood the sense of being just a human being. I need not try to analyze this change for my colored readers; they will understand in a flash what took place. For my white readers . . . I am afraid that any analysis will be inadequate, perhaps futile. . . . I was suddenly free; free from a sense of impending discomfort, insecurity, danger; free from the conflict within the Man-Negro dualism and the innumerable maneuvers in thought and behavior that it compels; free from the problem of the many obvious or subtle adjustments to a multitude of bans and taboos; free from special scorn, special tolerance, special condescension, special commiseration; free to be merely a man.

On the boat we had made some pleasant acquaintances from among our white compatriots. Of several of these I still have a distinct recollection. One was a West Point cadet; another was a young man going to Paris to study at the *Académie Julien*—the two were relatives, I think, and were traveling with two middle-aged ladies, who were aunts or something of that sort; a third was the fashion plate of the ship, a young man who seemingly had an inexhaustible supply of clothes and changed four or five times a day. It was this young man who strongly recommended that we put up in Paris at the Hotel Continental. We knew nothing of Paris hotels, and he appeared to know so much; we followed his advice. When we had registered and been assigned to our rooms, we found ourselves in possession of a suite of two bedrooms, sitting room, and bath, opening on the beautiful court. We were appalled in thinking of what the cost would be. What had they taken us for, South American millionaires or what? Bob and Rosamond were inclined to blame me, the one who knew the most about French, with letting the clerk or manager or whoever he was put it over on us. We decided that we should stay at the Continental a day or two for the sake of appearances, then look for a good *pension*.

When we had finished laying out this plan of action, it was near dinner time. We dressed and started out. As we stepped from our rooms a uniformed attendant standing at the door—waiting, it seemed for our exit—bowed low and said, "Messieurs." We walked toward the elevator, and there stood another uniformed attendant, who bowed low and said, "Messieurs." As we entered the elevator, the operator bowed low and said, "Messieurs." As we passed through the office, there came from various functionaries a chorus of "Messieurs." As we went out of the great gate, an attendant uniformed like a major general saluted and said, "Messieurs." We laughed heartily over all this when we got back to our rooms, and declared that whatever it cost to stay at the Continental, it was worth it.

In coming through the office we had been joined by a young man we had met on the ship. He knew his Paris, and we were glad to be taken in tow. After dinner, we went to see the performance at the Marigny; and after the theater our friend piloted us to Olympia. I was amazed at the size of the place, the size of the orchestra seated in the center, and the great gayety of the whole scene. We found a table and were seated. The next number played by the orchestra was *Under the Bamboo Tree*. We attached no particular importance to that; but when it was followed by *The Congo Love Song*, we took notice and sent our compliments to the leader with the request that he and his men order whatever they wished. Soon four girls joined our party; only one of them, a German girl with lovely dark eyes, being able to speak any English, and she knew only a few words. Nevertheless, they all chatted with and at us gayly while they sipped their beer or black coffee drunk from tall, thin glasses. All the while we were in Paris we generally ended up each evening at Olympia; and, generally, this same group of girls joined us at our table. I stopped trying to make an interpreter out of the German girl, and took my first plunge into the practical use of French. My ability to talk the language increased in geometrical progression. I had studied French at school, and had taken the Cortina course in New York, but Olympia proved to be the best school for learning French I ever attended.

A few days after our arrival we were invited to a studio party. Our hostess was an American singer at the Paris Opera House; her husband being the secretary, if I remember correctly, of the American Chamber of Commerce in Paris. Among the guests were the West Point cadet and the art student with their aunts. It was through them that we had received the invitation to the party. There were a number of artists of one kind or another present, and each who could did a turn. This party was our sole opportunity for a peep at Paris on the inside, but, in the short time we had, we saw about all that could be seen on the outside. However, we didn't make a business of seeing Paris; we made a pleasure of it. We looked with something like pity on tourist groups working on a schedule, being hustled from point to point, pausing only while their guide repeated his trite and hasty lecture on this building or that painting or the other monument. I was glad that on my first visit I was able to see what I did see leisurely; not forced to gulp it down but able to take the time to note the taste of it. I kept congratulating myself that I had declined the chance to visit Europe the summer after I graduated from Atlanta as a member of a tourist party of colored Baptist preachers. I quickly discovered that "historical points" interested me less than almost anything else; that a good picture and the facts well told were, generally, as satisfying as the actual sight. What I wanted most, and what cannot be gotten vicariously, was impressions from the life eddying round me and streaming by. I wanted to see people, people at every level, from an élite audience at the Opera House to a group of swearing fishmongers in the market.

Theodore Dreiser

Dreiser (1871–1945), author of *Sister Carrie* and *An American Tragedy*, remains famous as the good gray elephant of American letters, a clumsy, powerful, intelligent realist—and seems therefore an odd beast to respond to quick and mercurial Paris. But this 1913 report from *A Traveler at Forty* of his first visit to the city, when he was already fully formed, shows another side of Dreiser's talent, or, rather, shows Dreiser's true talent: a clear eye for things as they are, even in an "exotic" setting. Dreiser was a genuine realist, who resonated to whatever was real in front of him—or perhaps Paris just lights up even the darker spirits of the American mind. He couldn't write a graceful sentence if his life depended on it, but given that he saw so well and put down what he saw so bluntly, it never did.

----

from

A Traveler at Forty

As we neared Paris he had built this city up so thoroughly in my mood that I am satisfied that I could not have seen it with a realistic eye if I had tried. It was something—I cannot tell you what—Napoleon, the Louvre, the art quarter, Montmartre, the gay restaurants, the boulevards, Balzac, Hugo, the Seine and the soldiery, a score and a hundred things too numerous to mention and all greatly exaggerated. I hoped to see something which was perfect in its artistic appearance—exteriorly speaking. I expected, after reading George Moore and others, a wine-like atmosphere; a throbbing world of gay life; women of exceptional charm of face and dress; the bizarre, the unique, the emotional, the spirited. At Amiens I had seen enough women entering the trains to realize that the dreary commonplace of the English woman was gone. Instead the young married women that we saw were positively daring compared to what England could show—shapely, piquant, sensitive, their eyes showing a birdlike awareness of what this world has to offer. I fancied Paris would be like that, only more so; and as I look back on it now I can honestly say that I was not greatly disappointed. It was not all that I thought it would be, but it was enough. It is a gay, brilliant, beautiful city, with the spirit of New

York and more than the distinction of London. It is like a brilliant, fragile child—not made for contests and brutal battles, but gay beyond reproach.

When the train rolled into the Gare du Nord it must have been about eight o'clock. Barfleur, as usual, was on the qui vive for precedence and advantage. He had industriously piled all the bags close to the door, and was hanging out of a window doing his best to signal a facteur. I was to stay in the car and hand all the packages down rapidly while he ran to secure a taxi and an inspector and in other ways to clear away the impediments to our progress. With great executive enthusiasm he told me that we must be at the Hotel Normandy by eight-fifteen or twenty and that by nine o'clock we must be ready to sit down in the Café de Paris to an excellent dinner which he had ordered by telegraph.

I recall my wonder in entering Paris—the lack of any long extended suburbs, the sudden flash of electric lights and electric cars. Mostly we seemed to be entering through a tunnel or gully, and then we were there. The noisy facteurs in their caps and blue jumpers were all around the cars. They ran and chattered and gesticulated—so unlike the porters in Paddington and Waterloo and Victoria and Euston. The one we finally secured, a husky little enthusiast, did his best to gather all our packages in one grand mass and shoulder them, stringing them on a single strap. The result of it was that the strap broke right over a small pool of water, and among other things the canvas bag containing my blanket and magnificent shoes fell into the water. "Oh, my God," exclaimed Barfleur, "my hat box!"

"The fool ass," I added, "I knew he would do just that—My blanket! My shoes!"

The excited facteur was fairly dancing in anguish, doing his best to get the packages strung together. Between us we relieved him of about half of them, and from about his waist he unwrapped another large strap and strung the remainder on that. Then we hurried on—for nothing would do but that we must hurry. A taxi was secured and all our luggage piled on it. It looked half suffocated under bundles as it swung out into the street, and we were off at a mad clip through crowded, electric-lighted streets. I pressed my nose to the window and took in as much as I could, while Barfleur between calculations as to how much time this would take, and that would take, and whether my trunk had arrived safely, expatiated laconically on French characteristics.

"You smell this air—it is all over Paris."

"The taxis always go like this." (We were going like mad.)

"There is an excellent type—look at her."

"Now you see the chairs out in front—they are that way all over Paris."

I was looking at the interesting restaurant life which never really seems to be interrupted anywhere in Paris. You can always find a dozen chairs somewhere, if not fifty or a hundred, out on the sidewalk under the open sky, or a glass roof—little stone-topped tables beside them, the crowd surging to and fro in front. Here you can sit and have your coffee, your liqueur, your sandwich. Everybody seems to do it—it is as common as walking in the streets.

We whirled through street after street partaking of this atmosphere, and finally swung up in front of a rather plain hotel which, I learned this same night, was close to the Avenue de l'Opéra, on the corner of the Rue St. Honoré and the Rue de l'Echelle. Our luggage was quickly distributed and I was shown into my room by a maid who could not speak English. I unlocked my belongings and was rapidly changing my clothes when Barfleur, breathing mightily, fully arrayed, appeared to say that I should await him at the door below where he would arrive with two guests. I did so, and in fifteen minutes he returned, the car spinning up out of a steady stream that was flowing by. I think my head was dizzy with the whirl of impressions which I was garnering, but I did my best to keep a sane view of things, and to get my impressions as sharp and clear as I could.

I am quite satisfied of one thing in this world, and that is that the commonest intelligence is very frequently confused or hypnotized or over-persuaded by certain situations, and that the weaker ones are ever full of the wildest forms of illusion. We talk about the sanity of life—I question whether it exists. Mostly it is a succession of confusing, disturbing impressions which are only rarely valid. This night I know I was moving in a sort of maze, and when I stepped into the car and was introduced to the two girls who were with Barfleur, I easily succumbed to what was obviously their great beauty.

The artist Greuze has painted the type that I saw before me over and over—soft, buxom, ruddy womanhood. I think the two may have been twenty-four and twenty-six. The elder was smaller than the younger—although both were of good size—and not so ruddy; but they were both perfectly plump, round-faced, dimpled, and with a wealth of brownish-black hair, even white teeth, smooth plump arms and necks and shoulders. Their chins were adorably rounded, their lips red, and their eyes laughing and gay. They began laughing and chattering the moment I entered, extending their soft white hands and saying things in French which I could not understand. Barfleur was smiling—beaming through his monocle in an amused, superior way. The older girl was arrayed in pearl-colored silk with a black mantilla spangled with silver, and the younger had a dress of peach-blow hue with a white lace mantilla also spangled, and they breathed a faint perfume. We were obviously in beautiful, if not moral, company.

I shall never forget the grand air with which this noble company entered the Café de Paris. Barfleur was in fine feather and the ladies radiated a charm and a flavor which immediately attracted attention. This brilliant café was aglow with lights and alive with people. It is not large in size—quite small in fact—and triangular in shape. The charm of it comes not so much from the luxury of the fittings, which are luxurious enough, but from their exceeding good taste, and the fame of the cuisine. One does not see a bill of fare here that indicates prices. You order what you like and are charged what is suitable. Champagne is not an essential wine as it is in some restaurants—you may drink what you like. There is a delicious sparkle and spirit to the place which can only spring from a high sense of individuality. Paris is supposed to provide nothing better than the Café de Paris, in so far as food is concerned. It is as good a place to go for dinner as the city provides.

It amuses me now when I think of how the managerial ability of Barfleur had been working through all this. As the program had been arranged in his mind, I was to take the elder of the two ladies as my partner and he had reserved the younger for himself. As a matter of fact they were really equally pretty and charming—and I was interested in both until, after a few parleys and when I had exchanged a few laughing signs with the younger, he informed me that she was really closely tied up with some one else and was not available. This I really did not believe; but it did not make any particular difference. I turned my attention to the elder who was quite as vivacious, if not quite so forceful as her younger sister. I never knew what it meant before to sit in a company of this kind, welcome as a friend, looked to for gaiety as a companion and admirer, and yet not able to say a word in the language of the occasion. There were certain words which could be quickly acquired on an occasion of this kind, such as "beautiful," "charming," "very delightful," and so on, for which Barfleur gave me the French equivalent, and then I could make complimentary remarks which he would translate for all, and the ladies would say things in reply which would come to me by the same medium. It went gaily enough—for the conversation would not have been of a high order if I had been able to speak French. Barfleur objected to being used constantly as an interpreter, and when he became stubborn and chattered gaily without stopping to explain, I was compelled to fall back on the resources of looks and smiles and gestures. It interested me to see how quick these women were to adapt themselves to the difficulties of the situation. They were constantly laughing and chaffing between themselves—looking at me and saying obviously flattering things, and then laughing at my discomfiture in not being able to understand. The elder explained what certain objects were by lifting them up and insisting on the French name. Barfleur was constantly telling me of the compliments they made and how sad they thought it was that I could not speak French. We departed finally for the Folies-Bergère where the newest sensation of Paris, Mistinguett, was playing. She proved to be a brilliant hoyden to look upon; a gay, slim, yellow-haired tomboy who seemed to fascinate the large audience by her boyish manners and her wayward air. There was a brilliant chorus in spangled silks and satins, and finally a beautiful maiden without any clothing at all who was cloaked by the soldiery of the stage before she had half crossed it. The vaudeville acts were about as good as they are anywhere. I did not think that the performance was any better than one might see in one or two places in New York, but of course the humor was much broader. Now and then one of their remarkable *bons mots* was translated for me by Barfleur just to give me an inkling of the character of the place. Back of the seats was a great lobby or promenade where a fragment of the demimonde of Paris was congregated—beautiful creatures, in many instances, and as unconventional as you please. I was particularly struck with the smartness of their costumes and the cheerful character of their faces. The companion type in London and New York is somewhat colder-looking. Their eyes snapped with Gallic intelligence, and they walked as though the whole world held their point of view and no other.

From here at midnight we left for the Abbaye Thélème; and there I encountered the best that Paris has to show in the way of that gaiety and color and beauty and smartness for which it is famous. One really ought to say a great deal about the Abbaye Thélème, because it is the last word, the quintessence of midnight excitement and international *savoir faire*. The Russian and the Brazilian, the Frenchman, the American, the Englishman, the German and the Italian all meet here on common ground. I saw much of restaurant life in Paris while I was there, but nothing better than this. Like the Café de Paris it was small—very small—when compared to restaurants of similar repute in New York and London. I fancy it was not more than sixty feet square—only it was not square but pentagonal, almost circular. The tables, to begin with, went round the walls, with seats which had the wall for a back; and then, as the guests poured in, the interior space was filled up with tables which were brought in for the purpose; and, later in the morning, when the guests began to leave, these tables were taken out again, and the space devoted to dancing and entertainers.

As in the Café de Paris I noticed that it was not so much the quality of the furnishings as the spirit of the place which was important. This latter was compounded of various elements—success, perfection of service, absolute distinction of cooking, and lastly the subtlety and magnetism of sex which is capitalized and used in Paris as it is nowhere else in the world. I never actually realized until I stepped into this restaurant what it is that draws a certain moneyed element to Paris. The Tomb of Napoleon and the Panthéon and the Louvre are not the significant attractions of that important city. Those things have their value—they constitute an historical and artistic element that is appealing, romantic and forceful. But over and above that there is something else—and that is sex. I did not learn what I am going to say now until later, but it might as well be said here, for it illustrates the point exactly. A little experience and inquiry in Paris quickly taught me that the owners and managers of the more successful restaurants encourage and help to sustain a certain type of woman whose presence is desirable. She must be young, beautiful, or attractive, and above all things possessed of temperament. A woman can rise in the café and restaurant world of Paris quite as she can on the stage; and she can easily graduate from the Abbaye Thélème and Maxim's to the stage, though the path is villainous. On the other hand, the stage contributes freely to the atmosphere of Maxim's, the Abbaye Thélème, and other restaurants of their kind. A large number of the figures seen here and at the Folies-Bergère and other places of the same type, are interchangeable. They are in the restaurants when they are not on the stage, and they are on the stage when they are not in the restaurants. They rise or fall by a world of strange devices, and you can hear brilliant or ghastly stories illustrating either conclusion. Paris—this aspect of it—is a perfect maelstrom of sex; and it is sustained by the wealth and the curiosity of the stranger, as well as the Frenchman.

The Abbaye Thélème on this occasion presented a brilliant scene. The carpet, as I recall it, was a rich green velvet; the walls a lavender-white. From the ceiling six magnificently prismed electroliers were suspended—three glowing with a clear peach-blow hue and three with a brilliant white. Outside a small railing near the door several negro singers, a mandolin and a guitar-player, several stage dancers, and others were congregated. A perfect storm of people was pouring through the doors—all with their tables previously arranged for. Out in the lobby, where a January wind was blowing, you could hear a wild uproar of slamming taxi doors, and the calls of doormen and chauffeurs getting their vehicles in and out of the way. The company generally, as on all such occasions, was on the qui vive to see who else were present and what the general spirit of the occasion was to be. Instantly I detected a number of Americans; three amazingly beautiful English women, such as I never saw in England, and their escorts; a few Spaniards or South Americans; and, after that, a variety of individuals whom I took to be largely French, although it was impossible to tell. The English women interested me because, during all my stay in Europe, I never saw three other women quite so beautiful, and because, during all my stay in England, I scarcely saw a good-looking English woman. Barfleur suggested that they were of that high realm of fashion which rarely remains in London during the winter season—when I was there; that if I came again in May or June and went to the races I would see plenty of them. Their lovely hair was straw-colored and their cheeks and foreheads a faint pink and cream. Their arms and shoulders were delightfully bare, and they carried themselves with amazing hauteur. By one o'clock, when the majority of the guests had arrived, this room fairly shimmered with white silks and satins, white arms and shoulders, roses in black hair and blue and lavender ribbons fastened about coiffures of lighter complexion. There were jewels in plenty—opals and amethysts and turquoises and rubies—and there was a perfect artillery of champagne corks. Every table was attended by its silver bucket of ice; and the mandolins and guitars in their crowded angle were strumming mightily.

I speculated interestedly as we seated ourselves as to what drew all these people from all parts of the world to see this, to be here together. Barfleur was eager to come here first and to have me see this, without delay. I do not know where you could go, and for a hundred francs see more of really amazing feminine beauty. I do not know where for the same money you could buy the same atmosphere of lightness and gaiety and enthusiasm. This place was fairly vibrating with a wild desire to live. I fancy the majority of those who were here for the first time—particularly of the young—would tell you that they would rather be here than in any other spot you could name. The place had a peculiar glitter of beauty which was compounded by the managers with great skill. The waiters were all of them deft, swift, suave, good-looking; the dancers who stepped out on the floor after a few moments were of an orchid-like Spanish type—ruddy, brown, full-bodied, black-haired, black-eyed. They had on dresses that were as close fitting as the scales of a fish and that glittered with the same radiance. They waved and rattled and clashed castanets and tambourines and danced wildly and sinuously to and fro among the tables. Some of them sang, or voices accompanied them from the raised platform devoted to music.

After a while red, blue, pink and green balloons were introduced, anchored to the champagne bottles, and allowed to float gaily in the air. Paper parcels of small paste balls of all colors, as light as feathers, were distributed for the guests to throw at one another. In ten minutes a wild artillery battle was raging. Young girls were up on their feet, their hands full of these colored weapons, pelting the male strangers of their selection. You would see tall Englishmen and Americans exchanging a perfect volley of colored spheres with girls of various nationalities, laughing, chattering, calling, screaming. The cocotte in all her dazzling radiance was here—exquisitely dressed, her white arms shimmering, perfectly willing to strike up an understanding with the admirer who was pelting her.

After a time, when the audience had worn itself through fever and frenzy to satisfaction or weariness, or both, a few of the tables were cleared away and the dancing began, occasional guests joining. There were charming dances in costume from Russia, from Scotland, from Hungary, and from Spain. I had the wonder of seeing an American girl rise from her table and dance with more skill and grace than the employed talent. A wine-enthused Englishman took the floor, a handsome youth of twenty-six or eight, and remained there gaily prancing about from table to table, dancing alone or with whomsoever would welcome him. What looked like a dangerous argument started at one time because some high-mettled Brazilian considered that he had been insulted. A cordon of waiters and the managers soon adjusted that. It was between three and four in the morning when we finally left; and I was very tired.

It was decided that we should meet for dinner; and since it was almost daylight I was glad when we had seen our ladies to their apartment and returned to the hotel.

Edith Wharton

No American writer has ever known or understood Paris better than Edith
Wharton (1862–1937). She settled in Paris in the 1890s, in the wake of the dis-
solution of her marriage and her happy involvement with Morton Fullerton,
and she remained at 55, rue de Varenne until her death (although in her lovely
1934 memoir *A Backward Glance* she says, surprisingly, that she would have
preferred London). She used Paris as a setting less often than Henry James,
and though she had broad friendships among French writers and painters (and
clergymen, too), they tended to be with the second rank of "society" writers
and artists rather than with those we think of now as the real makers of modern French literature and art. Still, no American writer ever grasped quite so
well the dynamics of French society and the peculiar here-but-not-here role
of the American expatriate within it. She lived, as she said in her pages on
French society and French dinner parties, at the bottom of the table, but saw
what was going on at the top—and this makes her an ideal witness. She
remained in Paris long enough to see and record (in this chapter from *The War
on All Fronts*, 1919) the greatest of all European transformations, the changes
wrought by the Great War, one of whose famous side effects was the introduction into Paris of a whole generation of American doughboys. People who
wonder why American writers love to live in Paris might want to know that
Wharton's house in Paris bears a plaque celebrating her existence there, as
well as delicately explicating to passersby her relationship with Henry James.
There isn't a plaque like it anywhere in New York, her hometown.

The Look of Paris
(August, 1914—February, 1915)

I

AUGUST

On the 30th of July, 1914, motoring north from Poitiers, we had
lunched somewhere by the roadside under apple-trees on the edge
of a field. Other fields stretched away on our right and left to a border of
woodland and a village steeple. All around was noonday quiet, and the
sober disciplined landscape which the traveller's memory is apt to evoke

as distinctively French. Sometimes, even to accustomed eyes, these ruled-off fields and compact grey villages seem merely flat and tame; at other moments the sensitive imagination sees in every thrifty sod and even furrow the ceaseless vigilant attachment of generations faithful to the soil. The particular bit of landscape before us spoke in all its lines of that attachment. The air seemed full of the long murmur of human effort, the rhythm of oft-repeated tasks; the serenity of the scene smiled away the war rumours which had hung on us since morning.

All day the sky had been banked with thunder-clouds, but by the time we reached Chartres, toward four o'clock, they had rolled away under the horizon, and the town was so saturated with sunlight that to pass into the cathedral was like entering the dense obscurity of a church in Spain. At first all detail was imperceptible: we were in a hollow night. Then, as the shadows gradually thinned and gathered themselves up into pier and vault and ribbing, there burst out of them great sheets and showers of colour. Framed by such depths of darkness, and steeped in a blaze of mid-summer sun, the familiar windows seemed singularly remote and yet overpoweringly vivid. Now they widened into dark-shored pools splashed with sunset, now glittered and menaced like the shields of fighting angels. Some were cataracts of sapphires, others roses dropped from a saint's tunic, others great carven platters strewn with heavenly regalia, others the sails of galleons bound for the Purple Islands; and in the western wall the scattered fires of the rose-window hung like a constellation in an African night. When one dropped one's eyes from these ethereal harmonies, the dark masses of masonry below them, all veiled and muffled in a mist pricked by a few altar lights, seemed to symbolize the life on earth, with its shadows, its heavy distances and its little islands of illusion. All that a great cathedral can be, all the meanings it can express, all the tranquillizing power it can breathe upon the soul, all the richness of detail it can fuse into a large utterance of strength and beauty, the cathedral of Chartres gave us in that perfect hour.

It was sunset when we reached the gates of Paris. Under the heights of St. Cloud and Suresnes the reaches of the Seine trembled with the blue-pink lustre of an early Monet. The Bois lay about us in the stillness of a holiday evening, and the lawns of Bagatelle were as fresh as June. Below the Arc de Triomphe, the Champs Elysées sloped downward in a sun-powdered haze to the mist of fountains and the ethereal obelisk; and the currents of summer life ebbed and flowed with a normal beat under the trees of the radiating avenues. The great city, so made for peace and art and all humanest graces, seemed to lie by her river-side like a princess guarded by the watchful giant of the Eiffel Tower.

The next day the air was thundery with rumours. Nobody believed them, everybody repeated them. War? Of course there couldn't be war! The Cabinets, like naughty children, were again dangling their feet over the edge; but the whole incalculable weight of things-as-they-were, of the daily necessary business of living, continued calmly and convincingly to assert itself against the bandying of diplomatic words. Paris went on steadily about her midsummer business of feeding, dressing, and amusing the great army of tourists who were the only invaders she had seen for nearly half a century.

All the while, every one knew that other work was going on also. The whole fabric of the country's seemingly undisturbed routine was threaded with noiseless invisible currents of preparation, the sense of them was in the calm air as the sense of changing weather is in the balminess of a perfect afternoon. Paris counted the minutes till the evening papers came.

They said little or nothing except what every one was already declaring all over the country. "We don't want war—*mais il faut que cela finisse!*" "This kind of thing has got to stop": that was the only phrase one heard. If diplomacy could still arrest the war, so much the better: no one in France wanted it. All who spent the first days of August in Paris will testify to the agreement of feeling on that point. But if war had to come, then the country, and every heart in it, was ready.

At the dressmaker's, the next morning, the tired fitters were preparing to leave for their usual holiday. They looked pale and anxious—decidedly, there was a new weight of apprehension in the air. And in the rue Royale, at the corner of the Place de la Concorde, a few people had stopped to look at a little strip of white paper against the wall of the Ministère de la Marine. "General mobilization" they read—and an armed nation knows what that means. But the group about the paper was small and quiet. Passers by read the notice and went on. There were no cheers, no gesticulations: the dramatic sense of the race had already told them that the event was too great to be dramatized. Like a monstrous landslide it had fallen across the path of an orderly laborious nation, disrupting its routine, annihilating its industries, rending families apart, and burying under a heap of senseless ruin the patiently and painfully wrought machinery of civilization. . . .

That evening, in a restaurant of the rue Royale, we sat at a table in one of the open windows, abreast with the street, and saw the strange new crowds stream by. In an instant we were being shown what mobilization was—a huge break in the normal flow of traffic, like the sudden rupture of a dyke. The street was flooded by the torrent of people sweeping past us to the various railway stations. All were on foot, and carrying their luggage; for since dawn every cab and taxi and motor-omnibus had disappeared. The War Office had thrown out its drag-net and caught them all in. The crowd that passed our window was chiefly composed of conscripts, the *mobilisables* of the first day, who were on the way to the station accompanied by their families and friends; but among them were little clusters of bewildered tourists, labouring along with bags and bundles, and watching their luggage pushed before them on hand-carts—puzzled inarticulate waifs caught in the cross-tides racing to a maelstrom.

In the restaurant, the befrogged and red-coated band poured out patriotic music, and the intervals between the courses that so few waiters were left to serve were broken by the ever-recurring obligation to stand up for the Marseillaise, to stand up for God Save the King, to stand up for the Russian National Anthem, to stand up again for the Marseillaise. *"Et dire que ce sont des Hongrois qui jouent tout cela!"* a humourist remarked from the pavement.

As the evening wore on and the crowd about our window thickened, the loiterers outside began to join in the war-songs. *"Allons, debout!"*—and the loyal round begins again. "La chanson du départ!" is a frequent demand; and the chorus of spectators chimes in roundly. A sort of quiet humour was the note of the street. Down the rue Royale, toward the Madeleine, the bands of other restaurants were attracting other throngs, and martial refrains were strung along the Boulevard like its garlands of arc-lights. It was a night of singing and acclamations, not boisterous, but gallant and determined. It was Paris *badauderie* at its best.

Meanwhile, beyond the fringe of idlers the steady stream of conscripts still poured along. Wives and families trudged beside them, carrying all kinds of odd improvised bags and bundles. The impression disengaging itself from all this superficial confusion was that of a cheerful steadiness of spirit. The faces ceaselessly streaming by were serious but not sad; nor was there any air of bewilderment—the stare of driven cattle. All these lads and young men seemed to know what they were about and why they were about it. The youngest of them looked suddenly grown up and responsible: they understood their stake in the job, and accepted it.

The next day the army of midsummer travel was immobilized to let the other army move. No more wild rushes to the station, no more bribing of concierges, vain quests for invisible cabs, haggard hours of waiting in the queue at Cook's. No train stirred except to carry soldiers, and the civilians who had not bribed and jammed their way into a cranny of the thronged carriages leaving the first night could only creep back through the hot streets to their hotels and wait. Back they went, disappointed yet half-relieved, to the resounding emptiness of porterless halls, waiterless restaurants, motionless lifts: to the queer disjointed life of fashionable hotels suddenly reduced to the intimacies and make-shift of a Latin Quarter *pension*. Meanwhile it was strange to watch the gradual paralysis of the city. As the motors, taxis, cabs and vans had vanished from the streets, so the lively little steamers had left the Seine. The canal-boats too were gone, or lay motionless: loading and unloading had ceased. Every great architectural opening framed an emptiness; all the endless avenues stretched away to desert distances. In the parks and gardens no one raked the paths or trimmed the borders. The fountains slept in their basins, the worried sparrows fluttered unfed, and vague dogs, shaken out of their daily habits, roamed unquietly, looking for familiar eyes. Paris, so intensely conscious yet so strangely entranced, seemed to have had *curare* injected into all her veins.

The next day—the 2nd of August—from the terrace of the Hôtel de Crillon one looked down on a first faint stir of returning life. Now and then a taxi-cab or a private motor crossed the Place de la Concorde, carrying soldiers to the stations. Other conscripts, in detachments, tramped by on foot with bags and banners. One detachment stopped before the black-veiled statue of Strasbourg and laid a garland at her feet. In ordinary times this demonstration would at once have attracted a crowd; but at the very moment when it might have been expected to provoke a patriotic outburst it excited no more attention than if one of the soldiers had turned aside to give a penny to a beggar. The people crossing the square did not even stop to look. The meaning of this apparent indifference was obvious. When an armed nation mobilizes, everybody is busy, and busy in a definite and pressing way. It is not only the fighters that mobilize: those who stay behind must do the same. For each French household, for each individual man or woman in France, war means a complete reorganization of

life. The detachment of conscripts, unnoticed, paid their tribute to the
Cause and passed on. . . .

Looked back on from these sterner months those early days in Paris,
in their setting of grave architecture and summer skies, wear the light of
the ideal and the abstract. The sudden flaming up of national life, the
abeyance of every small and mean preoccupation, cleared the moral air as
the streets had been cleared, and made the spectator feel as though he
were reading a great poem on War rather than facing its realities.

Something of this sense of exaltation seemed to penetrate the throngs
who streamed up and down the Boulevards till late into the night. All
wheeled traffic had ceased, except that of the rare taxi-cabs impressed to
carry conscripts to the stations; and the middle of the Boulevards was as
thronged with foot-passengers as an Italian market-place on a Sunday
morning. The vast tide swayed up and down at a slow pace, breaking
now and then to make room for one of the volunteer "legions" which
were forming at every corner: Italian, Roumanian, South American,
North American, each headed by its national flag and hailed with cheer-
ing as it passed. But even the cheers were sober: Paris was not to be
shaken out of her self-imposed serenity. One felt something nobly conscious and voluntary in the mood of this quiet multitude. Yet it was a
mixed throng, made up of every class, from the scum of the Exterior
Boulevards to the cream of the fashionable restaurants. These people,
only two days ago, had been leading a thousand different lives, in indifference or in antagonism to each other, as alien as enemies across a frontier: now workers and idlers, thieves, beggars, saints, poets, drabs and
sharpers, genuine people and showy shams, were all bumping up against
each other in an instinctive community of emotion. The "people," luckily, predominated; the faces of workers look best in such a crowd, and
there were thousands of them, each illuminated and singled out by its
magnesium-flash of passion.

I remember especially the steady-browed faces of the women; and
also the small but significant fact that every one of them had remembered
to bring her dog. The biggest of these amiable companions had to take
their chance of seeing what they could through the forest of human legs;
but every one that was portable was snugly lodged in the bend of an
elbow, and from this safe perch scores and scores of small serious muzzles,
blunt or sharp, smooth or woolly, brown or grey or white or black or

brindled, looked out on the scene with the quiet awareness of the Paris dog. It was certainly a good sign that they had not been forgotten that night.

II

We had been shown, impressively, what it was to live through a mobilization; now we were to learn that mobilization is only one of the concomitants of martial law, and that martial law is not comfortable to live under—at least till one gets used to it.

At first its main purpose, to the neutral civilian, seemed certainly to be the wayward pleasure of complicating his life; and in that line it excelled in the last refinements of ingenuity. Instructions began to shower on us after the lull of the first days: instructions as to what to do, and what not to do, in order to make our presence tolerable and our persons secure. In the first place, foreigners could not remain in France without satisfying the authorities as to their nationality and antecedents; and to do this necessitated repeated ineffective visits to chanceries, consulates and police stations, each too densely thronged with flustered applicants to permit the entrance of one more. Between these vain pilgrimages, the traveller impatient to leave had to toil on foot to distant railway stations, from which he returned baffled by vague answers and disheartened by the declaration that tickets, when achievable, must also be *visés* by the police. There was a moment when it seemed that one's inmost thoughts had to have that unobtainable *visa*—to obtain which, more fruitless hours must be lived on grimy stairways between perspiring layers of fellow-aliens. Meanwhile one's money was probably running short, and one must cable or telegraph for more. Ah—but cables and telegrams must be *visés* too— and even when they were, one got no guarantee that they would be sent! Then one could not use code addresses, and the ridiculous number of words contained in a New York address seemed to multiply as the francs in one's pockets diminished. And when the cable was finally despatched it was either lost on the way, or reached its destination only to call forth, after anxious days, the disheartening response: "Impossible at present. Making every effort." It is fair to add that, tedious and even irritating as many of these transactions were, they were greatly eased by the sudden uniform good-nature of the French functionary, who, for the first time, probably, in the long tradition of his line, broke through its fundamental rule and was kind.

Luckily, too, these incessant comings and goings involved much walking of the beautiful idle summer streets, which grew idler and more beautiful each day. Never had such blue-grey softness of afternoon brooded over Paris, such sunsets turned the heights of the Trocadéro into Dido's Carthage, never, above all, so rich a moon ripened through such perfect evenings. The Seine itself had no small share in this mysterious increase of the city's beauty. Released from all traffic, its hurried ripples smoothed themselves into long silken reaches in which quays and monuments at last saw their unbroken images. At night the fire-fly lights of the boats had vanished, and the reflections of the street lamps were lengthened into streamers of red and gold and purple that slept on the calm current like fluted water-weeds. Then the moon rose and took possession of the city, purifying it of all accidents, calming and enlarging it and giving it back its ideal lines of strength and repose. There was something strangely moving in this new Paris of the August evenings, so exposed yet so serene, as though her very beauty shielded her.

So, gradually, we fell into the habit of living under martial law. After the first days of flustered adjustment the personal inconveniences were so few that one felt almost ashamed of their not being more, of not being called on to contribute some greater sacrifice of comfort to the Cause. Within the first week over two thirds of the shops had closed—the greater number bearing on their shuttered windows the notice "Pour cause de mobilisation," which showed that the "patron" and staff were at the front. But enough remained open to satisfy every ordinary want, and the closing of the others served to prove how much one could do without. Provisions were as cheap and plentiful as ever, though for a while it was easier to buy food than to have it cooked. The restaurants were closing rapidly, and one often had to wander a long way for a meal, and wait a longer time to get it. A few hotels still carried on a halting life, galvanized by an occasional inrush of travel from Belgium and Germany; but most of them had closed or were being hastily transformed into hospitals.

The signs over these hotel doors first disturbed the dreaming harmony of Paris. In a night, as it seemed, the whole city was hung with Red Crosses. Every other building showed the red and white band across its front, with "Ouvroir" or "Hôpital" beneath; there was something sinister in these preparations for horrors in which one could not yet believe, in the making of bandages for limbs yet sound and whole, the spreading of pillows for heads yet carried high. But insist as they would on the woe to come, these warning signs did not deeply stir the trance of Paris. The first days of the war were full of a kind of unrealizing confidence, not boastful or fatuous, yet as different as possible from the clear-headed tenacity of purpose that the experience of the next few months was to develop. It is hard to evoke, without seeming to exaggerate it, that mood of early August: the assurance, the balance, the kind of smiling fatalism with which Paris moved to her task. It is not impossible that the beauty of the season and the silence of the city may have helped to produce this mood. War, the shrieking fury, had announced herself by a great wave of stillness. Never was desert hush more complete: the silence of a street is always so much deeper than the silence of wood or field.

The heaviness of the August air intensified this impression of suspended life. The days were dumb enough; but at night the hush became acute. In the quarter I inhabit, always deserted in summer, the shuttered streets were mute as catacombs, and the faintest pin-prick of noise seemed to tear a rent in a black pall of silence. I could hear the tired tap of a lame hoof half a mile away, and the tread of the policeman guarding the Embassy across the street beat against the pavement like a series of detonations. Even the variegated noises of the city's waking-up had ceased. If any sweepers, scavengers or rag-pickers still plied their trades they did it as secretly as ghosts. I remember one morning being roused out of a deep sleep by a sudden explosion of noise in my room. I sat up with a start, and found I had been waked by a low-voiced exchange of "Bonjours" in the street. . . .

Another fact that kept the reality of war from Paris was the curious absence of troops in the streets. After the first rush of conscripts hurrying to their military bases it might have been imagined that the reign of peace had set in. While smaller cities were swarming with soldiers no glitter of arms was reflected in the empty avenues of the capital, no military music sounded through them. Paris scorned all show of war, and fed the patriotism of her children on the mere sight of her beauty. It was enough.

Even when the news of the first ephemeral successes in Alsace began to come in, the Parisians did not swerve from their even gait. The newsboys did all the shouting—and even theirs was presently silenced by decree. It seemed as though it had been unanimously, instinctively decided that the Paris of 1914 should in no respect resemble the Paris of 1870, and as though this resolution had passed at birth into the blood of millions born since that fatal date, and ignorant of its bitter lesson. The unanimity of self-restraint was the notable characteristic of this people suddenly plunged into an unsought and unexpected war. At first their steadiness of spirit might have passed for the bewilderment of a genera-tion born and bred in peace, which did not yet understand what war implied. But it is precisely on such a mood that easy triumphs might have been supposed to have the most disturbing effect. It was the crowd in the street that shouted "A Berlin!" in 1870; now the crowd in the street continued to mind its own business, in spite of showers of extras and too-sanguine bulletins.

I remember the morning when our butcher's boy brought the news that the first German flag had been hung out on the balcony of the Min-istry of War. Now, I thought, the Latin will boil over! And I wanted to be there to see. I hurried down the quiet rue de Martignac, turned the cor-ner of the Place Sainte Clotilde, and came on an orderly crowd filling the street before the Ministry of War. The crowd was so orderly that the few pacific gestures of the police easily cleared a way for passing cabs, and for the military motors perpetually dashing up. It was composed of all classes, and there were many family groups, with little boys straddling their moth-ers' shoulders, or lifted up by the policemen when they were too heavy for their mothers. It is safe to say that there was hardly a man or woman of that crowd who had not a soldier at the front, and there before them hung the enemy's first flag—a splendid silk flag, white and black and crim-son, and embroidered in gold. It was the flag of an Alsatian regiment—a regiment of Prussianized Alsace. It symbolized all they most abhorred in the whole abhorrent job that lay ahead of them; it symbolized also their finest ardour and their noblest hate, and the reason why, if every other rea-son failed, France could never lay down arms till the last of such flags was low. And there they stood and looked at it, not dully or uncomprehend-ingly, but consciously, advisedly, and in silence: as if already foreseeing all it would cost to keep that flag and add to it others like it: foreseeing the cost and accepting it. There seemed to be men's hearts even in the chil-dren of that crowd, and in the mothers whose weak arms held them up. So they gazed and went on, and made way for others like them, who gazed in their turn and went on too. All day the crowd renewed itself, and it was always the same crowd, intent and understanding and silent, who looked steadily at the flag, and knew what its being there meant. That, in August, was the look of Paris.

III
FEBRUARY

February dusk on the Seine. The boats are plying again, but they stop at nightfall, and the river is inky-smooth, with the same long weed-like reflections as in August. Only the reflections are fewer and paler: bright lights are muffled everywhere. The line of the quays is scarcely discernible, and the heights of the Trocadéro are lost in the blur of night, which presently effaces even the firm tower-tops of Notre-Dame. Down the damp pavements only a few street lamps throw their watery zig-zags. The shops are shut, and the windows above them thickly curtained. The faces of the houses are all blind.

In the narrow streets of the Rive Gauche the darkness is even deeper, and the few scattered lights in courts or "cités" create effects of Piranesi-like mystery. The gleam of the chestnut-roaster's brazier at a street corner deepens the sense of an old adventurous Italy, and the darkness beyond seems full of cloaks and conspiracies. I turn, on my way home, into an empty street between high garden walls, with a single light showing far off at its farther end. Not a soul is in sight between me and that light: my steps echo endlessly in the silence. Presently a dim figure comes around the corner ahead of me. Man or woman? Impossible to tell till I overtake it. The February fog deepens the darkness, and the faces one passes are indistinguishable. As for the numbers of the houses, no one thinks of looking for them. If you know the quarter you count doors from the corner, or try to puzzle out the familiar outline of a balcony or a pediment; if you are in a strange street, you must ask at the nearest tobacconist's—for, as for finding a policeman, a yard off you couldn't tell him from your grandmother!

Such, after six months of war, are the nights of Paris; the days are less remarkable and less romantic.

Almost all the early flush and shiver of romance is gone; or so at least it seems to those who have watched the gradual revival of life. It may appear otherwise to observers from other countries, even from those involved in the war. After London, with all her theatres open, and her machinery of amusement almost unimpaired, Paris no doubt seems like a city on whom great issues weigh. But to those who lived through that first sunlit silent month the streets to-day show an almost normal activity. The vanishing of all the motorbuses, and of the huge lumbering commercial vans, leaves many a forgotten perspective open and reveals many a lost grace of architecture; but the taxi-cabs and private motors are almost as abundant as in peace-time, and the peril of pedestrianism is kept at its normal pitch by the incessant dashing to and fro of those unrivalled engines of destruction, the hospital and War Office motors. Many shops have reopened, a few theatres are tentatively producing patriotic drama or mixed programmes seasoned with sentiment and mirth, and the cinema again unrolls its eventful kilometres.

For a while, in September and October, the streets were made pic-turesque by the coming and going of English soldiery, and the aggressive flourish of British military motors. Then the fresh faces and smart uni-forms disappeared, and now the nearest approach to "militarism" which Paris offers to the casual sight-seer is the occasional drilling of a handful of *piou-pious* on the muddy reaches of the Place des Invalides. But there is another army in Paris. Its first detachments came months ago, in the dark September days—lamentable rear-guard of the Allies' retreat on Paris. Since then its numbers have grown and grown, its dingy streams have percolated through all the currents of Paris life, so that wherever one goes, in every quarter and at every hour, among the busy confident strongly-stepping Parisians one sees these other people, dazed and slowly moving—men and women with sordid bundles on their backs, shuffling along hesitatingly in their tattered shoes, children dragging at their hands and tired-out babies pressed against their shoulders: the great army of the Refugees. Their faces are unmistakable and unforgettable. No one who has ever caught that stare of dumb bewilderment—or that other look of concentrated horror, full of the reflection of flames and ruins—can shake off the obsession of the Refugees. The look in their eyes is part of the look of Paris. It is the dark shadow on the brightness of the face she turns to the enemy. These poor people cannot look across the borders to eventual triumph. They belong mostly to a class whose knowledge of the world's affairs is measured by the shadow of their village steeple. They are no more curious of the laws of causation than the thousands overwhelmed at Avezzano. They were ploughing and sowing, spinning and weaving and minding their business, when suddenly a great darkness full of fire and blood came down on them. And now they are here, in a strange country, among unfamiliar faces and new ways, with nothing left to them in the world but the memory of burning homes and massacred children and young men dragged to slavery, of infants torn from their mothers, old men trampled by drunken heels and priests slain while they prayed beside the dying. These are the people who stand in hundreds every day outside the doors of the shelters improvised to rescue them, and who receive, in return for the loss of everything that makes life sweet, or intelligible, or at least endurable, a cot in a dormitory, a meal-ticket—and perhaps, on lucky days, a pair of shoes. . . .

What are Parisians doing meanwhile? For one thing—and the sign is a good one—they are refilling the shops, and especially, of course, the great "department stores." In the early war days there was no stranger sight than those deserted palaces, where one strayed between miles of unpurchased wares in quest of vanished salesmen. A few clerks, of course, were left: enough, one would have thought, for the rare purchasers who disturbed their meditations. But the few there were did not care to be disturbed: they lurked behind their walls of sheeting, their bastions of flannelette, as if ashamed to be discovered. And when one had coaxed them out they went through the necessary gestures automatically, as if mournfully wondering that any one should care to buy. I remember once, at the Louvre, seeing the whole force of a "department," including the salesman I was trying to cajole into showing me some medicated gauze, desert their posts simultaneously to gather about a motor-cyclist in a muddy uniform who had dropped in to see his pals with tales from the front. But after six months the pressure of normal appetites has begun to reassert itself—and to shop is one of the normal appetites of woman. I say "shop" instead of buy, to distinguish between the dull purchase of necessities and the voluptuousness of acquiring things one might do without. It is evident that many of the thousands now fighting their way into the great shops must be indulging in the latter delight. At a moment when real wants are reduced to a minimum, how else account for the congestion of the department store? Even allowing for the immense, the perpetual buying of supplies for hospitals and work-rooms, the incessant stoking-up of the innumerable centres of charitable production, there is no explanation of the crowding of the other departments except the fact that woman, however valiant, however tried, however suffering and however self-denying, must eventually, in the long run, and at whatever cost to her pocket and her ideals, begin to shop again. She has renounced the theatre, she denies herself the tea-rooms, she goes apologetically and furtively (and economically) to concerts—but the swinging doors of the department stores suck her irresistibly into their quicksand of remnants and reductions.

No one, in this respect, would wish the look of Paris to be changed. It is a good sign to see the crowds pouring into the shops again, even though the sight is less interesting than that of the other crowds streaming daily—and on Sundays in immensely augmented numbers—across the Pont Alexandre III to the great court of the Invalides where the German trophies are displayed. Here the heart of France beats with a richer blood, and something of its glow passes into foreign veins as one watches the perpetually renewed throngs face to face with the long triple row of German guns. There are few in those throngs to whom one of the deadly pack has not dealt a blow; there are personal losses, lacerating memories, bound up with the sight of all those evil engines. But personal sorrow is the sentiment least visible in the look of Paris. It is not fanciful to say that the Parisian face, after six months of trial, has acquired a new character. The change seems to have affected the very stuff it is moulded of, as though the long ordeal had hardened the poor human clay into some dense commemorative substance. I often pass in the street women whose faces look like memorial medals—idealized images of what they were in the flesh. And the masks of some of the men—those queer tormented Gallic masks, crushed-in and squat and a little satyr-like—look like the bronzes of the Naples Museum, burnt and twisted from their baptism of fire. But none of these faces reveals a personal preoccupation: they are looking, one and all, at France erect on her borders. Even the women who are comparing different widths of Valenciennes at the lace-counter all have something of that vision in their eyes—or else one does not see the ones who haven't.

It is still true of Paris that she has not the air of a capital in arms. There are as few troops to be seen as ever, and but for the coming and going of the orderlies attached to the War Office and the Military Government, and the sprinkling of uniforms about the doors of barracks, there would be no sign of war in the streets—no sign, that is, except the presence of the wounded. It is only lately that they have begun to appear, for in the early months of the war they were not sent to Paris, and the splendidly appointed hospitals of the capital stood almost empty, while others, all over the country, were overcrowded. The motives for this disposal of the wounded have been much speculated upon and variously explained: one of its results may have been the maintaining in Paris of the extraordinary moral health which has given its tone to the whole country, and which is now sound and strong enough to face the sight of any misery.

And miseries enough it has to face. Day by day the limping figures grow more numerous on the pavement, the pale bandaged heads more frequent in passing carriages. In the stalls at the theatres and concerts there are many uniforms; and their wearers usually have to wait till the hall is emptied before they hobble out on a supporting arm. Most of them are very young, and it is the expression of their faces which I should like to picture and interpret as being the very essence of what I have called the look of Paris. They are grave, these young faces: one hears a great deal of the gaiety in the trenches, but the wounded are not gay. Neither are they sad, however. They are calm, meditative, strangely purified and matured. It is as though their great experience had purged them of pettiness, meanness and frivolity, burning them down to the bare bones of character, the fundamental substance of the soul, and shaping that substance into something so strong and finely tempered that for a long time to come Paris will not care to wear any look unworthy of the look on their faces.

from

A Backward Glance

PARIS

A year or two after the publication of "The House of Mirth" my husband and I decided to exchange our little house in New York for a flat in Paris. My husband suffered increasingly from the harsh winds and sudden changes of temperature of the New York winter, and latterly we had spent the cold months in rather aimless drifting on the French and the Italian Rivieras. Alassio, San Remo, Bordighera, Menton, Monte Carlo, Cannes; we knew them all to satiety, and in none could I hope to find the kind of human communion I cared for. In none, that is, but Hyères, where we had begun to go nearly every year since the Paul Bourgets had acquired there a little peach-coloured villa above the peach-orchards of Costebelle. But even the companionship of these friends could not fill the emptiness of life in a Riviera hotel. A house and garden of my own, anywhere on the coast between Marseilles and Fréjus, would have made me happy; since that could not be, my preference was for a flat in Paris, where I could see people who shared my tastes, and whence it was easy to go south for sunshine when the weather grew too damp for my husband. On this, therefore, we decided in 1907, thereafter spending our winters in Paris, and going back to the Mount every summer. For two years we occupied an apartment sublet to us by American friends, in a stately Louis XIV *hôtel* of the rue de Varenne; then we hired a flat in a modern house in the same street, and there I remained till 1920, so that my thirteen years of Paris life were spent entirely in the rue de Varenne; and all those years rise up to meet me whenever I turn the corner of the street. Rich years, crowded and happy years; for though I should have preferred London, I should have been hard to please had I not discovered many compensations in my life in Paris.

I found myself at once among friends, both old and new. The Bourgets always spent a part of the winter in the quiet and leafy rue Barbet de Jouy, a short walk from our door; and in other houses of the old Faubourg I found three or four of the French girl friends I had known in my youth at Cannes, and who had long since married, and settled in Paris. Their welcome, and that of the Bourgets, at once made me feel at home, and thanks to their kindness I soon enlarged my circle of acquaintances. My new friends came from worlds as widely different as the University, the literary and Academic *milieux*, and the old and aloof society of the Faubourg Saint-Germain, to which my early companions at Cannes all belonged. As a stranger and newcomer, not only outside of all groups and coteries, but hardly aware of their existence, I enjoyed a freedom not possible in those days to the native-born, who were still enclosed in the old social pigeon-holes, which they had begun to laugh at, but to which they still flew back.

If in those days any authentic member of the Faubourg Saint-Germain had been asked what really constituted Paris society, the answer would undoubtedly have been: "There is no Paris society any longer—there is just a welter of people from heaven knows where." In a once famous play by Alexandre Dumas fils, "L'Etrangère", written, I suppose, in the 'sixties, the Duke (a Duke of the proudest and most ancient nobility) forces his equally proud and perfectly irreproachable wife to invite his foreign mistress (Mrs. Clarkson) to an evening party. The Duchess is seen receiving her guests in the high-ceilinged *salon* of their old *hôtel*, with tall French windows opening to the floor. Mrs. Clarkson arrives, elegant, arrogant and nervous; the Duchess receives her simply and courteously; then she rings for the major-domo, and gives the order: *"Ouvrez les fenêtres! Que tout le monde entre maintenant!"*

In the Paris I knew, the Paris of twenty-five years ago, everybody would have told me that those windows had remained wide open ever since, that *tout le monde* had long since come in, that all the old social conventions were tottering or already demolished, and that the Faubourg had become as promiscuous as the Fair of Neuilly. The same thing was no doubt said a hundred years earlier, and two hundred years even, and probably something not unlike it was heard in the more exclusive *salons* of Babylon and Ur.

At any rate, as I look back at it across the chasm of the war, and all the ruins since heaped up, every convention of that compact and amiable little world seems still to have been standing, though few were rigid enough to hinder social enjoyment. I remember, however, one amusing instance of this rigidity. Soon after coming to Paris my husband and I, wishing to make some return for the welcome my old friends had given us, invited a dozen of them to dine. They were all intimate with each other, and members of the same group; but, being new to the job, and aware of the delicate problems which beset the question of precedence in French society, I begged one of the young women I had invited to advise me as to the seating of my guests. The next day she came to me in perplexity.

"My dear, I really don't know! It's so difficult that I think I'd better consult my uncle, the Duc de D." That venerable nobleman, who had represented his country as Ambassador to one or two of the great powers, was, I knew, the final authority in the Faubourg on ceremonial questions, and though surprised that he should be invoked in so unimportant a matter, I gratefully awaited his decision. The next day my friend brought it. "My uncle was very much perplexed. He *thinks* on the whole you had better place your guests in this way." (She handed me a plan of the table.) "But he said: 'My dear child, Mrs. Wharton ought *never* to have invited them together'" —not that they were not all good and even intimate friends, and in the habit of meeting daily, but because the shades of difference in their rank were so slight, and so difficult to adjust, that even the diplomatist Duke recoiled from the attempt.

It took me, naturally, some time to acquire even the rudiments of this "unwritten law"; to remember, for instance, that an Academician takes precedence of every one but a Duke or an Ambassador (though what happens if he is both a Duke and an Academician I can't remember, if I ever knew); that the next-but-two most honoured guest sits on the right of the lady who is on the host's right; that a foreigner of no rank whatever takes precedence of every rank but that of an Academician, a Cardinal or an Ambassador (or does he? Again I can't remember!); and that, under the most exquisite surface urbanity, resentment may rankle for years in the bosom of a guest whose claims have been disregarded. As almost all the rules are exactly the opposite of those prevailing in England, my path was no doubt strewn with blunders; but such indulgence as may have been needed was accorded because of my girlish intimacy with a small group belonging to the inner circle of the Faubourg, and because I had written a successful novel, a translation of which had recently appeared, with a flattering introduction by Bourget. Herein lay one of the many distinctions between the social worlds of New York and Paris. In Paris no one could live without literature, and the fact that I was a professional writer, instead of frightening my fashionable friends, interested them. If the French Academy had served no other purpose than the highly civilizing one of linking together society and letters, that service would justify its existence. But it is a delusion to think that a similar institution could render the same service in other societies. Culture in France is an eminently social quality, while in Anglo-Saxon countries it might also be called anti-social. In France, where politics so sharply divide the different classes and coteries, artistic and literary interests unite them; and wherever two or three educated French people are gathered together, a *salon* immediately comes into being.

2

In the numberless books I had read about social life in France—memoirs, history, essays, from Sainte-Beuve to Jules Lemaître and after—I had been told that the *salon* had vanished forever, first with the famous *douceur de vivre* of the Old Régime, then with the downfall of the Bourbons, then with the end of the House of Orleans, and finally on the disastrous day of Sedan. Each of these catastrophes doubtless took with it something of the exclusiveness, the intimacy and continuity of the traditional *salon*; but before I had lived a year in Paris I had discovered that most of the old catch-words were still in circulation, most of the old rules still observed, and that the ineradicable passion for good talk, and for seeing the same people every day, was as strong at the opening of the twentieth century as when the *Précieuses* met at the Hôtel de Rambouillet. When I first went to live in Paris, old ladies with dowdy cashmere "mantles", and bonnets tied under their chins, were pointed out to me as still receiving every afternoon or evening, at the same hour, the same five or six men who had been the "foundation" of their group nearly half a century earlier. Though circles as small as these scarcely formed a *salon*, they were composed of the same elements, and capable of the same expansion. Occasionally even the most exclusive felt the need of a blood-transfusion, and more than once it happened to me to be invited, and as it were tested, by the prudent guardian of the hearth.

The typical *salon*, the *salon* in action, was of course a larger and more elastic organization. It presupposed a moderate admixture of new elements, judiciously combined with the permanent ones, those which were called *de fondation*. But these recognized *salons* were based on the same belief that intimacy and continuity were the first requisites of social enjoyment. To attain the perfection of this enjoyment the Parisian hostess would exercise incessant watchfulness over all the members of her own group, as well as over other groups which might supply her with the necessary new blood, and would put up with many whims and humours on the part of her chief performers; and I remember, when I once said to a French friend: "How can Madame A. endure the crotchets of Monsieur X.? Why doesn't she stop inviting him?" his astonished reply: *"Mais elle ne veut pas dégarnir son salon!"*

This continuity of social relations was what particularly appealed to me. In London, where another ideal prevailed, and perpetual novelty was sought for, the stream of new faces rushing past me often made me feel as if I were in a railway station rather than a drawing-room; whereas after I had got my bearings in Paris I found myself, as usual, settling down into a small circle of friends with whom, through all my years in the rue de Varenne, I kept up a delightful intimacy.

Paul Bourget was then at the height of his social popularity. He was one of the most interesting and versatile of talkers, and much in demand by ambitious hostesses; but he too preferred a small group to general society, and was always at his best among his intimates. Far more than I was aware of at the time, he smoothed my social path in Paris, bringing me into contact with the people he thought most likely to interest me, and putting me at once on a footing of intimacy in the houses where he was most at home.

Through all the changes which have since befallen us both, his friendship has never failed me; and in looking back at those mirage-like years I like to think how much of their happiness I owed to him and to his wife.

Early in our first winter he did me an exceptionally good turn. A new Academician—I forget who—was to be received under the famous "Cupola", and Bourget invited me to the ceremony. I had never seen an Academic reception—still one of the most unchanged and distinctive events of Parisian life—and was naturally delighted, as invitations are few, and much sought after if the candidate happens to be (as he was in this case) a familiar and popular Parisian figure. For some reason Minnie Bourget could not go with me, and as I had never been to the Institut, and did not know how to find my way in, or to manoeuvre for a seat, Bourget asked an old friend of his, the Comtesse Robert de Fitz-James, to take me under her wing. She invited me to luncheon, I think—or came to lunch with us; at any rate, before we had struggled to our places through the fashionable throng battling in the circuitous corridors of the Institut, she and I had become friends.

The widowed Comtesse de Fitz-James, known as "Rosa" among her intimates, was a small thin woman, then perhaps forty-five years old, with a slight limp which obliged her to lean on a stick, hair prematurely white, sharp features, eager dark eyes and a disarmingly guileless smile. Belonging by birth to the wealthy Viennese banking family of the Gutmanns, she had the easy cosmopolitanism of a rich Austrian Jewess, and though she had married early, and since her marriage had always lived in Paris, she spoke English almost perfectly, and was always eager to welcome any foreigners likely to fit into the carefully-adjusted design of her *salon*, which, at that time, was the meeting-place of some of the most distinguished people in Paris. There were still, among the irreducibles of the Faubourg, a few who held out, declined to risk themselves among such international promiscuities, and received the mention of the hostess's name with raised eyebrows, and an affectation of hearing it for the first time. But they were few even then, and now that the world we then knew has come to an end, even they would probably agree that in the last ten or fifteen years before the war Madame de Fitz-James' *salon* had a prestige which no Parisian hostess, since 1918, has succeeded in recovering.

When I first knew it, the *salon* in question looked out on the mossy turf and trees of an eighteenth century *hôtel* standing between court and garden in the rue de Grenelle. A few years later it was transferred to a modern building in the Place des Invalides, to which Madame de Fitz-James had moved her fine collection of eighteenth century furniture and pictures at the suggestion of her old friends, the Comte and Comtesse d'Haussonville, who lived on the floor above. The rue de Grenelle apartment, which had much more character, faced north, and her Anglo-Saxon friends thought she had left in search of sunlight, and congratulated her on the change. But she looked surprised, and said: "Oh, no; I hate the sun; it's such a bore always having to keep the blinds down." To regard the sun as the housewife's enemy, fader of hangings and devourer of old stuffs, is common on the continent, and Madame de Fitz-James' cream-coloured silk blinds were lowered, even in winter, whenever the sun became intrusive. The three drawing-rooms, which opened into one another, were as commonplace as rooms can be in which every piece of furniture, every picture and every ornament is in itself a beautiful thing, yet the whole reveals no trace of the owner's personality. In the first drawing-room, a small room hung with red damask, Madame de Fitz-James, seated by the fire, her lame leg supported on a foot-rest, received her intimates. Beyond was the big drawing-room, with pictures by Ingres and David on the pale walls, and tapestry sofas and arm-chairs; it was there that the dinner guests assembled. Opening out of it was another small room, lined with ornate Louis XV bookcases in which rows of rare books in precious bindings stood in undisturbed order—for Madame de Fitz-James was a book-collector, not a reader. She made no secret of this—or indeed of any of her idiosyncrasies—for she was one of the most honest women I have ever known, and genuinely and unaffectedly modest. Her books were an ornament and an investment; she never pretended that they were anything else. If one of her guests was raised to Academic honours she bought his last work and tried to read it—usually with negative results; and her intimates were all familiar with the confidential question: "I've just read So-and-So's new book. *Tell me, my dear: is it good?*"

This model hostess was almost always at home; in fact she very nearly realized the definition of the perfect hostess once given me by an old frequenter of Parisian *salons*. "A woman should never go out—*never*—if she expects people to come to her," he declared; and on my protesting that this cloistered ideal must, on merely practical grounds, be hard for a Parisian hostess to live up to, he replied with surprise: "But why? If a woman once positively resolves never to go to a funeral or a wedding, why should she ever leave her house?"

Why indeed? And Madame de Fitz-James, though she fell short of this counsel of perfection, and missed few funerals and weddings, and occasionally went to an afternoon tea, seldom lunched or dined out. When she did, she preferred big banquets, where the food and the plate were more interesting than the conversation. This, I am sure, was not because she was unduly impressed by the display of wealth, but because it was less of an effort to talk to the fashionable and the over-fed, and the crowd gave her the shelter of anonymity which she seemed to crave outside of her own doors. Occasionally—but very seldom—she came to dine with us; and these small informal parties, though always composed of her own friends, seemed to embarrass and fatigue her. She appeared to feel that she ought to be directing the conversation, signing to the butler to refill the wine-glasses, trying to reshape the groups into which the guests had drifted after dinner; and the effort to repress this impulse was so tiring that she always fled early, with an apologetic murmur. As with most of the famous hostesses I have known, her hospitality seemed to be a blind overpowering instinct, hardly ever to be curbed, and then only with evident distress. When I saw her in other people's houses she always made me think of the story of the English naturalist who kept two tame beavers, and one day, having absented himself for an hour or two, found on his return that the dear creatures had built a dam across the drawing-room floor. That is exactly what Madame de Fitz-James blindly yearned to do in other people's drawing-rooms.

3

She and Bourget had a real regard for each other, and it was thanks to him that I soon became an habitual guest at her weekly lunches and dinners. These always took place on fixed days; a dinner of fourteen or sixteen, with a small reception afterward, on a certain evening of the week, a smaller dinner on another, and on Fridays an informal and extremely agreeable luncheon, at which her accomplished cook served two *menus* of equal exquisiteness, one for those who abstained from meat on Fridays, the other for heretics and nonconformers. More than once, in the excitement and delight of the good talk, I have eaten my way unknowingly through the fat and the lean *menus*, with no subsequent ill-effects beyond a slight reluctance to begin again at dinner; and I was not the only guest whom intellectual enjoyment led into this gastronomic oversight.

Certainly, in my limited experience, I have never known easier and

more agreeable social relations than at Rosa de Fitz-James'. Lists of
names are not of much help in evoking an atmosphere; but the pre-war
society of the Faubourg Saint-Germain has been so utterly dispersed and
wiped out that as a group the frequenters of Madame de Fitz-James'
drawing-room have an almost historic interest. Among the Academicians—in such cases, I suppose, entitled to be named first—were, of
course, Bourget himself, the Comte d'Haussonville (Madame de Staël's
grandson and biographer), the two popular playwrights, Paul Hervieu and
the Marquis de Flers, the former gaunt, caustic and somewhat melancholy, the latter rotund, witty and cordial to the brink of exuberance; the
poet and novelist Henri de Régnier, and my dear friend the Marquis de
Ségur, a charming talker in his discreet and finely-shaded way, and the
author, among other historical studies, of a remarkable book on Julie de
Lespinasse. The Institut was represented by two eminent members, the
Comte Alexandre de Laborde, the learned bibliophile and authority on
illuminated manuscripts, whom his old friend, Gustave Schlumberger, has
characterized as "the most worldly of scholars, and the most scholarly of
men of the world"; the other, also a friend of mine, the Baron Ernest Seil-
lière, a tall quiet man with keen eyes under a vertical shock of white hair,
who had studied in a German University, and whose interest in the *Sturm-
und-Drang* of the German Romantics, and its effect on European culture,
has resulted in a number of erudite and interesting volumes.

Diplomacy (combined with the Academy) shone at Madame de Fitz-
James' in the person of the French Ambassador in Berlin, the wise and
witty Jules Cambon, whom I had known since his far-off days in Washington, and who was a much sought-for guest whenever his leave brought
him to Paris; by Maurice Paléologue, who, after filling important posts at
the Foreign Office, was to be the last French Ambassador at St Petersburg
before the war, and soon after its close to enter the Academy; by the German and Austrian Ambassadors, Prince Radolin and Count Czechen; by
don Enrique Larreta, the Argentine Ambassador, a real lover of letters, and
author of that enchanting chronicle-novel, "The Glory of Don Ramiro" (of
which Rémy de Gourmont's French version is a triumph of literary interpretation); and, among Secretaries of Embassy, by Mr. George Grahame,
attached to the British Embassy in Paris, the cultivated and indefatigably
brilliant Charles de Chambrun (now French Ambassador to the Quirinal),
and the gay and ironic Olivier Taigny, whose ill-health unfortunately
shortened his diplomatic career, but left him his incisive wit.

I have probably left out far more names than I have recorded; but I am impatient to escape from the seats of honour to that despised yet favoured quarter of the French dining-room, the *bout de table*. As I have already said, in France, where everything connected with food is treated with a proper seriousness, the seating of the guests has a corresponding importance—or had, at any rate, in pre-war days. In London, even in those remote times, though the old rules of precedence still prevailed at big dinners (and may yet, for all I know), they were relaxed on intimate occasions, and one of the first to go was that compelling host and hostess always to face each other from the head and foot of the table. In France, all this is reversed. Host and hostess sit opposite one another in the middle of the table (a rule always maintained, in my time, at whatever cost to the harmonious grouping of the party), and the guests descend right and left in dwindling importance to the table-ends, where the untitled, unofficial, unclassified, but usually young, humorous and voluble, are assembled. These *bouts de table* are at once the shame and glory of the French dinner-table; the shame of those who think they deserve a better place, or are annoyed with themselves and the world because they have not yet earned it; the glory of hostesses ambitious to receive the quickest wits in Paris, and aware that most of the brilliant sallies, bold paradoxes and racy anecdotes emanate from that cluster of independents.

The Parisian table-end deserves a chapter to itself, so many are the famous sayings originating there, and so various is the attitude of the table-enders. At first, of course, it is good fun to be among them, and a sought-after table-ender has his own special prestige; but as the years pass, he grows more and more ready to make way for the rising generation, and work upward to the seats of the successful. Not long ago I met at dinner a new Academician, elected after many efforts and long years of waiting, and who had risen without intermediate stages from the table-end to his hostess's right hand. As the guests seated themselves, an old and unpromoted table-ender, passing behind the new Academician, laid a hand on his shoulder, and said: "Ah, my dear B., after so many years of table-end I shall feel terribly lonely without my old neighbour!" Every one burst out laughing except the Academician, who silently unfolded his napkin with an acid smile, and the mistress of the house, who was flurried by this free-and-easy treatment of a guest now raised to the highest rank. A good story is told of the Comte A. de R., a nobleman known as a fierce stickler for the seat to which his armorial bearings entitled him, and who on one occasion was placed, as he thought, too near the table-end. He watched for a lull in the talk, and then, turning to the lady next to him, asked in a piercing voice: "Do you suppose, *chère Madame*, the dishes will be handed as far down the table as this?" (It was this same Comte de R. who, on leaving another dinner, said to a guest of equally aristocratic descent, who lived in his neighbourhood: "Are you walking home? Good! Let us walk together, then, *and talk of rank*.")

In those old days at Madame de Fitz-James' there were, I imagine, few malcontents at the table-ends, for the great rushes of talk and laughter that swept up from there sent a corresponding animation through all the occupants of the high seats. The habitual holders of the ends were the young André Tardieu, then the masterly political leader-writer of the *Temps*, his governmental honours still far ahead of him, the young André Chaumeix, in those days also of the *Temps*, Abel Bonnard, almost the only talker I have known in a French *salon* who was allowed to go on talking as long as he wanted on the same subject (the conventional time-allowance being not more than five minutes), Etienne Grosclaude, the well-known journalist and wit, and only a seat or two farther up (when the company was small) Alexandre de Gabriac, Charles de Chambrun, Taigny and the Marquis du Tillet, each alert to catch and send back the ball flung by their irrepressible juniors.

The whole *raison d'être* of the French *salon* is based on the national taste for general conversation. The two-and-two talks which cut up Anglo-Saxon dinners, and isolate guests at table and in the drawing-room, would be considered not only stupid but ill-bred in a society where social intercourse is a perpetual exchange, a market to which every one is expected to bring his best for barter. How often have I seen such transactions blighted by the presence of an English or American guest, perhaps full of interesting things to say, but unpractised in the accustomed sport, and blocking all circulation by imprisoning his or her restive but helpless neighbour in a relentless duologue!

At Madame de Fitz-James' the men always outnumbered the women, and this also helped to stimulate general talk. The few women present were mostly old friends, and *de fondation*; none very brilliant talkers, but all intelligent, observant and ready to listen. In a French *salon* the women are expected to listen, and enjoy doing so, since they love good talk, and are prepared by à long social experience to seize every allusion, and when necessary to cap it by another. This power of absorbed and intelligent attention is one of the Frenchwoman's greatest gifts, and makes a perfect background for the talk of the men. And how good that talk is—or was, at any rate— only those can say who have frequented such a *salon* as that of Madame de Fitz-James. Almost all the guests knew each other well, all could drop into the conversation at any stage, without groping or blundering, and each had something worth saying, from Bourget's serious talk, all threaded with golden streaks of irony and humour, to the incessant fire-works of Tardieu, the quiet epigrams of Henri de Régnier, the anecdotes of Taigny and Gabriac, the whimsical and half-melancholy gaiety of Abel Bonnard.

The creator of a French *salon* may be moved by divers ambitions; she may wish to make it predominantly political, or literary and artistic, or merely mundane—though the worldly *salon* hardly counts, and is, at any rate, not worth commemorating. Any hostess, however, who intends to specialize, particularly in politics, runs the risk of making her *salon* dull; and dullest of all is that exclusively devoted to manufacturing Academicians, an industry inexhaustibly fascinating to many Frenchwomen. Few can resist political or academic intrigues as an ingredient in their social mixture; but the great art is to combine the ingredients so that none predominates, and to flavour the composition with an occasional dash of novelty. The transients introduced as seasoning must not be too numerous, or rashly chosen; they must be interesting for one reason or another, and above all they must blend agreeably with the "foundation" mixture. In describing French society one has to borrow one's imagery from the French *cuisine*, so similar are the principles involved, and so equally minute is the care required, in preparing a *soufflé* or a *salon*.

Madame de Fitz-James chose her transients with exceptional skill. The few women she added now and then to her habitual group usually possessed some striking quality. The most stimulating and vivid was the Princesse Lucien Murat, and the two most charming were the daughter and the sister of famous poets; the subtle and exquisite Madame Henri de Régnier (one of the three daughters of Hérédia) and my dear friend Jeanne de Margerie, sister of Edmond Rostand, and an intimate of old days, for her husband, until recently French Ambassador in Berlin, had been for many years secretary of Embassy in Washington. Jeanne de Margerie's gifts were of a quieter order, but she was exceptionally quick and responsive, with an unfailing sense of fun; and when she died, not long after the war, a soft but warm radiance vanished from the Parisian scene, and from the lives of her friends.

I do not remember ever seeing Madame de Noailles, the poetess, at Madame de Fitz-James'. Poets are usually shy of *salons*, and so are monologuists like Madame de Noailles, whose dazzling talk was always intolerant of the slightest interruption. Among the women I met there by far the most remarkable was Matilde Serao, the Neapolitan novelist and journalist. She was an old friend of Bourget's, by whom she was first introduced to Madame de Fitz-James, who at once recognized her, in spite of certain external oddities, as an invaluable addition to her parties. Matilde Serao, for a number of years before the war, made an annual visit to Paris, and had many friends there. She was a broad squat woman, with a red face on a short red neck between round cushiony shoulders. Her black hair, as elaborately dressed as a Neapolitan peasant's, looked like a wig, and must have been dyed or false. Her age was unguessable, though the fact that she was accompanied by a young daughter in short skirts led one to assume that she was under fifty. This strange half-Spanish figure, oddly akin to the *Meniñas* of Velasquez, and described by Bourget as "Dr. Johnson in a ball-dress", was always arrayed in low-necked dresses rather in the style of Mrs. Tom Thumb's—I remember in particular a spreading scarlet silk festooned with black lace, on which her short arms and chubby hands rested like a cherub's on a sunset cloud. With her strident dress and intonation she seemed an incongruous figure in that drawing-room, where everything was in half-shades and semi-tones—but when she began to speak we had found our master. In Latin countries the few women who shine as conversationalists often do so at the expense of the rapid give-and-take of good talk. Not so Matilde Serao. She never tried to vaticinate or to predominate; what interested her was exchanging ideas with intelligent people. Her training as a journalist, first on her husband Edoardo Scarfoglio's newspaper, *Il Mattino*, and later as editor of a sheet of her own, *Il Giorno*, had given her a rough-and-ready knowledge of life, and an experience of public affairs, totally lacking in the drawing-room Corinnes whom she outrivalled in wit and eloquence. She had a man's sense of fair play, listened attentively, never dwelt too long on one point, but placed her sallies at the right moment, and made way for the next competitor. But when she was encouraged to talk, and given the field—as, alone with Abel Bonnard, she often was—then her monologues rose to greater heights than the talk of any other woman I have known. The novelist's eager imagination (two or three of her novels are masterly) was nourished on wide reading, and on the varied experience of classes and types supplied by her journalistic career; and culture and experience were fused in the glow of her powerful intelligence.

Another of Madame de Fitz-James' distinguished transients was Count Keyserling, who came often to her house when he was in Paris, as did his charming sister. There were also not a few agreeable Austrians, Count Fritz Hoyos and his sisters among them; none perhaps particularly interested in ideas, but all with that gift of ease and receptivity which made the pre-war Austrian so accomplished a social being. I remember, by the way, asking Theodore Roosevelt, at the end of his triumphal passage across Europe, what type of person he had found most sympathetic on his travels, and my momentary surprise at his unexpected reply: "The Austrian gentlemen."

Henry James was another outlander who, when he came to stay with us, at once became *de fondation*, as did Walter Berry and my friend Bernard Berenson; and from Rumania came Princess Marthe Bibesco and her cousin Prince Antoine (afterward Rumanian Minister in Washington)—but the list is too long to be continued. Instead, I wish to evoke at its close the figure of the most beloved, the kindliest and one of the wittiest of Madame de Fitz-James' "foundation" guests—the Abbé Mugnier (afterward made a Canon of Notre Dame), without whom no reunion at Rosa's would have been complete. The Abbé's sensitive intelligence was a solvent for the conflicting ideas and opinions of the other visitors, since no matter how much they disagreed with each other, they were one in appreciating "Monsieur l'Abbé", and at the approach of his small figure, with eyes always smiling behind their spectacles, and a tuft of gray hair vibrating flame-wise above his forehead, every group opened to welcome him.

Even for those who know the Abbé Mugnier well, it is not easy to define the qualities which thus single him out. Profound kindness and keen intelligence are too seldom blent in the same person for a word to have been coined describing that rare combination. I can only say that as vicar of the ultra-fashionable church of Sainte Clotilde, and then as chaplain of a convent in a remote street beyond Montparnasse, he seemed equally in his proper setting; and his quick sense of fun and irony is so lined with tender human sympathy that the good priest is always visible behind the shrewd social observer.

The Abbé Mugnier had an hour of celebrity when he converted Huysmans; he has since made other noted converts, and his concern for souls, and his wise dealings with them, cause him to be much sought after as the consoler of the dying, though those who have met him only in the world would not at first associate him with such scenes—at least not until they catch the tone of his voice in speaking of grief and suffering. His tolerance and sociability have indeed occasionally led people to risk in his presence remarks slightly inappropriate to his cloth; and it is good to see the quiet way in which, without the least air of offence, he gives the talk a more suitable turn.

His wise and kindly sayings—so quietly spoken that they sometimes escape the inattentive—are celebrated in Paris; but they have doubtless been recorded by many, and I will cite only two or three, which were said in my hearing. The Abbé, in spite of his social leanings, has a Franciscan soul, and is one of the few Frenchmen I have known with a genuine love of trees and flowers and animals. Before his sight began to fail he used to come out every year in June to my little garden near Paris, to see the long walk when the Candidum lilies were in bloom; and he really *did* see them, which is more than some visitors do, who make the pilgrimage for the same purpose. His tenderness for flowers and birds is so un-French that he might have imbibed it in the Thuringian forests where he used to wander on his summer holidays in the path of Goethe (Goethe and Châteaubriand, both forest-lovers, are his two literary passions); and it seems appropriate, therefore, that two of his sayings to me should be about birds.

We were speaking one day of the difficult moral problems which priests call *cas de conscience*, and he said: "Ah, a very difficult one presented itself to me once, for which I knew of no precedent. I was administering the Sacrament to a dying parishioner, and at that moment the poor woman's pet canary escaped from its cage, and lighting suddenly on her shoulder, pecked at the Host."

"Oh, Monsieur l'Abbé—and what did you do?"

"I blessed the bird," he answered with his quiet smile.

Another day he was talking of the great frost in Paris, when the Seine was frozen over for days, and of the sufferings it had caused among the poor. "I shall never forget the feeling of that cold. On one of the worst nights—or rather at three in the morning, the coldest hour of the twenty-four—I was called out of bed by the sacristan of Sainte Clotilde, who came to fetch me to take the viaticum to a poor parishioner. The sick man lived a long way off, and oh, how cold we were on the way there, Lalouette and I—the old sacristan's name was Lalouette (the lark)," he added with a reminiscent laugh.

The play on the name was irresistible, and I exclaimed: "Oh, how tempted you must have been, when he came for you, to cry out: ' 'Tis not the lark, it is the nightingale'—" I broke off, fearing that my quotation might be thought inappropriate; but with his usual calm smile the Abbé answered: "Unfortunately, Madame, we were not in Verona."

Once, in another vein, he was describing the marriage of two social "climbers" who had invited all fashionable Paris to their nuptial Mass, and had asked the Abbé (much sought after on such occasions also) to perform the ceremony. At the last moment, when the guests were already assembled, he discovered (what had perhaps been purposely slurred over), that the couple were in some way technically disqualified for a church marriage. "So," said the Abbé drily, "I blessed them in the sacristy, between two sterilized palms; and of course I could not prevent their assisting afterward at Mass with the rest of the company."

Another day we were lunching together at a friend's house, and the talk having turned on the survival in the French provinces of the old-fashioned village atheist and anti-clerical (in the style of Flaubert's immortal Monsieur Homais), our hostess told us that she had known an old village chemist near her father's place in the Roussillon who was a perfect type of this kind. His family were much distressed by his sentiments, and when he lay on his death-bed besought him to receive the parish priest; but he refused indignantly, and to his wife's question: "But what can you have against our poor *Curé*?", replied with a last gust of fury: "Your *curés*—your *curés*, indeed! Don't tell me! I know all about your *curés*—"

"But what do you know against them?"

"Why, I read in a history book long ago that ten thousand *curés* died fighting for the beautiful Helen under the walls of Troy."

A shout of mirth received this prodigious bit of history, and as our laughter subsided we heard the Abbé's chuckle, and saw the little flame-like tuft quiver excitedly on his crest.

"Well, Monsieur l'Abbé, what do you think of that?"

"Ah, would to heaven it were true!" the Abbé murmured sadly.

The war broke up that company of friendly people; death followed on war, and now the whole scene seems as remote as if it had belonged to a past century, and I linger with a kind of piety over the picture of that pleasant gray-panelled room, with its pictures and soft lights, and arm-chairs of faded tapestry. I see Bourget and James talking together before the fire, soon to be joined by the Abbé Mugnier, Bonnard and Walter Berry; Monsieur d'Haussonville, Hervieu and Larreta listening to Matilde Serao, and Chambrun, Berenson and Tardieu forming another group; and in and out among her guests Madame de Fitz-James weaving her quiet way, leaning on her stick, watching, prodding, interfering, re-shaping the groups, building and rebuilding her dam, yet somehow never in the way, because, in spite of her incomprehension of the talk, she always manages to bring the right people together and diffuses about her such an atmosphere of kindly hospitality that her very blunders add to the general ease and good humour.

Randolph Bourne

In his tragically short life, Randolph Bourne (1886–1918) did as much as any essayist can to define and inspire a generation. He made his reputation with the generation-defining, taboo-defying "Youth and Life" in 1909. After graduating from Columbia in 1913, he won a fellowship that took him to Paris just on the cusp of the Great War, where he fell in love with French civilization and, as he recounts here, at least one Frenchwoman. Reading Bourne's account (from *History of a Literary Radical*, 1920) of this oddly cerebral-sounding amour, it is probably worth recalling that he was terribly disfigured at birth by a ham-handed obstetrician with a forceps, and then, only four, was left hunchbacked and dwarfed by spinal tuberculosis.

Mon Amie

I

She was French from the crown of her head to the soles of her feet, but she was of that France which few Americans, I think, know or imagine. She belonged to that France which Jean-Christophe found in his friend Olivier, a world of flashing ideas and enthusiasms, a golden youth of ideals.

She had picked me out for an exchange of conversation, as the custom is, precisely because I had left my name at the Sorbonne as a person who wrote a little. I had put this bait out, as it were, deliberately, with the intention of hooking a mind that cared for a little more than mere chatter, but I had hardly expected to find it in the form of a young girl who, as she told me in her charmingly polished note, was nineteen and had just completed her studies.

These studies formed a useful introduction when she received me in the little old-fashioned apartment in the Batignolles quarter on my first visit. She had made them ever since she was five years old in a wonderful old convent at Bourges; and in the town had lived her grandmother, a very old lady, whom she had gone lovingly to see, as often as she could be away from the watchful care of the nuns. In her she had found her real mother, for her parents had been far away in Brittany. When the old lady died, my friend had to face an empty world, and to become acquainted all over again with a mother whom she confessed she found "little sympathetic." But she was a girl of *devoir*, and she would do nothing to wound her.

She told me one afternoon as we took our first walk through the dusky richness of the Musée Cluny, that the shock of death had disclosed to her how fleeting life was, how much she thought of death, and how much she feared it. I used the lustiness of her grandmother's eighty-four years to convince her as to how long she might have to postpone her dread, but her fragile youth seemed already to feel the beating wings about her. As she talked, her expression had all that wistful seriousness of the French face which has not been devitalized by the city, that sense of the near-ness of unutterable things which runs, a golden thread, through their poetry. Though she had lived away from Brittany, in her graver moments there was much in her of the patient melancholy of the Breton. For her father's people had been seafolk,—not fishermen, but pilots and navi-gators on those misty and niggardly shores,—and the long defeat and ever-trustful suffering was in her blood. She would interpret to me the homely pictures at the Luxembourg which spoke of coast and peasant life; and her beautiful articulateness brought the very soul of France out of the canvases of Cottet and Breton and Carrière. She understood these people.

But she was very various, and, if at first we plumbed together the pro-foundest depths of her, we soon got into shallower waters. The fluency of her thought outran any foreign medium, and made anything but her fly-ing French impossible. Her meager English had been learned from some curious foreigner with an accent more German than French, and we aban-doned it by mutual consent. Our conversation became an exchange of ideas and not of languages. Or rather her mind became the field where I explored at will.

I think I began by assuming a Catholic devotion in her, and implied that her serious outlook on life might lead her into the church. She scoffed unmitigatedly at this. The nuns were not unkindly, she said, but they were hard and narrow and did not care for the theater and for books, which she adored.

She believed in God. "Et le théâtre!" I said, which delighted her hugely. But these Christian virtues made unlovely characters and cut one off so painfully from the fascinating moving world of ideas outside. But surely after fourteen years of religious training and Christian care, did she not believe in the Church, its priesthood and its dogmas?

She repudiated her faith with indescribable vivacity. A hardened Anglo-Saxon agnostic would have shown more diffidence in denying his belief in dogma or the Bible. As for the latter, she said, it might do for children of five years. And the cutting sweep of that "enfants de cinq ans" afforded me a revealing glimpse of that lucid intelligence with which the French mind cuts through layers and strata of equivocation and compromise.

Most Frenchmen, if they lose their faith, go the swift and logical road to atheism. Her loss was no childish dream or frenzy; she still believed in God. But as for the Church and its priesthood,—she told me, with malicious irony, and with the intelligence that erases squeamishness, of a friend of hers who was the daughter of the priest in charge of one of the largest Parisian churches. Would she confess to a member of a priestly caste which thus broke faith? Confession was odious anyway. She had been kept busy in school inventing sins. She would go to church on Easter, but she would not take the Eucharist, though I noticed a charming lapse when she crossed herself with holy water as we entered Notre Dame one day.

Where had she ever got such ideas, shut up in a convent?—Oh, they were all perfectly obvious, were they not? Where would one not get them? This amazing soul of modern France!—which pervades even the walls of convents with its spirit of free criticism and its terrible play of the intelligence; which will examine and ruthlessly cast aside, just as my vibrant, dark-haired, fragile friend was casting aside, without hypocrisy or scruple, whatever ideas do not seem to enhance the clear life to be lived.

II

Accustomed to grope and flounder in the mazes of the intellect, I found her intelligence well-nigh terrifying. I would sit almost helplessly and listen to her sparkle of talk. Her freedom knocked into pieces all my little imagined world of French conventionalities and inhibitions. How could this pale, dignified mother, to whom I was presented as she passed hurriedly through the room one day, allow her to wander so freely about Paris parks and museums with a foreign young man? Her answer came superbly, with a flare of decision which showed me that at least in one spot

the eternal conflict of the generations had been settled: *"Je me permets!"*—
I allow myself. She gave me to understand that for a while her mother had
been difficult, but that there was no longer any question of her "living her
life"—*vivre sa vie*. And she really thought that her mother, in releasing her
from the useless trammels, had become herself much more of an independent personality. As for my friend, she dared, she took risks, she
played with the adventure of life. But she knew what was there.

The motherly Anglo-Saxon frame of mind would come upon me, to
see her in the light of a poor ignorant child, filled with fantastic ideals, all
so pitifully untested by experience. How ignorant she was of life, and to
what pitfalls her daring freedom must expose her in this unregenerate
France! I tried and gave it up. As she talked,—her glowing eyes, in which
ideas seemed to well up brimming with feeling and purpose, saying
almost more than her words,—she seemed too palpably a symbol of luminous youth, a flaming militant of the younger generation, who by her
courage would shrivel up the dangers that so beset the timorous. She was
French, and that fact by itself meant that whole layers of equivocation had
been cut through, whole sets of intricacies avoided.

In order to get the full shock of her individuality, I took her one afternoon to a model little English tea-room on the rue de Rivoli, where normal Britishers were reading *Punch* and the *Spectator* over their jam and
cake. The little flurry of disapprobation and the hostile stare which our
appearance elicited from the well-bred families and discreet young men
at the tables, the flaring incongruity of her dark, lithe, inscrutable personality in this bland, vacuous British atmosphere, showed me as could
nothing else how hard was the gem-like flame with which she burned.

As we walked in the Luxembourg and along the quays, or sat on the
iron chairs in the gardens of the Parc Monceau or the Trocadéro, our
friendship became a sort of intellectual orgy. The difficulty of following
the pace of her flying tongue and of hammering and beating my own
thoughts into the unaccustomed French was fatiguing, but it was the fascinating weariness of exploration. My first idle remarks about God
touched off a whole battery of modern ideas. None of the social currents
of the day seemed to have passed her by, though she had been immured
so long in her sleepy convent at Bourges. She had that same interest and
curiosity about other classes and conditions of life which animates us here
in America, and the same desire to do something effective against the misery of poverty.

I had teased her a little about her academic, untried ideas, and in grave reproof she told me, one afternoon, as we stood—of all places!—on the porch of the Little Trianon at Versailles, a touching story of a family of the poorest of the Parisian poor, whom she and her mother visited and helped to get work. She did not think charity accomplished very much, and flamed at the word "Socialism," although she had not yet had its program made very clear to her.

But mostly she was feminist,—an ardent disciple in that singularly uncomplicated and happy march of the Frenchwomen, already so practically emancipated, toward a definite social recognition of that liberation. The normal Frenchwoman, in all but the richer classes, is an economic asset to her country. And economic independence was a cardinal dogma in my friend's faith. She was already taking a secretarial course, in order to ensure her ability to make her living; and she looked forward quite eagerly to a career.

Marriage was in considerable disfavor; it had still the taint of the Church upon it, while the civil marriage seemed, with the only recently surrendered necessary parental consent, to mark the subjection of the younger to the older generation. These barriers were now removed, but the evil savor of the institution lingered on. My friend, like all the French intellectuals, was all for the "union libre," but it would have to be loyal unto death. It was all the more inspiring as an ideal, because it would be perhaps hard to obtain. Men, she was inclined to think, were usually *malhonnête*, but she might find some day a man of complete sympathy and complete loyalty. But she did not care. Life was life, freedom was freedom, and the glory of being a woman in the modern world was enough for her.

The French situation was perhaps quite as bad as it was pictured. Friendship between a girl and a young man was almost impossible. It was that they usually wished to love her. She did not mind them on the streets. The students—oh, the students!—were frightfully annoying; but perhaps one gave a *gifle* and passed rapidly on. Her parents, before she had become genuinely the captain of her soul, had tried to marry her off in the orthodox French way. She had had four proposals. Risking the clean candor of the French soul, I became curious and audacious. So she dramatized for me, without a trace of self-consciousness, a wonderful little scene of provincial manners. The stiff young Frenchman making his stilted offer, her self-possessed reluctance, her final refusal, were given in inimitable style. These incidents, which in the life of a little American *bourgeoise* would have been crises or triumphs, and, at any rate, unutterably hoarded secrets, were given with a cold frankness which showed refreshingly to what insignificance marriage was relegated in her life. She wished, she said, to *vivre sa vie*—to live her life. If marriage fitted in with her living of her life, it might take her. It should never submerge or deflect her. Countless Frenchwomen, in defiance of the strident Anglo-Saxon belief, were able both to keep a household and to earn their own living; and why not she also? She would always be free; and her black eyes burned as they looked out so fearlessly into a world that was to be all hers, because she expected nothing from it.

About this world, she had few illusions. To its worldlinesses and glitter she showed really a superb indifference. I brutally tried to trap her into a confession that she spurned it only because it might be closed to her through lack of money or prestige. Her eloquent eyes almost slew me with vivacious denial. She despised these "dolls" whose only business in life was to wear clothes. Her own sober black was not affectation, but only her way of showing that she was more than a *poupée*. She did not say it, but I quite appreciated, and I knew well that she knew, how charming a *poupée* she might have made.

Several of her friends were gay and worldly. She spoke of them with charming frankness, touching off, with a tone quite clean of malice, all their little worthlessnesses and futilities. Some of this world, indeed, shaded off into unimaginable *nuances*, but she was wholly aware of its significance. In the inimitable French way, she disdained to use its errors as a lever to elevate her own virtues.

III

Her blazing candor lighted up for me every part of her world. We skirted abysses, but the language helped us wonderfully through. French has worn tracks in so many fields of experience where English blunders either boorishly or sentimentally. French is made for illumination and clear expression; it has kept its purity and crispness and can express, without shamefacedness or bungling, attitudes and interpretations which the Anglo-Saxon fatuously hides.

My friend was dimly sensible of some such contrast. I think she had as much difficulty in making me out as I had in making her out. She was very curious as to how she compared with American girls. She had once met one but had found her, though not a doll, yet not *sympathique* and little understandable. I had to tell my friend how untranslatable she was. The Anglo-Saxon, I had to tell her, was apt to be either a school-child or a middle-aged person. To the first, ideas were strange and disturbing. To the second, they were a nuisance and a bore. I almost assured her that in America she would be considered a quite horrible portent. Her brimming idealism would make everybody uncomfortable. The sensual delight which she took in thinking, the way her ideas were all warmly felt and her feelings luminously expressed, would adapt her badly to a world of school-children and tired business men. I tried to go over for her the girls of her age whom I had known. How charming they were to be sure, but, even when they had ideas, how strangely inarticulate they sometimes were, and, if they were articulate, how pedantic and priggish they seemed to the world about them! And what forests of reticences and exaggerated values there were, and curious illogicalities. How jealous they were of their personalities, and what a suspicious and individualistic guard they kept over their candor and sincerities! I was very gay and perhaps a little cruel.

She listened eagerly, but I think she did not quite understand. If one were not frankly a doll, was not life a great swirl to be grappled with and clarified, and thought and felt about? And as for her personality, the more she gave the more she had. She would take the high risks of friendship.

To cross the seas and come upon my own enthusiasms and ideals vibrating with so intense a glow seemed an amazing fortune. It was like coming upon the same design, tinted in novel and picturesque colors of a finer harmony. In this intellectual flirtation, carried on in *musée* and garden and on quay throughout that cloudless April, I began to suspect some gigantic flattery. Was her enthusiasm sincere, and her clean-cutting ideas, or had she by some subtle intuition anticipated me? Did she think, or was it to be expected of me, that I should fall in love with her? But perhaps there was a touch of the too foreign in her personality. And if I had fallen in love, I know it would not have been with herself. It would have been with the Frenchness of her, and perhaps was. It would have been with the eternal youth of France that she was. For she could never have been so very glowing if France had not been full of her. Her charm and appeal were far broader than herself. It took in all that rare spiritual climate where one absorbs ideas and ideals as the earth drinks in rain.

She was of that young France with its luminous understanding, its personal verve, its light of expression, its way of feeling its ideas and thinking its emotions, its deathless loyalty which betrays only at the clutch of some deeper loyalty. She adored her country and all its mystic values and aspirations. When she heard I was going to Germany, she actually winced with pain. She could scarcely believe it. I fell back at once to the position of a vulgar traveler, visiting even the lands of the barbarians. They were her country's enemies, and some day they would attack. France awaited the onslaught fatalistically. She did not want to be a man, but she wished that they would let women be soldiers. If the war came, however, she would enlist at once as a Red Cross nurse. She thrilled at the thought that perhaps there she could serve to the uttermost.

And the war has come, hot upon her enthusiasms. She must have been long since in the field, either at the army stations, or moving about among the hospitals of Paris, her heart full of pride and pity for the France which she loved and felt so well, and of whose deathless spirit she was, for me, at least, so glowing a symbol.

Sherwood Anderson

From Winesburg, Ohio, to the Left Bank seems like a long way to go, but Anderson (1876–1941) turns out to be another of the "improbable" Americans in Paris, in the line of Catlin and Barnum—one of the primitive, or at least homespun, American writers who turned out to feel happier and more at home there than anyone might have expected. Anderson made his notes on Paris in 1921, and so is an early witness of the most famous of all American Parises—the Paris of the 1920s. It is one of the sad/delicious ironies of American letters that it would be his prodigal son, Ernest Hemingway—whom Anderson urged to go to Paris and who then mocked him at length in *The Torrents of Spring*—who would become the most famous resident of that Paris: proof, if more were needed, that we first knock down our fathers and then rifle their pockets. Though Anderson spells "Tuileries" as "Twilery" (the bizarre orthography in this excerpt is his) no one has ever seen the Parisian sky, or waiter, more happily, or described it, or him, more lucidly.

---

from

Paris Notebook, 1921

May 30
No one has ever written eloquently enough of French whiskers. Perhaps the thing cannot be done. There is sincere abandonment. One imagines a Frenchman going to an artist as an American about to build a house goes to an architect. The artist lays before him a thousand designs but he is not satisfied. A new design must be created.

For this there is an extra charge of 60 francs. "It does not matter. This is an important moment in life."

The American is afraid he will, in clothes, in manner of walking, in facial adornment, in the style of his hat, not quite conform to the accepted standards. He trembles lest someone stare at him on the street.

With the Frenchman it is not so. It is his passion to be an individual sharply defined, to stand forth among men.

The matter is not accomplished without a struggle. After a day in the streets of Paris nothing astonishes you. On every side are unbelievable fantastic whiskers, hats, trousers, coats.

A delightful sense of freedom is at once achieved. Deeply buried away within yourself is some passion for display. You have in secret hungered to wear a green feather in your cap, to adorn yourself with a red sash, to wear long fierce looking mustachios.

Being a born and bred American I have long looked forward to the coming of old age. "When the time comes that my work is done I shall become an old rascal, a charlatan," I have promised myself. My days shall be spent in swaggering about, in the telling of monstrous lies, in cheating. I have pictured myself reeling thro streets clad in red pants. My whiskers have grown long and white. I shout ribald songs, swear strange oaths.

This has been my secret dream. Now I shall have to give it up. There will be nothing original in anything I can do to make myself notorious and picturesque. Alas I am Anglo Saxon. The most humble Paris cab driver can outdo me without an effort.

I went to dine at a restaurant in old Paris, on the island. It is a place where boatmen from the Seine come to eat and drink and is called the "Marines." These little cafes are everywhere. There is a bench along the wall and a long table. Everywhere delicious food. A good dinner with wine tips and all, at the present rate of exchange costs about 60 or 70 cents in our money.

At the Marines I sat with a young French artist in prose and his misstress. They have lived together for 6 years although he is now but 24 and she a year younger. He was in the army for 4 years and in the meantime she worked, making her own living.

Now they are very poor and he is trying to make a living writing advertisments for stores.

What a sad, hurt sensitive face he has. His misstress is much younger but there is something finely maternal in her attitude toward him.

He tried to speak to me of the war but the little girl kept continually striving to change the subject. It is evident the matter has become a kind of insanity with him. One refrain kept running through all his talk. "They told us after the fighting we would have our chance, that a new life would begin."

He kept asking about places in America, wild places where life could be lived without money. There seemed a sort of dream of a golden land of fish, berries, cool streams, deep quiet forests.

Into the Marines came a jugler, a man of the streets. He entertained us by making little funnels of paper balancing them on his nose and burning them. When the paper funnel was burned he continued balancing the black delicate ash, continually talking the jargon on the streets. When someone applauded he said sharply, "Save your hands for the work of opening your purses."

At the opera the usher, an old French woman was dissatisfied with the tip given her for ushering us to our seats and began to grumble and scold. Another old woman—very neat and prim looking, who sat beside us answered her. A cloud of words filled the air. When the usher had fled the second old woman spoke to us. "Im from Baltimore and can't speak a word of French unless I'm mad through and through. Then I can give these old blackmailers as good as they send" she explained.

James Joyce the irishman came to see us, a long, somewhat gloomy, handsome man with beautiful hands. Everyone liked him at once. In conversation he is very witty and the smile that lights up his gloomy face when he has said a good thing is like a light brought suddenly into a dark room. His book Ulysses, that cannot be published in America or England is to be published in Paris by Joyce himself and Miss Beach who runs an American bookstore on the Rue here. Joyce has been at work on the book for seven years and that together with all his other writing has brought him in but a few pounds. He has a wife and children and for several years has lived far from his friends and no doubt often in great poverty in Italy and Switzerland. Among all modern writers his lot has perhaps been the hardest and it may well be that his Ulysses is the most important book that will be published in this generation.

Wherever one goes in the country here in France one has a tremendious feeling of man intimate connection and contact with the earth. It is as though every grain of dust in all France had been run through the fingers of some peasant's hands. One sees very little of farming with horse and power driven implements on the American plan. Everything is more intimate. The land is the son of the peasant and has been born out of the womb of the old peasant women who work in the fields.

The future of the stage does not lie with the French. The Germans or the English will in the end do better with that art. The French is the language of declamation and good plays must not be declaimed. Perhaps the French will only succeed in playing swaggering, romantic parts.

At noon in Paris the shops close for from 1½ to 2 hours. Luncheon is a function. Everyone goes to a restaurant and later to a cafe for coffee or liquer. Little shop girls parade the street. Clerks swagger with their sticks and become, for the moment boulevardiers. There is a charming and real break in the days work.

I have got me a place to sit in a little bare raised place above the Twillery Gardens, facing the Place de Concordat with the Rue de Rivoli at my right hand. Here no doubt the women of Paris came to knit stocking while the guillotine whacked off heads. One get a comfortable chair for the afternoon for 20 centimes and there is a broad flat wall that makes an ideal writing desk.

This has been a day of triumph for me. I have achieved a haircut. I wear my hair somewhat long and am vain about it. An American barber cuts it ruthlessly. He is determined you shall not be a dude or a sissy. Pleading is of no use. He insists your haircut shall be exactly like very other haircut in America.

I have little French and decided I must find a barber who spoke English. I spent hours looking in vain for such a place. Finally I plunged into a French shop.

A gentle quiet little old man led me to a low chair and dressed me in a white gown. We spent 10 minutes consulting. He cut a few hairs and we consulted again. Confidence grew in me. Peace stole in on my soul. "I am going to get the first real haircut of my life" I told myself. "It will cost me a fortune to have this artist at work on me but what care I."

The haircut cost me two frances, the equivalent of 14¢ at the present exchange. Someday a wise man will import a half dozen French barbers, start a france barber shop in Chicago and gain a fortune. He can charge almost any price. We cant all come to Paris just for a haircut.

There is a special kind of pearly clearness about French skies. Every American I see agrees with me about it. The clouds come down to you, beacon to you, something within you seems to be always on the point of floating away, into the skies. For one thing the low skyline in Paris makes the sky a more significant part of the life of the city dweller here. The pearly skies, the soft floating clouds and the fresh flowers for sale at marvelously low prices on every street corner give a constant and lovely sense of nature in the midst of the roar of the city.

June 2

Went to walk on the river bank. A whole life goes on down here regardless of the life above, in the streets. In a long barge there are more than a hundred women doing family washings. Other women kneel at the rivers edge beating the clothes on the stones with wooden paddles.

An industry has been set up. Men women and boys have gathered the cotton from the cottonwood trees that at this time of year carpet the streets of Paris. They are combing and cleaning it and making it into mattresses. Two dozen of them are at work in the shade of some great trees. It is a little outdoor factory with a foreman walking about looking important and smoking his pipe, boys running, the combers sitting at their machines and all busy and oblivious to the life of the river and the street above.

In the river boats and barges go up and down. On each barge lives a little family and the children play up and down on the flat decks, dogs bark, the bargemans wife is preparing dinner.

There are within sight a dozen painters, men and women with their easels and stools busily painting. In the distance up the river is Notre Dame, the bridges are black with people and vehicles, here there is something quiet, pastoral. What a contrast to the dark black shores of the rivers that flow thro our American cities.

The most lovely thing happened. My hotel is in a narrow street in the midst of the old city of Paris. Last night I awoke as a clock somewhere in the neighborhood was striking three. The whole city was silent. Suddenly from far off a nightingale began singing madly. It flew into our street and for a long time sat perched on some building near at hand. The clear lovely notes rang thro the narrow street. I heard window shutters opening. Others in the street were awake—listening. The lovely bird had united all of us. For ten minutes all in the street listened carried out of our self by the sweet song of the bird. Then it flew away, its song growing fainter and fainter as it floated away over the roofs of the city.

Dined with P on the sidewalk facing the river on the Quai d'Orsay. Working men went past along the sidewalk. He made two comments that have remained in my mind. First he spoke of the French talant for work. Except the niggers on rivers in Alabama, who sing as they work and who do an astonishing amount of hard labor without apparent effort, I have never seen any other people who take work for granted, as a part of the business of life as do the French. Here in Paris and in spite of the terrific suffering of the war one never sees the tired discouraged faces so caracteristic of American cities.

P also spoke of a sense of ownership of France in the French. It is true. It is like an immense stock company with big and little owners. Everyone is settled down here. Men stay in the place to which fate has assigned them. A certain freedom of action and of living is achieved. We at home have all been fed upon the notion that it is our individual duty to rise in the world. No doubt this philosophy has worked out with a certain splendor for a few individuals but on the other hand it may have much to do with our national weariness.

Take the case of writing in America. Why should the writer accept the standard of living of the business man. He does not deal in monies. Why should he expect to live by the standard set up by the dealers in monies and goods. On 1200 a year an American writer may live. To live and have leisure and freedom to work should be for him sufficient.

One gets, as P's remark suggests a sense of other standards here. It is perhaps because every Frenchman feels himself as in some way having a share in France. The country goes on. In the past beautiful things have been done. Even though a man is a waiter in a cafe under the shadow of the cathedral of Notre Dame he feels himself in some obscure way a part of the cathedral. Frenchmen built it. He is himself a Frenchman. He is a stockholder in the great company, that is France.

Everyone told me that because of the war, because of America's refusal to join in the peace, because of the action of some of the American soldiers here, for a hundred reasons I was to find the Frenchman resentful, ugly toward Americans.

It is not true. I have gone alone and with little French into all parts of Paris and into the country. Every where I have met with nothing but courtesy.

The philosophy of America, that every citizen may hope to rise to the highest estate has had a dreadful effect upon those who do not rise. There is a kind of deep resentment. The waiter in a restaurant where you try to buy as much food as possible for your money looks upon you with contempt. Here it is not so. Your desire to economize is understood by the men here who have made economizing a science. The waiter not being ashamed of his place in life is not contemptious of you because you are not rich.

In Paris there are as many bookstores as there were saloons in Chicago before prohibition. Imagine the 1st ward in Chicago with every saloon of the old days turned into a bookstore. The latin quarter here is like that.

Walked with P in the garden of the Palais Royal. We talked of America, both agreeing that while American cities were all comparatively ugly nothing could tempt us to come away to live permanently in a European city. We agreed that it was in some way a man's part to play the hand fate had delt him in life.

I wondered if—were a man born over here—his note in life would be essentially different. P thought not. "There is something men are striving for now that is bigger than nationalities" he said. "The effort to go down into the hidden parts of ourselves and find out about people down there hasn't much to do with nationalities."

Many French poets produce little poetry. They are forever sitting in cafes and develope marvelously the gift of conversation. Into the practice of that gift they pour themselves.

June 4

In the early morning went to walk in the narrow streets back of the Academy. Here are many little shops showing the work of younger painters for sale. A war had broken out between two unknown and obscure schools of painting. Four young men from one of the schools had come to attack certain advocates of an oposing school. The battle was fought out on one of the narrow streets. There young men had fortified themselves in a room on the second floor occupied by one of their members. They had as weapons to hurl at their opponents in the street eggs, oranges, pieces of furniture and dishes. The party in the street were supplied with similar munitients. The war raged furiously. Wild cries arose. One of the party in the street got hit fair on the breast with an egg. People from all the neighboring houses and from shops ran into the street and joined in the outcry. The battle lasted until practically all the furniture and dishes had been thrown out of the room above and the broken fragments had been fired back. Two windows were broken.

The battle ended in a handsome way. Two women came along the narrow street pushing a push cart. As there was nothing more to be thrown the man with the egg on his bosom ran into the street and threw up his hands. "Peace in the name of French womanhood" he shouted and the bystanders cheered.

Everywhere in France the spirit of Napoleon is alive. One feels so the man and his power on every street. In the bookstore windows everywhere ar prints, Napoleon making a victorious pease, Napoleon winning battles, signing papers, flourishing swords, riding fiery horses.

On the boat going to France I saw an American who once had a great name. In the smoking room I sat near him and listened to his conversation.

A devilish thought came. "Suppose after all Napoleon like that—made by advertising" I thought. I said something of the sort to a Frenchman. It was not a fortunate remark.

June 6

On a bridge over the Seine—a young working man with his sweetheart, a tall strong young daughter of France. They stood with arms about each other looking up the river. Occasionally they kissed oblivious to the thousands of people passing, seemingly equally oblivious of them. Very pretty. One sees lovers everywhere going straight on being lovers without self consciousness.

June 10

The splendid horses of Paris pulling the great wheeled carts. Great hogsheads of wine, grain piled high in brown sacks. The wheels of some of the carts are as high as the door of a church. Often the great horses are hitched tandem—three, four—six, ten. The horses are not castrated. There is fire and life in them. The drivers walk in the streets swinging their long whips which they crack like rifle shots.

O, the great horses. O the shrewd lunging sharp tongued drivers.

These are my people. There is the sharp acid smell of sweat. These men love the great breasted stallions as do I. They are not afraid. They do not castrate. Here is life more noble than anything machinery has yet achieved.

To stand on the Pont Arcole at night, when there is a new moon. In Paris in summer the darkness comes late falling softly. Along the wharfs boys are playing. Three tall boys are teaching a youngster to fight with his fists. They run laughing up and throwing down their arm dodge his blows. Their heads rock back and forth skillfully. Three girls from a house on the rue d'Arcole have come to stand beside me. They are young working girls in cheap dresses and join in the fun going on below. The boys are not unconcious of their presence. The little fellow strikes out more furiously. In the uncertain light the heads of the older boys, dodging the blows are like the heads of serpents. Suddenly a blow goes home with a sharp thud to the face. The little fellow dances with joy. The girls cry out with joy.

To the left but a short block away Notre Dame. The great bulk of it seems to lift itself up into the sky. It is a great floating body of lace woven of stone.

In front, to the left also the spire of Sainte Chapelle. In this soft glowing light the crown of thorns motif is accentuated. It is a growing thing, reaching up and up. It is almost dark now but in the fleecy clouds to the west the red still shows. Blood of Christ. The crown of thorns pressed down. The blood spurting. The spire is so lovely now, in this light the throat hurts.

Here is life all about. Little prostitutes decked out in cheap feathers hurry away out of streets behind you on the right bank. Men with their wives, fat wives come to lean on the railings and on the stone coping above the river. There is a drunken man whose wife is scolding. He laughs loudly.

Two prostitutes come close. There is a man with them, a striking young dandy. He is the pimp of the short fat prostitute. She is trying to tease him, playing clumsily. Perhaps the breath taking beauty of the place and the hour has awakened something. She pinces his arm and it hurt and whirling suddenly he kicks her on the buttocks, soundly.

She squeals with the pain of it but continues the play. Putting her two hands on the cheeks of her buttocks, she runs along the bridge squealing.

The other woman—she is tall and slender and wears her hat down over one ear and has no lover and is concious of me. She also puts her hands to her nether cheeks and squeals, looking back over her shoulder and laughing.

A night of love and love making. You go into the little park back of Notre Dame, you stand on many bridges, you go to see how that, when the moonlight falls on it, the Louvre looks a white frozen things. Everywhere lovers. Lips are being pressed to lips. Womens bodies are being pressed closely against the bodies of men. The lovers are in all the little dark places, on the bridges, on the stairway leading down to the dark river. A young girls body is held tightly against the trunk of a tree in the shadows of Notre Dame. A bearded man is holding it there. He presses his great body against it. The lovers are all silent.

When the workmen were building the great church to Our Lady of Paris nights came. Old fervors died and new fervors were born. The new fervor ran down into the fingers of workmen. It expressed itself in the gargoyles grinning down now at the lovers under the trees.

Notre Dame is too huge. The fervor could not run on. Only in Sainte Chapelle is the impulse quite pure and alone.

Two American college proffessor on the Q' d'Orsay. One is tall the other short. The short one has bad eyes and knocks against people and things. He presses close against his tall friend. They are talking of the effect of the coming of phiscoanalasys on art in America.

American cities have no Louvres, no Saint Chapelles, no Notre Dames, no Cluny but we have there a constant inflow of new people and impulses. Perhaps it would take a long time for a really new impulse to penetrate France.

Although America is inhabited by every race under the sun so that when one meets a fellow American he must always ask, "Of what blood are your people," we are peculiarly intolerant. Paris is the true cosmopolitan city. Here all races may meet and loose the sense of race. Just now the Germans are not looked on with favor but the Chinese, the negro, the Japannees, all these go about freely. One often sees negro dining in restaurants and walking in the streets with their white sweethearts. The sight attracts no attention. In an American city it would cause a riot. Perhaps being sure of its race lines the French can afford to be generous and careless.

One is constantly struck with the nearness of Parisian life to the country. Wagon loads of hay go thro the streets, peasants from the country are driving in in carts, the vegetables and fruits are peculiarly fresh and delicious. The morning dew is still on these berries now for sale from a little wheeled cart under my window.

I am charmed with the cries of the street vendors. Each has got a refrain, a skirl of music into his cry. It is sweet to lie in bed in the morning and hear the bird like voices crying regarding the shapening of knives, shining of shoes, selling of vegetables.

Americans make a great mistake in being timid and in staying about hotels where other Americans live. Here, as everywhere it is the common people who receive you most generously, who are delighted to help you in your difficulties with the language, who take you into their everyday life.

A Frenchman and his wife who have lived in America have been entertaining some wealthy American friends. The American men wanted to see the night life of Paris and have spent huge sums doing it. What they have got is a specially prepared stage set for them. They and their wives who have been in the big shops throwing money about have been cheated gloriously. My friend the Frenchman and his wife are rather pleased at what has happened to these Americans and I sympathise with their feeling.

When I visit the places about which Mark Twain wrote in his innocence Abroad and realize how he often made a laborously wrought joke of men's effort toward beauty in order to please and flatter American readers it is difficult for me to retain the love aroused in me by his writing of Huckelberry Finn.

When beauty comes off it seems to justify always the terrible cost. What would it mean if every American child could see Saint Chapelle, Chartres cathedral, the library in the palace at Fountainbleau. Those thousands of peasants coming up from the field, a kings desire being gratified, a hope of heaven where all men lead equally beautiful lives, stone laid on stone, beggars whining, stone on stone, thousands laboring terrible, stone being carved, the animal side of men coming out, the gargoyles carved, grinning things looking down on misery and on the strutting of kings, the mistresses of kings coming in carriages to look, driving in the morning with sleep heavy eyes after nights in heavy curtained beds, the men working silently perhaps, doggedly, thousands of men, crops being neglected, no sanitation, disease running among them. Stone on stone, years passing, now and then beautiful moments, stone carved beautifully with abandon, terror, and beauty, something to stand up for ages. Stone on stone. There is beauty achieved. Who shall say it is not all sacred, terrible, wonderful.

In a cafe again. There are two young negroes, with books in their hands talking with two white men students in the Boulevard Saint Germain, near the district of the great schools. Near me, at another table a white American woman—fat.

Her daughter, pale, with staring eyes. There is deep anger. "I saw a nigger with a white girl and the white girl's mother, walking openly in the street. My fingers itched to have hold of a gun and shoot—all them." The head of the fat mother nodding up and down. She agrees without thought, from habit.

A man, an artist, an American who has lived in Paris for 20 years. To dine with him. Three times during the evening he said the same thing. "A man is of no importance who hasn't his roots deep in his native soil" There was something tragic in his insistence. "Can't you go back?" I asked. "Not now. I have blown about too long. I'm an empty thing."

There was in his face something shrewd, yankee but his accent was English. All evening I kept remembering certain, dry, shrewd horse owners I knew long ago. He was like a man who has taken horses from track to track, all over the world, but has never won a race.

French writers are badly paid and from all I hear France is very provincial in its attitude toward outside men and outside ideas. The French writer, of the better sort (the artist) expects no profit from writing. Many are clerks or have government jobs. There is in the American attitude something much more generous, fine. Here the arts are honored but the better artists starve. In America there is little knowledge of what good art is but there is an eager generosity toward the artist.

June 13

To an upper class French home—the home of a French banker.—An Englishman with his French wife was present. I got down on the floor and tried to explain the game of baseball, the fame of Ty Cob, Babe Ruth and others. They were all polite and tried to speak English. Little cakes were served and the young Englishman played the violin. It was just such an evening as one might have spent in the home of a well to do banker in Iowa.

It apparently is not true, as I have often heard, that the French disliked the American soldiers. During the war and afterward the people all became sick of the sight of uniformed men. It was really war sickness. From all I have heard the common American soldier left a deep impressing of something rather fine. "They were the only soldiers that came who loved to play with our children" the French said. One hears that story everywhere. "The Americans loved our children."

> "The days were wonderful and
> the nights were wonderful
> and the life was pleasant."

"The spoon was set six. Eight was a biginning It began. Earrings are good to breed. Breed that."

Imagain a strong woman with legs like stone pillars sitting in a room hung thick with Picassos. Formerly there were many Matisse and —— too but except 2 —— these have gone.

The woman is the very symbol of health and streng. She laughs. She smokes cigaretts. She tell stories with an American shrewdness in getting the tang and the kick into the telling.

Gertrude Stein is perhaps 45 and for 10 or perhaps 15 years she has been sitting at a desk in the room writing such sentences as those above. When her first book Three Lives was published (at her own expense and later when Tender Buttons appeared a little flame of interest and amusement flared up in America. Newspaper paragraphers quoted her. It became for a time the thing, in smart literary circles to give readings from her works.

To dine is west. —

A great revolution in the art of words had begun and was being passed over with a laugh.

Gertrude Stein has always been laughed at. Years ago when her work first fell under my eyes and I was startled and profoundly stirred by its significants I made inquiry concerning her. Strange stories came out of Paris. She was a fat woman, very languid lying on a couch, people came into the room and she stared at them with strange cold eyes.

Carl Van Vechten

If the name Carl Van Vechten (1880–1964) means anything now to the American reader, it is probably because of his connection with the Harlem Renaissance and his early, alligatorish, slightly palm-frond appreciations of jazz. But he spent the memorable year of 1908 as the Paris correspondent of *The New York Times*, and his 1922 novel *Peter Whiffle: His Life and Works* is a revelation. An eccentric study of Paris bohemia, it not only gives a last hurrah to the 19th-century bohemian ideal of Paris—the *vie de Bohème, Trilby* world of garrets and eccentric artists—but also, in the person of the "conceptual" artist Whiffle, anticipates the more larksome world of Dada, with its love of mock-catalogues and private inventories. *Peter Whiffle* documents the transformation in the bohemian ideal from the essentially solitary world of the Symbolists and their imitators to the Cubist-inspired world of newspaper headlines and group manifestos, a transformation from the lonely poet to the militant group. The American Paris of the 1920s, hottest American Paris of all, really begins with this backward wave to the old bohemia.

---

from

Peter Whiffle

I was, as a matter of fact, in my twenties when I first went to Paris—my happiness might have been even greater had I been nineteen—and I was alone. The trip across England—I had landed at Liverpool—and the horrid channel, I will not describe, although both made sufficient impression on me, but the French houses at Dieppe awakened my first deep emotion and then, and so many times since, the Normandy cider, quaffed in a little café, conterminous to the railroad, and the journey through France, alive in the sunlight, for it was May, the fields dancing with the green grain spattered with vermilion poppies and cerulean cornflowers, the white roads, flying like ribbons between the stately poplars, leading away over the charming hills past the red-brick villas, completed the siege of my not too easily given heart. There was the stately and romantic interruption of Rouen, which at that period suggested nothing in the world to me but Emma Bovary. Then more fields, more roads, more towns, and at last, towards twilight, Paris.

Railroads have a fancy for entering cities stealthily through backyards and the first glimpses of Paris, achieved from a car-window, were not over-pleasant but the posters on the hoardings, advertising beer and automo-bile tires, particularly that of the Michelin Tire Company, with the picture of the pinguid gentleman, constructed of a series of pneumatic circles, seemed characteristic enough. Chéret was dead but something of his spirit seemed to glow in these intensely coloured affiches and I was young. Even the dank Gare Saint Lazare did not dismay me, and I entered into the novel baggage hunt with something of zest, while other busy passen-gers and the blue porters rushed hither and thither in a complicated but well-ordered maze. Naturally, however, I was the last to leave the station; as the light outside deepened to a rich warm blue, I wandered into the street, my porter bearing my trunk, to find there a solitary cocher mounted on the box of his carious fiacre.

An artist friend, Albert Worcester, had already determined my desti-nation and so I gave commands, Hôtel de la Place de l'Odéon, the cocher cracked his whip, probably adding a Hue cocotte! and we were under way. The drive through the streets that evening seemed like a dream and, even later, when the streets of Paris had become more familiar to me than those of any other city, I could occasionally recapture the mood of this first vision. For Paris in the May twilight is very soft and exquisite, the grey buildings swathed in a bland blue light and the air redolent with a strange fragrance, the ingredients of which have never been satisfactorily identi-fied in my nasal imagination, although Huysmans, Zola, Symons, and Cunninghame Graham have all attempted to separate and describe them. Presently we crossed the boulevards and I saw for the first time the rows of blooming chestnut trees, the kiosques where newsdealers dispensed their wares, the brilliantly lighted theatres, the sidewalk cafés, sprinkled with human figures, typical enough, doubtless, but who all seemed as unreal to me at the time as if they had been Brobdingnags, Centaurs, Griffins, or Mermaids. Other fiacres, private carriages, taxi-autos, carrying French men and French ladies, passed us. I saw Bel Ami, Nana, Liane de Pougy, or Otero in every one of them. As we drove by the Opéra, I am certain that Cléo de Mérode and Leopold of Belgium descended the steps. Even the buses assumed the appearance of gorgeous chariots, bear-ing perfumed Watteauesque ladies on their journey to Cythera. As we drove through the Tuileries Gardens, the mood snapped for an instant as I viewed the statue of Gambetta, which, I thought at the time, and have always thought since, was amazingly like the portrait of a gentleman hailing a cab. What could more completely symbolize Paris than the statue of a gentleman perpetually hailing a cab and never getting one?

We drove on through the Louvre and now the Seine was under us, lying black in the twilight, reviving dark memories of crime and murder, on across the Pont du Carrousel, and up the narrow Rue de Seine. The Quartier Latin! I must have cried aloud, for the cocher looked a trifle suspicious, his head turned the fraction of an inch. Later, of course, I said, the left bank, as casually as any one. It was almost dark when we drove into the open Place, flanked by the Odéon, a great Roman temple, with my little hotel tucked into one corner, as unostentatiously as possible, being exactly similar to every other structure, save the central one, in the Place. I shall stop tonight, I said to myself, in the hotel where Little Billee lived, for, when one first goes to Paris when one is young, Paris is either the Paris of Murger, du Maurier, or the George Moore of the Confessions, perhaps the Paris of all three. In my bag these three books lay, and I had already begun to live one of them.

The patron and a servant in a long white apron were waiting, standing in the doorway. The servant hoisted my trunk to his shoulder and bore it away. I paid the cocher's reckoning, not without difficulty for, although I was not ignorant of the language, I was unaccustomed to the simplicity of French coinage. There were also the mysteries of the pourboire to compute—ten per cent, I had been told; who has not been told this?—and besides, as always happens when one is travelling, I had no little money. But at length the negotiations were terminated, not to the displeasure of the cocher, I feel certain, since he condescended to smile pleasantly. Then, with a crack of his whip, this enormous fellow with his black moustaches, his glazed top-hat, and his long coat, drove away. I cast a long lingering look after him, apparently quite unaware that many another such teratological specimen existed on every hand. Now I followed the patron into a dark hallway and new strata of delight. He gave me a lighted candle and, behind him, I mounted the winding stairway to the first floor, where I was deposited in a chamber with dark red walls, heavy dark red curtains at the windows, which looked out over the Place, a black walnut wash-hand-stand with pitcher and basin, a huge black walnut wardrobe, two or three chairs of the same wood, upholstered with faded brocade, and a most luxurious bed, so high from the floor that one had to climb into it, hung with curtains like those at the window, and surmounted by a feather-bed. There was also another article of furniture, indispensable to any French bedroom.

I gave Joseph (all men servants in small hotels in Paris are named Joseph, perhaps to warn off prospective Potiphar's wives) his vail, asked for hot water, which he bore up promptly in a small can, washed myself, did a little unpacking, humming the Mattchiche the while, changed my shirt, my collar and my necktie, demanded another bougie, lighted it, and under the humble illumination afforded by it and its companion, I began to read again The Confessions of a Young Man. It was not very long before I was interrupted in the midst of an absorbing passage descriptive of the circle at the Nouvelle Athènes by the arrival of Albert Worcester, who had arranged for my reception, and right here I may say that I was lodged in the Hôtel de la Place de l'Odéon for fifty francs a month. Albert's arrival, although unannounced, was not unexpected, as he had promised to take me to dinner.

I was sufficiently emphatic. Paris! I cried. Paris! Good God!

I see you are not disappointed. But Albert permitted a trace of cynicism to flavour his smile.

It's too perfect, too wonderful. It is more than I felt or imagined. I'm moving in.

But you haven't seen it. . . .

I've seen enough. I don't mean that. I mean I've seen enough to know. But I want to see it all, everything, Saint Sulpice, the Folies-Bergère, the Musée de Cluny, the Nouvelle Athènes, the Comédie Française, the Bal Bullier, the Arc de Triomphe, the Luxembourg Gardens. . . .

They close at sundown. My expression was the cue for him to continue, They'll be open tomorrow and any other day. They're just around the corner. You can go there when you get up in the morning, if you do get up in the morning. But what do you want to do tonight?

Anything! Everything! I cried.

Well, we'll eat first.

So we blew out the candles, floated down the dark stairs—I didn't really walk for a week, I am sure—, brushing on our way against a bearded student and a girl, fragrant and warm in the semi-blackness, out into the delicious night, with the fascinating indescribable odour of Paris, which ran the gamut from the fragrance of lilac and mimosa to the aroma of horse-dung; with the sound of horses' hoofs and rolling wheels beating and revolving on the cobble-stones, we made our way—I swear my feet never touched the ground—through the narrow, crooked, constantly turning, bewildering streets, until we came out on a broad boulevard before the Café d'Harcourt, where I was to eat my first Paris dinner.

The Café d'Harcourt is situated near the Church of the Sorbonne on the Boulevard Saint Michel, which you are more accustomed to see spelled Boul' Mich'. It is a big, brightly lighted café, with a broad terrasse, partially enclosed by a hedge of green bushes in boxes. The hands of the clock pointed to the hour of eight when we arrived and the tables all appeared to be occupied. Inside, groups of men were engaged in games of checkers, while the orchestra was performing selections from Louis Ganne's operetta, Les Saltimbanques. On the terrasse, each little table, covered with its white cloth, was lighted by a tiny lamp with a roseate shade, over which faces glowed. The bottles and dishes and silver all contributed their share to the warmth of the scene, and heaping bowls of peaches and pears and apples and little wood strawberries, ornamenting the sideboards, gave the place an almost sumptuous appearance. Later I learned that fruit was expensive in Paris and not to be tasted lightly. Victor Maurel has told me how, dining one night with the composer of The Barber, he was about to help himself to a peach from a silver platter in the centre of the table when the frugal Madame Rossini expostulated, Those are to look at, not to eat!

While we lingered on the outer sidewalk, a little comedy was enacted, through the dénouement of which we secured places. A youth, with wine in his head and love in his eyes, caressed the warm lips of an adorable girl. Save for the glasses of apéritifs from which they had been drinking, their table was bare. They had not yet dined. He clasped her tightly in his arms and kissed her, kissed her for what seemed to be a very long time but no one, except me, appeared to take any notice.

Look! I whispered to Albert. Look!

Oh, that's all right. You'll get used to that, he replied negligently.

Now the kiss was over and the two began to talk, very excitedly and rapidly, as French people are wont to talk. Then, impulsively, they rose from their chairs. The man threw a coin down on his napkin. I caught the glint of gold. He gathered his arms about the woman, a lovely pale blue creature, with torrid orange hair and a hat abloom with striated petunias. They were in the middle of the street when the waiter appeared, bearing a tray, laden with plates of sliced cucumbers, radishes and butter, tiny crayfish, and a bottle of white wine. He stared in mute astonishment at the empty table, and then picked up the coin. Finally, he glanced towards the street and, observing the retreating pair, called after them:

Mais vous n'avez pas diné!

The man turned and shot his reply over his shoulder, Nous rentrons!

The crowd on the terrasse shrieked with delight. They applauded. Some even tossed flowers from the tables after the happy couple and we . . . we sat down in the chairs they had relinquished. I am not certain that we did not eat the dinner they had ordered. At any rate we began with the cucumbers and radishes and écrevisses and a bottle of Graves Supérior.

That night in Paris I saw no Americans, at least no one seemed to be an American, and I heard no English spoken. How this came about I have no idea because it never occurred again. In fact, one meets more Americans in Paris than one does in New York and most of the French that I manage to speak I have picked up on the Island of Manhattan. During dinner I began to suspect a man without a beard, in a far corner, but Albert reassured me.

He is surely French, he said, because he is buttering his radishes.

It would be difficult to exaggerate my emotion: the white wine, the bearded French students, the exquisite women, all young and smiling and gay, all organdie and lace and sweet-peas, went to my head. I have spent many happy evenings in the Café d'Harcourt since that night. I have been there with Olive Fremstad when she told me how, dressed as a serpent in bespangled Nile green, she had sung the finale of Salome to Edward VII in London, and one memorable Mardi-Gras night with Jane Noria when, in a long raincoat which covered me from head to foot, standing on our table from time to time, I shouted, C'est l'heure fatale! and made as if to throw the raincoat aside but Noria, as if dreading the exposure, always dragged me down from the table, crying, No! No! until the carnival crowd, consumed with curiosity, pulled me into a corner, tore the raincoat away, and everything else too! There was another night, before the Bal des Quat'z Arts, when the café was filled with students and models in costume, and costume for the Quat'z Arts in those days, whatever it may be now, did not require the cutting out of many handkerchiefs. But the first night was the best and every other night a more or less pale reflection of that, always, indeed, coloured a little by the memory of it. So that today, when sometimes I am asked what café I prefer in Paris and I reply, the d'Harcourt, there are those who look at me a little pityingly and some even go so far as to ejaculate, Oh, that! but I know why it is my favourite.

Even a leisurely dinner ends at last, and I knew, as we sipped our coffee and green chartreuse and smoked our cigarettes, that this one must be over. After paying our very moderate addition, we strolled slowly away, to hop into an empty fiacre which stood on the corner a block down the boulevard. I lay back against the seat and gazed at the stars for a moment as the drive began through the warm, fragrant Paris air, the drive back to the right bank, this time across the Pont Neuf, down the Rue de Rivoli, through the Place de la Concorde, where the fountains were playing, and up the Champs-Elysées. The aroma of the chestnuts, the melting grey of the buildings, the legions of carriages and buses, filled with happy, chattering people, the glitter of electricity, all the mystic wonder of this enchanting night will always stay with me.

We drove to the Théâtre Marigny where we saw a revue; at least we were present at a revue; I do not remember to have seen or heard anything on the stage. Between the acts, we walked in the open foyer, at this theatre a sort of garden, and admired the cocottes, great ladies of some distant epoch, they seemed to me, in their toilets from Redfern and Doucet and Chéruit and Callot Sœurs, their hats from the Rue de la Paix and the Place Vendôme, their exceedingly elaborate and decoratively artificial complexions. Later, we sipped cassis on the balcony. It was Spring in Paris and I was young! The chestnut trees were heavy with white blossoms and the air was laden with their perfume. I gazed down the Champs-Elysées, surely the true Elysian Fields, a myriad of lights shining through the dark green, the black, leaved branches. I do not think I spoke many words and I know that Albert did not. He may have been bored, but I think he derived some slight pleasure from my juvenile enthusiasm for, although Paris was old hat to him, he loved this particular old hat.

We must have stopped somewhere for more drinks on the way home, perhaps at Weber's in the Rue Royale, where there was a gipsy band. I do not remember, but I am sure that it was nearly four in the morning when we drove up before the little hotel in the Place de l'Odéon and when, after we had paid the driver and dismissed him, I discovered to my astonishment that the door was locked. Albert assured me that this was the custom and that I must ring for the concierge. So I pulled the knob, and even outside we could hear the distant reverberations of the bell, but no reply came, and the door remained closed. It was Joseph's job to open the door and Joseph was asleep and refused to awaken. Again and again we pulled the cord, the bell tinkling in the vast silence, for the street was utterly deserted, but still no one came. At last we desisted, Albert suggesting that I go home with him. We walked a few paces until we came to the iron fence surrounding the Luxembourg Gardens and there, lying beside it, I espied a ladder, left by some negligent workman.

But my room is on the first floor. The window is open; it looks over the Place. I can enter with the ladder, I cried.

Albert, amused, helped me carry it back. Set up, it just reached the window and I swiftly scaled it and clambered into the room, waving my hand back to Albert, who hoisted the ladder to his shoulder as he started up the street trying to whistle, Viens Poupoule! but laughing to himself all the time, so that the tune cracked. As for me, I lighted one of my candles, undressed, threw the feather-bed off to the floor, and climbed into bed. Then I blew out the candle and soon fell asleep. It was the tenth of May, 1907, that I spent my first night in Paris.

Malcolm Cowley

One of America's first and most consistently serious modernist literary critics, Cowley (1898–1989) was in France initially as part of the wave of American soldiers and ambulance drivers in the Great War. He returned to Paris in 1921, working on the avant-garde literary magazines *Broom* and *Secession*, and getting to know Hemingway, Pound, and Stein (the Tinker, Evers, and Chance of the American experience in Paris). But his experience of Paris was not simply mediated by his experience of modernist literature; it seems, on the evidence of these pages from his great *Exile's Return* (first published in 1933 and then revised and re-published in 1951), in some degree to have consisted of his reading. Like his great (and sporadically Francophile) contemporary Edmund Wilson, Cowley saw in French modernism something more searching and, in a complicated way, more "political" than any American writer had sensed in France before. Put in plain English: Cowley is perhaps the first important American writer who, in writing about Paris, does not tell us, and does not seem to care, if he had a good time.

Significant Gesture

During the last three weeks before sailing for America, I wrote no letters. I was much too excited to write letters; I had never, in fact, spent prouder, busier or more amusing days. I was being arrested and tried for punching a café proprietor in the jaw.

He deserved to be punched, though not especially by me; I had no personal grudge against him. His café, the Rotonde, had long been patronized by revolutionists of every nation. Lenin used to sit there, I was told; and proletarian revolts were still being planned, over coffee in the evening, by quiet men who paid no attention to the hilarious arguments of Swedish and Rumanian artists at the surrounding tables. The proprietor—whose name I forget—used to listen unobtrusively. It was believed, on more or less convincing evidence, that he was a paid informer. It was said that he had betrayed several anarchists to the French police. Moreover, it was known that he had insulted American girls, treating them with the cold brutality that French café proprietors reserve for prostitutes. He was a thoroughly disagreeable character and should, we felt, be called to account.

We were at the Dôme, ten or twelve of us packed together at a table in the midst of the crowd that swirled in the Boulevard Montparnasse. It was July 14, 1923, the national holiday. Chinese lanterns hung in rows among the trees; bands played at every corner; everywhere people were dancing in the streets. Paris, deserted for the summer by its aristocrats, bankers and politicians, forgetting its hordes of tourists, was given over to a vast plebeian carnival, a general madness in which we had eagerly joined. Now, tired of dancing, we sipped our drinks and talked in loud voices to make ourselves heard above the music, the rattle of saucers, the shuffle of feet along the sidewalk. I was trying, with my two hands on the table, to imitate the ridiculous efforts of Tristan Tzara to hop a moving train. "Let's go over," said Laurence Vail, tossing back his long yellow hair from his forehead, "and assault the proprietor of the Rotonde."

"Let's," I said.

We crossed the street together, some of the girls in bright evening gowns and some in tweeds, Louis Aragon slim and dignified in a dinner jacket, Laurence bareheaded and wearing a raincoat which he never removed in the course of the hot starlit night, myself coatless, dressed in a workman's blue shirt, worn trousers and rope-soled shoes. Delayed and separated by the crowd on the pavement, we made our way singly into the bar, which I was the last to enter. Aragon, in periodic sentences pronounced in a beautifully modulated voice, was expressing his opinion of all stool pigeons—*mouchards*—and was asking why such a wholly contemptible character as the proprietor of the Rotonde presumed to solicit the patronage of respectable people. The waiters, smelling a fight, were forming a wall of shirt fronts around their employer. Laurence Vail pushed through the wall; he made an angry speech in such rapid French that I could catch only a few phrases, all of them insults. The proprietor backed away; his eyes shifted uneasily; his face was a dirty white behind his black mustache. Harold Loeb, looking on, was a pair of spectacles, a chin, a jutting pipe and an embarrassed smile.

I was angry at my friends, who were allowing the situation to resolve into a series of useless gestures; but even more I was seized with a physical revulsion for the proprietor, with his look of a dog caught stealing chickens and trying to sneak off. Pushing past the waiters, I struck him a glancing blow in the jaw. Then, before I could strike again, I was caught up in an excited crowd and forced to the door.

Five minutes later our band had once more assembled on the terrace of the Dôme. I had forgotten the affair already: nothing remained but a vague exhilaration and the desire for further activity. I was obsessed with the idea that we should *changer de quartier*: that instead of spending the rest of the night in Montparnasse, we should visit other sections of Paris. Though no one else seemed enthusiastic, I managed by force of argument to assemble five hesitant couples, and the ten of us went strolling southeastward along the Boulevard Montparnasse.

On reaching the first café we stopped for a drink of beer and a waltz under the chestnut trees. One couple decided to return to the Dôme. Eight of us walked on to another café, where, after a bock, two other couples became deserters. "Let's change our quarter," I said once more. At the next café, Bob Coates consulted his companion. "We're going back to the Dôme," he said. Two of us walked on sadly. We caught sight of Montrouge—more Chinese lanterns and wailing accordions and workmen dancing with shopgirls in the streets—then we too returned to Montparnasse.

It was long after midnight, but the streets were as crowded as before and I was eager for adventure. At the Dôme I met Tristan Tzara, seized him by the arm and insisted that we go for a stroll. We argued the question whether the Dada movement could be revived. Under the chestnut trees we met a high-brown woman dressed in barbaric clothes; she was thought to be a princess from Senegal. I addressed her extravagant compliments in English and French; Tzara added others in French, German and his three words of Rumanian. "Go 'way, white boys," she said in a Harlem voice. We turned back, passing the crowded terrace of the Rotonde. The proprietor was standing there with his arms folded. At the sight of him a fresh rage surged over me.

"*Quel salaud!*" I roared for the benefit of his six hundred customers. "*Ah, quel petit mouchard!*"

Then we crossed the street once more toward the Dôme, slowly. But when I reached the middle of the tracks I felt each of my arms seized by a little blue policeman. "Come along with us," they said. And they marched me toward the station house, while Tzara rushed off to get the identification papers left behind in my coat. The crowds disappeared behind us; we were alone—I and the two *flics* and the proprietor of the Rotonde.

One of the two policemen was determined to amuse himself. "You're lucky," he said, "to be arrested in Paris. If you were arrested by those brutal policemen of New York, they would cuff you on the ear—like this," he snarled, cuffing me on the ear, "but in Paris we pat you gently on the shoulder."

I knew I was in trouble. I said nothing and walked peacefully beside him.

"Ah, the police of Paris are incomparably gentle. If you were arrested in New York, they would crack you in the jaw—like this," he said, cracking me in the jaw, "but here we do nothing; we take you with us calmly."

He rubbed his hands, then thrust his face toward mine. His breath stank of brandy.

"You like the police of Paris, *hein*?"

"Assuredly," I answered. The proprietor of the Rotonde walked on beside us, letting his red tongue play over the ends of his mustache. The other *flic* said nothing.

"I won't punch you in the nose like the New York policemen," said the drunken man, punching me in the nose. "I will merely ask you to walk on in front of me. . . . Walk in front of me, pig!"

I walked in front of him, looking back suspiciously under my armpit. His hand was on his holster, loosening the flap. I had read about people shot "while trying to escape" and began walking so very slowly that he had to kick me in the heels to urge me up the steps of the police station. When we stood at the desk before the sergeant, he charged me with an unprovoked assault on the proprietor of the Rotonde—and also with forcibly resisting an officer. "Why," he said, "he kicked me in the shins, leaving a scar. Look here!"

He rolled up his trouser leg, showing a scratch half an inch long. It was useless for me to object that my rope-soled shoes wouldn't have scratched a baby. Police courts in France, like police courts everywhere, operate on the theory that a policeman's word is always to be taken against that of an accused criminal.

Things looked black for me until my friends arrived—Laurence and Louis and Jacques Rigaut and my wife—bearing with them my identification papers and a supply of money. Consulting together, we agreed that the drunken policeman must be bribed, and bribed he was: in the general confusion he was bribed twice over. He received in all a hundred and thirty francs, at least four times as much as was necessary. Standing pigeon-toed before the sergeant at the desk and wearing an air of bashful benevolence, he announced that I was a pretty good fellow after all, even though I had kicked him in the shins. He wished to withdraw the charge of resisting an officer.

My prospects brightened perceptibly. Everyone agreed that the false charge was the more serious of the two. For merely punching a stool-pigeon, the heaviest sentence I could receive would be a month in jail. Perhaps I would escape with a week.

A preliminary hearing was held on the following evening, after a night in jail and a day spent vainly trying to sleep between visits from the police and telephone calls from anxious friends. I stopped at the Dôme to collect my witnesses; fortunately there was a party that evening and they were easy to find. They consisted of nine young ladies in evening gowns. None of them had been present at the scene in the Rotonde the night before, but that didn't matter: all of them testified in halting French that I hadn't been present either; the whole affair was an imposition on a writer known for his serious character; it was a hoax invented by a café proprietor who was a pig and very impolite to American young women.

The examining magistrate was impressed. He confided later to André Salmon that the proprietor of the Rotonde had only his waiters to support the story he told, whereas I had nine witnesses, all of them very respectable people, *des gens très bien*. That helped Salmon to get me out of the scrape, although he also brought his own influence to bear. He was a poet and novelist who was also a star reporter and covered all the important murder trials for *Le Matin*. Since magistrates liked to be on good terms with him, he managed to have my trial postponed from day to day and finally abandoned.

But the most amusing feature of the affair, and my justification for dealing with it at length, was the effect it produced on my French acquaintances. They looked at me with an admiration I could not understand, even when I reflected that French writers rarely came to blow and that they placed a high value on my unusual action. Years later I realized that by punching a café proprietor in the jaw I had performed an act to which all their favorite catchwords could be applied. First of all, I had acted for reasons of public morality; bearing no private grudge against my victim, I had been *disinterested*. I had committed an *indiscretion*, acted with *violence* and *disdain* for the law, performed an *arbitrary* and *significant gesture*, uttered a *manifesto*; in their opinion I had shown *courage*. . . . For the first time in my life I became a public character. I was entertained at dinners and cocktail parties, interviewed for the newspapers, asked to contribute to reviews published by the Dadaists in Amsterdam, Brussels, Lyon and Belgrade. My stories were translated into Hungarian and German. A party of Russian writers then visiting Paris returned to Moscow with several of my poems, to be printed in their own magazines.

The poems were not at all revolutionary in tone, but they dealt with a subject that, in those briefly liberal days of the New Economic Policy in Russia, had been arousing the enthusiasm of Soviet writers. They were poems about America, poems that spoke of movies and skyscrapers and machines, dwelling upon them with all the nostalgia derived from two long years of exile. I, too, was enthusiastic over America; I had learned from a distance to admire its picturesque qualities. And I was returning to New York with a set of values that bore no relation to American life, with convictions that could not fail to be misunderstood in a country where Dada was hardly a name, and moral judgments on literary matters were thought to be in questionable taste—in a city where writers had only three justifications for their acts: they did them to make money, or to get their name in the papers, or because they were drunk.

Matthew Josephson

Josephson (1899–1978) was one of the rare Americans to be entirely absorbed by a French milieu and live to tell the tale. *Life Among the Surrealists*, his sadly overlooked 1962 memoir of events almost a half century before, is one of the really golden studies of the intersection of French style and American energy in the 1920s. Josephson went to Paris, as he explains, intending to study the Symbolists and Realists—only to discover that they were, in the advanced French circles, quite *de trop*. Instead, the real energy in French artistic life lay with the near-nihilists of Dada, and by befriending them Josephson gained a front-row seat as Dadaist anarchy was transformed into the more artistically potent Surrealism. He became associate editor of the larksome *Broom*, and in a decade-long dance of ironies that Josephson had the luck to experience and the insight to understand, perhaps the greatest was that, while the Americans in Paris were drawn to French "civilization," the French avant-garde was drawn to American energy, advertising, and modernity. Josephson, with still one more irony, almost too rich to be credited, went back home at the height of the boom, became a stockbroker, made a fortune, and went back to France—only to find that he had been excommunicated by André Breton for insufficient surrealism. Josephson went on to write fine biographies of Zola and Rousseau, among other French writers, mostly of the 19th century, and to maintain his friendships with the Surrealists generally; he played host to Louis Aragon during World War II.

---

from

Life Among the Surrealists

At the time when Breton met with some of his younger disciples at my home he had talked, among other things, of a new project that was very dear to his heart; the organization of a sort of "congress" of intellectuals and artists to be held in Paris in the summer of 1922 with the object of inquiring into the principles of "modernism" in the arts. Part of its purpose would be "to determine the directives for the defense of the modern spirit." Eminent representatives of the avant-garde from all over

Europe would be invited to attend the Congress. André himself would preside over their assembly, whose proceedings would be released to the world's press and radio (something new). Roger Vitrac, then associated with Marcel Arland as an editor of the new literary review, *Aventure*, which had a very promising group of youthful contributors, at first gave his enthusiastic support to Breton's plan.

However, the most heated disputes soon burst forth among the Dadaists over this new and rather public-spirited enterprise. Breton had written Tzara, formally inviting him to serve as a member of the organizing committee, although these two principals were already rivals and intensely suspicious of each other's motives. Tzara wanted to keep Dada "pure"; that is, purely destructive in its action, always ready for a big joke, and keeping its powder dry for new surprise attacks. He did not want Dadaism associated with other schools and isms, such as Cubism and Futurism, and opposed holding a convention together with their spokesmen. "Dada is not modern," he used to say mystifyingly. He also made the grave accusation against Breton that he was "serious"; and in private, made mock of his schemes. For the record, however, Tzara wrote Breton a formal letter of declination.

> . . . I regret to say that the reservations I have felt about the very idea of the Congress would not be changed by my participating in it. I wish you, my friend, to believe that this is not an action of a personal nature directed against you or any others on the Committee, and I appreciate your desire to give representation to every tendency as I do the courtesy you have shown me.

As if to ward off further criticisms of his cherished project by the sharp-tongued Tzara, Breton quickly issued a press communiqué to one of the Paris newspapers (*Comoedia*, a widely read theatrical journal) published February 3, 1922, in which he warned the public against the machinations of a "certain personage who hailed from Zurich" and who was but "an impostor avid of publicity."

Breton's intemperate attack on Tzara was motivated in part by his domineering spirit and partly by his will to give a new and more positive direction to his following, in contrast with the negative spirit consistently manifested by Tzara. Dadaism and Tzara both must be destroyed. Dadaism had become futile, had been limiting itself to playing with velleities, and negated too many positive ideas and principles that Breton wished to fight for. He was en route toward a new faith that would be derived from the romantic traditions and the "proto-Surrealist" literature of France. For him, this episode marked the beginning of a life-long career of repeated "excommunications" of former friends and comrades.

Nevertheless, his sudden, venomous attack on the brilliant personality whom he had so eagerly invited to Paris two years before as "the new Rimbaud," and whom, a few days earlier, he had asked to join with him in the steering committee for his Congress, shocked the very persons whose support Breton solicited. The terms he had used in assailing Tzara (a Romanian Jew) as a *foreigner*, also suggested the xenophobe and the anti-Dreyfusard. Breton himself afterward admitted that he had been "inept."

The organizing committee for the Congress included the artists Fernand Léger, Robert Delaunay, and Amédée Ozenfant; also the composers Erik Satie and Georges Auric; and the poets Jean Paulhan and Roger Vitrac. In an open letter to the press a number of these men now accused Breton of having issued his public statement assailing Tzara without their authorization, and of having done this in the spirit of a "narrow nationalist" and "reactionary." They also announced a meeting to be held at the Closerie des Lilas, February 17, 1922, where the question of the proposed Congress would be fully investigated. Breton was invited to appear at this meeting, and in effect to stand trial. He came, of course.

More than a hundred people were on hand when I entered the upstairs banquet room of the old café. Virtually all of artistic and literary Paris was excited over the "trial" of Breton—though such periodic cataclysms were a familiar part of its life. I remember seeing the chunky, bright-eyed Pablo Picasso, together with Henri Matisse and the sculptor Constantin Brancusi; also Jean Cocteau and his young friend Raymond Radiguet, the precocious novelist; and a good many of the *Nouvelle Revue Française* clan, as well as members of the press. I had come without any clear notions of what the conflict was all about; after witnessing the most tempestuous verbal brawl I had ever seen or heard, I said to myself: "The Revolution is devouring its sons!"

Never in my experience were words of such passion and flame hurled at each other by men without coming to blows. (If they had been Americans, they would have butchered one another.) Several of Breton's close friends, including Soupault, Éluard, and Ribémont-Dessaignes, expressed disapproval of his action. Aragon, as ever, was at Breton's side, a pale and eloquent advocate. Breton spoke in rolling periods in his own defense; while Tzara, leaping to the attack, fairly screamed in his high voice, talking so fast that I could not follow him. Erik Satie, the comic spirit of modern music, a paunchy man with gold-rimmed pince-nez and a goatee, presided as "judge" and seemed to be laughing over the affair all the time. Philippe Soupault, in one very moving speech, strove in vain to reconcile the opposing parties. In the end—after all sorts of absurd charges had been hurled back and forth—the consensus of the meeting was expressed in a vote of nonconfidence in Breton and his proposed Congress of Paris—which thus, in its preparatory stages, collapsed. It was a humiliating reverse for the redoubtable man.

On the other hand, he had sounded the death knell for Dadaism, the beginning of whose agonies I witnessed at the Closerie des Lilas. After that day, Dada's bold lancers never rode to the fray again as of old, as a unified band. Perhaps, as some ventured to say at the time, Dada could triumph only by dying.

Intellectual Paris has always loved such imbroglios and takes them lightly. After it was over, several of us repaired to another café. There were with us Erik Satie, Tzara, Éluard, and Robert Delaunay. To my surprise, they rehashed the whole affair in very reasonable terms. Satie busied himself, in consultation with the others, in writing the terms of the majority resolution condemning Breton, which was to be handed to the press; he kept gurgling into his beard with amusement, as he selected some especially pompous phrases in the style in which André Breton delighted.

In March, 1922, Tzara published a little brochure called *Le Coeur à Barbe*, a polemic aimed at Breton. It was done on pink newspaper stock, illustrated with little pictures of steamships, balloons, camels, serpents, and even a urinal, done by Marcel Duchamp.

Among those who contributed satirical notes, epigrams, and doggerel to this pamphlet were Paul Éluard, Marcel Duchamp, Philippe Soupault, Erik Satie, and the "mysterious" Dr. Théodore Fraenkel, a young man of wit who had been the comrade of Breton and Aragon at medical school and in the Army. I, too, was guilty of some doggerel included in this brochure, and was promptly taken to task by Aragon, who assured me that I had not the least understanding of what I was doing. I replied that while I could not possibly follow all the raveled plots and counterplots of the warring factions, I did not believe they were serious, and, in any case, was resolved to live amongst them as a neutral party. This I managed to do for a long time, by meeting the "enemies" separately. In truth, they kept changing sides so rapidly that one could not distinguish friend from foe.

André Breton now revived the review *Littérature* (which had been suspended for several months) and in its April, 1922, issue published a memorable *envoi* to Dadaism. It had been, he declared, only a passing fashion, a "manner of sitting down." To be sure, it had been useful in fostering a certain "state of mind which served to keep us in a condition of readiness—from which we shall now start out, in all lucidity, toward that which calls to us." The call, it was hinted, would be uttered in good time by the prophet, André Breton.

He himself was preparing new ideas and new programs, which he was sure would be worth fighting and even dying for. In truth, he was turning back to old French traditions of esoteric romanticism and to the suggestions of "surrealism" left by Guillaume Apollinaire. This article of Breton's was entitled "Lâchez tout!" ("Abandon Everything!"), and had as its feature a remarkable epopee:

Abandon everything. Abandon Dada. Get rid of your wife. Give up your mistress. Give up your hopes and your fears. Sow your children out in the woods. Give up the substance for the shadow. Give up your easy way of life, and that which passes for a job with a future. Take to the roads. . . .

The war between the armies of Breton and Tzara did, after all, reach a stage of fisticuffs and bloodshed a year later, in 1923, when Tzara produced his play, *Le Coeur à Gaz*, at a Paris theater. A feature of the show was to be the reading of some poetry by Jean Cocteau, that melancholy dandy of the Right Bank, whom Breton regarded as his deadly enemy. Breton and his cohorts had threatened to start a riot if the play were put on; and Tzara, so it has been charged and also as stoutly denied, is said to have given the police warnings of their criminal intentions.

Breton and Aragon duly appeared in the orchestra of the theater; after they had heckled the actors awhile, both young men leaped to the stage, and Breton, wildly swinging his heavy knobbed cane, broke the arm of one of the players, the charming, pint-sized Pierre de Massot. Tzara hurled himself upon Breton and they rolled about the stage, while the audience was in a tumult, until the police arrived and threw Breton, Aragon, and their accomplices out into the street. Then, just as things had quieted down and the play had been resumed, Paul Éluard climbed up on the stage to create a new disturbance. But the distinguished poet was knocked about very rudely; during the melee he fell among the footlights, which exploded one by one and did some damage.

The next day the theater management sent a bailiff to Éluard with a bill for eight thousand francs. Thus the former brothers in Dadaism had reached the stage of waging lawsuits against each other!

Langston Hughes

One of the largest stories of the American experience in Paris is the black experience. From Langston Hughes (1902–1967) to Josephine Baker through Sidney Bechet (and Bud Powell and Bill Coleman too) to James Baldwin, the role of Paris as a refuge, asylum, and no-fire zone for African-American émigrés has been crucial. The belief, or myth, of Paris as a crucially non-racist city encouraged generations of black Americans to consider it a second home. (The intersection of the parallel universe of gay Paris made it all the more inviting for many writers who were both.) Here, in an exerpt from *The Big Sea* (1940), Hughes offers perhaps the first modern African-American account of what the city meant as an alternative to New York.

----

from

The Big Sea

MONTMARTRE

My ticket and the French visa had taken nearly all my money. I got to the Gare du Nord in Paris early one February morning with only seven dollars in my pockets. I didn't know anybody in the whole of Europe, except the old Dutch watchman's family in Rotterdam. But I had made up my mind to pass the rest of the winter in Paris.

I checked my bags at the parcel stand, and had some coffee and rolls in the station. I found that my high school French didn't work very well, and that I understood nothing anyone said to me. They talked too fast. But I could read French.

I went outside the station and saw a bus marked *Opéra*. I knew the opera was at the center of Paris, so I got in the bus and rode down there, determined to do a little sight-seeing before I looked for work, or maybe starved to death. When I got to the Opéra, a fine wet snow was falling. People were pouring out of the Métro on their way to work. To the right and left of me stretched the Grands Boulevards. I looked across the street and saw the Café de la Paix. Ahead the Vendôme. I walked down the rue de la Paix, turned, and on until I came out at the Concorde. I recognized the Champs Elysées, and the great Arc de Triomphe in the distance through the snow.

Boy, was I thrilled! I was torn between walking up the Champs Elysées or down along the Seine, past the Tuileries. Finally, I took the river, hoping to see the bookstalls and Notre Dame. But I ended up in the Louvre instead, looking at Venus.

It was warmer in the Louvre than in the street, and the Greek statues were calm and friendly. I said to the statues: "If you can stay in Paris as long as you've been here and still look O.K., I guess I can stay a while with seven dollars and make a go of it." But when I came out of the Louvre, I was tired and hungry. I had no idea where I would sleep that night, or where to go about finding a cheap hotel. So I began to look around for someone I could talk to. To tell the truth, I began to look for a colored person on the streets of Paris.

As luck would have it, I came across an American Negro in a doorman's uniform. He told me most of the American colored people he knew lived in Montmartre, and that they were musicians working in the theaters and night clubs. He directed me to Montmartre. I walked. I passed Notre Dame de Lorette, then on up the hill. I got to Montmartre about four o'clock. Many of the people there were just getting up and having their breakfast at that hour, since they worked all night. I don't think they were in a very good humor, because I went into a little café where I saw some colored musicians sitting, having their coffee. I spoke to them, and said: "I've just come to Paris, and I'm looking for a cheap place to stay and a job."

They scowled at me. Finally one of them said: "Well, what instrument do you play?"

They thought I was musical competition.

I said: "None. I'm just looking for an ordinary job."

Puzzled, another one asked: "Do you tap dance, or what?"

"No," I said, "I've just got off a ship and I want any kind of a job there is."

"You must be crazy, boy," one of the men said. "There ain't no 'any kind of a job' here. There're plenty of French people for ordinary work. 'Less you can play jazz or tap dance, you'd just as well go back home."

"He's telling you right," the rest of the fellows at the table agreed, "there's no work here."

But one of them indicated a hotel. "Go over there across the street and see if you can't get a little room cheap."

I went. But it was high for me, almost a dollar a day in American money. However, I had to take the room for that night. Then I ate my first dinner in Paris—*bœuf au gros sel*, and a cream cheese with sugar. Even with the damp and the slush—for the snow had turned to a nasty rain—I began to like Paris a little, and to take it personally.

The next day I went everywhere where people spoke English, looking for a job—the American Library, the Embassy, the American Express, the newspaper offices. Nothing doing. Besides I would have to have a *carte d'identité*. But it would be better to go back home, I was advised, because there were plenty of people out of work in Paris.

"With five dollars, I can't go back home," I said.

People shrugged their shoulders and went on doing whatever they were doing. I tramped the streets. Late afternoon of the second day came. I went back to Montmartre, to that same little café in front of my hotel, where I had no room that night—unless I paid again. And if I did take the same room again, with supper, I'd have scarcely four dollars left!

My bags were still checked at the station, so I had no clean clothes to put on. It was drizzling rain, and I was cold and hungry. I had had only coffee and a roll all day. I felt bad.

I slumped down at a table in the small café and ordered another *café crème* and a *croissant*—the second that day. I ate the croissant (a slender, curved French roll) and wondered what on earth I ought to do. I decided tomorrow to try the French for a job somewhere, maybe the Ritz or some other of the large hotels, or maybe where I had seen them building a big building on one of the boulevards. Perhaps they could use a hodcarrier.

The café had begun to be crowded, as the afternoon darkened into a damp and murky dusk. A tall, young colored fellow came in and sat down at the marble-topped table where I was. He ordered a *fine*, and asked me if I wanted to play dominoes.

I said no, I was looking for a cheap room.

He recommended his hotel, where he lived by the month, but when we figured it out, it was about the same as the place across the street, too high for me. I said I meant a *really* cheap room. I said I didn't care about heat or hot water or carpets on the floor right now, just a place to sleep. He said he didn't know of any hotels like that, as cheap as I needed.

Just then a girl, with reddish-blond hair, sitting on a bench that ran along the wall, spoke up and said: "You say you look at one hotel?"

I said: "Yes."

She said: "I know one, not much dear."

"Where?" I asked her. "And how much?"

"Almost not nothing," she said, "not dear! No! I will show you. Come."

She put on her thin coat and got up. I followed her. She was a short girl, with a round, pale Slavic face and big dark eyes. She had a little rouge on her cheeks. She had on a wine-red hat with a rain-wilted feather. She was pretty, but her slippers were worn at the heels. We walked up the hill in silence, across the Place Blanche and up toward the rue Lepic. Finally I said to her, in French, that I had very little money and the room would have to be very cheap or I would have nothing left to eat on, because I had no *travaille*. No *travaille* and no prospects, and I was not a musician.

She answered that this was the cheapest hotel in Montmartre, where she was taking me. *"Pas de tout cher."* But, as she spoke, I could tell that her French was almost as bad as mine, so we switched back to English, which she spoke passably well.

She said she had not been in Paris long, that she had come from Constantinople with a ballet troupe, and that she was Russian. Beyond that, she volunteered no information. The drizzling February rain wet our faces, the water was soggy in my shoes, and the girl looked none too warm in her thin but rather chic coat. After several turns up and down a narrow, winding street, we came to the hotel, a tall, neat-looking building, with a tiled entrance hall. From a tiny sitting room came a large French woman. And the girl spoke to her about the room, the very least dear, for *m'sieu*.

"Oui," said the woman, "a quite small room, by the week, fifty francs."

"I'll take it," I said, "and pay two weeks." I knew it would leave me almost nothing, but I would have a place to sleep.

I thanked the girl for bringing me to the hotel and I invited her to a cup of coffee with me next time we met at the café. We parted at the Place Blanche, and I went to the station to get my bags, now that I had some place to put them. After paying for the room and the storage of my bags, I had just about enough money left for coffee and rolls for a week—if I ate nothing *but* coffee and one roll a meal.

I was terribly hungry and it took me some time to get to the station by Métro. I got back to the hotel about nine that night, through a chilly drizzle. My key was not hanging on the hallboard, but the landlady pointed up, so I went up. It was a long climb with the bags, and I stopped on each landing to rest. I guess I was weak with hunger, having only eaten those two croissants all day. When I got to my room, I could see a light beneath the door, so I thought maybe I was confused about the number. I hesitated, then knocked. The door opened and there stood the Russian girl.

I said: "Hello!"

I didn't know what else to say.

She said: "I first return me," and smiled.

Her coat was hanging on a nail behind the door and a small bag sat beneath the window. She was barefooted, her wet shoes were beneath the heatless radiator, and her stockings drying on the foot of the bed.

I said: "Are you going to stay here, too?"

She said: "Of course! *Mais oui!* Why you think, I find one room?"

She had her hat off. Her red-blond hair was soft and wavy. She laughed and laughed. I laughed, too, since I didn't know what to say.

"I have no mon-nee nedder," she said.

We sat down on the bed. In broken English, she told me her story. Her name was Sonya. Her dancing troupe had gone to pieces in Nice. She had bought a ticket to Paris. And here we were—in a room that was all bed, just space barely to open the door, that was all, and a few nails in the barren wall, on which to hang clothes. No heat in the radiator. No table, no washstand, no chair, but a deep window seat that could serve as a chair and a place to put things on. It was cold, so cold you could see your breath. But the rent was cheap, so you couldn't ask for much.

We didn't ask for anything.

I put my suitcase under the bed. Sonya hung her clothes on the nails. She said: "If you have some francs I go *chez l'épicerie* and get white cheese and one small bread and one small wine and we have supper. Eat right here. That way are less dear."

I gave her ten francs and she went out shopping for the supper. We spread the food on the bed. It tasted very good and cost little, cheese and crisp, fresh bread and a bottle of wine. But I could see my francs gone in a few days more. Then what would we do? But Sonya said she was looking for a job, and perhaps she would find one soon, then we both could eat.

Not being accustomed to the quick friendship of the dispossessed, I wondered if she meant it. Later, I knew she did. She found a job first. And we both ate.

The day after I took the room, I wrote to my mother in McKeesport, requesting a loan. It was the first time I had ever written home asking for money. I told her that I was stranded in Paris, and would she or Dad please cable me twenty dollars. But I wondered how I would live the ten or twelve days I'd have to wait for the letter to reach America and the answer to come back. I was sure, however, that the money would come if my step-father had it. He was always generous and a good sport, my step-father.

Before I would have written my own father for a penny, I would have died in Paris, because I knew his answer would be: "I told you you should have listened to me, and gone to Switzerland to study, as I asked you!" So I would not write my father, though hunger reduced me to a skeleton, and I died of malnutrition on the steps of the Louvre.

Hunger came, too. Bread and cheese once a day couldn't keep hunger away. Selling your clothes, when you didn't have many, couldn't keep hunger away. Going to bed early and sleeping late couldn't keep hunger away. Looking for a job and always being turned down couldn't keep hunger away. Not sleeping alone couldn't keep hunger away.

Sonya did her stretching exercises on the bed every morning. There wasn't room to do them on the floor, and she wanted to keep in shape in case she got a job dancing. But Montmartre was full of Russian dancers—and no jobs.

She was twenty-four, older than I was. Her father had been on the wrong side in the Russian Revolution and had escaped to Turkey. He died in Roumania. Then Sonya danced in Bucharest, Budapest, Athens and Constantinople, Trieste, and Nice, where the troupe of dancers went to pieces because the manager fell ill, and contracts and working permits ran out. So Sonya, who, like me, had never seen Paris before, had packed up and come north.

Now, her costumes were all in pawn, and her best clothes, too. Still, she didn't look bad when she went out. She walked with her head up. And from the hands of the usurer she had managed to hold back one evening gown of pearl-colored sequins, hanging limp against our wall.

WORK

Sonya found work as a danseuse at Zelli's famous night club in the rue Fontaine. Not as a dancer in the show, but as a dancer with the patrons—a girl who sits at tables, dances with the guests and persuades them to order one more drink—and then another—usually champagne. She got no pay, but drew a commission on every bottle of champagne, beyond the first, she could persuade a guest to buy. Result, she drank a great many glasses of champagne every night, because the faster she could aid a bottle of champagne to disappear, the sooner a new one would appear, and like lightning, be opened by the attentive waiters, with an additional commission added in Sonya's column at the *caisse*

Most of the danseuses in the clubs did not really enjoy drinking champagne night after night, and they would dump it into the ice bucket if they got a chance, or the waiters would help them by carrying off each bottle half-emptied, if the guest was not observant. Then, with the bottle gone, the little danseuse would sigh: "It is so ver-ree warm this night. Couldn't we have just another one lee-tle drink champagne, please?" And if the guest was at all a good sport, he would naturally give the waiter the nod to open another 200-franc quart of *Cordon Rouge* that had already appeared like magic in the ice bucket on his table, waiting for the word for the cork to pop.

Some nights Zelli's did good business and some nights not, so Sonya's income varied greatly. It was never large, because it was a big club and Zelli had a great many girls working there, and it was not summer, with the American tourist trade to help out. So after a time, Sonya went to work in another smaller club, where there were only two danseuses. That was after we had known one another some three weeks, and I hadn't found a job yet, and most of my clothes were sold.

But one morning at daybreak, Sonya came home and woke me up with a joyous shout. "Loo-oo-ook-ee here!" she cried. She opened her pocketbook and it was full of money that fell out all over the bed.

"Where did you get it?" I asked sleepily.

"Took it," she said, "from a Danish who waste it anyhow."

It seems that a visiting Dane (in Paris for the first time) had got very drunk on the eight bottles of champagne Sonya helped him order. So when closing time came, Sonya kindly helped him pay his bill, too. And, in doing so, simply helped herself to a large handful of the Dane's francs.

"I deedn't take him all," she said, "just some lee-tle I need."

She was very happy to have money, and so was I. So we both dressed and went to the barber shop and got our hair cut. I got a shine, and Sonya, a manicure. Then we had luncheon at a café on the Place Pigalle. After that we went to a movie on the Boulevards, my first theater in Paris. And at dusk, we came back up to the little café on the rue Bruyère, where the

Montmartre performers hung out in the late afternoon, a place the Negroes called "The Flea Pit."

The café was crowded. We were sitting just inside the big window overlooking the street with our *fines*, when all of a sudden, Sonya went down under the table.

Startled, I thought she had fainted. But no; she had not fainted. She sat on the floor under the table, motioning everyone to be quiet and pay her no mind. She whispered to me that the big Dane was just passing the window outside! Fortunately, he didn't look in. He continued ambling along down the hill in the dusk, out of sight.

By now, I'd been in Paris a month and still had no job. At some of the places where I sought work, the French employees had almost run me away, particularly on one big construction job, where I thought the irate workmen, for a moment, intended to shower me with bricks.

"Salaud!" they screamed. *"Sale étranger!"*

It seems that there was a bitter anti-foreign feeling then among the French workers, because so many Italians and Poles had come to Paris and were working for even lower wages than the underpaid Frenchmen. I wasn't an Italian or a Pole, but they knew I was a foreigner of some kind, and they didn't like me, so they shouted insults.

And still there was no letter from my mother in McKeesport, much less a cable for twenty dollars. Finally, when a letter did arrive from home, it contained the longest list of calamities I have ever seen on one sheet of paper.

In the first place, my mother wrote, my step-father was seriously ill in the city hospital with pneumonia; she herself had no job and no money; my little brother had been expelled from school for fighting; and besides all that, the river was rising in McKeesport. The water was already knee-deep at the door, and if it got any higher she would have to get a rowboat and move out of the house. The Jewish people downstairs had fled to stay with relatives. But my mother had no place to go, and she couldn't even send me a two-cent stamp, much less twenty dollars. Besides, what was I doing way over there in France? Why didn't I stay home like decent folks, get a job, and go to work and help her— instead of galavanting all over the world as a sailor, and writing from Paris for money?

Well, I felt bad. I wondered how I would ever get back home, and how my mother would get along with so much trouble on her hands.

Fortunately, a few days after that letter came, I got a job myself. I had tried all the big night clubs in Montmartre, now I decided to try the little ones; so I started out early one evening. I noticed a little club in the rue Fontaine that had no doorman. I went in and asked for the owner. The owner turned out to be a colored woman, a *Martiniquaise*. I addressed her politely in my best French and asked if she needed a *chausseur*. She looked at me a moment, and finally said: *"Oui! Cinq francs et le dîner."* Naturally, I accepted.

Then and there, she showed me the way to the kitchen, where the cook fed me. And at ten o'clock that night, I took up my post outside the door on the rue Fontaine. The heavy dinner the cook gave me and the big bottle of wine that went with it made me so sleepy that I went to sleep standing up in the street outside the door. I couldn't help it. I slept almost all night.

I had no uniform, but the next day, at the Flea Market, I bought a blue cap with gold braid on it, which gave me an air of authority. My salary, five francs a night, was less than a quarter in American money, but it was a great help in Paris until I could do better.

Shortly after I began working for the Martinique lady, Sonya secured a contract to dance at Le Havre, so one rainy March afternoon I went to the Gare St. Lazare with her to say good-bye. She cried and I felt bad seeing her cry. She had been a swell friend and I liked her. She waved at me through the window as the long train pulled out. I waved back. And I never saw her any more.

That night I felt lonesome and sad standing outside the door of the little *boîte* in the cold, damp, winter night, my collar turned up and my cap with the gold braid pulled down as far over my ears as it would come. Every so often, I would step inside the door to get warm. Business was dull.

It was a very small night club of not more than ten tables and a tiny bar. There was a little Tzigane orchestra, and one entertainer. And a great many fights in the place.

Since they sold no cigarettes, the way I made my tips was largely by going to the corner to the *tabac* for packages of smokes for the guests. But whenever a fight would break out, I made an especial point of heading for the tabac so that I would not be called upon to stop it. I didn't know when I took the job that I was expected to be a bouncer as well as a doorman, and I didn't like the task of fight-stopping, because the first fight I saw there was between ladies, who shattered champagne glasses on the edge of the table, then slashed at each other with the jagged stems.

Madame's friend was a tall Roumanian girl, with large green circles painted on her eyes, who often came to the club in a white riding habit, white boots and hat, carrying a black whip. And madame herself would fight if the girl were insulted by any of the guests. For such a job, five francs was not enough, and the fights were too much, so I was glad when I found other work. Rayford Logan told me about an opening at a popular club on the rue Pigalle.

Rayford Logan is now a professor of history at Howard University in Washington. Then, he had been in France since the war, one of the Negro officers who stayed over there instead of coming home. That winter he was around Montmartre on crutches, having broken his leg in a bus accident. He received the *Crisis* all the time in Paris, and had read my poems, so when he knew I was a poet, he tried to help me find a job. One day he sent for me to tell me they needed a second cook at the Grand Duc, a well-known night club.

I couldn't cook, but I decided to say I could. Fortunately the title, second cook, really meant dishwasher, so I got the job. They fired another boy to give it to me. Strangely enough, the other boy happened to be from Cleveland, too, a tall brownskin fellow named Bob. He was discharged, the bosses said, because he came late to work, was unreliable, broke too many dishes, and cussed out the proprietors.

Gene Bullard, the colored manager, told me to be at work at eleven o'clock. Salary, fifteen francs a night and breakfast

I was coming up in the world.

Anita Loos

What a wonderful writer Anita Loos (1893–1981) can be, unbeknownst to most American readers. (Edmund Wilson was a notable exception to the general critical neglect of Loos's writing, while her reputation, like that of her contemporary Damon Runyon, whose career in many ways ran parallel to hers, is and always has been much higher in England.) Her *Gentlemen Prefer Blondes* (1925), however much its essential tartness has been sweetened by the movies (Marilyn Monroe plays Lorelei Lee as an innocent, which the real Lorelei is not, not a bit) is, or should be, a classic. Her ear for an American rhythm is amazing, her sympathy with her predatory belles contagious, and she is a master of one of the key American genres of the century, the extended faux-naïf. (She also handles the sex lives of her courtesans with remarkable candor for a pop writer of the period.) She gets down a show-girl and fashion-model Paris, centered on the Place Vendôme and the boîtes of Montmartre that, unlike most of that 1920s Paris, still exists. For style, this passage makes an interesting comparison with Gertrude Stein's own high modernist exercise in the faux-naïf in the pages that follow. Gertrude and Lorelei, defining extremes of American feminism, but voicing their wisdoms in the monosyllables of plain idiom, can sound, God knows, weirdly alike.

---

from

Gentlemen Prefer Blondes

April 27th:

Paris is devine. I mean Dorothy and I got to Paris yesterday, and it really is devine. Because the French are devine. Because when we were coming off the boat, and we were coming through the customs, it was quite hot and it seemed to smell quite a lot and all the French gentlemen in the customs, were squealing quite a lot. So I looked around and I picked out a French gentleman who was really in a very gorgeous uniform and he seemed to be a very, very important gentleman and I gave him twenty francs worth of French money and he was very very gallant and he knocked everybody else down and took our bags right through the custom. Because I really think that twenty Francs is quite cheap for a gentleman that has got on at least $100 worth of gold braid on his coat alone, to speak nothing of his trousers.

I mean the French gentlemen always seem to be squealing quite a lot, especially taxi drivers when they only get a small size yellow dime called a 'fifty santeems' for a tip. But the good thing about French gentleman is that every time a French gentleman starts to squeal, you can always stop him with five francs, no matter who he is. I mean it is so refreshing to listen to a French gentleman stop squeaking, that it would really be quite a bargain even for ten francs.

So we came to the Ritz Hotel and the Ritz Hotel is devine. Because when a girl can sit in a delightful bar and have delicious champagne cocktails and look at all the important French people in Paris, I think it is devine. I mean when a girl can sit there and look at the Dolly sisters and Pearl White and Maybelle Gilman Corey, and Mrs. Nash, it is beyond worlds. Because when a girl looks at Mrs. Nash and realizes what Mrs. Nash has got out of gentlemen, it really makes a girl hold her breath.

And when a girl walks around and reads all of the signs with all of the famous historical names it really makes you hold your breath. Because when Dorothy and I went on a walk, we only walked a few blocks but in only a few blocks we read all of the famous historical names, like Coty and Cartier and I knew we were seeing something educational at last and our whole trip was not a failure. I mean I really try to make Dorothy get eduated and have reverance. So when we stood at the corner of a place called the Place Vandome, if you turn your back on a monument they have in the middle and look up, you can see none other than Coty's sign. So I said to Dorothy, does it not really give you a thrill to realize that that is the historical spot where Mr. Coty makes all the perfume? So then Dorothy said that she supposed Mr. Coty came to Paris and he smelled Paris and he realized that something had to be done. So Dorothy will really never have any reverance.

So then we saw a jewelry store and we saw some jewelry in the window and it really seemed to be a very very great bargain but the price marks all had francs on them and Dorothy and I do not seem to be mathematical enough to tell how much francs is in money. So we went in and asked and it seems it was only 20 dollars and it seems it is not diamonds but it is a thing called "paste" which is the name of a word which means imitations. So Dorothy said "paste" is the name of the word a girl ought to do to a gentleman that handed her one. I mean I would really be embarrassed, but the gentleman did not seem to understand Dorothy's english.

So it really makes a girl feel depressed to think a girl could not tell that it was nothing but an imitation. I mean a gentleman could deceeve a girl because he could give her a present and it would only be worth 20 dollars. So when Mr. Eisman comes to Paris next week, if he wants to make me a present I will make him take me along with him because he is really quite an inveteran bargain hunter at heart. So the gentleman at the jewelry store said that quite a lot of famous girls in Paris had imitations of all their jewelry and they put the jewelry in the safe and they really wore the imitations, so they could wear it and have a good time. But I told him I thought that any girl who was a lady would not even think of having such a good time that she did not remember to hang on to her jewelry.

So then we went back to the Ritz and unpacked our trunks with the aid of really a delightful waiter who brought us up some delicious luncheon and who is called Leon and who speaks english almost like an American and who Dorothy and I talk to quite a lot. So Leon said that we ought not to stay around the Ritz all of the time, but we really ought to see Paris. So Dorothy said she would go down in the lobby and meet some gentleman to show us Paris. So in a couple of minutes she called up on the telephone from the lobby and she said "I have got a French bird down here who is a French title nobleman, who is called a veecount so come on down." So I said "How did a Frenchman get into the Ritz." So Dorothy said "He came in to get out of the rain and he has not noticed that it is stopped." So I said "I suppose you have picked up something without taxi fare as usual. Why did you not get an American gentleman who always have money?" So Dorothy said she thought a French gentleman had ought to know Paris better. So I said "He does not even know it is not raining." But I went down.

So the veecount was really delightful after all. So then we rode around and we saw Paris and we saw how devine it really is. I mean the Eyefull Tower is devine and it is much more educational than the London Tower, because you can not even see the London Tower if you happen to be two blocks away. But when a girl looks at the Eyefull Tower she really knows she is looking at something. And it would even be very difficult not to notice the Eyefull Tower.

So then we went to a place called the Madrid to tea and it really was devine. I mean we saw the Dolley Sisters and Pearl White and Mrs. Corey and Mrs. Nash all over again.

So then we went to dinner and then we went to Momart and it really was devine because we saw them all over again. I mean in Momart they have genuine American jazz bands and quite a lot of New York people which we knew and you really would think you were in New York and it was devine. So we came back to the Ritz quite late. So Dorothy and I had quite a little quarrel because Dorothy said that when we were looking at Paris I asked the French veecount what was the name of the unknown soldier who is buried under quite a large monument. So I said I really did not mean to ask him, if I did, because what I did mean to ask him was, what was the name of his mother because it is always the mother of a dead soldier that I always seem to think about more than the dead soldier that has died.

So the French veecount is going to call up in the morning but I am not going to see him again. Because French gentlemen are really quite deceeving. I mean they take you to quite cute places and they make you feel quite good about yourself and you really seem to have a delightful time but when you get home and come to think it all over, all you have got is a fan that only cost 20 francs and a doll that they gave you away for nothing in a restaurant. I mean a girl has to look out in Paris, or she would have such a good time in Paris that she would not get anywheres. So I really think that American gentlemen are the best after all, because kissing your hand may make you feel very very good but a diamond and safire bracelet lasts forever. Besides, I do not think that I ought to go out with any gentlemen in Paris because Mr. Eisman will be here next week and he told me that the only kind of gentlemen he wants to me to go out with are intellectual gentlemen who are good for a girls brains. So I really do not seem to see many gentlemen around the Ritz who seem to look like they would be good for a girls brains. So tomorrow we are going to go shopping and I suppose it would really be to much to expect to find a gentleman who would look to Mr. Eisman like he was good for a girls brains and at the same time he would like to take us shopping.

William Faulkner

While his customary rivals for the title of leading American novelist, 20th-century high-seriousness division (Hemingway and Fitzgerald particularly), have always been identified with Paris and took something crucial from it, the relation of Faulkner (1897–1962) to the city was far more fleeting. During his brief stay there in 1925, however, he wrote a series of letters home to his mother which, though touristy in orientation and unformed in style, still have, for their pep, observational skill, and essential sweetness ("I have come to think of the Luxembourg as my garden now."), a lot of life. Faulkner never penetrated even past the beautiful surface of life in Paris—but his letters, and particularly the passages about the "boat man," suggest that you may not have to in order to still "get" something crucial about French civilization.

———

Four Letters from Paris, 1925

To Mrs. M. C. Falkner
Sunday 16 Aug 1925   Paris
I've had a grand time today. Took a pacque-bot, a sort of marine trolley, that run up and down the river all day, and went down the river, past the barrier gates, on past Auteuil and Meudon, to Suresnes. The country there is hilly, with spires sticking out of the trees, and I crossed the river and walked through the Bois de Boulogne, up the avenue to the Place de l'Etoiles, where the Arch de Triomphe is. I sat there a while watching the expensive foreign cars full of American movie actresses whizzing past, then I walked down the Champs-Elysees to the Place de Concorde, and had lunch, an omelette, lettuce, cream cheese and coffee and a bottle of wine, at a restaurant where cabmen and janitors eat. Then I got the subway to the Bastille, looked about a while and then dived underground again to Père Lachaise, an old cemetery. Alfred de Musset is buried there, and all the French notables and royalty, as well as many foreigners. I went particularly to see Oscar Wilde's tomb, with a bas-relief by Jacob Epstein. Then I sat down at an 'ally catty on the corner' and had a glass

of beer and smoked my pipe, planning another article—I have finished two—and watching the people. The Latin peoples do their holidays so jolly, like Christmas with us, laughing and talking and wishing each other well.

I came back toward home, stopping at the Luxembourg Gardens to watch the children sailing boats on the pool. There is a man rents boats— toy ones—and even grown people sail them, while their friends look on. There will be a big man looking like a butcher and mustached like a brigand, with all his family along, holding yacht races with another gang like his, while both wives and all the children cheer. And there was an old old man, bent and rheumatic, sailing a boat too. He hobbled along around the pool, but he couldnt keep up with his boat, so other people would very kindly stop it and send it back across to him.

The cathedral of Notre Dame is grand. Like the cathedral at Milan it is all covered with cardinals mitred like Assyrian kings, and knights leaning on long swords, and saints and angels, and beautiful naked Greek figures that have no religious significance what ever, and gargoyles— creatures with heads of goats and dogs, and claws and wings on men's bodies, all staring down in a jeering sardonic mirth.

I have met one or two people—a photographer, and a real painter. He is going to have an exhibition in New York in the fall, and he sure can paint. I dont like the place I am living in. Its full of dull middle class very polite conventional people. Too much like being at a continual reception. Country folks are my sort, anyway. So I am going to move next week. I think that I can live cheaper than $1.50 per day.

My french is improving—I get along quite well now. Only I find after about 5 minutes that my opponent has been talking English to me. English spoken and American understood, you know. And—dont faint—I am growing a beard.

Billy

To Mrs. M. C. Falkner
Something August (Sunday) 1925   care American Express Co.,
Dear Moms—   11 rue Scribe, Paris
I wrote you, didn't I, about the old man who sails his boat in the pool in the Luxembourg gardens? He was there bright and early this morning when I came back from breakfast. It was a lovely day—(Paris weather is

overcast and grey, as a rule)—the sun was out and it was crisp and cool.
I saw him right away, hobbling along at top speed with his stick, sailing
his boat while people watched him in a sort of jolly friendliness. (This is
Sunday). There was another old man in a blue yachting cap with a toy
steam yacht. He was firing it up while about 6 people stood around giving
him advice. They are really beautiful boats—well made, of fine wood, and
all flagged and pennoned like big ones. Think of a country where an old
man, if he wants to, can spend his whole time with toy ships, and no one
to call him crazy or make fun of him! In America they laugh at him if he
drives a car even, if he does anything except play checkers and sleep in
the courthouse yard.

Then I went on and stopped to watch two old gray haired men, a
middle-aged man and a young boy play croquet. Croquet here is like
baseball at home, only every one plays it. Always a big crowd watching.
When my French gets better, I am going to take it up. They have another
game called Longue Paume (long hand) which they play with tennis rac-
quets but no net. The balls are dead, so you can hit them with all your
might but they dont go far. Its nice to watch. Even the old ladies play it.
And children everywhere. The French treat their children like they were
grown people, and even 5 year old children are as polite as grown people.
And here when you pay your fare on a street car the conductor says
'Thank you.' And as for buying something in a store—its like going to a
reception. Like this—

Good day, sir.

Good day, madam.

What will you have, sir?

Tooth paste, if you please, madam.

Thank you, sir. (gives you the toothpaste) Here it is, sir. Thank you.

Thank you, madam (give her a 5 franc note)

Thank you, sir (takes the note: gives you the change) Thank you, sir.

Thank you, madam (you take the change) Good day, madam.

Farewell, sir.

Good day, sirs (to every one else in the shop)

Good day, sir (they reply. You go out.)

These people believe in fresh air, even if they dont bathe. (It costs 25¢
to bathe even in a hotel in Europe) In America a woman will spend the
morning in her room reading or sewing in a dressing gown: here she gets
dressed and sits in the park, bringing the baby with her. And the cutest

babies. Think of little boys and girls Jimmy's age lisping French. Makes you feel awful uneducated.

I went out to Meudon this week, where Madame de Pompadour had a castle, where folks fought duels all over the place. And I have seen the chapel where James I of England was buried after both the French and English threw him out. Those poor Stewarts had an awful time.

Tomorrow I am going to Versailles—Marie Antoinette's hang-out,— and Fontainebleau.

Quite cool here. I am glad of my trench coat at night. Summer is almost gone. Lots of the trees are dying here, the elms about the Place d'Etoile and some of the old chestnut trees in the Luxembourg. American papers blame it on the Eiffel tower where there is a big wireless station and where they advertise automobiles by electric signs (and where Americans go and drink beer half way up) thats one thing I am looking forward to—September, when all the rich Americans will be gone. They are awful, the class that comes to Europe. Can you imagine going into a strange house and spitting on the floor? Thats the way they act.

                                                                Billy

————

To Mrs. M. C. Falkner
[postmarked 6 Sept. 1925]   Paris

I have just written such a beautiful thing that I am about to bust— 2000 words about the Luxembourg gardens and death. It has a thin thread of plot, about a young woman, and it is poetry though written in prose form. I have worked on it for two whole days and every word is perfect. I havent slept hardly for two nights, thinking about it, comparing words, accepting and rejecting them, then changing again. But now it is perfect— a jewel. I am going to put it away for a week, then show it to someone for an opinion. So tomorrow I will wake up feeling rotten, I expect. Reaction. But its worth it, to have done a thing like this.

I have over 20,000 words on my novel, and I have written a poem so modern that I dont know myself what it means.

Cold as [time?]: even the natives admit that it is quite cool. If the rainy season comes before I finish the novel I think I'll go back to Italy. Brisk and cool, but pleasant—in my trench coat—in the garden. I have come to think of the Luxembourg as my garden now. I sit and write there, and walk around to watch the children, and the croquet games. I always carry a piece of bread to feed to the sparrows.

There is the grandest marble in the Exposition gallery: a little fat boy about 1½ old in a sweater and knitted cap, bending over to pick up his ball. He is so fat and bundled up that he can hardly bend over, or straighten up again: you want to go and help him. In French a baby up to 4 or 5 is 'Le Petit' which means 'The Little.' You say "Look at the little" which is nice, I think.

Bill S. left for New York today. I went to the station with him at 6:30 this A.M. Paris is lovely then. They wash the streets every morning, it smells so good, and no traffic except market wagons full of fresh vegetables and flowers—violets, big chrysanthemums, dahlias—good healthy hardy flowers, not hothouse ones; and the Seine is still as a pond. It is not at all a big river, like you'd think. But everything here is small and quiet and cheerful—even the bridges are all gilt and tinselled, with carved figures and paintings and electric stars on them.

I have a new vice—bus rides. You can go as far as the bus goes for 60 centimes (3½ cents) and they go everywhere. Went up on Montmartre, the highest point in this part of France—(the county Paris is in is called the Isle of France, after the time when Norman and Saxon and German and Italian nobles owned the rest of it. It certainly was an island then, the water being principally blood) to see the lights of Paris come on in the dusk. Lovely. In almost every house there is a picture of Saint Genevieve, the patron saint of Paris, staring out over Paris at dusk. There is a beautiful one by Puvis de Chavannes in the Pantheon, where the unknown soldier's grave is. There is also in the Pantheon, on a blank panel of wall, a wreath to Guynemer, the aviator, beneath an inscription. There is also a street named for him. And near the cathedrals, in the religious stores, any number of inscriptions to dead soldiers, and always at the bottom: "Pray for him." And so many many young men on the streets, bitter and gray-faced, on crutches or with empty sleeves and scarred faces. And now they must still fight, with a million young men already dead between Dunkirk and the Vosges mountains, in Morocco. Poor France, so beautiful and unhappy and so damn cheerful. We dont know how lucky we are, in America.

My beard is coming along fine. Makes me look sort of distinguished, like someone you'd care to know.   Billy

———

To Mrs. M. C. Falkner

[postmarked 22 Sept. 1925]

Well, I'm off again today. My sport baggage is all packed and as you say, I can buy the old steed a package of pipe tobacco and a glass of what the Wildcat calls vang blink and gallop off in practically every direction. I think that expression is so good that I'm saving it for a story some day.

I saw Vannye several times. She took me to lunch twice, and when I saw her the last time she handed me an envelope. "For your birthday," she said when I had told her that I was off to the woods again. And when I looked in it, there was a thousand franc note. $50.00. So I taken part of it and bought her some hand-made handkerchiefs.

I'm glad to be getting away again. So much more fun not knowing where you'll be when night comes. Man here advises me to buy a map. But it isnt necessary—you are never over 2 kilometers from any village (and you never get closer than that to the one you think you want to reach. The best you can do is to keep up with them).

The Belgian Military Orchestra (all Continental bands are military and covered with epaulets and medals—for silence, probably—and swords) is in Paris and there is to be a musical combat between them and the French trombone battlers this afternoon. So I am staying over today to hear it. The bandstand is outdoors, in a grove of chestnut trees in the Luxembourg Gardens. It's lovely, the way the music sounds. And these people really love good music. The bands play Massenet and Chopin and Berlioz and Wagner, and the kids are quiet, listening, and taxi-drivers stop their cars to hear it, and even day laborers are there rubbing elbows with members of the Senate and tourists and beggars and murderers and descendants of the house of Orleans. You see often on the streets men who, had there been no Revolution, would now be dukes and princes, perhaps kings. There is still a Pretender in France, a man who should have been their king. And there really should be a king here. The other day I went to Vincennes, the first royal habitation. It is quite small—a chateau the size of the campus in a park 3 miles across. This was so small that the king moved to the Tuileries, which is on the Seine and includes the Louvre. It is smaller than the town of Oxford. Too small, so another king moved again, to Versailles this time, and built himself a regular city. But now the kings are dead, and the Republican government charges you 2 francs to look at their ruined splendor. But it would be grand to know that there *is* a king in the Tuileries, to go to the Place de la Concorde (where

Louis XVI and Marie Antoinette were guillotined) and see him drive out in his carriage with footmen in scarlet and gold and powdered hair.

Went to the Moulin Rouge last night. Anyone in America will tell you it is the last word in sin and iniquity. It is a music hall, a vaudeville, where ladies come out clothed principally in lip stick. Lots of bare beef, but that is only secondary. Their songs and dances are set to real music—there was one with not a rag on except a coat of gold paint who danced a ballet of Rimsky-Korsakoff's, a Persian thing; and two others, a man stained brown like a faun and a lady who had on at least 20 beads, I'll bet money, performed a short tone poem of the Scandinavian composer Sibelius. It was beautiful. Every one goes there—often you have to stand up.

They have plays here just for Americans. The suggestive lewd, where it is indicated that the heroine has on nothing except a bath robe, say. Then at the proper time the lights are all turned off and you are led to believe that the worst has happened. Nasty things. But Americans eat it up, stand in line for hours to get tickets. The French of course dont go to them at all. After having observed Americans in Europe I believe more than ever that sex with us has become a national disease. The way we get it into our politics and religion, where it does not belong anymore than digestion belongs there. All our paintings, our novels, our music, is concerned with it, sort of leering and winking and rubbing hands on it. But Latin people keep it where it belongs, in a secondary place. Their painting and music and literature has nothing to do with sex. Far more healthy than our way.

I can tell you about paintings when I get home. I have spent afternoon after afternoon in the Louvre—(that Carnegie was a hot sport) and in the Luxembourg; I have seen Rodin's museum, and 2 private collections of Matisse and Picasso (who are yet alive and painting) as well as numberless young and struggling moderns. And Cezanne! That man dipped his brush in light like Tobe Caruthers would dip his in red lead to paint a lamp-post. . . .

I expect I shall go to Belgium and Holland. The weather is sort of rainy, but not too much so, and fairly warm. When I think of home being 100 in the shade! Here it has been an unusually cool summer. Light overcoats at night, and sleeping under a comforter.

I did this* from a mirror my landlady loaned me. Didnt notice until

*Pen-and-ink sketch by Faulkner.

later that I was drawing on a used sheet. This part of 'Elmer.' I have him a half done, and I have put him away temporarily to begin a new one. Elmer is quite a boy. He is tall and almost handsome and he wants to paint pictures. He gets everything a man could want—money, a European title, marries the girl he wants—and she gives away his paint box. So Elmer never gets to paint at all.

My beard is getting along quite well. Vannye laughed at it, because she could see right through it to the little boy I used to be. Both the french language and the French people are incomprehensible to Vannye. She cant even get what she wants to eat. So the other day I took her to lunch and got her a steak, well done, fried potatoes and sliced tomatoes and a cup of coffee. In a restaurant where they specialize in paté and snails and such, and where every dish is a work of art. They looked at Vannye and me in amazement. In France you eat things one at a time. You have meat, then potatoes, then tomatoes, then coffee. But to have them all at one time, and all fried! Vannye doesn't even drink wine. I think that was the first time they ever saw anyone drink coffee with a meal. The wait-ress said to me: 'What will madam drink?' I say coffee. She says 'Pardon me?' I say coffee. She says 'But—coffee?' 'Of a truth,' I say, 'but certainly. Is it not so?' 'But yes,' she says, 'it is so. But—coffee. It is perhaps the wine of Anjou to which mister refers?' 'No no one thousand,' I say. 'Madam does not admire the wine. Madam would but of the coffee. This makes himself, is it not so?' 'Yes yes,' she says, 'of the coffee makes him-self here always. But—coffee.' 'Yes yes,' I say. 'Let to arrange himself for Madam the coffee.' 'Madam would that the coffee arrange himself during the march of the meal?' 'Yes yes, if one permits him.' 'Yes yes, mister. One permits him. But—coffee. It is perhaps——' So Vannye got her coffee. Coffee here is a general term which means nothing. Something black in a glass which authorizes you to sit in a cafe for an hour and watch the peo-ple pass. For breakfast you can get it, but most people take either a cup of chocolate or a glass of white wine. I prefer the chocolate. I was caught too late to drink wine before 12:00. And 1:00 o'clock is thirteen o'clock here. 10:00 P.M. is 22 o'clock.

E. E. Cummings

Exuberance is one of the themes of the American Paris in the 1920s—never any place or sound more exuberant, all that Gershwin—and who better to celebrate it than a poet whose whole gift was for exuberance. If at times E. E. Cummings (1894–1962) is to exuberance what a maitre d' is to a handshake—a bit too much of a pro to quite trust the sincerity—he deserves the popularity he has kept, without a break, since the 20s. (Just as Loos and Stein make an interesting high/low match or couple, so do Cummings and Cole Porter.) Here is his poem on a Paris sunset (from &, 1925) and his appreciation of Josephine Baker, first published in *Vanity Fair* in 1926.

---

from

Post Impressions

III

Paris;this April sunset completely utters;
utters serenely silently a cathedral

before whose upward lean magnificent face
the streets turn young with rain,

spiral acres of bloated rose
coiled within cobalt miles of sky
yield to and heed
the mauve
        of twilight(who slenderly descends,
daintily carrying in her eyes the dangerous first stars)
people move love hurry in a gently

arriving gloom and
see!(the new moon
fills abruptly with sudden silver

these torn pockets of lame and begging colour)while
there and here the lithe indolent prostitute
Night,argues

with certain houses

———

Vive la Folie!

In the old days—not the very old days either, but the long-lost days of a few years ago—your correspondent was no more addicted to the so-called "Serious drama" than he is at present. Although at that time, even as now, inhabiting Paris (which metropolis takes the serious drama super-seriously) he never willingly met an honest-to-God footlight face to face. But this does not mean that he neglected the theatre. Far from it! There were and are, in Paris, plenty of dishonest-to-God footlights, plenty of plotless dramas, plenty of "light" spectacles—and our article is devoted to a few of their many seductions and intricacies.

Be it added, that, to employ the adjective "light" with reference to the art of the *Concert Mayol*, the *Casino de Paris*, the *Moulin Rouge* and (last but far from least) the *Folies Bergère*, is to be guilty of a somewhat atrocious inaccuracy. For the type of spectacle which flourishes within said temples of mirth and amusement and which is universally designated by the word "revue" is extremely fundamental—no more light, forsooth, than the stupid trickeries and clumsy alexandrines of a *Théâtre Français* are dramatic. Nor do we speak as the scribes; having for some years, more or less, devoted ourselves to the glorious art of the plotless drama in general and the Parisian revue in particular.

During these highly agreeable years, we have frequently asked ourselves "what is the revue?" And justly so; since the revue, like everything else worth while, is constantly changing. In the aforesaid old days, for example, a typical Parisian revue was a jumble of extraordinarily ill-staged "sketches," of sumptuously indecent ditties, of highly confused convolutions on the part of a tastelessly costumed chorus and—finally—of incredibly immobile nudes, the least ponderous of whom looked as if she could very easily quell an eruptive volcano merely by sitting on it. What women!

Not even the Old Howard, of Boston, Mass., could furnish their rivals in ugliness, nor were Billy Watson's *Beef Trust* Beauties to be compared with them on the score of avoirdupois. One was reminded slightly of Rubens, more of the Eden Theatre in Madrid and most (ah, most) of the Oedipus Complex.

As a matter of fact, these old time nudes differed absolutely from the stupendous ladies in the canvases of Rubens; the essence of Rubens' females being their hurled weight, their velocity and momentum, whereas the essence of the Parisian nudes was their immobility. The naiads of Rubens' *Debarkation of Marie de Médicis*, for instance, copiously squirm as we watch them. The dryads of the old Parisian revue—and the woods were full of them—only stood around.

That was in the old days.

Et ça change. Gone are the snows of yesteryear. The hippopotami have melted: each has become a dozen fashionably formed and alluringly moving gazelles. Vivid, occasionally precise scenery has everywhere replaced the uncertain planes and flyspecked tones of the ancient music-hall scenery. That typically French, or rather Latin, rhythm, the 3/4 throb or waltz, is submerged in the 2/4 patter or riveter rhythm of *"le Jazz."* Maurice Chevalier (supported by *"les Dolly Sisters,"* who for some unknown reason think they can Charleston) sings many a song at the *Casino de Paris*, but the song which he sings best is unquestionably *"Pour être heureux"* (*Then I'll Be Happy*). The girls at the *Mayol*, who were always well above the average as to pulchritude, have improved 150% all over. Again, the marvellous Mistinguette and her Yankee dancing partner, awkward Earl Leslie, have promulgated a brand new eye tickler at the *Moulin Rouge* which, for splendour, size and nudity, knocks our American revues into a cocked hat.

But the latest and most astounding development of the Parisian revue is announced, by a Parisian journal, called *Eve*, in these terms:

"The Negro is more than ever in favour since the invasion of Jazz and American dances. In the new revue at the *Folies Bergère* called *La Folie du Jour*, there is a Negress, Josephine Baker, who is the great *vedette*. In truth, when one looks, one sees a mulatto with the sleek figure of the Anglo-Saxon, yet the face, the gestures, the dances, even the voice, retain all the rhythm and all the strangeness of her original race." And, as the immortal Bert Savoy would have said, "You don't know the half of it, dearie."

Josephine Baker will immediately suggest, to all addicts of the plotless drama, one peculiarly genuine spectacle entitled *The Chocolate Dandies*. For it was this revue which gave Miss Baker a microscopic, but notable, opportunity to "strut her stuff." As a member of the *Dandies* chorus, she resembled some tall, vital, incomparably fluid nightmare which crossed its eyes and warped its limbs in a purely unearthly manner—some vision which opened new avenues of fear, which suggested nothing but itself and which, consequently, was strictly aesthetic. It may seem preposterous that this terrifying nightmare should have become the most beautiful (and beautiful is what we mean) star of the Parisian stage. Yet such is the case. The black star, *"aux formes elancées d'Anglo-Saxonne,"* has accomplished precisely this transformation, and at the tender age of twenty.

Miss Baker, it seems, came to the *Folies Bergère* after participating in a Negro show which was taking Paris by storm. But when *les girls* of this show appeared "as is" and then "shook that thing" the good Parisians (than whom no people on earth can be more respectable) objected, and objected so strenously that *les girls* were compelled to don a respectable semi-nudity. At least so the story goes. Anyhow, Miss Baker escaped to the *Folies Bergère*. And at the *Folies Bergère*, as your humble servant can testify, there is nothing in the least respectable, semi-nude, or otherwise unsatisfactory about Miss Baker's getup—which consists of a few bananas and not too much jewelry. In brief, the *Folies Bergère* permits Josephine Baker to appear—for the first time on any stage—as herself.

Herself is two perfectly fused things: an entirely beautiful body and a beautiful command of its entirety. Her voice (simultaneously uncouth and exquisite—luminous as only certain voices are luminous) is as distinctly a part of this body as are her gestures, which emanate a spontaneous or personal rigidity only to dissolve it in a premeditation at once liquid and racial. She enters the show twice: first—through a dense electric twilight, walking backwards, on hands and feet, legs and arms stiff, down a huge jungle tree—as a creature neither infrahuman nor superhuman, but somehow both; a mysteriously unkillable Something, equally nonprimitive and uncivilized or, beyond time in the sense that emotion is beyond arithmetic. This stark and homogeneous glimpse is isolated, heightened and developed by a series of frivolously complicated scenes (*Whose Handkerchief Is It? The Language of Flowers, Oh the Pretty Sins, Bewitched* and *A Feast at Versailles*) whereby we are swiftly and surely conducted to that unique phenomenon of noise and naughtiness, the Intermission.

And still we find ourselves remembering the jungle.

Nor does the jungle release us from its enchantment until the middle of Act 2; when a vast egg very gradually descends from the topmost ceiling of the theatre to the level of the orchestra, opens, and emits a wand of golden flesh—a wand which struts and dances, a lithe and actual wand which blossoms unbelievably in authentic forms of love and death. Whereupon, from all parts of the audience, surges a gigantic wave of protest. Cries of "disgusting" mingle with gasps of "how shocking!" and wails of "how perfectly disgusting!" Horrified ladies cover their faces or hasten from the polluted environs. Outraged gentlemen shout, stamp or wave their arms angrily. And still Josephine Baker dances—a dance neither of doom nor of desire, but altogether and inevitably of herself.

Such, or nearly such, being the inexcusably alive protagonist of the revue at the *Folies Bergère*, we have at last found an answer to our question: "What is the revue?"

The revue is not (as Earl Carroll and most European producers think) a mammoth exhibition of boudoir-paintings-come-to-life and is not (as F. Ziegfeld, Jr., pretends to believe) a "glorification" of some type of female "beauty." By the laws of its own structure, which are the irrevocable laws of juxtaposition and contrast, the revue is a use of everything trivial or plural to intensify what is singular and fundamental. In the case of the *Folies Bergère*, the revue is a use of ideas, smells, colours, Irving Berlin, nudes, tactility, collapsible stairs, three dimensions and fire works to intensify Mlle. Josephine Baker.

And the sentiment which we beg to add is: Long live *la Folie*!

Charles Lindbergh

In the memory of the slightly too-literary minded, perhaps, the American Paris of the 1920s is the Paris of no-Prohibition and Hemingway at the wheel. By far the most significant public event, though, was the improbable arrival in the capital of a young midwesterner. Charles Lindbergh (1902–1974), as generations of revisionists have pointed out, was not the first aviator to manage the Atlantic—but he marked out a magic route between the two capitals of the period. His memoir *The Spirit of St. Louis* (1955) is a return to form for him, and a reminder that until he lost his son (and pieces of his mind) in the 30s, Lindbergh was a sensitive and exceptionally intelligent American original.

———

from
The Spirit of St. Louis

Down under my left wing, angling in from the north, winding through fields submerged in night, comes the Seine, shimmering back to the sky the faint remaining light of evening.

With my position known and my compass set, with the air clear and a river and an airway to lead me in, nothing but engine failure can keep me now from reaching Paris. The engine is running perfectly—I check the switches again.

The *Spirit of St. Louis* is a wonderful plane. It's like a living creature, gliding along smoothly, happily, as though a successful flight means as much to it as to me, as though we shared our experiences together, each feeling beauty, life, and death as keenly, each dependent on the other's loyalty. *We* have made this flight across the ocean, not *I* or *it*.

I throw my flashlight on the engine instruments. Every needle is in place. For almost thirty-three hours, not one of them has varied from its normal reading—except when the nose tank ran dry. For every minute I've flown there have been more than seven thousand explosions in the cylinders, yet not a single one has missed.

I'm leveled off at four thousand feet, watching for the luminosity in the sky ahead that will mark the city of Paris. Within the hour, I'll land. The dot on my map will become Paris itself, with its airport, hangars, and floodlights, and mechanics running out to guide me in. All over the ground below there are clusters of lights. Large clusters are cities; small ones, towns and villages; pin points are buildings on a farm. I can image that I'm looking through the earth to the heavens on the other side. Paris will be a great galaxy lighting up the night.

Within the hour I'll land, and strangely enough I'm in no hurry to have it pass. I haven't the slightest desire to sleep. My eyes are no longer salted stones. There's not an ache in my body. The night is cool and safe. I want to sit quietly in this cockpit and let the realization of my completed flight sink in. Europe is below; Paris, just over the earth's curve in the night ahead—a few minutes more of flight. It's like struggling up a mountain after a rare flower, and then, when you have it within arm's reach, realizing that satisfaction and happiness lie more in the finding than the plucking. Plucking and withering are inseparable. I want to prolong this culminating experience of my flight. I almost wish Paris were a few more hours away. It's a shame to land with the night so clear and so much fuel in my tanks.

I'm still flying at four thousand feet when I see it, that scarcely perceptible glow, as though the moon had rushed ahead of schedule. Paris is rising over the edge of the earth. It's almost thirty-three hours from my take-off on Long Island. As minutes pass, myriad pin points of light emerge, a patch of starlit earth under a starlit sky—the lamps of Paris—straight lines of lights, curving lines of lights, squares of lights, black spaces in between. Gradually avenues, parks, and buildings take outline form; and there, far below, a little offset from the center, is a column of lights pointing upward, changing angles as I fly—the Eiffel Tower. I circle once above it, and turn northeastward toward Le Bourget.

THE THIRTY-FOURTH HOUR
Over France

HOURS OF FUEL CONSUMED

NOSE TANK

¼ + ~~IIIII~~ I I I

LEFT WING	CENTER WING	RIGHT WING
¼ + I I I	¼ +	¼ + I I I I

FUSELAGE

~~IIIII~~ ~~IIIII~~ ~~IIIII~~ I I

Four fifty-two on the clock. That's 9:52, Paris time. Le Bourget isn't shown on my map. No one I talked to back home had more than a general idea of its location. "It's a big airport," I was told. "You can't miss it. Just fly northeast from the city." So I penciled a circle on my map, about where Le Bourget ought to be; and now the *Spirit of St. Louis* is over the outskirts of Paris, pointed toward the center of that circle.

I look ahead. A beacon should be flashing on such a large and important airport. But the nearest beacon I see is fully twenty miles away, and west instead of east of Paris. I bank slightly, so I can search the earth directly ahead. There's no flash. But I'm flying at four thousand feet. The beacon may be sweeping the horizon. I'm probably far above its beam. It's probably like the beacons on our mail route, set low to guide pilots wedging underneath clouds and storm, not for those who fly high through starlit nights. From my altitude, I shouldn't be hunting for a beacon, but for a darkened patch of ground, bordered by straight-lined, regularly spaced points of light, with a few green and red points among the yellow; that's how a landing field should look from four thousand feet.

Yes, there's a black patch to my left, large enough to be an airport. And there are lights all around it. But they're neither straight nor regularly spaced, and some are strangely crowded together. But if that's not Le Bourget, where else can it be? There's no other suitable grouping of lights—unless the location I've marked on my map is entirely wrong. I bank left to pass overhead. Are those floodlights, in one corner of the dark area? If they are, they're awfully weak. They're hardly bright enough to be for landing aircraft. But don't I see the ends of hangars over at one side? Or are they just the buildings of some factory?

It looks like an airport. But why would an airport be placed in such a congested section? There are thousands of lights along one side. They probably come from a large factory. Surely Le Bourget wouldn't have a factory that size right next to it. I'm almost overhead now. I can see no warning lights, no approach lights, and no revolving beacon. Looking straight down on a beacon, one can see the diffused light from its beam sweeping the ground under the tower. But those *are* floodlights, and they show the edge of a field. Maybe the French turn out their beacons when no planes are due, like that air-mail field at Cleveland. And even the people who think I have a chance of reaching Paris won't expect me here so soon. But why leave floodlights burning, and not the boundary lights and beacon? Of course I must remember I'm over Europe, where customs are strange.

This is right in the direction where Le Bourget ought to be; but I expected to find it farther out from the city. I'll fly on northeast a few miles more. Then, if I see nothing else that looks like an airport, I'll come back and circle at lower altitude.

Five minutes have passed. Only the lights of small towns and country homes break the blackness of the earth. I turn back on my course, throttle down slightly, and begin a slow descent.

The altimeter shows two thousand feet when I approach the lights again. Close to a large city in an unknown country, it's best not to fly too low. There may be hills with high radio towers on top of them. There are bound to be radio towers somewhere around Paris. I point my pocket flashlight toward the ground, and key out a message. There's no response.

I circle. Yes, it's definitely an airport. I see part of a concrete apron in front of a large, halfopen door. But is it Le Bourget? Well, at least it's a Paris airport. That's the important thing. It's Paris I set out for. If I land on the wrong field, it won't be too serious an error—as long as I land safely. I look around once more for other floodlights or a beacon. There are none—nothing even worth flying over to investigate. I spiral lower, left wing down, keeping close to the edge of the field. There aren't likely to be any radio towers nearby. I'll give those lights along the southern border a wide berth when I come in to land. There may be high factory chimneys rising among them.

From each changed angle, as I bank, new details emerge from night and shadow. I see the corners of big hangars, now outlined vaguely, near the floodlights—a line of them. And now, from the far side of the field, I see that all those smaller lights are automobiles, not factory windows. They seem to be blocked in traffic, on a road behind the hangars. It's a huge airport. The floodlights show only a small corner. It *must* be Le Bourget.

I'll drag the field from low altitude to make sure its surface is clear— that no hay-making machinery, cattle, sheep, or obstruction flags are in the way. After that, everyone down there will know I want to land. If they have any more lights, they'll switch them on. I shift fuel valves to the center wing-tank, sweep my flashlight over the instrument board in a final check, fasten my safety belt, and nose the *Spirit of St. Louis* down into a gradually descending spiral.

I circle several times while I lose altitude, trying to penetrate the shadows from different vantage points, getting the lay of the land as well as I can in darkness. At one thousand feet I discover the wind sock, dimly lighted, on top of some building. It's bulged, but far from stiff. That means a gentle, constant wind, not over ten or fifteen miles an hour. My landing direction will be over the floodlights, angling away from the hangar line. Why circle any longer? That's all the information I need. No matter how hard I try, my eyes can't penetrate the blanket of night over the central portion of the field.

I straighten out my wings and let the throttled engine drag me on beyond the leeward border. Now the steep bank into wind, and the dive toward ground. But how strange it is, this descent. I'm wide awake, but the feel of my plane has not returned. Then I must hold excess speed— take no chance of stalling or of the engine loading up. My movements are mechanical, uncoordinated, as though I were coming down at the end of my first solo.

I point the nose just short of the floodlights, throttle half open, flattening out slightly as I approach. I see the whole outline of the hangars, now. Two or three planes are resting in the shadows. There's no time to look for more details. The lighted area is just ahead. It's barely large enough to land on. I nose down below the hangar roofs, so low that I can see the texture of the sod, and blades of grass on high spots. The ground is smooth and solid as far as the floodlights show its surface. I can tell nothing about the black mass beyond. But those several pin points in the distance look as though they mark the far border. Since Le Bourget is a major airport, the area between is probably also clear—I'll have to take a chance on that; if I land short, I may stop rolling before I reach it.

I open the throttle and start a climbing turn. I don't dare pull the nose up steeply. I don't dare chandelle around the hangars to celebrate my arrival, as I often do coming in with the night mail at Chicago. I must handle the *Spirit of St. Louis* as I'd teach a student to fly.

I climb to a thousand feet. There are the lamps of Paris again, like a lake of stars. There's the dark area below, just as it was before. No one has turned on more lights. I level off for the downwind stretch. The wind sock hasn't changed—still bulged and angling across the line of hangars. The motorcars are still jammed in traffic. There's no sign of movement on the ground.

I'm a quarter-mile downwind now—— Back on throttle—— Bank around for final glide. Is my nose down far enough? Yes, the air speed's at ninety miles an hour. I'll overshoot if I keep on at this rate—— Stick back—— trim the stabilizer back another notch——close the throttle—— I can hardly hear the engine idling—is it too slow?—It mustn't stop now— The silence is like vacuum in my ears. I open the throttle for a quick burst—But I'm going much too fast.

In spite of my speed, the *Spirit of St. Louis* seems about to stall. My lack of feel alarms me. I've never tried to land a plane without feel before. I want to open the throttle wider, to glide faster, to tauten the controls still more. But—I glance at the dial—the needle points to eighty miles an hour. The *Spirit of St. Louis* is lightly loaded, with most of its fuel gone. Even at this speed I'll overshoot the lighted area before my tail skid strikes the ground. No, I'll have to pull the nose higher instead of pushing it down. I'll have to depend on the needle, on judgment more than instinct. I kick rudder and push the stick to one side, just to be sure—yes, controls are taut, there's plenty of speed. And feeling is not completely gone. I still have a little left. I can feel the skid and slip. But the edge of perception is dull, very dull. It's better to come in fast, even if I roll into that black area after I land. And it's better to come in high—there may be poles or chimneys at the field's edge—Never depend on obstruction lights—especially when you don't see any.

It's only a hundred yards to the hangars now—solid forms emerging from the night. I'm too high—too fast. Drop wing—left rudder— sideslip—— Careful—mustn't get anywhere near the stall. I've never landed the *Spirit of St. Louis* at night before. It would be better to come in straight. But if I don't sideslip, I'll be too high over the boundary to touch my wheels in the area of light. That would mean circling again—— Still too high. I push the stick over to a steeper slip, leaving the nose well down—— Below the hangar roofs now——straighten out—— A short burst of the engine—— Over the lighted area—— Sod coming up to meet me—— Deceptive high lights and shadows—Careful—easy to bounce when you're tired—— Still too fast—— Tail too high—— Hold off—— Hold off—— But the lights are far behind—— The surface dims—— Texture of sod is gone—— Ahead, there's nothing but night—— Give her the gun and climb for another try? —— The wheels touch gently—off again—No, I'll keep contact—Ease the stick forward—— Back on the ground—Off—Back—the tail skid too—— Not a bad landing, but I'm beyond the light—can't see anything ahead—Like flying in fog—Ground loop?—No, still rolling too fast—might blow a tire—The field *must* be clear—Uncomfortable though, jolting into blackness—Wish I had a wing light—but too heavy on the take-off—— Slower, now——slow enough to ground loop safely—left rudder—reverse it—stick over the other way—— The *Spirit of St. Louis* swings around and stops rolling, resting on the solidness of earth, in the center of Le Bourget.

I start to taxi back toward the floodlights and hangars—— But the entire field ahead is covered with running figures!

Waverly Root

Waverly Root (1903–1982), whose book *The Food of France* remains a classic, offers in his 1987 memoir *The Paris Edition* a lively retrospective account of Lindbergh's moment. Root lived in France for a long time, and is the type of the American Francophile newspaperman (a type that continues in our own day with R. W. Apple) who is a different sort than the American Paris journalist. The journalist writes about food; the newspaperman is there for the news, and eats on the side.

The Flying Fool

During my first days on the Paris Edition, I was still isolated from the matter-of-fact world by the euphoria of finding myself in Paris, above which I seemed to be floating without touching the ground. Oblivious to mundane matters I entered the office one morning in the first or second week of my employment by the *Chicago Tribune* to be met by unusual behavior on the part of Kospoth.

"The crazy fool," he said. "He'll never make it!"

"*Who'll* never make it?" I asked.

"Lindbergh," Kospoth answered.

"Who's Lindbergh?" I inquired.

By not knowing who Lindbergh was at 11:00 A.M. on May 21, 1927, I betrayed the fact that as a newspaperman I was being grossly overpaid at $15 a week. Nobody in the city room winced at my question, and Kospoth answered as if my ignorance were the most normal thing in the world: "Crazy young feller thinks he can fly the Atlantic. He'll never make it."

This exchange disposed of Lindbergh for the day, and we went about our routine with no consciousness that drama was occurring somewhere over the North Atlantic. I don't remember what I did that evening. It seems incredible that I would have stayed home during this period of exploring Paris, but quite as incredible that I could have roamed the streets without noticing that they had been more or less emptied. Subse-

318

quent reports put the number of Parisians who flocked out to Le Bourget to wait for Lindbergh as high as a million, which was a third of the total population of Paris at that time. Half a million would probably have been closer to the truth, but even that should have created a noticeable void in the streets and cafés. All Montparnasse seems to have moved to Le Bourget, but I had not yet found Montparnasse. It was therefore in complete ignorance that I strolled into the office at eleven the next morning.

"Where the hell you been?" Kospoth snarled. "Get over to the embassy as quick as you can for the press conference."

"What press conference?" I asked.

"Lindbergh's," said Kospoth. "He made it."

An absentee witness, I have to depend on what other journalists told me to reconstruct what happened on that historic night at the airfield of Le Bourget. They were not all in agreement with one another nor with the accounts that have been printed since, even including Lindbergh's. His book *The Spirit of St. Louis* is perhaps not to be accepted as gospel since it appeared twenty-six years after the event, time enough to play tricks with the memory. And, though Lindbergh signed it, I am inclined to wonder in what proportion he wrote it. Having done a good deal of ghostwriting myself, I think I can sense the telltale perfume of the ghostwriter, particularly during a passage in which Lindbergh described his sensations as he was being tossed perilously about by the crowd that was carrying him in triumph from his plane. As far as I can find out, this never happened.

The wild night at Le Bourget was a comedy of errors whose unifying characteristic was that nobody, including Lindbergh, had understood in advance the full amplitude of the event—except the public. The professionals—the diplomats, the airport authorities, the police, the journalists—were taken by surprise. Only the amateurs were sensitive enough to be kindled by the romance of Lindbergh's one-man exploit. It was the *people* who began flooding toward Le Bourget in a first wave when radio broadcasts announced that Lindbergh had been sighted over Ireland at 4:00 P.M., and when he was reported over England at 6:00 P.M., a second surge swelled the crowd and was still going strong even after Lindbergh had landed and left.

The great rush toward Le Bourget produced what was perhaps the first great traffic jam in history. We are accustomed to this sort of thing nowadays, but fifty years ago there were barely enough automobiles anywhere in the world to create such a phenomenon. Certainly no one would have believed that there were enough cars in Paris to fill the whole four miles of road from the city limits to Le Bourget. The French police—who apparently never even tried to do anything about the traffic jam, a hopeless task in any case—were not prepared to control the crowd at the airfield. They seem to have sent only one busload of officers to Le Bourget. I have forgotten the size of the police buses of those times, but this may have been somewhere between twenty and forty men to deal with half a million. When reinforcements turned up—a handful of policemen on bicycles—those who saw them arrive laughed. But bicycle police were not a bad idea; only bicycles could thread their way through the stalled cars on the road.

The American Embassy had been no more imaginative about what might happen if Lindbergh landed. Two weeks earlier a pair of French fliers, Charles Nungesser and François Coli, had taken off from Paris for, they hoped, New York, crossing the North Atlantic the hard way (its prevailing winds blow west to east), and were never heard from again. Ambassador Myron T. Herrick had cabled to Washington that under the circumstances the American aviators who were preparing to fly from New York to Paris should postpone their projects, for fear that an American triumph in the midst of French mourning would cause resentment in France. Perhaps he thought that this had put an end, for the moment, to transatlantic flying.

But it was too late for an ambassadorial admonition to check the momentum of the race that was getting under way for the $25,000 Raymond Orteig prize for the first direct nonstop flight between New York and Paris. Four planes that had been preparing for months to make the attempt were reaching the takeoff point at New York. Of the four, Lindbergh, the only one who planned to risk the crossing solo, seemed about the unlikeliest to get away first.

The news of his takeoff left the embassy as unperturbed as it had left the day staff of the Paris Edition. No plans were made for any reception. No doubt the diplomats, like Kospoth, believed he would never make it. If anyone gave a thought to the unlikely possibility that he might, he perhaps considered that the occasion might be marked sufficiently with a hastily organized cocktail party for a few French officials and prominent members of the American colony of Paris—visiting senator's treatment. While Lindbergh was pushing his way across the Atlantic, Ambassador Herrick was attending what he considered the most important event of the day: the doubles finals of the French international tennis championships at St. Cloud, between Tilden and Hunter for the United States and Borotra and Brugnon for France. He did not see its end (the French won, but it is probable that few Frenchmen noticed it, for the following day's papers had room for nothing but Lindbergh). It was in the middle of the match that a messenger brought to the ambassador the news that Lindbergh had been sighted over Ireland. The ambassadorial party left the stadium in considerable disarray. But if Herrick had been slow to anticipate the event, from the moment that it occurred he reacted with all the skill of a practiced diplomat to turn Lindbergh's personal exploit into a national triumph for the greater glory of the United States.

At Le Bourget, the airfield administration had been caught off balance like everybody else. I have purposely used the term airfield rather than airport for to have called the Le Bourget of 1927 an airport would have been a considerable exaggeration. This was before the days of regularly scheduled passenger services. Le Bourget was used mainly by military planes, whose hangars occupied one end of the field, while the civilian facilities, mostly for mail planes, were at the other. There were no runways—planes took off and landed on grass. The airfield had never been called on to deal with any such situation as it met with now, and reports vary on its unreadiness when the test came. Many witnesses insist that though the beacon on Mont Valérien, on the outskirts of Paris, had been lighted to guide Lindbergh to Paris, the landing lights at Le Bourget itself were not turned on until Lindbergh's motor was heard overhead. There could have been considerable confusion on this point, for military planes landing at the far end of the field had caused several false alarms.

All versions agree on one point: As Lindbergh touched down, an uncontrollable mob rushed toward his plane and he was barely able to cut his engine in time to avoid mowing a swathe through his well-wishers.

At this moment the only people who had correctly estimated what was likely to happen at Lindbergh's arrival played their largely unnoticed role. They were members of a small group of French pilots—three to my knowledge, but there may have been more—who had organized an unofficial reception committee. Fliers themselves, they had a practical appreciation of what a man who had spent thirty-three-and-a-half sleepless hours at the controls of a plane would need most—and it wasn't official ceremonies. They felt his most immediate need would be rest, and they had prepared a cot for him in the office of Major Pierre Weiss, commander of the bombers of the forty-third aviation regiment, based at Le Bourget. Two of the French fliers, Michel Détroyat, a military pilot, and "Toto" Delage (I do not know his real name), a civilian one, had placed themselves near the point where the plane came to a halt. When it did they were aided by a misunderstanding that everybody since has reported—Lindbergh's helmet, torn from his head or thrown into the crowd, was snatched by a young American who bore a slight resemblance to the flier and was accordingly borne off triumphantly by the crowd to Ambassador Herrick, waiting in the airfield's administrative building. One version of this story has either Delage or Détroyat clapping the helmet on the false Lindbergh's head, but this sounds almost too quick-witted to be true.

However it happened, the error gave the two French fliers time to hustle Lindbergh off to the haven they had prepared for him; the stories that say he was carried off on the shoulders of the crowd, including the account in his own book, seem not to have been true. Lindbergh was delivered to the cot in Major Weiss' office, too excited to sleep. He asked anxiously if he would have any difficulties because he had entered France without a visa, an idea that for a few moments rendered the French fliers speechless with laughter. Delage asked where he wanted to go and Lindbergh answered with a single word, "Ambassadeurs," the name of the hotel where the *New York Times* had reserved a room for him, underestimating the impact of the event to the extent of believing it could have an exclusive story by signing Lindbergh up to write his account of the flight. Delage understood him to mean the American Embassy and drove him there, getting through the traffic I don't know how. At the embassy an attempt was made to put him to bed for a second time, and the journalists who came pouring into the embassy were told that he was sleeping, exhausted, and could see no one until the next day. But Lindbergh was still too excited to sleep. About two in the morning he sent down word that he would see the press, and it was then that he gave his first brief interview, sitting on the edge of his bed, dressed in a pair of pajamas lent him by Herrick. It was no secret that the ambassador was portly, but the press was for once too respectful to expatiate on the elephantine effect his pajamas produced on a young man with the nickname of Slim.

When a big news story breaks, competition among correspondents of individual papers is frequently fierce and among correspondents of news agencies it is ferocious. I was thus able to believe a story about that night at Le Bourget, told me at the time, which I was unable to confirm later. I pass it on without guaranteeing its authenticity but it is not at all improbable. According to this account, the chief correspondents of the Associated Press and the International News Service arrived at Le Bourget to discover that their opposite number of the United Press had preceded them, distributing legal tender in the right places to such good effect that all the airfield's phone booths (there were only six, which until then had proved sufficient) were occupied by burly citizens instructed to keep the lines busy and to yield their places to no one not employed by the United Press. The representatives of the Associated Press and the International News Service decided on concerted action. Addressing themselves to taxi drivers who had brought customers to the field and were waiting to take them back again, they hired twelve bruisers who outweighed the United Press's men and assigned them to battle stations, with instructions not to act until the signal was given. There was no point in giving the enemy warning in time to permit a counteroffensive.

When the United Press bureau chief came pelting into the room and seized the telephone from one of his hirelings, the charge was sounded and the infantry gave assault. For a few hectic moments, a royal battle waged around the telephone booths. The one that contained the United Press correspondent was thrown to the floor, wires ripped from the wall, doorside down, with two men sitting on it. Inside its prisoner raged, shouted, swore, kicked, and threatened dire retribution but nobody paid any attention. In the struggle, all the telephone wires were torn out, and nobody was able to use the public phones that night.

In the offices of the *Chicago Tribune*, the Foreign News Service and the Paris Edition did not see eye to eye about the importance of the Lindbergh flight. Hank Wales knew he was faced with a big story, Bernhard Ragner did not. Like Ambassador Herrick, the editor of the Paris Edition felt that the important event of the day was the tennis match; unlike Herrick, he proved unable to shift gears when it became apparent that it was not. He assigned only one man to Le Bourget, Jules Frantz. William Shirer asked if he could go along to help. "If you want," Ragner said, "after you finish the tennis story. Whichever of you gets back first can write the story." This turned out to be Shirer. He beat the traffic jam by running three of the four miles from Le Bourget, until he was lucky enough to come upon a taxi driver who had been trying to get to the airfield and, discouraged, had decided to turn back. "OK," said Ragner. "You write the story. Keep it short."

Frantz arrived, breathing hard, forty minutes later. He had run the whole four miles to the first subway station at the city limits. He tore down to the composing room, where Ragner was just finishing the makeup of the first page. Shirer's story, or as much of it as Ragner had considered necessary to use, gleamed from the page in freshly composed metal, not yet touched by ink. There was a three-column headline on it.

"Three columns?" said Frantz. "Every paper in the world will put a banner on this story!"

"What for?" Ragner replied testily. "He landed. We've got the story. That's all there is to it."

Frantz offered to write a color story on the spectacle of the crowd at Le Bourget to supplement Shirer's story of the landing.

"It's too late to pull the paper apart and remake it now," Ragner said. "I have to catch my bus."

In desperation, Frantz proposed that he run over to Commercial Cables, where he knew Wales was writing his story, to bring back a carbon. For once even the dreaded name of the Foreign News Service boss failed to impress Ragner. "Go if you want," he said, "but we won't be able to use it."

Frantz went all the same. When he returned, Ragner had left and the table on which pages are made up in composing rooms was empty, with the last pages already trundled off to the stereotyping room. For a wild moment Frantz was tempted to mutiny: There was time to call the front page and an inside page back and remake the paper with, on the Lindbergh story, the eight-column headline it deserved. But Ragner, foresighted for once and obstinate as always, had left orders with the printers that under no circumstances was the paper to be remade.

Wales, meanwhile, had cabled his story to Chicago. He had cast it in the form of an exclusive interview with Lindbergh, undaunted by the handicap of never having set eyes on him nor heard his voice. Jay Allen, his assistant, had telephoned from the embassy a report of the brief 2:00 A.M. bedroom press conference, but everybody had that—only Wales dared promote it into a private interview. I heard envious correspondents say later that Wales had written most of it during the afternoon before Lindbergh arrived, which would not have been impossible. It was not difficult to imagine in advance some of the phrases that were bound to be uttered on such an occasion, including the sentiments the embassy would prompt Lindbergh to utter in the interests of French-American amity.

Wales was on excellent terms with Herrick and it wouldn't have been beyond him to acquaint Herrick with what he intended to write and make sure there would be no denial of it. Indeed he might even, as a friend of the ambassador, have served as a sort of unofficial adviser on what angles it would be politic to persuade Lindbergh to stress, in which case he could interview Lindbergh in absentia with a minimum of risk, for he would in essence be interviewing himself.

Whatever the mechanics of the affair, there arrived for Wales the next day a cable from Chicago: CONGRATULATIONS YOUR LINDBERGH EXCLUSIVE STOP MAILING FIVE HUNDRED BONUS. MCCORMICK.

Five hundred dollars was a lot of money in those days.

I had missed the historic arrival but for the rest of the time Lindbergh stayed in Paris, a week or two, I felt as though I were living in his pocket. I hardly let him out of my sight, unless he were in bed or the bathroom, about the only places where he could enjoy a little privacy. The adulation must have been more of an ordeal than the flight.

When I arrived at the embassy for Lindbergh's first formal press conference, I found the street outside the building besieged by hero-worshipers hoping to catch a glimpse of their idol as he passed in or out. The crowd would thin out as the days passed, but a hard core remained there as long as Lindbergh stayed in Paris.

As I entered the embassy, Lindbergh was descending the stairs between Herrick, who had imprisoned the flier's right arm under his own, and the representative of the Ryan airplane company, which had built the *Spirit of St. Louis*, in similar possession of his left arm. Lindbergh looked as if he were being led to the electric chair between two husky guards. He was, indeed, about to be thrown to the hounds—the pack of reporters who jammed the entrance hall. The first question came, idiotic but inevitable:

"What do you think of Parisian women?"

"I haven't seen any yet," Lindbergh said, which was his last contribution to the conversation except for the syllable "Uh." This I took to be in the nature of a clearing of the throat, preparatory to developing the theme further, but he was never given a chance to do so. If a question opened an opportunity to make political capital, Herrick answered for Lindbergh before he could get his mouth open. If it were technical, the Ryan man pounced on it. Between these answers, Lindbergh was helpless. Only once did a question stymie both of Lindbergh's custodians. It was his one chance to speak but he let it pass. The question had been put in the rasping voice of Hank Wales: "Say, Lindy, did you have a crapper on that plane?"

It was on that first day, I think, that I attended a lunch in Lindbergh's honor at the Clos Normand, a now-vanished restaurant on the edge of the Bois de Boulogne. Lindbergh was led to the place of honor, where he regarded with puzzled disbelief the forest of glasses rising behind his plate. I seem to remember that there were seven, for an aperitif, four wines, cognac, and even, the largest one, for mineral water. As Lindbergh sat down, the sommelier, all attention, sprang to his elbow, bottle cocked and ready to fire. Lindbergh pushed all the glasses back except the big one and requested water. It would have been polite for the rest of us to follow his example, but I do not recall that anyone did.

The days that followed were carbon copies of the first. There were two press conferences a day at the embassy because the reading public was mercilessly hungry for information and had to be fed. We followed Lindbergh through a succession of presentations of awards, official receptions, banquets, and laudatory speeches, reporting word after banal word. Never in human history had the name of Lafayette been so frequently brandished. Lindbergh was moved through this labyrinth of ceremony like a puppet, wearing a perpetual expression of bewilderment. He seemed to be wondering why everybody was making such a fuss about him; all he had done was what he had been accustomed to doing daily as a mail pilot—taking off from his point of departure and landing as planned at his point of destination. The press, which had started out by calling him the Flying Fool, had now shifted to Lucky Lindy. It was wrong both times, but as we watched him receive the accolades like a wide-eyed adolescent, we found it difficult to believe that he had achieved his exploit on purpose.

That was the impression, and it was completely wrong. He may have seemed helpless as he was guided through the unfamiliar political and social world, manipulated, apparently, by men more sophisticated, and more self-seeking, than himself, but in his own milieu he was complete master of his profession. His exploit was not the result of luck, it was the result of shrewd analysis of the factors making for failure or success, of unerring judgments in finding the best answers to the problems presented him, of courage in accepting the risk of applying those solutions, and of minute preparation for his flight.

Eight or ten of us found that out when we sat down with him at a lunch of the Anglo-American Press Association of Paris. It was a different Lindbergh who had come to eat with us, no longer the bewildered boy who had been promenaded helplessly through meaningless ceremonies, but a technician who knew precisely what he had done and why he had done it. Herrick was not with him. The Ryan representative was, but he hardly opened his mouth. This time Lindbergh did the talking. Why hadn't he taken a radio? Because, given the limited range and the cumbersome dimensions of the apparatus of those times, he had judged the added element of security insufficient to justify the expenditure of fuel required to transport its weight. Why did he alone dare fly solo? In a way, for the same reason: a copilot wasn't worth the gasoline it would take to carry him. What, after all, were the functions of a second man? First, to spell the first pilot when he became tired; second, by his presence to bolster the other's morale. Lindbergh judged he could keep awake long enough and maintain his morale without help from anyone else. Why, most important of all, had he taken off over the Atlantic on only one motor when all his rivals planned to use two? "Because," he said, "two engines meant twice as much chance of engine failure."

In case of trouble, a second engine might have saved his life, but it could not have carried him to Paris. His preoccupation was not with safety, but with success. And so he succeeded. During the next three years other pilots (with more men and more motors) would try to duplicate his feat but all of them failed. The first flight had been the perfect flight, and it has not been bettered since.

Ernest Hemingway

More than Henry James, more than Edith Wharton, more even than Janet
Flanner, the American writer whom most Americans identify with the city is
Ernest Hemingway (1899–1961). This is just a bit odd, because, aside from
the famous first chapters of *The Sun Also Rises* (1926), Hemingway rarely wrote
about the city. In fact, until the posthumous publication of *A Moveable Feast*
(1964) there is barely an extended section on Paris in his work, and what there
is tends to be narrowly American. Paris, or the American colony of Paris, was
his home, not his subject, and it was only in retrospect that it shone. Another
veteran of the ambulance corps, Hemingway settled in Paris in 1921, at
Sherwood Anderson's generous urging, working as the correspondent of the
Toronto Sun and living there off and on through the 1920s. His Paris memoir
includes much that is mean-spirited and score-settling and snobbish—a thing
made all the stranger and compulsive because Hemingway by then had far
outpaced and out-Nobeled every imaginable rival—but there is also much
that is surprisingly beautiful, and touchingly tender and domestic, given his
reputation (largely owed to some journalism and the lesser, later novels) as the
Charles Atlas of American letters. In these selections, Hemingway memorial-
izes what was, in his fine later words, "the city we loved, and learned, and
fought our way back into."

---

from

A Moveable Feast

SHAKESPEARE AND COMPANY

In those days there was no money to buy books. I borrowed books from
the rental library of Shakespeare and Company, which was the library
and bookstore of Sylvia Beach at 12 rue de l'Odéon. On a cold
windswept street, this was a warm, cheerful place with a big stove in
winter, tables and shelves of books, new books in the window, and photographs on the wall of famous writers both dead and living. The photographs all looked like snapshots and even the dead writers looked as

though they had really been alive. Sylvia had a lively, sharply sculptured face, brown eyes that were as alive as a small animal's and as gay as a young girl's, and wavy brown hair that was brushed back from her fine forehead and cut thick below her ears and at the line of the collar of the brown velvet jacket she wore. She had pretty legs and she was kind, cheerful and interested, and loved to make jokes and gossip. No one that I ever knew was nicer to me.

I was very shy when I first went into the bookshop and I did not have enough money on me to join the rental library She told me I could pay the deposit any time I had the money and made me out a card and said I could take as many books as I wished.

There was no reason for her to trust me. She did not know me and the address I had given her, 74 rue Cardinal Lemoine, could not have been a poorer one. But she was delightful and charming and welcoming and behind her, as high as the wall and stretching out into the back room which gave onto the inner court of the building, were shelves and shelves of the wealth of the library.

I started with Turgenev and took the two volumes of *A Sportsman's Sketches* and an early book of D. H. Lawrence, I think it was *Sons and Lovers*, and Sylvia told me to take more books if I wanted. I chose the Constance Garnett edition of *War and Peace*, and *The Gambler and Other Stories* by Dostoyevsky.

"You won't be back very soon if you read all that," Sylvia said.

"I'll be back to pay," I said. "I have some money in the flat."

"I didn't mean that," she said. "You pay whenever it's convenient."

"When does Joyce come in?" I asked.

"If he comes in, it's usually very late in the afternoon," she said. "Haven't you ever seen him?"

"We've seen him at Michaud's eating with his family," I said. "But it's not polite to look at people when they are eating, and Michaud's is expensive."

"Do you eat at home?"

"Mostly now," I said. "We have a good cook."

"There aren't any restaurants in your immediate quarter, are there?"

"No. How did you know?"

"Larbaud lived there," she said. "He liked it very much except for that."

"The nearest good cheap place to eat is over by the Panthéon."

"I don't know that quarter. We eat at home. You and your wife must come sometime."

"Wait until you see if I pay you," I said. "But thank you very much."

"Don't read too fast," she said.

Home in the rue Cardinal Lemoine was a two-room flat that had no hot water and no inside toilet facilities except an antiseptic container, not uncomfortable to anyone who was used to a Michigan outhouse. With a fine view and a good mattress and springs for a comfortable bed on the floor, and pictures we liked on the walls, it was a cheerful, gay flat. When I got there with the books I told my wife about the wonderful place I had found.

"But Tatie, you must go by this afternoon and pay," she said.

"Sure I will," I said. "We'll both go. And then we'll walk down by the river and along the quais."

"Let's walk down the rue de Seine and look in all the galleries and in the windows of the shops."

"Sure. We can walk anywhere and we can stop at some new café where we don't know anyone and nobody knows us and have a drink."

"We can have two drinks."

"Then we can eat somewhere."

"No. Don't forget we have to pay the library."

"We'll come home and eat here and we'll have a lovely meal and drink Beaune from the co-operative you can see right out of the window there with the price of the Beaune on the window. And afterwards we'll read and then go to bed and make love."

"And we'll never love anyone else but each other."

"No. Never."

"What a lovely afternoon and evening. Now we'd better have lunch."

"I'm very hungry," I said. "I worked at the café on a *café crème*."

"How did it go, Tatie?"

"I think all right. I hope so. What do we have for lunch?"

"Little radishes, and good *foie de veau* with mashed potatoes and an endive salad. Apple tart."

"And we're going to have all the books in the world to read and when we go on trips we can take them."

"Would that be honest?"

"Sure."

"Does she have Henry James too?"

"Sure."

"My," she said. "We're lucky that you found the place."

"We're always lucky," I said and like a fool I did not knock on wood. There was wood everywhere in that apartment to knock on too.

PEOPLE OF THE SEINE

There were many ways of walking down to the river from the top of the rue Cardinal Lemoine. The shortest one was straight down the street but it was steep and it brought you out, after you hit the flat part and crossed the busy traffic of the beginning of the Boulevard St.-Germain, onto a dull part where there was a bleak, windy stretch of river bank with the Halle aux Vins on your right. This was not like any other Paris market but was a sort of bonded warehouse where wine was stored against the payment of taxes and was as cheerless from the outside as a military depot or a prison camp.

Across the branch of the Seine was the Île St.-Louis with the narrow streets and the old, tall, beautiful houses, and you could go over there or you could turn left and walk along the quais with the length of the Île St.-Louis and then Notre-Dame and Île de la Cité opposite as you walked.

In the bookstalls along the quais you could sometimes find American books that had just been published for sale very cheap. The Tour D'Argent restaurant had a few rooms above the restaurant that they rented in those days, giving the people who lived there a discount in the restaurant, and if the people who lived there left any books behind there was a bookstall not far along the quai where the *valet de chambre* sold them and you could buy them from the proprietress for a very few francs. She had no confidence in books written in English, paid almost nothing for them, and sold them for a small and quick profit.

"Are they any good?" she asked me after we had become friends.

"Sometimes one is."

"How can anyone tell?"

"I can tell when I read them."

"But still it is a form of gambling. And how many people can read English?"

"Save them for me and let me look them over."

"No. I can't save them. You don't pass regularly. You stay away too long at a time. I have to sell them as soon as I can. No one can tell if they are worthless. If they turn out to be worthless, I would never sell them."

"How do you tell a valuable French book?"

"First there are the pictures. Then it is a question of the quality of the pictures. Then it is the binding. If a book is good, the owner will have it bound properly. All books in English are bound, but bound badly. There is no way of judging them."

After that bookstall near the Tour D'Argent there were no others that sold American and English books until the quai des Grands Augustins. There were several from there on to beyond the quai Voltaire that sold books they bought from employees of the left bank hotels and especially the Hotel Voltaire which had a wealthier clientele than most. One day I asked another woman stall-keeper who was a friend of mine if the owners ever sold the books.

"No," she said. "They are all thrown away. That is why one knows they have no value."

"Friends give them to them to read on the boats."

"Doubtless," she said. "They must leave many on the boats."

"They do," I said. "The line keeps them and binds them and they become the ships' libraries."

"That's intelligent," she said. "At least they are properly bound then. Now a book like that would have value."

I would walk along the quais when I had finished work or when I was trying to think something out. It was easier to think if I was walking and doing something or seeing people doing something that they understood. At the head of the Île de la Cité below the Pont Neuf where there was the statue of Henri Quatre, the island ended in a point like the sharp bow of a ship and there was a small park at the water's edge with fine chestnut trees, huge and spreading, and in the currents and back waters that the Seine made flowing past, there were excellent places to fish. You went down a stairway to the park and watched the fishermen there and under the great bridge. The good spots to fish changed with the height of the river and the fishermen used long, jointed, cane poles but fished with very fine leaders and light gear and quill floats and expertly baited the piece of water that they fished. They always caught some fish, and often they made excellent catches of the dace-like fish that were called *goujon*. They were delicious fried whole and I could eat a plateful. They were plump and sweet-fleshed with a finer flavor than fresh sardines even, and were not at all oily, and we ate them bones and all.

One of the best places to eat them was at an open-air restaurant built out over the river at Bas Meudon where we would go when we had money for a trip away from our quarter. It was called La Pêche Miraculeuse and had a splendid white wine that was a sort of Muscadet. It was a place out of a Maupassant story with the view over the river as Sisley had painted it. You did not have to go that far to eat *goujon*. You could get a very good *friture* on the Île St.-Louis.

I knew several of the men who fished the fruitful parts of the Seine between the Île St.-Louis and the Place du Verte Galente and sometimes, if the day was bright, I would buy a liter of wine and a piece of bread and some sausage and sit in the sun and read one of the books I had bought and watch the fishing.

Travel writers wrote about the men fishing in the Seine as though they were crazy and never caught anything; but it was serious and productive fishing. Most of the fishermen were men who had small pensions, which they did not know then would become worthless with inflation, or keen fishermen who fished on their days or half-days off from work. There was better fishing at Charenton, where the Marne came into the Seine, and on either side of Paris, but there was very good fishing in Paris itself. I did not fish because I did not have the tackle and I preferred to save my money to fish in Spain. Then too I never knew when I would be through working, nor when I would have to be away, and I did not want to become involved in the fishing which had its good times and its slack times. But I followed it closely and it was interesting and good to know about, and it always made me happy that there were men fishing in the city itself, having sound, serious fishing and taking a few *fritures* home to their families.

With the fishermen and the life on the river, the beautiful barges with their own life on board, the tugs with their smokestacks that folded back to pass under the bridges, pulling a tow of barges, the great elms on the stone banks of the river, the plane trees and in some places the poplars, I could never be lonely along the river. With so many trees in the city, you could see the spring coming each day until a night of warm wind would bring it suddenly in one morning. Sometimes the heavy cold rains would beat it back so that it would seem that it would never come and that you were losing a season out of your life. This was the only truly sad time in Paris because it was unnatural. You expected to be sad in the fall. Part of you died each year when the leaves fell from the trees and their branches were bare against the wind and the cold, wintry light. But you knew there would always be the spring, as you knew the river would flow again after it was frozen. When the cold rains kept on and killed the spring, it was as though a young person had died for no reason.

In those days, though, the spring always came finally but it was frightening that it had nearly failed.

Hart Crane

Were it not for the principle that a headnote should never exceed in size the excerpt it superintends, Hart Crane (1899–1932), the matchless metaphysical-rhetorical American poet of New York, who sums up in a single 1929 postcard the ebullient spirit of the American invasion in Paris at its height (and hints, too, at its then-"illicit" sexual attractions) would deserve a longer note than this one.

––––––

Postcard to Samuel Loveman

Dinners, soirées, poets, erratic millionaires, painters, translations, lobsters, absinthe, music, promenades, oysters, sherry, aspirin, pictures, Saphhic heiresses, editors, books, sailors. *And How!*

Harry Crosby

The muses are mean. Though hundreds of American writers of serious intent and high purpose passed through Paris in the 1920s, it was left to the weird and irresponsible and in many ways preposterous Harry Crosby (1898–1929) to make a record that does not just record the drinking but preserves some of the fizz. Crosby, well biographed by Geoffrey Wolff in his *Black Sun* (1976), wrote in a stream of intoxication whose apparently prescient virtues, like those of Gerald Murphy's paintings, can look almost accidental. (He anticipates the sound of the Beat writers of the 1950s, when American writing got high again.) The now-legendary murder-suicide that ended his life in 1929 and shut the Jazz Age with a slam only increases our sense of him as a madman who occasionally lucked out. But a strong case can be made, and has been, most notably by Edward Brunner, that, as an artist, Crosby knew exactly what he was and wasn't doing. In any case, he and Malcolm Cowley, crazy libertine and serious student, perform a nice Jazz Age variant on the ancient Franklin-Jefferson two step.

———

Paris Diaries

[August] 25 [1923]. Geraldine and champagne orangeades at the Ritz and afterwards to dance in the Bois and to dance in the Montmartre and finally at dawn to Les Halles where we were the only dancers. Seven o'clock and the end of the last bottle of champagne and a crazy bargain with a sturdy peasant to haul us to the Ritz in his vegetable cart and thus we reclined Geraldine in her silverness I in my blackness, upon the heaped-up carrots and cabbages while our poor man strained in the harness. A memorable ride with the strong summer Sun streaming through the streets, she frivolous and gay, I pale as her dress, with champagne eyes and tousled hair. The Ritz, and a gift to the cuisine of our vegetable cargo, and a paying off of our man (too early to eat at the Ritz) and then she to a warm bath and I home to a cold one. After which in a taxi-cab to the Bank. Is it to-morrow or yesterday? That is the way I feel.

———

December 18 [1923]. A long walk in the Bois and we came upon a stone house half-hidden by the trees, a house with a garden enclosed by a stone wall and guarded by a great iron gate. A handful of silver to the old crone and the gate was swung open. The Cimetière de l'Abbaye de Longchamp (had never heard of its existence) and we wandered among the graves, and the grass was tall and unkept and weeds everywhere and moss growing upon the wall and tombstones all leaning awry and by our side the aged crone mumbling and muttering. With her lean forefinger she indicated the grave of a danseuse du roi. Cypress trees grouped in a corner and the place overrun by cyclamen. A real burying place. We must be buried there.

———

April 5 [1924]. Removed a skull from the Catacombs ("horrible est la mort d'un pêcheur"). Is it the skull of a man or a woman, of a boy or a girl; is it the skull of a warrior or of a courtisane; of a princess or a thief? A princess perhaps whose hair was of sun and whose eyes were of fire. When did she flourish, what were her intimate thoughts, where did she die and how did she come to be buried in the Catacombs of Paris?

> "Why, if the soul can fling the Dust aside
> And naked on the Air of Heaven ride
> Were't not a shame—were't not a shame for him
> In this clay carcase crippled to abide?"

Astounding to consider that if everyone in Paris were to fall dead today the number of corpses would not equal the number of skulls interred in the catacombs.

Climbed afterwards to the top of the Tower of Notre Dame (376 steps) and after having crawled like snails through the dark dampness of underground, it gave me a certain splendor of the Sun, and the bridges this afternoon were like pearls upon a silver chain (where is the lost string of pearls) and there was a diminutive tug (a black smoke-plume issuing from her smokestack) towing a long line of low-lying, coal-burdened barges, coming upstream, butting against the current. And there was a red dory fastened to the rear barge that bobbed up and down like a cork, and afterwards we saw the gargoyles and no wonder C preferred the doves who fluttered in and out or else perched upon the rafters of the belfry.

———

May 18 [1924]. The Cluny and its Mediaevalness and I like the old suits of armor, the pikes and the lances, and the curious battlegear, and I like the old coaches and the frail Venetian glass, and the Dame à la Licorne, woven in gentle faded colors, and the Dutch faïence, and the carved woodwork, and the old-fashioned musical instruments, and the iron caskets; but above all the Sun that filtered through the stained glass windows in waves of yellow satin to color the precious metals and the faded embroideries. And afterwards to the chapel to say sun prayers and to the deserted garden to wander among the moss-covered statues

———

[July] 14 [1924]. Wild dancing in the streets all last night, grotesque couples whirling madly about to mournful dance music while paper lanterns swing to and fro between the drab buildings silhouetted against a lemon-colored sky. Departing day. The tragic sadness of the pleasures of the poor. Two boys revolving like tops, the earnest face of a man manœvring his woman through the crowd (Zorn), urchins upgazing in open-mouthed astonishment, two craintive maidens who cling to each other on the outskirts of the group and who timidly point to the pirouetting couples, and a crone, wizened and stooping, her white cap a patch of cleanliness among the dark shadows, and the old world face of the organ-grinder,—glimpses of the underworld, the restless, sweating underworld, the rabble seeking after happiness ("O Jesu make it stop") and how much more beautiful the full moon turning to silver the garden of the pavilion or the red Sun turning to autumn the garden of my soul.

———

[June] 17 [1926]. Tea at W.V.R.B.'s and we met Edith Wharton and everyone sat in the dining-room (where she wrote Ethan Frome, poor Ethan as she called him)—and there was Paul Morand of Ouvert and Fermé la Nuit and he was heavy and oriental with a pale opium face and there were the young Count and Countess (not *the* Countess) de Noailles, and a pretty Comtesse de Ganay and a Mrs. Hyde and last but not least a delightful Abbé Meugnier who said he wished that someone would invent another sin, he was so tired of always having to listen to the same ones, and who remarked when he saw Narcisse: "Mon coeur, c'est tout un jardin d'acclimatation."

[June] 18 [1926]. Preparations for the Quatz Arts and the students are building an enormous serpent in the Rue Allent, and tickets are being distributed "Femme donne ton Soleil en adoration aux Incas" and costumes are being prepared and C tries on hers and she is passionate with bare legs, bare breasts, and a wig of turquoise hair.

Many people undressing and painting for the ball. Ellen B in her garters, C in her chemise, Raymonde in a peignoir while Lord Lymington (Gerard) and Vicomte du Vignaux (Gérard) and Croucher and a Foreign Legion Man and two or three students and Mortimer and myself all naked rubbing red ochre all over ourselves. (my costume a frail red loin-cloth and a necklace of three dead pigeons).

At eight in the Library eighty students with their girls, and supper and a tremendous punch (forty bottles of champagne, five whiskey, five gin, five cointreau). And mad yells of Venez Boire and then pandemonium and more drinking and more and more and C and Raymonde were the most beautiful and C won the prize (twenty-five bottles of champagne) for the Atelier by riding (almost nude) around the ballroom in the jaws of the serpent while myriad students roared approval. I was ossified and was rescued by Raymonde who found me sprawled against a pillar and who was afraid of the mad antics and asked me to take her home or I her and there was a red blanket and the reek of dead pigeons and then complete oblivion.

————

[August] 31 [1926]. Paris. And all other lands and cities dwindle to Nothingness. Paris the City of the Sun.

————

[June] 10 [1927]. I buy ten live snakes on the Quays and take them home in a sack (this a preparation for the 4 Arts) and the house is in disorder (the Library stripped of its paintings and its Chinese porcelaines and all the bookcases turned to the wall) and the caterer man (harbinger of the fête) arrives and Narcisse sniffs the air (rats know before a shipwreck) and the Crouchers arrive and May appears and we go out for fard and perfume and I buy seven dead pigeons to wear as a necklace and then a hot bath May and I and C and afterwards with Lord L to put on green paint and it does not seem a year ago that we were doing exactly the same thing and at Eight the Students begin to appear—more and more and more and more (many more people than last year) and the Punch Bowl is filled and the Party has begun and soon everyone is Gay and Noisy Noisier and

Noisiest toward Ten O'Clock and seventy empty bottles of champagne rattle upon the floor and now straight gin Gin Gin Gin like the Russian refugees clamoring for bread and everyone clamored and the fire roared in the hearth (roared with the wine in my heart and the room was hot and reeked with cigarette and cigar smoke with fard and sweat and smell of underarms and we were all in Khmer Costume and there was Renée in yellow with her nombril showing and there was Raymonde in red and there was the Dark Princess and at Eleven we formed in line in the courtyard (I with the sack full of snakes) and marched away on foot ("perpetual girls marching to love" signed E. E. Cummings) and away on foot across the Concorde up the Champs Elysées to the Rond Point (stragglers disappeared into Footits Bar) down the Victor Emmanuel past the Piebald Horse ("when all white horses are in bed" signed E. E. Cummings) past the Piebald Horse and thank Christ I dont have to think of what they think back there and to the left and up the Faubourg Saint-Honoré and at last exhausted into the salle Wagram (snarling of tigers at the gate snarling of tigers inside) and up the ladder to the loge and up another ladder to an attic and up an imaginary ladder to and into the Sun and here I undid the sack and turned it upside down and all the snakes dropped down among the dancers and there were shrieks and cat-calls and there was a riot and I remember two strong young men stark naked wrestling on the floor for the honor of dancing with a young girl (silver paint conquered purple paint) and I remember a mad student drinking champagne out of a skull which he had pilfered from my Library as I had pilfered it a year ago from the Catacombs (O happy skull to be filled full of sparkling gold) and in a corner I watched two savages making love (stark naked wrestling on the floor) and beside me sitting on the floor a plump woman with bare breasts absorbed in the passion of giving milk to one of the snakes! Then the prize for warrior costumes and all the miraculous headgear and the black and white night and day of Zebra Skins and there was a man in a Leopard Skin and then the Prix de Beauté and the naked models ("fashioned very curiously of roses and of ivory" signed E.E.C.) ivory white against the blackness of the velvet curtain up and down the steps like girls of the Ziegfeld Chorus up and down the steps to the dais. And cheers and howls and searchlights and clangor of jazz. And gold of champagne. And a staggering out into the rain and it was cold and raining hard when we got home.

———

[June] 29 [1928]. Bal des 4 Arts (Hun costumes this year) and the usual smearing on of red ochre and the usual gathering of crowds in the street and the usual riotous dinner with a magnificent brandy punch manufactured by Mortimer in the most enormous bowl and there were ladies and models and tarts and a stampeding up and down stairs ("in the secret places of the stairs") and Lord L was there and Raymonde (the first time I have seen her this year) and Little Mrs. Hatmaker and Mme la Marquise and Merveilleux and Erik Doll and Barreto and the Rochefoucaulds and Ginetta and the Crouchers and at ten o'clock we rushed off on foot and in taxicabs (I sat with Raymonde on the roof of a taxicab) to the Salle Wagram and the costumes were magnificent this year and there was the usual pounding and stampeding and a climbing up and down ladders and queer scenes in the corners (one plump girl lying naked on the floor while three men color of red ochre made love to her et comment—a regular concours à la mort) and so home and to bed (many people in the house many people in bed but the best fun was painting girls' breasts (breasts by Crosby and Croucher) before the party.

———

[June] 30 [1928]. Awoke to find six of us (not counting Narcisse) in our bed and there was a strange man in a pale blue undershirt on the chaise longue who was playing the graphaphone the same tune again and again Paris c'est une Blonde and there was a knocking on the door and the Goof appeared with two coffees (vous pouvez descendre chercher encore cinq cafés) and afterwards hot baths à deux (my partner was little forget-me-not) and we had a hell of a time scrubbing off the paint and by luncheon time the bathroom looked like a pig-pen and the Goof and her sister appeared and announced they were leaving and I went on foot across the Tuileries and had luncheon (caviare and grapefruit and sherry cobblers) with the dark princess and came home and sat in the sun in the courtyard (while X was making love to Y up in the salon) and later a mad throwing of things mostly books into a suitcase and with C to the train (Ginetta and Erik Doll to see us off) and so a gentle rocking to sleep on the Orient Express clickety-click clickety-click clickety-clack clickety-click clickety-clack clickety-click clickety-click clickety-clack clickety-click clickety-clack clickety-clack clickety-click down the long rails towards Venice while I disappeared up invisible rails towards the Sun.

———

[January] 23 [1929]. Hart Crane for luncheon and he says he will let us edit his long poem on the Brooklyn Bridge fragments of which have appeared in the Criterion the Dial and Transition but it is not yet finished (he is thinking of going to Villefranche to finish it) and then he showed me a MSS of poems Blue Juniata by Malcolm Cowley and then the frotteurs came to frotter the floors and they made a great noise and broke a huge glass and I kicked them all out and CCC appeared and we talked in front of the fire and went to look at pictures on the Rue de Seine and at six o'clock I took a hot bath and went to bed and corrected proof sheets for Mad Queen which I have dedicated to

T.N.T.

never so mad a ladye.

————

May 15 [1929]. I see Joyce who has still another sentence to add to the Triangle (quand il n'y en a plus il y en a encore) and I go to see Brancousi who gives me the abstract portrait of Joyce and I take the abstract portrait of Joyce to show to Joyce and he has great difficulty in seeing it and Stuart Gilbert was there and Mrs Joyce and Miss Joyce and I took the picture to the graveur's and took back the other picture to Brancousi and then went with Croucher to the Bar on the corner of the Rue du Bac to read on the ticker that Elsa de Brabent had lost and while we were drinking our café-crèmes the ticker ticked again and I read that Golden Arrow had lost. Then home to the tea for Frans and May and there were already about twenty people and l hate tea-parties only there was no tea at this one nothing but champagne and C was very pretty in her gold tuxedo set off by the enormous orchid I had given her and more and more people kept stuffing in so I went out and walked around the block. Then back to the party again (I forgot to mention the object of the party which was to show Frans' paintings) and soon Eric arrived with a miraculous blonde. After this the tea-party from my point of view was a success and she (her name is Eva and she is Swedish and she likes Absinthe and Swedish Punch) and I and Eric all dined together Chez Fouquet caviare and caille and then to the Jungle to hold hands and drink whiskey and hear miraculous jazz.

————

[July] 10 [1929]. To the Black Sun Press (I am doing a second edition of Transit of Venus and a miniature edition of The Sun). Then to take a taxi to see McGowan about Hart Crane. I arrived in front of the Deux Magots and hailed a taxi. Just then McGowan stepped out of the café with Vitrac and a girl called Kitty Cannell. We drove off to the Palais de Justice. It was quarter to one. I had a date with Marks at the Ritz Bar so I rushed off and got him (we drank two cocktails) and brought him back with me to the trial. Hart was magnificent. When the Judge announced that it had taken ten gendarmes to hold him (the dirty bastards, they dragged him three blocks by the feet) all the court burst into laughter. After ten minutes of questioning he was fined 800 francs and 8 days in prison should he ever be arrested again. A letter from the Nouvelle Revue Française had a good deal to do with his liberation. They wouldn't let him out right away so I went with Marks to Le Doyen to eat and to drink sherry cobblers in the sun. We got tight and we went off to see Eugene O'Neill and I went to the bank. On my way back I started off towards the race-ticker bar on the Rue Cambon to see if Tornado had won, but on the way I saw a pretty American girl, so I talked to her and we went to the Ritz for a sherry cobbler (her name was Sheelah—I like it) but I had to rush off to the Conciergerie where I found Vitrac and Whit Burnett. Apparently Hart had been sent back to the Santé so Burnett and I drove over there (we saw a truck run over a cat) and here we had to wait and to wait from six until long after eight (we spent the time drinking beer and playing checkers and talking to the gendarmes). At last the prisoners began to come out, Hart the last one, unshaved hungry wild. So we stood and drank in the Bar de la Bonne Santé right opposite the prison gate and then drove to the Herald office where Burnett got out to write up the story for the newspaper, Hart and I going on to the Chicago Inn for cornbread and poached eggs on toast (Ginetta and Olivares were there and Ortiz) and Hart said that the dirty skunks in the Santé wouldn't give him any paper to write poems on. The bastards.

Cole Porter

Cole Porter (1891–1964), one of the five great American songwriters (Rodgers, Gershwin, Berlin, Arlen), came to Paris, like so many others in 1917 and returned regularly into the 1930s (which hit him less hard than most), luxuriating in what came later to be called Café Society. His occasional Parisian lyrics are at times tiresomely naughty, but his best early songs and, much later, his score for *Silk Stockings* (the musical adaptation of Ernst Lubitsch and Billy Wilder's fine, funny *Ninotchka*) helped fix in place the frou-frou but far from wishy-washy idea of Paris as the paradise of pleasure. "You Don't Know Paree" is from *Fifty Million Frenchmen* (1929).

———

You Don't Know Paree

VERSE
You come to Paris, you come to play;
You have a wonderful time, you go away.
And, from then on, you talk of Paris knowingly;
You may know Paris, you don't know Paree.

REFRAIN
Though you've been around a lot,
And danced a lot, and laughed a lot,
You don't know Paree.
You may say you've seen a lot,
And heard a lot, and learned a lot;
You don't know Paree.
Paree will still be laughing after
Ev'ry one of us disappears,
But never once forget her laughter
Is the laughter that hides the tears.
And until you've lived a lot,
And loved a lot, and lost a lot,
You don't know Paree,
You don't know Paree.

F. Scott Fitzgerald

Fitzgerald (1896–1940) spent relatively little time in Paris in the 1920s—the Riviera was his place, if anywhere was. But the author of *The Great Gatsby* and *Tender Is the Night*, though least good in good times, understood loss better perhaps than any American writer, and when Paris fell, he wrote its elegy. "Babylon Revisited" (which ought to be tweaked to fix the geography of the hero's path through Paris, here preserved, which takes him from the Right Bank to the Left Bank and back again) remains one of the finest, and saddest, of all American-in-Paris stories. (It first appeared in *The Saturday Evening Post* in February 1931.) Despite his reputation, Fitzgerald was never much good at a party—his flapper stories have passed away—but he was matchless on the morning after. His writing on Paris also includes a few lovely fragments, including this perfect, evocative, and plangent bit of American haiku from *The Crack-Up*: "Lying awake in bed that night, he listened endlessly to the long caravan of a circus moving through the street from one Paris fair to another. When the last van had rumbled out of hearing, the corners of the furniture were pastel blue with the dawn."

Babylon Revisited

"And where's Mr. Campbell?" Charlie asked.

"Gone to Switzerland. Mr. Campbell's a pretty sick man, Mr. Wales."

"I'm sorry to hear that. And George Hardt?" Charlie inquired.

"Back in America, gone to work."

"And where is the Snow Bird?"

"He was in here last week. Anyway, his friend, Mr. Schaeffer, is in Paris."

Two familiar names from the long list of a year and a half ago. Charlie scribbled an address in his notebook and tore out the page.

"If you see Mr. Schaeffer, give him this," he said. "It's my brother-in-law's address. I haven't settled on a hotel yet."

He was not really disappointed to find Paris was so empty. But the stillness in the Ritz bar was strange and portentous. It was not an American bar any more—he felt polite in it, and not as if he owned it. It had gone back into France. He felt the stillness from the moment he got out of the taxi and saw the doorman, usually in a frenzy of activity at this hour, gossiping with a *chasseur* by the servants' entrance.

Passing through the corridor, he heard only a single, bored voice in the once-clamorous women's room. When he turned into the bar he travelled the twenty feet of green carpet with his eyes fixed straight ahead by old habit; and then, with his foot firmly on the rail, he turned and surveyed the room, encountering only a single pair of eyes that fluttered up from a newspaper in the corner. Charlie asked for the head barman, Paul, who in the latter days of the bull market had come to work in his own custom-built car—disembarking, however, with due nicety at the nearest corner. But Paul was at his country house today and Alix giving him information.

"No, no more," Charlie said, "I'm going slow these days."

Alix congratulated him: "You were going pretty strong a couple of years ago."

"I'll stick to it all right," Charlie assured him. "I've stuck to it for over a year and a half now."

"How do you find conditions in America?"

"I haven't been to America for months. I'm in business in Prague, representing a couple of concerns there. They don't know about me down there."

Alix smiled.

"Remember the night of George Hardt's bachelor dinner here?" said Charlie. "By the way, what's become of Claude Fessenden?"

Alix lowered his voice confidentially: "He's in Paris, but he doesn't come here any more. Paul doesn't allow it. He ran up a bill of thirty thousand francs, charging all his drinks and his lunches, and usually his dinner, for more than a year. And when Paul finally told him he had to pay, he gave him a bad check."

Alix shook his head sadly.

"I don't understand it, such a dandy fellow. Now he's all bloated up—" He made a plump apple of his hands.

Charlie watched a group of strident queens installing themselves in a corner.

"Nothing affects them," he thought. "Stocks rise and fall, people loaf or work, but they go on forever." The place oppressed him. He called for the dice and shook with Alix for the drink.

"Here for long, Mr. Wales?"

"I'm here for four or five days to see my little girl."

"Oh-h! You have a little girl?"

Outside, the fire-red, gas-blue, ghost-green signs shone smokily through the tranquil rain. It was late afternoon and the streets were in movement; the *bistros* gleamed. At the corner of the Boulevard des Capucines he took a taxi. The Place de la Concorde moved by in pink majesty; they crossed the logical Seine, and Charlie felt the sudden provincial quality of the Left Bank.

Charlie directed his taxi to the Avenue de l'Opera, which was out of his way. But he wanted to see the blue hour spread over the magnificent façade, and imagine that the cab horns, playing endlessly the first few bars of *La Plus que Lent*, were the trumpets of the Second Empire. They were closing the iron grill in front of Brentano's Book-store, and people were already at dinner behind the trim little bourgeois hedge of Duval's. He had never eaten at a really cheap restaurant in Paris. Five-course dinner, four francs fifty, eighteen cents, wine included. For some odd reason he wished that he had.

As they rolled on to the Left Bank and he felt its sudden provincialism, he thought, "I spoiled this city for myself. I didn't realize it, but the days came along one after another, and then two years were gone, and everything was gone, and I was gone."

He was thirty-five, and good to look at. The Irish mobility of his face was sobered by a deep wrinkle between his eyes. As he rang his brother-in-law's bell in the Rue Palatine, the wrinkle deepened till it pulled down his brows; he felt a cramping sensation in his belly. From behind the maid who opened the door darted a lovely little girl of nine who shrieked "Daddy!" and flew up, struggling like a fish, into his arms. She pulled his head around by one ear and set her cheek against his.

"My old pie," he said.

"Oh, daddy, daddy, daddy, daddy, dads, dads, dads!"

She drew him into the salon, where the family waited, a boy and girl his daughter's age, his sister-in-law and her husband. He greeted Marion with his voice pitched carefully to avoid either feigned enthusiasm or dislike, but her response was more frankly tepid, though she minimized her expression of unalterable distrust by directing her regard toward his child. The two men clasped hands in a friendly way and Lincoln Peters rested his for a moment on Charlie's shoulder.

The room was warm and comfortably American. The three children moved intimately about, playing through the yellow oblongs that led to other rooms; the cheer of six o'clock spoke in the eager smacks of the fire and the sounds of French activity in the kitchen. But Charlie did not relax; his heart sat up rigidly in his body and he drew confidence from his daughter, who from time to time came close to him, holding in her arms the doll he had brought.

"Really extremely well," he declared in answer to Lincoln's question. "There's a lot of business there that isn't moving at all, but we're doing even better than ever. In fact, damn well. I'm bringing my sister over from America next month to keep house for me. My income last year was bigger than it was when I had money. You see, the Czechs——"

His boasting was for a specific purpose; but after a moment, seeing a faint restiveness in Lincoln's eye, he changed the subject:

"Those are fine children of yours, well brought up, good manners."

"We think Honoria's a great little girl too."

Marion Peters came back from the kitchen. She was a tall woman with worried eyes, who had once possessed a fresh American loveliness. Charlie had never been sensitive to it and was always surprised when people spoke of how pretty she had been. From the first there had been an instinctive antipathy between them.

"Well, how do you find Honoria?" she asked.

"Wonderful. I was astonished how much she's grown in ten months. All the children are looking well."

"We haven't had a doctor for a year. How do you like being back in Paris?"

"It seems very funny to see so few Americans around."

"I'm delighted," Marion said vehemently. "Now at least you can go into a store without their assuming you're a millionaire. We've suffered like everybody, but on the whole it's a good deal pleasanter."

"But it was nice while it lasted," Charlie said. "We were a sort of royalty, almost infallible, with a sort of magic around us. In the bar this afternoon"—he stumbled, seeing his mistake—"there wasn't a man I knew."

She looked at him keenly. "I should think you'd have had enough of bars."

"I only stayed a minute. I take one drink every afternoon, and no more."

"Don't you want a cocktail before dinner?" Lincoln asked.

"I take only one drink every afternoon, and I've had that."

"I hope you keep to it," said Marion.

Her dislike was evident in the coldness with which she spoke, but Charlie only smiled; he had larger plans. Her very aggressiveness gave him an advantage, and he knew enough to wait. He wanted them to initiate the discussion of what they knew had brought him to Paris.

At dinner he couldn't decide whether Honoria was most like him or her mother. Fortunate if she didn't combine the traits of both that had brought them to disaster. A great wave of protectiveness went over him. He thought he knew what to do for her. He believed in character; he wanted to jump back a whole generation and trust in character again as the eternally valuable element. Everything wore out.

He left soon after dinner, but not to go home. He was curious to see Paris by night with clearer and more judicious eyes than those of other days. He bought a *strapontin* for the Casino and watched Josephine Baker go through her chocolate arabesques.

After an hour he left and strolled toward Montmartre, up the Rue Pigalle into the Place Blanche. The rain had stopped and there were a few people in evening clothes disembarking from taxis in front of cabarets, and *cocottes* prowling singly or in pairs, and many Negroes. He passed a lighted door from which issued music, and stopped with the sense of familiarity; it was Bricktop's, where he had parted with so many hours and so much money. A few doors farther on he found another ancient rendezvous and incautiously put his head inside. Immediately an eager orchestra burst into sound, a pair of professional dancers leaped to their feet and a maître d'hôtel swooped toward him, crying, "Crowd just arriving, sir!" But he withdrew quickly.

"You have to be damn drunk," he thought.

Zelli's was closed, the bleak and sinister cheap hotels surrounding it were dark; up in the Rue Blanche there was more light and a local, colloquial French crowd. The Poet's Cave had disappeared, but the two great mouths of the Café of Heaven and the Café of Hell still yawned— even devoured, as he watched, the meager contents of a tourist bus—a German, a Japanese, and an American couple who glanced at him with frightened eyes.

So much for the effort and ingenuity of Montmartre. All the catering to vice and waste was on an utterly childish scale, and he suddenly realized the meaning of the word "dissipate"—to dissipate into thin air; to make nothing out of something. In the little hours of the night every move from place to place was an enormous human jump, an increase of paying for the privilege of slower and slower motion.

He remembered thousand-franc notes given to an orchestra for playing a single number, hundred-franc notes tossed to a doorman for calling a cab.

But it hadn't been given for nothing.

It had been given, even the most wildly squandered sum, as an offering to destiny that he might not remember the things most worth remembering, the things that now he would always remember—his child taken from his control, his wife escaped to a grave in Vermont.

In the glare of a *brasserie* a woman spoke to him. He bought her some eggs and coffee, and then, eluding her encouraging stare, gave her a twenty-franc note and took a taxi to his hotel.

II

He woke upon a fine fall day—football weather. The depression of yesterday was gone and he liked the people on the streets. At noon he sat opposite Honoria at Le Grand Vatel, the only restaurant he could think of not reminiscent of champagne dinners and long luncheons that began at two and ended in a blurred and vague twilight.

"Now, how about vegetables? Oughtn't you to have some vegetables?"

"Well, yes."

"Here's *épinards* and *chou-fleur* and carrots and *haricots*."

"I'd like *chou-fleur*."

"Wouldn't you like to have two vegetables?"

"I usually only have one at lunch."

The waiter was pretending to be inordinately fond of children. *"Qu'elle est mignonne la petite? Elle parle exactement comme une Française."*

"How about dessert? Shall we wait and see?"

The waiter disappeared. Honoria looked at her father expectantly.

"What are we going to do?"

"First, we're going to that toy store in the Rue Saint-Honoré and buy you anything you like. And then we're going to the vaudeville at the Empire."

She hesitated. "I like it about the vaudeville, but not the toy store."

"Why not?"

"Well, you brought me this doll." She had it with her. "And I've got lots of things. And we're not rich any more, are we?"

"We never were. But today you are to have anything you want."

"All right," she agreed resignedly.

When there had been her mother and a French nurse he had been inclined to be strict; now he extended himself, reached out for a new tolerance; he must be both parents to her and not shut any of her out of communication.

"I want to get to know you," he said gravely. "First let me introduce myself. My name is Charles J. Wales, of Prague."

"Oh, daddy!" her voice cracked with laughter.

"And who are you, please?" he persisted, and she accepted a rôle immediately: "Honoria Wales, Rue Palatine, Paris."

"Married or single?"

"No, not married. Single."

He indicated the doll. "But I see you have a child, madame."

Unwilling to disinherit it, she took it to her heart and thought quickly: "Yes, I've been married, but I'm not married now. My husband is dead."

He went on quickly, "And the child's name?"

"Simone. That's after my best friend at school."

"I'm very pleased that you're doing so well at school."

"I'm third this month," she boasted. "Elsie"—that was her cousin—"is only about eighteenth, and Richard is about at the bottom."

"You like Richard and Elsie, don't you?"

"Oh, yes. I like Richard quite well and I like her all right."

Cautiously and casually he asked: "And Aunt Marion and Uncle Lincoln—which do you like best?"

"Oh, Uncle Lincoln, I guess."

He was increasingly aware of her presence. As they came in, a murmur of ". . . adorable" followed them, and now the people at the next table bent all their silences upon her, staring as if she were something no more conscious than a flower.

"Why don't I live with you?" she asked suddenly. "Because mamma's dead?"

"You must stay here and learn more French. It would have been hard for daddy to take care of you so well."

"I don't really need much taking care of any more. I do everything for myself."

Going out of the restaurant, a man and a woman unexpectedly hailed him.

"Well, the old Wales!"

"Hello there, Lorraine. . . . Dunc."

Sudden ghosts out of the past: Duncan Schaeffer, a friend from college. Lorraine Quarrles, a lovely, pale blonde of thirty; one of a crowd who had helped them make months into days in the lavish times of three years ago.

"My husband couldn't come this year," she said, in answer to his question. "We're poor as hell. So he gave me two hundred a month and told me I could do my worst on that. . . . This your little girl?"

"What about coming back and sitting down?" Duncan asked.

"Can't do it." He was glad for an excuse. As always, he felt Lorraine's passionate, provocative attraction, but his own rhythm was different now.

"Well, how about dinner?" she asked.

"I'm not free. Give me your address and let me call you."

"Charlie, I believe you're sober," she said judicially. "I honestly believe he's sober, Dunc. Pinch him and see if he's sober."

Charlie indicated Honoria with his head. They both laughed.

"What's your address?" said Duncan sceptically.

He hesitated, unwilling to give the name of his hotel.

"I'm not settled yet. I'd better call you. We're going to see the vaudeville at the Empire."

"There! That's what I want to do," Lorraine said. "I want to see some clowns and acrobats and jugglers. That's just what we'll do, Dunc."

"We've got to do an errand first," said Charlie. "Perhaps we'll see you there."

"All right, you snob. . . . Good-by, beautiful little girl."

"Good-by."

Honoria bobbed politely.

Somehow, an unwelcome encounter. They liked him because he was functioning, because he was serious; they wanted to see him, because he was stronger than they were now, because they wanted to draw a certain sustenance from his strength.

At the Empire, Honoria proudly refused to sit upon her father's folded coat. She was already an individual with a code of her own, and Charlie was more and more absorbed by the desire of putting a little of himself into her before she crystallized utterly. It was hopeless to try to know her in so short a time.

Between the acts they came upon Duncan and Lorraine in the lobby where the band was playing.

"Have a drink?"

"All right, but not up at the bar. We'll take a table."

"The perfect father."

Listening abstractedly to Lorraine, Charlie watched Honoria's eyes leave their table, and he followed them wistfully about the room, wondering what they saw. He met her glance and she smiled.

"I liked that lemonade," she said.

What had she said? What had he expected? Going home in a taxi afterward, he pulled her over until her head rested against his chest.

"Darling, do you ever think about your mother?"

"Yes, sometimes," she answered vaguely.

"I don't want you to forget her. Have you got a picture of her?"

"Yes, I think so. Anyhow, Aunt Marion has. Why don't you want me to forget her?"

"She loved you very much."

"I loved her too."

They were silent for a moment.

"Daddy, I want to come and live with you," she said suddenly.

His heart leaped; he had wanted it to come like this.

"Aren't you perfectly happy?"

"Yes, but I love you better than anybody. And you love me better than anybody, don't you, now that mummy's dead?"

"Of course I do. But you won't always like me best, honey. You'll grow up and meet somebody your own age and go marry him and forget you ever had a daddy."

"Yes, that's true," she agreed tranquilly.

He didn't go in. He was coming back at nine o'clock and he wanted to keep himself fresh and new for the thing he must say then.

"When you're safe inside, just show yourself in that window."

"All right. Good-by, dads, dads, dads, dads."

He waited in the dark street until she appeared, all warm and glowing, in the window above and kissed her fingers out into the night.

III

They were waiting. Marion sat behind the coffee service in a dignified black dinner dress that just faintly suggested mourning. Lincoln was walking up and down with the animation of one who had already been talking. They were as anxious as he was to get into the question. He opened it almost immediately:

"I suppose you know what I want to see you about—why I really came to Paris."

Marion played with the black stars on her necklace and frowned.

"I'm awfully anxious to have a home," he continued. "And I'm awfully anxious to have Honoria in it. I appreciate your taking in Honoria for her mother's sake, but things have changed now"—he hesitated and then continued more forcibly—"changed radically with me, and I want to ask you to reconsider the matter. It would be silly for me to deny that about three years ago I was acting badly—"

Marion looked up at him with hard eyes.

"—but all that's over. As I told you, I haven't had more than a drink a day for over a year, and I take that drink deliberately, so that the idea of alcohol won't get too big in my imagination. You see the idea?"

"No," said Marion succinctly.

"It's a sort of stunt I set myself. It keeps the matter in proportion."

"I get you," said Lincoln. "You don't want to admit it's got any attraction for you."

"Something like that. Sometimes I forget and don't take it. But I try to take it. Anyhow, I couldn't afford to drink in my position. The people I represent are more than satisfied with what I've done, and I'm bringing my sister over from Burlington to keep house for me, and I want awfully to have Honoria too. You know that even when her mother and I weren't getting along well we never let anything that happened touch Honoria. I know she's fond of me and I know I'm able to take care of her and—well, there you are. How do you feel about it?"

He knew that now he would have to take a beating. It would last an hour or two hours, and it would be difficult, but if he modulated his inevitable resentment to the chastened attitude of the reformed sinner, he might win his point in the end.

Keep your temper, he told himself. You don't want to be justified. You want Honoria.

Lincoln spoke first: "We've been talking it over ever since we got your letter last month. We're happy to have Honoria here. She's a dear little thing, and we're glad to be able to help her, but of course that isn't the question——"

Marion interrupted suddenly. "How long are you going to stay sober, Charlie?" she asked.

"Permanently, I hope."

"How can anybody count on that?"

"You know I never did drink heavily until I gave up business and came over here with nothing to do. Then Helen and I began to run around with——"

"Please leave Helen out of it. I can't bear to hear you talk about her like that."

He stared at her grimly; he had never been certain how fond of each other the sisters were in life.

"My drinking only lasted about a year and a half—from the time we came over until I—collapsed."

"It was time enough."

"It was time enough," he agreed.

"My duty is entirely to Helen," she said. "I try to think what she would have wanted me to do. Frankly, from the night you did that terrible thing you haven't really existed for me. I can't help that. She was my sister."

"Yes."

"When she was dying she asked me to look out for Honoria. If you hadn't been in a sanitarium then, it might have helped matters."

He had no answer.

"I'll never in my life be able to forget the morning when Helen knocked at my door, soaked to the skin and shivering, and said you'd locked her out."

Charlie gripped the sides of the chair. This was more difficult than he expected; he wanted to launch out into a long expostulation and explanation, but he only said: "The night I locked her out—" and she interrupted, "I don't feel up to going over that again."

After a moment's silence Lincoln said: "We're getting off the subject. You want Marion to set aside her legal guardianship and give you Honoria. I think the main point for her is whether she has confidence in you or not."

"I don't blame Marion," Charlie said slowly, "but I think she can have entire confidence in me. I had a good record up to three years ago. Of course, it's within human possibilities I might go wrong any time. But if we wait much longer I'll lose Honoria's childhood and my chance for a home." He shook his head. "I'll simply lose her, don't you see?"

"Yes, I see," said Lincoln.

"Why didn't you think of all this before?" Marion asked.

"I suppose I did, from time to time, but Helen and I were getting along badly. When I consented to the guardianship, I was flat on my back in a sanitarium and the market had cleaned me out. I knew I'd acted badly, and I thought if it would bring any peace to Helen, I'd agree to anything. But now it's different. I'm functioning, I'm behaving damn well, so far as——"

"Please don't swear at me," Marion said.

He looked at her, startled. With each remark the force of her dislike became more and more apparent. She had built up all her fear of life into one wall and faced it toward him. This trivial reproof was possibly the result of some trouble with the cook several hours before. Charlie became increasingly alarmed at leaving Honoria in this atmosphere of hostility against himself; sooner or later it would come out, in a word here, a shake of the head there, and some of that distrust would be irrevocably implanted in Honoria. But he pulled his temper down out of his face and shut it up inside him; he had won a point, for Lincoln realized the absurdity of Marion's remark and asked her lightly since when she had objected to the word "damn."

"Another thing," Charlie said: "I'm able to give her certain advantages now. I'm going to take a French governess to Prague with me. I've got a lease on a new apartment——"

He stopped, realizing that he was blundering. They couldn't be expected to accept with equanimity the fact that his income was again twice as large as their own.

"I suppose you can give her more luxuries than we can," said Marion. "When you were throwing away money we were living along watching every ten francs. . . . I suppose you'll start doing it again."

"Oh, no," he said. "I've learned. I worked hard for ten years, you know—until I got lucky in the market, like so many people. Terribly lucky. It didn't seem any use working any more, so I quit. It won't happen again."

There was a long silence. All of them felt their nerves straining, and for the first time in a year Charlie wanted a drink. He was sure now that Lincoln Peters wanted him to have his child.

Marion shuddered suddenly; part of her saw that Charlie's feet were planted on the earth now, and her own maternal feeling recognized the naturalness of his desire; but she had lived for a long time with a prejudice—a prejudice founded on a curious disbelief in her sister's happiness, and which, in the shock of one terrible night, had turned to hatred for him. It had all happened at a point in her life where the discouragement of ill health and adverse circumstances made it necessary for her to believe in tangible villainy and a tangible villain.

"I can't help what I think!" she cried out suddenly. "How much you were responsible for Helen's death, I don't know. It's something you'll have to square with your own conscience."

An electric current of agony surged through him; for a moment he was almost on his feet, an unuttered sound echoing in his throat. He hung on to himself for a moment, another moment.

"Hold on there," said Lincoln uncomfortably. "I never thought you were responsible for that."

"Helen died of heart trouble," Charlie said dully.

"Yes, heart trouble." Marion spoke as if the phrase had another meaning for her.

Then, in the flatness that followed her outburst, she saw him plainly and she knew he had somehow arrived at control over the situation. Glancing at her husband, she found no help from him, and as abruptly as if it were a matter of no importance, she threw up the sponge.

"Do what you like!" she cried, springing up from her chair. "She's your child. I'm not the person to stand in your way. I think if it were my child I'd rather see her—" She managed to check herself. "You two decide it. I can't stand this. I'm sick. I'm going to bed."

She hurried from the room; after a moment Lincoln said:

"This has been a hard day for her. You know how strongly she feels—" His voice was almost apologetic: "When a woman gets an idea in her head."

"Of course."

"It's going to be all right. I think she sees now that you—can provide for the child, and so we can't very well stand in your way or Honoria's way."

"Thank you, Lincoln."

"I'd better go along and see how she is."

"I'm going."

He was still trembling when he reached the street, but a walk down the Rue Bonaparte to the quais set him up, and as he crossed the Seine, fresh and new by the quai lamps, he felt exultant. But back in his room he couldn't sleep. The image of Helen haunted him. Helen whom he had loved so until they had senselessly begun to abuse each other's love, tear it into shreds. On that terrible February night that Marion remembered so vividly, a slow quarrel had gone on for hours. There was a scene at the Florida, and then he attempted to take her home, and then she kissed young Webb at a table; after that there was what she had hysterically said. When he arrived home alone he turned the key in the lock in wild anger. How could he know she would arrive an hour later alone, that there would be a snowstorm in which she wandered about in slippers, too confused to find a taxi? Then the aftermath, her escaping pneumonia by a miracle, and all the attendant horror. They were "reconciled," but that was the beginning of the end, and Marion, who had seen with her own eyes and who imagined it to be one of many scenes from her sister's martyrdom, never forgot.

Going over it again brought Helen nearer, and in the white, soft light that steals upon half sleep near morning he found himself talking to her again. She said that he was perfectly right about Honoria and that she wanted Honoria to be with him. She said she was glad he was being good and doing better. She said a lot of other things—very friendly things—but she was in a swing in a white dress, and swinging faster and faster all the time, so that at the end he could not hear clearly all that she said.

IV

He work up feeling happy. The door of the world was open again. He made plans, vistas, futures for Honoria and himself, but suddenly he grew sad, remembering all the plans he and Helen had made. She had not planned to die. The present was the thing—work to do and someone to love. But not to love too much, for he knew the injury that a father can do to a daughter or a mother to a son by attaching them too closely: afterward, out in the world; the child would seek in the marriage partner the same blind tenderness and, failing probably to find it, turn against love and life.

It was another bright, crisp day. He called Lincoln Peters at the bank where he worked and asked if he could count on taking Honoria when he left for Prague. Lincoln agreed that there was no reason for delay. One thing—the legal guardianship. Marion wanted to retain that a while longer. She was upset by the whole matter, and it would oil things if she felt that the situation was still in her control for another year. Charlie agreed, wanting only the tangible, visible child.

Then the question of a governess. Charlie sat in a gloomy agency and talked to a cross Bérnaise and to a buxom Breton peasant, neither of whom he could have endured. There were others whom he would see tomorrow.

He lunched with Lincoln Peters at Griffons, trying to keep down his exultation.

"There's nothing quite like your own child," Lincoln said. "But you understand how Marion feels too."

"She's forgotten how hard I worked for seven years there," Charlie said. "She just remembers one night."

"There's another thing." Lincoln hesitated. "While you and Helen were tearing around Europe throwing money away, we were just getting along. I didn't touch any of the prosperity because I never got ahead enough to carry anything but my insurance. I think Marion felt there was some kind of injustice in it—you not even working toward the end, and getting richer and richer."

"It went just as quick as it came," said Charlie.

"Yes, a lot of it stayed in the hands of *chasseurs* and saxophone players and maîtres d'hôtel—well, the big party's over now. I just said that to explain Marion's feeling about those crazy years. If you drop in about six o'clock tonight before Marion's too tired, we'll settle the details on the spot."

Back at his hotel, Charlie found a *pneumatique* that had been redirected from the Ritz bar where Charlie had left his address for the purpose of finding a certain man.

DEAR CHARLIE: You were so strange when we saw you the other day that I wondered if I did something to offend you. If so, I'm not conscious of it. In fact, I have thought about you too much for the last year, and it's always been in the back of my mind that I might see you if I came over here. We *did* have such good times that crazy spring, like the night you and I stole the butcher's tricycle, and the time we tried to call on the president and you had the old derby rim and the wire cane. Everybody seems so old lately, but I don't feel old a bit. Couldn't we get together some time today for old time's sake? I've got a vile hang-over for the moment, but will be feeling better this afternoon and will look for you about five in the sweatshop at the Ritz.

Always devotedly,

LORRAINE.

His first feeling was one of awe that he had actually, in his mature years, stolen a tricycle and pedalled Lorraine all over the Étoile between the small hours and dawn. In retrospect it was a nightmare. Locking out Helen didn't fit in with any other act of his life, but the tricycle incident did—it was one of many. How many weeks or months of dissipation to arrive at that condition of utter irresponsibility?

He tried to picture how Lorraine had appeared to him then—very attractive; Helen was unhappy about it, though she said nothing. Yesterday, in the restaurant, Lorraine had seemed trite, blurred, worn away. He emphatically did not want to see her, and he was glad Alix had not given away his hotel address. It was a relief to think, instead, of Honoria, to think of Sundays spent with her and of saying good morning to her and of knowing she was there in his house at night, drawing her breath in the darkness.

At five he took a taxi and bought presents for all the Peters—a piquant cloth doll, a box of Roman soldiers, flowers for Marion, big linen handkerchiefs for Lincoln.

He saw, when he arrived in the apartment, that Marion had accepted the inevitable. She greeted him now as though he were a recalcitrant member of the family, rather than a menacing outsider. Honoria had been told she was going; Charlie was glad to see that her tact made her conceal her excessive happiness. Only on his lap did she whisper her delight and the question "When?" before she slipped away with the other children.

He and Marion were alone for a minute in the room, and on an impulse he spoke out boldly:

"Family quarrels are bitter things. They don't go according to any rules. They're not like aches or wounds; they're more like splits in the skin that won't heal because there's not enough material. I wish you and I could be on better terms."

"Some things are hard to forget," she answered. "It's a question of confidence." There was no answer to this and presently she asked, "When do you propose to take her?"

"As soon as I can get a governess. I hoped the day after tomorrow."

"That's impossible. I've got to get her things in shape. Not before Saturday."

He yielded. Coming back into the room, Lincoln offered him a drink. "I'll take my daily whisky," he said.

It was warm here, it was a home, people together by a fire. The children felt very safe and important; the mother and father were serious, watchful. They had things to do for the children more important than his visit here. A spoonful of medicine was, after all, more important than the strained relations between Marion and himself. They were not dull people, but they were very much in the grip of life and circumstances. He wondered if he couldn't do something to get Lincoln out of his rut at the bank.

A long peal at the door-bell; the *bonne à tout faire* passed through and went down the corridor. The door opened upon another long ring, and then voices, and the three in the salon looked up expectantly; Lincoln moved to bring the corridor within his range of vision, and Marion rose. Then the maid came back along the corridor, closely followed by the voices, which developed under the light into Duncan Schaeffer and Lorraine Quarrles.

They were gay, they were hilarious, they were roaring with laughter. For a moment Charlie was astounded; unable to understand how they ferreted out the Peters' address.

"Ah-h-h!" Duncan wagged his finger roguishly at Charlie. "Ah-h-h!"

They both slid down another cascade of laughter. Anxious and at a loss, Charlie shook hands with them quickly and presented them to Lincoln and Marion. Marion nodded, scarcely speaking. She had drawn back a step toward the fire; her little girl stood beside her, and Marion put an arm about her shoulder.

With growing annoyance at the intrusion, Charlie waited for them to explain themselves. After some concentration Duncan said:

"We came to invite you out to dinner. Lorraine and I insist that all this shishi, cagy business 'bout your address got to stop."

Charlie came closer to them, as if to force them backward down the corridor.

"Sorry, but I can't. Tell me where you'll be and I'll phone you in half an hour."

This made no impression. Lorraine sat down suddenly on the side of a chair, and focussing her eyes on Richard, cried, "Oh, what a nice little boy! Come here, little boy." Richard glanced at his mother, but did not move. With a perceptible shrug of her shoulders, Lorraine turned back to Charlie:

"Come and dine. Sure your cousins won' mine. See you so sel'om. Or solemn."

"I can't," said Charlie sharply. "You two have dinner and I'll phone you."

Her voice became suddenly unpleasant. "All right, we'll go. But I remember once when you hammered on my door at four A.M. I was enough of a good sport to give you a drink. Come on, Dunc."

Still in slow motion, with blurred, angry faces, with uncertain feet, they retired along the corridor.

"Good night," Charlie said.

"Good night!" responded Lorraine emphatically.

When he went back into the salon Marion had not moved, only now her son was standing in the circle of her other arm. Lincoln was still swinging Honoria back and forth like a pendulum from side to side.

"What an outrage!" Charlie broke out. "What an absolute outrage!"

Neither of them answered. Charlie dropped into an armchair, picked up his drink, set it down again and said:

"People I haven't seen for two years having the colossal nerve——"

He broke off. Marion had made the sound "Oh!" in one swift, furious breath, turned her body from him with a jerk and left the room.

Lincoln set down Honoria carefully.

"You children go in and start your soup," he said, and when they obeyed, he said to Charlie:

"Marion's not well and she can't stand shocks. That kind of people make her really physically sick."

"I didn't tell them to come here. They wormed your name out of somebody. They deliberately——"

"Well, it's too bad. It doesn't help matters. Excuse me a minute."

Left alone, Charlie sat tense in his chair. In the next room he could hear the children eating, talking in monosyllables, already oblivious to the scene between their elders. He heard a murmur of conversation from a farther room and then the ticking bell of a telephone receiver picked up, and in a panic he moved to the other side of the room and out of earshot.

In a minute Lincoln came back. "Look here, Charlie. I think we'd better call off dinner for tonight. Marion's in bad shape."

"Is she angry with me?"

"Sort of," he said, almost roughly. "She's not strong and——"

"You mean she's changed her mind about Honoria?"

"She's pretty bitter right now. I don't know. You phone me at the bank tomorrow."

"I wish you'd explain to her I never dreamed these people would come here. I'm just as sore as you are."

"I couldn't explain anything to her now."

Charlie got up. He took his coat and hat and started down the corridor. Then he opened the door of the dining room and said in a strange voice, "Good night, children."

Honoria rose and ran around the table to hug him.

"Good night, sweetheart," he said vaguely; and then trying to make his voice more tender, trying to conciliate something, "Good night, dear children."

V

Charlie went directly to the Ritz bar with the furious idea of finding Lorraine and Duncan, but they were not there, and he realized that in any case there was nothing he could do. He had not touched his drink at the Peters', and now he ordered a whisky-and-soda. Paul came over to say hello.

"It's a great change," he said sadly. "We do about half the business we did. So many fellows I hear about back in the States lost everything, maybe not in the first crash, but then in the second. Your friend George Hardt lost every cent, I hear. Are you back in the States?"

"No, I'm in business in Prague."

"I heard that you lost a lot in the crash."

"I did," and he added grimly, "but I lost everything I wanted in the boom."

"Selling short."

"Something like that."

Again the memory of those days swept over him like a nightmare—the people they had met travelling; then people who couldn't add a row of figures or speak a coherent sentence. The little man Helen had consented to dance with at the ship's party, who had insulted her ten feet from the table; the women and girls carried screaming with drink or drugs out of public places——

—The men who locked their wives out in the snow, because the snow of twenty-nine wasn't real snow. If you didn't want it to be snow, you just paid some money.

He went to the phone and called the Peters' apartment; Lincoln answered.

"I called up because this thing is on my mind. Has Marion said anything definite?"

"Marion's sick," Lincoln answered shortly. "I know this thing isn't altogether your fault, but I can't have her go to pieces about it. I'm afraid we'll have to let it slide for six months; I can't take the chance of working her up to this state again."

"I see."

"I'm sorry, Charlie."

He went back to his table. His whisky glass was empty, but he shook his head when Alix looked at it questioningly. There wasn't much he could do now except send Honoria some things; he would send her a lot of things tomorrow. He thought rather angrily that this was just money— he had given so many people money. . . .

"No, no more," he said to another waiter. "What do I owe you?"

He would come back some day; they couldn't make him pay forever. But he wanted his child, and nothing was much good now, beside that fact. He wasn't young any more, with a lot of nice thoughts and dreams to have by himself. He was absolutely sure Helen wouldn't have wanted him to be so alone.

Lincoln Kirstein

Lincoln Kirstein (1907–1996), best known now as the cofounder of the New York City Ballet and as a patron of representational painting, deserves to be remembered too as a poet (*Rhymes of a PFC*) and a memoirist. His diaries open up for us another pre-war Paris, in its way more potent than the familiar city of writers and collectors: the Paris of musicians and dancers, which would still be in dialogue with New York after the muses of painting had passed entirely to this side of the Atlantic.

From an Early Diary

June 3, 1933

Paris. Hôtel du Quai Voltaire, mainly to be next to Virgil Thomson's apartment, but also because Wagner stayed here during the first performances of *Tannhäuser* at the Opéra. Numerous automobiles with German license plates; refugees from Hitler. Dinner with Virgil. He says this year's chic is no longer American; it's German (exile), but will doubtless turn American again. Splits in the various ballet factions. Lifar at loose ends. Balanchine and Boris Kochno defect from René Blum's Ballet du Théâtre de Monte Carlo. Ballet must anticipate, direct, control, and continue fashion, like the big dressmakers. Key positions of two powerful women. Coco Chanel has given Balanchine and Kochno a considerable amount of money in secret (as she did Diaghilev). Misia Sert controls the appointment of *maître de ballet* at the Opéra, which Balanchine seems to have but which Lifar wants. Big mistake if Balanchine takes it. Main progressive line from Diaghilev is with Balanchine rather than Massine. Virgil spoke of possible American lyric repertory; an *opéra documentaire* on the subject of Andrew Johnson, his rise and fall. However, since this subject involves war, impossible to produce such a work here presently, since war is in everyone's thoughts yet no one wants to speak of it. I suggested a possible Yankee Clipper ballet; gave him my transcription of the manuscript of *Billy Budd* from the Widener Library; also *Benito Cereno*. He says these would overlap on Massine's *Matelots*; besides, neither has any ballerina

roles. The problem of opera is roles for a soprano; for ballet, roles for a ballerina. Preferred the notion of Pocahontas.

June 4

Passy: Musée des Archives de la Danse. Nijinsky's notations for *Faune*. At
Virgil's, Eugene Berman, a Russian painter trained as an architect, complaining non-stop; no one will let him design a ballet. Consoles himself by
knowing good painters don't take ballet seriously; only bad ones like
Bakst, Benois, and Bérard. Good ones, like Degas, had no interest in dancing; treated dancers like *natures mortes*. Diaghilev used painters as poster
artists; for fun or prestige on random occasions when he know his dancing
was less fetching than their decor. Berman would like to design big open-
air ceremonies; public funerals. Unhappy little man; hates everybody.

June 7

Rodin Museum, in search of drawings and/or sculpture of Nijinsky,
c. 1911. Masses of uncatalogued sketches. Conservateur vague; thinks
nothing exists; perhaps at the Meudon studio? Lunch with Romaine
Brooks, the portrait painter, and Mademoiselle Barney; they brought
Dolly Wilde, Oscar's niece; fascinating resemblance. Natalie Barney's lack
of interest in (contempt for) dressmaking (Chanel) and interior decoration
(Misia Sert). Are there no friendships in Paris? I asked. Miss Brooks said
Paris is a continent in itself; there are only alliances, no *amitiés*. I recalled
what Wilde said on his release from prison: "*Plus des amis, plusque des
amants.*" Dolly delighted; we did get on. Dinner with Estlin Cummings
and Marian Moorhouse; he spoke of attending rehearsals of *Les Noces*; La-
rionov took him backstage. Extreme professionalism of Russian dancers;
they would be talking to you, then dash onstage to counts of *raz, dva, tri,
chetyri*, then dash back, continuing the conversation as if there was no
stitch in the seam. Estlin is painting and writing a little every day. His own
ideas from some sort of an American ballet subject. To the Théâtre des
Champs-Élysées; premieres of *Les Ballets 1933*, sponsored by Edward
James, the young English *milord* (as Virgil says), husband of Viennese
dancer Tilly Losch. Balanchine and Bérard's *Mozartiana*; marvelous
tomato-red forecurtain; Mozart, the child prodigy at a clavichord, like a silhouette by Beardsley. Beautiful presentation of Tamara Toumanova, a
child dancer, in a nightmare funeral procession *adagio*; her four *porteurs*,
plumed like biped unicorns, carrying her hearse, which was herself alive.
Les Septs Péchés Capitaux, by two anti-Nazis, Bert Brecht and Kurt Weill.

Deliberate German horrors in the line of George Grosz, but brilliant. After it, organized but halfhearted demonstration: anti-Semitic, anti-Boche, anti-Communist. Estlin says that the Champs-Élysées Theatre has required demonstrations at ballet ever since *Le Sacre du Printemps*, but nothing has deserved it. *Les Songes*: a white cave by Derain; pretty clothes; Alice in Wonderland atmosphere. Too much Balanchine for one evening, but two out of three knockouts, not bad. Dolly Wilde said: "This is where we want to be; nowhere else; Paris is the only place; in Paris there is only Balanchine."

June 8

Virgil very much interested in Kurt Weill; he is writing a critique and has discovered his secret. He's a *Jewish* composer: his subject, remorse for the sorrowful history of the race; his theme, the Wailing Wall; general area, family life. Modigliani, Eugene Berman, Soutine, Kurt Weill, Aaron Copland: all brooders. Ernst Bloch and Marc Chagall are Jewish properties, but their attachment is essentially decorative, rhetorical, and affected. Jewish culture is always practical, concerned with action. The Jew, when he sins, apologizes; the Gentile has not only to repent but to send flowers if late for dinner. Gentile subject matter is War, Nationalism, Love. Jewish: the Home—its presence, absence, or loss. Gertrude Stein is an elementary mosaic of domestic detail. Virgil says I resist this separatist definition of Jewish art (I objected to his flowers-being-sent; I always send flowers), because I was brought up in a first generation without persecution, hence want to prove Jews are the same as everyone else. Dinner with Virgil, Maurice Grosser, and X. I was astonished at X, a miracle of health; the last time I saw him, he was on the point of death. The reason that Bébé Bérard has quarreled with him is not that his recent paintings show no Bérard influence, but that X has given up smoking: only a little coke last week. To the *vernissage* of drawings, costumes, and scenery for *Les Ballets 1933*. Dolly Wilde says Edward James is a natural son of Edward VII. He is small, delicate, elegant; no resemblance whatever to Tum-Tum.

June 9

Nine a.m. rehearsal of Pavel Tchelitchev's *Errante* at the Champs-Élysées Theatre. Sat with Bébé Bérard, who made a running commentary of preposterous fun poked at everything; finally I moved away. Maybe it is all bad; but he made me nervous. Balanchine's choreography: activated Tchelitchev drawings; no dancing, but some startling effects *à la* Loie

Fuller. Tilly Losch's ten-foot, sea-green-satin train; hard time managing it. Beautiful orchestration of Schubert's piano *Wanderer* fantasy by Charles Koechlin, a very handsome, gray-white bearded *vieux-maître*, kidding with Darius Milhaud. Stage carpenters were hammering in counterpoint to the orchestra; Koechlin to Milhaud: "It's your sort of music." Vicomtesse de Noailles with Edward James. *Le tout Paris*, which Virgil says consists not of 700 but of 70 people. Disappearance of Proust's *gratin*; no longer any real high society. Americans make the taste; Chanel's "poor girl" taste, really American. After the rehearsal, Esther Strachey took me to Mademoiselle Barney's, 20 rue Jacob. *L'Amazone* of Remy de Gourmont's letters, in a (Chanel?) white *tailleur*, showed me her house, once owned by Adrienne Lecouvreur. In the garden, an eighteenth-century *Temple de l'Amitié*; mottoes from La Rochefoucald embroidered on long white transparent linen curtains; she pointed out one: "Self-love is the greatest flatterer of all," which made me uncomfortable the rest of the afternoon. Conversation about Gloria Swanson in *Queen Kelly*, which has not been seen in the U.S. Mademoiselle Barney said Marian Moorhouse's clothes (by whom?) were like "the guts of a rainbow," and that the detestable Baron de Haussmann had planned a boulevard through her garden, but luckily died before it was done. Dinner with Estlin Cummings and Marian; repeated the guts-of-the-rainbow. Estlin says Miss B. does not like him because he is coarse and a man; story of his arrest for being a public nuisance, peeing (carefully) through the spokes of a fiacre. The judge: "*Monsieur, quand vous pissez sur Paris, vous pissez sur la France.*" To the Châtelet: Monte Carlo ballet; Massine's *Les Présages*, *Beau Danube*, *Matelots*. Entire delegation from rival *Ballets 1933*—James, Kochno, Tilly Losch, Bérard—leave ostentatiously after *Présages*. Dickie Ames took us all to Fouquet's, where he always went after the Diaghilev ballets; drank to the immortal memory. Dickie says there should be a national ballet theatre, independent of the Opéra; only way France can ever gain a proper company. Cummings, in the intermission after *Matelots*, started sketches in his program for an *Uncle Tom's Cabin* ballet. (Virgil says under no circumstances would he work with Cummings; his subject matter is boring, romantic, old-fashioned, always the same: the Artist, Love, Death; Cumming's ideal: Edmund Spenser, not Shakespeare.) Dickie Ames says everyone needs Diaghilev; there's no consolidating force around the considerable energy; split in tradition between Massine and Balanchine: Monte Carlo, reactionary; *Ballets 1933*, progressive; neither strong enough.

Drove home around three; horse protesting most of the way. Cold. Put my tuxedo coat around Dolly Wilde; *cocher* put his horse blanket around me.

June 10

With Dolly Wilde to Mademoiselle Barney's. Delightful young Chinese in colonel's dress uniform with decorations; six years fighting the Japanese; a girl! We shared admiration for Mei-lan Fang. At tea, sat next to Professor Mardrus, translator of the complete *Arabian Nights*. Said he had given Diaghilev the idea for *Schéhérazade* (!?!). Mardrus told the colonel his one great weakness as a scholar: he could not speak Chinese or Japanese, but only the seven (?) Semitic languages; he wore sort of an Arab caftan (?), horn-rimmed spectacles. To the Champs-Élysées Theatre; *Les Sept Péchés Capitaux*, with many details altered; Balanchine has left out the Mammy; considerably speeded up. No demonstration. *Errante*, stupendous climax with the falling chiffon cloud; Virgil says this is the private life of Pavel Tchelitchev: love, revolution, tempestuous love affairs, etc. Tchelitchev, looking like an angry, intelligent horse; with Edith Sitwell swathed in white chiffon, with a white-and-gold mobcap and huge gold plaque. She has just written a book on the English eccentrics; autobiography? With Dolly Wilde to elaborately simple new bar opened by Madame de Something-or-other, who has lost all her money but is brave and smart. Marvelously made-up, like a tiger lady in a discreet circus tamer evening gown (*not* Chanel). Victor Cunard came from correcting proof of Harold Nicolson's *Peacemaking*. Colonel Lawrence at Versailles; no one knew to whom he belonged, Faisal or Britain. A very old, sweet gentleman, seeing how fascinated I was with Madame de Something, told me in vast detail about the grand cocottes of *la belle époque*, and Emilienne d'Alençon, Chanel's first inspiration, as Liane de Pougy was Mademoiselle Barney's. I asked him about the story of Edward James and Edward VII; he said, "*Oh, bien possible*," without conviction. James, Tilly Losch, Tchelitchev, Edith Sitwell came in; great applause.

June 11

Interrupted Virgil, overpracticing for his concert. He asked how my education was proceeding; said if I spoke French better I'd get further. (I had not known that a *terrine* was on the menu at Michaud's.) With Peter and Nancy Quennel to Versailles; he wanted to know all about Edmund Wilson. Tried to describe the difference between literary inheritance of Harvard and Princeton; failed. Peter said in the early draft of Harold

Nicolson's *Peacemaking*, by some strange fluke, the name of Woodrow Wilson never appeared once, although everyone was thinking of nobody else. To a private concert at the home of Henry Cliquet-Pleyel; Virgil said it was like the annual recital of his music teacher in Kansas City. Paul Poiret, the ancient *couturier*, dithering with age and ague, a parrot made up as Henry VIII; recited three fables of La Fontaine, a famous parlor trick. During the music, he slept and shook. Argument with Maurice Grosser; I complained about the sensibility of Tchelitchev and Bérard; I am interested in subject matter, not sensibility. He said I was talking about preference, not taste. Taste was a serious business *dans tous les sens*, particularly in Paris. There was virtue in sensing and directing the mode, not alone in fashion, but in ideas and manners; the French had provided taste for the rest of the world for three centuries. Virgil said this was now over, and the next taste would be provided by America, having learned the trick in France. Maurice says I am simply put off Paris because I have never been part of it, and its social dimensions are beyond me. They are cutting great hunks out of their Gertrude Stein opera, Maurice imposing some sort of rationale on its action.

June 13
With Virgil and Philip Johnson, Deux Magots for lunch. Phil had just come from seeing Le Corbusier's new Swiss Pavilion at the Cité Universitaire; thinks Corbu has gone mad; too great fantasy, revealing he's now bored with real architecture. The real architecture is German, or Dutch (?). What mainly excited him was the graffiti left by the workers. Dinner with Alfred Barr, who showed incredible documents of what the Nazis have done to the arts; he wants to arrange a show of German Romantic painting (Caspar David Friedrich, Kaulbach, etc.) at the Museum of Modern Art, alongside publication of Hitler's taste—without comment.

June 14
Lunch with John Peale Bishop; he spoke of his novel, the sense of sin in America (his South); he said vice is appetite without desire. *What Maisie Knew* is a failure, because no child of that age could have conceivably known so much. Difficulties of narrative in the first person over the long haul. E. M. Forster says the novelist's great problem is the position of the narrator. Called for Katherine Anne Porter, 166 Boulevard Montparnasse; big seventh-floor apartment overlooking serene, green convent garden, which might have been miles in the country. She once wrote the libretto

of a ballet for Anna Pavlova, *Xochimilco*, with decor by the Mexican painter Adolfo Best-Maugard. She loved the idea for a New England doomsday ballet, a Calvinist hell. Spoke a long time on why it was American artists can't endure being, at one and the same time, men *and* women: Whitman, Melville, Henry James; most recently Hart Crane. She was with Crane his last six months in Mexico; horror; will never tell what happened to a living soul; years from now might compose it as a tragic history. She gave me the manuscript of her Cotton Mather book, of which I will publish at least the first chapter in *Hound & Horn*. To the Opéra: Lifar in *Spectre de la Rose*; perfect archaeological reconstruction of its physical frame; perfunctory performance. If I had not known something of what it had been would not have been interested. As Romola says: unrepeatable, jumps or no jumps.

June 15

At lunch, Janet Flanner (Genêt of *The New Yorker*) told me a lot of ballet background. La Comtesse de Polignac (Winaretta Sewing Machine Singer) furious because Igor Markevitch's ballet was refused by the Monte Carlo; gave a huge evening party with 500 invitations the night of Massine's opening, so that *le tout Paris* would be in absence and spoil it. Ballet activity is greater this year than at any time since Diaghilev's death, but there is no restraining or controlling influence; the dancers (choreographers?) are all too social and uppity; Diaghilev would have permitted none of this nonsense. I am undetermined as to whether to go off to Holland and help Romola finish the biography or stay here and somehow insert myself into a situation with Kochno-Balanchine, but there's small chance of even approaching them.

June 16

Lunch with Monroe Wheeler, Laurents, Avenue Gabriel. He gave me all the information I most wanted and needed, and tested my own aims. What did I actually want? What could I actually do? How much money did I actually have or could I raise? Kochno is not powerful enough to last as an impresario. Most of the control in the ballet world is bitten by fashion; or society, which is worse, since it has no real economic base. Everything cries out for Diaghilev to knock heads together. The true function of the impresario. Could not tell whether he was suggesting I try for this: "Self-love is the greatest flatterer of all." Self-doubt is the worst demon. What will happen in Paris is what always happens; either commercial exploitation or inconsequential chic; a dilution of dressmaking. With Monroe to the Galerie Pierre Colle; official salon of Sur-Realism. Enormous stuffed pink cotton cocks; a chair leaking into a glass of beer. To Virgil's. Conversation with Genia Berman. Sur-Realism: simply the most recent academy, with André Breton as its pope. A formulated but tedious development from the bankruptcy of Cubism. Picasso, among the older men; Tchelitchev, himself, Bérard among the younger ones, will have nothing to do with Sur-Realism; Salvador Dalí—*Avida Dollars*. At Mademoiselle Barney's collided with Professor Mardrus. I said I had been reading his excellent translation of the Koran. Indeed; why had I taken such trouble? Because I am interested. Indeed; what faith had I? *Israélite*. Oh, well then, of course; the Koran is the last book written by a Jewish prophet; nothing in it to which the rabbinate might object or deny. The Châtelet; beautiful *Sylphides*, Baronova, Riabouchinska; marvelous company. Sandy Calder and Isamu Noguchi in the interval. Filled with rage against both; Sandy is to do a ballet with Massine but made great fun of his dancing. Isamu said the whole thing was nothing but an *édition de luxe*, of no interest as stage decoration. Neither looked at the dancing. Ballet is hardly a serious thing; without permanence, an amusement. Agnes de Mille, fresh from her success in London.

June 17

Virgil, on French statuary; haste in documenting their past. Monuments at every *carrefour*; street names—a dictionary of national biography, on tap for constant reference; filed for use as the constant basis and reminder of a cohesive national culture. Virgil took me to Bébé Bérard's; lying enormous and rumpled on a chaise-longue with a horse blanket over him; unshaven, grubby, but comfy and nice. No chi-chi. Professionalism; room, a mess; obviously the confusion of work. Jasinky's beautiful costume in *Mozartiana*, taken from a photo of Serge Legat in a copy of the *Annual* of the Imperial Theatres which Diaghilev had given Kochno, who is furious because Bérard mucked up the page with paint. Showed them my Nijinsky photos from Romola. She now can't, or won't, come to Paris. I should meet her in Holland. *Ballets 1933* go to London for two weeks. Asked about Balanchine. Bérard says he is entirely mysterious, invisible offstage, unhealthy—TB; nobody seems to know him. He is held captive by a demon called Dimitriev, an ex-croupier, ex-singer, ex-soldier, most sinister type. Balanchine is in love with Tamara Toumanova, whose mother says he is old enough to be her father (at twenty-nine?). He never goes out or accepts invitations; there is simply no point in my trying to see him. He is slightly mad; really cares nothing for the ballet; is only interested in playing the piano; keeps taking music lessons from some old Russian lady, a pupil of Siloti and Rimsky; Virgil would know; he didn't. Dinner with Marian and Estlin Cummings. He cursed the Sur-Realists. Contrivance is the reverse of fantasy; "comes out of the tube, lies flat on the brush." "*Sur mesure et par commande.*" Systematic hysteria; Rimbaud gave all that crap up before he came of age. Fifteenth (?) wedding anniversary of the John Peale Bishops; much toast-drinking to Jeffersonian democracy. One nice old gentleman, a M. Gervais (?), lost an arm at Verdun; now on the General Staff, sure of imminent war with Germany; if not next year, the year after. He was quite serious; knew all of Robert E. Lee's moves into Pennsylvania before Gettysburg; learned at École Militaire; delighted John Bishop. Louis Bromfield with elaborate false nose and attached mustaches. John Bishop says Cummings holds his head like André Chenier on the guillotine.

Gertrude Stein

With Gertrude Stein (1874–1946) we come upon the resistant, the maddening, the inexplicable, and the necessary. The grande dame of American letters in Paris for more than thirty years, she oversaw with her companion Alice Toklas a salon on the rue de Fleurus that served as the hearth of the American occupation of Paris, particularly in the 1920s. She came to the city in 1903, in the wake of her brother Leo. "Paris was the place," she said, "that suited us who were to create the twentieth century art and literature." No one played a more vivid role in patronizing (if, at times, perhaps, in both senses) the masters of the new French painting. Both Picasso and Matisse benefited greatly from the presence of the Steins, and few players have ever placed their bets more decisively on the right horses. Her faux-naïf manner, though it surely played an essential role in simplifying the writing of Hemingway, among others, can sometimes in its longer stretches seem wearingly disingenuous, and in its longest stretches merely wearying. *The Autobiography of Alice B. Toklas* (1933) is a wonderful exception, however, as is her relatively late book *Paris France* (1940), which is filled with a heartfelt sense and more obvious shrewdness than this shrewd woman always allowed herself to show. More than any other writer, her work testifies to the force of the vision in which, as she wrote, employing a lovely Americanism: "America is my country, and Paris is my hometown."

———

from

The Autobiography of Alice B. Toklas

Gertrude Stein and I about ten days later went to Montmartre, I for the first time. I have never ceased to love it. We go there every now and then and I always have the same tender expectant feeling that I had then. It is a place where you were always standing and sometimes waiting, not for anything to happen, but just standing. The inhabitants of Montmartre did not sit much, they mostly stood which was just as well as the chairs, the dining rooms chairs of France, did not tempt one to sit. So I went to Montmartre and I began my apprenticeship of standing. We first

374

went to see Picasso and then we went to see Fernande. Picasso now never likes to go to Montmartre, he does not like to think about it much less talk about it. Even to Gertrude Stein he is hesitant about talking of it, there were things that at that time cut deeply into his spanish pride and the end of his Montmartre life was bitterness and disillusion, and there is nothing more bitter than spanish disillusion.

But at this time he was in and of Montmartre and lived in the rue Ravignan.

We went to the Odéon and there got into an omnibus, that is we mounted on top of an omnibus, the nice old horse-pulled omnibuses that went pretty quickly and steadily across Paris and up the hill to the place Blanche. There we got out and climbed a steep street lined with shops with things to eat, the rue Lepic, and then turning we went around a cor-ner and climbed even more steeply in fact almost straight up and came to the rue Ravignan, now place Emile-Goudeau but otherwise unchanged, with its steps leading up to the little flat square with its few but tender little trees, a man carpentering in the corner of it, the last time I was there not very long ago there was still a man carpentering in a corner of it, and a little café just before you went up the steps where they all used to eat, it is still there, and to the left the low wooden building of studios that is still there.

We went up the couple of steps and through the open door passing on our left the studio in which later Juan Gris was to live out his martyrdom but where then lived a certain Vailliant, a nondescript painter who was to lend his studio as a ladies dressing room at the famous banquet for Rousseau, and then we passed a steep flight of steps leading down where Max Jacob had a studio a little later, and we passed another steep little stairway which led to the studio where not long before a young fellow had committed suicide, Picasso painted one of the most wonderful of his early pictures of the friends gathered round the coffin, we passed all this to a larger door where Gertrude Stein knocked and Picasso opened the door and we went in.

He was dressed in what the french call the singe or monkey costume, overalls made of blue jean or brown, I think his was blue and it is a called a singe or monkey because being all of one piece with a belt, if the belt is not fastened, and it very often is not, it hangs down behind and so makes a monkey. His eyes were more wonderful than even I remembered, so full and so brown, and his hands so dark and delicate and alert. We went further in. There was a couch in one corner, a very small stove that did for cooking and heating in the other corner, some chairs, the large broken one Gertrude Stein sat in when she was painted and a general smell of dog and paint and there was a big dog there and Picasso moved her about from one place to another exactly as if the dog had been a large piece of furniture. He asked us to sit down but as all the chairs were full we all stood up and stood until we left. It was my first experience of standing but afterwards I found that they all stood that way for hours. Against the wall was an enormous picture, a strange picture of light and dark colours, that is all I can say, of a group, an enormous group and next to it another in a sort of a red brown, of three women, square and posturing, all of it rather frightening. Picasso and Gertrude Stein stood together talking. I stood back and looked. I cannot say I realised anything but I felt that there was something painful and beautiful there and oppressive but imprisoned. I heard Gertrude Stein say, and mine. Picasso thereupon brought out a smaller picture, a rather unfinished thing that could not finish, very pale almost white, two figures, they were all there but very unfinished and not finishable. Picasso said, but he will never accept it. Yes, I know, answered Gertrude Stein. But just the same it is the only one in which it is all there. Yes, I know, he replied and they fell silent. After that they continued a low toned conversation and then Miss Stein said, well we have to go, we are going to have tea with Fernande. Yes, I know, replied Picasso. How often do you see her, she said, he got very red and looked sheepish. I have never been there, he said resentfully. She chuckled, well anyway we are going there, she said, and Miss Toklas is going to have lessons in french. Ah the Miss Toklas, he said, with small feet like a spanish woman and earrings like a gypsy and a father who is king of Poland like the Poniatowskis, of course she will take lessons. We all laughed and went to the door. There stood a very beautiful man, oh Agero, said Picasso, you know the ladies. He looks like a Greco, I said in english. Picasso caught the name, a false Greco, he said. Oh I forgot to give you these, said Gertrude Stein handing Picasso a package of newspapers, they will console you. He opened them up, they were the Sunday supplement of american papers, they were the Katzenjammer kids. Oh oui, Oh oui, he said, his face full of satisfaction, merci thanks Gertrude, and we left.

We left then and continued to climb higher up the hill. What did you think of what you saw, asked Miss Stein. Well I did see something. Sure you did, she said, but did you see what it had to do with those two pictures you sat in front of so long at the vernissage. Only that Picassos were rather awful and the others were not. Sure, she said, as Pablo once remarked, when you make a thing, it is so complicated making it that it is bound to be ugly, but those that do it after you they don't have to worry about making it and they can make it pretty, and so everybody can like it when the others make it.

We went on and turned down a little street and there was another little house and we asked for Mademoiselle Bellevallée and we were sent into a little corridor and we knocked and went into a moderate sized room in which was a very large bed and a piano and a little tea table and Fernande and two others.

One of them was Alice Princet. She was rather a madonna like creature, with large lovely eyes and charming hair. Fernande afterwards explained that she was the daughter of a workingman and had the brutal thumbs that of course were a characteristic of workingmen. She had been, so Fernande explained, for seven years with Princet who was in the government employ and she had been faithful to him in the fashion of Montmartre, that is to say she had stuck to him through sickness and health but she had amused herself by the way. Now they were to be married. Princet had become the head of his small department in the government service and it would be necessary for him to invite other heads of departments to his house and so of course he must regularise the relation. They were actually married a few months afterward and it was apropos of this marriage that Max Jacob made his famous remark, it is wonderful to long for a woman for seven years and to possess her at last. Picasso made the more practical one, why should they marry simply in order to divorce. This was a prophecy.

No sooner were they married than Alice Princet met Derain and Derain met her. It was what the french call un coup de foudre, or love at first sight. They went quite mad about each other. Princet tried to bear it but they were married now and it was different. Beside he was angry for the first time in his life and in his anger he tore up Alice's first fur coat which she had gotten for the wedding. That settled the matter, and within six months after the marriage Alice left Princet never to return. She and Derain went off together and they have never separated since. I always liked Alice Derain. She had a certain wild quality that perhaps had to do with her brutal thumbs and was curiously in accord with her madonna face.

The other woman was Germaine Pichot, entirely a different type. She was quiet and serious and spanish, she had the square shoulders and the unseeing fixed eyes of a spanish woman. She was very gentle. She was married to a spanish painter Pichot, who was rather a wonderful creature, he was long and thin like one of those primitive Christs in spanish churches and when he did a spanish dance which he did later at the famous banquet to Rousseau, he was awe inspiringly religious.

Germaine, so Fernande said, was the heroine of many a strange story, she had once taken a young man to the hospital, he had been injured in a fracas at a music hall and all his crowd had deserted him. Germaine quite naturally stood by and saw him through. She had many sisters, she and all of them had been born and bred in Montmartre and they were all of different fathers and married to different nationalities, even to turks and armenians. Germaine, much later, was very ill for years and she always had around her a devoted coterie. They used to carry her in her armchair to the nearest cinema and they, and she in the armchair, saw the performance through. They did this regularly once a week. I imagine they are still doing it.

The conversation around the tea table of Fernande was not lively, nobody had anything to say. It was a pleasure to meet, it was even an honour, but that was about all. Fernande complained a little that her charwoman had not adequately dusted and rinsed the tea things, and also that buying a bed and a piano on the instalment plan had elements of unpleasantness. Otherwise we really none of us had much to say.

------

from

Paris France

Alice Toklas said, my grandmother's cousin's wife told me that her daughter had married the son of the engineer who had built the Eiffel Tower and his name was not Eiffel.

When were having a book printed in France we complained about the bad alignment. Ah they explained that is because they use machines now, machines are bound to be inaccurate, they have not the intelligence of human beings, naturally the human mind corrects the faults of the hand but a machine of course there are errors. The reason why all of us naturally began to live in France is because France has scientific methods, machines and electricity, but does not really believe that these things have anything to do with the real business of living. Life is tradition and human nature.

And so in the beginning of the twentieth century when a new way had to be found naturally they needed France.

Really not, french people really do not believe that anything is important except daily living and the ground that gives it to them and defending themselves from the enemy. Government has no importance except insofar as it does that.

I remember so well it was during the 1914 war and they were all french and they were talking about women voting and one of the women who was listening said, oh dear I have to stand in line for so many things coal and sugar and candles and meat and now to vote, oh dear.

After all it does not make any difference and they know it does not make any difference.

When I was first in Paris and for many years I had a servant, we were very good friends her name was Hélène. One day quite accidentally, I do not know how it happened because I was not at all interested, I said to her, Hélène what political party does your husband belong to. She always told me everything even the most intimate troubles with her family and her husband but when I said that, what party does your husband belong to, her face grew rigid. She did not answer. What is the matter with you Hélène I said, is it a secret. No Mademoiselle she answered it is not a secret but one does not tell it. One does not tell the political party one belongs to. Even I have a political party but I do not tell it.

There are always so many foreigners everywhere but particularly in France.

One day Gerald Berners and I were walking and he suggested that it would make a nice book to put in it all the aphorisms which were not true.

We thought of a great many and among them, familiarity breeds contempt and no man is a hero to his valet. We concluded that in fully ninety per cent of the cases it was the other way.

Familiarity does not breed contempt. On the contrary the more familiar it is the more rare and beautiful it is. Take the quarter in which one lives, it is lovely, it is a place rare and beautiful and to leave it is awful.

I remember once hearing a conversation on the street in Paris and it ended up, and so there it was that there was nothing for them to do, they had to leave the quarter. There it was, there was nothing else to do they had to leave the most wonderful place in the world, wonderful because it was where they had always lived.

Paris quarters were like that, we all had our quarters, to be sure when later we left them and went back to them they did look dreary, not at all like the lovely quarter in which we are living now. So familiarity did not breed contempt.

And then not being a hero to one's valet. Is there anybody in the world even yourself who is as pleased with your publicity as your servant certainly your french servant is pleased there is no doubt about that, past present and future servants all of them are pleased with that.

So then which quarters of Paris were important and when.

From 1900 to 1930, Paris did change a lot. They always told me that America changed but it really did not change as much as Paris did in those years that is the Paris that one can see, but then there is no remembering what it looked like before and even no remembering what it looks like now.

We none of us lived in old parts of Paris then. We lived in the rue de Fleurus just a hundred year old quarter, a great many of us lived around there and on the boulevard Raspail which was not even cut through then and when it was cut through all the rats and animals came underneath our house and we had to have one of the vermin catchers of Paris come and clean us out, I wonder if they exist any more now, they have disappeared along with the horses and enormous wagons that used to clean out the sewers under the houses that were not in the new sewerage system, now even the oldest houses are in the new system. It is nice in France they adapt themselves to everything slowly they change completely but all the time they know that they are as they were.

Belley the little country town now even all summer long eats grape fruits, they have concluded that grape fruits are a necessary luxury.

Our old servant Hélène who was with us before the war for many years, learned from us that children should be raised differently and more hygienically and raise it in that way she did but all the same one day I heard her talking to her six year old little boy and saying you are a good little boy, yes mother he said, and you love your mother very much, yes mother he said, and you will grow up loving your mother she said, yes mother he said and then she said you will be grown up and you will leave me for a woman will you not, yes mother he said.

I always remember too when the Titanic went down and everybody was so moved at the heroism and the saving of the women and children, I do not see anything sensible in that, said Hélène, what use are women and children alone in the world, what kind of life can they lead, it would have been lots more sensible, said Hélène, if they had drawn lots and saved a certain number of complete families much more sensible, said Hélène.

And that is what made Paris and France the natural background of the art and literature of the twentieth century. Their tradition kept them from changing and yet they naturally saw things as they were, and accepted life as it is, and mixed things up without any reason at the same time. Foreigners were not romantic to them, they were just facts, nothing was sentimental they were just there, and strangely enough it did not make them make the art and literature of the twentieth century but it made them be the inevitable background for it.

So from 1900 to 1930 those of us who lived in Paris did not live in picturesque quarters even those who lived in Montmartre like Picasso and Bracque did not live in old houses, they lived in fifty year old houses at most and now we all live in the ancient quarter near the river, now that the twentieth century is decided and has its character we all tend to want to live in seventeenth century houses, not barracks of ateliers as we did then. The seventeenth century houses are just as cheap as our barracks of ateliers were then but now we need the picturesque the splendid we need the air and space you only get in old quarters. It was Picasso who said the other day when they were talking about tearing down the insalubrious parts of Paris but it is only in the insalubrious quarters that there is sun and air and space, and it is true, and we are all living there the beginners and the middle ones and the older ones and the old ones we all live in old houses in ramshackle quarters. Well all this is natural enough.

Familiarity does not breed contempt, anything one does every day is important and imposing and anywhere one lives is interesting and beautiful. And that is all as it should be.

So it begins to be reasonable that the twentieth century whose mechanics, whose crimes, whose standardisation began in America, needed the background of Paris, the place where tradition was so firm that they could look modern without being different, and where their acceptance of reality is so great that they could let any one have the emotion of unreality.

Then there is their feeling about foreigners that helps a lot.

After all to the french the difference between being a foreigner and being an inhabitant is not very serious. There are so many foreigners and all who are real to them are those that inhabit Paris and France. In that they are different from other people. Other people find foreigners more real to them when they are in their own country but to the french foreigners are only real to them when they are in France. Naturally they come to France. What is more natural for them to do than that.

I remember an old servant invented a nice name for foreigners, they were Americans they existed because she was our servant and we were there, and then there was something she called a creole ecossais, we never did find out where that came from.

Of course they all came to France a great many to paint pictures and naturally they could not do that at home, or write they could not do that at home either, they could be dentists at home she knew all about that even before the war, Americans were a practical people and dentistry was practical. To be sure certainly, she was the most practical, because when her little boy was ill, of course she was awfully unhappy because it was her little boy but then also it was all to do over again because she did have to have one child, any french person has to have one child, and now after two years it was all to do again money and everything. And still why not of course why not.

So all this simple clarity in respect to seeing life as it is, the animal and social life in human beings as it is, the money value of human and social and animal life as it is, without brutality or without simplicity, what is it to-day a french woman said to me about an American writer, it is false without being artificial.

It did not take the twentieth century to make them say that as it has taken the twentieth century to make other people say that.

Foreigners belong in France because they have always been here and did what they had to do there and remained foreigners there. Foreigners should be foreigners and it is nice that foreigners are foreigners and that they inevitably are in Paris and in France.

They are beginning now at last, cinemas and the world war have slowly made them realise, what nationality the foreigners are. In a little hotel where we stayed some time they spoke of us as English, no we said no we are Americans, at last one of them a little annoyed at our persistance said but it is all the same. Yes I answered like the french and Italians all the same. Well before the war they could not have said that nor felt the unpleasantness of the answer. Then we had a Finnish maid here in the country, and once she came in all beaming, it is wonderful, she said, the milk woman knows Finland, she knows where Finland is, she knows all about Finland, why, said the Finnish maid, I have known very educated people who did not know where Finland was but she knew. Well did she know. No but she did have the ancient tradition of french politeness and that was that. They do, of course.

But really what they do do is to respect art and letters, if you are a writer you have privileges, if you are a painter you have privileges and it is pleasant having those privileges. I always remember coming in from the country to my garage where I usually kept my car and the garage was more than full, it was the moment of the automobile salon, but said I what can I do, well said the man in charge I'll see and then he came back and said in a low voice, there is a corner and in this corner I have put the car of Monsieur the academician and next to it I will put yours the others can stay outside and it is quite true even in a garage an academician and a woman of letters takes precedence even of millionaires or politicians, they do, it is quite incredible but they do, the police treat artists and writers respectfully too, well that too is intelligent on the part of France and unsentimental, because after all the way everything is remembered is by the writers and painters of the period, nobody really lives who has not been well written about and in realising that the french show their usual sense of reality and a belief in a sense of reality is the twentieth century, people may not have it but they do believe in it.

They are funny even now they are funny, all the peasants of the village, well not all but a number of them were eating their bread and wine, they do quite nicely now have jam on their bread, nice jam made of a mixture of apricots and apples, just how they happen at the same time I do not quite know, yes perhaps late apricots and early apples, it is very good.

So we were talking and they said to me, now tell me, why does the french chamber vote itself two more years of existence, and we, well of course we never do have anything to say but why do they, tell us. Well I said why not, you know it they know it, and beside if they are there why should not they stay there. Well said they laughing let's be like Spain. Let's have a civil war. Well said I what is the use, after all, after all their shooting each other up they are going to have their king again any way the king's son. Then for a change said they, why do not we have the king's nephew.

That is the way they feel about it, the only thing that is important is the daily life, and so the gangsters, so the twentieth century had really nothing to teach the french countryman therefore it was the proper background for the art and literature of the twentieth century.

The impressionists.

The twentieth century did not invent but it made a great fuss about series production, series production really began in the nineteenth century, that is natural enough, machines are bound to make series production.

So although there was more fuss made about machines and series production in the twentieth century than in the nineteenth of course it was a nineteenth century thing.

The impressionists and they were nineteenth century had as their aspiration and their ideal one painting a day, really two paintings a day, the morning painting and the afternoon painting actually it might have been the early morning and the early afternoon and the late afternoon. But after all there is a limit to the human hand after all painting is hand painting so actually even at their most excited moment they rarely did more than two more frequently one, and very often not one a day, most generally not one a day. They had the dream of a series production but as Monsieur Darantiere said about printing after all they had not the faults or the qualities of machines.

So Paris was the natural background for the twentieth century, America knew it too well, knew the twentieth century too well to create it, for America there was a glamour in the twentieth century that made it not be material for creative activity. England was consciously refusing the twentieth century, knowing full well that they had gloriously created the nineteenth century and perhaps the twentieth century was going to be too many for them, so they were quite self consciously denying the twentieth century but France was not worrying about it, what is was and what was is, was their point of view of which they were not very conscious, they were too occupied with their daily life to worry about it, beside the last half of the nineteenth century had really not interested them very much, not since the end of the romantic movement, they had worked hard, they always worked hard, but the last half of the nineteenth century had really not interested them very much. As the peasants always say every year comes to an end, and they like it when the bad weather does not keep them from working, they like to work, it is a pastime for them work is, and so although the last half of the nineteenth century did not interest them they did work. And now the twentieth century had come and it might be more interesting, if it was to be really interesting of course they would not work quite so much, being interested does sometimes stop one from working, work might then be even somewhat disturbing and distracting. So the twentieth century had come it began with 1901.

Henry Miller

Henry Miller (1891–1980) is a hinge figure in the history of Americans in Paris. He is popularly imagined as a kind of New Model Henry, marking the final transformation of the caricatured American in Paris from Henry James's timorous aesthete hovering on the fringe into the loutish bohemian, grabbing at whatever goes by. Yet Miller was in his way a kind of Jamesian too. "Just live!" was James's great exhortation, after all, and nobody just lived, or wrote with more dogged reverence for life-as-it-actually-is, than Miller. He came to Paris late for a writer of his generation, in 1930, the moment when Fitzgerald's generation were already saying a sad good-bye at the Ritz bar, and he stayed right through the worst decade of French history, a witness to the Great Depression and the breakdown of the Third Republic that led eventually to the black hole of the Occupation. Relatively little of this crisis appears in his work, however. Instead, making his life out on the poorer fringes of the city, a kind of Gauguin in reverse, he immersed himself in what he saw as the timeless culture of working-class Paris, sexually open and driven. (Like Gauguin in Tahiti, he was, apart from sexual adventures, also desperately lonely and isolated, and saw that as a subject.) Miller's instinct was not false; the world he describes, in a way, is more permanently Parisian, more familiar from the French realist masters Zola and Maupassant, than the hothouse world of Stein and even Hemingway. Miller's Paris seems, and is meant to be, the antithesis of everything Jamesian, a world of appetites filled and animal nature asserted as such. There is something inspired about his definition of Paris as "China," not the familiar capital but simply a world apart for an American escaping from America; something still thrilling in his willingness to confront the shit of Paris for what it was; and something permanent in his juxtaposition of coercive American niceness (all those terrible smiles!) with the hard French faces that he imagined bore the marks of history.

Walking Up and Down in China

Now I am never alone.
At the very worst I am with God!

In Paris, out of Paris, leaving Paris or coming back to Paris, it's always Paris and Paris is France and France is China. All that which is incomprehensible to me runs like a great wall over the hills and valleys through which I wander. Within this great wall I can live out my Chinese life in peace and security.

I am not a traveler, not an adventurer. Things happened to me in my search for a way out. Up till now I had been working away in a blind tunnel, burrowing in the bowels of the earth for light and water. I could not believe, being a man of the American continent, that there was a place on earth where a man could be himself. By force of circumstances I became a Chinaman—a Chinaman in my own country! I took to the opium of dream in order to face the hideousness of a life in which I had no part. As quietly and naturally as a twig falling into the Mississippi I dropped out of the stream of American life. Everything that happened to me I remember, but I have no desire to recover the past, neither have I any longings or regrets. I am like a man who awakes from a long sleep to find that he is dreaming. A pre-natal condition—the born man living unborn, the unborn man dying born.

Born and reborn over and over. Born while walking the streets, born while sitting in a café, born while lying over a whore. Born and reborn again and again. A fast pace and the penalty for it is not death simply, but repeated deaths. Hardly am I in heaven, for example, when the gates swing open and under my feet I find cobblestones. *How did I learn to walk so soon? With whose feet am I walking?* Now I am walking to the grave, marching to my own funeral. I hear the clink of the spade, the rain of sods. My eyes are scarcely closed, I have barely time to smell the flowers in which they've smothered me, when *bango!* I've lived out another immortality. Coming back and forth to earth this way puts me on the alert. I've got to keep my body in trim for the worms. Got to keep my soul intact for God.

Afternoons, sitting at La Fourche, I ask myself calmly: "Where do we go from here?" By nightfall I may have traveled to the moon and back. Here at the crossroads I sit and dream back through all my separate and immortal egos. I weep in my beer. Nights, walking back to Clichy, it's the same feeling. Whenever I come to La Fourche I see endless roads radiating from my feet and out of my own shoes there step forth the countless egos which inhabit my world of being. Arm in arm I accompany them over the paths which once I trod alone: what I call the grand obsessional walks of my life and death. I talk to these self-made companions much as I would talk to myself had I been so unfortunate as to live and die only once and thus be forever alone. *Now I am never alone. At the very worst I am with God!*

There is something about the little stretch from the Place Clichy to La Fourche which causes all the grand obsessional walks to bloom at once. It's like moving from one solstice to another. Supposing I have just left the Café Wepler and that I have a book under my arm, a book on Style and Will. Perhaps when I was reading this book I didn't comprehend more than a phrase or two. Perhaps I was reading the same page all evening. Perhaps I wasn't at the Café Wepler at all, but hearing the music I left my body and flew away. *And where am I then?* Why, I am out for an obsessional walk, a short walk of fifty years or so accomplished in the turning of a page.

It's when I'm leaving the Café Wepler that I hear a strange, swishing noise. No need to look behind—I know it's my body rushing to join me. It's at this moment usually that the shit-pumps are lined up along the Avenue. The hoses are stretched across the sidewalk like huge groaning worms. The fat worms are sucking the shit out of the cesspools. It's this that gives me the proper spiritual gusto to look at myself in profile. I see myself bending over the book in the café; I see the whore alongside me reading over my shoulder; I feel her breath on my neck. She waits for me to raise my eyes, perhaps to light the cigarette which she holds in her hand. She is going to ask me what I am doing here alone and am I not bored. The book is on Style and Will and I have brought it to the café to read because it's a luxury to read in a noisy café—and also a protection against disease. The music too is good in a noisy café—it augments the sense of solitude, of loneliness. I see the upper lip of the whore trembling over my shoulder. Just a triangular patch of lip, smooth and silky. It trembles on the high notes, poised like a chamois above a ravine. And now I am running the gauntlet, I and myself firmly glued together. The little stretch from the Place Clichy to La Fourche. From the blind alleys that line the little stretch thick clusters of whores leap out, like bats blinded by the light. They get in my hair, my ears, my eyes. They cling with bloodsucking paws. All night long they are festering in the alleyways; they have the smell of plants after a heavy rain. They make little plantlike sounds, imbecilic cries of endearment which make the flesh creep. They swarm over me like lice, lice with long plantlike tendrils which sponge the sweat of my pores. The whores, the music, the crowds, the walls, the light on the walls, the shit and the shit-pumps working valorously, all this forms a nebula which condenses into a cool, waking sweat.

Every night, as I head toward La Fourche, I run the gauntlet. Every night I'm scalped and tomahawked. If it were not so I would miss it. I come home and shake the lice out of my clothes, wash the blood from my body. I go to bed and snore loudly. *Just the right world for me!* Keeps my flesh tender and my soul intact.

The house in which I live is being torn down. All the rooms are exposed. My house is like a human body with the skin peeled off. The wallpaper hangs in tatters, the bedsteads have no mattresses, the sinks are gone. Every night before entering the house I stand and look at it. The horror of it fascinates me. After all, why not a little horror? Every living man is a museum that houses the horrors of the race. Each man adds a new wing to the museum. And so, each night, standing before the house in which I live, the house which is being torn down, I try to grasp the meaning of it. The more the insides are exposed the more I get to love my house. I love even the old pisspot which stands under the bed, and which nobody uses any more.

In America I lived in many houses, but I do not remember what any house was like inside. I had to take what was happening to me and walk the streets with it. Once I hired an open barouche and I rode down Fifth Avenue. It as an afternoon in the fall and I was riding through my own city. Men and women promenading on the sidewalks: curious beasts, half-human, half-celluloid. Walking up and down the Avenue half-crazed, their teeth polished, their eyes glazed. The woman clothed in beautiful garbs, each one equipped with a cold storage smile. The men smiled too now and then, as if they were walking in their coffins to meet the Heavenly Redeemer. Smiling through life with that demented, glazed look in the eyes, the flags unfurled, and sex flowing sweetly through the sewers. I had a gat with me and when we got to Forty-second Street I opened fire. Nobody paid any attention. I mowed them down right and left, but the crowd got no thinner. The living walked right over the dead, smiling all the while to advertise their beautiful white teeth. It's this cruel white smile that sticks in my memory. I see it in my sleep when I put out my hand to beg—the George C. Tilyou smile that floats above the spandangled bandanas at Steeplechase. America smiling at poverty. It costs so little to smile—why not smile as you ride along in an open barouche? Smile, smile. Smile and the world is yours. Smile through the death rattle—it makes it easier for those you leave behind. Smile, damn you! *The smile that never comes off!*

A Thursday afternoon and I'm standing in the Metro face to face with the homely women of Europe. There's a worn beauty about their faces, as if like the earth itself they had participated in all the cataclysms of nature. The history of their race is engraved on their faces; their skin is like a parchment on which is recorded the whole struggle of civilization. The migrations, the hatreds and persecutions, the wars of Europe—all have left their impress. They are not smiling; their faces are composed and what is written on them is composed in terms of race, character, history. I see on their faces the ragged, multicolored map of Europe, a map streaked with rail, steamship and airplane lines, with national frontiers, with indelible, ineradicable prejudices and rivalries. The very raggedness of the contours, the big gaps that indicate sea and lake, the broken links that make the islands, the curious mythological hangovers that are the peninsulas, all this strain and erosion indicates the conflict that is going on perpetually between man and reality, a conflict of which this book is but another map. I am impressed, gazing at this map, that the continent is much more vast than it seems, that in fact it is not a continent at all but a part of the globe which the waters have broken into, a land broken into by the sea. At certain weak points the land gave way. One would not have to know a word of geology to understand the vicissitudes which this continent of Europe with its network of rivers, lakes, and inland seas has undergone. One can spot at a glance the titanic efforts that were made at different periods, just as one can detect the abortive, frustrated efforts. One can actually feel the great changes of climate that followed upon the various upheavals. If one looks at this map with the eyes of a cartologist one can imagine what it will look like fifty or a hundred thousand years hence.

So it is that, looking at the sea and land which compose the continents of man, I see certain ridiculous, monstrous formations and others again which bear witness to heroic struggles. I can trace, in the long, winding rivers, the loss of faith and courage, the slipping away from grace, the slow, gradual attrition of the soul. I can see that the frontiers are marked with heavy, natural boundaries and also with light, wavering lines, variable as the wind. I can feel just *where* the climate is going to change, perceive as inevitable that certain fertile regions will wither and other barren places blossom. I am sure that in certain quarters the myth will come true, that here and there a link will be found between the unknown men we were and the unknown men we are, that the confusion of the past will be marked by a greater confusion to come, and that it is only the tumult and confusion which is of importance and that we must get down and worship it. As man we contain all the elements which make the earth, its real substance and its myth; we carry with us everywhere and always our changing geography, our changing climate. The map of Europe is changing before our eyes; nobody knows where the new continent begins or ends.

I am here in the midst of a great change. I have forgotten my own language and yet I do not speak the new language. I am in China and I am talking Chinese. I am in the dead center of a changing reality for which no language has yet been invented. According to the map I am in Paris; according to the calendar I am living in the third decade of the twentieth century. But I am in China and there are no clocks or calendars here. I am sailing up the Yangtsze in a dhow and what food I gather is collected from the garbage dumped overboard by the American gunboats. It takes me all day to prepare a humble meal, but it is a delectable meal and I have a cast-iron stomach.

Coming in from Louveciennes. . . . Below me the valley of the Seine. The whole of Paris thrown up in relief, like a geodetic survey. Looking across the plain that holds the bed of the river I see the city of Paris: ring upon ring of streets; village within village; fortress within fortress. Like the gnarled stump of an old redwood, solitary and majestic she stands there in the broad plane of the Seine. Forever in the same spot she stands, now dwindling and shrinking, now rising and expanding: the new coming out of the old, the old decaying and dying. From whatever height, from whatever distance of time or place, there she stands, the fair city of Paris, soft, gemlike, a holy citadel whose mysterious paths thread beneath the clustering sea of roofs to break upon the open plain.

In the froth and bubble of the rush hour I sit and dream over an *apéritif*. The sky is still, the clouds motionless. I sit in the dead center of traffic, stilled by the hush of a new life growing out of the decay about me. My feet are touching the roots of an ageless body for which I have no name. I am in communication with the whole earth. Here I am in the womb of time and nothing will jolt me out of my stillness. One more wanderer who has found the flame of his restlessness. Here I sit in the open street composing my song. It's the song I heard as a child, the song which I have lost in the new world and which I would never have recovered had I not fallen like a twig into the ocean of time.

For him who is obliged to dream with eyes wide open all movement is in reverse, all action broken into kaleidoscopic fragments. I believe, as I walk through the horror of the present, that only those who have the courage to close their eyes, only those whose permanent absence from the condition known as reality can affect our fate. I believe, confronted with this lucid wide-awake horror, that all the resources of our civilization will prove inadequate to discover the tiny grain of sand necessary to upset the stale, stultifying balance of our world. I believe that only a dreamer who has fear neither of life nor death will discover this infinitesimal iota of force which will hurtle the cosmos into whack—*instantaneously*. Not for one moment do I believe in the slow and painful, the glorious and logical, ingloriously illogical evolution of things. I believe that the whole world— not the earth alone and the beings which compose it, nor the universe whose elements we have charted, including the island universes beyond our sight and instruments—but the whole world, known and unknown, is out of kilter, screaming in pain and madness. I believe that if tomorrow the means were discovered whereby we might fly to the most remote star, to one of those worlds whose light according to our weird calculus will not reach us until our earth itself be extinguished, I believe that if tomorrow we were transported there in a time which has not yet begun we would find an identical horror, an identical misery, an identical insanity. I believe that if we are so attuned to the rhythm of the stars about us as to escape the miracle of collision that we are also attuned to the fact which is being worked out simultaneously here, there, beyond and everywhere, and that there will be no escape from this universal fate unless simultaneously here, there, beyond and everywhere each and every one, man, beast, plant, mineral, rock, river, tree and mountain *wills* it.

Of a night when there is no longer a name for things I walk to the dead end of the street and, like a man who has come to the end of his tether, I jump the precipice which divides the living from the dead. As I plunge beyond the cemetery wall, where the last dilapidated urinal is gurgling, the whole of my childhood comes to a lump in my throat and chokes me. Wherever I have made my bed I have fought like a maniac to drive out the past. But at the last moment it is the past which rises up triumphantly, the past in which one drowns. With the last gasp one realizes that the future is a sham, a dirty mirror, the sand in the bottom of the hourglass, the cold, dead slag from a furnace whose fires have burned out. Walking on into the heart of the Levallois-Perret I pass an Arab standing at the entrance to a blind alley. He stands there under the brilliant arc light as if petrified. Nothing to mark him as human—no handle, no lever, no spring which by a magic touch might lift him out of the trance in which he is sunk. As I wander on and on the figure of the Arab sinks deeper and deeper into my consciousness. The figure of the Arab standing in a stone trance under the brilliant arc light. The figures of other men and women standing in the cold sweat of the streets—figures with human contours standing on little points in a space which has become petrified. Nothing has changed since that day I first came down into the street to take a look at life on my own account. What I have learned since is false and of no use. And now that I have put away the false the face of the earth is even more cruel to me than it was in the beginning. In this vomit I was born and in this vomit I shall die. No escape. No Paradise to which I can flee. The scale is at balance. Only a tiny grain of sand is needed, but this tiny grain of sand it is impossible to find. The spirit and the will are lacking. I think again of the wonder and the terror with which the street first inspired me. I recall the house I lived in, the mask it wore, the demons which inhabited it, the mystery that enveloped it; I recall each being who crossed the horizon of my childhood, the wonder that wrapped him about, the aura in which he floated, the touch of his body, the odor he gave off; I recall the days of the week and the gods that ruled over them, their fatality, their fragrance, each day so new and splendorous or else long and terrifyingly void; I recall the home we made and the objects which composed it, the spirit which animated it; I recall the changing years, their sharp decisive edges, like a calendar hidden away in the trunk of the family tree; I recall even my dreams, both those of night and those of day. Since passing the Arab I have traversed a long straight road toward infinity, or at least I have the illusion that I am traversing a straight and endless road. I forgot that there is such a thing as the geodetic curve, that no matter how wide the deviation, there where the Arab stands, should I keep going, I shall return again and again. At every crossroads I shall come upon a figure with human contours standing in a stone trance, a figure pitted against a blind alley with a brilliant arc light glaring down upon him.

Today I am out for another grand obsessional walk. I and myself firmly glued together. Again the sky hangs motionless, the air stilly hushed. Beyond the great wall that hems me in the musicians are tuning up.

Another day to live before the debacle! Another day! While mumbling thus to myself I swing suddenly round past the cemetery wall into the Rue de Maistre. The sharp swing to the right plunges me into the very bowels of Paris. Through the coiling, sliding intestines of Montmartre the street runs like a jagged knife wound. I am walking in blood, my heart on fire. Tomorrow all this will perish, and I with it. Beyond the wall the devils are tuning up. Faster, faster, my heart is afire!

Climbing the hill of Montmartre, St. Anthony on one side of me, Beelzebub on the other. One stands there on the high hill, resplendent in his whiteness. The surface of the mind breaks into a choppy sea. The sky reels, the earth sways. Climbing up the hill, above the granulated lids of the roofs, above the scarred shutters and the gasping chimney pots. . . .

At that point where the Rue Lepic lies over on its side for a breathing spell, where it bends like a hairpin to renew the steep ascent, it seems as if a flood tide had receded and left behind a rich marine deposit. The dance halls, the bars, the cabarets, all the incandescent lace and froth of the electrical night pales before the seething mass of edibles which girdle the base of the hill. Paris is rubbing her belly. Paris is smacking her lips. Paris is whetting her palate for the feast to come. Here is the body moving always in its ambiance—a great dynamic procession, like the temple friezes of Egypt, like the Etruscan legend, like the morning of the glory of Crete. Everything staggeringly alive, a swarm of differentiated matter. The warm hive of the human body, the grape cluster, the honey stored away like warm diamonds. The streets swarm through my fingers. I gather up the whole of France in my one hand. In the honeycomb I am, in the warm belly of the Sphinx. The sky and the earth they tremble with the live, pleasant weight of humanity. At the very core is the body. Beyond is doubt, despair, disillusionment. The body is the fundament, the imperishable.

Along the Rue D'Orsel, the sun sinking. Perhaps it's the sun sinking, perhaps it's the street itself dismal as a vestibule. My blood is sinking of its own weight into the fragile, glassy hemorrhoids of the nerves. Over the sorrow-bitten façades a thin scum of grease, a thin green film of fadedness, a touch of dementia. And then suddenly, presto! all is changed. Suddenly the street opens wide its jaws and there, like a still white dream, like a dream embedded in stone, the Sacré Cœur rises up. A late afternoon and the heavy whiteness of it is stifling. A heavy, somnolent whiteness, like the belly of a jaded woman. Back and forth the blood ebbs, the contours rounded with soft light, the huge billowy cupolas taut as savage teats. On the dizzy escarpments the trees stick out like spiny thorns whose fuzzy boughs wave sluggishly above the invisible current that moves trance-like beneath the roots. Pieces of sky still clinging to the tips of the boughs— soft, cottony wisps dyed with an eastern blue. Level above level, the green earth dotted with bread crumbs, with mangy dogs, with little cannibals who leap out of the pouches of kangaroos.

From the bones of the martyrs the white balustrades, the martyred limbs still writhing in agony. Silk legs crossed in Kufic characters, maybe silk sluts, maybe thin cormorants, maybe dead houris. The whole bulging edifice with its white elephant skin and its heavy stone breasts bears down on Paris with a Moorish fatalism.

Night is coming on, the night of the boulevards, with the sky red as hell-fire, and from Clichy to Barbès a fretwork of open tombs. The soft Paris night, like a ladder of toothless gums, and the ghouls grinning between the rungs. All along the foot of the hill the urinals are gurgling, their mouths choked with soft bread. It's in the night that Sacré Cœur stands out in all its stinking loveliness. Then it is that the heavy whiteness of her skin and her humid stone breath clamps down on the blood like a valve. The night and Paris pissing her white fevered blood away. Time rolling out over the xylophones, the moon gonged, the mind gouged. Night comes like an upturned cuspidor and the fine flowers of the mind, the golden jonquils and the chalk poppies, are chewed to slaver. Up on the high hill of Montmartre, under a sky-blue awning, the great stone horses champ noiselessly. The pounding of their hoofs sets the earth trembling north in Spitzbergen, south in Tasmania. The globe spins round on the soft runway of the boulevards. Faster and faster she spins. Faster and faster, while beyond the rim the musicians are tuning up. Again I hear the first notes of the dance, the devil dance with poison and shrapnel, the dance of flaming heartbeats, each heart aflame and shrieking in the night.

On the high hill, in the spring night, alone in the giant body of the whale, I am hanging upside down, my eyes filled with blood, my hair white as worms. One belly, one corpse, the great body of the whale rotting away like a fetus under a dead sun. Men and lice, men and lice, a continuous procession toward the maggot heap. This is the spring that Jesus sang, the sponge to his lips, the frogs dancing. No trace of rust, no stain of melancholy. The head slung down between the crotch in black frenzied dream, the past slowly sinking, the image balled and chained. In every womb the pounding of iron hoofs, in every grave the roar of hollow shells. Womb and shell and in the hollow of the womb a full-grown idiot picking buttercups. Man and horse moving now in one body, the hands soft, the hoofs cloven. On they come in steady procession, with red eyeballs and fiery manes. Spring is coming in the night with the roar of a cataract. Coming on the wings of mares, their manes flying, their nostrils smoking.

Up the Rue Caulaincourt, over the bridge of tombs. A soft spring rain falling. Below me the little white chapels where the dead lie buried. A splash of broken shadows from the heavy lattice work of the bridge. The grass is pushing up through the sod, greener now than by day—an electric grass that gleams with horsepower carats. Farther on up the Rue Caulaincourt I come upon a man and woman. The woman is wearing a straw hat. She has an umbrella in her hand but she doesn't open it. As I approach I hear her saying—"*c'est une combinaison!*"—and thinking that *combinaison* means underwear I prick up my ears. But it's a different sort of *combinaison* she's talking about and soon the fur is flying. Now I see why the umbrella was kept closed. "*Combinaison!*" she shrieks, and with that she begins to ply the umbrella. And all the poor devil can say is—"*Mais non, ma petite, mais non!*"

The little scene gives me intense pleasure—not because she is plying him with the umbrella, but because I had forgotten the other meaning of "*combinaison.*" I look to the right of me and there on a slanting street is precisely the Paris I have always been searching for. You might know every street in Paris and not know Paris, but when you have forgotten where you are and the rain is softly falling, suddenly in the aimless wandering you come to the street through which you have walked time and time again in your sleep *and this is the street you are now walking through.*

It was along this very street that I passed one day and saw a man lying on the sidewalk. He was lying flat on his back with arms outstretched— as if he had just been taken down from the cross. Not a soul approached him, not *one*, to see if he were dead or not. He lay there flat on his back, with arms outstretched, and there was not the slightest stir or movement of his body. As I passed close to the man I reassured myself that he was not dead. He was breathing heavily and there was a trickle of tobacco juice coming from his lips. As I reached the corner I paused a moment to see what would happen. Hardly had I turned round when a gale of laughter greeted my ears. Suddenly the doorways and shopfronts were crowded. The whole street had become animated in the twinkling of an eye. Men and women standing with arms akimbo, the tears rolling down their cheeks. I edged my way through the crowd which had gathered around the prostrate figure on the sidewalk. I couldn't understand the reason for this sudden interest, this sudden spurt of hilarity. Finally I broke through and stood again beside the body of the man. He was lying on his back as before. There was a dog standing over him and its tail was wagging with glee. The dog's nose was buried in the man's open fly. That's why everybody was laughing so. I tried to laugh too. I couldn't. I became sad, frightfully sad, sadder than I've ever been in all my life. I don't know what came over me. . . .

All this I remember now climbing the slanting street. It was just in front of the butcher shop across the way, the one with the red and white awning. I cross the street and there on the wet pavement, exactly where the other man had lain, is the body of a man with arms outstretched. I approach to have a good look at him. It's the same man, only now his fly is buttoned *and he's dead*. I bend over him to make absolutely sure that it's the same man and that he's dead. I make absolutely sure before I get up and wander of. At the corner I pause a moment. What am I waiting for? I pause there on one heel expecting to hear again that gale of laughter which I remember so vividly. Not a sound. Not a person in sight. Except for myself and the man lying dead in front of the butcher shop the street is deserted. Perhaps it's only a dream. I look at the street sign to see if it be a name that I know, a name I mean that I would recognize if I were awake. I touch the wall beside me, tear a little strip from the poster which is posted to the wall. I hold the little strip of paper in my hand a moment, then crumple it into a tiny pill and flip it in the gutter. It bounces away and falls into a gleaming puddle. I am not dreaming apparently. The moment I assure myself that I am awake a cold fright seizes me. *If I am not dreaming then I am insane.* And what is worse, if I'm insane I shall never be able to prove whether I was dreaming or awake. But perhaps it isn't necessary to prove anything, comes the assuring thought. I am the only one who knows about it. I am the only one who has doubts. The more I think of it the more I am convinced that what disturbs me is not whether I am dreaming or insane but whether the man on the sidewalk, the man with arms outstretched, was myself. If it is possible to leave the body in dream, or in death, perhaps it is possible to leave the body forever, to wander endlessly unbodied, unhooked, a nameless identity, or an unidentified name, a soul unattached, indifferent to everything, a soul immortal, perhaps incorruptible, like God—who can say?

My body—the places it knew, so many places, and all so strange and unrelated to *me*. God Ajax dragging me by the hair, dragging me through far streets in far places—*crazy places* . . . Quebec, Chula Vista, Brownsville, Suresnes, Monte Carlo, Czernowitz, Darmstadt, Carnarsie, Carcassonne, Cologne, Clichy, Cracow, Budapest, Avignon, Vienna, Prague, Marseilles, London, Montreal, Colorado Springs, Imperial City, Jacksonville, Cheyenne, Omaha, Tuscon, Blue Earth, Tallahassee, Chamonix, Greenpoint, Paradise Point, Point Loma, Durham, Juneau, Arles, Dieppe, Aix-la-Chapelle, Aix-en-Provence, Havre, Nîmes, Asheville, Bonn, Herkimer, Glendale, Ticonderoga, Niagara Falls, Spartanburg, Lake Titicaca, Ossining, Dannemora, Narragansett, Nuremberg, Hanover, Hamburg, Lemberg, Needles, Calgary, Galveston, Honolulu, Seattle, Otay, Indianapolis, Fairfield, Richmond, Orange Court House, Culver City, Rochester, Utica, Pine Bush, Carson City, Southold, Blue Point, Juarez, Mineola, Spuyten Duyvil, Pawtucket, Wilmington, Coogan's Bluff, North Beach, Toulouse, Perpignan, Fontenay-aux-Roses, Widdecombe-in-the-Moor, Mobile, Louveciennes. . . . In each and every one of these places something happened to me, something fatal. In each and every one of these places I left a dead body on the sidewalk with arms outstretched. Each and every time I bent over to take a good look at myself, to reassure myself that the body was not alive and that it was not I but myself that I was leaving behind. *And on I went—on and on and on*. And I am still going and I am alive, but when the rain starts to fall and I get to wandering aimlessly I hear the clanking of these dead selves peeled off in my journeying and I ask myself—*what next?* You might think there was a limit to what the body could endure, but there's none. So high does the body stand above suffering that when everything has been killed there remains always a toenail or a clump of hair which sprouts and it's these immortal sprouts which remain forever and ever. So that even when you are absolutely dead and forgotten some microscopic part of you still sprouts, and be the past future so dead there's still some little part alive and sprouting.

It's thus I'm standing one afternoon in the broiling sun outside the little station at Louveciennes, a tiny part of me alive and sprouting. The hour when the stock report comes through the air—*over the air*, as they say. In the bistro across the way from the station is hidden a machine and in the machine is hidden a man and in the man is hidden a voice. And the voice, which is the voice of a full-grown idiot, says—American Can. . . . American Tel. & Tel. . . . In French it says it, which is even more idiotic. *American Can . . . American Tel. & Tel.* . . . And then suddenly, like Jacob when he mounted the golden ladder, suddenly all the voices of heaven break loose. Like a geyser spurting forth from the bare earth the whole American scene gushes up—American Can, American Tel. & Tel., Atlantic & Pacific, Standard Oil, United Cigars, Father John, Sacco & Vanzetti, Uneeda Biscuit, Seaboard Air Line, Sapolio, Nick Carter, Trixie Friganza, Foxy Grandpa, the Gold Dust Twins, Tom Sharkey, Valeska Suratt, Commodore Schley, Millie de Leon, Theda Bara, Robert E. Lee, Little Nemo, Lydia Pinkham, Jesse James, Annie Oakley, Diamond Jim Brady, Schlitz-Milwaukee, Hemp St. Louis, Daniel Boone, Mark Hanna, Alexander Dowie, Carrie Nation, Mary Baker Eddy, Pocahontas, Fatty Arbuckle, Ruth Snyder, Lillian Russell, Sliding Billy Watson, Olga Nethersole, Billy Sunday, Mark Twain, Freeman & Clarke, Joseph Smith, Battling Nelson, Aimee Semple McPherson, Horace Greeley, Pat Rooney, Peruna, John Philip Sousa, Jack London, Babe Ruth, Harriet Beecher Stowe, Al Capone, Abe Lincoln, Brigham Young, Rip Van Winkle, Krazy Kat, Liggett & Meyers, the Hallroom Boys, Horn & Hardart, Fuller Brush, the Katzenjammer Kids, Gloomy Gus, Thomas Edison, Buffalo Bill, the Yellow Kid, Booker T. Washington, Czolgosz, Arthur Brisbane, Henry Ward Beecher, Ernest Seton Thompson, Margie Pennetti, Wrigley's Spearmint, Uncle Remus, Svoboda, David Harum, John Paul Jones, Grape Nuts, Aguinaldo, Nell Brinkley, Bessie McCoy, Tod Sloan, Fritzi Scheff, Lafcadio Hearn, Anna Held, Little Eva, Omega Oil, Maxine Elliott, Oscar Hammerstein, Bostock, The Smith Brothers, Zbysko, Clara Kimball Young, Paul Revere, Samuel Gompers, Max Linder, Ella Wheeler Wilcox, Corona-Corona, Uncas, Henry Clay, Woolworth, Patrick Henry, Cremo, George C. Tilyou, Long Tom, Christy Mathewson, Adeline Genee, Richard Carle, Sweet Caporals, Park & Tilford's, Jeanne Eagles, Fanny Hurst, Olga Petrova, Yale & Towne, Terry McGovern, Frisco, Marie Cahill, James J. Jeffries, the Housatonic, the Penobscot, Evangeline, Sears Roebuck, the Salmagundi, Dreamland, P. T. Barnum, Luna Park, Hiawatha, Bill Nye, Pat McCarren, the Rough Riders, Mischa Elman, David Belasco, Farragut, The Hairy Ape, Minnehaha, Arrow Collars, Sunrise, Sun Up, the Shenandoah, Jack Johnson, the Little Church

Around the Corner, Cab Calloway, Elaine Hammerstein, Kid McCoy, Ben Ami, Ouida, Peck's Bad Boy, Patti, Eugene V. Debs, Delaware & Lackawanna, Carlo Tresca, Chuck Connors, George Ade, Emma Goldman, Sitting Bull, Paul Dressler, Child's, Hubert's Museum, The Bum, Florence Mills, the Alamo, Peacock Alley, Pomander Walk, The Gold Rush, Sheepshead Bay, Strangler Lewis, Mimi Aguglia, The Barber Shop Chord, Bobby Walthour, Painless Parker, Mrs. Leslie Carter, The Police Gazette, Carter's Little Liver Pills, Bustanoby's, Paul & Joe's, William Jennings Bryan, George M. Cohan, Swami Vivekananda, Sadakichi Hartman, Elizabeth Gurley Flynn, the Monitor and the Merrimac, Snuffy the Cabman, Dorothy Dix, Amato, the Great Sylvester, Joe Jackson, Bunny, Elsie Janis, Irene Franklin, The Beale Street Blues, Ted Lewis, Wine, Woman & Song, Blue Label Ketchup, Bill Bailey, Sid Olcott, In the Gloaming Genevieve and the Banks of the Wabash far away. . . .

Everything American coming up in a rush. And with every name a thousand intimate details of my life are connected. What Frenchman passing me in the street suspects that I carry around inside me a dictionary of names? and with each name a life and death? When I walk down the street with a rapt air does any frog know *what* street I'm walking down? Does he know that I am walking inside the great Chinese Wall? Nothing is registered in my face—neither suffering, nor joy, nor hope, nor despair. I walk the streets with the face of a coolie. I have seen the land ravaged, homes devastated, families uptorn. Each city I walked through has killed me—so vast the misery, so endless the unremitting toil. From one city to another I walk, leaving behind me a grand procession of dead and clanking selves. *But I myself go on and on and on.* And all the while I hear the musicians tuning up. . . .

Last night I was walking again through the Fourteenth Ward. I came again upon my idol, Eddie Carney, the boy whom I have not seen since I left the old neighborhood. He was tall and thin, handsome in an Irish way. He took possession of me body and soul. There were three streets— North First, Fillmore Place and Driggs Avenue. These marked the boundaries of the known world. Beyond was Thule, Ultima Thule. It was the period of San Juan Hill, Free Silver, Pinocchio, Uneeda. In the basin, not far from Wallabout Market, lay the warships. A strip of asphalt next to the curb allowed the cyclists to spin to Coney Island and back. In every package of Sweet Caporals there was a photograph, sometimes a soubrette, sometimes a prize-fighter, sometimes a flag. Toward evening

Paul Sauer would put a tin can through the bars of his window and call for raw sauerkraut. Also toward evening Lester Reardon, proud, princely, golden-haired, would walk from his home past the baker shop—an event of primary importance. On the south side lay the homes of the lawyers and physicians, the politicians, the actors, the firehouse, the funeral parlor, the Protestant churches, the burlesk, the fountain; on the north side lay the tin factory, the iron works, the veterinary's, the cemetery, the school-house, the police station, the morgue, the slaughterhouse, the gas tanks, the fish market, the Democratic club. There were only three men to fear—old man Ramsay, the gospel-monger, crazy George Denton, the peddler, and Doc Martin, the bug exterminator. Types were already clearly distinguishable: the buffoons, the earth men, the paranoiacs, the volatiles, the mystagogues, the drudges, the nuts, the drunkards, the liars, the hypocrites, the harlots, the sadists, the cringers, the misers, the fanat-ics, the Urnings, the criminals, the saints, the princes. Jenny Maine was hump for the monkeys. Alfie Betcha was a crook. Joe Goeller was a sissy. Stanley was my first friend. Stanley Borowski. He was the first "other" person I recognized. He was a wildcat. Stanley recognized no law except the strap which his old man kept in the back of the barber shop. When his old man belted him you could hear Stanley screaming blocks away. In this world everything was done openly, in broad daylight. When Silberstein the pants maker went out of his mind they laid him out on the sidewalk in front of his home and put the strait jacket on him. His wife, who was with child, was so terrified that she dropped the brat on the sidewalk right beside him. Professor Martin, the bug exterminator, was just returning home after a long spree. He had two ferrets in his coat pockets and one of them got away on him. Stanley Borowski drove the ferret down the sewer for which he got a black eye then and there from Professor Martin's son Harry who was a half-wit. On the shed over the paint shop, just across the street, Willie Maine was standing with his pants down, jerking away for dear life. "Bjork" he said. "Bjork! Bjork!" The fire engine came and turned the hose on him. His old man, who was a drunkard, called the cops. The cops came and almost beat his old man to death. Meanwhile, a block away, Pat McCarren was standing at the bar treating his cronies to cham-pagne. The matinee was just over and the soubrettes from The Bum were piling into the back room with their sailor friends. Crazy George Denton was driving his wagon up the street, a whip in one hand and a Bible in the other. At the top of his crazy voice he was yelling "Inasmuch as ye do it unto the least of my brethren ye do it unto me also," or some such crap. Mrs. Gorman was standing in the doorway in her dirty wrapper, her boobies half out, and muttering "Tch tch tch!" She was a member of Father Carroll's church on the north side. "Good marnin' father, fine marnin' this marnin'!"

It was this evening, after the dinner, that it all came over me again— I mean about the musicians and the dance they are making ready. We had prepared a humble banquet for ourselves, Carl and I. A meal made entirely of delectables: radishes, black olives, tomatoes, sardines, cheese, Jewish bread, bananas, apple sauce, a couple of liters of Algerian wine, fourteen degrees. It was warm outdoors and very still. We sat there after the meal smoking contentedly, almost ready to doze off, so good was the meal and so comfortable the hard chairs with the light fading and that stillness about the rooftops as if the houses themselves were quietly breathing through the fents. And like many another evening, after we had sat in silence for a while and the room almost dark, suddenly he began to talk about himself, about something in the past which in the silence and the gloom of the evening began to take shape, not in words precisely, because it was beyond words what he was conveying to me. I don't think I caught the words at all, but just the music that was coming from him—a kind of sweet, woody music which came through the Algerian wine and the radishes and the black olives. Talking about his mother he was, about coming out of her womb, and after him his brother and his sister, and then the war came and they told him to shoot and he couldn't shoot and when the war was over they opened the gates of the prison or the lunatic asylum or whatever it was and he was free as a bird. How it happened to spill out this way I can't remember any more. We were talking about *The Merry Widow* and about Max Linder, about the Prater in Vienna—and then suddenly we were in the midst of the Russo-Japanese war and there was that Chinaman whom Claude Farrère mentions in *La Bataille*. Something that was said about the Chinaman must have sunk to the very bottom of him for when he opened his mouth again and started that speech about his mother, her womb, the war coming on and free as a bird I knew that he had gone far back in the past and I was almost afraid to breathe for fear of bringing him to.

Free as a bird I heard him say, and with that the gates opening and other men running out, all scot-free and a little silly from the confinement and the strain of waiting for the war to end. When the gates opened I was in the street again and my friend Stanley was sitting beside me on the little step in front of the house where we ate sour bread in the evening. Down the street a ways was Father Carroll's church. And now it's evening again and the vesper bells are ringing, Carl and I facing each other in the gathering gloom, quiet and at peace with each other. We are sitting in Clichy and it is long after the war. But there's another war coming and it's there in the darkness and perhaps it's the darkness made him think of his mother's womb and the night coming on, the night when you stand alone out there and no matter how frightful it gets you must stand there alone and take it. "I didn't want to go to the war," he was saying. "Shit, I was only eighteen." Just then a phono began to play and it was *The Merry Widow* waltz. Outside everything is so still and quiet—just like before the war. Stanley is whispering to me on the doorstep—something about God, the *Catholic* God. There are some radishes in the bowl and Carl is munching them in the dark. "It's so beautiful to be alive, no matter how poor you are," he says. I can just barely see him sticking his hand into the bowl and grabbing another radish. So beautiful to be alive! And with that he slips a radish into his mouth as if to convince himself that he is still alive and free as a bird. And now the whole street, free as a bird, is twittering inside me and I see again the boys who are later to have their heads blown off or their guts bayoneted—boys like Alfie Betcha, Tom Fowler, Johnny Dunn, Sylvester Goeller, Harry Martin, Johnny Paul, Eddie Carney, Lester Reardon, Georgie Maine, Stanley Borowski, Louis Pirosso, Robbie Hyslop, Eddie Gorman, Bob Maloney. The boys from the north side and the boys from the south side—all rolled into a muck heap and their guts hanging on the barbed wire. If only one of them had been spared! But no, not one! Not even the great Lester Reardon. The whole past is wiped out.

It's so beautiful to be alive and free as a bird. The gates are open and I can wander where I please. But where is Eddie Carney? Where is Stanley?

This is the Spring that Jesus sang, the sponge to his lips, the frogs dancing. In every womb the pounding of iron hoofs, in every grave the roar of hollow shells. A vault of obscene anguish saturated with angel-worms hanging from the fallen womb of a sky. In this last body of the whale the whole world has become a running sore. When next the trumpet blows it will be like pushing a button: as the first man falls he will push over the next, and the next the next, and so on down the line, round the world, from New York to Nagasaki, from the Arctic to the Antarctic. And when man falls he will push over the elephant and the elephant will push over the cow and the cow will push over the horse and the horse the lamb, and all will go down, one before the other, one after the other, like a row of tin soldiers blown down by the wind. The world will go out like a Roman candle. Not even a blade of grass will grow again. A lethal dose from which no awakening. Peace and night, with no moan or whisper stirring. A soft, brooding darkness, an inaudible flapping of wings.

John Dos Passos

Doomed to be taken, however unfairly, as one of the great failed promises of American letters, Dos Passos (1896–1970) came to France for the first time in 1917 as part of the great wave of American ambulance drivers of World War I. Although never really a member of the Parisian cohort of the 1920s, his reputation in France became, and ironically remains, higher than perhaps almost any other American writer of his generation. The impersonal logic of his literary method and its distinguishing note of dry irony, a kind of willed and slightly humorless desire to locate his subjects in neatly defined networks of history and social change—achieved most famously in his masterpiece *U.S.A*, but on view too in this passing view of a Parisian month, from *Journey Between Wars* (1938)—appeals to the orderly, system-loving side of the French imagination. Sartre, no less, called him a better writer than Faulkner or Kafka, and saw in his method something close to the one right, or responsible, way to write fiction, using material from the world as it is without being a mere photographer. "Dos," as he was known, keeps his temper, and cool, even in Paris, even in the 1930s.

——

A Spring Month in Paris

*M*ontmartre *Revisited*
Running up the grimy steps of the metro at the Place de Clichy, it was hard not to feel in my ears the different ring the name had had other times, ten years back, twenty years back, the longago Paris-on-leave ring of barroom chatter, funny stories, comic prostitutes, all the sidewalk café Saturdaynight jingle that went with the gone mythological sound of Montmartre. But twenty years from war to war have somewhat eroded the venereal mount of martyrs of bidet and makeupbox, and taken the glitter out of the last lingering tinsel of nineteenth-century whoopee. Those days the metro and the taxis stopped running early in the evening and after supper we used to walk up the steep cobbled streets and then the unlit stone stairs, past houses that reminded us of the stageset for the last act of *Louise*, to see the airraids from the top of the hill. Moonlight nights were the best. We would wait out of breath on the terrace in front of the

lividlooking church, with its narrow domes that looked so naked in the moonlight, and wait for the Gothas to come over. Under the silvery haze the unlit city would stretch like an iceflow in tiers and ridges from under our feet into the long past (Lutetia, Julian the Apostate, Villon, St. Bartholomew, Henri Quatre's white plume at Ivry, the Bastille and the singing mobs, the wall of the Communards, the days of the grand dukes) and far away to the north an antiaircraft gun would start barking. The sirens would chill the spine and the whole ring of the barrage would go into action. Shrapnel would sparkle tinsely overhead, and gradually through the din the sound of airplane motors would fill our ears humming now soft now loud. Very soon would come the shriek and the red flare and the shattering growl where the bombs had hit. One time something made a flame and fluttered down like a piece of burning paper far to the east. The barrage would slacken, everything would get still, and as we'd start the long walk home to the hotel, we'd hear the *breloque*, merry quacking little fireengine, hurrying up and down the black streets announcing that the raid was over. The next morning Monsieur Poincaré with his derby and his gloves and his cutaway coat buttoned high under his little beard would be photographed felicitating the survivors or beaming on the wounded.

This is March, 1937. I'm headed for a different Clichy, the industrial town outside the city limits of Paris. It's a long walk from the Place de Clichy, out a long crowded thoroughfare of little gimcrack stores, rundown movietheatres, jerry-built bars and cafés that blow a stale breath of *pernod* in your face as you pass, and haberdashers and noveltyshops shoddier than Fourteenth Street and not so much fun. It's a long walk out to Clichy. Where the Franco-Prussian War fortifications used to be there are weedy buildinglots. Now Paris's fortifications are the Maginot line along the north frontier. The street crosses a temporary bridge of unpainted wood. Big trucks slither through the coating of mud on the pavement. The glum darkgrey buildings of a factory town close in on either side. The sidewalks fill up with soberlooking middleaged men coming home from work. In skimpy meatmarkets broadbeamed women are counting out the change to buy the family supper. People look sober and their clothes are drab, but they are not down yet. The young girls aren't pretty but their eyes are bright, and sturdyseeming young men skim in and out among the trucks and the big green buses on their bicycles. The talk you hear has the throaty drawl of the workingclass suburbs.

The street opens up into a square set with young trees. Across it stands the grey townhall, looking like every other townhall in every other French small town. This is where the riot was and the shooting that gave this new resonance to the name of Clichy, Under the stunted barelybudding trees the square is thick with knots of workingmen. In the middle of each knot a couple of men are arguing, soberly enough, or else an eyewitness is telling for the hundredth time his story. Not many women, a few families that have come, kids and all, from other parts of Paris to see for themselves. Hardly anybody is excited. People listen gravely to what others have to say. One tall man with a red hatchet face is making a speech, that doesn't go so well with the crowd, about how the workingclass must arm and answer bullets with bullets. The older men have all been through one war. They know about bullets. Now and then a man nudges another man and whispers, "Look out for provocateurs."

There's a feeling of uneasiness in the crowd. People are trying to work out the story for themselves. They look at the broken windows and the bulletmarks on the grey stone of the townhall, and at the boardedup corner café and the butchershop wrecked by the crowd during the scrimmage. That was the window over the tobaccostore the shooting started from. No, the first shots were fired from the roof of the movingpicture theatre. No, this is how it happened.

They point out the broken windows and the scars where police bullets made little pits in the grey stone walls. People shake their heads. They don't talk much. They'd rather let the other fellow speak first. People feel insecure. It's only two nights ago at this time that nothing had happened yet; the wounded were still walking around feeling good, the young blood was pumping through the bodies of the dead.

That night Mr. Léon Blum, the parliamentary medicineman whose spells had so far kept off civil war, had dressed himself in his best soup and fish and had gone to the opera to hear the London Philharmonic play a Haydn symphony. *Perfide Albion.* He is called out of the concert by the news that a firstclass riot is going on at Clichy. A crowd has tried to storm the Olympia movietheatre where the Fiery Crosses, under their new name of French Social Party, are giving each other the creeps with speeches about the Moscow menace. The police have fired into the crowd.

While Mr. Blum went home to his quiet literary man's apartment on the Ile St. Louis to change into an outfit more suitable for the occasion, his secretary, Mr. Blumel, and his bearded Minister of the Interior, Mr. Marx Dormoy, were trying to quell the storm. The Fiery Crosses had given up their meeting and had been shepherded by the police out of the movietheatre by the back door at the first catcalls and were by this time well on their way to their respectable homes. Mr. Blumel was shot down by the police as he stood in the middle of the fracas with his arms raised trying to get a hearing, and both the mayor of Clichy and Mr. Marx Dormoy got their heads broken. The crowd took cover in the townhall; the police took the townhall by storm. At last, the shock troops tired of beating up the townspeople, the wounded were taken to hospitals, the dead went to the morgue, newspapermen staggered groggy out of their telephonebooths, the presses started clanking out the story, and the battle was history.

Two days later the people of Clichy are still talking it over gravely, standing in knots, shivering a little in the chill of the gathering twilight. The truce has been broken; no telling now; anything can happen now. People begin to scatter to their suppers. The last little groups of arguers break up shaking their heads as they go.

Front Populaire

The French are great hands for a funeral. The next Sunday the funeral procession of the young men shot down at Clichy crossed the northern quarters of Paris. We saw the head of it start from near the Gare de l'Est at ten in the morning, with the plumed hearses and the cars full of flowers and the red goldlettered tradeunion flags and the lettered streamers of crafts and trades and political parties, and at seven in the evening the tail of it was still pouring through the square in front of the townhall at Clichy five miles away. Young men, old men, young women, families, the great sober middleaged mass of the French people. They are not handsome, they're not very lively, even the young people have an old look, but it's hard not to feel that they embody, just as they did twenty years ago during the frenzy of wholesale war, a stubborn, unfanatical, live-and-let-live habit of mind, a feeling in every man and woman of the worth of personal dignity that is, for better or for worse, the unique contribution of Western Europe to the world. Twenty years ago seeing Frenchmen during gasattacks, under shellfire, in dressing stations, in bombarded cities, standing grumblingly in line, bumbling helplessly like flies in flypaper in the effortdestroying gum of their governmental red tape, I used to have the same feeling of respect. Now, walking all day under the leaden sky in the slowmoving unhurried crowds, even listening to the speeches of the popular leaders that ranted out of the loudspeakers (all for the popular front, down with the Fascists, support the exposition, boys) I couldn't help feeling with a certain relief (these are days when a man wonders sometimes how long any spot on the globe will be left fit to live in) that this would be a tough people to wipe out. It's easy to forget how central the French people are in everything we mean when we say Europe.

Croix de Feu

The next time I climbed up the stairs at the Place de Clichy metro station it was again late afternoon. I was on my way out to see a member of the French Social Party, the converted Fiery Crosses, a nicemannered young man who was managing his family trucking and warehousing business. When I got there a quavery middleaged lady was in his office talking about the cause. She was a charity worker who helped on the social service end. Handouts, distribution of old clothes, medicine and tracts for the sick, a little cash for the deserving; it turned out that some of the deserving had been unmasked as communists in sheep's clothing and as money was none too plentiful there had been suggestions from higher up that only the faithful be relieved. The deserving poor. They'd damn well better be deserving. Afterwards my friend took me upstairs to a dark middleclass diningroom that had the look of the family being away for the summer, although it was not summer, and rummaged in a big old walnut sideboard to find me a drink. He found a bottle of kümmel and poured me but a small glass. For himself he put a few drops in a glass of water. I couldn't help thinking that whoever had arranged this stiff room devoted to proper heavy meals, properly served at the proper time by a maid in a starched apron, would not have approved of our sitting there drinking the wrong drink at the wrong time. My friend spoke lovingly of *Le Patron* as he called the good colonel Casimir de la Rocque, spoke of the need for a moral revaluation, for the spiritual resurgence of France etcetera, etcetera, said politicians were disgusting. There I agreed with him. The Fiery Crosses were opposed to class hatred; Le Patron had supporters in all walks of life; he was for the union of all Frenchmen. Especially the small artisans were for him. As for Blum and the Front Populaire, they were ruining business. They were endangering the franc. They were the lackeys of Moscow. The firm's profits had been cut in half. The packers and the truckdrivers kept demanding more wages. The forty-hour week. Paid vacations, good God. He hadn't been able to buy a new car. There was a trip to America he'd been planning that he hadn't been able to take. True Frenchmen understood that that sort of thing had to stop. What was the use of raising wages if the price of living went up faster than the increased purchasing power? It was time the working classes got it through their heads that their standard of living was too high already. It would be the ruin of business.

He was perfectly rational, hardly violent; again and again he denied that the P.S.F. had started the shooting at Clichy, and he was certainly telling the truth so far as he knew it. But my friend had not a suspicion in the world that big profits for him were not also the best possible thing for the workingclass, la belle France, civilization and the human race in general.

At the office of *Flambeau*, the good colonel Casimir's newspaper, where I went the next afternoon to enquire for an editor I'd been recommended to, things didn't seem so rational. There was nobody in the vestibule but the doorman and a little redeyed hunchback in a derby hat who looked madhatter mad. The doorman didn't look any too sane either. He opened the door by inches when I knocked and closed it after me with a bang and turned the key. "That's orders," he said mysteriously. No, the editor wasn't there, nobody was there. Except enormous poster photographs of the good colonel Casimir hung around the vestibule. "Le Patron, le voilà!" he shouted with a sweep of his arm. "Magnificent," he said, rubbing his hands. "Magnificent," said the hunchback in the derby hat. Then like alarmclocks going off they started in, one into each ear, on the regular line; nobody but Le Patron could save France from Blum and the other Jews and the thieving freemasons and the communists, who were going to take everybody's property away, ruin the franc, burn the churches, rape the nuns and your wife and mine, turn the French farmer over to the minions of Moscow to be collectivized and his daughters nationalized and everything sold to the Jews, murderers, thieves, Jews. That's the first thing; they'd have to drive out the Jews. It was hard to get them to stop talking long enough to unlock the door and let me out. Before they let me go they pointed again to the huge hawknosed haughty-looking face on the poster. "Remember his face! Go to hear him speak. He's the savior of France," they shrieked.

Odysseus Among the Shades

We went in through the dank cobbled court of an eighteenth-century house on the Left Bank near the river. Across the court we went through a carriage gate with boxtrees in tubs on either side into an open garden very green in the drizzly gaslight. At the back was a little stone house with tall shuttered windows. We stepped from the dark hall into a feebly lit room with a big coal fire. There, among potted palms and little curleycue tables and burnished brass and silver objects with complicated surfaces that caught the firelight, over Dresden coffeecups, sat politely benign the characters in a novel Henry James unluckily didn't live long enough to write, one of those chronicles of gradually diminishing interest, of the marriage of the prejudices and inhibitions of Back Bay with those of the Faubourg St. Germain. The talk was about the Spanish Civil War. Voices were gradually growing more tense. The last warmth in these fading fictions that had unhappily survived their inventor was in their hatred. It was natural enough that they should be for Franco because they were people well along in life and encrusted with dividends and possessions that they felt only policing armies could hold for them against the rising hordes of the workingclass. As for the cost of the policing, that would be taken out of the hides of the wageslaves once they'd been taught manners again. What was surprising, as it is always surprising, was the bloody personal violence of their feelings. They were gentle and refined people, the sort of people who would be moved by finding a hurt cat, or even a hurt child, in the street, and would probably put themselves out to find a remedy. Their quiet and assured lives seemed as far from the bloody fighting round Madrid as the ghosts Odysseus visited in the underworld were far from the cities and the pitchblack ships and the oarsmen and the booty that were his seaman's life. A woman who bore the name of a nineteenth-century literary figure was retailing the stories of a Spanish lady of title who had recently escaped from the embassy at which she had taken refuge in Madrid with not only her life but a large sum of money and the family jewels. As bloody atrocity of the Reds followed bloody atrocity, these fading lady and gentleman ghosts from a world that the deaths of James and Proust have left without a master, began to swell and grow warm and ruddy with life, like the ghosts that Odysseus that crafty navigator poured out the blood for. Odysseus kept the ghosts off him with a sword. He was a wise man, because the only life of those dead was hatred of life. A curious thing about atrocity stories is that they mirror, instead of the events they purport to describe, the extent of the hatred of the people that tell them.

Still, you can't listen unmoved to tales of misery and murder. You know that only too many of them are true, and women who see those they love butchered before their eyes suffer the same whether they are duchesses or the wives of bankers or trolleyconductors. I was beginning to feel pretty nightmarish when they shifted to the chapter of the destruction of art by the Reds. A story was unfolded that seemed to be covering events and people vaguely familiar. It was about how the Reds were selling the arttreasures of Spain, and about an American woman who was an international Red of the bloodiest type and the mistress of the American ambassador who was a Red too (a Democrat is the same as a Red). She had recently arrived in Paris with a trunkload of stolen Grecos to sell to the highest bidder. By that time it was hard not to laugh. The nightmare figures sank back into the innocent dodder of the perpetually misinformed. The Red adventuress was an innocent and extraordinary kindly spinster whom I had known years ago in Madrid and who was helping get up an artexhibition for the benefit of Spanish hospitals. But was there any use in trying to explain? What could Odysseus say to the shades?

Workers' Housing

Out in Suresnes, the working people's suburb beyond the Bois de Boulogne, I had been walking around one morning with the mayor, Henri Sellier, who has been the leader of a newdealish program of municipal housing that in ten years has transformed the living standards of a whole section of Paris suburbs. He's a stocky sanguine bearded man with the bluff unassuming manners of an army doctor. He had taken us out of the townhall the back way to avoid the crowd of constituents waiting to see him on various matters, and we had been walking round the town visiting his apartment houses, his old people's village, the new theatre and auditorium that was building, the schools, the beautiful school for tuberculous children on the hill above the town. "They say we spend too much money," he said. "But we are saving the cost of poverty and sickness and ignorance. . . . That's worth something, isn't it? And our bonds are perfectly sound. We pay our interest without any difficulty. . . . If we ran a bank for profit they'd think we were wonderful."

All the time we were walking around the model suburb, with its patches of park and its new freshlooking airy buildings, there kept coming to the tip of my tongue something I dared not say. "Vienna. That's how they did it in Vienna." How many years ago was it that we were walking round the municipal apartments in Vienna? In Vienna they shelled the workers out of their fine apartments. "Where are your bombproof cellars? Where are your machinegun nests? How are you going to defend yourselves when the owners decide to attack?"

The Game of Parliament

No, the cost of living has not yet wiped out the increase in wages, Mr. Blum said categorically, leaning across his desk. He proceeded to quote figures with telling effect, shaking his finger a couple of times with a slightly professorial air. It was Saturday afternoon in his apartment on the Quai de Bourbon with its ancient scrubbed panelling and its parquet floor giving off a light scent of furniture polish, and its elderly pleasant-faced maid to open the door, on the shady unfashionable side of the Ile St. Louis. I had had to wait only a moment. Mr. Blum walked in from an inside room wearing dressinggown and blue pajamas, a tall man with a healthy lightbrown skin, taller and younger than he looks in the Chamber, an air of vigor about him that you don't expect in the Parisian literary man who wrote such urbane drama criticism in *Comædia*, in the amateur in politics. Outside the window, beyond the long lace curtains you could look out at the Seine, olivegreen with the spring mud flowing swift under the old old Pont Marie. Opposite there was a big new landing for cement barges and building stone that stood out raw against the mellow encrusted buildings of the old city.

Mr. Blum, after apologizing for not being dressed (he'd been resting up after a hard session of the Chamber) started talking in a physician's tone with a manner not exactly domineering but definitely firm. He's a clear clever talker, is always ahead of you with some other lead when your lips start to form the word Spain. Finally you leave him temporarily accepting his diagnosis, but when you've gone out through the group of pallidlooking secretservice men in the little stone court of the ancient apartmenthouse and step out on the quay into the spring sunshine coming through the young leaves of the trees you start remembering questions that got left unasked, like the symptoms you forgot to tell the physician about. The unasked question this time, as it so often is when you are talking to a politician who's not a pure charlatan, was: Why didn't you have the common decency to resign when you knew you had failed?

To see Léon Blum really in action you have to see him in the Chamber of Deputies. It's like watching a firstrate billiardplayer. They say that he's the only Left politician that old Poincaré admired as a speaker. The session about the events at Clichy a couple of days before I saw him was quite a show. This spring the debates in the Chamber were something Paris turns out for, even on a rainy afternoon; a long cue of people with umbrellas and raincoats was waiting on the pavement.

After your card has gotten you past the guards you climb a great many stairs to the tribune in the gallery. The seats are as uncomfortable as those in the gallery at the opera. The whole air of the building makes you think of it as one of the French state theatres, the gilding, the allegorical figures in flowing draperies on the ceiling, the hard seats, the bad ventilation, the malevolence of the attendants, the difficulty in hearing what goes on. This afternoon the proceedings have the character of an exhibition match because it is wellknown that the vote of confidence has been all sewed up beforehand. The deputies are talking for their constituents.

The Right attacks. Mr. Ybarnégaray talks for the French Social Party, he's the mouthpiece of Colonel Casimir. He brings out the Moscow bogey that is the Right's only stock in trade at the moment. The Front Populaire has sold the country out to the Kremlin. The new social legislation is going to ruin the small businessman. He talks on and on amid the cheers of his supporters and an increasing racket from the Left. Old man Herriot, the president of the Chamber, who towers over the deputies from his high desk in the middle, a loosepaunched huge pale man with a teddybear haircut who leans from side to side over his desk like a figure in a Punch-and-Judy show, glaring or smiling at his charges with the manner of an indulgent schoolmaster, has to rap more and more for order. Under the heckling and jeering from the Left Mr. Ybarnégaray loses his head and finally lets a big indiscreet cat out of the bag. "Berlin will never allow communism in France," he shouts. Pandemonium.

This gives Mr. Blum his chance to do the handsome thing and to get to his feet and suggest that the gentleman from the Pyrenees can't mean what he seems to mean. Mr. Blum can handle his opponents in the Chamber with one hand tied behind his back. Mr. Ybarnégaray finishes his speech under Mr. Blum's protection. It is obvious that he has made a fool of himself.

After supper the stage is all set for Mr. Blum's speech in defense of his policies. The speech is clear, to the point and seemingly frank; there's no doubt but that Mr. Blum has more brains than his colleagues. His speaking is rather spoiled for me by the almost whining apologetic tone of his voice. He has a curious trick of clasping and unclasping his hands when he speaks, and then bringing them together as if to shake hands with himself, but instead clasping and unclasping each one separately. But in his speech there are moments of unexpected dignity and force. You remember that people of all parties have told you that Mr. Blum is no Ramsay MacDonald. After all there's nothing in France that corresponds to a Duchess. At the end of his speech Mr. Blum let loose a little trial balloon in the shape of a slip of the tongue in which he called the Front Populaire the Front Nationale. I guess the Front Nationale is the Duchess.

The Key Word is National

The significance of the phrase came to me sharply when a newspaperman who was playing Virgil to my Dante among French politicians took me to see the editor of the official Socialist Party paper, who was minister without portfolio with his office in the Ministry of Justice next to the Ritz on the Place Vendôme. He was a small brown wryfaced man with a bush of white hair. When we were ushered in he was talking over the telephone at his desk in the middle of his huge ancient régime office, arguing in a sour meridional voice with someone at the other end of the line. We couldn't help hearing what he was saying, "*Amis ou non, il faut les mettre dédans.* . . . Put them in the cooler whether they're friends or not. No, confiscation is better, saves the trouble of a lawsuit." "After all," he said, looking sharply at us as he laid down the receiver, "we've got to govern." When we got outside we found out what he must have been talking about. The police had just confiscated an issue of *Jeune Garde*, the young socialist paper, at the same time as they confiscated an issue of *Flambeau*, the good colonel Casimir's sheet. National seems often to be a key word when a new group of politicians attain power. All the time he talked to us about the program of the Socialist Party, Monsieur le Ministre was playing with little gold paper seals out of a box he had on his desk, the gold paper seals that are affixed to the bottom of official documents.

Paname

But Paris in the spring is pleasant as a song in a musical comedy, if you can get away from the chore of interviewing politicians and waiting for them in their gloomy antechambers where the furniture and carpets and the palefaced attendants with not very clean starched shirts and white ties and unbrushed liveries look as if they hadn't been changed since the days of the Sun King. The horsechestnuts are sprouting. It's spring. Now and then the sun comes out. Rosytinted clouds mass and scatter little showers of rain in the broad sky above the Place de la Concorde and then roll away again. It's not the keyedup international Paris, capital of the world, of the great days of the Peace Conference, or the old Ville Lumière of the grand dukes, that they are trying to bring back to life with artificial respiration for the Exposition, but it's an agreeable chilly springlike Paris that has the cosy feeling of every old much lived in city. The city gives you the feeling of being something stable and permanent in a changing world of violence. It's almost the mediaeval feeling of a city protected by its walls. The feeling of being encrusted with the vagaries of generations of Parisians. In the Tuileries gardens one Sunday we met an elderly conciergelooking woman leading a fox on a string. An old yellow dog ran beside the fox keeping the other dogs off him. At the Samaritaine department store they sell anacondas by the meter. In one window there was a large sign, LES VAMPIRES SONT ARRIVES. "Bats are lovely pets," said a lady we were lunching with; "they fold up like little umbrellas. *C'est tellement gentil.*"

Paris, March, 1937.

Anne Morrow Lindbergh

Anne Morrow Lindbergh (1906–2001), unfairly typed now as a gentle essayist of the old-fashioned kind, deserves to be remembered for a lot more than that. She had a sharp eye and a steely pen, and her diary of the years of the Lindbergh family trauma (*Locked Rooms and Open Doors*) is, in its way, a kind of milestone in the history of "confessional" writing. As Alfred Kazin once pointed out, Anne Lindbergh was perfectly positioned to have the right "point of view" on modern mass media—an old-style American stoic confronting new-style American hysteria, though one doubts that she would have found the literary achievement worth the price in personal suffering. Here, in an excerpt from *The Flower and the Nettle* (1976), her diaries of 1936–39, she braves two of the Parisian scene's more formidable institutions: the *haute couturier* and Gertrude Stein.

———

from

The Flower and
the Nettle

Thursday, January 5th. Sunshine, morning

Go for Jon and we walk down Avenue Victor Hugo. In one drugstore Jon is given a hydrogen balloon. He carries it carefully home, pulling at the leash in the air above him.

After lunch Jon, C., and I go up the Eiffel Tower. Jon goes to the far corner of the platform and watches the trains going over the bridges, over the sunset-lit Seine far below us.

Sixteen trains!

Tea at home with Land. Land is very fretful, but he has no cold left. I think it is his teeth. I am worn out putting him to bed, by his continuous fretful cry.

Jon goes to bed happy. "What a day!" I say. "Yes," smiles Jon. "Sixteen trains and a balloon!"

———

Wednesday, January 18th

After lunch I go down and try to find a black dress—a very pretty one pictured in *Vogue* at Robert Piguet. After passing the door three times I finally go in and ask about it. Up marble stairs into a room done in cherry satin and blue with blue hyacinths the exact shade in flower pots—terribly swell.

I try not to show how scared I feel.

Several women come in dressed to the teeth. Models come in and parade around. A leisurely air of a sanctuary (a clothes sanctuary), a world in which nothing matters except clothes. All the priestesses of the cult hover about.

I want to know the price of the dress (which is a business—you have to see all the dresses first and then wait a long time while they go out and consult a book and then come back and give it to you from the notebook, as though it had just been decided upon after consultation, which it probably was!) and finally get it.

It is very expensive but not fabulous. It would be if the franc were not so low. How do people get *all* their clothes from a place like this?

I say I will try on the dress Friday (if I have courage enough to go back!).

Go out and walk to Aux Trois Quartiers for dishcloths at the white sale—*torchons de cuisine* (what a comedown!)—and look for sweaters for Jon.

Home for tea.

C. comes in unexpectedly, loaded with coat, brown bundles, the paraphernalia of flying, looking blown and outdoors—lovely surprise. The house comes to life; bustle, excitement, and purpose again. Evidently a very successful visit, though short. Among other things he introduced Mr. Rublee to Merkel, whom he liked (of course he would), and he talked about Mr. Rublee to several people. I do hope it helps. Mr. Rublee has a difficult task. I feel happy and proud of C.

———

Friday, January 20th

Talk to Soeur Lisi about leaving the children with her. Call Despiau. Go to have my hair done and try on a black cloth coat at Caroline's with velvet collar and cuffs for winter and spring, very inexpensive—$31.

No one in Paris ever wears rubbers (in the snow they wear high boots).

They all look at mine in astonishment. And yet the streets and sidewalks are *always* wet. It rains a lot and the streets never get really dry, as the weather, even if clear, is too damp. Have they got wet feet all the time? Nothing is so damaging to the shoes or one's disposition as perpetually wet feet.

After lunch I put on my Paris suit, which is too tight around the hips but the *only* smart thing I have, a blue blouse and hat with the blue feather, and set out for Piguet's. For a while I sit alone in the room with the cerise-satin sofas and the periwinkle-satin chairs (on painted pale green legs) with white walls and valentine trimmings on the doors and windows.

Then a rich woman—fat, powdered, and veiled—comes in with her spoiled daughter in an astrakhan suit—gold hair up under a ribboned hat.

They are brought a sketch M. Piguet has just drawn for a dress for the daughter. She looks at it critically and then complains that it is *odinaire* and has no distinction. Then she shows her mother the wool dress I saw the other day (which I think is about 2700 francs) for ordinary occasions, a simple little dress, and they agree it will do quite well for her, though not of course for anything more than a simple day dress!

Then my dress comes in. From the way everyone recognizes it, I gather it has had a *succès fou*, which means everyone will either have it or a copy of it.

However, I try it on and order it. I gather from the glance the powdered Mama gave me that I do not look too badly (in my suit, hat, etc.), except for my umbrella. No one in their class ever carries an umbrella because of course they never walk in the rain. In rain they travel in limousines, to hotels or grand shops, and the chauffeur or doorman has an umbrella to guide them from car to door!

But going down the carpeted, mirrored stairs I catch a glimpse of myself in the mirror. It is no use; even at my best, I always look like a little girl—a nice little girl sometimes—but I will *never* be smart!

Home for tea with Land and Jon, Land in his rocking horse, Jon on the chair next to me. Land always says *au 'voir* to C. whenever he comes into the room. Whether because he *wants* him to leave, or because C. is always leaving, I don't know.

Telegram from Mother. Margot has a fine boy—both doing well! I feel moved and excited. I pray all goes well. Dear Margot and Mother. Mother must be so relieved and happy.

I think of Elisabeth and wish I could share it with her—how happy she would be. I wonder about the miracle of that new life. Is there some of Elisabeth in that little boy?

Write Mother and pack. C. reads to Jon. Out to post letters after supper.

To bed early. There is a "deep depression to the west of Ireland" as usual. Will we be able to go tomorrow?

———

Sunday, February 5th

C. and I go for a long walk in the Bois. It is a lovely day—clear, not cold, and a delicious sun—with the smells of spring, The Bois on Sunday is superb. It is all of Paris. I felt part of something monumental today as I walked through it—a great slice of French life. Children on roller skates, whole families trailing around the lake, men talking politics, girls in high-heeled shoes with their beaux, fathers playing football with their little boys. Boy-scout troops in bright kerchiefs and brown uniforms, shouting and running through the trees. Baby carriages. Couples embracing, or being photographed hand in hand, men selling peanuts, streams of cars, crowds of people at certain points, women in their best clothes, strolling. And all in the mild sunlight and all pleasantly happy and enjoying it. Trailing home in the late afternoon are scooters, dragged children, baby carriages, new hats, high heels, men in overcoats.

Jon and Land play a game of hide-and-go-seek after tea, Jon hiding and calling to Land. Land staggering in, flushed and gay: "Where's Jon?" Much shouting and laughter. It is almost the first time they have really played together. Watching Jon's face is a great satisfaction—what it means to him to have Land. He says several times at supper, smiling, "Land can really play now. He isn't a baby any more."

———

Monday, February 13th

C. and I out after lunch, to the "*hôtel*" Comtesse de Noailles to see the Berman portrait (for Mother). The dealer from whom we got the Vlaminck is there and his wife. The huge house is full of museum pieces and one small hall hung solid with old masters, with Rouault and Chirico and Dali among them. The dealer thinks this is a fine idea as good things of all ages go together. Maybe so. I thought the old masters made the moderns look pretty tacky. But did not say so.

The portrait of the Comtesse by Berman is not yet hung but we see it against the wall. It is beautifully painted in unhealthy colors—violent pinks and yellows. In a sense it is perfectly conventional and conventionally painted. But at the same time I am struck by a violent lack of health and sanity in the portrait. I feel sure it would not do for Mother.

We see three beautiful Goyas, especially one man in gray (the most beautiful Goya I have ever seen). A Degas boy, a Delacroix portrait of a woman, which are lovely too.

She has a number of Dali, Braque, and Picasso, Dali seeming to be the favorite. A large one over the mantel in a modern salon (which also contains a Rubens covering a whole wall). C. points out a Dali, one of those beautifully painted super-vivid small scenes which has always something so horrible in it that you feel struck in the face—no, not struck in the face but insulted somewhere deeply inside. This one had a man with an elongated head like a huge tumor which hung pendulous on a tripod by his side. It made me ill.

The dealer says he does not like Dali; whether this is to please us or not I don't know. He says we should meet Derain.

We are, however, greatly relieved to get out of the house. I feel oppressed by the sickly abnormal atmosphere of those modern painters. I feel, in a strange way, violently puritan—that there is wickedness there, Sodom and Gomorrah, yet why, I could not say. Picasso seems to me a brilliant genius—overintellectual, spiritual even in his insanity—but these people are physical, super-physical. And their things smell of mortality.

I feel I must see something else to get the taste out of my mouth. So we go to the Orangerie and look at the exhibit of eighteenth-century *gravures*, which is like listening to Mozart.

Then we walk up toward the Louvre—a lovely cold light on the bare trees, an evening light, but cool, almost autumnal.

———

Monday, March 6th

C. still has a temperature; stays in bed all day. He has eaten nothing—doesn't like the vegetable bouillon and doesn't like anyone to come in and fuss around him.

I go out between 12 and 1 with Jon. On the way back I buy a can of meat bouillon for C., also rush into a flower store to get some white violets for Mrs. Miller's birthday "party" tonight.

I go down to Mrs. Miller's car waiting for me. It is raining hard. The violets are soaking wet (because I put them in water). C. said they looked like old crushed white tissue paper!

When I get there Jo and Gertrude Stein and Alice B. Toklas are there. Jo comes up gallantly and makes me feel at home. Mrs. Miller puts on my violets, which drip all over her black velvet sash. Jo has brought her a watercolor. And I see a new flower painting by Vlaminck.

I meet Gertrude Stein. A stocky, solid, middle-aged person with stubbly gray hair cut like a man's; a squarish face, a good chin, aquiline nose, and curious little hard brown eyes, near together. She has on a kind of long-skirted brown crash suit with a white uniform blouse (which looks as if she had made it herself in a fit of independence), clipped at the throat with a very beautiful old paste (no—probably diamond) pendant pin, and old diamond cuff-links. Except for these signs of luxury the dress looks like a costume for a "Mädchen in Uniform" matron. But her face is strong—simple and very American.

Alice B. Toklas (I really never *believed* in her, but there she was!) was more conventionally dressed in black taffeta with a modern Chanel (pink stone) flower necklace around her high-necked dress. This managed to look very old-fashioned and so did she. She had very dark hair combed into a low bang over her forehead, dark sympathetic and intelligent eyes, rather elegant hook nose, altogether a gracious, intelligent, and kind face.

Jo was bantering Gertrude Stein (who talks in a loud, rather harsh mannish voice) on her getting a dog—a new dog after her old one had died. (She got one as much the same as possible, immediately, and named it the same.)

"Oh, how *could* you!" said Jo.

"But it's the only thing to do!" she parried. *"Le Roi est mort—vive le Roi!"*

(She likes to be different, I thought instinctively.)

The Lin Yutangs arrive, he looking around disappointedly for C. I explain about the cold.

We go in to supper, I sit between Gertrude Stein and Lin Yutang.

Gertrude Stein is easy to talk with because she does not want anything from you. She *delivers*—and very well. I found myself pinned down by what she was saying, about Americans (Louis Bromfield in this case) going home and excitedly "discovering" America. "There seems to me something indecent in it, like 'discovering' you love your mother and father or your husband."

I say it's like being afraid you'll "forget" someone who's died.

We got onto memory and she says that when she is asked why there are so few geniuses she always says the same thing. She went into a rather profound definition of genius and its connection to a *time sense*. In other words (I cannot quote her—I was so intent on understanding her that I lost the words) that it was only *the now* which should be written, what you felt and were *now*. The trouble was that many writers looked back or forward. So few could write *the now*. (This is sloppily stated. She said it concisely, and it cut deep; but, as always, abstractions are difficult to quote.) I gathered that it was the same thing, said *philosophically*, that Rilke said *poetically* of writing poetry, "even to have memories is not sufficient. If there are many of them one must be able to forget them, and one must have the great patience to wait till they return. For the memories *themselves are not yet what is required. Only if they become blood within us, sight and gesture, nameless and no longer distinguishable from ourselves*, only then is it possible, in some very rare hour, for the first word of a verse to arise in their midst—to proceed from them" [*Journal of My Other Self*].

After an intense and absorbing conversation with her I turn to the delightful and *not* intense Lin Yutang. We talk about C. chiefly: his life on the farm, his school, his wanting to go into pure science, etc. Lin Yutang is a most sympathetic person. We talked of the soundness one has if one has a basic connection with the land.

After dinner I find (the ladies segregating) that I am again listening to Gertrude Stein, completely absorbed, trying very hard, sitting on the edge of my chair, to memorize those clear chiseled and profound statements.

"Life," she said, with one of her magnificently careless gestures, "is just one thing—just one thing—very simple, that's all it is: we are living here in a *finite* world, a finite universe, with limits. Even in flying there are limits. One lives in a *finite* world and one is able to *conceive* of the Infinite." (She is sitting down squarely, her legs slightly apart, like a man, her strong firm hands cupping a "finite world" on her lap.) Now—leaving out the disquieting murmur inside me that probably a scientist like du Noüy would dispute the statement that the world is finite—still that is a magnificent statement.

She went on to illustrate what pain, what complexities, what inevitable difficulties arose from this paradox, this lame state of man. "Even

Hitler and Mussolini . . . they conceive of the infinite. They want to make the finite (race, nation, etc.) become the infinite. Every world conqueror has dreamed of doing this, but it is doomed to failure . . . carries the seeds of its own death. You are sure to wake up one morning like Alexander brokenhearted because 'there are no more worlds to conquer.' "

She goes on and gives other examples. I am reminded of Christ's "Render unto Caesar the things that are Caesar's." I tell her this and she agrees. "*He* only tried to do it *here*." She tapped the brain. (The Kingdom of God.)

I am quite excited by this idea and am well off down the road it has opened up in my mind. But she goes right on—about *humanitarianism*: "I know. It's the fashion in America." Much overrated, she felt, in industrial and other fields. "Mankind on the whole is pretty contented with life, otherwise it wouldn't live."

"But," I said, "that doesn't mean one shouldn't try to *better* conditions?"

"Who is to say what is *better*?" she said.

A long discussion of "dull" lives. "Everyone's life is dull looked at from the outside."

How did we get onto Munich and Louis Bromfield again? "Louis got excited in September because Europe didn't go to war and he wanted it to go to war. Well, Europe didn't *want* to go to war, that's all. Czechoslovakia—yes, that was too bad, but Europe didn't *want* to go to war for it."

She went on to tell me a beautiful story about a peasant in the south of France, a simple uneducated man. She asked him if there were going to be a war.

"No," he said, "there isn't going to be a war."

"Why not?" she asked.

"*Ce n'est pas logique,*" he said simply (very French, she pointed out).

"Why not?" she asked again.

"Well," he said, "you see, Mademoiselle, I am forty-two. And I fought in the last war and here I am about to fight in another war. And my son is eighteen and he would fight in this war. *Ce n'est pas logique.* If I were *sixty* and it was my grandson who was eighteen, *then* there might be a war. But now, *ce n'est pas logique.*"

I do think this is superb. We were still talking when the men came back. About Munich and Chamberlain, whom she was for, oddly enough (since most artistic, literary, and "intellectuals" are against him). She said that he was arranging things in a common-sense way, as a housewife arranges squabbles in her kitchen.

We go into the studio and I talk with Mrs. Lin Yutang, a vigorous, earnest woman who teaches her children Chinese in the morning, works at a China Relief office all afternoon, and takes French lessons besides! She is a little hard to understand and I spend so much time concentrating on the words as they rush out, bubble out over each other, that I sometimes miss the meaning.

Gertrude Stein and Lin Yutang—or rather Gertrude Stein—had a conversation on Catholicism and the young French Catholic Party that I wanted to hear. She said no one could understand France without understanding Catholicism.

And then suddenly we were going. Alice B. Toklas standing up—stooped and small and black—looked like the frail little old maid she is. And Gertrude Stein put a small round felt cap on her head (of no particular shape or size; it stuck on the top of her head and did not fit, having the same impetuous homemade look as the brown crash suit) and suddenly looked absurd. They both seemed to me pathetic at that moment—sad old women going home. Though I suppose this isn't true. I think they are probably very happy and contented with life.

And I go home to C. in bed. I get him some cornflakes and milk and myself some too and sit on the bed and try to describe Gertrude Stein to him. I have the feeling that she is quite a big person of this age—*not* for her literary "pioneering," her own "daring" experiments in writing, as she no doubt thinks, but as a great personality nurturing, encouraging, and stimulating a whole body of writers. The Dr. Johnson of this age. The Mme de Staël. I kept thinking of the Yeats' poem:

"They came like swallows and like swallows went,
  And yet a woman's powerful character
  Could keep a swallow to its first intent;
  And half a dozen in formation there,
  That seemed to whirl upon a compass-point,
  Found certainty upon the dreaming air. . . ."

Oscar Hammerstein II

Hammerstein (1895–1960), a man of "limited talent and unlimited soul," in Stephen Sondheim's phrase, was the chief lyricist of the American operetta (not quite the same thing as the American musical) from the time of *Showboat* in the 1920s through the stately ocean liners of the Rodgers & Hammerstein musicals of the 1940s. In 1941, after Paris fell to the Germans, Hammerstein used the occasion to write a song lyric for a film version of *Lady, Be Good*. Set to a plangent Jerome Kern tune, it still catches the heartfelt (if slightly self-interested—Americans having a hard time grasping the point that things more significant than taxi-horns were being extinguished) American feeling about that fall. (Tony Martin recorded it, and had a hit with it, that same year.) It has become an anthem of all lost Parises.

————

The Last Time I Saw Paris

A lady known as Paris,
Romantic and charming,
Has left her old companions and faded from view.
Lonely men with lonely eyes are seeking her in vain.
Her streets are where they were,
But there's no sign of her—
She has left the Seine.

    The last time I saw Paris,
    Her heart was warm and gay.
    I heard the laughter of her heart in ev'ry street café.
    The last time I saw Paris,
    Her trees were dressed for spring
    And lovers walked beneath those trees
    And birds found songs to sing.
    I dodged the same old taxicabs that I had dodged for years;
    The chorus of their squeaky horns was music to my ears.
    The last time I saw Paris,

Her heart was warm and gay—
No matter how they change her, I'll remember her that way.

I'll think of happy hours
And people who shared them:
Old women selling flowers in markets at dawn,
Children who applauded Punch and Judy in the park,
And those who danced at night and kept their Paris bright
Till the town went dark.

The last time I saw Paris,
Her heart was warm and gay.
I heard the laughter of her heart in ev'ry street café.
The last time I saw Paris,
Her trees were dressed for spring
And lovers walked beneath those trees
And birds found songs to sing.
I dodged the same old taxicabs that I had dodged for years;
The chorus of their squeaky horns was music to my ears.
The last time I saw Paris,
Her heart was warm and gay—
No matter how they change her, I'll remember her that way.

Sylvia Beach

Booksellers, like art dealers, receive abuse from many, and contribute more than most. No bookseller more than Sylvia Beach (1887–1962), who is remembered today as the publisher of the first edition of Joyce's *Ulysses* but who also provided in her famous bookshop Shakespeare and Company a salon for everyone from T. S. Eliot to Paul Valéry. A woman of undaunted ingenuous enthusiasm, massive patience, and quiet courage, she recalls, in this excerpt from her lovely and haunting 1959 memoir, Parisian life under Nazi occupation.

---

from

Shakespeare and Company

WAR AND THE OCCUPATION

Up in Savoy at the end of the summer of 1939, posters summoned all the young men to join their regiments, and there was great mourning in all of the families. I took the last bus down the mountain before the young driver was mobilized and the bus requisitioned. The station at Chambéry was crowded with soldiers carrying their equipment. I managed to get on a train to Paris. In the same compartment was a young Englishwoman with her baby and her nurse. They were hurrying home to England. The husband had said good-by on the platform. He would follow his family soon, but he didn't believe we'd have war.

Shakespeare and Company remained open. The war went on. Then suddenly the Germans swept over France. As they came nearer and nearer to Paris, the population fled or tried to flee. Day and night, people streamed through the rue de l'Odéon. People camped, and slept, in front of the railway stations in the hope of getting on a train. Some left in their cars—which had to be abandoned along the roadsides for lack of gas. Most of them fled on foot, carrying babies and baggage, or pushing baby carriages or wheelbarrows. Some had bicycles. Meanwhile, a constant stream of refugees from the north and northeast, including Belgium—people uprooted from their farms and towns—flowed through the city toward the west.

Adrienne and I did not join the exodus. Why flee? My Canadian student assistant, Ruth Camp, did try to get away. She was machine-gunned in the ditches, and was later interned in spite of her efforts.

A lovely June day in 1940. Sunny with blue skies. Only about 25,000 people were left in Paris. Adrienne and I went over to the Boulevard Sébastopol and, through our tears, watched the refugees moving through the city. They came in at the East Gate, crossed Paris by way of the Boulevard Saint Michel and the Luxembourg Gardens, then went out through the Orléans and Italie gates: cattle-drawn carts piled with household goods; on top of them children, old people and sick people, pregnant women and women with babies, poultry in coops, and dogs and cats. Sometimes they stopped at the Luxembourg Gardens to let the cows graze there.

From the windows in the hospital where I had lunch with my old friend Dr. Bertrand-Fontaine, we watched the last of the refugees pouring in. Close on their heels came the Germans. An endless procession of motorized forces: tanks and armored cars and helmeted men seated with arms folded. The men and the machines were all a cold gray, and they moved to a steady deafening roar.

There were a few Nazi sympathizers in Paris, called "*Collabos*," but they were the exception. Everybody we knew was for resistance. Dr. Bertrand-Fontaine was an active member of the Resistance. Her son Rémi died at twenty in one of the worst prison camps, Mauthausen in Austria.

Parisians who survived the exodus came back, and my French friends were delighted to find Shakespeare and Company still open. They fairly stuffed themselves on our books, and I was busier than ever. I had a volunteer helper, a young Jewish friend, Françoise Bernheim. A student of Sanscrit, but now excluded from the Sorbonne by the Nazi laws, she was encouraged by her professor to copy the notes taken by her non-Jewish friends, and, with his help and theirs, she was persevering in her studies.

I had resisted all the efforts of my Embassy to persuade me to return to the United States. (The route was through Lisbon, and the alluring rates for transportation included the item: "a parrot, six dollars.") Instead,

I had settled down to share life in Nazi-occupied Paris with my friends. Also, as I went about with Françoise, I shared with her some of the special restrictions on Jews—though not the large yellow Star of David that she wore on her coat or dress. We went about on bicycles, the only form of transportation. We could not enter public places such as theatres, movies, cafés, concert halls, or sit down on park benches or even on those in the streets. Once, we tried taking our lunch to a shady square. Sitting on the ground *beside* a bench, we hurriedly ate our hard-boiled eggs and swallowed the tea in our thermos bottles, looking around furtively as we did so. It was not an experience that we cared to repeat.

SHAKESPEARE AND COMPANY VANISHES

When the United States came into the war, my nationality, added to my Jewish affiliations, finished Shakespeare and Company in Nazi eyes. We Americans had to declare ourselves at the Kommandatur and register once a week at the Commissary in the section of Paris where we lived. (Jews had to sign every day.) There were so few Americans that our names were in a sort of scrapbook that was always getting mislaid. I used to find it for the Commissaire. Opposite my name and antecedents was the notation: "has no horse." I could never find out why.

My German customers were always rare, but of course after I was classified as "the enemy," they stopped coming altogether—until a last outstanding visit ended the series. A high-ranking German officer, who had got out of a huge gray military car, stopped to look at a copy of *Finnegans Wake* that was in the window. Then he came in and, speaking perfect English, said he would buy it. "It's not for sale." "Why not?" My last copy, I explained. I was keeping it. For whom? For myself. He was angry. He was so interested in Joyce's work, he said. Still I was firm. Out he strode, and I removed *Finnegans Wake* from the window and put it safely away.

A fortnight later, the same officer strode into the bookshop. Where was *Finnegans Wake*? I had put it away. Fairly trembling with rage, he said, "We're coming to confiscate all your goods today." "All right." He drove off.

I consulted my concierge. She opened an unoccupied apartment on the third floor. (My own apartment was on the second floor.) My friends and I carried all the books and all the photographs upstairs, mostly in clothesbaskets; and all the furniture. We even removed the electric-light fixtures. I had a carpenter take down the shelves. Within two hours, not a single thing was to be seen in the shop, and a house painter had painted out the name, Shakespeare and Company, on the front of 12 rue de l'Odéon. The date was 1941. Did the Germans come to confiscate Shakespeare and Company's goods? If so, they never found the shop.

Eventually, they did come to fetch the proprietor of Shakespeare and Company.

After six months in an internment camp, I was back in Paris, but with a paper stating that I could be taken again by the German military authorities at any time they saw fit. My friends agreed that, instead of waiting to be sent back, I should "disappear." Miss Sarah Watson undertook to hide me in her Foyer des Etudiantes (Students' Hostel) at 93 Boulevard Saint Michel. I lived happily in the little kitchen at the top of the house with Miss Watson and her assistant, Madame Marcelle Fournier. With the card I was given as a member of the Foyer, I felt as though I was back in my student days. The Germans had made several attempts to take over the Foyer, but, though Miss Watson herself was interned for a time, Madame Fournier performed the miracle of keeping the place open and full of students going on with their studies. It was American, with an American head, but, since it was attached to the University of Paris, the Recteur obtained the release of Miss Watson from the internment camp and she continued at her post.

I visited the rue de l'Odéon daily, secretly, heard the latest news of Adrienne's bookshop, saw the latest volume of the clandestine Editions de Minuit. The Midnight Editions, which had a wide underground circulation, were published by my friend Yvonne Desvignes at terrible risk. All of the prominent writers in the Resistance appeared in it. Eluard used to deliver the little volumes.

Janet Flanner

Janet Flanner (1892–1978), who for fifty years wrote *The New Yorker*'s "Letter from Paris," is remembered for her longevity and reach, but she deserves to be remembered as a stylist who in the last part of her writing life moved beyond style. She came to Paris in 1921 and began writing letters home, of such distinction that when they came to the attention of Harold Ross (who gave her the pen name Genêt, thinking it sounded more French), he offered to publish them. Much of her writing in the 1920s was concerned with the American colony in the city. In highly, at times wonderfully mannered prose she profiled Isadora, Picasso, Gertrude, and the rest. But it was when bad times came, and the Americans largely fled or were forced home by their creditors, that she flourished. At a moment before CNN or the Internet brought hard news into every home as it happened, she had an advantage of distance. Rewriting the local news in a matchlessly cool, precise, and pointed prose, she made cameo engravings of Parisian conditions that, for at least two generations of American readers, *were* Paris. She spent the war years in America, but returned for the liberation, the Fourth Republic, and the rise, fall, and return of de Gaulle, always first among her heroes. These later dispatches—such as her quietly poignant account of the Parisian reaction to the death of FDR, published in the April 28, 1945, *New Yorker*—show that she could write quiet as well as she did festive, and that her sharp was as strong as her shimmer. (She spent the last twenty years of her residence at the Ritz, still writing home, until her retirement in 1975.)

Letter from Paris

April 19 (by wireless)

The death of President Roosevelt caused a more personal grief among the French than the deaths of their own recent great men. On the demise of both Papa Clemenceau and Marshal Foch, their grief was a nationalistic, patriotic emotion, since these men, the one with his sabre-sharp tongue, the other with his sword, had saved France. The sorrow the French felt at losing Roosevelt seemed like someone's private unhappiness multiplied by millions. Friday morning, when the news was first known here, French men and women approached the groups of Americans in uniform standing on street corners and in public places and, with a mixture of formality and obvious emotion, expressed their sorrow, sometimes in French, sometimes in broken English. On the Rue Scribe, a sergeant in a jeep held up traffic while he received the condolences of two elderly French spinsters. In the Jardin des Tuileries, an American woman was stopped beneath the white-flowering chestnut trees by a French schoolboy who, with trembling voice, spoke for his father, a dead Army officer, to express his father's love for the dead President. At the outdoor flower stalls of the Place de la Madeleine, a patriarchal flower vendor gave a passing and startled paratrooper a free pink tulip, with the statement "Today they will be sending beautiful flowers for your great man. How sad." A café waitress naïvely touched the sublime when she said of his death, *"C'est ennuyeux pour toute l'humanité."*

On Friday morning, the Germans' Stuttgart radio, the first enemy station to show signs of life that day, interrupted a hysterical patriotic harangue to announce Roosevelt's death, without comment. By Saturday it had worked out its new anti-American propaganda line. It no longer mentioned the man it had consistently heckled as President Rosenfeldt, but declared that President Truman was already viewed with skepticism by the United States and that if he fulfilled his promise to follow those White House policies which had started this second World War, he would have the distinction of starting the third.

Since the American system for filling the Presidential chair when it is left vacant by death was unknown to most French citizens, the journals here carried an official explanatory paragraph headed *"Monsieur Truman Sera Président Jusqu'en 1948"* and quoted our Constitution. The Paris press wrote of F.D.R. with sober magnificence and sincere superlatives. Under the spirited Gallic headline *"Vive Roosevelt!,"* the *Libération-Soir* spoke of "the unjust destiny and yet the ancient grandeur of the event." *Le Monde*, in an editorial entitled *"Après Roosevelt,"* began by saying, "The great voice which directed American political destinies has been hushed, but its echo continues in French souls." In conclusion, it praised "his charm, his beautiful and great words," and said, "Let us weep for this man and hope that his wise and generous conception of the human communities remains like a light to brighten the path for all men of good will." De Gaulle's Minister of Foreign Affairs said, "It is not only appropriate but necessary to express the depth of the sadness of the government and of the French people. Roosevelt was one of the most loved and venerated men in France. He takes with him the tenderness of the French nation." Which is true.

The increasing malaise, now that Roosevelt must be absent from the peace, and the unexpected return last Saturday of thousands of French prisoners liberated from Germany, juxtaposed fear and happiness in a way Parisians will probably always remember in recalling that historic weekend. On Saturday, eight thousand French male prisoners were flown back from Germany in American transport planes, which afterward tumultuously circled the city while the men were being unpacked from trucks outside the newly decorated reception center in the Gare d'Orsay. On its walls these weary men saw an astonishing series of modernistic bas-reliefs depicting their welcome return to the freedom of what explanatory signs called *"la liberté d'aimer"* and the liberty to play, to sleep, to work, to eat, to drink, and to breathe freely. Few of the prisoners, in their hasty flight from the German Army and their later flight with the Americans in the skies, had heard our sad news. When they did hear it, one thin, bitter blond Frenchman said, *"Voyez-vous.* We've come home too late."

The next day, the first contingent of women prisoners arrived by train, bringing with them as very nearly their only baggage the proofs, on their faces and their bodies and in their weakly spoken reports, of the atrocities that had been their lot and the lot of hundreds of thousands of others in the numerous concentration camps our armies are liberating, almost too late. These three hundred women, who came in exchange for German women held in France, were from the prison camp of Ravensbrück, in the marshes midway between Berlin and Stettin. They arrived at the Gare de Lyon at eleven in the morning and were met by a nearly speechless crowd ready with welcoming bouquets of lilacs and other spring flowers, and by General de Gaulle, who wept. As he shook hands with some wretched woman leaning from a window of the train, she suddenly screamed, *"C'est lui!,"* and pointed to her husband, standing nearby, who had not recognized her. There was a general, anguished babble of search, of finding or not finding. There was almost no joy; the emotion went beyond that, to something nearer pain. So much suffering lay behind this homecoming, and it showed in the women's faces and bodies.

Of the three hundred women whom the Ravensbrück *Kommandant* had selected as being able to put up the best appearance, eleven had died en route. One woman, taken from the train unconscious and placed on a litter, by chance opened her eyes just as de Gaulle's color guard marched past her with the French tricolor. She lifted an emaciated arm, pointed to the flag, and swooned again. Another woman, who still had a strong voice and an air of authority, said she had been a camp nurse. Unable to find her daughter and son-in-law in the crowd, she began shouting "Monique! Dominique!" and crying out that her son and husband had been killed fighting in the resistance and now where were those two who were all she had left? Then she sobbed weakly. One woman, six years ago renowned in Paris for her elegance, had become a bent, dazed, shabby old woman. When her smartly attired brother, who met her, said, like an automaton, "Where is your luggage?," she silently handed him what looked like a dirty black sweater fastened with safety pins around whatever small belongings were rolled inside. In a way, all the women looked alike: their faces were gray-green, with reddish-brown circles around their eyes, which seemed to see, but not to take in. They were dressed like scarecrows, in what had been given them at camp, clothes taken from the dead of all nationalities. As the lilacs fell from inert hands, the flowers made a purple carpet on the platform and the perfume of the trampled flowers mixed with the stench of illness and dirt.

The Ravensbrück prisoners were only an unexpected addition to a day of memorable gloom in Paris. An hour before their arrival, a brief and dramatic memorial service for our President had been held in Notre Dame. Great crowds of silent Parisians thronged the *Parvis* before the cathedral. Inside, behind the high altar, taps was sounded by a trumpet. "The Star-Spangled Banner" was played slowly as a dead march, and a prayer of intercession to the Virgin Queen of Heaven for the soul of a Democratic, Episcopalian President and the "Kyrie Eleison" were splendidly chanted, in fine diction, into a microphone by an Army chaplain. At the conclusion, the Garde Républicaine, in white breeches and gold helmets, made a semicircle inside the cathedral and an honor line outside its door, through which marched the cameo-faced Parisian Cardinal Suhard, with his ebony cane; a purple-robed Bishop; Madame L'Ambassadrice Américaine, with His Excellency; and General de Gaulle, followed by his Cabinet, including its assembly speaker, Le Père Blanc Carrière, white-haired, white-socked, and in his religious order's hooded white-wool robe.

The death of a global figure like Roosevelt produces a political vacuum. It is already being filled here by an inrush of worldly suppositions. These are diverse. According to them, de Gaulle will benefit from

Roosevelt's death, bourgeois France will lose, Republican France will gain by coming closer, through her alliance with Russia and against England, to her goal of a nonmonarchial Latin bloc—a non-Fascist, kingless Italy, Spain, Portugal, and France, which will establish an anti-Queen Victorian Mediterranean. Churchill, London, and all royalty, including the Greek, will lose insofar as their old-fashioned balance-of-power notion of a controlled Europe will suffer. Germany will lose, because Roosevelt was her worthy enemy; Germany will gain, because the international and local rich he fought will revive Germany's cartelized industrial power. Europe as a whole, these speculations continue, will gain, insofar as it will settle its own fate, free of the too carefully guiding White House hand and the power of the Downing Street cigar. These notions, too, are tributes to that rare American figure who has, on the Continent, left his own great mark— a void.

Elizabeth Bishop

One of the rare American poets whose reputation, high enough in her own lifetime, continues to climb untroubled after her death, Elizabeth Bishop (1911–1979) came to Paris for the first time in 1935. She stayed for several months in a seven-room, seventh-floor apartment at 58 rue de Vaugirard filled with antiques and its owners' clock collection—an ambient that likely inspired her "Paris, 7 A.M." (from *North & South*, 1946) in which the pattern of streets radiating on the Right Bank from the Etoile are superimposed on the pattern of a clock's moving hands, and become a metaphor for time itself.

Paris, 7 A.M.

I make a trip to each clock in the apartment:
some hands point histrionically one way
and some point others, from the ignorant faces.
Time is an Etoile; the hours diverge
so much that days are journeys round the suburbs,
circles surrounding stars, overlapping circles.
The short, half-tone scale of winter weathers
is a spread pigeon's wing.
Winter lives under a pigeon's wing, a dead wing with damp
        feathers.

Look down into the courtyard. All the houses
are built that way, with ornamental urns
set on the mansard roof-tops where the pigeons
take their walks. It is like introspection
to stare inside, or retrospection,
a star inside a rectangle, a recollection:
this hollow square could easily have been there.
—The childish snow-forts, built in flashier winters,
could have reached these proportions and been houses;
the mighty snow-forts, four, five, stories high,

437

withstanding spring as sand-forts do the tide,
their walls, their shape, could not dissolve and die,
only be overlapping in a strong chain, turned to stone,
and grayed and yellowed now like these.

Where is the ammunition, the piled-up balls
with the star-splintered hearts of ice?
This sky is no carrier-warrior-pigeon
escaping end/less intersecting circles.
It is a dead one, or the sky from which a dead one fell.
The urns have caught his ashes or his feathers.
When did the star dissolve, or was it captured
by the sequence of squares and squares and circles, circles?
Can the clocks say; is it there below,
about to tumble in snow?

Ludwig Bemelmans

Ludwig Bemelmans (1898–1962) is remembered today, and well he should be, as the inventor and illustrator of the life of Madeline, the smallest girl of the twelve who walk every day in two straight lines from their ivy-covered Paris boarding school. The *Madeline* books (which are, oddly, almost completely unknown in Paris) have probably done more than any other literature to imprint a vision of Paris on the American imagination. But Bemelmans also deserves to be known, as he was in his lifetime, as a travel writer whose charming, acid prose gives exact meaning to the critic's abused word "bittersweet." (English wasn't his first language, and though one senses it, one doesn't mind it, either. There is a kind of Ernst Lubitsch accent to his sentences, just discernible and still delightful.) His 1948 book *The Best of Times*, an account of a trip to a Europe largely ruined yet recovering, is a remarkable collection of drawings and writings, in which his faux-Fauve style finds an equivalent in his prose. No one wrote with more acerbity about French restaurant manners or with more insider's pleasure about French food.

No. 13 Rue St. Augustin

My once fragile and nervous Paris underworld friend Georges thrived on the Germans while they occupied his city.

He says loudly, and with pride, that by operating alone and unofficially, he dispatched more of them to hospitals than he could possibly have put there had France allowed him to put on a uniform and shoulder a musket.

He has become respectable. The once thorny individual and hard hunter, who walked fast, on thin soles, constantly looking in back of him, who watched the reflection of the street in the shop windows that darkness turned into mirrors, now saunters along with a cane and in the center of the street.

The decay is evident also in the loudness of his talk, the steady look in his eye, in his genuine pearl stickpin, and the general air of martial bourgeoisie that he exhibits in his clothes.

There are others now, who freeze and sweat on his behalf, and move along the walls of the houses, looking back. You find them along the Faubourg St. Honoré, the Rues Royale and Castiglioni, and two of them share in the business of the Place Vendôme.

The contacts they make are ushered into a floating office that is located today in this bistro and tomorrow in that. The grand advantage of this arrangement is that there is no office rent and that is complicates matters for the gendarmes. For in the back room of the bistro the dollar is exchanged at a rate more realistic than that officially paid.

This service is supplemented by a kind of traveler's aid. The amateur, newly arrived in Paris and looking for amusements, is not left to his own helpless fumbling, but is taken by the hand and properly guided.

An ever-widening circle of grateful and steady clients testifies to the reputation of the enterprise and the sound principles on which it is run.

Georges has come by his eminence after a slow, grim battle, up from sleeping in caves with *clochards* and under bridges, up from the narrow cots of the mean and hungry girls of the Boulevard Sébastopol, and from horse steak and the hard plotting of complicated games of confidence.

"It won't be grand and noble company," he said to me on a Thursday afternoon, holding his hand over the mouthpiece of the telephone.

"I warn you that one will stay long at the table, and the food will be so-so, because they are not *eingerichtet* for that kind of entertaining." Georges had learned German during the war and occasionally used words like *"eingerichtet,"* which means furnished, or equipped.

"The wine I can vouch for," he continued. "But there will be *heulen und Zähneknirschen*, which means howling and gnashing of teeth, because this is the sad day on which this establishment, which is one of the oldest and most reputable in Paris, will be closed by law. I must explain to you what happened," said Georges. "For the first time in history the women of France vote, and their deputy is one Marthe Richard. The first proposition she offered was a vote on the abolition of establishments such as Numéro Treize, and every woman in France, except the keepers of such houses and the inmates thereof, voted to close them. The women voted one hundred per cent, naturally. I can promise you that it will be interesting."

He took his hand away from the mouthpiece and asked Mademoiselle Geneviève if he could bring a friend, and with metallic sharpness her voice recorded through the room as from a trumpet: *"Mais venez donc, avec votre ami, mais ça nous fait treize à table."*

"I hope you attach no importance to numbers," said Georges. "The house is Number Thirteen, Rue St. Augustin, and there will be thirteen at the table. You may, however, if this upsets you, stop trembling, because we are invited to this little family celebration by Mademoiselle Geneviève, and her patron saint, Ste. Geneviève, is, as you perhaps know, the protector of Paris."

After a very short ride from the Hôtel de France et Choiseul, the taxi stopped, not in an obscure and somber alley or in a hypocritically genteel location, but in the center of a busy thoroughfare lined by respectable shops und businesses, all located in solid houses. There was no hidden entrance: the door of Number Thirteen, with the number boldly lettered on it, was heavy and oaken, carved, and had immense polished brass knobs for handles. It was still light, and the street was filled with people. Part of Number Thirteen was occupied by a firm that sold filing equipment, and the brunette young women in black who stood there waiting for customers looked at us without any kind of expression on their faces other than that with which people look out into a street in which nothing of particular interest happens. While we waited for the bell to be answered, there were also women who came out of a grocery store, and children who seemed to belong in the street. While it is a curious feeling to stand and wait outside an establishment of the reputation of Numéro Treize and wait a long while to be let in, it seemed to bother nobody. We were not even taken notice of.

The foyer was burnished with a blue Oriental rug, stained-window background, and a table on which stood an artificial palm. There was a seascape, two matching Japanese silk screens, and at the foot of the stairs, looking upward and holding a cluster of light fixtures above her head, was a more than life-size marble statue of a nude woman of the degree of artistry and voluptuousness of the one that stands in a similar place and pose at the exclusive Travellers' Club on the Avenue des Champs Elysées. This latter statue, however, has been worn away in places by the hold the older members take on her as they support themselves mounting to the upper rooms.

"We wait here for the signal to go up," said Georges. While waiting I opened the stained-glass door beyond which there was the usual Parisian courtyard, with light like that in a good studio. Two of the walls in this yard were lined with six rows of empty champagne bottles stacked eight feet high, the longer wall made up of quart bottles, the side wall of pint sizes—all of the Veuve Clicquot. Opposite the pint bottles was a curious French toilet. There hung dozens of towels to dry and bed linen, and from a window even with the ground came the warm vapor smell of a laundry. Warm soap-water smell is rare now in Paris.

"Here is where you formerly left your hat and coat," said Georges, indicating a small *garde-robe*, when I had returned from my inspection of the courtyard.

"And you waited for the signal to go up. I don't see the need for that any more," he said. So we climbed the stairs to the first floor, where in a second foyer, as elaborate as a Fifth Avenue shoe salon, we were received by the Gouvernante of the house. I did not hear her name as I was being introduced because her face and person accosted me with an old and shocking familiarity, and later, all the while I was being presented to several other ladies, I sought to place the Gouvernante.

The ladies present on that evening seemed to have been singled out for this honor by the length of their service and their loyalty to the house. The Gouvernante, as she is called, who wore the same costume as the rest, is comparable to the sergeant of an infantry company in her closeness to her charges and absolute authority over them. The dresses they wore were of the kind of couture in which the ladies' orchestra indulge—cloth cut from the same bolt of old-rose satin with a pattern like that of hardwood paneling woven into it. It was somewhat faded and soiled. From much undoing and putting on, the hooks and eyes were strained along the opening under the arm down to the waist, where the dresses were especially stained and worn, as in the case of the ladies' orchestra, where the costumes are stain-streaked on the side of the violinist's fiddling arm, and ravaged also at the knees where the instrument is gripped by the cellist.

With a gracious smile, and holding a welty arm and pudgy, rosy hand in the direction of a small salon, the Gouvernante asked me to enter and, with a lion tamer's look, turned to the ladies, who thereupon turned around and made excuses, saying that they would busy themselves with the last preparations for the dinner.

The Gouvernante, sitting on the edge of a tufted satin chair, under an obscene painting, started a polite conversation with me. She sat erect and directly opposite me, and looked down on the carpet while arranging some ribbons that were embedded in the yellow lace on her collar. Her body was a puffy sack that seemed filled with small objects of rounded and oval shapes. She had pulled up the wide skirt showing two upside-down-bottle-shaped legs crossed, and broad feet in discolored satin slippers modestly half-hidden in the tassels that hung from the bottom of the chair. She later brought her hands down from the lace and placed them one above the other, palms up in her lap, and kept on talking and sweetly smiling. The wrist watch which she wore on a black, silken cordlike strap was like a string tied about a sausage, and the whole arrangement, with the exception of the painting in back of her, closely resembled a pose in the atelier of a photographer thirty years ago.

As I looked at this scene a bizarre emotion came suddenly upon me, a condition of the mind that rides along with fevers and gives you a reverse clairvoyance which you lack when well—you see sharply as into a long black box, back into your life; and as if on the most marvelous and clearest stereopticon slides, forgotten scenes appear and live afresh, while at the same time the person you look at, the table before you, and the chair on which you sit, are only half there.

The scene that had come back and lit up was from my childhood in Regensburg. Among the people I knew then was a distant relative, a Fraülein Käthchen, who visited us every week, and sat often in our garden, mostly in a blue satin dress, with snow-white lace on her sleeves and throat, or white ribbons tied in a bow on an institutional collar. She looked like Renoir's paintings of sweet young women. She walked through the city with upraised head, and would smile at me. I was happy when she visited us and spent an evening embroidering or playing the piano.

Sweet Käthchen worked as a receptionist and retoucher for a photographer, an artistic individual who wore a beard and Bohème cravat, and embossed all the portraits he took with the golden coats of arms of the King of Bavaria and the Duke of Thurn and Taxis, whom he had also photographed, and was therefore privileged to add the word "Hofphotograph" to the shield of his firm on his visiting cards and letterheads. It was hoped in Regensburg that he would marry Käthchen and make her the Frau Hofphotográphin. He was the city's best photographer, and Käthchen was envied until the day it was discovered that the Hofphotograph had taken pictures of women in the nude. Although he swore that he had done his evil posing on Sundays, behind locked doors, and that he had never taken any pictures of Käthchen, that she had never retouched any of the Sunday pictures and had no idea of their existence, it was all over. The ribbons and white lace and the beauty of her face were of no avail. Poor Käthchen was dropped by the ladies of Regensburg—no one asked her any more to eat napoleons and drink chocolate with whipped cream at the Schürnbrandt Konditorei on the Neupfarrplatz, which is the Café de la Paix of Regensburg. Poor Käthchen soon disappeared.

After this excursion into the past my mind came back to the room in which I sat opposite the Gouvernante of Numéro Treize. The only meaning I got from the last of many words that she had spoken while I was away was that it was about the closing of the house, and I observed that her French was weighted down with German inflection and mispronunciation.

I answered, *"Ja, es ist schrecklich."* I was certain by then that before me, as the Gouvernante of Numéro Treize in soiled lace and satin, sat poor Käthchen. She looked past me to another obscene still life and said, *"Ja furchtbar ist es—"* and with the expression of one recently bereaved, she added, *"Entschuldigen sie bitte,"* and ran out of the room to greet a new arrival. She stood out there, surrounded by the ladies of the house, who were wiping their hands on the towels they had tied around themselves to protect their satin costumes, and smiled down the stairs. It was all exactly the same in shape, color, and light as Toulouse-Lautrec has painted it—vile, warm, and sad. I have always thought that to partake of the offerings in such places is to do the most painful and desperate act of charity there is. "Only the Senator is missing," said the Gouvernante, "and then we will sit down."

I walked out into the stair hall. The bell rang after a while, and there was below again a scene as in a photographer's studio. The man who was referred to as the "Senator" arrived. He was in black with a high stiff collar, a very flat derby, the thin ends of long white mustaches sticking out left and right beyond his checks. He had very long legs which he employed in the fashion of a crab, lifting them extraordinarily high as if they were feelers. He put his arm around the waist of the nude and began to mount the steps, after for a moment having held his cane and hat in vain in the direction of the small room at the foot of the stairs where he usually was relieved of them. He entered the salon with that expression of the acceptance of the unavoidable which was already on everybody's face.

The soup was on the table in a room to which two maids had opened the mirrored doors. It was decorated in the monotonous aphrodisiac school of the rest of the house. My mood was further bent when Georges, after bringing Käthchen's pudgy hand to his lips, said that after endless apprenticeship and ardent devotion in this and other establishments, by application and hard work Käthchen had risen to her present position of importance, and that he, for one, would see to it that she would not suffer by the change of things. The Gouvernante thanked him and put her hands around Georges. She motioned to the door and said that Mademoiselle Geneviève wanted everyone to sit down and not let the soup get cold, and that she would be with us presently.

I reached for the chair that was indicated to me and stood between the places of the Patronne of the house, Mademoiselle Geneviève, and that of the Gouvernante. The Senator had the place of honor at the head of the table.

"To put at ease any who suffer from superstition," said Käthchen, "the thirteenth we have invited will not come—it is Marthe Richard."

A voice rich in contempt, of low register and carrying through the corridor into the dining room, repeated the name "Marthe Richard," and a second after as the guests arose, Mademoiselle Geneviève entered the room, circled the table, and then sat down.

Mademoiselle Geneviève tilted her head and attached an enormous pendant of antique design to her left perforated earlobe. She then unfolded her napkin and looked serenely and with authority over the table.

A servant poured Bâtard Montrachet from a magnum bottle, the conversation was fit for the ears of the Pope, and the manners and small pleasantries of handing around the bread and smiling across the table were as frequent as are only those of the small bourgeoisie when invited out.

I forgot how good or bad the Poulet Grandmère was on that evening: there was too much to observe. I was brought back when, with a push of her arm and a nod, because her mouth was full and she could not speak, Käthchen offered me the use of the small extra plate on which she was depositing her bones.

After the chocolate soufflé and the coffee, Napoleon inhalers were half filled with brandy. The Senator dipped one end of his napkin carefully into the crystal bowl that held the flowers, and then wiped his mustache and that part of his beard that was under his lips. He slapped himself on the chest and stood up, glass in hand, facing Mademoiselle Geneviève.

He lifted his glass and started to speak. He reviewed the history of the house, and also that of France and mankind. He went back to Paradise and Adam and Eve, and returned to the world at the time of the end of the First World War. His speech was too long to report in full but passages from it deserve to be rescued:

"We French," he said, "are the only nation who have had the courage to recognize life and deal with it without hypocrisy and to the benefit of everyone.

"We are ridiculed for our humanity, and our own government now bows its head to political expedience and rewards those who have paid heavy taxes with expropriation—and such as our beloved Mademoiselle Geneviève, who have served it well and beyond the call of duty, are rewarded with threats of imprisonment.

"Does anyone in the government remember, for example, Mademoiselle Geneviève came to the aid of the Republic after the last war, when on the occasion of the glorious visit of the distinguished foreign statesmen, she took upon herself the delicate task of arranging some quiet diversions for those men who were so beloved and honored!"

"*Oh, ils éaient charmants!*" said Käthchen.

"*Des vrais amis de la France—*" broke in one of the ladies.

"*C'était épatant,*" said Mademoiselle Geneviève.

"That, of course, is something the world has forgotten about—just as they have forgotten what you did for the Allies in this war, Geneviève," said the Senator, looking at Mademoiselle.

"I did not do it with any thought of reward," said that one, and looked sadly into the flowers.

He came to the end after that, saying, "While everything sank all about us in scenes of infinite desolation, *cette fée merveilleuse*"— he lifted his glass and everybody stood up—"made it possible for us to find in this sequestered retreat some consolation, and lifted from us, for golden hours, the dreadful burden that life had become.

"Marthe Richard, who is responsible for this—Marthe Richard, opportunist, swindler, collaborator, and a woman so conveniently forgetful of her own beginnings—what does she hope to accomplish in her small time? *Révolutionner le monde?* Bah—!"

Amidst violent headshaking and murmuring from the people seated at the table, the Senator sat down and waited for the applause to end. Then he got up once more and recited:

> Dans le gazon d'Avril où nous irons courir,
> Est-ce que les oiseaux se cachent pour mourir?

Mademoiselle Geneviève looked at me with interest while she kept turning one of the three rings on the ring finger of her left hand, exactly as my mother did before she asked someone an important question or said something of great consequence.

She said finally, "*Non*, they won't hide, neither will they die, nor will the ladies who have consecrated themselves to this *affaire* enter into a convent. It has been orderly up to now and properly regulated, and, as the Senator said, everyone has been benefited thereby. We had a philosophy about it. But from now on everyone will suffer. It can easily become vicious."

A maid passed a box of exquisite long cigars from which Mademoiselle Geneviève took one and lit it, holding it away from herself, watching the flame while slowly turning the cigar.

"I take the distant view," said Mademoiselle Geneviève, and asked me about America. "You had a problem somewhat like this one in America—you had *La Prohibition* for a while?"

"Yes, it lasted several years."

"Did it work?"

"No, it did not work."

"It never works to forbid pleasure to people. And is it not true that many Americans who did not drink before Prohibition started to drink just because it was forbidden, and that the cost of drinking doubled?"

"That is right."

"*Alors*," she said, looking through the smoke of the cigar, with half-closed eyes. "*Alors*, it is then perhaps not the catastrophe we think it is. We are now stunned and lying helpless on our backs like flies that have been swatted, but that will change—it all may be for the best—it may turn into a really big thing—if intelligently done."

The Senator took Mademoiselle Geneviève by the arm and made her comfortable in the small salon under the obscene painting. There was a tour of the *maison* under the guidance of poor Käthchen.

"How strange to find all the doors, otherwise tightly shut, open," said Georges in the corridor. Inside the rooms the beds had been dismantled; here and there a mattress, worn as the dresses of the ensemble, was leaning against a wall sagging like someone hard hit in the stomach.

"The excuse for taking even our house from us," said Käthchen, "is that people need homes. *Alors*, this is going to make a fine nursery, *par exemple!*" she said, pointing into a room that was decorated with a frieze showing the intimate acrobatics of satyrs and wood nymphs. This décor was repeated with Egyptian, Moorish, and Parisian personnel in the other apartments. There was always a large mirror on the ceiling, and some of the de-luxe suites had mosaic decorations in the baths, and one—the most ornate—offered a miniature swimming pool and Roman couch between its pillars.

On the first floor there was a small theater. The salon in which we had eaten was where the ladies of the house were usually presented to the clients. This was equipped, for those who were considerate, bashful, or had a desire for anonymity, with a single-view, plate-glass pane, the size of a shop window, which was mirrorlike on the side of the ladies, in which they could see themselves pose, while the buyer sat on the other side, nodding his approval, pointing at this or that one, or saying "Thank you."

Protected by this device, which is usually employed to observe the behavior of babies and children in various institutions dedicated to research, the selection was made in the comfort of deeply upholstered *fauteuils*, with champagne and without embarrassment to either the ladies of the house or to the client.

"This mirrored glass pane, whose name is Argus, which was made in America, has cost us a fortune. We shall take it with us," said Käthchen, after she had turned off all the various trick lighting effects that were controlled from behind the marvelous mirror. We examined a mild kind of torture chamber and a lacy, virginal bedroom.

"You have seen it all," said the Gouvernante.

The Senator was out on the staircase, as we came down, with his hat, cane, and coat.

"But you're not going?" said Käthchen.

"Ah, no—" he said, and went downstairs followed by one of the maids. He left the house—and a second later as everybody upstairs watched, he rang the bell outside and came in the door again. He handed his things to the maid, who now stood in the *garde-robe*, and he waited for the signal.

"*On peut monter?*" piped the maid, and falling immediately into her role, Käthchen upstairs sang out, "*Le passage est libre—on peut monter,*" meaning "The passage is free, one may come up." That is the way people are asked to come upstairs, so that their identity remains protected.

To this trumpet call and signal to advance, the old carcass below trembled, and the bug legs took the steps two at a time.

The ladies, who had been honored with attending this last night, received the Senator with tears and led him into the salon. Their soiled costumes shone in the amber light, there was laughter and dancing.

Mademoiselle Geneviève stood with a handkerchief pressed to her eyes.

"*Ah, les enfants préfèrent toujours le jeu à l'étude,*" she said. "Children always prefer play to study."

A few weeks later after a long ride in a sleigh, I was back in Tyrol and sat with my back against the big oven in my mother's three-hundred-year-old house.

She smoked her after-dinner cigar, and I thought it was a good moment to ask her. I said— "Mother, whatever became of poor Käthchen?"

My mother turned the center one of the three rings she wore on the ring finger of her left hand slowly, and then looked at the white ash of the Ramon Allones I had brought her from America. She held it away from herself and blew the smoke toward the paneled ceiling into which the former pious owners of the house had set an azure medallion showing the Holy Ghost. She half closed her eyes, and said,

"Poor Käthchen! After that terrible scandal she left Regensburg, and she married another photographer, who also turned out to be no good. She moved to Dresden, and now she lives in what is left of it in the Russian Zone."

"She couldn't possibly be in Paris?" I asked.

"Oh, no, somebody heard from her only a week ago. You must send her a little fat when you get back to America."

Richard Wilbur

Richard Wilbur (b. 1921), whose translations of Molière and Racine have probably done more to expand American understanding of French literature than any other translations in our time, came to France for the first time in the wake of World War II and searched in Parisian scenes for signs of restoration amid the ruins of European culture. Those who love his poetry love it for the exactness, lucidity, and wit with which he deals with even the most resistant subjects, as in this study (from *The Beautiful Changes*, 1947) of whores and soldiers in the Place Pigalle.

———

Place Pigalle

Now homing tradesmen scatter through the streets
Toward suppers, thinking on improved conditions,
While evening, with a million simple fissions,
Takes up its warehouse watches, storefront beats,
By nursery windows its assigned positions.

Now at the corners of the Place Pigalle
Bright bars explode against the dark's embraces;
The soldiers come, the boys with ancient faces,
Seeking their ancient friends, who stroll and loll
Amid the glares and glass: electric graces.

The puppies are asleep, and snore the hounds;
But here wry hares, the soldier and the whore,
Mark off their refuge with a gaudy door,
Brazen at bay, and boldly out of bounds:
The puppies dream, the hounds superbly snore.

Ionized innocence: this pair reclines,
She on the table, he in a tilting chair,
With Arden at ease; her eyes as pale as air
Travel his priestgoat face; his hand's thick tines
Touch the gold whorls of her Corinthian hair.

"Girl, if I love thee not, then let me die;
Do I not scorn to change my state with kings?
Your muchtouched flesh, incalculable, which wrings
Me so, now shall I gently seize in my
Desperate soldier's hands which kill all things."

Dawn Powell

Dawn Powell (1896–1965), the Jane Austen of Greenwich Village, who after a miserable childhood in Ohio made her way to New York to write, among other novels, *Turn*, *Magic Wheel* and *Angels on Toast*—still, with Howells', the best social comedies to arise from Manhattan manners—had a natural feel for city life, and it didn't desert her in Paris. Her letters from her first trip in 1950 reveal a bemused, and very hard-drinking, outsider's perspective on what was still a poor and just-recovering city. It is fun to see what this driest observer of New York manners makes of Parisian ones, and pleasing to find a bemusement more tender than savage. Her eye for a telling detail never is more in evidence than in her confusion (which generations of Americans have shared, and no Parisian can understand) over how the Rue Jacob can become the Rue de Université *right in the middle of the block*, without anyone questioning whether these two streets are not, in plain geographic fact, if not in Parisian geographic fancy, just one.

———

Three Letters

TO JOSEPH GOUSHA

> *Tuesday, October 24 [1950], 5 p.m.*
> *or 17 hrs. or 12 o'clock high*
> *in your money*

Cher maître (must remember not to say *cher merde* unless it's a very dear old friend)—

I am overlooking the *toits* of Paris at the same time eating the remains of a 500-franc breakfast (a cold *jambon* enough for three, brioche and soluble Nestlé tea and soluble Zeeman's rye in same). I had the breakfast in bed so I would be able to work which was very successful though expensive. I usually wander around for break around 11 after an early instant coffee, but my stomach is still queasy from *mal de mer* and cannot endure any more wine for breakfast which is rather necessary in these very cheap places where the whole thing is only about 150 francs anyway. Besides, as soon as I get out I can't stop walking. This is distinctly your city as an old waterfront man and I try to lay it out for your future visit.

Everything is working out as I planned so far. I have seen nobody and have not tried to. I celebrate my loneliness and this is a wonderful city to be alone in and I trust you will have that privilege. I mean it is so overwhelming that to have somebody with you trying to talk about how Elsie has her hair fixed now or what kind of car your wife likes best would be just like an interruption while reading the most galloping mystery. However, in a few days I will probably be wishing for an evening of sensationally silly conversation with remarkably silly people or even relations.

The maid pleaded for the room about 2:30 so I dressed and took my first Autobus (no. 68—20 francs) across the same bridge I covered yesterday past the rue de l'Université, Louvre and on to the Avenue de l'Opera whence I trickled over to the rue Scribe to the American Express Company which was very empty indicating the lack of Americans in Paris, I guess, at present, as I had been warned you had to stand in line for hours. Then I spotted the Galeries aux Lafayettes next to the Café de l'Opera (all these familiar outdoor cafés including Floré look rather seedy and Coney boardwalk-ish right now, though in the Floré neighborhood my eye was taken by one Café Royal because it had an enormous round bar inside). I found the people outside these places looked sort of pathetic and certainly chilly though I daresay after being here long enough there is always the hope of seeing somebody from Duluth ambling along with a wad in their hands. . . .

The room is pleasant and light, very quiet except for the dining-room orchestra, which stops before 10:30 and is not at all tempting as it only has eight pieces and a strictly metronomic beat, inspiring an old soldier to the march, perhaps, but no mad lust to the ballroom. The chambermaid, waiter and *valet du chambre* are lovely and thoughtful and helpful and jolly, but everywhere else the conduct of business is no smiling matter. Even a mere cashing of checks is an exchange of military insults, grim and solemn. You laugh when you are on the picnic, in the theater, playing with the *bébés*, but not when money is being exchanged, I gather. Courtesy and respect, yes, but let's not horse around with Our Lady of the Bourse.

There are three little buttons on the wall phone, one each for *valet du chamber*, *femme du chambre* and *maître d'hôtel*. Whichever one you ring, an old Edison Record cracked voice wheezes, "*Vous faites mepris*, go crochet yourself." So you crochet yourself and presently someone knocks on the door and all is well. The cutest thing is the little glass mail chute which suddenly has a sound like chimney swifts fluttering around in the chimney and there is a letter in it for you, blown in from goodness knows where, but it's very clever and Fagin would love it. The bidet is a fine thing, too, but your feet hang out (us big California girls). I don't know where you Americans get the idea we have no toilet paper in France, we have plenty of it and nothing ordinary either, it's made of the finest isinglass, in fact a Dupont product I think. I'm making some lackluster contact lenses out of it.

The loveliest place I have seen is the Hôtel Voltaire on the Quai Voltaire which both Esther and Dos recommended. Opposite the Louvre on the Seine and small. When Jack's young friend Marcel Clarin wrote me, he found it full up for four months. I daresay it is without these Hotel Taft conveniences but in another week I may not be able to stand this busy place. The Voltaire is very convenient because it is the last stand before going over the Seine but you can get the Boulevard Raspail bus going back to Montparnasse, etc.

This break indicates a telephone call and who was it but Monsieur Jolas downstairs. He just came up for a few minutes, looking very distinguished and faunish (stout faunish) and much gray hair. This is my first human contact and I was very pleased. I will dine with him and Maria tomorrow night, if I can remember how to act after my last social life with Miss Daly of Boston. He wished you were here. Said he was just back from Germany two months and had turned down a big job at big money (this is his 6th year with OWI or whatever it is) but he wanted to do his own writing. Said he was doing so very well and Maria had bought an apartment on the black market for $2000 not far from here (the rue Bonaparte) and both daughters were married, one with baby and another one coming up. I still had an untouched bottle of the Frankenberg-Flynn brandy and Wheelock's Bonded Beam and some Carstairs but he said he did not indulge in those Americanisms which was just as well as we would probably both end up in the St. James jail. . . .

I may move to a cheaper place if I find any next week, as Gene says this is a bad, cooperationist hangout, though he and Maria have often lived here. I think there will be strange mystery taxes on the regular bill since no one charges or presents bills at the time.

Much love and take care of Fagin and Louise and write me about your mother. Have dinner for the boys.

Dawn

TO EDMUND WILSON

[*ca. November 17, 1950*]

Dear Wig . . .

I just cashed my last ten dollars and was economizing on lunch at the same time disposing of—*alors*, let us say I am the Count of Monte Cristo and the world is mine, at least it feels as if somebody had bashed it over my ears like an old silk hat. Anyway, it would be a hangover in any other country, though in any other country what I drank would be regarded as mere civilized drinking and I wouldn't be *having* a hangover—so the waiter shortchanged me a hundred francs. With that hundred francs I could have lived like a prince for as long as I cared to in my present mood.

The mood is due to three *amer picons* with M. Jolas (who cleverly was having martinis), an Alsatian *beaucoup* wine dinner at a brasserie on Champs-Elysées with both Jolases, myself longing for less raw French meat and eternal French fried, souffléed, allumetted *pommes*—who would have dreamed that they really did have French fried potatoes in France?—and finally a delicate grog with Maria at Deux Maggots (I never dreamed decent people went there anymore, either), Gene having left. The reason he left was my remark that Sartre was the Hopalong Cassidy of France, and he said I should be more humble before French letters, though he himself is not a Sartre admirer. I returned that this view was not—as he held—the stupid view of America toward France, but my own and based not on my brief but not brief enough stay in Paris but on Sartre as a commercial enterprise like cornflakes or Shirley Temple—that is (and he does make the trains run on time) restaurants, hotels, magazines, theaters, real estate thrive on his okay, just as our Hopalong Cassidy boots, breakfast foods, etc. Furthermore, he might be the big frog in Boston but Elyria would still believe Louis Bromfield was the country's leading mind, Carolina would be astounded to learn that there was anybody but Paul Green, New Orleans would have or have had Roark Beadford, and of course there is a group that calls Ben Hecht Ben. Anyway you can see those Uncle Sam pants getting too long. . . .

Margaret probably told you Koestler came with Jim Putnam to my deportation party and gave me his wife's address then as he thought I should look her up. Maria says she's been very sick with asthma. I cannot look up anybody till my finances get more financial. I knew exactly what this would be like but rather fancied my fortunes might change with an ocean voyage.

I would like Paris better if I had any deep feeling for what they like, but I really dislike the pallid, watery-eyed churchly old-whore sentimentality of their limpid pastoral novels—Maurois, Hemon and that school. I find Sartre's work (novels) cutouts from Colette, Aragon, Roger-the-Thibaults'-man, and every other leading novelist, and I hate the rather insanitary tidiness of the people—the newspapers folded just so, their enjoyment in all their little chores, their fixed ideas—the way the newsman is horrified that I want different newspapers every day, and more than one. "But Madame took *Le Figaro* yesterday and so she is a *Figaro* reader, how can she take *Humanité* and *Paris-Presse* too?" Also, I cannot get anyone to admit that rue Jacob is a continuation of rue de l'Université or Boulevard des Italiens is a continuation of Boulevard des Capucines. No. These streets have nothing to do with each other. No, Madame, it is not the same street under a different name, it is an entirely different street. And Fourth Avenue is *not* the lower end of Park Avenue. It is, on the contrary, completely different, in fact it leaves off at 34th Street, whereas, you must admit, Park Avenue only *begins* at 34th Street. Good God, Madame has put her stamps on the letter upside down. The Post Office will not accept. Madame must buy fresh stamps and put the blue one here, so, the red one there, so, and the other one here. This is the order in which it is done.

I do love the tiny little noises in the morning, the autos squeaking *oui oui*, and birds peeping *oui oui* and the whole hotel *oui oui*. The radios go on and I have such a good ear for language that I have picked up one favorite song I hear. It goes:

> LAUNDREE—*come you to me once more*
> Laundree—*what did I pay you for*
> (*parlando*) *You went away*
> (*sing*) *one summer day*
> *Occur this way, s'il vous plaît*
> *Laundree, come sleep with me ce soir.*

Maria says Joyce's son comes in from Zurich only to get Pop's checks to drink up. She also states that many Americans who entertained Sartre and Beauvoir lavishly in America and rather expected some return favors here have been surprised to find them rather grudgingly given one cassis at de Floré café and briskly shoved off. Maria said that the French were really very hospitable, only their hospitality consisted in allowing people to have as many men in their hotel as they liked or allowing them to bring their pets into restaurants.

Most people here seem irritated and surprised that America has so much war talk. However, Gene, who has been on the Frankfurt *Zeitung* for some years (now through with it) says a new war seems certain. . . .

The New Yorker almost bought a story of mine but unluckily decided it would be dated by the time I had made some changes they wanted. I enjoy walking from one end of the Right Bank over bridges and under and over the Left Bank and I like the newspapers and little bakeries. I don't like the cafés because a gentlewoman can't go prancing around alone in them unless she's expecting her group, and the stores have an enormous amount of junk at high price, and in the main I think this is a good place to study to be a dope fiend. I haven't been so abysmally sunk (though I did expect it) since I was making $1000 a week in Hollywood. I have found that money does not bring happiness but neither does the lack of it. (Doesn't that have the old Gallic touch, though, my brave?)

My best (which hardly seems good enough) to Elena and Rosalind and tell the Givenses to get over here for Halloween. Tell everybody and I will meet them at the boat with my hat in my hand. (French courtesy.)

Fondly,
Dawn

—————

TO JOSEPH GOUSHA

Friday Paris a.m. Rain.
In Lutetia brasserie
waiting for omelette
jambon brunch having
had tea and stale
delicious bun in room
[ca. December 15, 1950]

Dear American friend—

Behold a wreck. . . . Thought to soothe interim with view of Paris rain from gargoyles of Notre Dame. Interior is like walking into a sapphire— incredibly breathtaking. Go outside church to spiral up (30 francs) an ancient dungeonlike stone stairs lit by wedges of light and narrow and when you give up you can't go down or up so you have to continue gasping and spiraling while schoolboys and a pair of girls pass you. On last (I thought) roof I was only afraid I would drop into the gargoyles from spiraling and puff, but smell of cooking cabbage drew me on, emerging evidently from tiny cell atop Notre Dame (probably true of Eiffel Tower too) and a bright-eyed and beaming little woman materialized—scarf over head, leather oilskins, mittens, boots—and beckoned me.

I gasped, "No more, please!" but she beamishly insisted and we crossed a gargoyle ledge to the awful horror of God's own garden—saints and monsters all perched on air or dangling vertigo-making sidewise—and suddenly no church underneath. Two French girls cheered me on to follow this merry witch who refused my "Non, j'y reste" with a "Montez, madame, montez!" and I pitched behind her on up dark wooden stairs of an atticlike unsafety where the Bell itself sat. She bonged it to show it was 2nd finest in Paris—then came the Descent!!! The dungeon chill, the sense of stepping into infinity of B.C. and Ad Infinitum—left me chilled and in a sweat. The witch stayed aloft. I had already seen her black cat asleep among the lower Chimeres with Gene one dusky walk.

After that the young du Bois couple restored me. He had $100 a week from Viking to do (illustrate and write) children's books. . . . My great need is simply music (and I don't mean *good*, in fact *any*) and Jane's passion is Maurice Chevalier, who, she said, stares straight at her if she sits down front. We went to theater where he packs them in nightly—got usual seats, which they immediately changed to front row through 100-franc tip to usher, and Maurice appeared. They know it all by heart and I don't care much and I was largely concerned with desire to pee— due to frozen theaters, no dinner yet. Then we went to wonderful joint Chez Inez on rue Champollon (near Sorbonne), Inez being a handsome colored character with an Indo-Chinese gent, both singers and black. . . . Her songs are splendid—super-Fiske as no holds are barred. One song "Everybody's Pissing in the Bidet 'Cause It's Cold Down There in the Hall." Another one "Who Took Me Home Last Night?" with a guess in it that it was a guy who was French from the top of his head to the toes of her feet. . . .

Maria tells me Faulkner is in Lutetia as ideal place for celebrated anonymity. She also said the newsman of *Le Monde* got him out at Floré and he got off some remarks on the negro that (says Maria) Finishes Him with France. This is bushwa—as I can well understand anybody's reaction to that superignorant sentimentality Europe and England have about the negro. You don't see the people who scold about it having any permanent black connections—they love them in the slumming way as Entertainers. Billy du Bois said sports announcers on radio described Ray Sugar (as they say here) in his fight with Stouck as a fashion show and the announcers and reporters cried "Voilà! Ray Sugar appears in tres bean white—but beautiful—robe, his hair perfect, the crowd is going wild, now the beautiful robe white goes and—Mon Dieu!—the beautiful blue satin trunks—the crowd already accepts him as victor! Now Stouck in a dirty old brown robe—hair disheveled—he removes unfortunate robe and *dommage*! Dirty brown trunks. What kind of fighter is it?" Theory is that Ray Sugar killed him with embarrassment.

Love and again thank you!

Art Buchwald

A genuinely beloved humorist, Buchwald (b. 1925) was throughout the 1950s a bright light of the American Paris. He arrived in 1948, having come to study French on the G.I. Bill, and quickly talked his way into a job on the Paris edition of the New York *Herald Tribune*. The job soon became a column, and the column eventually became a fixture, syndicated throughout the United States and collected in *Art Buchwald's Paris* (1954), from which this excerpt is taken. He eventually returned to America and a full-time career as a Washington satirist, but he has returned to the Parisian subject often since, publishing his memoir *I'll Always Have Paris* in 1966. It is customary to say of a humorist that he really has a darker side, and though Buchwald later confessed to many dark moments in his life, his view of the city remains beguilingly bright. Like Irwin Shaw, Buchwald helped define a moment of very nearly pure American happiness in Paris: the war won, the Marshall Plan in place, the city still nearly intact, and Americans still nearly innocent, or thinking themselves so.

---

from

First Days in Paris

The question everyone usually gets around to asking me is, "Why did you come to Paris?" I always seem to be at a loss for an answer. Unlike many of my friends who came to paint the world's greatest picture or write the great American novel, or others who came to escape nagging parents, unhappy love affairs, and suburban boredom, I actually had no reason for making the trip.

For three years, from June, 1945 until June, 1948, I was happily enrolled at the University of Southern California, and was collecting the then very respectable sum of seventy-five dollars a month. Previous to that I had done time in the Marine Corps—17 months in the Central Pacific—and I knew nothing about Paris, France or Europe in general. Any information I had on the subject came from exaggerated stories of ex-GI's who had served in that theater and who indicated the streets of Paris were paved with mattresses, and for a package of cigarettes or a cake of soap the world was yours.

Thoughts of Paris hadn't entered my mind until early in 1948, when I discovered the good citizens of New York State had voted to give each and every one of its sovereign sons a bonus for serving in the Armed Services during the "troubles," as we liked to call it. The sum was staggering: two-hundred-fifty dollars, tax free. It came so unexpectedly that I had not already spent it before it arrived.

In discussing what to do with it in the offices of the *Daily Trojan*, the school newspaper, I was informed that for one hundred and seventy-five dollars I could buy a one-way ticket from New York to Paris. Someone else told me that I could also study under the GI Bill of Rights in Paris, and that seventy-five dollars went much farther there than it did in Southern California. There was no telling how much wine, women and song you could purchase with your government check.

It didn't take me long to make my decision. I decided at the end of June term to invest the entire sum of two hundred and fifty dollars in a one-way European trip, and through the GI Bill of Rights to become a very well-rounded, educated man. (So far after six years I've accomplished part of my plan. I am now very well-rounded.)

I hitch-hiked to New York at the end of June, 1948, and announced my plans to my father, whose only response was, "What do you want to go to Paris for? Stay in New York and learn a good trade."

I bought a steerage ticket on a student ship called the *Marine Jumper* and left New York amidst a flurry of tearful good-bys (my sisters thought I was really going to join the French Foreign Legion), two salamis and a bottle of Scotch—my father's contribution to a *bon voyage*. The trip took ten days and was uneventful except for some Quaker students in charge of entertainment who wouldn't release any films except documentaries. After a brief revolt and several editorials in the ship's newspaper, Betty Hutton was let out of the film can and an impending mutiny was avoided.

We arrived in France July 28. During the trip I had made the pleasant acquaintance of three young ladies from the Parsons School of Design who were going to Paris to study for the summer. Jeanie, Margie and Maurie apparently knew a porter when they saw one, and, although they had been cool toward me during the voyage, things started warming up a bit as soon as their luggage was put on deck.

After unloading the girls' baggage as well as my own, we took the boat train to Paris. We arrived in Paris at ten o'clock, but the people who were supposed to meet my three girls never arrived. They spoke no French (neither did I), had no hotel reservations and were at a loss to know what to do. Pretty soon the tears started to come down and I promised the trio I wouldn't desert them.

But since the responsibility was a heavy one, I became tough. "All right," I said, "I'll take care of you, but you have to do what I say."

They agreed. The first thing I did was find a hotel. It was late so I decided any hotel would do. We went into the first one we saw and demanded three rooms. Two girls would bunk together in one, another girl would bunk alone in the second, and I'd take the third.

The rooms were on the fifth floor and as the girls were unpacking a heavy-set rouged lady stopped by the door. She said in broken English: "What are you kids doing here?"

"Why?" asked Margie.

"Don't you know what this hotel is?"

They said they didn't.

"It's a brothel," and laughing she walked away.

As soon as the girls were unpacked we went to eat. We entered the first café we saw, ordered ham sandwiches and beer (we had been warned not to drink the water), and sat watching a pair of winos getting into a fight. Finally Marge broke down and cried.

"My first night in Paris," she said, "and I'm eating in a gin mill and sleeping in a whorehouse."

The girls all moved into one room when we got back to the hotel and stacked all the furniture except the beds against the door.

I went to sleep but woke up around six in the morning and heard scuffling in the hall. I opened my door and the only thing I saw was a nude Chinaman running down the hall.

At breakfast later I casually said to the girls:

"Say, did any of you see a nude Chinaman running down the hall this morning?"

This time all three of them started crying.

I unloaded the girls at the American Express and, with the responsibility off my hands, went about getting settled in Paris.

I looked up a friend from school. He was living at the time in a small apartment which belonged to a French girl friend, near the Place Clichy.

My friend was an artist and was going away for the summer. He offered to rent me the apartment for fifteen hundred francs (about four dollars) a month, and I gladly accepted.

The apartment, consisting of a kitchen, a dining room and a bedroom, was perfect for a poor American bachelor who had disembarked in France with only eighty dollars in his pocket, and I could have it for three months. I moved in immediately and proceeded to get myself registered in some school, any school, so I could collect the seventy-five dollars a month.

I chose the Alliance Française, a French-language school on the Boulevard Raspail, where I discovered after a few weeks that I could bribe the girl who took attendance, and could devote myself to the more exciting things that Paris had to offer. In the summer of 1948 I also discovered that an American was entitled to gas coupons whether he owned a car or not. These coupons could be sold on the black market for as much as fifteen thousand francs (about forty dollars) a month, a fine supplementary income for all students of the time. With the gasoline coupons and the government check I was doing fine.

When my friend came back from the country I gave up the Place Clichy apartment and moved over to the Boulevard Montparnasse, famed in Hemingway lore, song and story. The hotel I selected was called the Hotel des Etats-Unis and was certainly misnamed. It was a Polish cooperative and its forty-some odd rooms were filled with every nationality under the sun. At the time there were several Americans staying at the hotel including Gary Davis, the boy who became a world citizen and then asked for his American passport back. My room cost me seventy-five cents a day, and I ate one meal in the bar in the evening for the same price. The other meal I usually ate at a restaurant called Henriette's, and it averaged thirty-five cents a day.

The Hotel des Etats-Unis had a wonderful bar which was the meeting place of all the guests as well as neighborhood drinkers and Polish stockholders from the hotel.

There were about fifty Poles involved in the ownership of the hotel, and fortunately they all had saints' days, which meant free vodka on the house for all.

Davis at the time had made his dramatic gesture of handing in his passport and was the hero of the hour. The Poles, who were always holding board meetings and leaving notes in our boxes concerning our rent, were also delighted with Davis's notoriety and even more impressed when bags of mail kept pouring in from all over the world. At the time the self-styled citizen of the world had many advisors and workers. The first idea they sold the Poles was that they planned to make the Hotel des Etats-Unis global headquarters for the World Citizen Movement, and so wanted to take over all the rooms immediately.

The board of directors were enchanted with the idea, especially when they were informed that the World Citizens would pay a higher rent on each room. The Poles started a campaign to get all the non-world citizens out of the hotel. We refused to leave, and for a month things became tense. Then when the Davis group failed to meet their rent for one floor for just one month, the Poles changed their minds. They insisted we stay and the Davis people go.

Most of the people who lived at the hotel were sympathetic to Gary Davis and what he was trying to do. We all admired his courage and we certainly liked the one-world concept. We even went so far as to lick envelopes or stick on stamps and occasionally, when the police raided the hotel, we ran interference for some of the stateless citizens they were looking for.

Therefore, although the movement was forced to move, our hearts were still with it. It was quite a shock a year and a half ago to run into Gary again. By this time he had been allowed back in the United States, had played on Broadway in *Stalag 17*, was married and separated and had become a completely changed person.

I always thought we were good friends, so when he came to Paris I called him up and asked him if we could have a drink together.

He said over the phone: "How much is it worth to you?"

I thought he was kidding and asked him to come to the Hotel California on the Rue de Berri across from the *Herald-Tribune* offices.

When he arrived he said again: "How much is this worth to you?"

I said I just wanted to have a talk and he replied: "Look, my time is valuable. If you don't want to pay to talk to me I'll be going."

I became angry and said "Okay, go," and he said:

"How about paying my taxi fare to get over here? It's five hundred francs."

I gave him five hundred francs and watched him hurry out the door, a broken and disillusioned man. The next month he was arrested in England for trying to break into Buckingham Palace to speak to the queen.

Although neither the French nor American newspapers were in agreement on the Gary Davis movement, they all seemed to be in agreement on the hotel. *Time* magazine called it sleazy and smelling of stale potatoes. The *Herald-Tribune* said it was dark and shabby, and many of the journals referred to it as a "Left Bank hole-in-the-wall." But to those of us who lived there the Hotel des Etats-Unis was home.

The bar of the hotel, where most of the respectable activity took place, was usually crowded every night with Negro musicians, Montparnasse prostitutes, Polish refugees, American college students, French artists and occasional Swedish tourists who came down from Sweden in large buses to be lodged in the hotel for one or two nights as part of an all-inclusive Sweden-to-Paris tour.

Bad cognac, cheap beer and vodka were the most popular beverages, and most of the guests of the hotel were usually blind before the bar closed at four o'clock in the morning.

The hotel had its share of strange people. Besides the world citizens (who rarely drank), we had a chronic alcoholic—an American young lady who used to start screaming at three and four in the morning that there were mice in her room. This of course was entirely possible, and many sober people complained of the same thing, but her protests woke everybody in the building. When we tried to calm her down, Sarah threatened to kill all of us, and one of us would have to take her out to another bar to make her forget her troubles. She was taken to a French hospital twice, and finally the American Embassy arranged to have her sent back to America. Only those of us who lived at the hotel could back her story that she really saw mice at night.

A Spanish dancer, very pro-Franco as well as oversexed, lived in the next room, and since the walls were paper thin I was treated to both Spanish music and loud love affairs. One evening I was trying to go to sleep when I heard her playing with castanets. First there was a series of castanet clacks and then the bed would squeak—then the castanets and then the squeaking bed. Finally I heard a deep male voice shout:

"For Chris' sakes. Put down those God damn castanets."

Sexes naturally mixed freely in such an atmosphere, and I constantly kept bumping into strange women going in and out of friends' rooms. One American friend had a misfortune with a young lady from one of the better eastern colleges, and we all were delighted to be invited to a lavish but unexpected wedding. Another friend who found himself in the same situation took the easier way out and reenlisted in the American army. The last I heard of him he was sent to Korea, where I'm sure he regretted the folly of his impulsive escape.

People at the Hotel des Etats-Unis were sleeping together, painting pictures, writing books and getting drunk. Paris apparently wasn't any different for us than it was for thousands of students who had been there before us and would probably come after us.

James Baldwin

James Baldwin (1924–1987), the African-American essayist and novelist
whose genius for realism could almost always trump an occasional weakness
for rhetoric, like so many others came to Paris for the first time in 1948
and remained in France off and on for the rest of his life. His was a classic
American voyage, a black (and gay) man seeking refuge and space in a place
promised as color-blind. Unlike many of his contemporaries, Baldwin would
see clearly, and presciently, that persecution was a function of circumstance
rather than fixed mental corruption, as he dramatizes in this sequence from
Notes of a Native Son (1955) about being truly down and out and arrested
in Paris. Of all Americans in Paris, Baldwin may be the most intelligently
disabused, or disillusioned. He had a clear sense of his own distance, as an
émigré American, from anything quite real in France, and where his '50s contemporaries Shaw and Buchwald, among others, found this distance comic
and liberating, it left Baldwin—for whom all distance always had in it a hint
of cruelty yet to come—deeply disturbed. In Paris, Baldwin discovered that
the American racism he had fled was simply a subset of a larger and inevitable
human indifference to suffering. His discovery in Paris, dramatized here in
what he concedes is an episode of comic opera imprisonment, is not that the
French are particularly malignant, but that human existence everywhere proceeds through a series of ineluctable oppressions. As he says, the laughter that
he heard in the French courtroom is "the laughter of those who consider
themselves to be at a safe remove from the wretched, for whom the pain of
living is not real." This laughter, for Baldwin, is universal and never stilled.

Equal in Paris

On the 19th of December, in 1949, when I had been living in Paris for
a little over a year, I was arrested as a receiver of stolen goods and
spent eight days in prison. My arrest came about through an American
tourist whom I had met twice in New York, who had been given my name
and address and told to look me up. I was then living on the top floor of a
ludicrously grim hotel on the rue du Bac, one of those enormous dark,
cold, and hideous establishments in which Paris abounds that seem to

breathe forth, in their airless, humid, stone-cold halls, the weak light, scurrying chambermaids, and creaking stairs, an odor of gentility long long dead. The place was run by an ancient Frenchman dressed in an elegant black suit which was green with age, who cannot properly be described as bewildered or even as being in a state of shock, since he had really stopped breathing around 1910. There he sat at his desk in the weirdly lit, fantastically furnished lobby, day in and day out, greeting each one of his extremely impoverished and *louche* lodgers with a stately inclination of the head that he had no doubt been taught in some impossibly remote time was the proper way for a *propriétaire* to greet his guests. If it had not been for his daughter, an extremely hardheaded *tricoteuse*—the inclination of *her* head was chilling and abrupt, like the downbeat of an ax—the hotel would certainly have gone bankrupt long before. It was said that this old man had not gone farther than the door of his hotel for thirty years, which was not at all difficult to believe. He looked as though the daylight would have killed him.

I did not, of course, spend much of my time in this palace. The moment I began living in French hotels I understood the necessity of French cafés. This made it rather difficult to look me up, for as soon as I was out of bed I hopefully took notebook and fountain pen off to the upstairs room of the Flore, where I consumed rather a lot of coffee and, as evening approached, rather a lot of alcohol, but did not get much writing done. But one night, in one of the cafés of St. Germain des Près, I was discovered by this New Yorker and only because we found ourselves in Paris we immediately established the illusion that we had been fast friends back in the good old U.S.A. This illusion proved itself too thin to support an evening's drinking, but by that time it was too late. I had committed myself to getting him a room in my hotel the next day, for he was living in one of the nest of hotels near the Gare St. Lazare, where, he said, the *propriétaire* was a thief, his wife a repressed nymphomaniac, the chambermaids "pigs," and the rent a crime. Americans are always talking this way about the French and so it did not occur to me that he meant what he said or that he would take into his own hands the means of avenging himself on the French Republic. It did not occur to me, either, that the means which he *did* take could possibly have brought about such dire results, results which were not less dire for being also comic-opera.

It came as the last of a series of disasters which had perhaps been made inevitable by the fact that I had come to Paris originally with a little over forty dollars in my pockets, nothing in the bank, and no grasp whatever of the French language. It developed, shortly, that I had no grasp of the French character either. I considered the French an ancient, intelligent, and cultured race, which indeed they are. I did not know, however, that ancient glories imply, at least in the middle of the present century, present fatigue and, quite probably, paranoia; that there is a limit to the role of the intelligence in human affairs; and that no people come into possession of a culture without having paid a heavy price for it. This price they cannot, of course, assess, but it is revealed in their personalities and in their institutions. The very word "institutions," from my side of the ocean, where, it seemed to me, we suffered so cruelly from the lack of them, had a pleasant ring, as of safety and order and common sense; one had to come into contact with these institutions in order to understand that they were also outmoded, exasperating, completely impersonal, and very often cruel. Similarly, the personality which had seemed from a distance to be so large and free had to be dealt with before one could see that, if it was large, it was also inflexible and, for the foreigner, full of strange, high, dusty rooms which could not be inhabited. One had, in short, to come into contact with an alien culture in order to understand that a culture was not a community basket-weaving project, nor yet an act of God; was something neither desirable nor undesirable in itself, being inevitable, being nothing more or less than the recorded and visible effects on a body of people of the vicissitudes with which they had been forced to deal. And their great men are revealed as simply another of these vicissitudes, even if, quite against their will, the brief battle of their great men with them has left them richer.

When my American friend left his hotel to move to mine, he took with him, out of pique, a bedsheet belonging to the hotel and put it in his suitcase. When he arrived at my hotel I borrowed the sheet, since my own were filthy and the chambermaid showed no sign of bringing me any clean ones, and put it on my bed. The sheets belonging to *my* hotel I put out in the hall, congratulating myself on having thus forced on the attention of the Grand Hôtel du Bac the unpleasant state of its linen. Thereafter, since, as it turned out, we kept very different hours—I got up at noon, when, as I gathered by meeting him on the stairs one day, he was only just getting in—my new-found friend and I saw very little of each other.

On the evening of the 19th I was sitting thinking melancholy thoughts about Christmas and staring at the walls of my room. I imagine that I had sold something or that someone had sent me a Christmas present, for I remember that I had a little money. In those days in Paris, though I floated, so to speak, on a sea of acquaintances, I knew almost no one. Many people were eliminated from my orbit by virtue of the fact that they had more money than I did, which placed me, in my own eyes, in the humiliating role of a free-loader; and other people were eliminated by virtue of the fact that they enjoyed their poverty, shrilly insisting that this wretched round of hotel rooms, bad food, humiliating concierges, and unpaid bills was the Great Adventure. It couldn't, however, for me, end soon enough, this Great Adventure; there was a real question in my mind as to which would end soonest, the Great Adventure or me. This meant, however, that there were many evenings when I sat in my room, knowing that I couldn't work there, and not knowing what to do, or whom to see. On this particular evening I went down and knocked on the American's door.

There were two Frenchmen standing in the room, who immediately introduced themselves to me as policemen; which did not worry me. I had got used to policemen in Paris bobbing up at the most improbable times and places, asking to see one's *carte d'idenitité*. These policemen, however, showed very little interest in my papers. They were looking for something else. I could not imagine what this would be and, since I knew I certainly didn't have it, I scarcely followed the conversation they were having with my friend. I gathered that they were looking for some kind of gangster and since I wasn't a gangster and knew that gangsterism was not, insofar as he had one, my friend's style, I was sure that the two policemen would presently bow and say *Merci, messieurs*, and leave. For by this time, I remember very clearly, I was dying to have a drink and go to dinner.

I did not have a drink or go to dinner for many days after this, and when I did my outraged stomach promptly heaved everything up again. For now one of the policemen began to exhibit the most vivid interest in me and asked, very politely, if he might see my room. To which we mounted, making, I remember, the most civilized small talk on the way and even continuing it for some moments after we were in the room in which there was certainly nothing to be seen but the familiar poverty and disorder of that precarious group of people of whatever age, race, country, calling, or intention which Paris recognizes as *les étudiants* and sometimes, more ironically and precisely, as *les nonconformistes*. Then he moved to my bed, and in a terrible flash, not quite an instant before he lifted the bed-spread, I understood what he was looking for. We looked at the sheet, on which I read, for the first time, lettered in the most brilliant scarlet I have ever seen, the name of the hotel from which it had been stolen. It was the first time the word *stolen* entered my mind. I had certainly seen the hotel monogram the day I put the sheet on the bed. It had simply meant noth-ing to me. In New York I had seen hotel monograms on everything from silver to soap and towels. Taking things from New York hotels was practi-cally a custom, though, I suddenly realized, I had never known anyone to take a *sheet*. Sadly, and without a word to me, the inspector took the sheet from the bed, folded it under his arm, and we started back downstairs. I understood that I was under arrest.

And so we passed through the lobby, four of us, two of us very clearly criminal, under the eyes of the old man and his daughter, neither of whom said a word, into the streets where a light rain was falling. And I asked, in French, "But is this very serious?"

For I was thinking, it is, after all, only a sheet, not even new.

"No," said one of them. "It's not serious."

"It's nothing at all," said the other.

I took this to mean that we would receive a reprimand at the police station and be allowed to go to dinner. Later on I concluded that they were not being hypocritical or even trying to comfort us. They meant exactly what they said. It was only that they spoke another language.

In Paris everything is very slow. Also, when dealing with the bureau-cracy, the man you are talking to is never the man you have to see. The man you have to see has just gone off to Belgium, or is busy with his fam-ily, or has just discovered that he is a cuckold; he will be in next Tuesday at three o'clock, or sometime in the course of the afternoon, or possibly tomorrow, or, possibly, in the next five minutes. But if he is coming in the next five minutes he will be far too busy to be able to see you today. So that I suppose I was not really astonished to learn at the commissariat that nothing could possibly be done about us before The Man arrived in the morning. But no, we could not go off and have dinner and come back in the morning. Of course he knew that we *would* come back—that was not the question. Indeed, there was no question: we would simply have to stay there for the night. We were placed in a cell which rather resembled a chicken coop. It was now about seven in the evening and I relinquished the thought of dinner and began to think of lunch.

I discouraged the chatter of my New York friend and this left me alone with my thoughts. I was beginning to be frightened and I bent all my energies, therefore, to keeping my panic under control. I began to realize that I was in a country I knew nothing about, in the hands of a people I did not understand at all. In a similar situation in New York I would have had some idea of what to do because I would have had some idea of what to expect. I am not speaking now of legality which, like most of the poor, I had never for an instant trusted, but of the temperament of the people with whom I had to deal. I had become very accomplished in New York at guessing and, therefore, to a limited extent manipulating to my advantage the reactions of the white world. But this was not New York. None of my old weapons could serve me here. I did not know what they saw when they looked at me. I knew very well what Americans saw when they looked at me and this allowed me to play endless and sinister variations on the role which they had assigned me; since I knew that it was, for them, of the utmost importance that they never be confronted with what, in their own personalities, made this role so necessary and gratifying to them, I knew that they could never call my hand or, indeed, afford to know what I was doing; so that I moved into every crucial situation with the deadly and rather desperate advantages of bitterly accumulated perception, of pride and contempt. This is an awful sword and shield to carry through the world, and the discovery that, in the game I was playing, I did myself a violence of which the world, at its most ferocious, would scarcely have been capable, was what had driven me out of New York. It was a strange feeling, in this situation, after a year in Paris, to discover that my weapons would never again serve me as they had.

It was quite clear to me that the Frenchmen in whose hands I found myself were no better or worse than their American counterparts. Certainly their uniforms frightened me quite as much, and their impersonality, and the threat, always very keenly felt by the poor, of violence, was as present in that commissariat as it had ever been for me in any police station. And I had seen, for example, what Paris policemen could do to Arab peanut vendors. The only difference here was that I did not understand these people, did not know what techniques their cruelty took, did not know enough about their personalities to see danger coming, to ward it off, did not know on what ground to meet it. That evening in the commissariat I was not a despised black man. They would simply have laughed at me if I had behaved like one. For them, I was an American.

And here it was they who had the advantage, for that word, *Américain*, gave them some idea, far from inaccurate, of what to expect from me. In order to corroborate none of their ironical expectations I said nothing and did nothing—which was not the way any Frenchman, white or black, would have reacted. The question thrusting up from the bottom of my mind was not *what* I was, but *who*. And this question, since a *what* can get by with skill but a *who* demands resources, was my first real intimation of what humility must mean.

In the morning it was still raining. Between nine and ten o'clock a black Citroën took us off to the Ile de la Cité, to the great, gray Préfecture. I realize now that the questions I put to the various policemen who escorted us were always answered in such a way as to corroborate what I wished to hear. This was not out of politeness, but simply out of indifference—or, possibly, an ironical pity—since each of the policemen knew very well that nothing would speed or halt the machine in which I had become entangled. They knew I did not know this and there was certainly no point in their telling me. In one way or another I would certainly come out at the other side—for they also knew that being found with a stolen bedsheet in one's possession was not a crime punishable by the guillotine. (They had the advantage over me there, too, for there were certainly moments later on when I was not so sure.) If I did *not* come out at the other side—well, that was just too bad. So, to my question, put while we were in the Citroën—"Will it be over today?"—I received a *"Oui, bien sûr."* He was not lying. As it turned out, the *procès-verbal* was over that day. Trying to be realistic, I dismissed, in the Citroën, all thoughts of lunch and pushed my mind ahead to dinner.

At the Préfecture we were first placed in a tiny cell, in which it was almost impossible either to sit or to lie down. After a couple of hours of this we were taken down to an office, where, for the first time, I encountered the owner of the bedsheet and where the *procès-verbal* took place. This was simply an interrogation, quite chillingly clipped and efficient (so that there was, shortly, no doubt in one's own mind that one *should* be treated as a criminal), which was recorded by a secretary. When it was over, this report was given to us to sign. One had, of course, no choice but to sign it, even though my mastery of written French was very far from certain. We were being held, according to the law in France, incommunicado, and all my angry demands to be allowed to speak to my embassy or to see a lawyer met with a stony *"Oui, oui. Plus tard."* The *procès-verbal* over, we were taken back to the cell, before which, shortly, passed the owner of the bedsheet. He said he hoped we had slept well, gave a vindictive wink, and disappeared.

By this time there was only one thing clear: that we had no way of controlling the sequence of events and could not possibly guess what this sequence would be. It seemed to me, since what I regarded as the high point—the *procès-verbal*—had been passed and since the hotelkeeper was once again in possession of his sheet, that we might reasonably expect to be released from police custody in a matter of hours. We had been detained now for what would soon be twenty-four hours, during which time I had learned only that the official charge against me was *receleur*. My mental shifting, between lunch and dinner, to say nothing of the physical lack of either of these delights, was beginning to make me dizzy. The steady chatter of my friend from New York, who was determined to keep my spirits up, made me feel murderous; I was praying that some power would release us from this freezing pile of stone before the impulse became the act. And I was beginning to wonder what was happening in that beautiful city, Paris, which lived outside these walls. I wondered how long it would take before anyone casually asked, "But where's Jimmy? He hasn't been around"—and realized, knowing the people I knew, that it would take several days.

Quite late in the afternoon we were taken from our cells; handcuffed, each to a separate officer; led through a maze of steps and corridors to the top of the building; finger-printed; photographed. As in movies I had seen, I was placed against a wall, facing an old-fashioned camera, behind which stood one of the most completely cruel and indifferent faces I had ever seen, while someone next to me and, therefore, just outside my line of vision, read off in a voice from which all human feeling, even feeling of the most base description, had long since fled, what must be called my public characteristics—which, at that time and in that place, seemed anything but that. He might have been roaring to the hostile world secrets which I could barely, in the privacy of midnight, utter to myself. But he was only reading off my height, my features, my approximate weight, my color—that color which, in the United States, had often, odd as it may sound, been my salvation—the color of my hair, my age, my nationality. A light then flashed, the photographer and I staring at each other as though there was murder in our hearts, and then it was over. Handcuffed again, I was led downstairs to the bottom of the building, into a great

enclosed shed in which had been gathered the very scrapings off the
Paris streets. Old, old men, so ruined and old that life in them seemed
really to prove the miracle of the quickening power of the Holy Ghost—
for clearly their life was no longer their affair, it was no longer even their
burden, they were simply the clay which had once been touched. And
men not so old, with faces the color of lead and the consistency of oat-
meal, eyes that made me think of stale *café-au-lait* spiked with arsenic,
bodies which could take in food and water—any food and water—and
pass it out, but which could not do anything more, except possibly,
at midnight, along the riverbank where rats scurried, rape. And young
men, harder and crueler than the Paris stones, older by far than I, their
chronological senior by some five to seven years. And North Africans, old
and young, who seemed the only living people in this place because they
yet retained the grace to be bewildered. But they were not bewildered
by being in this shed: they were simply bewildered because they were
no longer in North Africa. There was a great hole in the center of this
shed, which was the common toilet. Near it, though it was impossible to
get very far from it, stood an old man with white hair, eating a piece of
camembert. It was at this point, probably, that thought, for me, stopped,
that physiology, if one may say so, took over. I found myself incapable of
saying a word, not because I was afraid I would cry but because I was
afraid I would vomit. And I did not think any longer of the city of Paris
but my mind flew back to that home from which I had fled. I was sure
that I would never see it any more. And it must have seemed to me that
my flight from home was the crudest trick I had ever played on myself,
since it had led me here, down to a lower point than any I could ever in
my life have imagined—lower, far, than anything I had seen in that
Harlem which I had so hated and so loved, the escape from which had
soon become the greatest direction of my life. After we had been here an
hour or so a functionary came and opened the door and called out our
names. And I was sure that this was my release. But I was handcuffed
again and led out of the Préfecture into the streets—it was dark now, it
was still raining—and before the steps of the Préfecture stood the great
police wagon, doors facing me, wide open. The handcuffs were taken off,
I entered the wagon, which was peculiarly constructed. It was divided by
a narrow aisle, and on each side of the aisle was a series of narrow doors.
These doors opened on a narrow cubicle, beyond which was a door which
opened onto another narrow cubicle: three or four cubicles, each private,

with a locking door. I was placed in one of them; I remember there was a small vent just above my head which let in a little light. The door of my cubicle was locked from the outside. I had no idea where this wagon was taking me and, as it began to move, I began to cry. I suppose I cried all the way to prison, the prison called Fresnes, which is twelve kilometers outside of Paris.

For reasons I have no way at all of understanding, prisoners whose last initial is A, B, or C are always sent to Fresnes; everybody else is sent to a prison called, rather cynically it seems to me, La Santé. I will, obviously, never be allowed to enter La Santé, but I was told by people who certainly seemed to know that it was infinitely more unbearable than Fresnes. This arouses in me, until today, a positive storm of curiosity concerning what I promptly began to think of as The Other Prison. My colleague in crime, occurring lower in the alphabet, had been sent there and I confess that the minute he was gone I missed him. I missed him because he was not French and because he was the only person in the world who knew that the story I told was true.

For, once locked in, divested of shoelaces, belt, watch, money, papers, nailfile, in a freezing cell in which both the window and the toilet were broken, with six other adventurers, the story I told of *l'affaire du drap de lit* elicited only the wildest amusement or the most suspicious disbelief. Among the people who shared my cell the first three days no one, it is true, had been arrested for anything much more serious—or, at least, not serious in my eyes. I remember that there was a boy who had stolen a knitted sweater from a *monoprix*, who would probably, it was agreed, receive a six-month sentence. There was an older man there who had been arrested for some kind of petty larceny. There were two North Africans, vivid, brutish, and beautiful, who alternated between gaiety and fury, not at the fact of their arrest but at the state of the cell. None poured as much emotional energy into the fact of their arrest as I did; they took it, as I would have liked to take it, as simply another unlucky happening in a very dirty world. For, though I had grown accustomed to thinking of myself as looking upon the world with a hard, penetrating eye, the truth was that they were far more realistic about the world than I, and more nearly right about it. The gap between us, which only a gesture I made could have bridged, grew steadily, during thirty-six hours, wider. I could not make any gesture simply because they frightened me. I was unable to accept my imprisonment as a fact, even as a temporary fact. I could not, even for a moment, accept my present companions as *my* companions. And they, of course, felt this and put it down, with perfect justice, to the fact that I was an American.

There was nothing to do all day long. It appeared that we would one day come to trial but no one knew when. We were awakened at seven-thirty by a rapping on what I believe is called the Judas, that small opening in the door of the cell which allows the guards to survey the prisoners. At this rapping we rose from the floor—we slept on straw pallets and each of us was covered with one thin blanket—and moved to the door of the cell. We peered through the opening into the center of the prison, which was, as I remember, three tiers high, all gray stone and gunmetal steel, precisely that prison I had seen in movies, except that, in the movies, I had not known that it was cold in prison. I had not known that when one's shoelaces and belt have been removed one is, in the strangest way, demoralized. The necessity of shuffling and the necessity of holding up one's trousers with one hand turn one into a rag doll. And the movies fail, of course, to give one any idea of what prison food is like. Along the corridor, at seven-thirty, came three men, each pushing before him a great garbage can, mounted on wheels. In the garbage can of the first was the bread—this was passed to one through the small opening in the door. In the can of the second was the coffee. In the can of the third was what was always called *la soupe*, pallid paste of potatoes which had certainly been bubbling on the back of the prison stove long before that first, so momentous revolution. Naturally, it was cold by this time and, starving as I was, I could not eat it. I drank the coffee—which was not coffee—because it was hot, and spent the rest of the day huddled in my blanket, munching on the bread. It was not the French bread one bought in bakeries. In the evening the same procession returned. At ten-thirty the lights went out. I had a recurring dream, each night, a nightmare which always involved my mother's fried chicken. At the moment I was about to eat it came the rapping at the door. Silence is really all I remember of those first three days, silence and the color gray.

I am not sure now whether it was on the third or the fourth day that I was taken to trial for the first time. The days had nothing, obviously, to distinguish them from one another. I remember that I was very much aware that Christmas Day was approaching and I wondered if I was really going to spend Christmas Day in prison. And I remember that the first trial came the day before Christmas Eve.

On the morning of the first trial I was awakened by hearing my name called. I was told, hanging in a kind of void between my mother's fried chicken and the cold prison floor, *"Vous préparez. Vous êtes extrait"*—which simply terrified me, since I did not know what interpretation to put on the word *"extrait,"* and since my cellmates had been amusing themselves with me by telling terrible stories about the inefficiency of French prisons, an inefficiency so extreme that it had often happened that someone who was supposed to be taken out and tried found himself on the wrong line and was guillotined instead. The best way of putting my reaction to this is to say that, though I knew they were teasing me, it was simply not possible for me to totally *dis*believe them. As far as I was concerned, once in the hands of the law in France, anything could happen. I shuffled along with the others who were *extrait* to the center of the prison, trying, rather, to linger in the office, which seemed the only warm spot in the whole world, and found myself again in that dreadful wagon, and was carried again to the Ile de la Cité, this time to the Palais de Justice. The entire day, except for ten minutes, was spent in one of the cells, first waiting to be tried, then waiting to be taken back to prison.

For I was *not* tried that day. By and by I was handcuffed and led through the halls, upstairs to the courtroom where I found my New York friend. We were placed together, both stage-whisperingly certain that this was the end of our ordeal. Nevertheless, while I waited for our case to be called, my eyes searched the courtroom, looking for a face I knew, hoping, anyway, that there was someone there who knew *me*, who would carry to someone outside the news that I was in trouble. But there was no one I knew there and I had had time to realize that there was probably only one man in Paris who could help me, an American patent attorney for whom I had worked as an office boy. He could have helped me because he had a quite solid position and some prestige and would have testified that, while working for him, I had handled large sums of money regularly, which made it rather unlikely that I would stoop to trafficking in bed-sheets. However, he was somewhere in Paris, probably at this very moment enjoying a snack and a glass of wine and as far as the possibility of reaching him was concerned, he might as well have been on Mars. I tried to watch the proceedings and to make my mind a blank. But the proceedings were not reassuring. The boy, for example, who had stolen the sweater *did* receive a six-month sentence. It seemed to me that all the sentences meted out that day were excessive; though, again, it seemed that all the people who were sentenced that day had made, or clearly were going to make, crime their career. This seemed to be the opinion of the judge, who scarcely looked at the prisoners or listened to them; it seemed to be the opinion of the prisoners, who scarcely bothered to speak in their own behalf; it seemed to be the opinion of the lawyers, state lawyers for the most part, who were defending them. The great impulse of the court-room seemed to be to put these people where they could not be seen—and not because they were offended at the crimes, unless, indeed, they were offended that the crimes were so petty, but because they did not wish to know that their society could be counted on to produce, probably in greater and greater numbers, a whole body of people for whom crime was the only possible career. Any society inevitably produces its criminals, but a society at once rigid and unstable can do nothing whatever to alleviate the poverty of its lowest members, cannot present to the hypothetical young man at the crucial moment that so-well-advertised right path. And the fact, perhaps, that the French are the earth's least sentimental people and must also be numbered among the most proud aggravates the plight of their lowest, youngest, and unluckiest members, for it means that the idea of rehabilitation is scarcely real to them. I confess that this attitude on their part raises in me sentiments of exasperation, admiration, and despair, revealing as it does, in both the best and the worst sense, their renowned and spectacular hard-headedness.

Finally our case was called and we rose. We gave our names. At the point that it developed that we were American the proceedings ceased, a hurried consultation took place between the judge and what I took to be several lawyers. Someone called out for an interpreter. The arresting officer had forgotten to mention our nationalities and there was, therefore, no interpreter in the court. Even if our French had been better than it was we would not have been allowed to stand trial without an interpreter. Before I clearly understood what was happening, I was handcuffed again and led out of the courtroom. The trial had been set back for the 27th of December.

I have sometimes wondered if I would *ever* have got out of prison if it had not been for the older man who had been arrested for the mysterious petty larceny. He was acquitted that day and when he returned to the cell—for he could not be released until morning—he found me sitting numbly on the floor, having just been prevented, by the sight of a man, all blood, being carried back to *his* cell on a stretcher, from seizing the bars and screaming until they let me out. The sight of the man on the stretcher proved, however, that screaming would not do much for me. The petty-larceny man went around asking if he could do anything in the world outside for those he was leaving behind. When he came to me I, at first, responded, "No, nothing"—for I suppose I had by now retreated into the attitude, the earliest I remember, that of my father, which was simply (since I had lost his God) that nothing could help me. And I suppose I will remember with gratitude until I die the fact that the man now insisted: "*Mais, êtes-vous sûr?*" Then it swept over me that he was going *outside* and he instantly became my first contact since the Lord alone knew how long with the outside world. At the same time, I remember, I did not really believe that he would help me. There was no reason why he should. But I gave him the phone number of my attorney friend and my own name.

So, in the middle of the next day, Christmas Eve, I shuffled downstairs again, to meet my visitor. He looked extremely well fed and sane and clean. He told me I had nothing to worry about any more. Only not even he could do anything to make the mill of justice grind any faster. He would, however, send me a lawyer of his acquaintance who would defend me on the 27th, and he would himself, along with several other people, appear as a character witness. He gave me a package of Lucky Strikes (which the turnkey took from me on the way upstairs) and said that, though it was doubtful that there would be any celebration in the prison, he would see to it that I got a fine Christmas dinner when I got out. And this, somehow, seemed very funny. I remember being astonished at the discovery that I was actually laughing. I was, too, I imagine, also rather disappointed that my hair had not turned white, that my face was clearly not going to bear any marks of tragedy, disappointed at bottom, no doubt, to realize, facing him in that room, that far worse things had happened to most people and that, indeed, to paraphrase my mother, if this was the worst thing that ever happened to me I could consider myself among the luckiest people ever to be born. He injected—my visitor—into my solitary nightmare common sense, the world, and the hint of blacker things to come.

The next day, Christmas, unable to endure my cell, and feeling that, after all, the day demanded a gesture, I asked to be allowed to go to Mass, hoping to hear some music. But I found myself, for a freezing hour and a half, locked in exactly the same kind of cubicle as in the wagon which had first brought me to prison, peering through a slot placed at the level of the eye at an old Frenchman, hatted, overcoated, muffled, and gloved, preaching in this language which I did not understand, to this row of wooden boxes, the story of Jesus Christ's love for men.

The next day, the 26th, I spent learning a peculiar kind of game, played with match-sticks, with my cellmates. For, since I no longer felt that I would stay in this cell forever, I was beginning to be able to make peace with it for a time. On the 27th I went again to trial and, as had been predicted, the case against us was dismissed. The story of the *drap de lit*, finally told, caused great merriment in the courtroom, whereupon my friend decided that the French were "great." I was dulled by their merriment, even though it was meant to warm me. It could only remind me of the laughter I had often heard at home, laughter which I had sometimes deliberately elicited. This laughter is the laughter of those who consider themselves to be at a safe remove from all the wretched, for whom the pain of the living is not real. I had heard it so often in my native land that I had resolved to find a place where I would never hear it any more. In some deep, black, stony, and liberating way, my life, in my own eyes, began during that first year in Paris, when it was borne in on me that this laughter is universal and never can be stilled.

Irwin Shaw

Irwin Shaw (1913–1984) began his career as a writer with several extraordinary short stories in *The New Yorker* and *Esquire* ("The Girls in Their Summer Dresses" among them) and moved to Europe in 1950 after the success of his first novel, *The Young Lions*. Though his critical reputation would shrink in the 1950s and 60s, his legend as an American who really got Europe, a second Hemingway of the ski slopes, only grew. His gifts as a reporter shine through even his lesser work. If this evocation, from *Holiday* magazine, of a slightly idealized Paris as experienced by well-off Americans in the 50s has elements of cliché, what is nonetheless striking in Shaw's Paris is how organic and heartfelt the clichés once were.

---

from

Remembrance of Things Past

You start at a café table because everything in Paris starts at a café table. You are waiting for the girl you love.

She is young and American and perfect. She has straight legs and an enormous appetite and solid low-heeled shoes and she likes to walk and she has just arrived in the city for the first time in her life and she likes to listen to you talk and she is imaginary. She is late, of course, because you have been so conditioned by the women you have known that even the ones you invent can't meet you on time. You have invented her because you have been daydreaming; you have been playing with the idea of pleasure, and it has occurred to you that there could be few things more pleasurable in this sad world than to roam Paris for a day hand in hand with such a girl.

You sit there, glowing with the prospect of unfolding Paris for the first time to this superb, unreal, and uninitiated creature.

It is summer or autumn or winter or spring and it is sunny and raining and there is snow on the statues and bits of ice in the Seine and the trees are all in full blossom and the swimmers are diving into the purified water in the wooden pools along the river banks and it is early in the morning

482

and late at night and the President is giving a ball and the Garde Républicaine is out in breastplates and horsehair tails and the North Africans are rioting for autonomy at the Place de la République and all the policemen have dents in their shining steel helmets.

Mass is being celebrated at Saint-Sulpice and they are burying an actor in Père Lachaise. There are long lines outside the mail windows at the American Express. The young lieutenants are leaving for Indochina. There is a fair on the Esplanade des Invalides and the phrenologists are doing well next to the shooting galleries. They are selling perfume on the Rue de la Paix and the wine merchants are worried about this year's Burgundy and a thousand deep baskets of watercress are being stacked at Les Halles. The buses are coming in from Orly airfield to the Gare des Invalides with the passengers from New York and South Africa and Warsaw and the trains going south have whole cars filled with bicycles for the vacationers en route to the Côte d'Azur. It is August and half the shops are closed, with their iron shutters down, and it is February and the porters wait with wheelchairs at the Gare de l'Est for the skiers with broken legs.

On the gray islands in the river they are turning out four hundred fifty buglike, four-horsepower Renaults a day and the Communists are painting "Americans Go Home" on the iron bridges. They are selling canaries near the Hôtel de Ville and putting out newspapers on the Rue Réaumur and the headlines show that the Premier is worried about the price of butter, that French football has suffered another catastrophe at Colombes, and that a young woman with an Algerian lover has walled up her landlady in the cellar. The butchers are putting lilacs in their windows and everybody at the flea market is guaranteeing that everything is over a hundred years old. A carousel calliope is playing under the elevated structure on the Boulevard Garibaldi and children are getting rides in goat carts near the American Embassy. There is a new middleweight fighting at the Palais des Sports who will never make anyone forget Marcel Cerdan. A pensioner has committed suicide because he was afraid the inflation would deprive him of his tobacco and there is a banquet planned for the millers who are accused of driving a whole town mad with flour tainted by ergot, the event organized by the flour manufacturers who wanted to demonstrate their solidarity with their unlucky colleagues.

It is Sunday and the couples are sprawled all over the Bois and the lions are roaring for the crowds across the deep moats in the Vincennes zoo. It is the fourteenth of July, and there are parades and the placing of wreaths in the memory of the dead and the memory of the Bastille and the memory of the unfortunate Foullon, whose head was carried on a pike up the Rue Saint-Martin in 1789, his mouth stuffed with grass because he had said of the people of Paris, "*Eh bien*. If this riffraff has no bread, they'll eat hay." There is also the sound of jets flying in formation over the city, and there is dancing in the streets and in the gardens of the great houses, and there are fireworks in the sky behind the cathedral and marshals of France standing at attention while the bands play the anthem, whose words include, "To arms, citizens!"

It is a workday, and the open platforms of the buses are crowded with people who breathe deeply of the gasoline fumes on their way to their offices. It is market day, and the housewives push through the stalls under the trees at the Place de l'Alma, next to the Salon Nautique, looking at the prices of the chickens and the cheeses and the celery root and complaining that life is too expensive.

There is a smell of freshly baked bread in the air and the streets are full of people hurrying home with long, unwrapped loaves under their arms. In the crowded *charcuteries* there are a dozen different kinds of pâté on the counters and Alsatian *choucroute* and *gnocchi* and snails and *coquilles Saint-Jacques*, ready to be put into the oven, and the salesgirls sound like a cageful of flutes as they call out the prices to the customers. In the Métro there is an experimental train that runs on rubber tires, to alleviate the nervous agony of being alive in the twentieth century. In the Berlitz classrooms the activities of the family Dupont are carefully followed as they say good morning to each other, open and close doors, and lay various objects on a table. On the Ile Saint-Louis the owner of an American convertible finds its top slashed for the seventh time and decides he will have to buy a closed car.

In the lobbies of the big hotels, sharp-eyed men are whispering to each other, making deals to import and export vital materials, and an American at the bar of the George V says to his business associates, "I don't like to boast, but I am very close to the Virginia tobacco industry."

The all-girl orchestras are tuning up for their afternoon programs of waltzes in the big, bare cafés on the Boulevard Clichy, and in the *bals musettes* shopgirls dance with clerks under the paintings of thugs and apaches. There are thousands of people lined up at the Porte Saint-Cloud to watch a bicycle race, and everybody is going to Deauville for the weekend.

The fountains are playing at the Rond-Point, casting a fine spray over the flower borders, and Notre Dame is illuminated and looks as light as a dream on its stone island, and the streets are empty and the traffic heavy, and you sit there planning this limitless, all-seasoned, perfect day with your perfect girl in the city that is the Jerusalem of many strange pilgrimages and the capital of nostalgia and that you can never leave without tasting a faint, bitter flavor of exile.

You sit at the table on land that has been rented from the municipality for four thousand francs a square meter a year, and you remember that there is a rumor that the government, in a typically indirect and tactful attempt to limit alcoholism, is going to raise the price of its sidewalks to make drinking less general or at least more expensive. You are sipping a Cinzano because gin is so dear and it is too early for brandy. Behind you, on the wall of the café, there is a yellowed copy of the law to suppress public drunkenness. The law was passed during World War I but is still in effect, and you admire the men who could worry about things like that with Germans only a few miles away and dropping shells every twenty minutes into the city from the long-range gun that they called Big Bertha and that was trained on Paris from the Saint-Gobain Forest, eighty-two miles distant.

You lift your eyes above the rim of your glass and read that anyone who is found for the first time in a state of manifest drunkenness in the streets, roads, cafés, cabarets, or other public places can be fined between one and five francs, which at the present rate would range between one-quarter of a cent and a penny. But if you get caught manifestly drunk twice, the results, according to the proclamation, promise to be more grave: For two years you lose the right to vote, the right to serve as a juror or in the administration of the government, and the right to carry arms, and you are deprived, according to the small print, of your paternal powers over your children and your descendants.

You sip soberly at your drink and peer out at the passers-by for the bright American head that is bound to look a little artless and unpremeditated among the clever, artificially streaked short hair of the Parisian women on the boulevard. The girl you love has not yet arrived, and you half-close your eyes and plan the first step.

First, there should be a general, bird's-eye view of the city, and the best place for that is the top of the Eiffel Tower. From there, the city lies embraced by its winding river and flows in a silvery haze over its moderate hills and its central plain. You can look out over the homes and the shops and the cemeteries and places of worship of three million people, and you can see the hill in Montmartre where the Temple of Mercury used to stand and where Saint-Denis was beheaded. You can trace the course of the river and see where the canals join it and the Marne, and you can tell the girl about the Norsemen who sailed up the river in their oared galleys in the ninth century, jovially axing the farmers and the city dwellers along the banks, as was the custom of travelers in that time.

There is one drawback about the tower, though—the elevator makes you nervous. You know that you are unreasonable. You know that since it opened for business in 1889, it has carried millions of people safely up to the top. But you suffer a little from vertigo, and every time you get into the creaking, slightly tilted car you regret, with unreasonable chauvinism, being that high in the air and dependent for your life on French machinery. You would depend unhesitatingly on French courage to get you out of danger, on French medicine to cure a stomach ache, on French wit to make you laugh or a French wife to make you happy—but all that cable, all those girders, all those grinding gears . . . You decide to settle for a more moderate eminence: the top of the Arc de Triomphe is quite high enough for a young girl's first view of Paris, and its elevator is comfortably enclosed in a stone shaft.

Anyway, you will tell her, Paris is not a city of heights. Its architects, out of respect for man, have made certain that man is not dwarfed by his works here. It is a city built to human scale, so that no man should feel pygmied here. Parisians are devoted to their sky and have passed a set of complicated laws designed to keep the height of buildings at a modest level, so that the sky, soft, streaked, gentle, beloved by painters, can be a constant, intimate presence above the roofs and the treetops. In defense of their sky, Parisians can be outlandishly fierce. A builder in Neuilly who put up an apartment house taller than the legal limit was ordered by the court to tear down the top two stories, although they had been leased in advance and there is a crucial housing shortage. In addition, the builder was forced to pay a whopping fine for every day that the offending twenty feet of construction loomed above the skyline. And then, as an aesthetic afterthought, the judge sentenced him to jail. Oh, you think, remembering the caged and distant sky above your native city, if only there were more builders in Sing Sing.

From the top of the monument, staring out at the city, your girl doesn't say anything because she is perfect. The great avenues—which Baron Haussmann, Napoleon III's prefect of police, created to get the mob of Paris out into the open where he could use cavalry on them when they wanted a raise in salary or wished to murder a minister—sweep out to all points of the compass.

The boulevards are named after victories and soldiers, and on the arch itself are the names of one hundred and seventy-two battles chiseled into the stone. Many of the streets of Paris are labeled for battlefields on which Frenchmen have conquered, and you wonder what it must do to the spirit of the citizens of a city to have the sound of triumph on their lips every time they give an address to a taxi driver, and whether they would be different today if, along with the Avenue Wagram and the Avenue de Friedland, there were a Boulevard Sedan, a Rue Waterloo, and a Place of the Surrender.

Although statistically Paris has the least green space per citizen of any major city in Europe, there are so many trees that when they are in foliage and seen from above, much of the metropolis seems to be built in a giant park. Close by, the city leans against the green escarpments of Saint-Cloud and Saint-Germain, across the bending river, reminding you that Paris is more intimate with and more accessible to the countryside than any other great city in the world. The slate, jumbled world of the rooftops is pewter and lavender, Paris's own colors, and there is the gleam of innumerable studio windows, facing north. The pinkish Carrousel past the other end of the Champs Elysées is like a distant and frivolous reflection of the arch on whose peak you are standing, and the wind up here carries a frail leaf-and-mold smell of the river with it. The white dome of the Sacré-Coeur speaks of nineteenth-century religion on the heights of Montmartre, and you can see the gray, medieval stone tower of Saint-Germain-des-Prés rising on the opposite bank from its nest of cafés.

Standing there, with the whole city spread around you, its palaces and spires and statues glistening in the damp sunlight, you reflect aloud to the girl on how wise Parisians are to have had ancestors who were ruled by tyrants, because tyrants are egotists with an itch to build monuments to themselves. Then after a while you get rid of the tyrants and are left with the Louvre and the Tuileries and the obelisk and the Place Vendôme and the brave, sculptured horses and the great boulevards that were built because someone was ruthless enough and powerful enough to tear down acre after acre of people's homes and pave what used to be somebody's kitchen and plant chestnut trees in somebody else's bedroom. You reflect on the selfishness of being alive in your own time. You are delighted with what Louis XIV did to the city with the taxes he squeezed from the poor, and with what Napoleon built on the blood of a generation of young Frenchmen, though you would struggle to the death against a new Louis or a later Napoleon, no matter how many arches and palaces he guaranteed for your descendants to enjoy on their visit from America a hundred years from now.

You remember the first time you climbed to the top of the arch, which was just after the Liberation, when the Twenty-eighth Division marched past to show Paris the Americans were really here. You remember the noise the tanks made on the Champs Elysées, and the massed, weary, pleasant young faces of the soldiers, and the absence of music because they were all going to fight that night at Saint-Denis and they had no time for bands. And you realize that every time you think of the city, there is something of that time in your feeling for it.

It is difficult not to love a city you have seen for the first time on the day it was liberated. And Paris was liberated in just the right way. It hadn't been bombed, except on the outskirts, and all the bridges were still standing, and the inhabitants themselves had spent the last five days firing off small arms and feeling heroic, and the weather was sunny and warm and all the girls wore their best dresses, and there were enough Germans left to put up a show of war and give the local boys an opportunity to behave martially in front of good audiences before the final surrender.

Everybody was thin from the war, but not starving, and you kept hearing the "Marseillaise," and the smoke from a few small fires rose unimportantly here and there, and for an afternoon it felt as though the war had ended and it couldn't have ended in a better place. The word was that von Sholtitz had spared the city, against Hitler's orders, and the Parisians felt, Of course, who could have the heart to blow up Paris? There was blood against some of the walls, and the next day they were piling flowers there for the dead and everybody was kissing everybody else and there was a considerable amount of free wine.

Travelers are always telling you their favorite times for seeing a city for the first time: Rome at Easter, London in June, New York in October, Pittsburgh at five o'clock in the morning. And you tell the girl to make sure to see Paris the next afternoon it is liberated. It is a city that takes gratefully to a mixture of riot, celebration, and bloodshed. The citizens are experts at putting up and tearing down barricades, at killing each other, and at greeting and firing upon troops. The streets are admirably arranged for mass demonstrations, parades, and the maneuvering of armor. The buildings are solid and made of stone and merely chip when hit by shells, and in a year or two the damp, benevolent air ages the scars so that they are indistinguishable from the precious marks of the centuries before. There are monuments everywhere that lend an atmosphere of significance to acts performed in their vicinity, and when people die in front of them in the belief that they are preserving civilization, civilization takes on a tangible and satisfactory presence.

You tell something of this to the girl whose hair is blowing and whose eyes are shining here above the jumble of stone and memory and history, and she squeezes your hand and says, "Isn't it time for lunch? I'm dying."

Then you begin a ritual that is one of the most pleasant in the world— deciding slowly and carefully which place in all the city of Paris is the one place you wish to lunch at that day. You can go to the run-down old hotel on the hill at Saint-Cloud, which has a terrace overlooking some tennis courts, with the river down at the bottom of the slope and the city lost beyond its trees just three hundred yards away on the opposite bank, and you can sit out there getting sunburned, feeding off the tableful of hors d'oeuvre, watching the French play tennis. (The French play a crafty, deft game, slow and full of lobs and chops and angles, and unless you're Sedgman or McGregor, it is less tantalizing to eat lunch and watch them than play against them.) The hotel used to be a club for American airborne officers in the hilarious summer just after the war and cognac used to be ten cents a glass and everybody used to mix it with Coca-Cola and there was a pretty waitress there who decided one night she was wildly in love with an airborne major who weighed a hundred and thirty-five pounds and who was working for the National Broadcasting Company in Chicago the last time you heard about him.

Or, since it is the girl's first day in town and you feel limitlessly wealthy in her presence, you might take a taxi out to the Bois and eat in the restaurant under the glass chandeliers that are swung from the trees and order trout and a bottle of wine and take a walk later and watch the ceremonious ladies and gentlemen cantering around the bridle paths as though nothing had happened since 1900. And you could walk in the forest, which is amazingly like a real forest for a tract of land so close to a large city, and imagine how it must have looked when the troops of Wellington and the Czar were encamped there in 1815 after Napoleon had had his final bad time.

If it is a gray, autumnal day, you can walk on over to Auteuil with her and wander around the almost empty stands and watch the steeplechase races, buying the odds from dusty men in the paddock who have them written down on flimsy strips of yellow paper and putting your bets down, as usual, on the horse that falls at the last hedge, but enjoying the stretching deep green infield and the inconsequent way the horses vanish behind trees, carrying your money with them into obscurity. And you can regret the decline of jump racing in America and the lack of variety in the dirt tracks of Saratoga and Arlington and Santa Anita, where the horses always run the same way, like wooden mounts on a merry-go-round and where your money is always painfully visible as it is being lost.

But if your girl doesn't feel like open air her first afternoon, you can be less enterprising and walk through the eighth, or American, arrondissement, so-called because at certain moments it looks as though the French had moved out and the Americans moved in, and go to a small restaurant that has grapevines planted all along its sliding glass windows, so that everyone is reflected in shimmering green above the tablecloths. It is not your favorite restaurant, but you were witness there to a meal that was not so much a lunch as a ceremony, an act of devotion, a celebration of the mystic nature of food, a reverent wallowing in gluttony that erased for two hours all memory of the drugstore sandwiches and hasty milk shakes of your native land.

The meal was eaten by four grave-faced businessmen, obviously men of importance and economic power, and they started with *pâté de foie gras*, pink and fatty, and went on to *quenelles de brochet*—river fish, flaked and mixed with soaked bread and crumbs, kidney fat, and eggs, and covered with a sauce of mushrooms and cream. The four gentlemen—talking in subdued, polite voices of taxes, labor policies, import difficulties, and the necessity for expanding plants—ate solidly and industriously, washing the *quenelles* down with a half-bottle of Chablis apiece. Then they moved on to slablike Chateaubriands, blue and bloody and complete with fried potatoes and Bordelaise sauce and two bottles of Nuits-Saint-Georges. Then, of course, there was salad and cheese, Brie and Camembert and plump chunks of pale Gruyère, with another bottle of Nuits-Saint-

Georges, and fruit and crêpes, flaming with liqueurs, and finally coffee and two brandies apiece, after which they solemnly rose from the table, shook hands, and went back to their offices to oversee the manufacture of automobiles or the transfer of stock.

You walk past the shop where you can buy a silver-handled umbrella for ninety dollars and past the doorway where a ragged, shapeless old lady, wrapped in newspapers, slept all winter, as though she had a lease on the space, past the big hotels where the Hollywood people stay and in front of which the Cadillacs are parked. You go past the corner where a squarely built, rubber-booted, peasantlike flower girl, with bright red cheeks and wearing a fluttering apron, offers lilacs and violets and gladiolas, which she brings each morning in a taxi, whose driver she tips handsomely. You skirt the religious school behind its wall, where the eight-year-old boys arrive bare-legged and chilled each morning and gravely shake hands with each other before going in to their catechism. You walk past the café with the inviting name of La Belle Ferronnière, at whose tables sit the mannequins from the nearby fashion houses, and American soldiers, and a number of Rumanians and Hungarians speaking in their native tongues. The café is dominated by a coffee machine only a little smaller than a locomotive boiler, and the man who tends it leaps from lever to lever and wheel to wheel like a nervous engineer trying to run a dynamo that is slightly out of order. The coffee is black and, contrary to the usual slander, delicious, and if you want it *au lait*, the man behind the counter pours some milk into a copper pitcher and shoots steam into it with a roaring, hoarse noise and serves your coffee frothy and bubbled.

You arrive at the restaurant but the four heroes are not there that afternoon, and you decide to prolong the ecstasy of choosing a place to eat and you saunter down toward the river, and if it is spring the chestnuts are in bloom, pink and white, and even if your girl had never been to Paris before she has read enough about the chestnuts of Paris so that you don't have to say anything about them. But if it is late spring, the blossoms drift thickly along the curbs, swirling up in pink and white clouds with the wind of passing automobiles, and the young girls float across the streets in leafy light and shadow, going to and coming from First Communion in their trailing white veils like frail, light-footed, grave-eyed brides.

Tied up at the stone river banks are the oil barges and the pleasure craft, which can be berthed by payment of a nominal rental to the city and which then can boast what must certainly be the most attractive address in the world, "The River Seine, just a little east of the Pont Alexandre III."

You pass the Grand Palais, where the big exhibitions are held and where the scandal of the Salon d'Automne unfolded, when some propaganda paintings by Communists were hung, then taken down, then hung again, and you remember one in particular, which was called "The Good Health of Comrade Thorez." Comrade Thorez was the head of the French Communist Party; he was in Moscow at the time being treated for a stroke, and the painting showed a band of uniformly smiling workers dancing and registering pleasure while a rosy young woman held up, in the foreground, a newspaper that carried a headline announcing Comrade Thorez's recovery, and it was hard to see whom the picture could damage, except possibly Comrade Thorez, and then only if he were an art critic.

You cross the Pont de la Concorde and stare at the Chambre des Députés. There seem to be dozens of policemen on duty there, in front of the statues, as though the legislators half-expected a rush of citizens to flood past the gates in a berserk desire to vote. Inside, the government is probably falling, and deputies are almost certainly making speeches denouncing each other for their behavior at the time of Munich, or at the signing of the Nazi-Soviet Pact, or during the Occupation, and the Right and the Left are insulting each other and voting together against the government on every proposal. The deputies, in their red-plush amphitheater, do not have the look of ponderous, fleshy well-being of our own congressmen. They seem small, quick, intellectual, and poised for flight, and they have an air of restrained irritation with each other, like passengers in a crowded elevator that has been stuck between floors for a long time. And you remember what a French friend said to you about the then current Premier. "If that man is to be a success," he said, "he must make the French eat worse next year. Anyone can demand austerity in England and get away with it. But in France it takes character."

It was in this chamber that Clemenceau, when he was Premier, came out with one of the most invigoratingly candid statements ever pronounced by the head of a state. "I am against all governments," he growled, "including my own."

You wonder how far the old man would have gotten in an American election with talk like that.

S. J. Perelman

S. J. Perelman (1904–1979) was the matchless rococo stylist and poet of Hollywood vulgarity and New York neuroses; his great subject was always the mismatch between the romantic images of the world he had absorbed as a boy reading in Providence, Rhode Island, and the messy and venal reality those images turned out to conceal. He loved the exquisite side of French sensibility—he liked to call himself, in the French manner, a "feuilletoniste," a "writer of little leaves" (to use his own literal translation of the common French term for a comic essayist)—and wrote about Paris often, particularly during the long stretches of the 1950s and 60s when he took the indignities of modern travel perhaps too single-mindedly as a subject. Paris seems to have represented in his personal cosmology a kind of anti-Hollywood, not the appalling capital of cheap vulgarity but the bewildering capital of feckless high style. If his Paris, as in this bitterly funny casual first collected in *The Road to Miltown* (1957), is no more "real" than his London or Hollywood, a Perelmanian symbol more than an observed place, it is still, as a representation of a particular kind of American bafflement at Parisian manners, as achieved as any photograph.

The Saucier's Apprentice

The last place I would have expected to run into Marcel Riboflavin, *sous-inspecteur* of the Police Judiciaire—which is to say, the *Sûreté*—was the Sunday-morning bird market in Paris, but then Marcel's vagaries have long since ceased to surprise me. Stoop to tie your shoelace in Baton Rouge or Bombay, in Dublin or Dar es Salaam, and like as not you will find Marcel confronting you with an owlish eye and nibbling a meditative praline. Where he gets all those meditative pralines from—or why, since they attract a veritable canopy of flies—the Lord only knows; nonetheless, there he is in rusty bourgeois black, patiently following up some infinitesimal clue, or like as not just nibbling a praline. I was standing in the hurly-burly of the bird market three Sundays ago, lost in admiration of two little doves in georgette blouses who would have rounded out any boy's aviary, when an unmistakable voice sounded in my ear.

"*Doucement, mon vieux,*" it warned. "We old roosters must be cautious. Don't try to outwit your arteries."

Startled, I turned to behold Marcel, an indulgent smirk on his face, wagging his forefinger at me. It was quite apparent what he was thinking, and I hastened to disabuse him. "The fact is," I explained, "the smaller of that pair—the helpless-looking one—reminds me of a teacher of mine at grammar school, a Miss Floggerty. She had taffy-colored hair, as I recall—"

"*Bien sûr, bien sûr,*" he said sympathetically. "I, too, have those symptoms of senility. Tragic but inescapable. Come, let us link arms and stroll through the complex of alleys fringing the Quartier Latin." As we linked arms and strolled, genially updating each other on our activities since our last meeting, I noticed a strangely familiar magazine protruding from my friend's coat pocket.

"You have symptoms of gentility also," I remarked. "Since when have you taken to reading *Harper's Bazaar*? Or do your investigations extend into the gilded salons of the *haute couture*?"

Marcel's face, or at least that portion of it visible through the flies, suddenly became cryptic. "In my post, one is called on to unravel many tangled skeins," he said evasively. "By the way, this café we are nearing is reputed to have the worst anisette in Paris. Shall we try it?" We did, and it was unspeakable. After a moment, Marcel withdrew a praline from a recess in his clothing and nibbled it meditatively. I am not overly intuitive, but I have learned that when sub-inspectors of the Sûreté with dickty fashion magazines protruding from their pockets invite one to share an apéritif, curious stories ofttimes unfold, and so it proved.

"As you are doubtless aware," began Marcel, drawing on his praline, "*Harper's Bazaar* not only prognosticates the mode but frequently publishes news of consuming interest—you will pardon the play on words— to gourmets. Such was the arresting article you see here." He spread out the periodical and indicated a piece entitled "Sauces from the Source," by Rosamund Frost. At first glance, it did not seem particularly cataclysmic. Maxim's, the celebrated Paris restaurant, had confected five basic frozen sauces calculated to tease the American palate. It was the secrecy attending their manufacture, however, and the abnormal precautions adopted to guard the creators, that riveted my attention. "Seat of the production," wrote Miss Frost, conspiratorially turning up the collar of her typewriter, "is Seabrook Farms in New Jersey, the well-known purveyors of frozen fruit and vegetables. But because M. and Madame Vaudable, owners of the Paris Maxim's, have a deep distrust of American cooking methods, they have evolved their own system of preparation. For each large batch of sauces, a head chef, an assistant, and several *sauciers* are flown over from Paris, to be held virtually incommunicado in New Jersey until the batch is finished. They are then flown home before they have had any chance to be contaminated by such ill practices as thickening with flour."

I lifted my eyes slowly to Marcel's, the question I was almost afraid to put into words muted to a whisper. "You mean . . ." I asked.

"Precisely," he said, dislodging a grain of sugar from his denture. "Scarcely a month after this information appeared, the chief of our Bureau Culinaire, the section specializing in food outrages, sent for me in a state of pronounced agitation. A few nights earlier, faint but indisputable traces of flour had been detected in a pipkin of sauce béarnaise served at Maxim's."

"It could have been pure coincidence," I objected. "A harassed scullion, a sudden avalanche of orders—"

"In France," Marcel said with wintry dignity, "accidents occur in the bedroom, not the kitchen. No, it was all too plain that this was a deliberate, predetermined *coup de main*, a perfidious assault on the very citadel of our national cuisine. The victim of the atrocity, it appeared, was a distinguished artist of the Comédie-Française and one of its foremost tragedians, Isidor Bassinet. Providentially, Bassinet realized the implications of his discovery in time to avert a panic that might easily have wrought havoc among the clientele. Summoning the maître d'hôtel, he cuttingly suggested that the sauce was more suitable for calking a boat, tweaked the man's nose, and retired. The headwaiter, of course, relayed the gibe to the chef, who instituted a probe forthwith and immediately gave us the alert."

"I hesitate to denigrate an actor," I said, hesitating almost a full second, "but might not Bassinet himself have insinuated flour into the sauce as the pretext for a histrionic outburst?"

"We did not discount the possibility," said Marcel. "A clandestine search was made of his rooms that yielded naught incriminating gravy-wise; his erotic photomurals, his collection of whips, and the jar of candied hashish by his bedside could have belonged to any floorwalker in the Bon Marché. The longer I pondered the problem, the more convinced I became it was an inside job. Someone on the kitchen force—whether a madman or a cold, diabolic intelligence I was not yet prepared to say—had engineered the deed, and I knew that, encouraged by success, he would strike again. My theory was vindicated all too swiftly. Two evenings later, Alexander Satyriasis, the Greek shipping magnate, was dining at Maxim's with his wife and his mistress. The occasion was their silver wedding anniversary, and Satyriasis, an epicurean, had left no spit unturned to insure a gastronomical triumph. The hors d'oeuvres, the soup, the roast—all were transcendent. Then, as the trio expectantly attacked the salad, Paradise crumbled about their ears. Under their forks lay the ultimate annihilation, the final obscenity—a canned pear stuffed with cream cheese and walnuts, garnished with cole slaw and Russian dressing."

"Good God!" I exclaimed. "At the Fig 'n Thistle, yes; at the Mumble Shop and a thousand Stygian tearooms, yes; but in the Rue Royale—"

Marcel repressed an involuntary shudder. "It was appalling," he admitted. "When I got there, the table was cordoned off and Satyriasis had not yet recovered consciousness. He came around eventually, but, *entre nous*, the man will never be the same. I instantly fell to work and grilled the entire personnel, from the head sommelier down to the doorman. Nobody would even hazard a guess at the origin of the salads; apparently they had been slipped onto the service tray while the waiter's back was turned, and beyond that not a vestige of a clue. Those were dark days, I can tell you," Marcel went on somberly. "The knowledge that we were powerless to combat him exhilarated our mysterious adversary, spurring him on to new and more gruesome excesses. Under the management's very nose, patrons were assailed with baked grapefruit topped with maraschino cherries, fried clams encapsulated in deep fat, mashed potatoes pullulating with marshmallow whip. The nadir of bestiality was reached one night when cards were surreptitiously pinned to the menu inviting diners to have their tea leaves read by a gypsy palmist."

"Forgive me for underscoring the obvious," I said. "Surely it must have occurred to you that a woman, and patently an American, was at the bottom of all this?"

"Naturally," said Marcel with a shade of impatience. "The crucial question, though, was where was she and how was she effecting her depredations? Five of the restaurant's employees, as you saw from the magazine account, had been flown to New Jersey and held there incommunicado. Plainly, one of their number—younger and more impressionable than the rest—had evaded his custodians and succumbed to some harpy who had lured the fatuous boy to a drive-in like those Howard Monsoon places that line your roads, and there, befuddled by viscous malted drinks and chicken-in-the-basket, he had been persuaded to betray his birthright. In all likelihood, I reasoned, the seductress had followed him to Paris to gloat over her handiwork; perhaps, if I could ferret out the cat's-paw, he might lead me to her. Acting on my presentiment, I at once attached myself to the kitchen in the guise of an assistant pastry chef and proceeded to elicit what I could about the quintet who had been overseas."

"And your hypothesis bore fruit?"

"In a fashion I never anticipated," replied Marcel. "Four of them were prosaic, stodgy types, family men whose world revolved around their thimbleful of Pernod and their game of bowls. The youngest, however, was an altogether different piece of work. A mere novice entrusted with handling condiments, he was a shy, secretive lad with long eyelashes and a curiously girlish aspect. Whenever the badinage among his mates grew ribald, he flushed deeply and made himself scarce, and once or twice I surprised him examining his complexion in a compact. The conviction that our little colleague was a masquerader emboldened me to experiment. Utilizing the test that had unmasked Huckleberry Finn, I casually asked the youth to thread a needle. As I expected, he brought the thread to the needle instead of vice versa. Then I shied an egg beater at him without warning—that is, without warning that I was shying an egg beater at him—and, sure enough, he automatically spread the knees under his apron to form a lap. The evidence was too damning to be ignored. That night, when my suspect let himself into his modest furnished room in the Saint-Germain-des-Prés quarter, stripped off his mess jacket, and disclosed a brassière, I emerged from an armoire and sprang the trap."

"You might have waited a moment or two for confirmation," I remonstrated.

"As a reader of *Harper's Bazaar*, I am reasonably *au courant* with the subject," said Marcel tartly. "Besides, I had all the proof necessary to stamp the creature as the perpetrator of the crimes. Simmering on the gas stove was a dish of salmon croquettes flanked by carrots and peas, and, in the oven beneath, a graham-cracker pie. Overcome by remorse, yet grateful that the suspense had ended, the fair culprit dissolved in tears. Her name, she confessed, was Gristede Feigenspan, and she was a feature writer for *Effluvia*, a periodical circulated gratis by supermarkets in your country. To dramatize the pre-eminence of American cookery, her editors

had abducted the youngest member of the French contingent, had substituted Gristede, and were planning to publicize her exploits under the
title 'I Was a Fake Saucier at Maxim's.' "

I drew a long breath. "A singular tale," I commented. "I take it she
paid the inevitable price for her audacity?"

"That," said Marcel, with an enigmatic smile, "is a matter of opinion."
He hoisted himself cumbrously to his feet as a dynamic young woman in
black jodhpurs, with a bag slung over her shoulder, gravitated toward our
table. "I don't think you know my wife," he said. "Gristede, allow me to
present an old *copain* from the States—a journalist, like yourself."

"Too, too fantastic," she trilled, extending her hand. "How long are
you staying in Paris? You must come to dinner."

"I—er—I'm just en route to Beirut," I stammered. "I mean I'm off to
a fiesta in Trieste—"

"Don't be an Airdale," she said forcefully. "We'll give you a real home-
cooked meal. Hasn't Marcel told you about my noodles Yankee Doodle,
smothered in peanut butter and mayonnaise?"

I looked at Marcel, but his face, flies and all, had turned to stone.
That's the trouble with these garrulous French detectives—they're
unpredictable. One moment they wring their dossiers inside out for you,
and then—*pouf!*—they shut up like a clam.

May Sarton

May Sarton (1912–1995), the still slightly under-appreciated essayist and poet, spent only a single isolated year in Paris, but in this little-known memoir of that year (from *The Reporter*, April 1956), she captures magically well the combination of aching joy and equally aching loneliness that overcomes the good student in Paris: the park, the books, and the children watched. (Bookends of our literature as they may seem to be, lesbian exquisitist and Gothic novelist, she and William Faulkner had remarkably similar experiences, and recorded similar feelings, in their Parisian *sejours*.)

———

Good-by to a World

I look back on that winter in Paris as one might look back on a period of illness or even insanity, or perhaps simply as one looks back on oneself at nineteen. It was the winter of 1931–32, and my parents were to spend it in Beirut at the American University, while I was by my own choice left in Paris to fend for myself, to study theater, and (it was supposed) to take advantage of the monuments of civilization that lay all around me. There they were, the Sorbonne where I might have studied, the museums, the libraries, the cemeteries—I stood before them like a cat with one paw raised, unwilling to step into cold water. I did nothing wise or sensible. I simply lived in Paris. I wandered about, ardent and hungry, picking up whatever was accidentally brought to my attention, tasting it and then wandering on, casual and solitary, always it seemed on pavements with a film of damp over them, my feet half frozen, wearing my only respectable garment, a purple corduroy suit, with a copy of Baudelaire—bought for five francs at a stall—in my purse. I read this, as perhaps it should be read, on benches here and there, in cafés where I was suddenly too tired to walk another step. Whatever I learned, I learned, as Henry James put it, from the "rich ripe fruit of perambulation." It was Paris by osmosis.

Of course I had to live somewhere, and the somewhere turned out to be Montrouge, a workman's quarter, just beyond the Porte d'Orléans, for a friend sublet me his apartment there, on the Place Jules Ferry, where there were a few blocks of modern apartment buildings. My place, in one of these, was like that whole winter, curiously empty and curiously crowded. It was chiefly a studio, empty except for a large glass bottle made into a lamp, a mattress on the floor beside it, a phonograph, and some records—my friend was a dancer. The living quarters were on a small balcony above this chill vacuum, and they were extremely crowded, containing as they did a bed, a desk, bookshelves, chairs, a fireplace, all in a small space. A tiny kitchen and bath opened off on one side of this balcony, and on the other side it gaped draftily onto the unheated studio. This strange apartment was on the ground floor, and I lived there acutely aware of every footstep on the pavement outside. I was lonely at first, and frightened.

The chief trouble with living in this quarter was simply that the Métro shut down at midnight, and if I went to the theater or was out with friends, there was nothing for it but to take taxis, and my budget hardly allowed for such extravagance. But living on the Place Jules Ferry had one great advantage. There was market once a week, just outside my door. On that day I woke to the sound of wooden trestles being put up and the harsh cheerful cries of the vendors, and I woke up in a village. And as in all such markets, you could buy anything from rubber boots or a sweater to cheese, vegetables, meat, and fish. When I emerged with my basket, it was into a friendly busy talkative village scene, and I was welcomed. "*Hé, mon p'tit, v'la le meilleur p'tit tricot vous verrez de vot' vie—ça tient, tu sais, ça ne s'use pas,*" the ever-hopeful sweater woman yelled from across the square. My best friend was the egg man who handed his customers a little basket and said in the softest voice, "*Choisissez, Mademoiselle—un p'tit oeuf à la coq rien de meilleur, n'est-ce pas?*" I was fond also of the cheese woman, with whom I had long talks about which was superior, La Vache Qui Rit or La Vaché Sérieuse at twenty centimes more. It was 1931, and the franc, believe it or not, was at roughly thirty-five to the dollar. I bought eggs, cheese, sardines, tomatoes, and always a bunch of flowers—bunches of cheap marigolds or daisies, and once in a great while, early in the month, roses.

What astonishes me now, surrounded as I am, as we all are, by a network of responsibilities, is the utter freedom of that year, the freedom not to do as well as the freedom to do. I spent hours listening to records, writing poems and letters, keeping a rather helter-skelter journal, or just lying on the mattress in the studio, feeling happy, feeling unhappy, romantic, directionless, ready to veer with any breeze. I was, of course, making vague attempts to learn about theater. I got permission, for instance, to visit the rehearsals of the Compagnie des Quinze, then in its first burst of glory, and preparing for a season that would include Obey's famous *Noé*, and to visit rehearsals of the Pitoëffs whom all Paris adored, though I, insensitive perhaps, could not share the enthusiasm for Ludmilla. I saw a great many plays, for Jouvet and Valentine Tessier were playing at the Champs Elysées and Dullin at his "Atelier" (in a wonderful production of *Volpone*). I went back three times to see the haunting, hieratic Marguerite Jamois in Gantillon's production of *Maya*, the prostitute who became the incarnation of each man's secret dream of woman. But the thing was, of course, that I was burning to act myself, not just watch others perform, watching them as I did with the sour, absolute, critical eye of inexperience. "Where is the theater?" I cried disconsolately, brushing all these riches aside.

I wanted to break in myself. Secure in the armor of ignorance, I cooked up a wild scheme and dashed off a letter to Lugné-Poë. I supposed that Lugné-Poë at that time might have been compared to a combination of Belasco and the entire Theatre Guild board of directors rolled into one: Entrepreneur, director, actor, it was he who had first introduced Paris to Ibsen, who had founded and directed the Oeuvre Theatre, and who even then kept consistently in the *avant-garde*, discovering a new playwright or a new star each season. His name was still magic in the Paris theater. It was magic to me for a rather curious reason. For I had, three or four years earlier, fallen in love with the tiny Vuillard portrait of Lugné as a young man, the face bending over a desk, the cap of black hair, and the whole stance (only the shoulders, head, and hands being visible) suggesting intensity of a very high voltage. I knew also that he had played Solness in Ibsen's *Master Builder*, and my letter was a barefaced request that he revive it and allow me to play Hilda opposite him.

Of course I never really expected any result from this piece of effrontery. It was the kind of letter you write when you are nineteen and suspect your grandiose schemes of being exactly what they are, screens against despair. It was like the poems I was writing at the time, a way of persuading myself that I existed. So when the public phone in the hall rang a few days later, I went quite calmly to answer it. A deep masculine voice asked for me by name and then said, *"Mademoiselle, vous êtes folle,"* but then invited the mad demoiselle to come and have a talk at his office in the Rue Turgot; it was, of course, Lugné-Poë.

The Rue Turgot was in a section of Paris I had not yet explored, and to get there I had to change two or three times in the Métro, so it seemed quite an expedition when I set out the next morning. I suppose that if I were to choose one single thing that would restore Paris to the senses, it would be that strangely sweet, unhealthy smell of the Métro, so very unlike the dank cold or the stuffy heat of subways in New York. The smell of the Métro is more than a smell: it is an aura, an emanation as powerful and unlike any thing else as is the breath of a cow, and to a lover of Paris it is intoxicating. I was properly intoxicated when I finally emerged into that warm sunny November day, into a quarter I did not know, on my way to meet the man of Vuillard's portrait. The Rue Turgot is a dingy little street with the usual cold façades that open into courtyards, the usual little shops, shoemakers, or mustard vendors, and when I came to the number I had been given, I looked twice because nothing here had the faintest resemblance to a theatrical producer's offices.

A little boy in a black apron and sabots was playing with a bucket and shovel in the courtyard. I peered up a dingy staircase and then turned back to ask where I could find Lugné-Poë. "M. Lugné is not here yet," the little boy answered in a high soprano. It was warm, and I was tired. I sat down on the stoop beside him, and for some reason I have forgotten put the pail on my head for his amusement. I was sitting there in that ludicrous position when the child nudged me and said, *"Voilà!"* Lugné-Poë wore a large black hat and seemed enormous and formidable. He did not look amused as he glanced at us. He was followed by a male secretary carrying two briefcases, and they disappeared up the dingy staircase while I received the full impact of my own foolishness and arrogance and would have liked to melt away. But the whole thing had been a dare to myself and I had to take it. I followed them up the narrow dirty stairway to the second floor. The door was open. It was always open, for the office was so small and so packed with books, papers, magazines, and files that there was barely room for Lugné-Poë in his big black leather armchair and for his roll-topped desk stacked with piles of dusty telegrams. (They were all from Duse, relics of Lugné's management of her South American tour, as I learned later.)

I sat down without courage and endured a long piercing glance from those black eyes. Then we both laughed, and I found myself talking with him, quite frankly, quite simply, as if he were an old friend. It was an examination, but at a certain point in the examination I knew that I had, for some quite unknown and perhaps fantastic reasons, passed. During the course of it, he told me that I had the face of a writer, but not, he would think, that of an actress; he had found out that I wrote poems and demanded that I send him some within a few days; he had told me that if I was determined to try the theater he would see if he could get me a walk-on somewhere, and meanwhile that we would keep in touch, that he would not forget me. While we talked, the secretary popped in and out from the back room, getting more and more exasperated, because he was trying to reach Ruth Draper for Lugné, and had been given a wrong number. "Try 92-91," Lugné would say, and then when that did not work, "Well, try 19-29," and while they worked at this hit-or-miss system, I could look at the big man who sat so relaxed in his armchair and who did not resemble the Vuillard portrait at all. The young man Vuillard caught thinking would never open a huge mouth and laugh that formidable, devouring laugh; nor did the man in the picture look like an elephant, as Lugné-Poë, with his great sensitive nose, his immense forehead and small sardonic eyes, certainly did. He was altogether smaller and tighter, the man in the portrait, than this creature on a huge scale, so avid for life, so generous in his welcome to it in whatever form, even in the arrogance of the young.

When finally I was out on the street, I did not know whether I felt more deflated, reassured, befriended or challenged, but surely some of the loneliness had been lifted away. He did not forget me, for he had, as I was to learn through the year, a genius for "keeping in touch" with those he had chosen, or who had chosen him, all over the world. And what a company it was, international by the accident of birth, but closely allied in that they were all actors, playwrights, poets, all in need of his laconic "Bravo!" telegraphed from Oran to New York, or his "Look here, my child, despair is not our genre. Besides, you cannot disappointment. We have work to do, you and I."

He did not forget me in that first winter of our still tentative friendship. I was summoned to attend a dress rehearsal with him, or just for a talk in the little office, or for his suddenly shy, always perspicacious comment

on a poem. I would not admit that I was to be a writer and not an actress—
that would take six more years—but since I would not admit it, he was
willing to wait and believe in what life itself would do. And meanwhile
he was educating me, thrusting a play in manuscript into my hands, insisting that I read and perhaps even translate Lenormand, always divin-
ing the moment when the little donkey I was needed a carrot.

And I was learning in sudden flashes. I had never heard the word
"surrealism" when I went to the first showing of Cocteau's film
"Le Sang d'un Poète," but the shock of beauty and strangeness produced in me a riot of conflicting emotions that were acted out before my
astonished eyes by that first audience in no uncertain terms. All during
the film people shouted insults at each other, got into actual fist fights,
subsided, whispered furiously, walked out, came back, by the intermission were mortal enemies, and by the end were magnetized by their
quarrels into knots of gesticulating furies in the lobby. I had not realized
what a passion for art and for ideas exists in France until that evening,
and it was exhilarating, though the film itself continued to trouble me,
and still does.

By the middle of the winter, I had established certain relationships and
had a few real friends. One was Mary Chilton, who lived in a pension on
the Rue Notre Dame des Champs, where I had stayed briefly before getting settled in Montrouge. Mary Chilton was studying at the Sorbonne.
She was seventeen, shy, intensely serious, and studied late into the night.
I used to pass by the pension on my way home from discussions at the
Café du Dôme a few blocks away, and if Mary's light was still on, I would
throw pebbles at her window and she would come down and unbolt the
door and let me in. Then, at midnight and into the small hours of the
morning we would sit and talk by her open fire. I admired her tremen-
dously. She was, I sensed, a true intellectual. She had the distinction of
extreme sensitivity with a harsh, disciplined core. We enjoyed each other
because we were so different. She was following a definite program of
reading, for instance, while I picked up books here and there in the stalls,
and made sudden discoveries that I could share with her. When I think of
that winter in Paris, it is Mary who first floats before my eyes, the stillness
of the night, her soft voice, her dreadful pallor, for she was actually seriously ill, though we did not know it. Our two solitudes never quite
merged perhaps, but accepted each other gratefully. She represented for

me a kind of innocence and depth that I, in my new-found sophistication, so unsophisticated really, felt I had already and forever lost.

For while she studied, I danced, or went to the theater or to the Médrano Circus with others less dedicated friends. The Fratellinis were playing that winter. Who will ever forget them? One was the classic clown straight out of the *commedia dell' arte*, tragic and beautiful, with his stark white face under the white conical cap, red tragic mouth, surprised doleful eyes, his brilliant spangled suit with a round white collar, his white shoes and socks. Their act began with his entrance on a prolonged trumpet fanfare. Then suddenly he was standing before us, absolutely still, and slowly lifted his arms straight out in a wide stylized gesture of—was it acknowledgment of the roar of applause or a kind of ovation to the joy of what was to follow, this grave, this noble gesture? It made a kind of tremor run through the audience and on the current of that tremor the two other brothers, the grotesque ones, ran in, one in the guise of a horse perhaps, his immense plopping shoes showing beneath, the other in a worn top hat playing a tiny violin. They had the indefinable magic quality I have only seen once again, in Harpo Marx. They came from another world, dancing and playing and inventing their preposterous jokes, and whatever they did was magic.

My other great friend was also American, a young stage designer whom I had known at the Civic Repertory Theatre where we had both worked the year before. She lived in an attic room at the Hôtel Foyot. It had a slanting roof and its window opened onto the tower of the Palace in the Luxembourg Gardens and its comforting clock face. When we had been out too late for me to catch the last Métro, I sometimes stayed the night with—let us call her Helen. We ordered scrambled eggs and coffee sent up from the restaurant downstairs, where we could never afford to eat a real meal. Always short of money, we used quite often to have supper at a café near the Odéon, eggs again and a salad. Then we would make a brief appearance at the Cochon de Lait next door, and order (to the undisguised horror of the waiter) nothing except coffee and mousse au chocolat. What barbarians we must have seemed, and in fact were! Our idea of a really good drink was that perfect period piece, the Alexander cocktail.

We were enamoured of another period piece, the indestructible Stroeva, who sat on a high stool, in a tuxedo with glittering studs, and sang sentimental French songs in a heavy Russian accent, accompanying herself on a guitar. We were a little late, for she had enchanted Scott Fitzgerald's generation and it was they who hummed those tangos—"Tu Sais," for instance. During that winter Stroeva sometimes appeared at music halls like Bobino's, which we could afford, but more often at an intimate night club on the Right Bank near the Opera, which was outside our sphere in every way. It must have been embarrassing to her to see us arrive night after night during the period of our infatuation, in the same suits, one purple, one bright green (everyone else in evening dress, of course), take the same table, pay the minimum charge for a bottle of champagne, and sit in an intoxicating silence, broken only by our frantic applause at the end of each number. But we were Americans, and Americans were scarce that winter. We were treated with admirable courtesy.

There were less embalmed evenings when we danced to an accordion in the joints on the Rue de la Montagne, where the customers were not Americans but regular Parisian toughs and their girls, leading from the hip and bending their *mômes* far back in the tangos we all loved. There I went with a Dutchman, bespectacled and earnest, who watched me and the French with a cool eye of an anthropologist at large, and whom I remember with gratitude because he gave me as a parting gift his heavily underlined copy of Gide's *Nourritures Terrestres*. ("All the tiredness in your head, Nathanaël, come from the diversity of your riches. You don't even know which among them all to choose, and you don't understand that the only riches is life itself. Nathanaël, you must burn in you all the books.")

There were moments of immense excitement when after spending an hour browsing under the arches of the Odéon bookstall, I ran off with my prize "to burn it in myself" in the Luxembourg Gardens—a worn copy of Colette, Péguy, or Stendhal, or Joubert, the leather binding falling apart, or the poems of an unknown who turned out to be well known and whose name was Valéry. There I sat in the shade of chestnut trees, late into the autumn, while the leaves whirled up in eddies around me, cutting the pages, stopping to look out at the high plume of the fountain and the children sailing their boats in the round pond at its feet. I cannot ever go back without remembering that here I first read Stendhal, here Péguy. Everything I saw around me flowed in and out of the printed page, the wide sandy paths where mothers and children and old men take their places and become part of the formal pattern as if they were kings and the mothers and children of kings, the serrated palaces of leaves in the air over those truncated busts of the Queens of France, and over it all the ever-changing mountains of cloud, the Alpine scene which melts and reforms all day over Paris.

Like so many other Americans and English who have made up a Paris of their own, this was my Paris but it hardly was a Frenchman's, and I knew almost no French people at that time. Like nearly all Americans that year, I was poor, for it was 1932. Our personal letters were full of sinister news of jobs lost, businesses closing down, of men selling apples in the streets. But by curious stroke of fate, I did not lose a job that year but was offered one, as general organizer (I had no title and invented my duties as best I could) of the apprentice group at the Civic Repertory Theatre. The small salary was more than I had ever had to spend, and seemed a munificent prospect. Besides it was what I most wanted to do, and I could go to Lugné-Poë in triumph and tell him that it was, after all, to be the theater.

But the job was still a half year away, and at the end of each month Helen and I were always flat broke, always in debt, and cooking up schemes for existing until next month's check arrived from our families at home. One of these schemes has stayed in my mind as, in some way, the essence of that irresponsible winter. In a moment of desperation, we decided to pawn the various objects of value that Helen's admirers had given her over the years. In Paris where life is so highly individualized, it came as a shock to discover that pawning was official business, conducted by the government in an institution that resembles both a prison and a bank. The walls were bare; there was nothing to relieve apprehension except a row of *guichets* that looked like ticket windows in a small New England railroad station. All around the walls sat silent pale-faced people who might have been prisoners about to go on trial. They waited with tickets in their hands. We were subdued at once by the atmosphere and took a last hunted look at the gold compact, the cigarette case, the silver mesh bag that we hoped would make us solvent again. They were duly passed in by Helen to a man at a ticket window, and we sat down clutching our tickets and feeling more and more like criminals. Presumably while we waited some bureaucrat noted down the objects in a great ledger, pausing with his pen in the air, as they all do, and for some reason fashioning each letter just above where it would go down before writing it in. Presumably several corridors away someone else in a Prince Albert coat put a magnifying glass in his eye and assessed the value of each object. At any rate, whatever was going on behind the blank wall took an unconscionable time. But at last our number was called and we were filled with a wave of hope.

What was the clerk telling us? And in such a severe tone of voice, too. "These are worth nothing, Madame. I am sorry."

"But the silver mesh?" Helen managed to protest.

"An imitation."

"The gold compact?"

"Silver gilt."

We gathered up the poor familiar objects which had lost all their glitter in an instant and slunk out of the door. Then Helen laughed, a bit ruefully no doubt, but she did manage to laugh.

We came out into the early spring air, the damp streets, the flower woman at the corner selling narcissus and mimosa in those flat reed baskets from the south of France. We came out into the trembling rainbow atmosphere, and it all swept over us as if we were seeing it for the first time. John and Arthur, or whatever their names were, those faithless swains who had given Helen silver gilt for gold, were brushed aside, and we consoled ourselves by buying a small bag of marrons glacés with the last few francs. After all, we were in Paris, and it was a lovely day.

The other image which remains with me as an essence of that time is quite a different one. It was a day of national mourning, the day of Briand's funeral. Whatever his blunders, his sentimentality, his old-fashioned sense of the destiny of France as a civilizing power, his belief that war could be "outlawed" by a pact that rested on the moral force of world opinion, when he died even such ignorant, self-absorbed young people as we were felt a kind of premonition, the shadow over the sun.

All along the Champs Elysées the lamps were lit, and each shrouded in black gauze. All along the Champs Elysées the people gathered. People who had made expeditions from the suburbs with their children, people who just happened to be passing by, people moved by the desire to see a parade, foreigners, French, we all waited restlessly as the traffic was detoured and the wide avenue became suddenly empty and still. For such a crowd, we were curiously silent. We shuffled, we waited, a father scolded a little boy who wanted to be picked up—*"Mais, voyons, il n'y a rien à voir."* Then far off, we heard the drums, then the slow march as the bands began to play. The Garde Républicaine's helmets caught the light and flashed in the distance, then went by, the guards holding their horses at a walk, the bits jangling. Battalions of soldiers followed, still in horizon blue (it was the last time we were to see it), and finally the casket itself, draped in the tricolor, moving slowly enough so that the dignitaries walking at its side could keep in step, the French President and the Cabinet, the foreign ambassadors, the generals. Each time as the casket itself reached a group on the sidewalks, a kind of sigh went over. We were saying good-by to a world, and strangely enough, for that brief moment, we knew it.

The Paris of that winter seemed empty to me, and I felt for years afterward that I had wasted it. Now it seems very full. It is already the past, the irrevocable past. Mary Chilton died that spring, quite suddenly; Lugné-Poë, just before the fall of France; the last of the Fratellinis has gone. Good-by, my Paris. But who is nineteen now, sitting in the Luxembourg Gardens, creating a world within that world and testing the rich ripe fruit of perambulation in the ancient ever-renewed and renewing city.

Paul Zweig

Paul Zweig (1935–1984) was best known in his own lifetime as a poet and critic of American literature, but the works of his that seem likely to live, and for a long time, are the autobiographical essays collected in the 1977 *Three Journeys* and the beautiful posthumous *Departures* (1986). Zweig, an enigmatic figure for one who lived so recently, clearly had a gift for belief, for losing himself in a new faith or identity: one of the finest chapters in *Three Journeys* concerns his newfound enthusiasm for the Indian guru Muktananda (who is also the subject of his 1977 *Muktananda: Selected Essays*). Nowhere was his will to believe put to more astonishing use than in France. Born a poor Jewish boy in Brighton Beach, his most intense and self-emancipating journey was to Paris, where, by an extraordinary act of will, he seems to have been able to entirely lose his American identity and take on that of an engagé French radical at the time of the near civil war in France over Algeria. This piece of self-abnegation, or even imposture, and the loves and compulsions that led him to it, are the subject of this excerpt from *Departures*. He later dropped his "French" identity and returned to New York, where he remarried, had a daughter, and taught at Queens College. He died, tragically young, of a form of cancer of the blood, and wrote about that too, wonderfully well.

---

from

Departures

During my first year in Paris, I lived in a small residence hotel on the Rue de Tournon, near the Luxembourg Gardens. I had a long, narrow room, with pink wallpaper and a *porte-fenêtre* that took up all of the exterior wall. There was a stained sink, an armoire with a mirror on it, a skinny bed, a desk and chair; and, facing me out the window, a skyline made of chimney pots and steeples, attics, gray slanting rooftops silhouetted against the sky like a line of script.

I lived in a formidable isolation. For weeks I walked all over the city, whispering my couple of French words in grocery stores and restaurants.

As the weeks passed, I forgot what it was like to speak in complete sentences. This was a new kind of solitude. I began to have a fantasy that if I looked into a mirror, I wouldn't see anyone there.

During these weeks, my only human contact was with a group of young Arabs who hung out in a café on the Boulevard Saint Michel. They were immigrants from Morocco or Algeria; most of them were unemployed, their families left behind while they looked for work. One day, I sat down in their café. Somehow they seemed more accessible than the fast-talking French. I mumbled *"Parlez-vous anglais?"* to one of them, and he answered with a friendly twitter and a handshake. He and his friends sounded out slow French syllables for my benefit. They showed me a couple of restaurants with trestle tables and paper tablecloths where I could eat for a few francs. We sat on the curb of the boulevard and looked at photographs of their wives and children, still living in their home villages in the mountains of the Kabylia, in Algeria, or in the Rif Mountains of Morocco. They let me know that they weren't Arabs, but Berbers, mountain people. North Africa had been theirs before the Arabs got there. I barely know what Algeria was—a crescent of fertile valleys and mountains, lined with pure white beaches, clinging to the northern rim of the Sahara.

Those weeks in Paris were a turning point. I felt stripped of every comfort; my wordlessness was a kind of invisibility that, oddly, made me feel conspicuous: one of Notre Dame's grotesques, with a thick tongue and a ludicrous body. Living less hadn't gotten me very afar; I was stupefied by a world gone slightly awry.

And then something happened that was overwhelming, although curiously uneventful. I had no name for it. Little by little I began to make sense out of the French I heard in cafés and restaurants, on the radio, in fleeting conversations. Much of it I still didn't understand, but I began to notice that it was language, expressed by the voices of these people with tight lips who seemed to talk through me with spars and splinters of sound.

I started to spend hours every day reading the newspapers with a dictionary. I carried around a pale blue school pamphlet of Paul Valéry's poems. I still own it, although it is brown with food stains and dirt now. I recited the poems over and over to myself. And as I did, they took on a thickness, a layered life that was the life of language. I acquired a kind of tunnel vision. French words walked in my sleep, masculine, feminine;

a sexual throb invaded the little explosions of the consonants, the compressed intonations, particularly the stranglings of the *r*'s, that stamp of true initiation into the street theater and persistent fakery of sounding French.

My solitary life became a form of heroism. I wasn't like those other Americans sitting at the Café de Tournon, across the street from my hotel. All evening they talked English and drank coffee or wine in the pink neon that lit a rectangle of sidewalk in front of the café. I could see them from the opening of my window, where I sat for hours, leaning against a worn wooden rail. I could hear the laughter, the excited voices, the intellectual discussions. Women gathered in the pink light wearing thin dresses, their long hair falling onto their shoulders.

Don't go in there, I warned myself with a determination that seemed to have come from nowhere and given no warning. I found myself wanting desperately to be a foreigner, an alien; I wanted to be walled in by my lucidity. For the first time in my life, I wanted something with all my heart, and what was it? To step across a brink, vanish into a peculiar unsympathetic realm, where I would be a secret visitor, a perfect construction of the will, almost a windup doll, making only the right movements, saying only foreign things to foreign people. America, New York, even my own language, had become like dead skins to me. After a month or so, I started trying to read French novels: Voltaire's *Candide*, then some Balzac, some Flaubert. For a long time there was no enjoyment in it, except maybe the enjoyment of wading in thick space lit by occasional glows of sense. I read with my lips, trying to unravel the clipped sounds, discover where the lengths of sentence hinged on verbs or came to earth solidly on immovable nouns. Often I had to look up almost every word.

Even as I worked, I was aware that I had never thrown myself into something so completely this way before. I longed to expand into whole sentences again. I discovered—it was a trick of physiology—that my accent was perfect. I made those strangled *r*'s as if I had been born to it. The stars which had given me birth on July 14, Bastille Day, twenty-one years before, had decided I would become master of the ultimate disguise. I would become a creature in one of those parallel worlds science-fiction writers love to invent. In one world, I was a poet born in Brooklyn, shy, conservative, but given to irruptions of strange behavior; in another, I was the same man, but French.

The isolation was probably driving me a little crazy. I had become a watcher. I watched little boys in blue uniforms sail their model boats on the pond in the Luxembourg Gardens, and the low tumbling clouds that poured over the treeline across the park. I watched the tired faces of the intellectuals at the Old Navy Café on the Boulevard Saint Germain, around the corner from my hotel. Their weariness seemed to be the expression of terrible knowledge. This was the somber petering out of the existentialist movement. A gloom was concentrated behind the cream-colored wooden front of the café that could not be dispelled by coffee and strong cigarettes, or by the women with adolescent breasts who circulated among the tables.

I watched girls in pert, threadbare coats kissing their friends on two cheeks, or squeezed into a doorway with a lover. I watched the crowds coming up out of the Métro; and the *charbonniers*, their faces gleaming with black dust, delivering sacks of coal from the two-wheeled carts they pushed down the middle of narrow streets. I walked in streets that were dingy and full of smells: the Rue Gît-le-Coeur, the Rue Xavier Privas, the Rue Maître Albert: strips of pure Zola that were grim and damp. The century hadn't yet swept them into its noisy life. They were quiet, morose.

That fall, the Russians invaded Hungary, and Paris seemed to go wild with indignation and fear. Posters went up all over the city: COMMUNIST MURDERERS, FREE HUNGARY. Suddenly I saw what a tiny place Europe was. Paris was only a tank ride from Budapest. This was the continent where armies crashed across borders, and wars were fought in picture-book fields lined with poplars. The last war had ended only eleven years before. Every day, I passed marble plaques bearing the names of young men killed fighting the Nazis. The plaques often had wilted flowers placed on the sidewalk beneath them. They were fresh deaths. In some crowded apartment up too many flights of stairs, they were still mourned: by a mother, a lover, a wife; or else, dutifully, by the local Communist Party cell, commemorating the Party's heroic role in the Resistance.

War belonged to the city's history; the streets reverberated with it. There were angry rallies at the Maubert Mutualitié, a neighborhood meeting hall where, only a few years later, I would listen to political speeches and croon the rousing stanzas of the Internationale. Brigades of anti-Communist youths were preparing to fight the Russians in Hungary. They wore black leather and chains, and looked cruelly earnest.

I looked on, feeling dread, but also curiosity for these political passions which were as foreign to me as French itself. I had been brought up in the political consciousness of the 1940s. I knew that my mother had once been involved with communism, and during the McCarthy years the spines of certain books were turned to the wall. Politics had seemed treacherous, full of betrayals. But the cold war remained a dim noise that had no bearing on the backyard barbecues and fraternity parties. Even the Rosenberg trial hadn't broken through my visceral distrust of everything public.

But now the passions of French public life disoriented me. The streets roared with demonstrations. Black symbols were painted on walls, with anti-Semitic slogans under them, or YANKEE GO HOME, or some revolutionary outcry I didn't understand.

Toward the end of September I met a girl in a *cave* on the Rue de la Huchette. The *cave* was in a Gothic basement down a flight of stairs. There was a hot musty smell of damp stone walls mingled with cigarette smoke and spilled wine. We danced to loud Dixieland music played by a group of bearded Frenchmen wearing existentialist black sweaters. The girl's name was Nicole. She had dull brown hair falling neatly onto her neck, and unhealthy-looking skin. Between her few words of English and my few words of French, we managed to understand each other. She had just spent a year living in a small village in the Spanish Pyrenees, she told me, because the doctors had found a tubercular spot on her lungs.

Nicole was operatic in the quietest possible way. She was a mouse, winsome and forlorn. We made a pair. She was virtuous and intense, soulful, usually silent. Her eyes expressed quiet hurt. When she laughed, she touched her lips, as if to excuse herself. I found Nicole's reserve incredibly attractive. On our meetings in the Luxembourg Gardens beside the boat pond, or in my shadowy room lying on the bed, barely touching, there was a distance between us. When I tried to undress her, she winced or gave a nervous laugh. And as the weeks passed, I understood that Nicole intended to remain chaste. Kisses were all right; so were slow, hesitant talks in the privacy of my room, with our hands touching, and a few wispy caresses. But no sex. I accepted this; I think I liked it. It gave our friendship a forlorn halo, as in an artistic photograph: two people in silhouette on a foggy afternoon. It preserved the abstract quality of my feelings, as if my life were a line drawing.

Nicole lived at home with her parents in a tiny apartment in Montparnasse, with the toilet outside in the hall, and no shower. Her mother was a dental assistant. She usually wore brightly colored dresses with lots of beads and rings, and she had a throaty laugh that seemed to bounce off the walls of the tiny living room. With her mother present, Nicole was even more silent than usual; almost as silent as her stepfather, an old man with a wide, creviced face, who usually sat on the couch holding a crumpled beret in his hands. He was a carpenter, but from the ironic nods of the mother and daughter, I gathered his business didn't prosper.

Nicole and her mother enjoyed teaching me French. They would point at objects, and name them with a precise, slightly pompous tone, as if I were a little simpleminded; and I would talk back at them in my clinking French, swallowing my words, giving them wrong genders. I took on the role of an earnest idiot. Nicole's mother adopted me as her project. While Nicole sat on the couch leafing through *Elle*, her mother made throaty flourishes and fed me foods that bewildered me. I remember Nicole's brooding smile when I was defeated by a leathery green blossom that sat on my plate beside a dish of melted butter. I tried to stick my knife into it. I picked it up and put it down quickly with scalded fingertips. I had never seen an artichoke before, and required instruction.

Nicole's self-contained sadness became a part of my life. We circled around each other mildly. I think she was frightened of me. That was my problem: my invisibility, my living less. But I never saw—never could see—the nomadic glimmers of the homunculus self; the complex loops of the fugitive atom, alone, alone. Nicole probably didn't see it either, at least not in so many words. She simply sensed that I wasn't all there; a foreigner within a foreigner who, despite his relentless good manners, was, probably unbeknownst to himself, fundamentally a wild man.

By now I had a student card, and was able to eat in a student restaurant near my hotel. The meals were served on steel trays: There was usually a watery stew, some vegetables, soup, thin yogurt, and lots of bread. I got into the habit of stuffing my pockets with the bread and munching the crusts late at night while reading in bed.

I had managed to get a job teaching English for a few hours a week in a commercial high school; it was enough to pay the rent and buy restaurant tickets. Now and then I had a real meal at a restaurant in the Rue de Seine, or made a midnight foray across the river to the glass-and-cast-iron sheds of Les Halles, the central produce market, for a bowl of thick onion soup crusted over with cheese. I walked home over the Pont Neuf. The equestrian statue of Henri IV stood in the middle of the bridge, with the empty river behind it. Along one side stood the dark palisade of the Louvre; on the other, the buoyant dome of the Académie Française seemed to float like a bubble. Paris late at night was a dead city. The Métro shut down at one o'clock; the cafés were closed; a faint night light glowed over the zinc counters as I walked past.

All fall I read Pascal's *Pensées*, at first in a Modern Library translation and then, with a feeling of cool daring, in French. As I read the self-mortifying prose and the bleak aphorisms, I was filled with abstract excitement. I longed to be virtuous and pure. On those nights, munching hard bread and hearing an occasional car rumble down the cobbled street outside my window, I could feel the great vacuum—"the silence of those infinite spaces"—and perceive myself standing on a thin line between two infinities: the starlit one out there and the whirling sub-atomic one within. Pascal was a genius of insecurity; I read him avidly, as one reads a horror story. I followed Pascal in his terrible desire to make man comfortless and exposed. I learned that I was a machine of deli-quescing internal parts. When he explained his famous bet, I wanted to bet too: Maybe God exists, maybe He doesn't; but it makes sense to bet that He does, because what do you have to lose? If He exists, you win; if He doesn't, you lose anyway. I tried to bet, I lay awake method-ically casting the dice; but I never actually bet. I could strip down, almost gleefully; I could become less; I had a talent for it. But the bet left me cold. I didn't have it in me. The story of the piece of folded paper that Pascal carried around with him recording a night of mystical perception (on the paper he had written: "fire fire fire") made me skep-tical and a little disrespectful. I suspected it was an illusion, the result of indigestion or a fever.

Meanwhile, I wrote insufferable letters to my parents exhorting them to be moral and good, to have elevated ambitions, to stop being dis-honest and merely sociable. When I turned off the light and tried to sleep, I heard my heart beating against the mattress; it was breakable, a clock of death. I shifted until the mattress became silent. Only then could I fall asleep.

My cold excitement matched the weather. December was chilly, and it rained every day. Paris became darker under the lid of clouds. With the cold weather, Nicole seemed to withdraw into herself. She was always cold. Often she seemed to be listening to something, her head slightly bent, as if I were scolding her. We saw each other less and less frequently.

I think this was her choice. She was, after all, a middle-class young woman thinking of the future. Her gypsy mother had sniffed me out, while skipping around the apartment to keep me entertained. She was a practical woman, and Nicole's melancholy required measures. It became obvious that I was not going to marry her daughter. I was temporary, a man without a future or with too much future. More like a tropical scavenger who had swung down to earth and was likely to disappear again just as quickly, stealing the fruit in the bowl.

As Nicole became less available, her place in my life was taken by an overpowering desire.

One day in early December I opened up a paperback novel by Françoise Mauriac, *Thérèse Desqueyroux*, placed my French-English dictionary beside it, and got ready for several hours of the labor that, at times, resembled plowing the ocean: learning French. Every day for months, I had been making a place in my brain and equipping it with syntax, vocabulary, fractions of sentences. I had worked my fat diphthongs into musical vowels. I had collected bits of language, colloquialisms, slang. I had wrestled with subtleties, degrees of intimacy and impersonality in the various forms of personal address: *tu, vous*. My mind was full of voices, lilts of conversation, a babble of French intonations.

I began reading Mauriac: the gloomy pine forests of the Landes in southwestern France; a creaking silence that pierced the heart of his characters; the thin vein of religious exaltation, amid a hunger for self-sacrifice and self-mutilation. The novel was relentless, a kind of hallucination that was deepened by the straining of my attention as I tried to stare meaning into the barely familiar words and sentences.

After a while I found myself drifting into the story. I leafed through my dictionary and underlined words in the text, hardly noticing what I was doing. The novel's dour language enveloped me; I savored and smelled it. It wasn't Mauriac—whom I didn't know anything about—but French. The nasal definiteness of the *passé simple*, turning memory into a sentence of immutability; the needlelike phrases. It dawned on me that I wasn't studying now. I was reading, as if I had crossed a line through a membrane and found myself in a new, unheard-of place full of intense forms that were almost familiar, almost ordinary. Here was the world as I had always known it: the trees and clouds; fathers and daughters; destructive passions and the secrets of souls; but expressed in a syncopated medium, as if I had stumbled on a reality that resembled my own in every way, except for an immaterial glow letting me know that, appearances to the contrary, I was at the opposite end of space.

It took a while for my discovery to take hold: I could read now. French wasn't simply a discipline, it had become a pleasure.

James Thurber

James Thurber (1894–1961) came to Paris as a code clerk during World War I, and returned sporadically throughout his life, particularly in the 1930s. He brought Harold Ross to Paris long enough to record Ross's perfectly American comment on the Sainte-Chapelle: "Stained glass is damned embarrassing." Though Thurber spoke little French—a few of his funniest pieces begin in the misunderstandings generated by his mistakes—no American writer has ever loved more what he called "the most beautiful surface of manners in the world." His starved Ohio heart leapt at the intricately ceremonial nature of French life; he was in awe of the complexities involved in just borrowing orange juice, and the glass to put it in, from a café. Here—in a piece from *Alarms and Diversions* (1957)—he tells us something about how that love began.

———

The First Time I Saw Paris

What I saw first of all was one outflung hand of France as cold and limp as a dead man's. This was the seacoast town of Saint-Nazaire, a long while ago. I know now that French towns don't die, that France has the durability of history itself, but I was only twenty-three then, and seasick, and I had never been so far from Ohio before. It was the dank, morose dawn of the 13th of November, 1918, and I had this first dismal glimpse of *France la Doulce* from the deck of the U.S. Transport *Orizaba*, which had come from the wintry sea like a ship out of Coleridge, a painted ship in an unreal harbor. The moist, harsh light of breaking day gave the faces of the silent staring gobs on deck a weird look, but the unreality was shattered soon enough by the raucous voice of a boatswain bawling orders. I had first heard this voice, strong enough to outshout a storm, snarling commands at "abandon ship" drill: "Now, light all lanterns!" and "Now, lower all lifeboats!" I had been assigned to a life raft that was rusted to the deck and couldn't be budged. "Now, what's the matter with Life Raft Number Six?" the boatswain had roared. A sailor next to me said, "She's stuck to the deck, sir." The boatswain had to have the last word and he had it. "Now, leave her lay there!" he loudly decreed.

The *Orizaba* had taken a dozen days zigzagging across the North Atlantic, to elude the last submarines of the war, one of which we had sighted two days before, and Corcoran and I felt strange and uncertain on what seemed anything but solid land for a time. We were code clerks in the State Department, on our way to the Paris Embassy. Saint-Nazaire was, of course, neither dead nor dying, but I can still feel in my bones the gloom and tiredness of the old port after its four years of war. The first living things we saw were desolate men, a detachment of German prisoners being marched along a street, in mechanical step, without expression in their eyes, like men coming from no past and moving toward no future. Corcoran and I walked around the town to keep warm until the bistros opened. Then we had the first cognac of our lives, quite a lot of it, and the day brightened, and there was a sense of beginning as well as of ending, in the chilling weather. A young pink-cheeked French army officer got off his bicycle in front of a house and knocked on the door. It was opened by a young woman whose garb and greeting, even to our inexperienced eyes and ears, marked her as one of those females once described by a professor of the Harvard Law School as "the professionally indiscreet." Corcoran stared and then glanced at his wristwatch. "Good God!" he said. "It isn't even nine o'clock yet."

The train trip down to Paris was a night to remember. We shared a sleeping compartment with a thin, gloved, talkative Frenchman who said he was writing the history of the world and who covered his subject spasmodically through the night in English as snarled as a fisherman's net, waking us once to explain that Hannibal's elephants were not real, but merely fearful figments of Roman hallucination. I lay awake a long time thinking of the only Paris I knew, the tranquil, almost somnolent city of Henry James's turn-of-the-century novels, in which there was no hint of war, past or approaching, except that of the sexes.

Paris, when we finally got there, seemed to our depressed spirits like the veritable capital city of the Beginning. Her heart was warm and gay, all right, but there was hysteria in its beat, and the kind of compulsive elation psychiatrists strive to cure. Girls snatched the overseas caps and tunic buttons from American soldiers, paying for them in hugs and kisses, and even warmer coin. A frightened Negro doughboy from Alabama said, "If this happened to me back home, they'd hang me." The Folies Bergères and the Casino de Paris, we found a few nights later, were headquarters of the New Elation, filled with generous ladies of joy, some offering their charms free to drinking, laughing and brawling Americans in what was left of their uniforms. At the Folies a quickly composed song called "*Finie la Guerre*" drew a dozen encores. Only the American MP's were grim, as they moved among the crowds looking for men who were AWOL, telling roistering captains and majors to dress up their uniforms. Doughboy French, that wonderful hybrid, bloomed everywhere. "*Restez ici* a minute," one private said to his French girl. "*Je* returny *après cet* guy partirs." *Cet* guy was, of course, a big-jawed military policeman set on putting a stop to non-regulation hilarity.

"I do not understand the American," a Casino girl told me. "They fight at night with each other, they break mirrors, they become bloody, they say goddamn everybody, and the next day what do you think? They are in the Parc Monceau on all fours giving little French children a ride on their backs. They are marvelous. I love them."

The Americans have never been so loved in France, or anywhere else abroad, as they were in those weeks of merriment and wild abandon. When, late in 1919, most of our soldiers had sailed back home, *La Vie Parisienne* had a full-page color drawing of an American officer over whose full-length figure dozens of lovely miniature French girls were rapturously climbing, and the caption ruefully observed: "The hearts of our young ladies have gone home with the Americans."

My trunk had stayed on the *Orizaba*. Corcoran and I had been the only two civilians on board, and transports were not used to unloading non-military baggage. All I had was the clothes I wore—my hat had been claimed as a souvenir—and I set about the considerable task of buying a wardrobe, paying what amounted to five dollars for B.V.D.'s at the Galeries Lafayette. A suit I bought at a shop deceptively called "Jack, American Tailor" is packed away in the modest files of secret memory. It might have been made by the American Can Company. I tried on hats for an hour in a shop on the Avenue de l'Opéra, upon whose civilian stock the dust of four years of war had settled. There were narrow-brimmed hats, each with a feather stuck on one side, that made me look like Larry Semon, movie comic of the silent days, and some that would have delighted that great connoisseur of funny hats, Mr. Ed Wynn. They were all placed on my head with an excited "*Voilà!*" by the eager salesman, and they were all too small, as well as grotesque. In one of the famous black, broad-brimmed hats, long and lovingly associated with the painters and poets of Bohemian Paris, I looked like a baleful figure attending the funeral of Art. I nearly broke the salesman's heart when I turned down a ten-gallon white Stetson he had dug up out of the cellar. So I went through that cold, dank Paris winter without a hat.

I had bought a cane, which in Columbus would have identified me as a lounge lizard of dubious morals, and I acquired enough boulevard French to say, "*Où est la Place de la Concorde?*" and to reply to "*Voulez-vous une petite caresse?*" My *tout ensemble* was strange, but not strange enough to deceive doughboys and gobs wandering along the Champs Elysées, homesick and disconsolate after the elation died down. I helped them decipher the small red-and-black French-English dictionaries they carried and told them that, contrary to their invariable conviction, they would not be stuck in "this god-forsaken city" forever. Once I translated, for a puzzled demoiselle, a mysterious note she had got through the mails from a doughboy who had returned to her one day before *cet* guy had partired. It began, "I am in a place I cannot leave." I managed to explain to her that her boy had been jailed for being absent without leave. I gathered that he had been, when on the loose, a great lover, fighter and piggy-back rider, like the others. "I wish to cry on your shirt," his girl friend told me, and she cried on my shirt. That astonished shirt, stained with Lacrimae Puellae 1919, must have cost a lot, but all I remember is that the amazing French shirttail reached to my knees.

When I got to France, the franc was worth almost a quarter, but pretty soon you could get fourteen francs for your dollar, and since prices didn't rise as rapidly as the franc fell, the $2,000 annual salary of a code clerk began to mean something. One amateur speculator among us, certain that the franc would come back with all the resilience of Paris, bought up francs and was wiped out when *la chute* continued. In my nearly forty years off and on in France I have seen this coin of a thousand values vary from 5.30 to 350. "It will be as worthless as dandelions," a dour concierge predicted in 1919, but she was wrong.

"Ah, *ces américaines*," sighed a Folies girl one evening. "*Quels hommes!* They are such good bad boys. They wish to spend the night, even the weekend." She went on to explain how this complicated the economic structure of one in her profession. She was used, in the case of other foreigners, to a nightly transference of paid affections as neatly maneuvered as the changing of partners in a square dance. "These Americans are men born to marry," my informant went on. Many of them—thousands, I believe—did marry French girls and took them home to an astonished

Brooklyn, a disapproving Middle West, and occasionally more amiable regions. I read somewhere in 1928 that about 75 per cent of these wartime marriages had ended in the return of the brides to France. One of those who stayed wrote me a letter a quarter of a century ago in which she said, dolorously, "There is not the life in Detroit. It is not Paris. Can you send me some books in French?" She had married a great big good bad American Army lieutenant. I sent her, among other books in French, the poems of Mallarmé and the book Clemenceau wrote after the war. I often wonder what finally became of another girl who married a sailor and went to live in Iowa, and what they thought of her English out there. She had learned it all from the plays of Shakespeare and it was quaint and wonderful to hear, but definitely not for Iowa. "How goes the night?" she asked me once, straight out of *Macbeth*, to which I was proudly able to reply, "The moon is down. I have not heard the clock." This Gallic Elizabethan had given up working for a few francs a week in a garment factory for a more lucrative and less monotonous career. Once I met her by appointment, and in pursuit of my sociological studies, on the terrace of the Café de la Paix, where, over vermouth cassis, she explained that she was going to meet, in half an hour, an American captain whom she had comforted one night long ago when he didn't have a sou. It seems he had promised to meet her at the café and pay his debt of gratitude, and he had written her from somewhere and fixed an hour. "He will be here," she said confidently, and she was right. A quiet, almost shy good bad boy, he slipped her a sealed envelope while I studied the passing throng in which, true prophecy has it, you will see everybody you know if you sit at your table long enough. I still remember that what he ordered was chocolate ice cream.

The City of Light, during most of 1919, was costumed like a wide-screen Technicolor operetta, the uniforms of a score of nations forming a kind of restless, out-of-step finale. The first Bastille Day celebration after the war was a carnival that dazzled the eye and lifted the heart. Chairs at windows of buildings along the route of march cost as much as fifty dollars, and stepladders on the crowded sidewalks could be rented for fifteen dollars. At night, in a thousand "tin bars," as our men called bistros, and in more elaborate *boîtes de nuit*, the Americans often changed the prewar pattern of Paris night life by fighting among themselves, or singly, in pairs, or in groups, the Anzacs, the waiter, the management, the *gendarmerie*, or whoever was looking for action. Chairs and bottles were thrown, and mirrors cracked from side to side. There was a conviction among Americans, more often false than true, that they were always over-charged, and this was the chief provocation for trouble, but high spirits, the irritating factor of unfamiliarity, triple sec, and a profound American inability to pick up foreign languages easily, often led to roughhouse. A civilian I knew who hailed from New Jersey, and constantly and profanely wished he were back there, asked me one morning how to say in French, "I demand the release of these Americans." It turned out that no Ameri-cans he knew were in durance anywhere. My unilingual companion sim-ply planned to go out on the town that night with some compatriots and wanted to be prepared, in case his detachment was overwhelmed by the authorities in some bar. Like me, he worked at the Embassy, then on the Rue de Chaillot, and he had a code-room pass which he proposed to wave while shouting his command. I told him the French were always aroused, never intimidated, by civilians shouting orders, especially if they flaunted mysterious and doubtful official credentials. He would be taken, I told him, for that most despised of creatures, the *mouchard*, or police spy. Not the next morning, but a few days later, he showed up with bruised knuckles and a swollen jaw. "You were right," he admitted meekly.

Paris had been down on her knees, but now she got back on her feet, surely and resolutely, in the noble tradition of the world's most spirited city. Montmartre, when I first walked down its deserted silent streets, had seemed down and out for good, but by New Year's Eve, 1918, it had begun to function, and before long the Moulin Rouge and the Chat Noir were gaily crowded again. Excellent food, the great pride of Paris, was naturally slow in reaching the tables of the famous restaurants, but I took an Amer-ican Red Cross girl to Voisin's not many weeks after I arrived, and it seemed to have gone through the war as if nothing worse than a storm had passed. This was the quietly elegant restaurant celebrated for its calm, almost austere, survival of the Siege of Paris in the war with Prussia, when, undaunted by dwindling supplies, it served up the tender cuts of some of the more edible animals of the zoo. I remember being shown one of the remarkable and touching menus of those war years. I have forgotten just when it closed its doors forever, but in 1938, while accompanying my wife on a shopping trip, I was suddenly overcome by a curious and haunting sense of the past in a woman's glove store. Recognition flowed back like a film developing, and I realized that I stood within a few feet of where the American girl and I had sat for lunch one day. It was like meeting an old beloved friend who has undergone a sorrowful change and no longer knows who you are.

Paris during the months of the Peace Conference would have delighted Hadrian, Playboy of the Roman Empire, who enjoyed colorful spectacles brought together from the corners of the world. When President Wilson drove down the Champs Elysées, more people watched and cheered, more flags were waved, more eyes were bright, than I have ever seen in one place at a time. The way from there had to be down, because there was no higher place to reach, and the international highway of acclaim never runs straight and smooth very far. There had been, even on the day of armistice, voices that did not shout "*Finie la guerre!*" but solemnly warned, "*Maintenant ça commence.*" But these prophets of predicament and peril were lost sight of in the carnival. I didn't hear them myself; I was too busy, between coding and decoding telegraphic messages, watching Premier Paderewski arriving at his hotel, catching glimpses of Herbert Hoover sitting erect in the back seat of his big Cadillac, identifying the impressive head of Lloyd George at one of the restaurants in the Bois de Boulogne. At the Casino de Paris, the famous straw hat and lower lip of Maurice Chevalier, not long before turned thirty, attracted crowds as his rising star dimmed a little the light of the great Mistinguette. He did a wonderful burlesque of an American gob, by turns melancholy and gay, excited and bewildered, taking the edge off Mistinguette's singing of "For Me and My Gal," a song the French loved. The Americans, of course, were singing "Smiles" and "Hindustan," and then a song of which someone had sent me a recording from America, "Dardanella." I remember taking the Red Cross girl to dinner at Noël Peters, where a trio of piano, violin and cello played many pieces, only one of them American. After brandy I had requested an American song, and the pianist finally dug up the sheet music of "Goodbye My Bluebell."

Everybody went out to Versailles, where the famous fountains had been turned on for the first time in years. All kinds of devices were used to get into the Hall of Mirrors. Never had so many fake passes been so elaborately contrived, but few of them worked. And through it all the Battle of Paris went on. Souvenir hunting by Americans reached a high point. They took things out of niches and tried to pry things loose from plinths, to add to the relics of war brought back from the front, including ornamental vases made by French soldiers out of the casings of French 75's. I got one of these at Fort Vaux outside Verdun, which had been stormed and taken and retaken so many times. Verdun had been the farthest north reached by me and another Embassy clerk in the week before Christmas, 1918. We had gone by train as far as the town of Vierzy, where my companion searched vainly for the grave of a friend from Illinois who had been a marine. Another marine from the Embassy guard, talking and dreaming of his ranch in Montana, had gone with us as far as Vierzy, mainly to find an open space in which he could practice firing a Luger he had picked up somewhere, but he would have no part of our plan to walk through the battlefields, day after day, as far as Soissons and Verdun. Up there we paid our way into Fort Vaux and the underground city of Verdun with American cigarettes. I often consume again, in fantasy, the light omelet, *pain de famille*, and good white wine served to us by a young French farmer and his wife who were bravely rebuilding their home in one of those landscapes of destruction so poignantly painted by the late English artist Paul Nash. It took long argument to persuade the couple to take money for the meal.

In our trek through the battlefields, with the smell of death still in the air, the ruined and shattered country scarred with ammunition dumps and crashed planes, we came upon the small temporary cemeteries arranged by the Graves Registration Service, each with a small American flag, such as the children of Paris waved at President Wilson, nailed to a post and faded by the rain and wintry weather. In one of these cemeteries my companion, a Tennessee youth, only a little taller than five feet, began singing "The Star-Spangled Banner" with his hat over his heart, and went on singing it in a sudden downpour of rain, for the anthem, once started, must be finished. He was loaded down with junk on our way back, most of which he had to abandon. He mourned his failure to wrench an ornamental iron gate from the entrance to a shattered château. The only thing I brought back, besides the vase, was the identification papers of an Algerian soldier named A. Mokdad, which were lying on the ground, punctured by two machine-gun bullets. Detachments of French labor battalions were trying to clear up the wreckage here and there, a task that seemed hopeless. But the French soldiers were tough, determined men. By the light of a Very shell one night in Soissons we had seen a company of *poilus* marching through the mud, singing "Madelon." In the muzzles of some of their carbines flowers from God knows where had been stuck. The soldiers looked enormous and indomitable, and it is good to know that one or two French painters of the time did justice to their stature, painting them to look like the rocks they were. Contrary to the prewar American notion of French-men as small and dapper, there were scores of d'Artagnans in the armies of France for every Aramis—and he was tough enough himself.

Back in Paris, I made a brief survey of the souvenirs collected by Americans I knew. One man had brought from somewhere a machine gun, which he kept in his hotel room and left there when he went home. Leg-end had it that the upraised sword of the equestrian statue of George Washington in the Place d'Iéna had been replaced nine times, and one overenthusiastic vandal had been arrested while attempting to take one of the gilt cherubs from the superstructure of the bridge of Alexandre III across the Seine. A sailor I know collected, with the aid of chisel and screwdriver, ornate locks from old doors and gates, and his trophies must have weighed a good hundred pounds. A doughboy who fancied bronze and marble busts in museums was less successful. It was rumored, in the days of the Great Hunt, that not more than five servicemen were admit-ted to Napoleon's tomb at one time. Everybody heard, and retold, the wonderful myth of the bold and enterprising soldier in the Louvre who had got away with the arms of the Venus de Milo and the head of the Winged Victory.

I have nothing tangible to remind me of those tangled days, the Ver-dun vase and the papers of A. Mokdad having long since disappeared. The vase, wherever it is, must still bear the deathless hammered-out name "Verdun." From a separate trip to Rheims I brought back nothing but chill memories that still turn up now and then in nightmares. I see the vacant staring space from which the rose window of the cathedral had been carefully removed in time, and the gaping hole in one wall of the edifice, made by a shell hit. This great city of the Champagne country was all but deserted when I was there, and a walk through its streets was a walk on the moon. The disappearance of one wall had revealed a bedroom that looked like a dismal abandoned stage set. The works of a printing shop, its machines and type, were scattered across a street. The façade of a theater had been ripped off, revealing a crumbling stage, while empty seats and boxes, unharmed except by weather, gave the beholder the feel-ing that cast and audience had fled in horror during the showing of some kind of extravaganza in hell. And in Paris, so near in space, seemingly so far away in time, morbid visitors, looking for the effects of war, asked where they could find the church upon which a shell from Big Bertha had made its terrible direct hit.

All of us went to the grand opera many times, my own first visit being to hear "Aïda" and to see the *haut monde* of Paris once again in evening clothes, glittering up and down the marble staircases between acts. Someone pointed out René Fonck in the crowd, and I still remember the ribbon of the great airman's croix de guerre, as long as a ruler to accommodate all the palms he had won. There is a timelessness about grand opera in Paris, and except for the uniforms, there was no hint that the greatest war in history had come so recently to an end. I paid a dollar that night for a pack of American cigarettes, but this was not my most memorable financial transaction. A week or two after our arrival Corcoran and I had paid a dollar apiece for fried eggs, and almost as much for marmalade.

I sometimes ate with the doughboys, who never got used to French food, and groused about American Army grub. In Verdun one day we ate Army beans and the rest of the rations, using borrowed mess kits. "Look at them guys eat that stuff," one private said. "I'll be damned if they don't like it." We also liked the wheat cakes with genuine maple sirup served at an Army kitchen set up in the basement of the Crillon, the de luxe hotel in the heart of Paris which had been taken over by the Americans.

I saw no doughboys or gobs at the opera, but they crowded into the cinemas when they opened, to watch the American films of three actors popular with the French—W. S. Hart ("*le roi du ranch*"), Harold Lloyd, known as "*Lui*," and Douglas Fairbanks *père*, lovingly called "Doogla" by the French.

When I finally sailed back home, sixteen months had elapsed since the Armistice, and the Brave New World was taking on its disillusioning shape. Theodore Roosevelt had died in 1919, which marked in its way the end of an era, and Woodrow Wilson had come down from his dizzy pinnacle of fame and hope, and was on his way to his own dismayed and frustrated end. Before long a celebrated room was to be filled with smoke out of which a political magician named Harry M. Daugherty would produce the shadowy figure of Warren Gamaliel Harding and the misleading motto of "Return to Normalcy" in a period of flagpole sitting, nonstop dancing, Channel swimming, ocean flying, husband murder, novels of disenchantment, and approaching financial chaos. I reached New York still without a hat. It was March and blustery in New York, and one of the first things I did was to buy one. It fitted my head, and seemed to my repatriated eye extremely becoming. It wasn't until later that day that I looked inside the hat to see the mark of the maker. I quote from a piece I wrote in 1923 for the Columbus, Ohio, Sunday *Dispatch*: "Something inside the crown caught my eye. I looked more closely. '*Fabriqué par Moissant et Amour, 25 Avenue de l'Opera, Paris,*' it said."

Paris, City of Light and of occasional Darkness, sometimes in the winter rain seeming wrought of monolithic stones, and then, in the days of its wondrous and special pearly light, appearing to float in mid-air like a mirage city in the Empire of Imagination, fragile and magical, has had many a premature requiem sung for the repose of its soul by nervous writers or gloomy historians who believe it is dying or dead and can never rise again. Paris, nonetheless, goes right on rising out of war, ultimatum, occupation, domestic upheaval, cabinet crises, international tension, and dark prophecy, as it has been in the habit of doing since its residents first saw the menacing glitter of Roman shields many centuries ago. Recently in the New York Sunday *Times* John Davenport sang sorrowfully of the Paris of today as a dying city, a city of ghosts, but his funeral arrangements were laughed off by, among others, a South Carolina reader who protested, "It is not Paris but an Anglo-American myth that is dying."

The Americans and English have never become an integral part of the anatomy of the city, which is forever French. Its visitors come and go, hopeful or despondent, comfortable or uneasy, looking in the wrong places for the throb of its heart. I have been in and out of Paris half a dozen times from 1920 to 1955, and I have had my moments of depression and worry about the great city, but I have never felt that I was sitting up at night with a fatally sick friend. I have seen her moods shift from confidence to despond, for Paris is a lady of temperament and volatility, but I have never felt she was mortally languishing, like a stricken heroine of grand opera.

I enjoy arguing with Parisian friends about the true gender of their fair city, pointing out that "feminine," in my lexicon, means neither frail nor frivolous, neither capricious nor coquettish, but female, and summing up with this sound paraphrase of Kipling: "The female of the cities is far tougher than the male." In my observation, the female of any species is not, in Simone de Beauvoir's pallid phrase, the Second Sex, but the First Sex, of which the Second is luckily born. Frenchmen jump too easily to the inference that "lady," when applied to Paris, means *poule de luxe*, or that what we feminists have in mind is the gay figure evoked when Monsieur Chevalier sings "*Paris, elle est une blonde.*" What we really mean is Woman in the sense and stature, the sign and symbol, in which she is represented everywhere you look in Paris, from the celebrated statue of the fighting French woman called "*Quand Même*," in the Tuileries, to the monumental figure on one side of the Arch of Triumph. Or take the statues in the Place de la Concorde representing eight great provincial cities of France, all of which are depicted as women. Perhaps the finest, that of Strasbourg, was shrouded in black when I first beheld it, but I was happily on hand when the lady was joyously stripped of her mourning after Strasbourg had been restored to France.

Street rioting has broken out in the streets of Paris from time to time, for Paris does not repress her anger any more than she suppresses her desires, and windows are smashed and buildings are burned, and now and then someone is killed. Once in a while the United States has been the object of Parisian wrath—thirty years ago I witnessed a *rixe* or two, but never a real *bagarre*—because of our failure to write off the French war debt. There were those at the time who feared that demonstrators might overturn the statue in the Place des Etats-Unis of Washington and Lafayette shaking hands. It has been marked with chalk, but it will never be overthrown. Not far from these sculptured hands across the sea stands an equally solid monument to the 118 Americans who lost their lives in the service of France during the First World War, sixty-one of them in the Lafayette Escadrille. The granite tribute contains the indestructible names of Raoul Lufbery, Norman Prince, Kiffin Rockwell, Victor Chapman and Alan Seeger.

This is the American quarter of Paris that I knew so well in the months after the Armistice. In front of what was once the chancellery of our Embassy at 5 Rue de Chaillot, a statue of Rochambeau salutes the mounted image of George Washington in the Place d'Iéna not far away. It was indeed *bien américain* the time of my first visit, for Woodrow Wilson lived at No. 11 Place des Etats-Unis, and a short walk from there was the Avenue du Président Wilson and a *pension* filled with Americans from the Embassy. The streets were loud with American voices and bright with our uniforms, and marines sometimes played baseball in the Rue de Chaillot. A bar advertised "American cocktails" and Yanks sang our war songs, including the one with the line "I'll bring you a Turk and the Kaiser, too," which may have inspired the wild notion in some of our men to invade Doorn and bring old Wilhelm back to America as the souvenir of souvenirs. Nearly twenty years ago I made a pilgrimage to the old Yank district, meeting French friends of mine who were still there, and reading the tablet placed near the door of the former chancellery by the Paris Post of the American Legion, a small memorial perpetuating the myth that the late Myron T. Herrick was our Ambassador during the war of 1914–18. Actually he had been replaced in December, 1914, by the late William G. Sharp, who served during all but four months of the war, but has gone unremembered and unmarked. Legend made Myron Herrick our wartime ambassador, and legend, from Barbara Frietchie to Mr. Herrick, is more durable than fact.

The last time I saw Paris, or heard and sensed the city, since I was no longer able to see the old landmarks, was in the late summer of 1955, and I didn't get around to the once familiar places which, if you are there and interested in such a ramble, you can find most easily by following the Avenue Kléber out of the Place de l'Etoile toward the Seine and the Eiffel Tower. Here are the permanent pages of history, written in bronze and stone, of America in Paris, and they are worth a morning's walk and an hour's meditation.

The second time I saw Paris, in 1925, she wore a new gown and a different mood. The Americans had taken over the Left Bank from the Deux Magots to the Dome and the Rotonde, and there were almost as many writers and artists as there had been doughboys and gobs. It was the era of Hemingway, Scott Fitzgerald and John Dos Passos in Paris, and over the restless new American hive Gertrude Stein, prophetess of the Lost Generation, presided like a modernistic queen bee. But that is another memory, for another time.

A *bientôt*.

Sidney Bechet

After several happy tours and longer visits, the soprano sax virtuoso Sidney Bechet (1897–1959) moved to France for good in 1950; he was revered there as something like a national cultural treasure, a reception far beyond anything he could have found in America. (Did the ringing romantic vibrato of his playing put the French in mind of their own popular music, recalling that same piercing vibrato common to Django and Piaf?) In this excerpt from his posthumously published memoir *Treat It Gentle* (1960), he gives us a taste of the jazz life in Paris as he experienced it, and suggests by implication why Paris was, and to a degree remains even in these jazz-poor days, the Great Good Place for jazz musicians.

———

Trouble in Paris

Some of what came to me, there was a good feeling to it, and some, it was poor. When I was playing at Chez Florence the second time, after Noble Sissle had gone back to America, I got myself into real trouble on account of bad feeling. I got into a gunfight and I went to jail for it.

In those days it was really something the way things went on. Times just aren't like that any more. Any time you walked down the street you'd run into four or five people you knew—performers, entertainers, all kinds of people who had a real talent to them. Everywhere you'd go you'd run into them; you couldn't help yourself. And everybody had a kind of excitement about him. Everyone, they was crazy to be *doing*. Well, you'd start to go home, and you'd just never get there. There was always some singer to hear or someone who was playing. You'd run into some friends and they were off to hear this or to do that and you just went along. It seemed like you just *couldn't* get home before ten or eleven in the morning.

It was almost like Prohibition up there in Montmartre in those days. It was almost like back in the days when you'd get a bottle of essence of garden gin and some seed alcohol and some distilled water and pour it into your bathtub. You'd start out with four people waiting in the other room and when you looked out again there be ten or a dozen. One of them, he'd come into the bathroom. "Here let's taste some of that," he'd say. Then first thing you'd know you'd have a consultation. "No, it's not right yet," somebody would say when he'd tasted it. "Not enough gin." And there'd go some more of the Gardens. Somebody else, he'd try it, and he'd decide it needed some. There'd go the rest of the Gardens. By that time you were gone too. When you come out of the bathroom with a jug of that stuff, there wouldn't be more than room enough to stand up for the crowd, everybody playing the piano, talking, drinking, fooling around, everybody full of a kind of excitement, a kind of waiting for something big to happen.

That's the way it was in Montmartre in 1928, except that there wasn't any need to be making your own gin. And just like there was the Prohibition mobs in New York, there was that kind of mob around Montmartre, too. There were always men there who had rackets. They were making a lot of money by getting paid off by the owners of the clubs and cabarets, just so they could stay open. It was a kind of protective association they called it, but it was really just a shakedown. And to run a racket like that, you need a certain kind of person, a thug like. There were a lot like that around in those days and sometimes when one of them got drunk, it wasn't safe around them. So what happened as a result of things like that, nearly everybody, he carried a gun. You could be surer if you had a gun on you. There was tough times back there.

We musicianers, the ones I knew the most about, we'd meet when we were off work. We had regular places where we could expect to find one another. Mostly it was in one little café off rue Fontaine. We'd sit in the back room of this cafe and we'd joke, play a few cards, or someone would take out his instrument, or we'd just talk. Pretty soon you'd begin to see those saucers piling up.

One night a fellow named Mike McKendrick was there. He was the one I had the trouble with, and the trouble was really brought on by a fellow who was supposed to be his friend, Glover Compton. Glover was a piano player. He was from Chicago and he was always talking about being a Northerner. He really liked to talk big; whatever he had to say, he talked like he expected everyone else to listen and be mighty ready to shake in their boots while they was doing it. It was like he was looking for a reputation as a bad man, as someone really evil. He wasn't no one in any big-time way, but he was trying to cut in as much as he could. He was always acting like he wanted to stir up trouble, like he wanted to be known as a place where trouble started.

For some time before this night he'd been getting after Mike, telling him this and that about me, getting to see if he could start an argument between us, get some kind of a feud going. Mike was just a kid then. He was playing banjo somewhere in one of those cabarets. I don't know nothing about his wanting to be any trouble-maker; but this night he started coming at me with a lot of stories he told me this Glover had passed on to him, and I wasn't in any mood for that kind of thing. So finally we had an argument. It didn't really amount to anything right then, and we both had to leave to go to work after a while; but all the same there had been this argument.

The same night—it was morning by then—I was walking home from work and I passed this cabaret. I was about to go inside, but just as I got to the door I saw Glover. He had a whole party with him and I knew if I went in there he'd be only too happy to start some more trouble, so I stayed out. I just turned around and started to walk off, but Glover had seen me and he sent Mike out after me. That was his way, that Glover . . . he wasn't the kind to do anything himself if he could get someone else to do it for him, especially when it was trouble he was wanting.

So Mike came hurrying up after me and he said, "Sidney, come on inside. My friend wants to see you." Well I knew better than that; that was only a ruse like. If I went in there and sat down at their table, there'd be a whole lot of baiting and there was only one way that could end up. So I said, "You tell your friend I'm not special about seeing him." But Mike started insisting. He'd drunk some—quite a bit, in fact—and he wouldn't listen to anyone saying "No." Finally I just told him, why didn't he smarten up some? "What you doing getting mixed up in something like that Glover?" I said. "Don't you have anything better to do?"

Right away he started in talking like this Glover. Mike, he was from Chicago, too, and he'd picked up these big ideas about being a Northerner. "I don't think I like you," he said. "I don't think I like the way you look, Dixie-boy. You want to see what we do to people like you in Chicago?"

Well, it's one of those things I know something about. I'd heard that all before. Northern musicianers, they start themselves going sometimes. There's something jealous-like about them when another musicianer, he's from the South. So now this one, he's going to show me some of Chicago!

I didn't want to mess with him. I didn't want any trouble and just so long as he didn't go too far I didn't want anything at all to do with him.

So I turned to go on, and just as soon as I turned my back he began to shout out, all excited. Maybe it was just that he was waiting for me. "My friend won't like that," he said, and he pulled out a gun and fired two shots at me. I pulled out my own gun then—he hadn't hit me—and my first bullet grazed his forehead. Then Glover heard the shots and he came running out, and one of my bullets got him in the leg, and another hit a girl, and one ricochetted off a lamp-post and, what's really unfortunate, hit some Frenchwoman who was passing on the other side of the street on her way to work.

It was something, the way it happened . . . something hard to make it clear. It's like there's somebody else inside a man, somebody that's not really that man, and when a thing happens, an anger like I had then, that other person takes over. That's not to make excuses. I know well enough it's me all the time. That's just to try to tell you what feeling there was to it, standing there on the street, not even giving a goddamn how many shots they're sending back at me, not even seeming to know whether or not they're shooting at all, just standing there pumping my gun and wanting to see everyone of them dead in front of me.

And all the time, I don't like it. There's a kind of disgust to it. I'm not for covering up any part of what's true: I can be mean. It takes a awful lot; someone's got to do a lot to me. But when I do get mean, I can be powerful mean. That's the way I was right then on the street outside that cabaret. I'm busting mean. If someone was to change the world into glass and throw it up in front of me, I was in a mood then to just smash it right there. I would have smashed any damn thing.

And then, after it was over, the mood was gone from me. All I'd got left was disgust. I started walking away then. I was on my way over to the police, to give myself up and explain to them what had happened. But before I no more than got started, I was identified by some bystanders who pointed me out to a policeman who came up from behind me. He wanted to know what the trouble was. He told me the people had pointed me out. Right off I told him I wasn't denying any part of it; I told him exactly what had gone on. I wasn't afraid of anything serious happening. I'd had nothing to do with starting it; all I did, I was acting in self-defence. There was that girl who had been with Glover, she'd gotten a scratch, but I didn't give a damn about her; and at that time I didn't know about the Frenchwoman. But it was right there that the real trouble started. That Frenchwoman had had to go to hospital, and just the fact that she *was* a

Frenchwoman and I a foreigner and I had sent her to the hospital—that put it into a whole new jurisdiction like.

The police took me and Mike McKendrick in, and right away our friends started raising some money for us. Mike had got some very influential friends who got him a lawyer, and a lot of people pooled some money together and got a lawyer for me. Gene Boulard put out a lot of money to help me. Gene was a real man about Paris; he had a way. He was a man—well, the only way I can say it, he was what Glover Compton would have liked to have been in regards to making a name for himself. Except Gene had no meanness in him. If someone needed help, he did more than any Salvation Army could do with a whole army; and what he wanted to do for himself, he could do in a smooth, smart way. He'd made himself the kind of man people around Paris had a need for. The cabarets, the clubs, the musicianers—when there was some trouble they couldn't straighten out by themselves, they called on Gene. He was a man you could count on.

Gene could almost have fixed this. It would have been just a fight among musicianers. But this Frenchwoman who was hit, that took it out of the law of being simply something that Americans were involved in. Gene just couldn't get it quieted down and Mike and I both had terms to serve; we both got sentenced.

So there we were off to prison together, and when we got to the prison they put us in the detention cell while they're fixing up our regulations, making out papers for what cells we're to have, and all that official business. We were locked up together there for a while. Mike kept coming over to tell me how sorry he was. "I wish it had never happened," he told me. "I'm sorry for the whole business, Sidney. If it hadn't been for that Glover it never *would* have happened. He's the one who told me to get after you. If I hadn't listened to him. . . ."

He went on like that all the time we were together. What could I answer? You know what you'd think. There's only one thing you can answer: it's happened and it's too late. There's nothing left for it but just to forget the whole thing.

But that Glover, he *still* wasn't ready to forget it. It was in 1928 I went to prison. I was in jail for eleven months, and when I came out I had no rights, it wasn't even legal for me to stay in France. And yet even then, I found out later, this fellow Glover was working at his lawyer, planning some way he could arrange for me to have more time to serve, some action he could bring. The day I was coming out of prison, he was still trying to get up an action to keep me there, trying to get his lawyer to put out a warrant for me, urging him to figure out some case he could bring against me. When I ran into him later, I told him he'd better watch out for that other leg; I was tired of the whole thing, and I wasn't fixing to take any more of what he was giving out. I was really close to getting God-almighty sick of it all and of him too. But this Gene Boulard, he could see there was maybe trouble coming. He took this Glover aside. "You stay away," he told him, "you really better stay away." And he made him do it. I never had any bother from Glover after that.

That was all a long time ago, but it's not a thing a man can forget. Twenty, twenty-one years later, I was in Paris at the Préfecture, getting my visa arranged, and the Commissioner started talking about it. "That wasn't your fault," he said. "If that had been your fault, you couldn't have come back to France. That was self-defence; it was your right."

I couldn't very well tell him it was a little late for figuring that out, but that trial I got was a hell of a thing. Even that eleven months I spent in a French jail made less impression on my mind than what I kept thinking about that trial. I had that inside me for a long time.

There was two things about it. The first, it was that Frenchwoman. That part of it, it's still the same today: I don't care who you are, if you go to France and you get into some trouble where there's a Frenchman mixed up in it, that court don't care what's right, it don't care what's wrong. If there's a Frenchman and a foreigner mixed up in it together, the foreigner, he's in the wrong. Whether it's justice or injustice don't matter: the Frenchman, he's the one that counts.

But there was another thing, too. I sat there in that court watching my lawyer, watching the judge, watching the people. My lawyer was supposed to be representing me, but after a while you'd have got the impression that it was not a man that was being represented, but his money. It really came right down to that: there wasn't enough money. A deal had to be made.

Like I said, my lawyer was supposed to be representing me, but he was so busy working with Mike's lawyer, it's as if I've just been forgotten. To save themselves trouble, those lawyers decided they'd make it easier on *both* of us by kind of sharing the guilt. They had it all figured out: it was just a couple of foreigners mixed up in this thing and somebody had got to pay for hurting a Frenchwoman, so they'd work it for both of us to pay up some time and that way it would all be cleared up. No question of right or wrong or who shot first or who shot in self-defence: just a question of a couple of foreigners. The easy way was to treat them all alike.

So they got together and they told us to say what they had prepared. We were to tell the court it was just an argument that had got started somehow, that we were very sorry about it all but we had been drinking and we hadn't known what we was doing. All that kind of talk. Instead of having me cleared and one of us going free, they fixed it so that both of us should serve time, and that way Mike would get less and neither one of us would get a whole lot, and the whole business would be cleared up.

The day they had that all fixed, my lawyer got up and began saying that to the jury. "Here's a man," he says, "who admits to doing wrong. You who are in the jury, you can feel how that is; give this man your under-standing. He knows he's done wrong. He recognizes his mistake and asks for sympathy. . . ." There was a whole lot like that.

And all of a sudden Gene understood what they were doing, and he jumped up right there in court where he was with the spectators. He called out from where he was and then he came hurrying up before the court and he told them no, that wasn't the way it had happened. He explained all he could . . . what he knew about it, what the witnesses had said.

Well, it was like he'd gone crazy. It was like the whole court had gone crazy. There was one lawyer shouting one thing and another lawyer shout-ing something else, and this court official pounding here and that court official pounding there and before anybody understood what-all was going on, the court got recessed.

After that Gene, my lawyer and me talked for hours about what was to be done, and what it all came down to was that Gene and me, we just couldn't raise the money. It would cost a certain amount more to present the case the way it should have been, and we just couldn't get that much money together.

That's the thing. Not being able to stand up the way you are to have the right to say what's the fair thing, what's the real thing that happened. That was the wrong.

A. J. Liebling

A. J. Liebling (1904–1963), whose 1962 *Between Meals: An Appetite for Paris* remains for many of us the finest and funniest book ever written by an American in or about Paris, came to the city (as he explains in the book's opening chapters) for the first time as a small child. He was to return often, most memorably with the American and French liberation armies of 1944, a journey he recorded in *The Road Back to Paris*. *Between Meals* came at the end of Liebling's life, but from the top of his form. After a relatively slow start at *The New Yorker* in the 1930s, where his wise-guy newspaper "feature" mode at first sat uneasily with the magazine's inclination to Yankee understatement, he hit his stride during the war, when he reported from North Africa and was present in the Channel on D-Day. The experience of the war sharpened his prose without simplifying it, and for the nearly twenty years after his return home he wrote, at home and abroad, a series of essay-collections masquerading as books—*The Earl of Louisiana*, *The Sweet Science*, *The Honest Rainmaker*. These became, and remain, the bedrock of the New Journalism, or for that matter of any American reporting that inhabits, or at least haunts, the old form of the comic personal essay. In these selections from *Between Meals* Liebling recalls the Paris he knew best, the Paris of the 1920s seen not from fashionable Montparnasse but from the viewpoint of a hungry and isolated American student. The Restaurant des Beaux-Arts, by the way, persisted until 2001, when it finally succumbed to the commercial pressures of the Saint-Germain neighborhood and became a boutique.

————

from

Between Meals:
An Appetite for Paris

JUST ENOUGH MONEY

If, as I was saying before I digressed, the first requisite for writing well about food is a good appetite, the second is to put in your apprenticeship as a feeder when you have enough money to pay the check but not enough to produce indifference to the size of the total. (I also meant to say,

539

previously, that Waverley Root has a good appetite, but I never got around to it.) The optimum financial position for a serious apprentice feeder is to have funds in hand for three more days, with a reasonable, but not certain, prospect of reinforcements thereafter. The student at the Sorbonne waiting for his remittance, the newspaperman waiting for his salary, the freelance writer waiting for a check that he has cause to believe is in the mail—all are favorably situated to learn. (It goes without saying that it is essential to be in France.) The man of appetite who will stint himself when he can see three days ahead has no vocation, and I dismiss from consideration, as manic, the fellow who will spend the lot on one great feast and then live on fried potatoes until his next increment; Tuaregs eat that way, but only because they never know when they are going to come by their next sheep. The clear-headed voracious man learns because he tries to compose his meals to obtain an appreciable quantity of pleasure from each. It is from this weighing of delights against their cost that the student eater (particularly if he is a student at the University of Paris) erects the scale of values that will serve him until he dies or has to reside in the Middle West for a long period. The scale is different for each eater, as it is for each writer.

Eating is highly subjective, and the man who accepts say-so in youth will wind up in bad and overtouted restaurants in middle age, ordering what the maître d'hôtel suggests. He will have been guided to them by food-snob publications, and he will fall into the habit of drinking too much before dinner to kill the taste of what he has been told he should like but doesn't. An illustration: For about six years, I kept hearing of a restaurant in the richest shire of Connecticut whose proprietor, a Frenchman, had been an assistant of a disciple of the great Escoffier. Report had it that in these wilds—inhabited only by executives of the highest grade, walking the woods like the King of Nemi until somebody came on from Winnetka to cut their throats—the restaurateur gave full vent to the creative flame. His clients took what he chose to give them. If they declined, they had to go down the pike to some joint where a steak cost only twelve dollars, and word would get around that they felt their crowns in danger— they had been detected economizing. I finally arranged to be smuggled out to the place disguised as a *Time-Life* Executive Vice-Publisher in Charge of Hosannas with the mission of entertaining the advertising manager of the Hebrew National Delicatessen Corporation. When we arrived, we found the Yale-blue vicuña rope up and the bar full of couples in the hundred-thousand-dollar bracket, dead drunk as they waited for tables; knowing that this would be no back-yard cookout, they had taken prophylactic anesthesia. But when I tasted the food, I perceived that they had been needlessly alarmed. The Frenchman, discouraged because for four years no customers had tasted what they were eating, had taken to bourbon-on-the-rocks. In a morose way, he had resigned himself to becoming dishonestly rich. The food was no better than Howard Johnson's, and the customers, had they not been paralyzed by the time they got to it, would have liked it as well. The *spécialité de la maison*, the unhappy *patron* said when I interrogated him, was jellied oysters dyed red, white, and blue. "At least they are aware of that," he said. "The colors attract their attention." There was an on-the-hour service of Brink's armored cars between his door and the night-deposit vault of a bank in New York, conveying the money that rolled into the *caisse*. The wheels, like a juggernaut's, rolled over his secret heart. His intention in the beginning had been noble, but he was a victim of the system.

The reference room where I pursued my own first earnest researches as a feeder without the crippling handicap of affluence was the Restaurant des Beaux-Arts, on the Rue Bonaparte, in 1926–27. I was a student, in a highly generalized way, at the Sorbonne, taking targets of opportunity for study. Eating soon developed into one of my major subjects. The franc was at twenty-six to the dollar, and the researcher, if he had only a certain sum—say, six francs—to spend, soon established for himself whether, for example, a half bottle of Tavel *supérieur*, at three and a half francs, and braised beef heart and yellow turnips, at two and a half, gave him more or less pleasure than a *contre-filet* of beef, at five francs, and a half bottle of *ordinaire*, at one franc. He might find that he liked the heart, with its strong, rich flavor and odd texture, nearly as well as the beef, and that since the Tavel was overwhelmingly better than the cheap wine, he had done well to order the first pair. Or he might find that he so much preferred the generous, sanguine *contre-filet* that he could accept the undistinguished *picrate* instead of the Tavel. As in a bridge tournament, the learner played duplicate hands, making the opposite choice of fare the next time the problem presented itself. (It was seldom as simple as my example, of course, because a meal usually included at least an hors d'oeuvre and a cheese, and there was a complexity of each to choose from. The arrival, in season, of fresh asparagus or venison further complicated matters. In the first case, the investigator had to decide what course to omit in order to fit the asparagus in, and, in the second, whether to forgo all else in order to afford venison.)

A rich man, faced with this simple sumptuary dilemma, would have ordered both the Tavel *and* the *contre-filet*. He would then never know whether he liked beef heart, or whether an *ordinaire* wouldn't do him as well as something better. (There are people to whom wine is merely an alcoholized sauce, although they may have sensitive palates for meat or pastries.) When one considers the millions of permutations of foods and wines to test, it is easy to see that life is too short for the formulation of dogma. Each eater can but establish a few general principles that are true only for him. Our hypothetical rich *client* might even have ordered a Pommard, because it was listed at a higher price than the Tavel, and because he was more likely to be acquainted with it. He would then never have learned that a good Tavel is better than a fair-to-middling Pommard— better than a fair-to-middling almost anything, in my opinion. In student restaurants, renowned wines like Pommard were apt to be mediocre specimens of their kind, since the customers could never have afforded the going prices of the best growths and years. A man who is rich in his adolescence is almost doomed to be a dilettante at table. This is not because all millionaires are stupid but because they are not impelled to experiment. In learning to eat, as in psychoanalysis, the customer, in order to profit, must be sensible of the cost.

There is small likelihood that a rich man will frequent modest restaurants even at the beginning of his gustatory career; he will patronize restaurants, sometimes good, where the prices are high and the repertory is limited to dishes for which it is conventionally permissible to charge high prices. From this list, he will order the dishes that in his limited experience he has already found agreeable. Later, when his habits are formed, he will distrust the originality that he has never been constrained to develop. A diet based chiefly on game birds and oysters becomes a habit as easily as a diet of jelly doughnuts and hamburgers. It is a better habit, of course, but restrictive just the same. Even in Paris, one can dine in the costly restaurants for years without learning that there are fish other than sole, turbot, salmon (in season), trout, and the Mediterranean *rouget* and *loup de mer*. The fresh herring or sardine *sauce moutarde*; the *colin froid mayonnaise*; the conger eel *en matelote*; the small fresh-water fish of the Seine and the Marne, fried crisp and served *en buisson*; the whiting *en colère* (his tail in his mouth, as if contorted with anger); and even the skate and the *dorade*—all these, except by special and infrequent invitation, are out of the swim. (It is a standing tourist joke to say that the fishermen on the quays of the Seine never catch anything, but in fact they often take home the makings of a nice fish fry, especially in winter. In my hotel on the Square Louvois, I had a room waiter—a Czech naturalized in France— who used to catch hundreds of *goujons* and *ablettes* on his days off. He once brought a shoe box of them to my room to prove that Seine fishing was not pure whimsey.) All the fish I have mentioned have their habitats in humbler restaurants, the only places where the aspirant eater can become familiar with their honest fishy tastes and the decisive modes of accommodation that suit them. Personally, I like tastes that know their own minds. The reason that people who detest fish often tolerate sole is that sole doesn't taste very much like fish, and even this degree of resemblance disappears when it is submerged in the kind of sauce that patrons of Piedmontese restaurants in London and New York think characteristically French. People with the same apathy toward decided flavor relish "South African lobster" tails—frozen as long as the Siberian mammoth— because they don't taste lobstery. ("South African lobsters" are a kind of sea crayfish, or *langouste*, but that would be nothing against them if they were fresh.) They prefer processed cheese because it isn't cheesy, and synthetic vanilla extract because it isn't vanillary. They have made a triumph of the Delicious apple because it doesn't taste like an apple, and of the Golden Delicious because it doesn't taste like anything. In a related field, "dry" (non-beery) beer and "light" (non-Scotchlike) Scotch are more of the same. The standard of perfection for vodka (no color, no taste, no smell) was expounded to me long ago by the then Estonian consul-general in New York, and it accounts perfectly for the drink's rising popularity with those who like their alcohol in conjunction with the reassuring tastes of infancy—tomato juice, orange juice, chicken broth. It is the ideal intoxicant for the drinker who wants no reminder of how hurt Mother would be if she knew what he was doing.

The consistently rich man is also unlikely to make the acquaintance of meat dishes of robust taste—the hot *andouille* and *andouillette*, which are close-packed sausages of smoked tripe, and the *boudin*, or blood pudding, and all its relatives that figure in the pages of Rabelais and on the menus of the market restaurants. He will not meet the *civets*, or dark, winy stews of domestic rabbit and old turkey. A tough old turkey with plenty of character makes the best *civet*, and only in a *civet* is turkey good to eat. Young turkey, like young sheep, calf, spring chicken, and baby lobster, is a pale preliminary phase of its species. The pig, the pigeon, and the goat—as suckling, squab, and kid—are the only animals that are at their best to eat when immature. The first in later life becomes gross through indolence; the second and third grow muscular through overactivity. And the world of tripery is barred to the well-heeled, except for occasional exposure to an expurgated version of *tripes à la mode de Caen*. They have never seen *gras-double* (tripe cooked with vegetables, principally onions) or *pieds et paquets* (sheep's tripe and calves' feet with salt pork). In his book, Waverley Root dismisses tripe, but he is no plutocrat; his rejection is deliberate, after fair trial. Still, his insensibility to its charms seems to me odd in a New Englander, as he is by origin. Fried pickled honeycomb tripe used to be the most agreeable feature of a winter breakfast in New Hampshire, and Fall River, Root's home town, is in the same cultural circumscription.

Finally, to have done with our rich man, seldom does he see even the simple, well-pounded *bifteck* or the *pot-au-feu* itself—the foundation glory of French cooking. Alexandre Dumas the elder wrote in his *Dictionary Cuisine*: "French cooking, the first of all cuisines, owes its superiority to the excellence of French bouillon. This excellence derives from a sort of intuition with which I shall not say our cooks but our women of the people are endowed." This bouillon is one of the two end products of the *pot*. The other is the material that has produced it—beef, carrots, parsnips, white turnips, leeks, celery, onions, cloves, garlic, and cracked marrowbones, and, for the dress version, fowl. Served *in* some of the bouillon, this constitutes the dish known as *pot-au-feu*. Dumas is against poultry "unless it is old," but advises that "an old pigeon, a partridge, or a rabbit roasted in advance, a crow in November or December" works wonders. He postulates "seven hours of sustained simmering," with constant attention to the "scum" that forms on the surface and to the water level. ("Think twice before adding water, though if your meat actually rises above the level of the bouillon it is necessary to add boiling water to cover it.") This supervision demands the full-time presence of the cook in the kitchen throughout the day, and the maintenance of the temperature calls for a considerable outlay in fuel. It is one reason that the *pot-au-feu* has declined as a chief element of the working-class diet in France. Women go out to work, and gas costs too much. For a genuinely good *pot-au-feu*, Dumas says, one should take a fresh piece of beef—"a twelve-to-fifteen-pound rump"—and simmer it seven hours in the bouillon of the beef that you simmered seven hours the day before. He does not say what good house-keepers did with the first piece of beef—perhaps cut it into sandwiches for the children's lunch. He regrets that even when he wrote, in 1869, excessive haste was beginning to mar cookery; the demanding ritual of the *pot* itself had been abandoned. This was "a receptacle that never left the fire, day or night," Dumas writes. "A chicken was put into it as a chicken was withdrawn, a piece of beef as a piece was taken out, and a glass of water whenever a cup of broth was removed. Every kind of meat that cooked in this bouillon gained, rather than lost, in flavor." *Pot-au-feu* is so hard to find in chic restaurants nowadays that every Saturday evening there is a mass pilgrimage from the fashionable quarters to Chez Benoit, near the Châtelet—a small but not cheap restaurant that serves it once a week. I have never found a crow in Benoit's *pot*, but all the rest is good.

A drastically poor man, naturally, has even less chance than a drastically rich one to educate himself gastronomically. For him eating becomes merely a matter of subsistence; he can exercise no choice. The chief attraction of the cheapest student restaurants in my time was advertised on their largest placards: *"Pain à Discrétion"* ("All the Bread You Want"). They did not graduate discriminating eaters. During that invaluable year, I met a keen observer who gave me a tip: "If you run across a restaurant where you often see priests eating with priests, or sporting girls with sporting girls, you may be confident that it is good. Those are two classes of people who like to eat well and get their money's worth. If you see a priest eating with a layman, though, don't be too sure about the money's worth. The fellow *en civil* may be a rich parishioner, and the good Father won't worry about the price. And if the girl is with a man, you can't count on anything. It may be her kept man, in which case she won't care what she spends on him, or the man who is keeping her, in which case she won't care what he spends on her."

Failing the sure indications cited above, a good augury is the presence of French newspapermen.

The Restaurant des Beaux-Arts, where I did my early research, was across the street from the Ecole des Beaux-Arts, and not, in fact, precisely in my quarter, which was that of the university proper, a good half mile away, on the other side of the Boulevard Saint-Germain. It was a half mile that made as much difference as the border between France and Switzerland. The language was the same, but not the inhabitants. Along the Rue Bonaparte there were antiquarians, and in the streets leading off it there were practitioners of the ancillary arts—picture framers and book-binders. The bookshops of the Rue Bonaparte, of which there were many, dealt in fine editions and rare books, instead of the used textbooks and works of erudition that predominated around the university. The students of the Beaux-Arts were only a small element of the population of the neighborhood, and they were a different breed from the students of the Boulevard Saint-Michel and its tributaries, such as the Rue de l'Ecole de Médecine, where I lived. They were older and seemingly in easier circumstances. I suspected them of commercial art and of helping Italians to forge antiques. Because there was more money about, and because the quarter had a larger proportion of adult, experienced eaters, it was better territory for restaurants than the immediate neighborhood of the Sorbonne. I had matriculated at the Faculté des Lettres and at the Ecole des Chartes, which forms medievalists, but since I had ceased attending classes after the first two weeks, I had no need to stick close to home. One of the chief joys of that academic year was that it was one long cut without fear of retribution.

I chanced upon the Restaurant des Beaux-Arts while strolling one noon and tried it because it looked neither chic nor sordid, and the prices on the menu were about right for me: *pâté maison*, 75 centimes; sardines, 1 franc; artichoke, 1.25; and so on. A legend over the door referred to the proprietor as a M. Teyssedre, but the heading of the bill of fare called him Balazuc. Which name represented a former proprietor and which the current one I never learned. I had a distaste for asking direct questions, a practice I considered ill-bred. This had handicapped me during my brief career as a reporter in Providence, Rhode Island, but not as much as you might think. Direct questions tighten a man up, and even if he answers, he will not tell you anything you have not asked him. What you want is to get him to tell you his story. After he has, you can ask clarifying questions, such as "How did you come to have the ax in your hand?" I had interrupted this journalistic grind after one year, at the suggestion of my father, a wise man. "You used to talk about wanting to go to Europe for a year of study," he said to me one spring day in 1926, when I was home in New York for a weekend. "You are getting so interested in what you are doing that if you don't go now you never will. You might even get married."

I sensed my father's generous intention, and, fearing that he might change his mind, I told him that I didn't feel I should go, since I was indeed thinking of getting married. "The girl is ten years older than I am," I said, "and Mother might think she is kind of fast, because she is being kept by a cotton broker from Memphis, Tennessee, who only comes North once in a while. But you are a man of the world, and you understand that a woman can't always help herself. Basically . . ." Within the week, I had a letter of credit on the Irving Trust for two thousand dollars, and a reservation on the old *Caronia* for late in the summer, when the off-season rates would be in effect. It was characteristic of my father that even while doing a remarkably generous thing he did not want to waste the difference between a full-season and an off-season passage on a one-class boat. (He never called a liner anything but a boat, and I always found it hard to do otherwise myself, until I stopped trying. "Boat" is an expression of affection, not disrespect; it is like calling a woman a girl. What may be ships in proportion to Oxford, where the dictionary is written, are boats in proportion to New York, where they nuzzle up to the bank to feed, like the waterfowl in Central Park.)

While I continued to work on the Providence paper until the rates changed, Father, with my mother and sister, embarked for Europe on a Holland-American boat—full-season rate and first class—so that my sister might take advantage of her summer holiday from school. I was to join them for a few days at the end of the summer, after which they would return to the United States and I would apply myself to my studies. Fortunately, I discovered that the titulary of a letter of credit can draw on it at the issuing bank as easily as abroad. By the time I sailed, I was eight hundred dollars into the letter, and after a week in Paris at a hotel off the Champs-Elysées I found, without astonishment, that I had spent more than half of the paternal fellowship that was intended to last me all year. The academic year would not begin until November, and I realized that I would be lucky to have anything at all by then. At this juncture, the cotton broker's girl came to my rescue in a vision, as an angel came to Constantine's. I telegraphed to my parents, who were at Lake Como, that I was on my way to join them. From my attitude when I got there—reserved, dignified, preoccupied—my father sensed that I was in trouble. The morning after my arrival, I proposed that we take a walk, just the two of us, by the lake. Soon we felt thirst, and we entered the trellised arbor of a hotel more modest than ours and ordered a bottle of rustic wine that recalled the stuff that Big Tony, my barber in Providence, used to manufacture in his yard on Federal Hill. Warmed by this homelike glow, I told my father that I had dilapidated his generous gift; I had dissipated in

riotous living seventy-two per cent of the good man's unsolicited bene-
faction. Now there was only one honorable thing for me to do—go back
to work, get married, and settle down. "She is so noble that she wouldn't
tell me," I said, "but I'm afraid I left her in the lurch."

"God damn it," he said, "I knew I should never have given you that
money in one piece. But I want you to continue your education. How
much will you need every month?"

"Two hundred," I said, moderately. Later, I wished I had asked for
fifty more; he might have gone for it. "You stay in Paris," he said—he
knew I had chosen the Sorbonne—"and I'll have the Irving send you two
hundred dollars every month. No more lump sums. When a young man
gets tangled up with that kind of women, they can ruin his whole life."

That was how I came to be living in Paris that academic year in a financial situation that facilitated my researches. Looking back, I am sure my
father knew that I wanted to stay on, and that there was no girl to worry
about. But he also understood that I couldn't simply beg; for pride's sake,
I had to offer a fake *quid pro quo* and pretend to myself that he believed
me. He had a very good idea of the value of leisure, not having had any
until it was too late to become accustomed to it, and a very good idea of
the pleasure afforded by knowledge that has no commercial use, having
never had time to acquire more than a few odd bits. His parents had
brought him to America when he was eight years old; he went to work at
ten, opened his own firm at twenty-one, started being rich at thirty, and
died broke at sixty-five—a perfect Horatio Alger story, except that Alger
never followed his heroes through. At the moment, though, he had the
money, and he knew the best things it would buy.

The great day of each month, then, was the one when my draft arrived
at the main office of the Crédit Lyonnais—the Irving's correspondent
bank —on the Boulevard des Italiens. It was never even approximately
certain what day the draft would get there; there was no air mail, and I
could not be sure what ship it was on. The Crédit, on receiving the draft,
would notify me, again by ordinary mail, and that would use up another
day. After the second of the month, I would begin to be haunted by the
notion that the funds might have arrived and that I could save a day by
walking over and inquiring. Consequently, I walked a good many times
across the river and the city from the Rue de l'Ecole de Médecine to the
Boulevard des Italiens, via the Rue Bonaparte, where I would lunch at the
Maison Teyssedre or Balazuc. There were long vertical black enamel

plaques on either side of the restaurant door, bearing, in gold letters, such information as "Room for Parties," "Telephone," "Snails," "Specialty of Broils," and, most notably, "Renowned Cellar, Great Specialty of Wines of the Rhone." The Great Specialty dated back to the regime of a proprietor anteceding M. Teyssedre-Balazuc. This prehistoric *patron*, undoubtedly an immigrant from Languedoc or Provence, had set up a bridgehead in Paris for the wines of his region of origin.

The wines of the Rhone each have a decided individuality, viable even when taken in conjunction with *brandade de morue*—a delightful purée of salt codfish, olive oil, and crushed garlic—which is their compatriot. *Brandade*, according to Root, is "definitely not the sort of dish that is likely to be served at the Tour d'Argent." "Subtlety," that hackneyed wine word, is a cliché seldom employed in writing about Rhone wines; their appeal is totally unambiguous. The Maison Teyssedre-Balazuc had the whole gamut, beginning with a rough, faintly sour Côtes du Rhône—which means, I suppose, anything grown along that river as it runs its three-hundred-and-eighty-mile course through France. It continued with a Tavel and then a Tavel *supérieur*. The proprietor got his wines in barrel and bottled them in the Renowned Cellar; the plain Tavel came to the table in a bottle with a blue wax seal over the cork, the *supérieur* in a bottle with a purple seal. It cost two cents more a pint. I do not pretend to remember every price on the card of the Restaurant des Beaux-Arts, but one figure has remained graven in my heart like "Constantinople" in the dying Czar's. A half bottle of Tavel *supérieur* was 3.50; I can still see the figure when I close my eyes, written in purple ink on the cheap, grayish paper of the *carte*. This is a mnemonic testimonial to how good the wine was, and to how many times I struggled with my profligate tendencies at that particular point in the menu, arguing that the unqualified Tavel, which was very good, was quite good enough; two cents a day multiplied by thirty, I frequently told myself, mounted up to fifteen francs a month. I don't think I ever won the argument; my spendthrift palate carried the day. Tavel has a rose-cerise *robe*, like a number of well-known racing silks, but its taste is not thin or acidulous, as that of most of its mimics is. The taste is warm but dry, like an enthusiasm held under restraint, and there is a tantalizing suspicion of bitterness when the wine hits the top of the palate. With the second glass, the enthusiasm gains; with the third, it is overpowering. The effect is generous and calorific, stimulative of cerebration and the social instincts. "An apparently light but treacherous rosé," Root calls it, with a nuance of resentment that hints at some old misadventure.

Tavel is from a place of that name in Languedoc, just west of the Rhone. In 1926, there were in all France only two well-known wines that were neither red nor white. One was Tavel, and the other Arbois, from the Jura—and Arbois is not a rose-colored but an "onion-peel" wine, with russet and purple glints. In the late thirties, the rosés began to proliferate in wine regions where they had never been known before, as growers discovered how marketable they were, and to this day they continue to pop up like measles on the wine map. Most often rosés are made from red wine grapes, but the process is abbreviated by removing the liquid prematurely from contact with the grape skins. This saves time and trouble. The product is a semi-aborted red wine. Any normally white wine can be converted into a rosé simply by adding a dosage of red wine* or cochineal.

In 1926 and 1927, for example, I never heard of Anjou rosé wine, although I read wine cards every day and spent a week of purposeful drinking in Angers, a glorious white-wine city. Alsace is another famous white-wine country that now lends its name to countless cases of a pinkish cross between No-Cal and vinegar; if, in 1926, I had crossed the sacred threshold of Valentin Sorg's restaurant in Strasbourg and asked the sommelier for a rosé d'Alsace, he would have, quite properly, kicked me into Germany. The list is endless now; flipping the coated-paper pages of any dealer's brochure, you see rosés from Bordeaux, Burgundy, all the South of France, California, Chile, Algeria, and heaven knows where else. Pink champagne, colored by the same procedure, has existed for a century and was invented for the African and Anglo-Saxon trade. The "discovery" of the demand for pink wine approximately coincided with the repeal of prohibition in the United States. (The American housewife is susceptible to eye and color appeal.) In England, too, in the same period, a new class of wine buyer was rising with the social revolution. Pink worked its miracle there, and also in France itself, where many families previously limited to the cheapest kind of bulk wine were beginning to graduate to "nice things."

Logically, there is no reason any good white- or red-wine region should not produce equally good rosé, but in practice the proprietors of

*"Some [peasants] will give you a quick recipe for rosé which shall not pollute these pages."—The late Morton Shand's classic, A Book of French Wines, Jonathan Cape, Ltd., London, 1960 edition.

the good vineyards have no cause to change the nature of their wines; they can sell every drop they make. It is impossible to imagine a proprietor at Montrachet, or Chablis, or Pouilly, for example, tinting his wine to make a Bourgogne *rosé*. It is almost as hard to imagine it of a producer of first-rate Alsatian or Angevin wines. The wines converted to *rosé* in the great-wine provinces are therefore, I suspect, the worst ones—a suspicion confirmed by almost every experience I have had of them. As for the *rosés* from the cheap-wine provinces they are as bad as their coarse progenitors, but are presented in fancy bottles of untraditional form—a trick learned from the perfume industry. The bottles are generally decorated with art labels in the style of Robida's illustrations for Rabelais, and the wines are peddled at a price out of all proportion to their inconsiderable merits. There is also behind their gruesome spread the push of a report, put out by some French adman, that while white wine is to be served only with certain aliments, and red wine only with certain others, *rosé* "goes with everything," and so can be served without embarrassment by the inexperienced hostess. The truth is, of course, that if a wine isn't good it doesn't "go" with anything, and if it is it can go in any company.* Tavel though, is the good, the old, and, as far as I am concerned, still the only worthy *rosé*.†

At the Restaurant des Beaux-Arts, the Tavel *supérieur* was as high on the list as I would let my eyes ascend until I felt that the new money was on its way. When I had my first supersensory intimation of its approach, I began to think of the prizes higher on the card—Côte Rôtie, Châteauneuf-du-Pape, and white as well as red Hermitage, which cost from three to five francs more, by the half bottle, than my customary Purple Seal. Racing men like to say that a great horse usually has a great name—impressive and euphonious—and these three wines bear similar

---

*Mr. Frank Schoonmaker, a writer on wine and a dealer in it who has done much to diffuse *rosé* in this country, wrote to me after the first appearance of this statement that I "surely wouldn't want to serve a good claret with sardine or a Montrachet with roast beef." To this I must answer that I wouldn't serve a Montrachet or any other good wine of *any* color with sardines, since they would make it taste like more sardines. Beer might be a better idea, or in its default, *rosé*, and I offer, without charge, the advertising slogan "*Rosé*, the perfect companion for fish oil."

†The eminent Shand, in 1960 (*A Book of French Wines*), wrote with more authority but no less bitterness of the Pink Plague: "Odd little *rosés* were belatedly exhumed from a more than provincial obscurity to set before clamorous foreign holiday parties; or if none such had ever existed steps were speedily taken to produce a native *rosé*."

cachets. The Pope's new castle and the Hermitage evoke medieval pomp and piety, but the name Côte Rôtie—the hillside roasted in the sun—is the friendliest of the three, as is the wine, which has a cleaner taste than Châteauneuf and a warmer one than Hermitage. Châteauneuf often seems to be a wine that there is too much of to be true, and it varies damnably in all respects save alcoholic content, which is high. Red Hermitage is certainly distinguished; as its boosters like to say, of all Rhone wines it most resembles a great Burgundy, but perhaps for that reason it was hardest for a young man to understand. It was least like a *vin du Rhône*. As for the scarce white Hermitage, of which I haven't encountered a bottle in many years, it left a glorious but vague memory. Côte Rôtie was my darling. Drinking it, I fancied I could see that literally roasting but miraculously green hillside, popping with goodness, like the skin of a roasting duck, while little wine-colored devils chased little nymphs along its simmering rivulets of wine. (Thirty years later, I had a prolonged return match with Côte Rôtie, when I discovered it on the wine card of Prunier's, in London. I approached it with foreboding, as you return to a favorite author whom you haven't read for a long time, hoping that he will be as good as you remember. But I need have had no fear. Like Dickens, Côte Rôtie meets the test. It is no Rudyard Kipling in a bottle, making one suspect a defective memory or a defective cork.)

On days when I merely suspected money to be at the bank, I would continue from the Restaurant des Beaux-Arts to the Boulevard des Italiens by any variation of route that occurred to me, looking in the windows of the rare-book dealers for the sort of buy I could afford only once a month. Since on most of my trips I drew a blank at the Crédit Lyonnais, I had plenty of time for window-shopping and for inspection of the bookstalls on the quays. To this I attribute my possession of some of the best books I own—the *Moyen de Parvenir*, for example, printed at Chinon in the early seventeenth century, with the note on its title page: "New edition, corrected of divers faults that weren't there, and augmented by many others entirely new."

On the *good* day, when I had actually received the notification, I had to walk over again to collect, but this time I had a different stride. Simply from the way I carried myself when I left my hotel on the Rue de l'Ecole de Médecine, my landlord, M. Perès, knew that I would pay my bill that night, together with the six or seven hundred francs I invariably owed him for personal bites. He would tap cheerfully on the glass of the window that divided his well-heated office and living quarters from the less well-heated entrance hall, and wave an arm with the gesture that he had probably used to pull his company out of the trenches for a charge at Verdun. He was a *grand blessé* and a Chevalier of the Legion of Honor, *à titre militaire*, with a silver plate in his head that lessened his resistance to liquor, as he frequently reminded Madame when she bawled him out for drinking too much. "One little glass, and you see how I am!" he would say mournfully. In fact, he and I had usually had six each at the Taverne Soufflet, and he convived with other lodgers as well—notably with an Irishman named O'Hea, who worked in a bank, and a spendthrift Korean, who kept a girl.

At the restaurant, I would drink Côte Rôtie, as I had premeditated, and would have one or two Armagnacs after lunch. After that, I was all business in my trajectory across Paris, pausing only nine or ten times to look at the water in the river, and two or three more to look at girls. At the Crédit, I would be received with scornful solemnity, like a suitor for the hand of a miser's daughter. I was made to sit on a bare wooden bench with other wretches come to claim money from the bank, all feeling more like culprits by the minute. A French bank, by the somber intensity of its addiction to money, establishes an emotional claim on funds in transit. The client feels in the moral position of a wayward mother who has left her babe on a doorstep and later comes back to claim it from the foster parents, who now consider it their own. I would be given a metal check with a number on it, and just as I had begun to doze off from the effects of a good lunch, the Côte Rôtie, the brisk walk, and the poor ventilation, a *huissier* who had played Harpagon in repertoire at Angers would shake me by the shoulder. I would advance toward a grille behind which another Harpagon, in an alpaca coat, held the draft, confident that he could riddle my pretensions to the identity I professed. Sometimes, by the ferocity of his distrust, he made me doubt who I was. I would stand fumbling in the wrong pocket for my *carte d'identité*, which had a knack of passing from one part of my apparel to another, like a prestidigitator's coin, and then for my passport, which on such occasions was equally elusive. The sneer on Harpagon's cuttlefish bone of a face would grow triumphant, and I expected him to push a button behind his grille that would summon a squad of detectives. At last, I would find my fugitive credentials and present them, and he would hand over the draft. Then he would send me back to the bench, a *huissier* would present me with another number, and it all had to be done over again—this time with my Kafka impersonation enacted before another Harpagon, at another grille, who would hand out the substantive money. Finally, with two hundred times twenty-six francs, minus a few deductions for official stamps, I would step out onto the Boulevard des Italiens—a once-a-month Monte Cristo. "Taxi!" I would cry. There was no need to walk back.

PASSABLE

Following the publication of some of the foregoing papers I had an avalanche of letters—perhaps a half dozen—asking scornfully whether, in my student days in Paris, I did nothing but eat. I tried conscientiously to think of what I did between meals in the years 1926–7, when I was twenty-two-three, and it seems to have been quite a lot. For one thing, in those days young men liked women. We did not fear emasculation. We had never heard of it. This would today be considered a subliterary approach, but there it was. Havelock Ellis was the sage who made authority in the dormitories. Freud had not yet seeped down to the undergraduate level. Molly Bloom was the pin-up girl of the *nouvelle vague*, and we all burned to beat out Blazes Boylan.

Women offered so much fun from the beginning that further possibilities appeared worth investigating. For this we considered acquaintance, or even marriage, with an undergraduate of the opposite sex insufficient. We assumed, perhaps overoptimistically, that the possibilities of the subject were limitless. They may not be, but no finite man will ever be able to brag that he has exhausted them.

For the beginning student of all essential subjects, the Latin Quarter was an ideal school. The Restaurant des Beaux-Art, as I have indicated, was a great place to learn to eat because the items on the menu were good but simple. The cafés on the Boulevard Saint-Michel offered self-instruction of another kind, but similarly within the grasp of the beginner. You could find any feature of a beauty queen in our cafés, but they were all on different girls. A girl who was beautiful all over would pick a better neighborhood. So, just as at the restaurant, you had to choose a modest but satisfying agenda. In doing that you learned your own tastes.

It was trickier than that because a woman, unlike a *navarin de mouton*, has a mind. A man may say, when he begins to recognize his tastes, "Legs, on a woman, are more important to me than eyes." But he has to think again when he must choose between a witty woman with good eyes and a dull one with trim legs. Give the witty woman a bad temper and the dull one constant good humor and you add to the difficulty of the choice. To multiply the complexity the woman, unlike the *navarin*, reacts to you. She may be what you want, but you may not be what she wants. In such a case she will turn out to be not what you wanted at all.

The unimaginative monogamist has none of these perplexities, but I doubt that he has fun either. I attribute the gloom of many young novelists to an adolescent mistake made at a church Afterward belated curiosity clashes with entrenched ignorance and produces that *timor mundi* which is the *mal de siècle*. "Ain't It Awful, Mabel?" is their strange device, instead of "Up in Mabel's Room."

The girls would arrive at their customary tables soon after lunch, in late afternoon, and establish themselves with a permanent *consommation*, something inexpensive and not tempting, for they would make it last until somebody treated them to something better. This might be a long time, and they had a skill in husbanding the drink that would have stood them in good stead if they had been airmen downed in the Sahara. When treated, they exhibited another desert talent, the opportunism of the camel. They drank enough to last them to the next oasis.

They spent the afternoon writing on the house stationery. If the waiter caught them doodling or doing ticktacktoes he would cut off their supply. With the hour of the *apéritif* came animation and hope. After the dinner hour, if they had not been invited to eat, there remained animation. It could always happen that, if they kept up their spirits, some late customer would offer them a sandwich. The girls were like country artisans; they took money for their services, but only when they felt like working. On occasion they would accept payment in kind—a dinner or a pair of stockings—but then, as often as not, they would ask you to lend them their current week's room rent.

I suppose some of them had sweet men, but these must have been *dilettanti* too. No protector worthy of the name would have tolerated such irregularity. He would have said the girls of the Boulevard Saint-Michel were not serious. And he would have starved on a percentage of their earnings, like a literary agent who depended on poets. All the girls were young. It was easy to comprehend that this was a phase without a future; there was no chance to accumulate. Where they went after they disappeared from the Quarter I do not know. They were brisk rather than chic, and they made up without exaggeration. My memory is not tenacious in matters of dress, but I am sure the girls wore short skirts—I remember the legs. One girl helped me select a hat for a woman in America, and this would not have been possible except in a period when all hats were essentially alike. It was the age of the face *sous cloche*.

The *cloche* was an enlarged skull cap, jammed down on the head like an ice-cream scoop on a ball of vanilla. For the rest, their clothes were not elaborate, with the short skirt, a short blouse and short jacket, and underneath a *soutien-gorge* and *pantalon*. Having the *points de repère* once well in mind, one saw at a glance what was what.

Sometimes a girl would enter *en ménage* with a student, usually a Romanian or an Asiatic. If it was one of the latter, with an allowance from home, the girl would disappear from her customary café for a while or appear there only with him. If it was a Romanian, she would be on the job more regularly than before. Often a girl would make such an arrangement to gain the status of a kept woman, which would protect her from the jurisdiction of the *police des moeurs*.

Once the cops of this unsavory group picked up a girl without visible means of support they would force her to register. Then they would give her a card that subjected her to a set of rules.

"Once a girl has the card she is bound to infract the rules," the girls said. "We are all so lazy. She misses a couple of visits; she is subject to heavy penalties. Then comes blackmail. The police put her to work for chaps who give them a cut. *Hop*, then, no more chattering with student friends who have no money.

"It's the pavement for her, and turn over the receipts to the mackerel at five o'clock in the morning. The police have opened another account."

I was glad to know how things were. It made me feel like an insider, and it helped me understand cops, who run to form everywhere.

Our girls were not intellectuals. None was a geisha primed with poems, nor were there hetaerae who could have disputed on equal terms with Plato, or even with Max Lerner. But all served as advisers on courses of study. They knew the snaps and the tough ones in all faculties, which professors were susceptible to apple polishing and which the most resolutely *vache*. Above all, they had anticipated a theory that was to be imparted to me later as a great original discovery by T. S. Matthews, an editor of *Time*, who told me that the content of communication was unimportant. What did count, Matthews said, was somebody on one end of a wire shouting, "My God, I'm alive!" and somebody on the other end shouting, "My God, I'm alive too!"

It was a poor prescription for journalism, but a good program for conversation between the sexes. (The girls did not keep us at the end of a wire.)

To one I owe a debt the size of a small Latin American republic's in analysts' fees saved and sorrows unsuffered during the next thirty-odd years. Her name was Angèle. She said: *"Tu n'es pas beau, mais t'es passable."* ("You're not handsome, but you're passable.")

I do not remember the specific occasion on which Angèle gave me the good word, but it came during a critical year. I am lucky that she never said, *"T'es merveilleux."* The last is a line a man should be old enough to evaluate.

My brain reeled under the munificence of her compliment. If she had said I was handsome I wouldn't have believed her. If she had called me loathsome I wouldn't have liked it. *Passable* was what I hoped for. *Passable* is the best thing for a man to be.

A handsome man is so generally said by other men to be a fool that in many cases he must himself begin to believe it. The superstition that handsome men are dull is like the prejudice that gray horses quit. Both arose because their subjects were easy to follow with the eye. The career of the late Elmer Davis, a handsome but intelligent man, was made more difficult by his good looks. Favored with a less prepossessing appearance, he would have won earlier acceptance. There are homely fools too, and quitters of all colors.

Women who are both randy and cautious, and therefore of the most profitable acquaintance, avoid handsome lovers because they are conspicuous. He who is *passable* escapes attention. To be *passable* is like a decent suit. It gets you anywhere. *Passable* and *possible* are allied by free association. A young man wants desperately to be considered at least a possibility. But it is the only game in which there is no public form, and he can't present a testimonial from his last employer. He is like a new player in a baseball league where there are no published batting averages. To be *passable* gets him in the ball park without arousing inflated expectations. The ugly man is the object of a special cult among women, but it is relatively small. He runs well only in limited areas, like a Mormon candidate in Utah.

A heartening fact, if you are *passable*, is that there are more *passable* women than any other kind, and that a *passable* man establishes a better rapport with them. Very pretty girls are preferable, of course, but there are never enough to go around. Angèle was *passable* plus—a woman who looks pretty at her best and *passable* at her worst. Her legs, though well-tapered, were a trifle short and her round head a trifle large for good proportion with her torso, in which there was no room for improvement. It was solid Renoir. Her neck was also a bit short and thick—a good point in a prizefighter but not in a swan. She had a clear skin and a sweet breath, and she was well-joined—the kind of girl you could rough up without fear of damage. Angèle had a snub nose, broad at the base, like a seckel pear tilted on its axis.

It was a period when the snub nose enjoyed high popular esteem. The fashions of the day called for a gamine, and a gamine cannot have a classic profile. A retroussé nose, for example, looked better under a cloche. The cloche made a girl with an aquiline nose look like the familiar portrait of Savonarola in his hood. It gave her the profile of that bigot or a spigot.

I had an early belief that I could get along with any woman whose nose turned up. This proved in later life to have been a mistake based on a brief series of coincidences, but when I knew Angèle it still influenced me. Among snub-nosed idols in the United States we had Mary Pickford, Marion Davies, Mae Murray, and Ann Pennington, to name a few I remember. The last two were dancers, and when they kicked, the tips of their noses and their toes were in a straight line. In France they had Madge Lhoty and a girl named Lulu Hegoboru.

Here memory, furtive and irrelevant, interpolates a vision of La Hegoboru taking a refrain of "Tea for Two" in English, in the Paris production of *No, No, Nanette*: "I will back a sugar cack—" as she jumped right, kicked left.

We have no such artists today. The profession of ingenue exists no longer. There was a girl in *Little Mary Sunshine* who had the gist of it, but she will have no chance to develop. In her next job she may have to play an agoraphobic Lesbian in love with her claustrophobic brother. The tragic siblings will be compelled to tryst in a revolving door. It is the kind of play people like to write now, because it can be done in one set, in this case the door.

Angèle had large eyes with sable pupils on a pale-blue field, and a wide mouth, and a face wide at the cheekbones. Her hair was a black soup-bowl bob, as if she had put a cloche on and let a girl friend cut around it. (Girls in the United States went to barber shops for their haircuts.) The corners of her mouth were almost always turned up because Angèle was of a steady, rough good humor. Angèle was a Belgian; half the girls in Paris were Belgians then, and all of them said their parents had been shot by the Germans in World War I.

I met Angèle at Gypsy's Bar on the Rue Cujas, a late place outside the circle of tranquil cafés in which I usually killed my evenings. Most of the time I tried to live like a Frenchman, or, rather, like my idealized notion, formed at home, of how a Frenchman lived. The notion included moderation: I would drink only wine and its distillates, cognac, Armagnac and marc. I did not class French beer among alcoholic drinks. In the United States I had been accustomed to drink needle beer, reinforced with alcohol; a six-ounce glass for twenty-five cents hit as hard as a shot of whiskey for half a dollar.

I did not get drunk as long as I followed what I imagined was the French custom. I thought a sedentary binge effeminate. Now and then, though, I would suffer from a recurrent American urge to stand up and tie one on. It was like the *trouvère*'s longing to hear the birds of his own province:

> The little birds of my country,
> They sing to me in Brittany;
> The shrill-voiced seagulls' cries among
> Mine ears have heard their evensong,
> And sweet, it was of thee.

When this yearning struck during the solvent week of my month— the first after receiving my allowance—I would go to Gypsy's and drink Scotch. The bar was in the Quarter but not used by students. It was too dear. There were even gigolos there—what student would tip a gigolo? I shall not try at this distance in time to guess the nature of Gypsy's sustaining clientele. There may have been a *spécialité de maison*, but I never learned what. I would stand at the bar and think my own thoughts, clear and increasingly grandiose as the level dropped in the bottle. People whose youth did not coincide with the twenties never had our reverence for strong drink. Older men knew liquor before it became the symbol of a sacred cause. Kids who began drinking after 1933 take it as a matter of course.

For us it was a self-righteous pleasure, like killing rabbits with clubs to provide an American Legion party for poor white children. Drinking, we proved to ourselves our freedom as individuals and flouted Congress. We conformed to a popular type of dissent—dissent from a minority. It was the only period during which a fellow could be smug and slopped concurrently.

Angèle impinged on my consciousness toward the end of one of these reveries. She said that I needed somebody to see me home. In Tours the previous summer, a girl making a similar offer had steered me into the hands of two incompetent muggers. Angèle was of a more honorable character. She came home with me. In the morning, when we had more opportunity to talk, we found that we were almost neighbors. She had a room in the Hôtel des Facultés, where the Rue Racine and the Rue de l'Ecole de Médecine form a point they insert in the Boulevard Saint-Michel. My room, one of the pleasantest of my life, was in the fifth (by French count) floor, front, of the Hôtel Saint-Pierre, 4 Rue de l'Ecole de Médecine, next door to a Chinese restaurant that had dancing. At night, while I read, the music from the dancing would rise to my window and a part of my brain would supply the words to the tune as I tried to maintain interest in the *Manual of Provençal Documents* of Monsieur Maurice Prou. One that recurred often was *"Oh, les fraises et les framboises, le bon vin qu'nous avons bu,"* from *Trois Jeunes Filles Nues*, one of Mirande's great hits.

It was an atmosphere not conducive to the serious study of medieval history, which was my avowed purpose in the Quarter.

Angèle not only lived by day on the same street, but frequented by night the same cafés I did—the Taverne Soufflet, La Source, the Café d'Harcourt, all strung along the Boulevard Saint-Michel. She made her headquarters in the d'Harcourt, where it was the merest chance that she had not remarked me, she said. She had so many friends, she explained, there was always somebody engaging her attention.

I said that in any case I spent most of my time in the Soufflet, where the boss was a pal of my landlord. But after that I would go to the d'Harcourt whenever I wanted to see her. It had a favorable effect on her standing if I bought her a drink there, and none on mine if I took her to the Soufflet. If she was not at her post, her waiter would take her messages. He would also tell her to dress warmly in winter and not get her feet wet, to take sufficient nourishment to keep up her strength, and not to be beguiled by clients who had to his experienced eye the aspect of muscle-men recruiting for a brothel. It was a relationship already familiar to me from New York, where a waiter was the nearest thing to a mother lots of girls had.

When we had established the similarity of our *frequentations*, Angèle and I marveled that we had to go all the way to Gypsy's, a good fifty meters from the Boulevard, to find each other. We sounded like the traditional New Yorkers who inhabit the same apartment house but meet for the first time in Majorca.

After that I was with her often. I do not know if she had a heart gold, but she had what I learned long years later to call a therapeutic personality. She made you feel good.

When I took her out in the evening we sometimes strayed from the Quarter. This was like taking a Manhattan child to the Bronx Zoo. Girls did not shift about in Paris. Clienteles were localized, and so were usages. Montparnasse, although not a long walk away from the Quarter, had all the attributes of a foreign country, including, to a degree, the language.

In Montparnasse the types in the cafés spoke English, American, and German. The girls there had to be at least bilingual. In the Quarter, the languages, besides French, were Vietnamese, Spanish, Czech, Polish and Romanian. But the specimens of all these nationalities spoke French at least passably. The girls consequently could remain resolutely monolingual. The clients were students, or simulated students, at the University. Those were the days of the Little Entente, and France set the cultural and military pattern for the East Europe that is behind the Curtain now. Romanian students came to French universities as freely as if they had done their secondary work in France.

The pre-eminence of the University of Paris was acknowledged as it had been in the Middle Ages. All the tribes rescued from the Austro-Hungarian and Turkish Empires flocked there—Serbs and Croats, Egyptians, Greeks, Armenians, along with Haitians and Koreans, Venezuelans and Argentines. There were also, of course, the North Africans. It would have been a great place to form friendships that would serve in the convulsive years to come. But I thought, if I thought about it at all, that regional convulsions were as out-of-date as *écriture onciale* or horse armor.

Our foreignness made each more confident of his speech than he would have been among the French. From my first appearance in the Quarter, my French was no worse than that of a White Russian or a Czech, and I rose rapidly and successively through the grades of being mistaken for a Hungarian, German Swiss, Alsatian, and Belgian from the Flemish-speaking provinces. Beyond that point I have not since progressed, except in Algeria, where I am mistaken for an old lag of the Foreign Legion who has all kinds of accents so inextricably mixed that it is hopeless to attempt to disassociate them.

Angèle did not like Montparnasse. Neither did I. I had come to France for the same reason that at home I would go out to a beach and swim out just beyond the breakers. There I could loaf. Lying on my back, I would paddle just enough to keep out of the pull, and draw my knees up to my chin and feel good. The Americans in Montparnasse, sitting at their tables in front of Le Sélect and talking at each other, reminded me of monkeys on a raft. They were not in the water at all. One reason I didn't think I liked them was that they had all decided they were writers, or painters, or sculptors, and I didn't know what I was. During my residence in the Hôtel Saint-Pierre I never heard of Gertrude Stein, and although I read *Ulysses*, I would as soon have thought of looking the author up as of calling on the President of the Republic.

Angèle disliked Montparnasse because the people looked at the same time too prosperous and too bizarre. The American women, she said, did not look like Frenchwomen and the Frenchwomen did not look like other Frenchwomen. There were no serious bookstores stacked with doctoral dissertations and tributes to deceased savants. (She herself was not a reader, but she liked academic surroundings.) The types appeared smug and possibly addicted to narcotics. The waiters in the cafés were insolent and Italian, and the *consommations* were overpriced. There were too many fairies and they gave her *drôles* of looks. Let them not fear, she was not in competition. We wound up our tour at the Closerie des Lilas, the border post, at the corner of the Boulevard Montparnasse and our own Boulevard Saint-Michel. The Montparnassiens occupied the post—its tariff was too high for the Quarter. I offered her a whiskey there, but she said it smelled of bedbugs. Now all the French drink Scotch.

Angèle could not get back to the d'Harcourt with sufficient celerity, but once there, it pleased her to have voyaged. She talked as if she were home from a world cruise. But when we went to Montmartre, she was in her glory. She had talked all her life about the *nuits blanches* of Montmartre but had never been there. I took her to Zelli's and we drank several bottles of champagne. She was a solid drinker. All her appetites were robust. In bed she was a kind of utility infielder. She made me buy half a dozen flashlight photographs of us and the bottles, like sportsmen and sailfish, to serve as documentation when she recounted our adventure. Her room, in the prow of a ship-shaped building, was barely wide enough for a single bed. I was there only once, in September of 1927, when she was ill. Half of the mirror was covered with photographs of us at Zelli's.

Aside from her concession that I was passable, which is wrapped around my ego like a bulletproof vest riveted with diamonds, I retain little Angèle said. The one other exception is a report so vivid that I sometimes confuse it with a visual memory.

Angèle told me one morning that she and a number of her colleagues had been playing cards in her room. There were a couple of girls sitting on her bed, a couple more on the bureau, one on the only chair and another on her trunk, when one took off her shoes.

A second girl said, after a moment, "It smells of feet in here!" The shoeless girl said, "Say that once more and you will say *Bon jour* to the concierge."

"You get it?" said Angèle. "The concierge is on the ground floor, we are on the sixth. She will throw her down the stairs. The other comrade who commenced says again, 'It smells of feet.'

"So the other hooks on and drags her out on the landing, and they roll down the stairs together, interscratching with all claws. On the fifth, two law students, interrupted in their studies, pull them apart from each other. The girls couldn't work for three nights afterward.

"One student took up for the girl he had pulled upon, and the other took up for the adversary. Now the students have quarreled, and the girl whose feet smelled has moved in with one of them at the Facultés, while the other student has moved in with the girl whose nose was delicate. It is romance in flower."

Life in the Quarter was a romance that smelled of feet.

I am afraid that I do not succeed in making Angèle's quality come clear. To attempt a full description of a woman on the basis of a few fragmentary memories is like trying to reconstruct a small, endearing animal from a few bits of bone. Even some of the bits are not much help. My arms try to remember her weight—I should say 118, give or take two pounds.

It makes me wince, now, to recall that she used to butt me in the pit of the belly, quite hard, and that we both thought it chummy. My point of view has changed with the tone of my muscles.

Yet she existed. The proof is that my old landlord, Perès, remembers her well. I sometimes meet Perès at a brasserie called l'Alsace à Paris. The proprietor there is M. Perès' old friend, the former owner of the Taverne Soufflet, which failed in 1931 because he had a wife who did not keep her mind on the business. (It is too much to expect the *patron* of a café to keep his mind on the business himself.) Now M. Robert, whose last name I have not learned in thirty-six years of greeting him, has an excellent wife who does not have to keep her mind on the business. It goes as if on rollers.

M. Perès, who retired from the management of the Hôtel Saint-Pierre shortly after World War II, continues to live in the Quarter because, he says, it keeps him young. He has recently been made an Officer of the Legion of Honor. He was a Chevalier, *à titre militaire*, as I have said before, when I first came to live under this roof in 1926, having distinguished himself by courage in World War I. I always suspected him of trying to give the impression, however, that he had won the ribbon for some discovery in Aramaic intransitive verbs or the functioning of the gall bladder. This would have been more chic in his neighborhood. During World War II he served as a captain of infantry, at fifty-one, and distinguished himself again.

"I was a bit put out," he said to me when I congratulated him on his new rosette, "because my promotion was slow in arriving. A man of seventy in the vicinity of the University who has only the ribbon has the air of a demifailure. But the delay was occasioned by the nature of my business. The Chancellery of the Legion is cautious in awarding the higher grades to hotelkeepers, because the hotel may be a *maison de passe*. Once I announced my retirement, the rosette was not long on the way."

M. Perès, in thirty years at the Saint-Pierre, lodged an infinity of students. It makes him think of himself as a housemaster. "One of our fellows is raising the question of confidence in the Chamber today," he may say when you meet him, meaning a Deputy who used to live at the Saint-Pierre as a student. "He has gone farther than I would have predicted." Or, "One of our fellows is now the leading internist in Port-au-Prince— I had a card last week." Or, "One of our chaps who is the professor of medieval history at the University of Jerusalem has, it appears, achieved a remarkable monograph on secular law in the Latin kingdom of Acre. He had your room about ten years after you left. He, at least, worked from one time to another." It is M. Perès' contention that I was a *farceur*, a do-nothing, because we sneaked out so often for a drink at the Soufflet when his wife was in bad humor.

The Anciens de l'Hôtel Saint-Pierre is the sole alumni association of which I would willingly attend a reunion; unhappily it does not exist. If it did, it would include the ladies' auxiliary, *bien entendu*; the girl who lived with the Korean on the floor below me, the mistress of the Dane upstairs, Angèle and subsequent and preceding Angèles of all promotions, and the two little maids from Dax, Lucienne and Antoine, who led the way to the bathroom, which was on the third floor, when the client had ordered a bath. They then allowed themselves to be trapped long enough for an invigorating tussle.

M. Perès remembers Angèle almost as well as if she had made a name for herself as a comparative zoologist in Peru.

She died in the winter of 1927–28, not of a broken heart, but flu. I was no longer in Paris, but in Providence, Rhode Island, where I had returned to a job on the Providence *Journal* and *Evening Bulletin*, and Perès included word of her death, along with other neighborhood news, in a letter that he sent me.

"She had a felicity of expression," he said of her one day thirty years later. "Once she said to me, 'Head of a ruin, how much do you extort for your cubicles?' There wasn't a sou's worth of harm in her. What a pity that she had to die. How well she was built!" he said in final benison.

"She was *passable*," I said.

I could see that M. Perès thought me a trifle callous, but he did not know all that *passable* meant to me.

Virgil Thomson

Virgil Thomson (1896–1989), genial master of American music criticism, lived in Paris for a truly long time, from 1925 until the outbreak of the war in 1940, and while there he wrote with Gertrude Stein the memorable and still-performed opera *Four Saints in Three Acts*. But he never put on airs, either: "I wrote in Paris," he tells us, "music that was always, in one way or another, about Kansas City." Like every true Parisian of the time, he learned the joy of social life in compressed spaces—a pleasure better known after the war to New Yorkers—as in this account from his 1966 memoir *Virgil Thomson* of an apartment on a memorable block near the river. (Thomson's local canteen, the Voltaire, is still flourishing too.)

———

17 quai Voltaire

The quai Voltaire is a row of eighteenth-century houses standing between the rue des Saints-Pères and the rue du Bac and looking across the Seine to the Louvre. Just above it sits the seventeenth-century Institut de France, arms open like a miniature Saint Peter's for receiving daily its college of lay cardinals, the forty "immortals" of l'Académie Française. A farther short walk upstream brings the medieval world—the Conciergerie, Sainte-Chapelle, and Notre-Dame. Downstream one passes the 1900 Gare d'Orsay and the eighteenth-century Hôtel de Salm (Palais de la Légion d'Honneur) and looks across to the Tuileries Gardens before arriving at the Chamber of Deputies and Place de la Concorde, both dominating from on high excellent swimming-baths that sit in the Seine without using its water. The situation could not be more central or more historical.

Number 17, where I went to live in 1927 (permanently, as it has now turned out), consists of two houses, each with its courtyard and concierge, plus a three-story pavilion known as *l'atelier d'Ingres*, where the grandmother of our concierge's husband was said to have posed for *La Source*. In the second of the larger houses, dating from 1791 and built over the ruins of the fifteenth-century Abbaye des Théatins, I occupied, five stories up, a furnished studio complete with bath and with a view that included Louvre, Opéra, and Sacré-Coeur. The concierge of the first house, Madame Jeanne, took care of it. She took care of me too, washing my woolens, receiving my messages, ordering anthracite coal for my *salamandre*, and in general looking to my comfort. Her sister, Madame Elise, concierge of the second house, came later to cook for me (and first class she was); but at this time I had no kitchen, only an alcohol stove for making coffee or tea.

The first house was L-shaped; and my landlord, Dr. Ovize, though not its owner, lived there with his wife on the top floor behind a twelve-foot-wide terrace dominating three fourths of the city. The second house, where I lived, was also L-shaped; and, completed by the Ingres studio, it enclosed three sides of a generous courtyard, turning the back of its principal wing to the Hôtel du Quai Voltaire, at number 19. Madame Elise, my concierge, only slept in this house; she spent her days helping out Madame Jeanne and preparing sumptuous meals for Madame Jeanne's husband, a bonded messenger for the Bank of France. And as if to bind further the two houses, their cousin Berthe (as a live-in servant she could not be called Madame) was maid to my next-door neighbor, the poet Lucie Delarue-Mardrus; and Madame Mardrus herself, ex-wife of an Arabic scholar, Dr. Jesus-Christ Mardrus, was the close friend of Madame Ovize. As a further connection, she shared literary and feministic consanguinities with my friends Miss Natalie Barney and Elisabeth de Gramont, Duchesse de Clermont-Tonnerre.

Berthe, costumed in black, was a schooled servant who addressed one in the third person. When I knocked on her kitchen door one day to ask how to make a mayonnaise, she began, "Monsieur will take a bowl and an egg. Monsieur will break his egg and put into his bowl the yellow only." Though forty or more, she was not afraid of stairs, always running down to find Madame Mardrus a taxi, then climbing back by the steep circular service stairs. Dark men from the Auvergne carried fifty-pound sacks of coal up that stairway too.

Madame Elise was tall, heavy, and beautiful, with blue eyes and white hair. She smiled constantly, unless cooking. Then she would hover, fluttering like a hen and barely breathing, as out of her left hand she would take with three fingers of her right a pinch of something and throw it in, then wait still breathless, as if listening, till she divined the gesture a success. When I began to cook she told me many secret things; and occasionally

I taught her an American dish. This she would never put into repertory until her brother-in-law had pronounced it good. And she did not think it right not to eat soup. Thus I discovered that no dinner was too much work if I allowed her to make soup also—which she did well, cooking it always very slowly, while she mended, tending her sister's lodge.

The studio was octagonal and twenty feet tall, with high windows on the north and northeast facets, which were covered at night by rose-colored floor-length curtains, padded to keep the cold out. The walls and carpet were a golden tan; chairs, table, and dish-cabinet, all from Louis-Philippe times, were of mahogany. A velvet-covered plain couch was my bed. At the top of some long stairs were a balcony and a very large bath-dressing room. This had two windows (one with my finest view), its own heat (gas), and its mechanism (also gas) for heating water, plus a clothes-closet. I had brought with me some Chinese water colors and a Persian chess table (gifts of Mary Butts) and the abstract sculpture by Arp (gift of Philip Lasell). Almost immediately too there was a large Bérard, a man's portrait much larger than life painted in almost-black blues over candle-wax modeling (a gift from Bérard out of his first one-man show). There was Chinese tea from Boston (via Mrs. Lasell). I acquired a rented piano from Pleyel. And I had new clothes, the first in several years, for with the first gift of money from Mrs. Lasell, before she put me on allowance, I had ordered at Lanvin three suits, an overcoat, and six poplin shirts with matching underdrawers. I paid for these in cash, made friends, forever after having credit there.

I said one day to Gertrude, "We are poor as anything and feeling quite bohemian, and yet we all wear suits and ties and hats. What did Picasso and Max Jacob wear when they were young?" But she did not remember, and so she asked Picasso. "Caps," he replied, "and sweaters, except for Max, who was a dude," then remembering further, "but we bought our sweaters at Williams's [British sport shop]."

Madame Jeanne, my caretaker, had black hair and flashing eyes; and though less monumental than her sister, was more striking. I have seen her image on the portal of an eleventh-century church (Saint-Lô), along with those of Anatole France and of an ever remembered old French taxi driver. She was in fact as basically French as anyone I ever knew; she *was* France. She could barely read; she believed America to have been discovered by Lafayette; and the store called Old England she would write phonetically in French as Olden Gland. All the same, reciting the injustices of Madame Ovize toward her sister, she was Sarah Bernhardt, Réjane, Marie Bell. She was also Corneille and Racine, for what is the language of these at its most lapidary but the basic French of kings and concierges? *"J'admire ton courage et je plains ta jeunesse,"* says the monarch to the hero of *Le Cid* ("I admire your bravery and pity your youth"). And the young Oreste in *Andromaque* confesses, *"Mon innocence enfin commence à me peser"* ("My innocence begins to be a weight").

Of my sculpture by Arp Madame Jeanne had asked, reasonably enough, what it represented. And when I answered that I had no clue, she settled the matter with, *"C'est une idée d'artiste."* And when to her inquiry about a crystal that looked like pink flowers, I answered that such forms, found in the Sahara, were known as *"roses du désert,"* she observed philosophically, putting it back on the shelf, *"C'est intéressant tout de même la nature."* For humane understanding she was Madame Langlois's equal; and in her mastery of the tactful remark she could match my mother.

In my first week some composer had been playing me his newest piece, a long, loud, and highly discordant work. The next morning a letter came from my poet-neighbor Lucie Delarue-Mardrus that was a cry of pain. I answered with an invitation to tea, and she accepted. Tall and dark-haired, with soft brown eyes, she was a Norman from Honfleur, poet, painter, even something of a musician. It was around her music making that we made our pact. She liked to practice the violin from twelve to one; and I agreed not to mind music at that hour, since I would surely be shaving, bathing, and dressing to go out. During the earlier morning, when I might be using the piano, she agreed to do her writing in a room from which she could not hear my music. Early afternoons we both were out. Late afternoons she would tolerate whatever she might hear, since she now knew that what came through my walls would always be some dialect of music. I proposed not playing evenings after ten, but she said that music could not be heard from where she slept. So we became friends and began to visit, sometimes at her flat when all six of her tall dark sisters would arrive from Honfleur, sometimes at mine when there were literary people, still oftener at Dr. Ovize's, where there would be lunches lasting for hours, with music afterwards. Here I would play and sing my own, or I would play two-piano Mozart with Madame, a chihuahua-size Jewess from Algiers with deep shadows under green eyes and a mop of bright red hair teased into a headlight.

On November first I had taken possession; on November second I began Act One. Very shortly after, I composed my first song in French, a setting of four poems by Georges Hugnet that were not related to one another save by their lilting metrics. Henri Sauguet gave it the title of *La Valse grégorienne*, on account of its chant-like intonings and archaic harmony. The French found in it no prosodic fault, insisted I sing it for them all the time. It was so successful, in fact, that I went no farther just then with setting French. I had my *Four Saints* to be getting on with.

In the early Boulanger days I had trained myself to write music without instrumental aid, had come indeed to prefer working that way. For the opera I found myself working differently. With the text on my piano's music rack, I would sing and play, improvising melody to fit the words and harmony for underpinning them with shape. I did this every day, wrote down nothing. When the first act would improvise itself every day in the same way, I knew it was set. That took all of November. Then I wrote it out from memory, which took ten days. By mid-December I had a score consisting of the vocal lines and a figured bass, a score from which I could perform.

On Christmas night I performed Act One for close friends only. The party that went along with this performance grew out of a Christmas box sent at the request of Mrs. Lasell by Rosa Lewis, King Edward VII's former cook, owner of the Cavendish Hotel, clubhouse for London's millionaire bohemia. It contained three massive objects—a *fois gras en croûte*, a Stilton cheese, and a plum pudding. By having sent in to go along with these a salad of apples and peeled walnuts, an aspic of chicken, and some champagne, I managed to offer a lap supper to twelve people. What effect my music made I was not sure. Gertrude Stein was pleased, of course, and Alice too. Everybody, in fact, seemed buoyed up by the opera's vivacity. Tristan Tzara told Hugnet he had been deeply impressed by a music at once so "physical" and so gay. I had wondered whether a piece so drenched in Anglican chant (running from Gilbert and Sullivan to Morning Prayer and back) could rise and sail. But no one else seemed bothered by its origins. On the contrary, they had all undergone a musical and poetic experience so unfamiliar that only their faith in me (for they were chosen friends) had allowed them to be carried along, which indeed they had been, as on a magic carpet.

What gave this work so special a vitality? The origin of that lay in its words, of course, the music having been created in their image. Music, however, contains an energy long since lost to language, an excitement created by the contest of two rhythmic patterns, one of lengths and one of stresses. A pattern made up of lengths alone is static, and the stuttering of mere stresses is hypnotic. But together, and contrasted, they create tension and release; and this is the energy that makes music sail, take flight, get off the ground. By applying it to the text of Gertrude Stein, I had produced a pacing that is implied in that text, if you wish, but that could never be produced without measured extensions. Speech alone lacks music's forward thrust.

The theme of *Four Saints* is the religious life—peace between the sexes, community of faith, the production of miracles—its locale being the Spain Gertrude remembered from having traveled there. The music evokes Christian liturgy. Its local references, however, are not to Spain, which I had never seen, but rather to my Southern Baptist upbringing in Missouri. It does not do, this music, or attempt to do, any of the things already done by the words. It merely explodes these into singing and gives them shape. Poetry alone is always a bit amorphous; and poetry as spontaneously structured as Gertrude Stein's had long seemed to me to need musical reinforcement. I do not mean that her writing *lacks* music; I mean that it *likes* music. Much of it, in fact, lies closer to musical timings than to speech timings. The rigamarole ending of *Capital Capitals*, for instance, I have always felt to have small relation to Spenser, Shakespeare, Milton, or Keats; but I do recognize in its peroration-by-repetition the insistences of a Beethoven finale.

If it is the relation of music to words that makes opera in two senses moving, it is the relation of instrumental accompaniment to vocal line that makes an opera resemble its epoch. The singing line from Monteverdi to Alban Berg shows surprisingly little change, because with conscientious composers the words-and-music factor, even through language differences, is a constant. You have only to think of Purcell's *Dido and Aeneas*, Mozart's *Don Giovanni*, Wagner's *Tristan und Isolde*, Bizet's *Carmen*, and Stravinsky's *The Rake's Progress* to realize that the history of the lyric stage is largely the history of its changing instrumental accompaniment.

Now the *Four Saints* accompaniment is as odd as its text, so odd, indeed, that it has sometimes been taken for childish. In fact, many persons not closely involved with either poetry or music but mildly attached to all contemporary artwork by the conviction that it is thrifty to be stylish have for more than thirty years now been worried by my use of what seems to them a backward-looking music idiom in connection with a forward-looking literary one. That worry can only be argued against by denying the assumption that discord is advanced and harmoniousness old-fashioned. Not even the contrary is true, though the production of complete discord through musical sounds (the only kind of discord that is not just noise) has been practiced since before World War I. The truth is that only artists greedy for quick fame choose musical materials for their modishness. In setting Stein texts to music I had in mind the acoustical support of a trajectory, of a verbal volubility that would brook no braking. My skill was to be employed not for protecting such composers as had invested in the dissonant manner but for avoiding all those interval frictions and contrapuntal viscosities which are built into the dissonant style and which if indulged unduly might trip up my verbal speeds. Not to have skirted standard modernism would have been to fall into a booby trap. On the contrary, I built up my accompaniments by selecting chords for their tensile strength and by employing in a vast majority of cases only those melodic elements from the liturgical vernacular of Christendom, both Catholic and Protestant, that had for centuries borne the weight of long prayers and praises and of that even longer fastidiously fine-printed and foot-noted contract that we called the Creed.

I set all of Stein's text to music, every word of it, including the stage directions, which were so clearly a part of the poetic continuity that I did not think it proper to excise them. And for distributing all these parts among the singers I assumed a double chorus of participating saints and two Saint Teresas (not alter egos, just identical twins); and I added as non-saintly commentators, or "end men," a *compère* and a *commère*. Though I had Gertrude's permission to repeat things if I wished, I no more took this freedom than I did that of cutting. She was a specialist of repetition; why should I compete? I simply set everything, exactly in the order of its writing down, from beginning to end.

Act Two was composed and written out by the end of February; and Acts Three and Four (for *Four Saints in Three Acts* is merely a title; actually there are thirty or more saints and four acts) were finished by summer and written out in July. Generally I worked mornings, sometimes also in the late afternoon. Always I went out for lunch and usually for dinner, unless I had a guest or two, in which case I had *cordon bleu* food sent in from the Hôtel de l'Université. This was a good quarter of a mile from door to door; but a dainty waitress would trip it twice, bearing her platter up five flights with soup and roast, a second time with dessert. When I had grippe a nearer restaurant would send a waiter up four times a day, twice to take the order and twice to deliver it. Otherwise, once out of the house and down my stairs, I usually stayed out till five or so on errands or walks.

Lunch was likely to be at a bistro on the rue Jacob called La Quatrième République, its title an irony left over from immediate post-war idealism. There one encountered almost always the singer Victor Prahl, usually Janet Flanner and her novelist companion Solita Solano, sometimes the reporter Vincent Sheean. The food, excellent and very cheap, was served downstairs by a portly *patron*, upstairs by a domineering waitress who had no fatigue in her as she ran up the circular staircase, or patience in her busy life for Americans who dallied over menus. *"Yvonne la terrible,"* Janet would call her. When one young man, mixing his salad, put in a whole teaspoonful of mustard, she teased him harshly, "You must be in love."

My walks that winter were chiefly with Russell Hitchcock, who had come to live near by in the rue de Lille and who was writing his first works on architectural history. Just as earlier and later I walked with Maurice Grosser in the woods outside of Paris from the forests of Rambouillet and Saint-Cloud clean round to the Bois de Vincennes, I walked the city itself, every quarter of it, with Hitchcock. I had done this by myself years earlier, looking for a lodging, but now I saw it from another view, for he could read it like a history book. This is not easy, since French house design has changed little since the seventeenth century. But ornament has changed with almost every decade; and a particular treatment of stone—smooth, rusticated, or vermiculated, with or without indentations—has marked the larger epochs of style. Involved at this time with Romantic architecture, Russell would love to point out, in contrast to the airy neo-classical design under Louis XVI of the customs barriers at the Porte de la Chapelle, the willful heaviness in the same epoch of Saint-Philippe-du-Roule, almost as massively weighted for romantic expressivity as the Napoleonic Place du Caire, with its trophylike sphinx façade, and the Chapelle Expiatoire, pious Restoration memorial to the executed monarch Louis XVI and his Queen Marie-Antoinette.

Red-bearded and not slender, speaking loudly because he was himself a little deaf, and always dressed with flamboyance, Russell attracted considerable attention; but he pleased the French by his knowledge of their country, by his elegant manners, which were formal without being lugubrious, and by his air, at once *bon enfant* and *gros jouisseur*, of having a wonderful time. He interested very little Gertrude Stein, more Georges Hugnet, who translated his early brochures for publication, a great deal Madame Langlois, who could spot a proper scholar when she saw one. It was through Russell that I first knew the academician Louis Gillet and his wife, who, having young ones themselves, liked other young ones to be about and who had as country house (except Sundays, three to five, when it was on show) the Château de Challis, near Ermenonville, which belonged to the Académie Française and of which Monsieur Gillet was curator. It was there, in fact, that Louise Gillet was married in the medieval chapel to music of mine. The residence itself had been a moated castle till its eighteenth-century owner, romantically attached to contemplating the Gothic but less so to living in it, had it transformed by dynamite into a ruin and then built himself a modern (Louis XV) house, from which his guests could view in comfort the ivy-clad reminder of times past.

With Henri Sauguet I also walked, but more for poking around slums than for mastering history. We showed each other our music, shared adventures and addresses, bound ourselves together by an unspoken credo (based on Satie) that forbade us to be bogus either in our music or in our lives. In the spring of 1927, coming from Villefranche with Lasell and Mary Butts, I had joined Sauguet at Monte Carlo, where Diaghilev was putting on *La Chatte*, his first ballet. Georges Hugnet too I saw constantly—also Henri Cliquet-Pleyel and his wife Marthe-Marthine. Cliquet was hollow-cheeked and looked Hispanic, save for the large, soft eyes, which could be only French. His wife was plumpish, blond, the classical soubrette, alert and sex-minded, also a singer of remarkable musicianship. With Hugnet and Kristians Tonny—blond, muscular, and Dutch, with the sea at the back of his eyes—we constituted a *petite famille* for dinners and laughter. Cliquet was a pianist of unusual facility, a sight reader of renown, and a composer of willful banality. His music was a tender parody, his life a slavery to pot-boiling jobs. Marthe too was not ever to be prosperous; she had thrown away her singing career for marriage in Rumania, and she could not fight her way back. She and Cliquet, though attached relentlessly, did each other no good. He would go into tantrums in which he burned his manuscripts or destroyed pictures with razors (*"colères de faiblesse,"* Madame Langlois called them) and she would take to red wine, quarts of it a day. Yet they remained for me gentle companions and colleagues of impeccable solidarity. Around 1928, Hugnet wrote a long poem about the Emperor Commodus, which Cliquet made into a cantata. Cliquet also composed an operetta with book and lyrics by Max Jacob, *Les Impôts*. This was a parody of every operetta in the world, and both verses and music were exquisite. When Cliquet died at seventy, in 1963, he had just completed a work called (actually) *Concerto posthume*. The earlier large works such as *Commode* and *Les Impôts*, not yet found, may have been destroyed by him in some frenzied fury.

Hugnet that winter went on publishing, usually poetry books. Tonny continued to draw and to experiment with paint. The three of us together made a gift for Gertrude which was a set of poems by Georges put to music by me and bound up in a cover that Tonny had drawn on silver paper by stylus pressure only. The full title of the offering was *Le Berceau de Gertrude Stein, ou le mystère de la rue de Fleurus, huit poèmes de Georges Hugnet mis en musique par Virgil Thomson sous le titre de Lady Godiva's Waltzes*. Godiva was Gertrude's private name for her Ford, of which the cough and tripping rhythms dominate the piece. Marthe-Marthine first sang it publicly at a concert of my works in May of '28. Georges also made a film that spring in collaboration with a Belgian nobleman, the Comte d'Ursel. It was called *La Perle* and is a Dadalike fantasy that prefigured the surrealist films of Luis Buñuel. For its appearance at the cinema Aux Ursulines I arranged my *Valse grégorienne*, to please d'Ursel, for the five-piece orchestra that accompanied the show.

Lots of people came in and out of my flat that first year, and sometimes there were large parties. For one of these Bernard Fay invited a galaxy of literary stars and aged princesses. At another, Scott Fitzgerald stood up on my anthracite-burning *salamandre* with such shaky balance that both he and the stove just missed decline and fall. The novelists Marcel Jouhandeau and André Gide used to appear. Also León Kochnitzky, poet and professional traveler. Not Antheil, who was in America. Nor Ernest Hemingway, whom I never asked. He was part of a Montparnasse hard-liquor set which, though thoroughly fascinated by itself, was less interesting to people not also drinking hard liquor. Robert McAlmon I did find interesting; I also esteemed him as a writer; but just like Hart Crane, who was around for a while and whom I also admired, he was too busy drinking and getting over it to make dates with. Both were better when casually encountered. Mary Reynolds, the queen of American Montparnasse, came often, also Olga Dahlgren, a Philadelphian abroad, and my own painters, of course—Kristians Tonny, Bérard, and Leonid and Eugene

Berman. Also a Swiss writer unbelievably impoverished, not always clean, not always sober, his mind ingenious, his talk both learned and funny— Charles-Albert Cingria, who lived in an unheated garret room with a fifteenth-century spinet, a bicycle, and five hundred books and who wrote in the most beautiful French prose small brochures about large historical questions, such as the rights of rhythm in Gregorian chant.

So what with parties and people, with new clothes and stable measurements (for I patronized a Russian gymnast who could keep me at 135 pounds), and with the opera advancing by leaps, time stopped once more. Nothing seemed to be going on, because everything was going right. In April Mrs. Lasell appeared, wholly recovered from her mastoiditis, returning with her brother and sister-in-law from an African trip. She was pleased with my flat and with my general industriousness, as well she might have been. Never before had I worked so fast or so well as I was doing in this comfortable place and with enough money to live more easily than before (just a little more easily, but that made the difference). Anyone could see that I was in phase, that my guardian angel was on the job, and that 17 quai Voltaire was not only the "strange packet ship" that Lucie Mardrus called it; it was for me in every way a magic locale. I did not tell Jessie Lasell that Gertrude's Chicago millionairess Mrs. Emily Chadbourne Crane had at Gertrude's extreme insistence also become temporarily my patron. But that was in part why I was doing so nicely— so nicely indeed that I thought it about time I gave a concert of my works. And I proposed this to Mrs. Lasell; it would cost $500. She thought the idea sound, gave me the money, went home happy. I had also promised to visit her in America at Christmas.

Jack Kerouac

Jack Kerouac (1922–1969), author of *On the Road* and *The Dharma Bums* and inventor of the "spontaneous" manner in American writing, came to Paris in 1966 as a bohemian pleasure seeker and inebriate very much in the Henry Miller manner, but wrote about the city with a kind of breezy sweetness that the harder-minded older man would never have much liked. If his account in *Satori in Paris* (1966) is almost too brightly registered and has a slightly dated beatnik-and-bongos rhythm to it, still it captures the Paris that generations of students and backpackers still seek. (Kerouac makes an interesting, surprising pair with Irwin Shaw, another 1950s icon whose writing about Paris, for all the difference in social class and literary "polish," has a similar kind of good-hearted ingenuousness, reminding us that one of the things that Americans have in common with the French, and share not at all with the suspicious English, is a readiness to *like* things.) Kerouac's American awe at the wonderful simplicity of *choucroute* is not unlike the reciprocal French awe at the wonderful simplicity of Kerouac.

---

from

Satori in Paris

P aris is a place where you can really walk around at night and find what you dont want, O Pascal.

Trying to make my way to the Opera a hundred cars came charging around a blind curve-corner and like all the other pedestrians I waited to let them pass and then they all started across but I waited a few seconds looking the other charging cars over, all coming from six directions— Then I stepped off the curb and a car came around that curve all alone like the chaser running last in a Monaco race and right at me—I stepped back just in time—At the wheel a Frenchman completely convinced that no one else has a right to live or get to his mistress as fast as he does—As a New Yorker I run to dodge the free zipping roaring traffic of Paris but Parisians just stand and then stroll and leave it to the driver—And by God

577

it works, I saw dozens of cars screech to a stop from 70 M.P.H. to let some stroller have his way!

I was going to the Opera also to eat in any restaurant that looked nice, it was one of my sober evenings dedicated to solitary studious walks, but O what grim rainy Gothic buildings and me walking well in the middle of those wide sidewalks so's to avoid dark doorways—What vistas of Nowhere City Night and hats and umbrellas—I couldn't even buy a newspaper—Thousands of people were coming out of some performance somewhere—I went to a crowded restaurant on Boulevard des Italiens and sat way at the end of the bar by myself on a high stool and watched, wet and helpless, as waiters mashed up raw hamburg with Worcestershire sauce and other things and other waiters rushed by holding up steaming trays of good food—The one sympathetic counterman brought menu and Alsatian beer I ordered and I told him to wait awhile—He didnt understand that, drinking without eating at once, because he is partner to the secret of charming French eaters:— they rush at the very beginning with *hors d'oeuvres* and bread, and then plunge into their entrees (this is practically always before even a slug of wine) and then they slow down and start lingering, now the wine to wash the mouth, now comes the *talk*, and now the second half of the meal, wine, dessert and coffee, something I cannae do.

In any case I'm drinking my second beer and reading the menu and notice an American guy is sitting five stools away but he is so mean looking in his absolute disgust with Paris I'm afraid to say "Hey, you American?"—He's come to Paris expecting he woulda wound up under a cherry tree in blossom in the sun with pretty girls on his lap and people dancing around him, instead he's been wandering the rainy streets alone in all that jargon, doesnt even know where the whore district is, or Notre Dame, or some small cafe they told him about back in Glennon's bar on Third Avenue, *nothing*—When he pays for his sandwich he literally throws the money on the counter "You wouldnt help me figure what the real price is anyway, and besides shove it up your you-know-what I'm going back to my old mine nets in Norfolk and get drunk with Bill Eversole in the bookie joint and all the other things you dumb frogs dont know about," and stalks out in poor misunderstood raincoat and disillusioned rubbers—

Then in come two American schoolteachers of Iowa, sisters on a big trip to Paris, they've apparently got a hotel room round the corner and aint left it except to ride the sightseeing buses which pick em up at the door, but they know this nearest restaurant and have just come down to buy a couple of oranges for tomorrow morning because the only oranges in France are apparently Valencias imported from Spain and too expensive for anything so avid as quick simple *break* of *fast*. So to my amazement I hear the first clear bell tones of American speech in a week:— "You got some oranges here?"

"*Pardon?*"—the counterman.

"There they are in that glass case," says the other gal.

"Okay—see?" pointing, "two oranges," and showing two fingers, and the counterman takes out the two oranges and puts em in a bag and says crisply thru his throat with those Arabic Parisian "r's":—

"*Trois francs cinquante.*" In other words, 35¢ an orange but the old gals dont care what it costs and besides they dont understand what he's said.

"What's *that* mean?"

"*Pardon?*"

"Alright, I'll hold out my palm and take your kwok-kowk-kwark out of it, all we want's the oranges" and the two ladies burst into peals of screaming laughter like on the porch and the cat politely removes three francs fifty centimes from her hand, leaving the change, and they walk out lucky they're not alone like that American guy—

I ask my counterman what's real good and he says Alsatian Choucroute which he brings—It's just hotdogs, potatos and sauerkraut, but such hotdogs as chew like butter and have a flavor delicate as the scent of wine, butter and garlic all cooking together and floating out a cafe kitchen door—The sauerkraut no better'n Pennsylvania, potatos we got from Maine to San Jose, but O yes I forgot:— with it all, on top, is a weird soft strip of bacon which is really like ham and is the best bite of all.

I had come to France to do nothing but walk and eat and this was my first meal and my last, ten days.

But in referring back to what I said to Pascal, as I was leaving this restaurant (paid 24 francs, or almost $5 for this simple platter) I heard a howling in the rainy boulevard—A maniacal Algerian had gone mad and was shouting at everyone and everything and was holding something I couldnt see, very small knife or object or pointed ring or something— I had to stop in the door—People hurried by scared—I didn't want to be *seen* by him hurrying away—The waiters came out and watched with me—He approached us stabbing outdoor wicker chairs as he came—The headwaiter and I looked calmly into each other's eyes as tho to say "Are we together?"—But my counterman began talking to the mad Arab, who was actually light haired and probably half French half Algerian, and it became some sort of conversation and I walked around and went home in a now-driving rain, had to hail a cab.

Romantic raincoats.

M.F.K. Fisher

M.F.K. Fisher (1908–1992), a great American miniaturist in prose, could achieve an almost Vermeer-like clarity and lucidity in her portraits of places and plates. She came to France for the first time in the 1930s, a journey she recorded in her *Long Ago in France*. Paris was not, it seems, her primary French place—Provence and Burgundy held her heart. But here, in a piece from *As They Were* (1982), she writes about the still extant (and still magnificent-looking, if not always palate-delighting) restaurant in the Gare de Lyon with the passion and precision she brought to all her writing about food. "When I write of hunger, I am really writing about love and the hunger for it," she once wrote memorably, in words that became a kind of motto for subsequent generations of American writers who, obsessed with French food and French restaurants, also believed themselves obsessed with something more. Forming with Liebling one of the two pillars of higher food writing, they make an interesting pair of opposites-of-appetite, hers for a perfect plate, his for a full one.

———

Gare de Lyon

Paris fairs and expositions, always attempted and sometimes realized on a grand scale, have been beset, at least in the twentieth century, by strikes, riots, floods, and other natural and man-made hindrances to such minor goals as opening on time. In the same way, they have left something strong and beautiful behind them, whether tangible or in men's minds and hearts.

In 1937, for instance, there was the Internationale. Strikes were an almost stylish necessity of life in those quaintly distant days before all hell broke loose, and the fair lagged in summer heat while opulent or simply eager tourists marked time in the cafés and museums; outlandish buildings were put up and torn down and picketed and sabotaged. I was there from Switzerland to meet my parents, who loved great fairs, as do most Midwesterners reared on St. Louis and Chicago and even San Francisco shivarees, and my father was excited by the violent scornful unrest in that year's Parisian air, as he had never been at home by giant mechanical toys like roller coasters.

We walked every day in the purlieus of the Exposition, to guess when a pavilion might possibly be opened or bombed. At night we looked at the lighted revolving statue of bright gold in the U.S.S.R. exhibit, but Father did not want to visit it, for vaguely political reasons. Once we went on the Seine in a *bateau-mouche*, and he was thrilled when every window in the Citroën plant was filled with striking beleaguered workers saluting us with raised fists. Nothing like that at home!

But from that fair, which never really came to life for us who waited, rose one bright star, the Guernica mural by Picasso. It was there. It was on view. It was well guarded. It was moving and terrible, and we went perhaps five times to look slowly at it, close up, far off, not talking. It was a difficult experience for my father, but one he faced with an almost voluptuous acceptance, so that we began to return compulsively to the long room where the painting unrolled itself. There were piles of rubble and discarded tools on the unfinished paths outside the building, but inside people walked silently up and down, finding parts of themselves in Guernica, even from Iowa and California.

Backwards to 1931, there was a fair called the Exposition Coloniale. As far as I know, some of it opened more or less on schedule, at least in time to assemble peculiar exotic hints of the imminent collapse of French attempts to keep their own sun shining around the clock on territorial land grabs. What else could it try to demonstrate? Why else would a reputedly thrifty nation spend hundreds of thousands of francs re-creating African villages and Indo-Chinese temples for visitors to gape at? From now in Time, it all seemed then to have some of the luminous gaiety of a terminal cancer patient's final defiant fling. I lurched about on camels, and watched silent backs squatting in front of their phony huts to carve cabalistic masks. Everywhere there was a heady perfume of leather, of raw silk and wool, of unknown spicy foods. As in the Internationale that came so few years afterwards, the Coloniale had a dappled green magic, under the summer leaves, and left behind it more than its rare polished woods and supple cloth.

But both those fairs seemed unreal. They were *there*, in spite of strikes and riots and general political uncertainty, but where are their physical traces? Where is the cardboard Angkor Wat by now? The painting of Guernica still exists, but where is the long shady building that harbored it? Where is the golden statue that revolved seductively, almost lewdly, above the Soviet pavilion? In the end, where are the dreams and wars that spawned all that pomp?

It was perhaps different in 1900. The hunger and shame of the Franco-Prussian War had been half forgotten by a new generation, and the Dreyfus Affair seemed temporarily under wraps. Paris needed and indeed deserved a circus. Architects were appointed, perhaps subconsciously, who could evoke all the rich weightiness of the Third Empire, before the late and current troubles, and they put together some pleasure domes for their fair that still enchant us: two palaces, the Grand and the Petit; the bridge across the Seine named for Alexander the Third; best of all, to some at least, the Gare de Lyon.

It happened before my time, and the French accounts are understandably vague about how and when that World's Fair finally ground into action. It seems natural, by now, that the enormous glassy station was formally inaugurated a year late, but it is still there to prove that in 1901, on April 17, the President of the Republic and countless international notables gathered in it to declare that the Gare de Lyon was indeed a reality.

No doubt other very solemn things have happened there in almost a century, like treaty signings and top-level hanky-panky connected with both railroads and people, and municipal banquets, but it is hard to imagine that they did not contain a certain element of enjoyment, in that magical place. Surely the ceremonial toasts tasted better there. . . .

As far as I can know or learn, no other railroad station in the world manages so mysteriously to cloak with compassion the anguish of departure and the dubious ecstasies of return and arrival. Any waiting room in the world is filled with all this, and I have sat in many of them and accepted it, and I know from deliberate acquaintance that the whole human experience is more bearable at the Gare de Lyon in Paris than anywhere else. By now the public rooms on the train level are more plastic-topped, chromium-benched, than in the first days of wood everywhere, with iron and brass fittings. But the porters seem to stay sturdy and aware, and there is a near-obsolete courtesy at the "snack bars," even five minutes before commute time.

For me, it began to come to life in 1937. I was there often, from 1929 on, always one more ant scuttling for a certain track, a cheap train south to Dijon, a luxury train to Lausanne. The station was something to run through. It was a grimy glass tunnel, and I felt glad when we pulled out and headed south.

But in 1937, when I could meet my parents in La Ville Lumière, I grew almost shockingly aware of the station. I went there early that twilight, to wait for their train. On the quai that looked far out under the glass roof and along all the gleaming tracks was a café, part of the big noisy bar-brasserie inside. There were little trees in long boxes, to sweeten the air and catch the soot, and the tables were of that grey-white marble that apparently was created by Nature solely for cafe tabletops. I sat waiting, drinking a brandy and water, realizing suddenly that I was not in a station, but in a place.

My family arrived, worn after a rough crossing, and it was not for perhaps ten days that I went back. My father was going down to Nice. For the first of countless times I cunningly arranged our getting around Paris so that we would have to *wait* for the train to slide in under the glass roof along the silver track, so that I could be there . . . in the place.

It was one of the pleasantest times I'd ever known with a man I'd always respected and loved. We were two people, suddenly. We sat behind the boxes filled with gritty treelings, and although it was only late morning we drank slowly at brandy again, with water and casual talk and mostly a quiet awareness of the loveliness of the great station.

It was not noisy. It was not stuffy. People did not look sad or even hurried. Trains whistled and chugged in and out, slid voluptuously toward us and then stopped. Big boards lit up here and there, high above the tracks, telling people where to go, when. A porter came to tell me that it was time for the gentleman to board.

"This is the way to do it! How can a railroad station be so beautiful?" my father asked happily, and I knew that I had marked off another mile in my life.

Then there was a war, and when I went back to Paris in the early fifties, I scuttled through without more than a shy shamed look at the glassed roof that the Occupiers had found too essential to destroy. I did not permit the station's magic to take hold again until about the mid-sixties, when I went alone to Paris, for the first time in my life: no husbands—lovers—parents—children . . . I was on a writing assignment, and I asked to be lodged in the attic of a hotel on the Seine in a room I liked most. My husband and I had planned, before the War and he died, to rent two little connecting rooms there and make a kind of pied-à-terre, a place where we could leave books and be warmer than in Switzerland. This all turned impossible, and when I went back so much later I felt scared, so that I asked to take one of those familiar rooms. And in the other, to my astonishment, lived a person I admired deeply named Janet Flanner. It was fine. My husband would have liked it.

And so it happened that I reported, that summer, to my friend about my love affair with the Gare de Lyon, and she in turn decided to take her own look, her view she admitted had always been sketchy in spite of some forty years in Paris, and with due reflection she reported the whole thing to André Malraux, who then controlled the governmental wires that could declare a French relic or monument legitimately "historical," and therefore supposedly immune to further human destruction.

Malraux had a rare and passionate belief in "the redemptive power of beauty," and seemed to know that a minor living art form is far more vital than a major dead one. From what I have been told, he started at once to safeguard the shabby old restaurant in the Gare de Lyon, so that by now it is a twinkling *Monument Historique*, worthy of all that was opulently cheerful, generously vulgar and delightful, about *la Belle Époque*.

Things were different from my lives before, in the mid-sixties. The job demanded that I go between Paris and the South quite often, and I was looked at as freakish because I insisted on taking the Mistral train from the station instead of flying. A waste of time, of energy, I was told by my bosses. But nobody could understand how totally renewing of many strengths it was for me to go there at least two hours before the beautiful train pulled out, to eat a slow breakfast, and then slide southward through the forests and farms and into Burgundian vineyards and then suddenly, like an explosion, into the Midi below Lyon . . . and on down, through poignantly familiar towns like Avignon to the spot past the Étang de Berre, just before the Quartier de St. Louis in Marseille, where there is a mysterious flash of gold from the tiny needle of Notre Dame de la Garde.

From then on it was less emotional sailing, with cliffs and twisted pines and strange villas, until I got to the familiar little station in Cannes and the resumption of my professional life, but always I felt brave enough for it, after the private meal in Paris.

The main room of the First-Class Restaurant-Buffet at the Gare de Lyon seems to run the whole length of what to us Americans is the second floor. Actually, if one enters by way of the noble staircase from the inside quai of the station, there are several rooms of varying importance to the left, closed and reserved for board meetings and other mysterious gatherings. Mostly, pundits and tycoons heading for them use a smaller staircase that goes up under the Clock Tower, and never set foot in the enormous Restaurant. (The Big Ben Bar and the cloakrooms are conveniently to their right as they enter.)

To the rest of us travelers, going up the staircase from the quai is much more exciting than the handy little "back stairs," and the huge room sweeps out, dream-like and yet inviting, and across from us the lace curtains move faintly in the drafts from the great square below.

Down at the far end, to our right, the Train Bleu is properly hushed and somewhat more elegant, if that is possible, than what any traveler can expect in the main room, only tacitly separated from its little offshoot. Service is swift or slow, according to one's logistical needs, and there is a comfortable feeling of *bourgeois* polish and sparkle everywhere: clean linen and brass, waxed floors, good plain food as well as a few fastuous dishes. Madame Maigret would approve of it. So, I feel sure, would Brillat-Savarin, if it were not some 150 years too late. . . .

It is one of the most amazing public dining rooms I have ever seen, or even imagined. The ceiling is very high and elaborate. The windows are tall, looking on one side upon a goodly part of Paris, and then to the right into and under the endless stretch of grey glass roof over all the tracks that come to a dead stop down below . . . Switzerland, Italy, Spain, the Near East, all France to the south. . . .

The walls, between and above the great lace-hung windows, are covered with more than forty huge murals of every possible scenic delight that the Paris-Lyon-Mediterranean trains could offer their travelers at the turn of the century, mostly peopled by plump Edwardian diplomats in top hats, and famous divas and courtesans in filmy garden frocks or even bathing dresses, all frolicking discreetly against breath-taking landscapes.

By now, the paintings have been cleaned, and their elaborate frames retouched. The lace curtains have been mended and starched and rehung, and the three monumental ceilings with their "crammed and gorgeous" paintings have been pulled back to life in our comparatively clean air, after years of collecting soot from the old steam trains below. And all the elegant *bancs* and chairs, comfortable in dark soft leather, have been refurbished, along with the sumptuous but functional brass racks for luggage and hats, and the tall lampstands along the middle aisle.

Perhaps best, at least for the waiters, is that the endless polished floors underfoot have been strengthened or repaired, so that there is no longer the steady creaking that I first noticed, when I listened there in the sixties.

I am not sure, by now, why I first decided to go to this station two hours before train time. Perhaps I wanted to sit where I had once been with my father. Perhaps I wanted to ready my spirit for the new job in the South. A porter (oh, a fine man, an angel in a blue soft blouse! I remember him clearly tall, past middle age, oddly protective of me as was exactly right on that day . . .) told me when I asked to follow him to the café on the inside quai that he thought I would be better off upstairs, where he would come for me in ample time before the Mistral left. I felt docile, and followed him under the Clock Tower and past the end of the big noisy brasserie-cafe on the ground floor and up some back stairs, into the shrouded silent corridors of the First-Class Restaurant. I had never been there before.

He pounded on ahead of me with my luggage, and a waiter who knew him came from somewhere past the deserted old Big Ben Bar. My porter went straight down the middle aisle of what seemed like a silent gaudy cathedral to me, and stopped toward the far end, which as I remember was being remodeled for the new Train Bleu section.

"Madame is hungry," he said in a mild way to his friend. "She is taking the Mistral. I'll be back." I felt helpless but undismayed. This was part of important private history, I sensed.

The waiter was surprisingly young to be working in such an awesome monument. He gave me a menu, and l settled myself in the huge sunny temple while he went down to the newsstand where I had planned to sit in all the sooty racket behind a spindly box tree, drinking *café au lait*. When he came up again with two very solemn dailies, I told him that I would like bread and butter, Parma ham, and a half-bottle of a *brut* champagne that seemed quite expensive to me and that is no longer on the excellent wine list. He looked pleased, and scudded off, with the floor under him making a fine high racket in the emptiness.

In 1967 or whenever that was, I felt dismal about the state of bread in Paris, and had not yet found that it would be almost as bad everywhere, and I decided then that the fresh loaf served at the Gare de Lyon was the best I had tasted since before World War II. (It still is.) The butter was impeccable, not something from a tinfoil wrapping marked with either optimism or blasphemy *Beurre d'Isigny*. The ham was genuine, perhaps tasting of violets on the wishful tongue. The champagne seemed one of the best I had ever drunk.

The waiter saw that I was more interested in where I was than in where the grim newspaper editorials were telling me to be, and he stood tactfully beside the table while I asked him about some of the murals. He knew a lot, in a controlled but fervent way that I had long recognized in devotees. Now and then he flicked at one of my crumbs, to stay professional.

Then the handsome, thoughtful, strong, blue-bloused, honest, punctual porter beckoned to me from the gigantic doorway that opened onto cloakrooms and the Big Ben Bar and the far closed doors of a Belle Époque palace, and I left without sadness, knowing that I would return. I turned back at the end of the corridor, and the waiter lifted the bottle of champagne where I had left one glassful, and bowed and smiled. I felt fine about everything, even my job . . . generous, warm, floaty.

The next time that I cannily arranged to be in Paris so that I would have to take the Mistral again, I went somewhat earlier to the station. I forget whether there were only two waiters that morning, or whether it was later on, when I suddenly looked up from my habitual little meal and saw four or five of them drifting around the table. Mostly they were young, but there were some old ones, too, and they had decided they knew me, and what they had apparently decided to share with me was horrendous.

The Restaurant, they said, was doomed. *"One"* (*"they"* in our lingo) had decided that it was too old to live. The famous lace curtains were in tatters. The paintings were out of date, and filthy with some seventy years of soot and general neglect and pollution. The floors buckled under the weight of the men's trays. Yes, a promising young chef, probably a madman like them all, had opened the Train Bleu. But who but stunned starved travelers would come up to such a drab old wreck as this? "It is a crime of neglect," they said furiously, very quietly, as they stood around my table. "It must not happen. This beautiful thing must not be condemned to death . . ."

I looked at them, so proud, and at the gleaming glass and silver and linen and at my little meal, and then past all of it to the bedraggled lace, the dim dirty light, the flaking gold leaf above us. I would like to think that I said firmly, "Something will be done." The truth is that I probably whimpered a little as I let the men bustle me down the stairs to the train for the South.

I talked about all this, though, with my Paris neighbor, Janet. I told her about how passionately concerned the waiters were. And it went on from there. And by now the Gare de Lyon is in comparatively fine fettle, no way an aging beauty revived by hormones, but rather a mature female who has survived some unpredictable if foregone setbacks with good health and gracefulness.

Much is going on under the five storeys of the mansarded structure of 1900 (". . . a fairly discreet evocation of the Belle Époque," one government document describes it with equal discretion), and within a few years most of suburban Paris will commute from six deep layers of artful stations being burrowed out, for various environmental reasons. Currently, ridiculous bright-orange awnings in a garishly scooped shape have been placed over the seven majestic windows on the "Paris" side of the Restaurant floor, but doubtless they will fade, and fall off.

The interior style of this giant station is "pure 1900," whatever that may mean. On the ground floor thousands of people push in and out, buying tickets and meeting uncles and going somewhere, and the café-brasserie is always open and crowded. On the "train" side, the little trees in front of the marble-topped tables were sparse or gone when I last saw them in 1974, and the newsstand did not have its old inky glamour. This could be partly because I too was older and Colette and Simenon had stopped churning out their paperbacks, and partly because travelers do not feel as leisurely as they did when I once sat there with my father. By now there are snack-bar counters inside the busy buffet, and people drink and eat hastily. But a graceful stairway still leads upward, under the glass sky, and instead of one's being alone in the bright huge Restaurant, there seem always to be some *people*. They read newspapers or talk quietly at odd hours like my own; the place buzzes gently, like a rococo hive, all carvings and paintings and gilt.

Conceivably gentlemen throng at proper hours around the Big Ben Bar, where "all the cocktails of the Belle Époque" are said to be served . . . along with the British (and by now international) substitute of whiskey and water for the sweet pinkish drinks of 1900. (I have never seen a barman there, but then, neither have I seen more than a few travelers in the Restaurant at nine-thirty in the morning . . .)

Once in the seventies I ate an early lunch rather than a late breakfast in the Grande Salle. It was moderately filled with middle-class people who looked as if they were going somewhere soon, which of course they were. They ate quickly but seriously, in general the *plat du jour*, and read newspapers or peeked at their watches, or talked quietly with Aunt

Matilda, who was going to see her first grandchild in Montélimar. The waiters glided miles and miles on the gleaming new floors. The incredibly long lace curtains pushed in and out over half-open windows onto the square, but there seemed little city noise. The ceiling with its three enormous murals looked somewhat lower since it had been cleaned, and the walls glowed richly. I walked about, looking at the paintings I liked best, sipping a "Kir au Chablis," and the waiters smiled at me as if they knew we shared a fine secret, which of course they did not know at all. Or did they?

I drank a Grand Cru Chablis, three years in bottle, feeling as extravagant as one of the well-kept women in the glamorous murals high above me, and ate a fine little soufflé of shellfish and mushrooms. Wood strawberries were listed, and their mysterious perfume would have suited the sudden sensuality of the meal, but the waiter shook his head. So I ate dark small raspberries with the rest of the wine, and leaned back to look at the ceiling crammed with color, in carved gilded curlicues, high above the incredible walls covered with their gaudily leering murals, all gold-scarlet-blue, a gigantic jumble of snowy Alps, fishing boats, trains, women, politicians, vineyards . . .

Even in its dingier days since 1901, the Gare de Lyon had stayed alive, I thought beautifully, and had made tired travelers stretch and smile. It had, one baffled but delighted writer said, "great harmony in spite of its decadent extravagance."

Yes, that was it: a strange massive *harmony*!

I thought of my friend Janet, who had grown angry with herself after she went there to lunch quietly alone, a double wonder for a person of her gregarious volatility. She felt baffled about not using, ever in her long years in Paris, more than the quick dashes through the station and onto the quais for trains going south to Lyon and then east and west and on further. She groaned, and scolded helplessly at human blindness.

Often people try to keep secret the charm of a tiny restaurant one thousand light-years from nowhere around the corner, in case there will not be a free table the next time they are hungry for its inimitable broth or brew. But who can hide the secret of a colossus like the Gare de Lyon, where thousands of people rush or amble through every day, according to the trains they must catch or leave or even think about?

Inside, under the misty glass, in the music of wheels and horns and whistled strange signals, there are signs guiding passengers to the toilets, the newsstand, the café, the Buffet, the upstairs Restaurant, the Train Bleu. There is no attempt to hide any of this vital and perhaps aesthetic information.

It comes down, I suppose, to a question of where one really chooses to be, and for how long. This is of course true of all such traffic hubs as railway stations, but nowhere is there one with a second floor like that of the Gare de Lyon, so peculiarly lacy and golden. It has, in an enormous way, something of the seduction of a full-blown but respectable lady, post-Renoir but pre-Picasso, waiting quietly in full sunlight for a pleasant chat with an old lover . . .

Glen Ellen, 1979

Diana Vreeland

Diana Vreeland (1903–1989), the leading fashion editor of her time, was actually born in Paris, and came to the United States only in 1911. Her most memorable French journeys, though, were those she made as a representative of *Harper's Bazaar*, and of the triumphant American fashion market (and, soon, fashion industry) at the time of the reopening of the French collections after World War II. Her voice and manner, captured beautifully (with the help of George Plimpton) in her autobiography *D. V.* (1984), were those of one who dictated, with more irony than was always understood, French lessons to American women.

from

D. V.

I remember the night Reed and I arrived in Paris right after the war. Oh, how it had changed! Potato flour. To think that one was eating French bread, the great French triumph, made of potatoes! Everyone was in wooden shoes. *Clack clack clack.* You could tell the time of day from your hotel room by the sound of wooden soles on the pavement. If there was a great storm of them, it meant that it was lunch hour and people were leaving their offices for the restaurants. Then there'd be another great clatter when they returned to the office, et cetera et cetera. . . . The day we arrived it just happened to be Bastille Day, although we hadn't planned it that way. The fountains on the place de la Concorde were playing for the first time since the liberation. And we drove all over Paris. We went everywhere—Chaillot, St. Denis . . . I forget the names of the *quartiers* above Montmartre, but we went to all of them. Every little square had the most ghastly little band playing the same ghastly little tune.

Strangers were dancing with strangers. Girls were dancing with girls. Strange young men who looked haunted—as if they hadn't been out of a cellar in years—were dancing with fat old women. It was raining. No one was speaking. It was hideous—and marvelous.

At what must have been four o'clock in the morning, I suddenly realized I was hungry. So we picked this little street above Montmartre, and on it was a restaurant that looked awfully nice, but the shutters were closed. So we banged and banged on the shutters until a man came out.

"We've had nothing to eat," I said. "We've just arrived from America and we've been spending this wonderful night in Paris, but we're so *hungry*."

"*Mais entrez, madame et monsieur!*" the man said. "*Entrez! C'est une auberge!*"

I've never forgotten that, because, for me, France has always been an *auberge*—for feelings, for emotion, and for so many other things. Reed and I spoke of that experience for years after. The man opened up the door so wide that he could not have made a greater gesture if it had been the Hall of Mirrors!

Paris! I was so excited. But Paris had changed. The world had changed.

I realized this when I went for my fittings. You don't know what a part of life fittings once were. Remember I told you that before the war I used to have three fittings on a *nightgown*—and I'm not *that* deformed.

After the war you were no longer fitted for nightgowns.

Other things had changed. Couture before the war wasn't that expensive. It was hard to pay more than two hundred dollars for a dress. I had been what was known as a *mannequin du monde*—meaning "of the world"—because I was out every night in every nightclub, seen, seen, seen. . . . I was always given by the *maison de couture* for being a *mannequin du monde* what was known as a *prix jeune fille*—that is to say, they would give me the dress to wear and keep. The phrase no longer exists in the French vocabulary. The first thing I asked after the war was: "Does it still exist—as an expression?" I wasn't hinting around.

"Absolutely not!" I was told. "It's as dead as mud."

*   *   *

There's no such thing as a slack French face. Haven't you ever noticed that? I've given this a lot of thought, and I think it's because the French have to exercise their jaws and the inside of their mouths so much just to get the words *out*. The vowels demand so much. In fact, the French language has a lot to do with the handsomeness and the beauty of the French face. Talk one line in French and the whole inside of your face moves, whereas the English language leaves you a bit slack. I'll give you an example: Look in the mirror. Now say *"Ché-rie!"* Did you see what your face just did? Did you see all the exercise you got? Now try "Dear." No exercise there. You're really on a dead horse. Don't you love that phrase? A friend of mine and I once got out of a movie house across from Bloomingdale's and we stepped into a taxi standing there at curbside. A guy leaned in the back window and said, "Hey, you're on a dead horse. No driver." We looked, and sure enough there wasn't anybody in the front seat. Heaven knows where he was. In the movie house? Perhaps he was off having a hamburger.

But to get on with it, there never was a more French face than de Gaulle's. France was . . . de Gaulle. And, as you know, the French like the French very much. De Gaulle was full of the old *amour-propre*, all right—he *loved* himself. And he was my hero, as he was for much of France and much of the world for many, many years.

In the middle sixties he'd fallen out of favor. I'd just arrived in Paris to cover the collections, and I was dining with the young married set—all very charming but rather *comme il faut*, shall we say. I was full of my own worth. So I said, "You know, when anything extraordinary happens here, you can't take it. Now take de Gaulle—"

"Oh!" They went to pieces. "You're not going to try and sell us *de Gaulle?*"

"I'm not selling," I said, "I'm only telling you."

"But we're thinking of our *country!*"

"I am, too. I don't live here, but I know heroes. You've got to have a hero. You've got to have a face. You've got to have a leading man. I'll give you an example: If *everyone* at this table was responsible for ordering the dinner, would we ever get a bite to eat?"

Then I went on: "How many people will come through the corridors—through the *bloodstream*—of history in the last fifty years the way de Gaulle will? Who fought so that France would continue to exist? When there was no place for him to fight here, who went to London and waited like an errand boy for Churchill to listen to him? Why, I don't understand why you're treating him the way you are. Do you think that whatever is bourgeois and ordinary and 'so what?' is great? Anything *extra*ordinary . . . that's really what France stands for—the supreme logic of the extraordinary!"

I really gave them a bit of what for!

The next day I got a call from one of the chaps at the table.

"Diana, we believe in desire and passion. When anyone loves with your passion, they should be closer to the person they love, so I've arranged for you to go to his press conference. I will hold your seat for you. Come as soon as you can."

As soon as I'd hung up the phone, I turned to Reed and told him what had happened. I said to Reed, "Chanel is opening this afternoon at three-thirty—I can't possibly do it!"

"Why?" he said.

"Well," I said, "because Chanel is . . . I mean, after all, I'm *paid* to cover these collections."

I had the most marvelous husband. He was always on the right side. He always knew what to do and what to say to me.

"You *are*? What's the matter with you? You're so cracked about this fellow de Gaulle, and you get this unique opportunity, everything arranged for you, and you bring up *Chanel*, whose clothes you've only been looking at since 1925!"

So I sent a message to Mademoiselle Chanel saying that, unfortunately, I'd broken a tooth on a piece of bread (which was a very good excuse—all Americans *do* on French crusts) and that I couldn't attend.

Well, I went to the press conference. I arrived at the Elysée Palace, but I didn't have my passport. *"Passeport, madame, passeport!"* the gendarmes said. It was rather windy, so their capes sort of blew this way and I sort of went that way and went right on in. How could they keep me out?

I took my seat in the second row. And then, in the most beautiful voice—trained, I have no doubt, by the Comédie Française—my hero said, *"Mesdames, messieurs. . . ."*

I mean, the *beauty* of the language! The *pleading* for the morals! He had the most beautiful diction. And he had the hands of the Comédie Française, too—the hands of a leader, the hands, almost, of a messiah. It was the most thrilling experience.

I also made a great discovery. In the usual photograph you see of de Gaulle from the sixties he's almost totally bald. When I saw him I realized that his hairline was much closer to his face—a very distinguished hairline framing a small, completely refined, totally French face. Now, obviously, he wasn't done up for the photographs—this is the general of an army and the President of France! There was no monkey business *there*.

When I got back to the Crillon, where we were staying, after these splendid hours of being a part of this glorious man, my hero, there were

red roses waiting for me—red red roses. They were from Coco Chanel—
the kind Chanel always sent, the kind that open, not the kind that shrivel
up into a little walnut and die—and amongst them was the most charming note in Mademoiselle's own hand: *"Chère Diane, My plane waits for you
at Le Bourget. It will take you to Lausanne, where you will see my dentist, the
greatest in the world."*

Of course, I immediately had to send my own flowers and a note saying what a charming thought it had been on her part and that in the tooth
department it hadn't been as bad as I had originally thought, et cetera, et
cetera, and I would be able to come and see her show the next afternoon.

The next day she'd forgotten all about the tooth. I didn't have to
explain *anything*. Which was fortunate. Chanel could not abide de Gaulle
and shouted it from every rooftop.

Coco Chanel always fitted me in her private atelier six flights up in the
house on the rue Cambon. First, there was the beautiful rolling staircase
up to the salon floor—the famous mirrored staircase—and after that, you
were practically on a *stepladder* for five more flights. It used to kill me. As
soon as I'd arrive at the front door of the house, there'd be someone waiting, saying, *"Mademoiselle vous attend, madame."*

My God, I used to get up there so breathless! And then I'd get fitted.
Coco was a nut on armholes. She never, ever got a armhole quite, *quite* perfect, the way she wanted it. She was always snipping and taking out
sleeves, driving the tailors absolutely crazy. She'd put pins in me so I'd be
contorted, and she'd be talking and talking and giving me all sorts of
philosophical observations, such as "Live with rigor and vigor" or "Grow
old like a man," and I'd say, "I think most men grow old like women,
myself," and she'd say, "No, you're wrong, they've got logic, they've got
a reality to them"—with my arm up in the air the whole time! Then if
she *really* wanted to talk, she'd put pins in under both arms so I simply
couldn't move, much less get a word in!

She watched the collections from the top of the mirrored stairs. She
used to crouch there all alone, and when you went up to see her afterward,
she knew exactly what you thought.

She was extraordinary. The *alertness* of the woman! The *charm*! You
would have fallen in love with her. She was mesmerizing, strange, alarming, witty . . . you can't compare anyone with Chanel. They haven't got
the *chien*! Or the chic. She was French, don't forget—totally French!

Where she came from in France is anyone's guess. She said one thing one day and another thing the next. She was a peasant—and a genius. Peasants and geniuses are the only people who count, and she was both.

The Duke of Westminster and Grand Duke Dmitri were the two men in her life. Between them she learned everything there is to know about luxury, and no one's ever had a greater sense of luxury than Coco Chanel.

The Grand Duke Dmitri was *the* handsomest . . . the hang of his suits! His leg in a *boot!* Oh *God!* He was more interested in fishing and shooting—like all Russian men—but he was a beauty! Now, whether he killed Rasputin or not, who knows? He never lived out of his father's palace until he came to Paris, and then I don't think he had a bed to himself, he was so poor. Chanel discovered him and reinstated him; she got him beautiful rooms and wonderful valets and marvelous flannels and all the things that a gentleman likes. And from him she learned all about great jewels and great living. Then she went off with the Duke of Westminster. He was desperately in love with her, but she refused to marry him. She pointed out that there had already been three Duchesses of Westminster, but there would always be just one Coco Chanel. She learned about afternoon teas from him and about magnificently maintained country houses. She rode with him and became a splendid horsewoman. The Duke had about seven properties in England, the greatest property owner in the world save the Russians in the days of the Czars. Such elegance! Every inch a Duke! He had his shoelaces ironed every day. Insisted on it. But then that's nothing. Shoelaces were nothing to iron.

He was named after a horse—Bendor, who won the Derby. Lots of people were named after horses. One of my great friends in London was Lady Morvyth Menson. I asked, "For goodness' sakes, where'd you get this name Morvyth?" She said, "Well, you see, my father was off racing somewhere when I was born. My mother was dying, and there was no one in charge but the servants. 'We've got to name this child *something.*'" So they called her Morvyth after one of the polo ponies. Terribly pretty Welsh name, isn't it?

Well, most people get most things from something—I don't say *everything*, but most things. From the English, and from her life with the Duke of Westminster, Chanel learned luxury, and she copied the clean turnout of Eton boys and the men at shoots. And from Russia she copied the Romanov pearls. Dmitri got out of Russia the way you'd get out of a fire— but he had the pearls. He gave them to her, and she made copies of them which the women of the world have known and worn ever since, whether artificial or cultured—that long, long string. . . .

And the Russian clothes! I remember now that Coco used to go to Moscow quite regularly in the thirties. When I was there a few years ago with Tom Hoving, arranging the show of Russian costumes for the Metropolitan, I went to the Historical Museum, where I saw all the rich peasant dresses. When I got back to the hotel, Tom asked me what I'd seen. "Well," I said, "I saw a lot of marvelous clothes—most of which I've worn myself." He looked at me as if I were demented. "Actually," I said, "*literally*. . . . These were Chanel's clothes of the thirties—the big skirts, the small jackets, the headdresses. . . ."

A woman dressed by Chanel back in the twenties and the thirties— like a woman dressed by Balenciaga in the fifties and sixties—walked into a room and had a dignity, an authority, a thing beyond a question of taste.

I'm not speaking of the late Chanel, who amused herself by dressing the streets of Paris. When she reopened after the war, she wanted to see her suits all over the place. They say she showed the clothes to the copyists before she showed them to the customers or the press. She had reached the point in life where she'd done everything—*everything*—and she had to amuse herself.

These postwar suits of Chanel were designed God knows *when*, but the tailoring, the line, the shoulders, the underarms, the *jupe*—never too short, never making a fool of a woman when she sits down—is even today the right thing to wear.

When I first became friends with her in the middle thirties, Coco was extraordinarily good-looking. She was a bright, dark gold color—wide faced, with a snorting nose, just like a little bull, and deep Dubonnet-red cheeks. Before the war she lived in a house on the Faubourg St. Honoré. It had an enormous garden with fountains, the most beautiful salons opening on the garden, and something like fifty-four Coromandel screens shaping these rooms into the most extraordinary *allées* of charm. There she received the *world*. It was a proper society she had around her—artists, musicians, poets—and everyone was fascinated by her. Cocteau adored her, Bébé Bérard adored her, Picasso . . . who in those days drove around Paris with his latest mistress by his side in a bright yellow Hispano-Suiza with a hammer and sickle painted on the side. Definitely part of the scene!

Coco Chanel became a figure in all of this—Paris society—entirely through wit and taste. Her taste was what you'd call *formidable*. She was

irresistible. Absolutely. About a year before she died, I got I an invitation
to dine with her at her apartment on the rue Cambon. It was for the Duke
and Duchess of Windsor. Niki de Gunzburg had called me up and said,
"Did you get this invitation from Coco? Well, then, I'll take you, because
we're only going to be six, and we'll have a wonderful time."

I'd been so often in that marvelous drawing room of hers, that splendid dining room. The fire was burning. Wonderful bronze animals on
the floor.

I had never seen those rooms the way they were that night. Everything was in a glow. The fire was discreet because it wasn't that cold, but
it was Paris and therefore damp. Niki and I were the first to arrive. Then
the Windsors were announced. Coco went forward, and I had never seen
a woman look at a man the way she welcomed him. I can't put it into
words. Their drinks were brought to them. They never looked away from
each other. The Duke was just as absorbed as she was.

They went and sat on a sofa, and in low, completely joyous mono-
tones they talked to each other. No one else existed for them. The rest of
us could have been out on the street for all they cared. Time went by.
Finally Hervé Mille, a charming man who was one of the six, said, "Coco,
I thought we were all invited here to *dine*."

Coco turned from the Duke—the first time—and batted her eyes at
the butler, and we proceeded into the dining room. She was on his right
at dinner . . . and they started to talk again. Obviously, they had once had
a great romantic hour together. Well, I mean, it was clear to the dullest
eye. I have never seen such intensity in my life.

The next morning I was sleeping a little late. When I asked the operator "Are there any calls?" she said, *"Oui, Madame la Duchesse de Windsor a
téléphoné cinq fois, madame."* She'd been calling since eight o'clock in the
morning; you know, she never sleeps at all. When I reached her, she said,
"My God, Diana, will we ever see the likes of that dinner again!"

The Duchess wasn't at all disturbed. She couldn't wait to get me on
the phone in the morning to have a good talk about it.

When Chanel died—she had never been taken ill; she'd finished her
collection two or three weeks before—her secretary approached Susan
Train of French *Vogue* with a little black velvet bag and a note that read:
"Pour Mme Vreeland de la part de Mademoiselle."

In the bag were the pearl earrings Chanel always wore. These were
real—though she seldom wore real jewels. Actually, on the day she died,

as far as we know, her *great* collection of jewels—including the famous Romanov pearls Dmitri had given her—disappeared off the *face of the earth*.

Isn't it curious, though, that she gave these earrings to me? I'd always been *slightly* shy of her. And of course she was at times *impossible*. She had an utterly malicious tongue. Once, apparently, she'd said that I was the most pretentious woman she'd ever met. But that was Coco—she said a lot of things. So many things are said in this world, and in the end it makes no difference. Coco was never a *kind* woman . . . she was a *monstre sacré*. But she was the most interesting person *I've* ever met.

One night Coco was going to stay in New York on her way to Paris from Hawaii. I said, "Would you like to come for dinner on your way through?" She said, "No, no, no. Too strenuous. I'm too tired. I'm too bored! I can't wait to get back to Paris." Then there was a phone call saying, "Mademoiselle would love to come for dinner if she doesn't have to talk." I said there would be only four of us; she didn't even have to come to the table—but I would so love to see her. She didn't come often to this country; I think she came three times in all. In those days the French seldom crossed the Atlantic. I have no idea why the French complain about travel. Of course, they complain about everything . . . including France.

Dorothea Tanning

Born in Galesburg, Illinois, which she described as a place "where nothing ever happens except the wallpaper," Dorothea Tanning (b. 1910) is the perfect American avant-garde pilgrim, gifted Midwest girl division. Becoming in the 1940s one of the leading American surrealist painters, her relationship with and eventual marriage to the artist Max Ernst brought her right into the center of the French avant-garde at one of its highest periods. In this excerpt from her lovely memoir *Birthday* (1986) she conjures up that world as seen not from its curiosity-seeking fringe, as in almost every other American case, but from its living center. Note her perfect sentence about Dada founder Tristan Tzara: "He refutes his poverty with that monocle." Note also that her favorite haunt, the restaurant Aux Charpentiers, is still alive and kicking and more or less intact, all these decades later. Paris really is sometimes a perfectly still feast.

---

from

Birthday

The Paris winter of that first year is stringent. Poets and peasants alike, hunched in stiff, hard overcoats, haunt the café, hoping to hear of a room, half a room, somewhere, anywhere except the hotel. The hotel too is hunched and stiff with cold. We are lent an apartment with studio on the quai Saint-Michel. It has damask *tentures* and handsome rugs. From its lofty balcony we look down at the superb sweep of the Seine, flowing between us and the Cathedral of Notre Dame.

This stylish pad that we were privileged to inhabit for two months, January and February, was dependent for heat on two delicate porcelain stoves, pretty little things called *mirus*, which had a distressing way of simply going out instead of burning the coal we heaped into them. Outdoors, on the side of our number thirteen, a tall column of yellow ice (from the top-floor toilet) clung like a painted waterfall. As pipes burst so did our bubble. Braving the icy studio, Max's hand did not thaw enough to grasp a brush.

In the salon we sit tight on the satin chairs, bundled in sweaters, coats, boots, a cold marble chessboard between us. Mirrors sparkle like ice cubes while in the kitchen drops of grease congeal white on the pans. We make tèa, gallons of hot tea and Max scratches a hole in the frost on the windowpane. Yes, the Seine is frozen over.

"*Allons! Les misérables.*" There she is, our *concierge*, our life line who, a week later, wangles us our own space: two tiny rooms under the *mansarde*, with comfy stove and lumpy bed. Our first Paris home. Attained, they would say, by means of five flights of stairs. Not minded at all, especially going down, for it meant that we would sit in the warm café glassed in for winter, with stove, stovepipe, chessboards (you brought your own pieces) and gray, milky coffee.

Soon Marcel Z., a chess-playing friend, will arrive. Handshakes all around. We play and he defeats me with ease and much gloating. The hot smell of damp overcoats huddled in the corner like sheep out of the rain. The lovely, steamy silence broken only by hard-thinking sighs or my opponent drumming (unfairly, I think) with his fingers on the formica table. The short winter afternoon gives up trying; lights go on in the boulevard and go out in the boutiques across the street where tradesmen, coming out, bring down their iron curtains with a grinching crash, lock them at the bottom, and walk away.

Time for dinner, more handshakes, *au revoir* and the Restaurant Charpentier around the corner, a place of high understanding and low prices. Our own Man Ray is there. American in *béret basque*, our wedding twin, hovered by his Julie, soft-spoken sprite, light of his life. "They smashed the window," he sadly tells us. A little gallery had been showing his objects. The by-now famous metronome, the housewife's iron sprouting tacks, the *Pain peint*, a loaf of French bread painted blue. And in the Paris night hooligans had destroyed them. DEGENERATE, they had scrawled. "My things utterly ruined," said Man. He always said "my things": objects, photographs, paintings.

Scion of this restaurant dynasty and whirlwind waiter was Ern*est*, who knew everything, it would seem, about the U.S.A.—mountains, populations, rivers, presidents, the sort of information found in almanacs and reburied in them at once. "*Tiens, connaissez-vous les capitals?*" And he would duck his head to my ear as he set down the steaming ragout, to reel off the names of the capitals of our states, thus embarrassing us all who knew not. He would go there one day, he said. Perhaps he is here now.

On the boulevard Saint Germain those soft evenings rarely failed to bring their surprises. There, lit by the glow of café terraces and cruising cars would loom the face of some friend, Wifredo Lam, Roland Penrose, in town for a day, Sam Francis or Man Ray. Thus would begin for us all an unexpected evening, over *couscous* or *pot-au-feu*, it didn't matter; with or without tablecloths, but always supplied with wine and the antic story.

It can be said with truth that I learned my French from Madame Guyot, our *concierge*. With her dovelike voice, her immense gentleness, her superb *blanquette*, her expert way of finding the flea in the bed, she quite literally kept us alive.

In fact, she is to me only one in a vast sisterhood of heroic human beings: the French *concierges*. I have never understood why these patient, defeated women, glued to their miserable *loges* day and night, at the beck and call of a great houseful of tenants, fallen upon and vilified at every *con-tretemps*, torn from their sleep by late arrivals and early departures—are doomed by fate to remain in their *merde* forever; maligned and ridiculed by worldly travelers and pompous asses who never seem to speak of them as anything but disheveled witches to be borne with. They are, willy-nilly, figures in a Punch and Judy, *bizarre*.

For a while I went daily to paint in a studio on the rue Saint-Andrés-des-Arts, really a small apartment. I can close my eyes and see her before me, my studio *concierge*. *Oui, vous*, Madame Turpin, with your great phlebitic legs, your glistening white arms that end in little hands like butterflies, are you still there in the jaws of your recliner, behind the window that looks out on nothing save damp cobblestones and courtyard windows? Does your husband still come home from the weekly cross-country grind of his truck-driving haul to make your bed and tell you that you are still his beauty and his light? Reader, let us thank heaven for the TV.

Madame Deleuze has a white odorous dog. Madame Bertin has three cats. Madame Guyot has one too, a real monster that loves her. That is, there is no other way to explain his behavior when Monsieur Guyot comes home (he too is a truck driver) and Kiki jumps up on the table and urinates in his soup. *"Il fallait le faire couper,"* ("We had to neuter him") sighs gentle Madame Guyot.

Every morning she padded into our aerie to light the fire and grind the coffee while we struggled out of heavy sleep, reluctant to affront the shivering day. At last April, a rudimentary spring. We went to the movies. And there found the famous Paris fleas, *les puces.* "They live mostly in the Champs-Elysées cinemas," said friend Marcel. Madame G. was inclined to agree. Sure enough, it was usually after an evening at the movies that I would thrash the night away in an uneven battle with the wretched beasts. Not Max, who remained superbly asleep and unbitten. Fleas. That summer we knew slightly a writer of novels, the Parisian kind: Menilmontant at night, plenty of *argot,* Paris' brawny, untranslatable slang, and girls who wait. He was the sort of macho fellow seen in French films of yore: tight suit, bedroom eyes, white teeth in view, who had written a heroic and hilarious chapter on these insects. At a *vernissage* I shook hands with him. "Why did he scratch the inside of my hand?" I asked Max. And he, laughing, "Maybe because he is so used to scratching his fleas." So saying he takes me to the other side of the room.

When you are young you are out. When you live in an attic you are out. That is what it means, coming out. They might have said going out. For it is an outgoing process, innocent, the need to know the others. In our case, the need to escape the two slanting little rooms with their stove-burning *boulettes* to warm us, the gas plate where savory ethnic dishes got put together by friends, the cold-water basin that kept us clean.

Behind the wealth of crackled dormers and crumbling walls any corner of which could deliver to the eager eye copious samples of Leonardo's visions, except that for horses, battles, processions, landscapes, we of the glorious present might distinguish drifting up through the flaky surface like photographs wavering in a watery developer, monsters of outer space, rockets, bombs, devastated cities. Behind their frail facades, then, are the poor poets, always the first victims of upheaval, *éboulement.* Living out their uncertain lives in houses that lean, on leaky top floors, *les mansardes,* with water faucets on dim brown hall landings, in rooms formerly occupied by servants and reached by flight after flight of tilting spiral stairs, complete with clammy handrail, broken-hearted hollows in the steps, bare bulbs over the doors. Poor poet, poor Tzara. He refutes his poverty with that monocle. Like all of them behind their abject walls, he dreams big, and all externals fall away before his thundering poem. He had fathered dada in Zurich. Now Paris hides him, a card-carrying embarrassment three flights up a murky staircase.

Or so I think.

We pressed the bell, heard the tinkle. The door opened and a maid in frilly black and white made way for us to pass into the salon. A blaze of eighteenth-century rooms of inordinate height (ah, those stairs) where winter sunshine played with the chandeliers and caused lavender-yellow-rose beams to tremble on the worn seraglio carpet. Long windows gave way to a sepia garden conversed with the bare tops of ancient trees.

In a library of leaves: pamphlets, tracts piled high, magazines, catalogues, manuscripts, boxes on boxes, gray-labeled, albums, papers, books—not ancient ones, he cared not—standing among his treasures as if in a paper nest, there was Tzara, amazing Tzara, just as I had wanted him to be. His knitted *gilet* bore a hero's darns and spots. From his thatch of pepper-and-salt hair to the baggy tweed pants there was nothing, I felt, that could ever be changed. He wore, not a monocle, but shell-rimmed glasses.

African carvings hung high on the walls along with Papuan spears, Polynesian masks; a collection living in harmony with pale Louis Seize chairs and an ormolu desk.

"Le déjeuner est servi."

We sat just us three at a round table graced with fanciful Bohemian glassware and placed, curiously, in the big entry hall. We ate sardines and drank wine served by the pretty *soubrette*, and after our spartan lunch we looked at mementos, drawings, letters, poems on ruled paper and a number of those sketchy sketches on paper table-covers. There was a well-known formula for the assiduous scavenger-collector: after the jolly bistro dinner, toward the end of the talk, the wine, the laughing, the antics, at some point there appeared from nowhere a pen, a pencil or even colored crayons. *"Allons, Pablo, comment était ce drôle de flic, comment il t'a montré du doigt."* ("Come on Pablo, draw that dumb cop, the way he pointed at you.") Everyone drew and wrote and signed. *"C'est ton tour, Alberto, hah, regarde, Portrait d'un cloche."* ("Your turn, Alberto, hah, Look! Portrait of a Bum.") When the bill was paid (a great bluster here) and chairs pushed back and leaves taken, someone during the merry bustle would turn quickly and tear the "tablecloth," the drawings, signatures and doodles landing safely in his pocket, why not, instead of in the restaurant garbage or restaurant pockets. Tzara's beloved collection, what will become of it?

Full of ferocious wit he could also be cruel. To a fellow poet passing the café where he sat: "Ah, *mon cher ami*, I found a rare book of yours, *rarissisme—all* the pages were cut." (Publishers always left it to the reader to cut the book's pages.)

Now his dada charm had turned to communist clout, and in *Fuite*, one of his plays, I heard the actor say: "Better my chosen chains than a found liberty." Max was not *d'accord*.

It doesn't take very long then to realize that left-bank Paris, where everything, for us, seemed to happen, wears her rags and tags on the outside. A perpetual carnival where disguise and discretion are one and the same. As the caliph of Baghdad donned pauper's tatters to ride among his people, so the Paris street wears its uniform of humble grays that add up to pearl and amethyst, precious as a patina.

So that was it. They all lived behind scarred walls and leaning stairs. Imitation wood-grain varnish everywhere, sticky smelling, better than none at all. Terrifying little elevators into which you squeezed your fatalism and your elbows with the others, saucy Madames de, Monsieur le Préfet, the radical countess, the silent museum director. *"Pardon, madame." "Ooh là-là."* "Five!" "Are we not too many?" Someone leans to squint at the notice. "Three hundred kilos capacity," he reads on the brass plate. General laughter among the ladies, who are of course so svelte. Safely delivered, we are let into the rooms which, as they appeared to my American eye, so often resembled Versailles.

A peculiarly Parisian tendency among a few of its inhabitants was nostalgia for the perfect princely past. That it had been far from perfect does not deter these dreamers from their airless play-acting. But no matter. They are harmless in the main, no more dangerous than children building sand castles on the beach, bless their little hearts.

One is perplexed, however, to see an occasional artist join in the game. What is he up to? Or rather, what is he? His faery world of power melts European history into a sticky mass of titles and brocade dressing gowns. He is in deadly earnest about the gilded past in which he places a few of his ancestors and about his preeminence in the present, all of which works admirably, providing he doesn't go outdoors. And he has learned how to turn himself off if he does.

I have seen not a few of such people at art openings or luncheons. They see nothing. Or if they do, it is with disdain. Once a painter whose avowed turf was little girls spat like a cat at the mention of Nabokov's *Lolita*, new on the Paris literary scene. "I *hated* that book. I hated it. He has no *right*. Only a highborn artist should be allowed to handle that subject."

Our fief was of course Saint-Germain-des-Prés, with sallies to Montparnasse where another nostalgia is the prevailing malady. It is utterly impossible to walk along the boulevard Montparnasse on a brightly brave autumn day without seeing on its café terraces the petulant ghosts of former denizens haloed by that determined glamour that only intervening time can confer. *Montparnos* of old, French flavored with American, hang around the wicker chairs, sociable spooks full of droll stories but spooks all the same. Even in spring the place looks autumnal with its pale new leaves and paler sun, and some fragile survivor eager to talk about Hemingway or Henry Miller, or Man Ray's Kiki.

One sat at a table for hours, a forgotten glass of something paying the way. Tattered poets drank *café-crèmes* to keep warm. Seedy youngish men with exploded hair wrote in smudged notebooks. When they looked up, which they did rather often, they did not see you. When they looked down again, their pencils scribbled self-consciously. Sometimes they were joined by girls in heavy makeup and thin jackets.

According to street names we were in a city of saints with an occasional profane. The rue Guillaume Apollinaire was a subject of much jesting among literary buffs and artists who would point out to you its doll-like length occupied by two massive gray buildings *sans* numbers, *sans* entrances, these being located around the corners on its two busy right-angle streets. You could *walk* on the rue Guillaume Apollinaire but you could not *live* there. Max said Apollinaire would have laughed and loved his phantom street. In any case, he soon had to lie back in his tomb. The subject was so unmercifully taken up and elaborated in disrespectful sheets like *Le Canard Enchaîné* that a few years later the city fathers got busy when no one was looking and had a couple of doors punched in the side of their building—it belonged to the town—and numbers conspicuously added to dress them up.

Now, with the slow tread of this summer night, memory serves me ill. Try, try to remember at least some of the thirty-four times three hundred and sixty-five nights. They are the ones to be cherished. Try, try to remember them and the same number of days to match, all shine and midnight blue, before they turn to black. For it is not always possible to notice when you are in orbit. Moments snowball to years. I watch them whirl around us with their processions and silences, their peripheral nebulae, famous and infamous, mortal and wistfully immortal.

Sources and Acknowledgments

Great care has been taken to locate and acknowledge all owners of copyrighted material included in this book. If any such owner has inadvertently been omitted, acknowledgement will gladly be made in future printings.

Benjamin Franklin, Letter to Mary Stevenson: *The Papers of Benjamin Franklin*, vol. XIV, Leonard W. Labaree, ed. (New Haven: Yale University Press, 1970). Reprinted by permission of the Papers of Benjamin Franklin, Yale University Library.

Abigail Adams, Letters from Auteuil: *Letters of Mrs. Adams, the Wife of John Adams* (Boston: Wilkins, Carter, 1848).

Thomas Jefferson, Two Letters: *The Memoirs, Correspondence and Private Papers of Thomas Jefferson*, Thomas Jefferson Randolph, ed. (London: H. Colburn & R. Bentley, 1829).

Gouverneur Morris, *from* A Diary of the French Revolution: *A Diary of the French Revolution* (Boston: Houghton Mifflin, 1939).

Thomas Paine, Shall Louis XVI. Have Respite?: *The Writings of Thomas Paine*, Moncure Conway, ed. (New York: G.P. Putnam's Sons, 1895).

James Gallatin, *from* The Diary of James Gallatin: *The Diary of James Gallatin*, Count Gallatin, ed. (New York: Charles Scribner's Sons, 1916).

George Ticknor, *from* Life, Letters, and Journals: *Life, Letters, and Journals of George Ticknor* (Boston: James R. Osgood, 1877).

Henry Wadsworth Longfellow, Letter to Stephen Longfellow, Jr.: *The Letters of Henry Wadsworth Longfellow*, vol. I, Andrew Hilen, ed. (Cambridge: Harvard University Press, 1966). Reprinted by permission of Harvard University Press. Copyright © 1967 by the President and Fellows of Harvard College.

Ralph Waldo Emerson, *from* Journal, 1833: *The Journals and Miscellaneous Notebooks of Ralph Waldo Emerson*, vol. IV, Alfred R. Ferguson, ed. (Cambridge: The Belknap Press of Harvard University Press, 1964). Reprinted by permission of Harvard University Press. Copyright © 1964 by the President and Fellows of Harvard College.

Nathaniel Parker Willis, *from* Pencillings by the Way: *Pencillings by the Way* (London: John Macrone, 1835).

James Fenimore Cooper, *from* Gleanings in Europe: *Gleanings in Europe* (Philadelphia: Carey, Lea and Blanchard, 1837).

P. T. Barnum, *from* Struggles and Triumphs; or, Forty Years' Recollections: *Struggles and Triumphs; or, Forty Years' Recollections* (Hartford: J. B. Burr, 1869).

George Catlin, *from* Catlin's Notes of Eight Years' Travels and Residence in Europe: *Catlin's Notes of Eight Years' Travels and Residence in Europe* (London: George Catlin, 1848).

Margaret Fuller, *from* Things and Thoughts in Europe: *New-York Daily Tribune*, May 15, 1847.

Harriet Beecher Stowe, *from* Sunny Memories of Foreign Lands. *Sunny Memories of Foreign Lands* (Boston: Phillips, Sampson, 1854).

Nathaniel Hawthorne, *from* The French Notebooks: *The French and Italian Notebooks*,

Thomas Woodson, ed. (Columbus: Ohio State University Press, 1980). Reprinted by permission of Ohio State University Press.

Mark Twain, *from* The Innocents Abroad: *The Innocents Abroad* (Hartford, Connecticut: American Publishing, 1869).

Elihu Washburne, The Proclamation of the Republic: *Recollections of a Minister to France, 1869–1877*, vol. I (New York: Charles Scribner's Sons, 1889).

Henry James, Occasional Paris: *The Galaxy*, January 1878; "The Velvet Glove": *The English Review*, March 1909.

Frederick Douglass, Letter from Paris: *Amistad*, August 1985.

Henry Adams, Letter to John Hay: *The Letters of Henry Adams*, vol. III: 1886–1892, J. C. Levenson, Ernest Samuels, Charles Vandersee, and Viola Hopkins Winner, eds. (Cambridge: Harvard University Press, 1982). Reprinted by permission of Harvard University Press. Copyright © 1982 by the Massachusetts Historical Society.

Richard Harding Davis, *from* The Show-Places of Paris: *About Paris* (New York: Harper & Brothers, 1895).

Isadora Duncan, *from* My Life: *My Life* (New York: Boni & Liveright, 1927). Copyright © 1927 by Horace Liveright, Inc., renewed © 1955 by Liveright Publishing Corporation. Used by permission of Liveright Publishing Corporation.

Edward Steichen, *from* A Life in Photography: *A Life in Photography* (Garden City: Doubleday, 1963). Copyright © 1963 by Edward Steichen. Used by permission of Doubleday, a division of Random House, Inc.

James Weldon Johnson, *from* Along This Way: *Along This Way* (New York: Viking Press, 1933). Copyright © 1933 by James Weldon Johnson, renewed © 1961 by Grace Nail Johnson. Used by permission of Viking Penguin, a division of Penguin Group (USA) Inc.

Theodore Dreiser, A Traveler at Forty: *A Traveler at Forty* (New York: Century, 1913).

Edith Wharton, The Look of Paris: *Fighting France, from Dunkerque to Belport* (New York: Charles Scribner's Sons, 1919); *from* A Backward Glance: *A Backward Glance* (New York: D. Appleton Century, 1934). Reprinted with the permission of Scribner, an imprint of Simon & Schuster Adult Publishing Group. Copyright © 1933, 1934 by The Curtis Publishing Group, copyright renewed © 1961, 1962 by William R. Tyler.

Randolph Bourne, Mon Amie: *History of a Literary Radical, and Other Essays* (New York: B. W. Huebsch, 1920).

Sherwood Anderson, *from* Paris Notebook, 1921: *France and Sherwood Anderson: Paris Notebook, 1921*, Michael Fanning, ed. (Baton Rouge: Louisiana State University Press, 1976.) Reprinted by permission of Harold Ober and Associates Incorporated. Copyright © 1976 by Eleanor Anderson.

Carl Van Vechten, *from* Peter Whiffle: *Peter Whiffle* (New York: Modern Library, 1929). Reprinted by permission of the Carl Van Vechten Trust.

Malcolm Cowley, Significant Gesture: *Exile's Return: A Literary Odyssey of the 1920s* (New York: Viking Press, 1951). Copyright © 1934, 1935, 1941, 1951 by Malcolm Cowley. Used by permission of Viking Penguin, a division of Penguin Group (USA) Inc.

Matthew Josephson, *from* Life Among the Surrealists: *Life Among the Surrealists* (New York: Holt, Rinehart & Winston, 1962). Reprinted by permission of Harold Ober Associates Incorporated. Copyright © 1962 by Matthew Josephson.

Langston Hughes, *from* The Big Sea: *The Big Sea: An Autobiography* (New York: Alfred A. Knopf, 1940). Copyright © 1940 by Langston Hughes. Copyright renewed © 1968 by Arna Bontemps and George Houston Bass. Reprinted by permission of Hill and Wang, a division of Farrar, Straus and Giroux, LLC.

Anita Loos, *from* Gentlemen Prefer Blondes: *"Gentlemen Prefer Blondes": The Illuminating Diary of a Professional Lady* (New York: Boni & Liveright, 1925). Copyright © 1925 by Anita Loos, renewed 1952 by Anita Loos Emerson. Copyright © 1963 by Anita Loos. Used by permission of Liveright Publishing Corporation.

William Faulkner, Four Letters from Paris, 1925: *Selected Letters of William Faulkner*, Joseph Blotner, ed. (New York: Random House, 1977). Copyright © 1977 by Jill Faulkner Summers. Used by permission of Random House, Inc.

E. E. Cummings, *from* Post Impressions: *Complete Poems: 1904–1962*, George J. Firmage, ed. (New York: W.W. Norton, 1994), copyright © 1923, 1925, 1951, 1953, © 1991 by the Trustees for the E. E. Cummings Trust. Copyright © 1976 by George James Firmage, used by permission of Liveright Publishing Corporation; Vive la Folie!: *Vanity Fair*, September 1926. Copyright © 1926, 1954 by the Trustees for the E. E. Cummings Trust. Used by permission of Liveright Publishing Corporation.

Charles Lindbergh, *from* The Spirit of St. Louis: *The Spirit of St. Louis* (New York: Charles Scribner's Sons, 1953). Reprinted with the permission of Scribner, an imprint of Simon & Schuster Adult Publishing Group. Copyright © 1953 by Charles Scribner's Sons; copyright renewed © 1981 by Anne Morrow Lindbergh.

Waverly Root, The Flying Fool: *The Paris Edition: The Autobiography of Waverly Root, 1927–1934*, Samuel Abt, ed. (San Francisco: North Point Press, 1987).

Ernest Hemingway, *from* A Moveable Feast: *A Moveable Feast* (New York: Charles Scribner's Sons, 1964). Reprinted with permission of Scribner, an imprint of Simon & Schuster Adult Publishing Group. Copyright © 1964 by Ernest Hemingway Ltd. Copyright renewed © 1992 by John H. Hemingway, Patrick Hemingway, and Gregory Hemingway.

Hart Crane, Postcard to Samuel Loveman: *The Letters of Hart Crane, 1916–1932*, Brom Weber, ed. (Berkeley: University of California Press, 1952). Reprinted by permission of Hart Crane Papers, Rare Book and Manuscript Library, Columbia University.

Harry Crosby, Paris Diaries: *Shadows of the Sun: The Diaries of Harry Crosby*, Edward Germain, ed. (Santa Barbara: Black Sparrow, 1977).

Cole Porter, You Don't Know Paree: *The Complete Lyrics of Cole Porter* (New York: Alfred A. Knopf, 1983). Copyright © 1929 by Warner Bros. Inc. Rights for Extended Renewal Term in U.S. controlled by the Estate of Cole Porter (administered by WB Music Corporation). All rights reserved. Used by permission.

F. Scott Fitzgerald, Babylon Revisited: *The Short Stories of F. Scott Fitzgerald: A New Collection*, Matthew J. Bruccoli, ed. (New York: Charles Scribner's Sons, 1989). Reprinted with permission of Scribner, an imprint of Simon & Schuster Adult Publishing Group. Copyright © 1931 by Curtis Publishing Co. Copyright renewed © 1959 by Frances Scott Fitzgerald Lanahan.

Lincoln Kirstein, From an Early Diary: *By With To & From: A Lincoln Kirstein Reader*, Nicholas Jenkins, ed. (New York: Farrar, Straus & Giroux, 1991). Copyright © 1991 by Lincoln Kirstein. Reprinted by permission of Farrar, Straus and Giroux, LLC.

Gertrude Stein, *from* Autobiography of Alice B. Toklas: *The Autobiography of Alice B. Toklas* (New York: Harcourt, Brace, 1933). Copyright © 1933 by Gertrude Stein and renewed © 1961 by Alice B. Toklas. Used by permission of Random House, Inc.; *from* Paris France: *Paris France* (New York: Charles Scribner's Sons, 1940). Reprinted by permission of Stanford G. Gann, Jr., Literary Executor, Estate of Gertrude Stein.

Henry Miller, Walking Up and Down in China: *Black Spring* (New York: Grove Press, 1963). Copyright © 1937 by Henry Miller; copyright © 1991 by The Estate of Henry Miller. Used by permission of Grove / Atlantic, Inc.

John Dos Passos, A Spring Month in Paris: *Journey Between Wars* (New York: Harcourt, Brace, 1938). Copyright © 1938 by John Dos Passos. Reprinted by permission of Lucy Dos Passos Coggin.

Anne Morrow Lindbergh, *from* The Flower and the Nettle: *The Flower and the Nettle: Letters and Diaries of Anne Morrow Lindbergh, 1936–1939* (New York: Harcourt Brace Jovanovich, 1976). Copyright © 1976 by Anne Morrow Lindbergh, reprinted by permission of Harcourt, Inc.

Oscar Hammerstein II, The Last Time I Saw Paris: *Lyrics* (New York: Simon & Schuster, 1949). Copyright © 1941. All rights reserved. Used by permission of Universal-Polygram International Publishing, Inc.

Sylvia Beach, *from* Shakespeare and Company: *Shakespeare and Company* (New York: Harcourt, Brace, 1959). Copyright © 1959 by Sylvia Beach and renewed © 1987 by Frederic Beach Dennis, reprinted by permission of Harcourt, Inc.

Janet Flanner, Letter from Paris: "Letter from Paris," *The New Yorker*, April 28, 1945. Copyright © William Murray. Reprinted by permission of William Murray.

Elizabeth Bishop, Paris, 7 A.M.: *North & South* (Boston: Houghton Mifflin, 1946). Copyright © 1979, 1983 by Alice Helen Methfessel. Reprinted by permission of Farrar, Straus and Giroux LLC.

Ludwig Bemelmans, No. 13 Rue St. Augustin: *The Best of Times: An Account of Europe Revisited* (New York: Simon & Schuster, 1948). Reprinted with permission of Simon & Schuster Adult Publishing Group. Copyright © 1947 by Ludwig Bemelmans. Copyright © 1948 by Simon & Schuster and Artists and Writers Guild, Inc.

Richard Wilbur, Place Pigalle: *The Beautiful Changes and Other Poems* (New York: Reynal and Hitchcock, 1947). Copyright © 1947 and renewed © 1975 by Richard Wilbur, reprinted by permission of Harcourt, Inc.

Dawn Powell, Three Letters: *Selected Letters of Dawn Powell, 1913–1965*, Tim Page, ed. (New York: Henry Holt, 1999). Reprinted by permission of the Estate of Dawn Powell.

Art Buchwald, *from* First Days in Paris: *Art Buchwald's Paris* (Boston: Little, Brown, 1954). Copyright © 1952, 1953, 1954 by Art Buchwald. Reprinted by permission of the author.

James Baldwin, Equal in Paris: *Notes of a Native Son* (Boston: Beacon Press, 1955). Copyright © 1955, renewed 1983, by James Baldwin. Renewed by permission of Beacon Press, Boston.

Irwin Shaw, *from* Remembrance of Things Past: *Paris! Paris!* (New York: Harcourt, Brace, 1977). Copyright © Irwin Shaw. Reprinted by permission. All rights reserved.

S. J. Perelman, The Saucier's Apprentice: *The Road to Miltown* (New York: Simon and Schuster, 1957). Reprinted by permission of Harold Ober Associates Incorporated.

First published in *The New Yorker*. Copyright © 1956 by S. J. Perelman. Copyright renewed © 1984 by Abby and Adam Perelman.

May Sarton, Good-by to a World: *The Reporter*, April 19, 1956. Copyright © 1956. Reprinted by permission of Russell & Volkening, Inc.

Paul Zweig, *from* Departures: Memoirs: *Departures: Memoirs* (New York: Harper & Row, 1986). Copyright © 1986 by the Estate of Paul Zweig. Reprinted by permission of Georges Borchardt, Inc., for the author.

James Thurber, The First Time I Saw Paris: *Alarms & Diversions* (New York: Harper and Brothers, 1957). Copyright © 1942 by Rosemary A. Thurber. Reprinted by arrangement with Rosemary A. Thurber and The Barbara Hogenson Agency. All rights reserved.

Sidney Bechet, Trouble in Paris: *Treat It Gentle: An Autobiography* (New York: Hill and Wang, 1960). Copyright © 1960 by Twayne Publishers and Cassell & Company, Ltd. Reprinted by permission of Hill and Wang, a division of Farrar, Straus and Giroux, LLC.

A. J. Liebling, *from* Between Meals: An Appetite for Paris: *Between Meals: An Appetite for Paris* (New York: Simon & Schuster, 1962). Copyright © 1962. Reprinted by permission of Russell & Volkening, Inc.

Virgil Thomson, 17 quai Voltaire: *Virgil Thomson* (New York: Alfred A. Knopf, 1966). Copyright © 1966 by Virgil Thomson. Used by permission of Alfred A. Knopf, a division of Random House, Inc.

Jack Kerouac, *from* Satori in Paris: *Satori in Paris* (New York: Grove Press, 1966). Copyright © 1966 by Jack Kerouac. Reprinted by permission of Sterling Lord Literistic, Inc.

M.F.K. Fisher, Gare de Lyon: *As They Were* (New York: Alfred A. Knopf, 1982). Copyright © 1982 by M.F.K. Fisher. Reprinted by permission of Alfred A. Knopf, a division of Random House Inc.

Diana Vreeland, *from* D.V.: *D.V.*, George Plimpton, ed. (New York: Alfred A. Knopf, 1984). Copyright © 1984. Reprinted by permission of the Diana Vreeland Estate.

Dorothea Tanning, *from* Birthday: *Birthday* (San Francisco: Lapis, 1986). Copyright © 1986 by Dorothea Tanning. Reprinted by permission of the author.